METHOD AND THEORY FOR INVESTIGATING THE PEOPLING OF THE AMERICAS

METHOD AND THEORY FOR INVESTIGATING THE PEOPLING OF THE AMERICAS

EDITED BY:
Robson Bonnichsen
D. Gentry Steele

PEOPLING OF THE AMERICAS PUBLICATIONS
Edited Volume Series

CENTER FOR THE STUDY OF THE FIRST AMERICANS
Oregon State University
Corvallis, Oregon

METHOD AND THEORY FOR INVESTIGATING THE PEOPLING OF THE AMERICAS
© 1994 Center for the Study of the First Americans. All rights reserved.
No part of this book may be reproduced, projected, stored in a retrieval system, or transmitted, for whatever purpose, in any form or by any means, whether electronic, mechanical, magnetic, photographic, laser, or otherwise, without the prior written permission of the publisher: Center for the Study of the First Americans, Department of Anthropology, Oregon State University, Corvallis, OR 97331.

C & C Wordsmiths of Blue Hill, Maine, typeset all copy and prepared camera-ready masters for most of the graphics in this book.
Printed in the United States of America by Thomson-Shore, Inc., Dexter, MI.
This book is printed on 100% acid-free paper.

ISBN: 0-912933-09-7

THE CENTER FOR THE STUDY OF THE FIRST AMERICANS

The Center for the Study of the First Americans is an affiliate of the Department of Anthropology at Oregon State University. It was established in July 1981 by a seed grant from Mr. William Bingham's Trust for Charity. The Center's goals are to encourage research about Pleistocene peoples of the Americas, and to make this new knowledge available to both the scientific community and the interested public. Toward this end, the Center staff is developing research, public outreach, and publications programs.

The Center's Peopling of the Americas publication program focuses on the earliest Americans and their environments. This program includes: (1) a monograph series presenting primary data on sites in North and South America, which are more than 10,000 years old; (2) a process series presenting new methods and theories for interpreting early remains; (3) an edited volume series presenting topical papers and symposia proceedings; (4) a popular book series making the most significant discoveries and research available to the general public; and (5) a bibliographic series.

In addition, the Center publishes a quarterly newspaper called the *Mammoth Trumpet*. The newspaper is written for both a general and a professional audience. The Center also publishes an annual journal, *Current Research in the Pleistocene*. The journal presents note-length articles about current research in the interdisciplinary field of Quaternary studies as they relate to the field of the Pleistocene peopling of the Americas.

MANUSCRIPT SUBMISSIONS

BOOKS

The Center solicits high-quality original manuscripts in English. For information write to: Robson Bonnichsen, Center for the Study of the First Americans, Department of Anthropology, Oregon State University, Corvallis, OR 97331 or call (503) 737-4596.

CURRENT RESEARCH IN THE PLEISTOCENE

Researchers wishing to submit summaries in this annual serial should contact editor Bradley T. Lepper, Newark Earthworks State Memorials, 99 Cooper Ave., Newark, OH 43055 (614/344-1920) or request Information for Contributors from the Center. The deadline for submissions is January 31 of each calendar year; early submission is suggested.

MAMMOTH TRUMPET

News of discoveries, reports on recent conferences, book reviews, and news of current issues are invited.

ADDITIONALLY . . .

Authors are encouraged to submit reprints of published articles or copies of unpublished papers for inclusion in the Center's research library. Exchanges of relevant books and periodicals with other publishers is also encouraged. Please address contributions and correspondence to the Center's library.

PEOPLING OF THE AMERICAS PUBLICATIONS

OTHER TITLES

UNDERSTANDING STONE TOOLS: A COGNITIVE APPROACH
David E. Young and Robson Bonnichsen
ISBN: 0-912933-00-3

ARCHAEOLOGICAL SEDIMENTS IN CONTEXT
Julie K. Stein and William R. Farrand, Editors
ISBN: 0-912933-01-1

ENVIRONMENTS AND EXTINCTIONS:
MAN IN LATE GLACIAL NORTH AMERICA
Jim I. Mead and David J. Meltzer, Editors
ISBN: 0-912933-02-x

NEW EVIDENCE FOR THE PLEISTOCENE PEOPLING OF THE AMERICAS
Contributions in English, Spanish, and Portuguese with extensive English abstracts
Alan L. Bryan, Editor
ISBN: 0-912933-03-8

TAPHONOMY: A Bibliographic Guide to the Literature
Christopher Koch, Compiler
ISBN: 0-912933-05-4

BONE MODIFICATION
Robson Bonnichsen and Marcella H. Sorg, Editors
ISBN: 0-912933-06-2

CLOVIS: ORIGINS AND ADAPTATIONS
Robson Bonnichsen and Karen L. Turnmire, Editors
ISBN: 0-912933-08-9

In recognition of Alan Lyle Bryan and Ruth Gruhn's many outstanding contributions to First American Studies,   we are pleased to dedicate this volume in their honor.

Contents

Introducing First Americans Research
    Robson Bonnichsen and D. Gentry Steele 1

The Discovery of Deep Time:
A History of Views on the Peopling of the Americas
    David J. Meltzer 7

Radiocarbon Dating of Bone Using Accelerator Mass
Spectrometry: Current Discussions and Future Directions
    R. E. Taylor 27

Accelerator C-14 Dating of Human Fossil Skeletons:
Assessing Accuracy and Results on New World Specimens
    Thomas W. Stafford, Jr. 45

The Role of Geoarchaeology in Paleoindian Research
    C. Reid Ferring 57

Pleistocene Peoples of China and
The Peopling of the Americas
    Wu Xinzhi 73

Origins and Affinities of the Native Peoples of Northwestern
North America: The Evidence of Cranial Nonmetric Traits
    Nancy S. Ossenberg 79

Modelling Ancient Population Relationships from
Modern Population Genetics
    Emőke J. E. Szathmary 117

Relating Eurasian and Native American Populations Through
Dental Morphology
    Christy G. Turner II 131

Paleobiological Evidence of the Peopling of the Americas:
A Morphometric View
    D. Gentry Steele and Joseph F. Powell 141

Molecular Approaches to the Isolation and Analysis of
Ancient Nucleic Acids
    David L. Andrews 165

Linguistic Evidence for the Peopling of the Americas
    Merrit Ruhlen 177

The History and Classification of American Indian Languages:
What are the Implications for the Peopling of the Americas?
    Ives Goddard and Lyle Campbell 189

Low-Range Theory and Lithic Technology:
Exploring the Cognitive Approach
    David E. Young, Robson Bonnichsen, Diane Douglas, Jill McMahon, and Lise Swartz 209

An Application of Nitrocellulose Membrane for the Identification
of Blood Residues on Artifactual Materials
    David C. Hyland, Jean M. Tersak, James M. Adovasio and Michael I. Siegel 239

The Pacific Coast Route of Initial Entry: An Overview
    Ruth Gruhn 249

General Index 257

Introducing First Americans Research

ROBSON BONNICHSEN
*Center for the Study of the First Americans
and the Department of Anthropology
Oregon State University
Corvallis, OR 97331*

D. GENTRY STEELE
*Department of Anthropology,
Texas A&M University
College Station, TX 77843-4352*

INTRODUCTION

One of the most interesting and important unsolved questions in New World prehistory is the initial peopling of the Americas. It is of interest because that first colonization of the Americas represents the ultimate pioneering event, the landing of a brave new people in a brave New World, a world never before inhabited by humans. Unquestionably adding to the fascination of this event is that these pioneers faced and adapted to a New World far different than we inhabit today. During glacial times, glacial ice and snow dominated the terrain of northern latitudes. Wildlife encountered by Pleistocene people included mammoths, mastodons, ground sloths, camels, and horses, the likes of which humans of the Holocene were never to see. But to archaeologists worldwide, the most important attraction of the peopling of the Americas is that it probably represented one of the last steps in the colonization of the world by humans.

Although the search for American origins has been a focus of scientific inquiry for more than a century, the scientific community has failed to reach a consensus of opinion concerning when initial populations reached the Americas, and how many separate colonization events occurred. Some of the factors contributing to the present diversification of opinions include the overwhelming scope of the problem, the antiquity of the initial event, the lack of common scientific goals and objectives of the investigating scholars, and language barriers among investigators from different nations.

There is agreement on one point. Investigators are virtually unanimous in their agreement that the founding American populations came from Northeast Asia, Thus, an understanding of the cultural, biological, and environmental factors in Asia and Beringia that were responsible for this dispersal is essential for a complete understanding of the colonization of the Americas. Yet, syntheses integrating research results from Asia and the Americas have been slow to develop. This is true because of differences in scientific methods used by investigators on different continents. When syntheses are attempted, problems invariably arise from lack of standardized methods, differences in classification nomenclature, and reporting procedures. Because of these differences, it has been difficult to move beyond the description of individual sites to answer broader questions important to developing a through understanding of the process(es) that led to the peopling of the Americas.

Another stumbling block is what has become known as the pre-Clovis debate. Potential pre–12,000-year-old sites in North America and South America are few in number, widely scattered, and the data from most of these sites are scanty and controversial. This controversy on the timing of the initial peopling of the Americas is particularly acute in North America. One school of thought advocates late-entry colonization by Clovis big-game hunters. Opposing this view is a group of scholars who represent a far less cohesive view. They agree that the initial colonization of the Americas predates Clovis peoples, but how much earlier, and how many intervening colonization events occurred is hotly contested.

In many respects, the debate over the timing of the peopling of the Americas is a problem of communication as well as one of science. Critics of the pre-Clovis hypothesis challenge claims for the Pleistocene occupation of the Americas by presenting alternative interpretations not considered by site investigators. This has been a very effective method of shifting the burden of proof back to the principle investigator.

This has not always been as productive as desired. Many of the arguments advanced regarding claims for pre-Clovis antiquity of American sites are reasonable arguments. Yet, by necessity, most critics base their counter-claims on the published literature, some of which occur in languages other than English, without the actual benefit of having a first-hand knowledge of early Asian and American sites and artifacts.

Explanations which seek to account for the initial peopling of the Americas are by necessity based on descriptive site reports. Although the need for quality site reports cannot be over-emphasized, it is almost impossible for a principal investigator to anticipate all counter-arguments that may be raised by critics. To anticipate possible criticisms, principal investigators should consider some of the more plausible alternative interpretations of the site. Pre-publication field conferences of invited archaeologists and allied specialists to the site to view site stratigraphy and artifacts before back filling might sharpen the focus of key issues to be addressed in final reports and for eliminating nonproductive debate. Conversely, scholars critically reviewing site data and interpretations should consider the full context in which the site exists, and base their criticisms on a solid foundation of knowledge about the site, its environs, and the significance of the site in broader issues of archaeology.

FOCUSING FIRST-AMERICANS STUDIES

There is a need to move beyond the present period of controversy. While there is probably no single resolution that will lead to scientific advancement in Paleoindian studies, we can begin by examining the principal long-term goal of this field. The search for American origins should develop viable scientific models that explain the dispersal of humans across Asia, North America, and South America. It should search for causes—a search for an understanding of the cultural and biological forces and environmental contexts that allowed humans to move across the northern hemisphere and onto America's southern hemisphere.

From its inception more than 10 years ago, the Center for the Study of the First Americans (formerly the Center for the Study of Early Man) has been committed to stimulating and focusing scientific and public interest on the peopling of the Americas. The Center's unique objectives have been to serve as a catalyst to coordinate, integrate, and synthesize relevant lines of evidence, and to incorporate scholarly works from the international community with alternative viewpoints into the more traditional literature.

With the objective of moving the field forward, three problem areas were recognized that could be addressed by convening an international conference of specialists. The First World Summit Conference on the peopling of the Americas was convened at the University of Maine, Orono, during May of 1989. Problem areas this conference addressed included: (1) The need for a common approach for investigating early American and Asian sites; (2) The need for a synthesis of what is known about the peopling of the Americas; and (3) The need for a bridge between the scientific community and the public.

As implied by the first problem area, one of the most important identifiable issues is the lack of a common intellectual approach for investigating early human prehistory. Some first-Americans scholars have training in anthropological theory but lack training in the Quaternary sciences. We propose that the proper intellectual framework for first Americans studies involves the use of the multidisciplinary approach and integrates anthropological theory and the Quaternary sciences. The present volume seeks to draw together some of the most common multidisciplinary themes used in constructing models that seek to explain the peopling of the Americas.

To fully evaluate the significance of a Paleoindian site requires a knowledge of the Paleoindian record from North America, South America, and Asia. Our second step for forwarding the studies of the peopling of the Americas has been to provide a systematic coverage of regional archaeological studies that pertain to the peopling of the Americas. These studies have also consistently identified those areas meritorious of future research. This synthesis, the most comprehensive effort to date, is based upon papers delivered at Summit '89, (CSFA), and on papers solicited after the conference.

Toward this end, one of us (R. Bonnichsen) began by acquiring a first-hand knowledge of key sites, artifact and faunal collections, and the scholars in the field. This step was deemed necessary for several reasons. First, publication may lag discovery by as much as 10 years in some cases, making it very difficult to track developments taking place on several continents. Furthermore, some important sites are not reported, or if they are, they may occur in languages difficult to access. And last but not least, the visitation approach provided a means of identifying who was really doing the work and was a way to become acquainted with young and relatively unknown scholars. In this process, over 30 institutions housing early archaeological and Paleontological collections in the United States and Canada were visited. Additionally, sites and collections were reviewed in Mexico (1982–1983), China (1985), South America (1987), and Russia (1990). Although many individuals have made worthy contribution to our understanding of the dispersal of Asian populations into the Americas, it has been impossible to include everyone. Nonetheless, one of the key objectives in developing these volumes has been to present as wide an array of views on the topic as possible and from as large an international body of scholars as possible. The Center's Scientific Council and several external peer-review panels collaborated in shaping the product that has emerged. Because of the scope and the amount of material involved, we felt that the only way we could manage this volume of information would be by having a specialist provide a regional synthesis. These data will appear in the forthcoming volumes: *Ice Age Peoples of North America* and *Ice Age Peoples of South America*.

The third step for advancing First American Studies involves bridging the gap between scientific and public archaeology. The focus in first-Americans studies on scientific debate has overshadowed other considerations of site significance such as their social, political, and economic importance. Local and regional authorities, who are responsible for preservation of the archaeological record and public education, need to be informed of site significance. Dr. Ruthann Knudson organized a special symposium at Summit '89 called "Our Public Trust." This area focuses on the legal, educational, and funding issues important to conserving our earliest archaeological remains and educating the world's citizens about the cultural heritage of America. This effort has resulted in a volume to appear in this series titled *The Public Trust and The First Americans*.

THE METHOD AND THEORY VOLUME

The methods and theories of the study of the first Americans represent a unique blend of disciplines and multidisciplinary expertise. In developing this volume, we have not attempted to cover conventional anthropological theory, which focuses on topics relating to hunter-gatherer adaptive strategies, and is covered elsewhere in the literature (Dillehay, and Meltzer 1991; Stanford and Day 1992). Rather, we have attempted to provide overviews of topical areas important to first-Americans research and model building. The first volume, *Method and Theory for Investigating the Peopling of the Americas*, focuses on issues important in understanding the history of the field, chronology, geoarchaeological, biological and linguistic anthropology, as well as issues concerning the analysis of material cultural remains. Additionally, one paper by Ruth Gruhn, which presents a coastal-entry model of the peopling of the Americas, has been included as one illustration of how various lines of evidence can be integrated in a model explaining the peopling of the Americas.

The methodological and theoretical underpinnings one uses to corroborate the archaeological record is, at least in part, dependent upon the problem that one is seeking to solve, and because of this, models constructed by Paleoindian researchers share a number of features. Most Clovis and pre-Clovis models designed to explain how people and ideas moved from Asia to the Americas incorporate human biological, linguistic, and/or archaeological methods of analysis organized into specific temporal frameworks. Given these themes, our goal in this volume is to draw attention to more recent developments occurring in the above mentioned fields, which may be critical for the construction of models of how the Americas were colonized.

We have begun this volume most appropriately with David Meltzer's paper documenting a view of the history of the peopling of the Americas. As Meltzer illustrates, some of our approaches to understanding the peopling of the New World are based upon modern technological advances and are unique to the twentieth century. Other approaches, which we use today, are remarkably similar to the approaches of the nineteeth century, and an examination of these approaches used by scholars spanning these two centuries helps illuminate the process of scientific controversy and its resolution. This understanding may in turn help enhance scholarly communication today.

The development of reasonable models of human colonization, settlement, and subsistence and cultural change all entail a temporal dimension. The placement of human occupation in appropriate environmental context requires independent dates on archaeological and environmental remains. During the early 1950s, the development of radiocarbon dating revolutionized our understanding of the antiquity of human occupation in the Americas. We are now experiencing a second revolution with the introduction of accelerator mass spectrometer (AMS) dating, which allows very small samples of organic remains to be precisely dated.

AMS ^{14}C dating represents an important advance in dating methodology, as it permits a reduction of several orders of magnitude in sample size, along with a decrease in counting time. The development of realistic models which seek to explain the peopling of the Americas must be based on well-dated archaeological and environmental records from specific archaeological and localities, and AMS ^{14}C dating holds great promise for increasing the reliability of bone dating. Taylor in this volume carefully sets forth current issues influencing accuracy-of-dating precision in obtaining ^{14}C determinations on bone. The most important issues discussed include: (1) sample provenance factors; (2) sample composition factors: (3) constraints imposed by nature that influence the means by which ^{14}C concentrations are measured; and (4) factors involving consideration of reservoir of secular variation. In addition to problems affecting dating, Taylor outlines the fundamental principles of how AMS technology works.

Stafford in his contribution emphasizes that direct dating of human skeletal remains is a crucial line of investigation to establish a chronology of the appearance of humans in the New World. He presents problems and solutions of dating human skeletons, reviews literature summarizing allegedly early human skeletal remains recently dated by the AMS technique, and interprets ^{14}C dates on human skeletal remains from the Del Mar skull, California, the skeletons from the Anzick site, Montana, and the Texpexan skeleton from the Texpexan site, Mexico.

As previously noted, many scholars believe that the dispersion of Asian populations into the Americas either was effected by, or linked to, environmental changes which occurred during the Pleistocene. Therefore, paleoclimatic and environmental models of the Pleistocene are considered critical in understanding the peopling of the Americas. In the case of North America, this topic has been recently synthesized by Porter (1989) and Ruddiman and Wright (1987), so the decision was made not to duplicate these efforts. Paleoclimatic information is included in the South America volume.

Reid Ferring provides an overview of geoarchaeological topics and illustrates how earth sciences can be integrated into archaeological research strategies. Geoarchaeology is the application of methods and concepts from the earth sciences to archaeological problems. Ferring indicates that the geoarchaeology of the Paleoindian period is unique due to the rapid change from the Pleistocene to the Holocene and is characterized by rapid and dramatic changes in landscape and biotic communities. Ferring's review of geoarchaeological approaches draws primarily from Central Plains examples. Paleoindian archaeological case-studies illustrate differences in scale and range from regional analysis of site distributions and paleoenvironmental reconstruction to within-site study of site-formation process and concepts.

In considering the biological evidence of the peopling of the Americas, it was realized that no comprehensive collection of papers reviewing the biological evidence had been published since Laughlin and Harper's (1979) landmark volume. (While this volume was in production a special 1992 issue of *Human Biology* on the biological anthropology of New World populations was published.) Therefore, an effort was made to provide an expanded coverage of human biological papers which relate to the peopling of the Americas.

The first human biological paper is Wu Xinzhi's review of the Pleistocene peoples of China and the peopling of the Americas. Wu Xinzhi first summarizes the Pleistocene *Homo erectus* and *Homo sapiens* osteological remains recovered from China, and emphasizes those morphological traits which characterize Asian populations. Based upon this survey, Wu Xinzhi draws two conclusions. His first conclusion is that there has been a gradual morphological change in the *Homo* lineage in China through time. His second conclusion is that some of the Asian features, such as the presence of Inca bones, shovel-shaped incisors, and a broad and flat upper face, are of great antiquity and clearly link the American populations with those of Asia.

Three of the six physical anthropological contributions to the present volume share a common methodological approach in evaluating the biological nature of the first Americans and estimating when these earliest colonizations occurred. Ossenberg, Szathmary, and Turner's research contributions compare relatively recent populations, one to another, and on the basis of their structure and/or genetic similarities, infer their phylogenetic relationships, and when they first diverged one from another. This preponderant reliance on relatively recent samples (Archaic to extant populations) to infer an ancient event is justified by the need for large samples for meaningful comparisons.

Nancy S. Ossenberg in her presentation concentrates upon interpreting the origins and affinities of the native peoples of northwestern North America on the basis of cranial nonmetric traits. Her presentation concurs with those of Turner and Szathmary that North American populations are closest to Asians, and typically northern Asians. However, in contrast to the widely published view of a strong genetic alliance of Aleuts and Eskimo, and a marked genetic distinction of these populations from North American Indians, Ossenberg's data support the view that the Aleuts are more closely allied with northern American Indians, and that all three of these northern American populations are closely allied to one another. In the final portion of her presentation, Ossenberg provides her interpretation of the evolutionary history of these northern Americans.

Emöke J. E. Szathmary in her contribution has addressed the most specific topic of human biologists. She critically evaluates the Gm haplotype data which have been interpreted as supporting the three-migration model of the peopling of the New World proposed by Greenberg et al. (1986). This model proposes that all modern American indigenous populations can trace their ancestry to either the Paleoindians, Na-Dene, or Eskimo-Aleuts, and that the Paleoindians were the first colonizers that arrived, probably sometime more recently than 15,000 years ago. Szathmary concludes that the Gm data do not support this model any more closely than they support Ossenberg's model.

As important as Szathmary's review of the Gm haplotype data are, her evaluation of evolutionary models is based on distance matrices of compared anatomical structures or genetic data. She accepts that dendrograms reflect structural relations, but cautions that to identify such dendrograms as phylogenetic trees presumes there have been constant rates of change in the structures or genes, that no gene flow has occurred between the populations since their initial separation, and that the traits considered accurately reflect the entire genome. These are major presumptions too commonly glossed over in our interpretation of evolutionary models. Szathmary goes on to clearly document how sensitive distance matrices are to changes in the traits and shapes considered, and uses Gm haplotype examples to caution against over-interpretation of dendrograms based on too few traits, on too small a sample, and on ill-defined populations.

Christy G. Turner II in his contribution to *Method and Theory for Investigating the Peopling of the Americas* presents an interesting twist to his well-published three-migrations model for the peopling of the New World. In addition to clearly documenting the dental similarities of the northern Asians and the American Indians, he proposes that the peoples of the world can be divided into two basic groups, Asians and non-Asians. This view challenges the view of Cavalli-Sforza and colleagues, which proposes that modern human populations can be subdivided into sub-Saharan Africans and non-Africans, a dichotomy supporting the hypothesis that anatomically modern humans evolved in Africa and spread from there to colonize the world. Turner infers that if Cavalli-Sforza's data support the African origin of our species, then his own data must support the view of an Asian origin for our species. Turner concludes his paper with a critique of the data sets supporting these two phylogenetic models, and champions the greater value of the dental data that he has amassed.

Rather than compare relatively modern populations, Steele and Powell provide the most recent review of the earliest human skeletal samples known in North America. These samples support the model of an Asian origin for the American populations, but do not provide enough evidence to determine whether these remains are descendants from northern Asian populations of modern aspect, or from an earlier, more generalized northern Asian population. A review of the medical disorders apparent in these remains documents the presence of traumatic and dental disorders typical of more recent American hunters and gatherers.

The newest area of research into the evolutionary relationships of human populations and their origins relies on the comparison of genetic similarities and dissimilarities between nuclear and mitochondrial DNA recovered from ancient human samples. The newness and the complexity of technique of the method, however, are themselves major difficulties. Interpretations of population relationships are being made based on this new evidence, and are starting to be incorporated into larger synthetic models on the peopling of the world without a thorough and critical understanding of the limitations of the method as well as its potential. David L. Andrews, in his article "Molecular Approaches to the Isolation and Analysis of Ancient Nucleic Acids," provides an explanatory overview of the method.

Twentieth-century scholars interested in first-Americans studies have not traditionally drawn on linguistics to understand the initial peopling of the Americas. With the publication of Greenberg's (1987) and Greenberg's et al. (1986) proposal that linguistic, genetic, and dental evidence independently support an interpretation that the Americas were populated by three independent migrations, linguistics was brought to the forefront. Our objectives concerning linguistics in this volume are to further discussion and to represent the range of opinion on this controversial topic.

Merritt Ruhlen in "Linguistic Evidence for the Peopling of the Americas" supports the view of Greenberg (1987) and Greenberg et al. (1986). Greenberg classifies all languages of the western hemisphere into just three groups: Eskimo-Aleut, Na-Dene, and Amerindian. The smallest of these, Eskimo-Aleut, is restricted to the Arctic region of North America and is believed to belong to a large Eurasian phylum, which he identifies as Eurasiatic. Na-Dene includes closely related Athabascan languages, Eyak, Tlingit, and Haida. The last and most controversial groups, Amerindian, includes all the remainder of the North and South American Indian languages.

On the basis of this classification, Ruhlen, following Greenberg, concludes that the American language taxa represent three separate and independent immigrations to the Americas. The first to arrive was the Amerindian group, followed by Na-Dene, followed by speakers of Eskimo-Aleut. The putative three-migration hypothesis is said to be supported by evidence from dentition, and in genetics based on genetic markers such as the Gm haplotype. (For a dissenting view, see Szathmary's paper in this volume). These authors also feel that this threefold classification can be linked to the archaeological record. Amerindian supposedly represents the Clovis migration, thought to have occurred about 11,500 yr B.P.; Na-Dene equates with the Paleoarctic tradition that first appeared in Alaska about 10,500 yr B.P., and with Eskimo-Aleut, which first appeared at Anagula, Alaska, approximately 10,000 yr B.P. Goddard and Campbell in "History and Classification of American Indian Languages: What are the Implications for the Peopling of the Americas?" summarize the arguments that do not support the proposed linkage between linguistic, genetic, and anatomical data, and disagree with Ruhlen's methodology for determining phyletic relationships between linguistic groups.

Material-culture studies are an essential aspect of Paleoindian research and for linking sites into proposed migration routes and tracing human development through time. David E. Young and his collaborators in this volume propose that stone-tool classifications, which rely on normative classifications for categorizing form, are valuable for descriptive purposes but are poorly suited for explaining cultural change. If early immigrants to the Americas modified the shape of their tools to accommodate changing ecological conditions, or in moving from one ecological region to another, formal classification will result in tools being placed in different morphological groupings. Another problem of normative classifications is that artifacts with similar forms, regardless of manufacturing procedure, will be grouped together. For example, the concept of the Clovis style of point may have diffused across populations; however, its form may lead to the conclusion that a single human group migrated from one region to another.

The Young and Bonnichsen's cognitive approach seeks to augment traditional formal classifications. With its emphasis on production technology, the cognitive approach provides an independent means for assessing intra- and inter-site variability of lithic assemblages. Because it is possible to make many artifact shapes with the same production grammar, rapid change can occur in the types of tools produced by an individual or group. By classifying flake scars (morpho-units), relating them to the behaviors responsible for their creation (behavior-units), and determining the sequencing of these units, it is possible to get at the grammar (repertoire of units plus rules) used to make artifacts. In making reconstructions, the cognitive approach draws upon experimental analogies in which behavior and morphology have been linked. The principal value of the cognitive approach, in respect to the general question of the peopling of the Americas, lies in its ability to assess variability. It allows informed inferences to be made regarding factors responsible for variability in the archaeological record.

D. C. Hyland and his collaborators, in "An Application of Nitrocellulose Membrane for the Identification of Blood Residues on Artifactual Materials," review four previously established techniques for identifying the species of animal represented by blood residue left on prehistoric tools, and introduce the new technique of enzyme immunoassay as a fifth technique developed by the cultural Resource Management program at the University of Pittsburgh. The technique's advantages are that it is relatively inexpensive and can be conducted in the field. Its principal disadvantage is that the destruction of residue limits the number of comparisons that can be made with the sample. While the method of blood residue analysis on lithic is in its infancy, its importance to the study of the colonizing of the Americas is that it will allow scholars to consider another aspect of the life styles of the first Americans.

The concluding paper exemplifies the use of the multidisciplinary approach to construct a testable model of how the Americas were peopled. Gruhn proposes in her coastal-entry-route model that humans entered the New World from Asia along the Pacific Rim in middle-Wisconsinan time. In seeking to demonstrate her hypothesis, she draws on the environmental record from the North Pacific coastal zone, ethnographic, archaeological, and historical linguistic data. The coastal-entry model is certainly a viable alternative to the conventional model of an early interior route and can be tested against the archaeological record.

In summary, the goal of first American studies is to develop quality site reports and realistic models that explain the events responsible for the peopling of the Americas. To achieve this goal requires a multidisciplinary approach and a critical, but unbiased, examination of all available data. The following papers represent some of the new scientific frontiers most likely to enhance our understanding of American origins.

REFERENCES CITED

Bonnichsen, R.
    1989 Introduction. *Abstracts: The First World Summit Conference on the Peopling of the Americas*, edited by R. Bonnichsen and J. Tomenchuk, pp. vii-vii. Center for the Study of the First Americans, University of Maine, Orono.

Dillehay, T., and D. Meltzer (editors)
    1991 *The First Americans: Search and Research.* CRC Press, Boston.

Greenberg, J. H.
    1987 *Language in the Americas.* Stanford University Press, Stanford.

Greenberg, J. H., C. G. Turner II, and S. L. Zegura
    1986 The Settlement of the Americas: A Comparison of the Linguistic, Dental, and Genetic Evidence. *Current Anthropology* 27:477–497.

Laughlin, W. S., and A. B. Harper, eds.
    1979 *The First Americans: Origins, Affinities and Adaptations,* Gustav Fischer, New York, Inc., New York.

Porter, S. C.
    1989 Landscapes of the Last Ice Age In North America. In *Americans Before Columbus: Ice-Age Origins,* edited by R. C. Carlisle, pp. 1–23. Ethnology Monograph Series Number 12, Department of Anthropology, University of Pittsburgh.

Ruddiman, W. F., and H. E. Wright, Jr., editors
    1987 *North America and Adjacent Oceans During the Last Deglaciation: The Geology of North America,* v. k-3. Geological Society of America, Boulder.

Stanford, D. J., and J. S. Day (editors)
    1992 *Ice Age Hunters of the Rockies.* University of Colorado Press, Niwot, CO.

The Discovery of Deep Time:
A History of Views on the Peopling of the Americas

DAVID J. MELTZER
Department of Anthropology
Southern Methodist University
Dallas, Texas 75275

The attempt to answer the question of when the first people came to America took on its modern shape in the 1860s when, spurred by the discoveries in Europe of a *pre*history, Americans sought evidence that the past on this continent had also begun in the dim recess of the Pleistocene. By the 1870s, artifacts reminiscent of ancient European Paleolithic tools were being widely reported, and by 1889 this evidence for an "American Paleolithic" was widely accepted. Yet, scarcely a year later the American Paleolithic was under withering attack. And the controversy that began in the spring of 1890 grew bitter, ranged widely, and went unresolved for nearly four decades. Only with the Folsom discoveries would proof emerge that humans had been in North America since at least the latest Pleistocene.

Looking back at the efforts to demonstrate a deep human antiquity in the Americas is fascinating for its own sake, but it also reveals that while some of our modern efforts to resolve the controversy are radically different from approaches taken by our archaeological forebears, some are surprisingly unchanged. We still rely on linguistic and anatomical evidence from modern native North American populations to inform on the number, timing, and antiquity of migrations to the Americas. We still have strong disagreements about central issues of artifact identity and context. We still bring quite different theoretical baggage to the problem. Thus we can still, much as our forebears did, look at precisely the same evidence and draw precisely opposite conclusions.

Peering into the window of history helps us understand the process of scientific controversy and its resolution, allows us to see why some strategies may succeed in resolving this problem while others are doomed to fail, and reveals in stark highlights why for the last century the question of human antiquity in the New World has been among the most unruly problems in American archaeology.

INTRODUCTION

Late in life Julian Steward recalled that when he attended the American Anthropological Association meetings in Denver in 1931, he heard E.B. Renaud "proclaim the presence of pure paleolithic culture in America." Steward then added, "That these meetings were opened with a prayer I presume to be purely coincidental" (Steward 1973:40).

Steward could look with bemusement at Renaud, for by 1931 the American Paleolithic—championed in the struggle to establish a deep human antiquity in America—had been cast aside. The Folsom discovery had proven what Paleolithic proponents had been claiming—that the earliest Americans arrived during the Pleistocene. But Folsom was so different from anything previously seen and so unlike the European Paleolithic it rendered the American Paleolithic obsolete. To Steward, Renaud was like the last survivor of a species going extinct.

Nearly sixty years later we tend to view the American Paleolithic much as Steward did: a bemusing but ultimately misguided affair. Yet, a closer look at efforts before 1927 to establish human antiquity in America shows that this dispute cut to the conceptual core of early American archaeology and forced it to confront and clarify methodological and theoretical ambiguities; it revealed in harsh tones the professional porousness of the field and the difficulty of distinguishing the elite from the amateur (Hinsley 1985:69); it involved a range of ancillary sciences and thus exposed the vulnerability of archaeological interpretation to non-archaeological data and disputes; and, most importantly, it held the time depth of American prehistory in the balance (Kidder 1936:143).

In fact, that dispute was not all that different from the controversy as it stands today. Perhaps the only significant difference between then and now is that we don't open our meetings with a prayer.

In this chapter I provide a narrative of the pre-1927 effort to establish human antiquity in America, then draw from that history lessons relevant to the current dispute. There is nothing in this history that offers a *solution* to today's impasse over the existence of a pre-12,000 yr B.P. human occupation, but there is much in that history that sheds light on why we do what we do, and why this problem so stubbornly resists resolution.

THE CONTROVERSY OVER HUMAN ANTIQUITY IN AMERICA, 1492–1927

Overture

The discovery of the Americas was a profound jolt to European thinkers. Of its people, the Biblical narratives—then the prime historical source—said nothing. Even so, the native Americans had to be accounted for in historical terms. As Samuel Haven (1806–1881) noted in his mid-century review of *Archaeology of the United States*:

> On the presumption that all the varieties of the human race were descended from a single pair, and that after the flood the earth was indebted solely to the ark of Noah for the replenishment of man and beast, the manner in which these reached the western world became to scholars and divines a subject of anxious inquiry (Haven 1856:3).

Thus, the ancestral roots of the American Indian were sought in historically known or imagined peoples, among them:

> Tyrian Phoenicians, Assyrians, ancient Egyptians, Canaanites, Israelites, Trojans, Romans, Etruscans, Greeks, Scythians, Tartars, Chinese Buddhists, Hindus, Mandingoes or other Africans, Madagascans, the early Irish, Welsh, Norsemen, Basques, Portuguese, French, Spaniards, Huns, or survivors of the Lost Continents of Mu or Atlantis (Wauchope 1962:3).

If there was a consensus among speculators and historians, it was that the native Americans were the Ten Lost Tribes of Israel (Hallowell 1960:4–5). There appeared to be "corroboration in the customs and traditions of the Indians" (Haven 1856:5) with those of the ancient Israelites, although Wauchope makes the trenchant observation that in those early years Hebrew ethnology as described in the Old Testament "was about the only well-documented "primitive" way of life known and therefore the first to occur to a seeker of Indian relationships" (Wauchope 1962:3). Nonetheless, identifying the native Americans as long-wandering Israelites had two undeniable virtues: it explained why those tribes had become lost, and it provided a ready explanation for the native Americans.

While the Lost Tribes of Israel theory would ultimately fall into disfavor (but only after enjoying a nearly 300-year run) the Old World origin of native Americans was undeniable. The puzzle of how the Ten Lost Tribes or any other Old World group reached America was resolved as early as 1590 by Fray Joseph de Acosta (1539–1600). In a remarkable display of acuity, he argued that the ancestors of native Americans had to have come across in an overland migration, somewhere in the far north where he inferred (but certainly could not confirm) that the Old and New Worlds were close or connected (de Acosta 1590, summarized in Jarcho 1959:435). Even so, it would take another 200 years before Thomas Jefferson was able to report that:

> The late discoveries of Captain Cook, coasting from Kamchatka to California, have proved that, if the two continents of Asia and America be

separated at all, it is only by a narrow streight [Jefferson [1787] 1975:142].

Prior to the mid-19th century, determining *who* the native Americans were, would attract far more controversy than *when* they had arrived, for no one suggested their antiquity was greater than the 6000 years allotted in either Biblical or secular histories (e.g., Haven 1856:153). Even so, the native Americans spoke a baffling number of languages, showed surprising variation in physical type, and displayed an array of distinct cultural practices, all of which implied a long period of divergence from a single source (Gossip 1869; Jefferson [1787] 1975).

Looking for Deep Time

The controversy over the antiquity of the native Americans only began after 1860, with the discoveries in Europe of human remains in association with extinct Pleistocene mammals (Grayson 1983; Gruber 1965). Those discoveries of humans in *deep* time (Gould 1987:2), time earlier and unknown to history, abruptly created *pre*history independent of the chronology and context of the Biblical and historical records. Scientists now confronted the vexing problem of telling time from artifacts and the earth itself. The chronology of the human past would never be so clear as it once was.

With the Biblical and Pleistocene barriers for human antiquity broken in Europe, a vigorous search began for an American Paleolithic (Meltzer 1983:5–6). The belief there was a general synchronism of geological beds between Europe and the United States (Whittlesey 1869:271–272), along with the emerging evolutionary theory, buttressed the claim that Paleolithic human ancestors "*must* have existed in the Pliocene period" of Europe and America (Wallace 1887:667).

Armed with such expectations, it was no surprise that by the mid-1870s "Paleolithic" artifacts, apparently identical to those discovered in Europe (as illustrated in Evans 1872), were being found in North America. It was physician-naturalist Charles Abbott (1843–1919) whose work in the Delaware Valley first called attention to these artifacts (Abbott 1872, 1873), and who argued they were not the mere handiwork of native Americans, but of an older, Paleolithic race, much as had once lived in Europe (Abbott 1876). After all, "had the Delaware River been a European stream, the implements found in its valley would have been accepted at once as evidence of the so-called *paleolithic man*" (emphasis in original) (Abbott 1881a:126–127).

These discoveries attracted Frederic Ward Putnam (1839–1915) of the Peabody Museum of Archaeology and Ethnology (Harvard), an institution whose benefactor had specified in his deed of gift that were implements of an earlier geological period than the present found, "especial attention be given to their study" (Putnam 1881:147–148). Putnam first visited Abbott at Trenton in September of 1876, where together they found two "rude" specimens in situ. Putnam was impressed. He saw "no reason to doubt the general conclusion [Abbott] has reached in regard to the existence of man in glacial times on the Atlantic Coast of North America" (quoted in Abbott 1881a:127). With funding from the Peabody Museum, Abbott continued his research (Abbott 1877, 1878).

There was general agreement these "rude" implements were artifacts and not naturally broken stones, although Abbott carefully considered the latter (Abbott 1877:31–32, 1878:228–229; also Haynes 1881:133–135; Shaler 1889:24–25; Wadsworth 1881:146; Wright 1889a:507–512; but see Holmes 1893d:153). As WJ McGee (1853–1912), geologist for the United States Geological Survey (USGS) testified, "the series is not from the certainly natural to the doubtfully artificial, but from the certainly artificial to the doubtfully natural" (McGee 1888b:36).

Yet, the age of the artifacts was difficult to ascertain, save that they seemed to be contemporary with those of the European Paleolithic. Abbott thought they might reach back to pre-glacial times (Abbott 1883:359), but geologist Henry C. Lewis (1853-1888), who named the deposit in which they were found (Lewis 1880), thought the Trenton gravels were deposited "immediately following the final retreat of the glacier" (Lewis 1884:21). The geologist Reverend George Frederick Wright (1838–1921), who with British archaeologist W. Boyd Dawkins had visited Abbott in November of 1880, and had accompanied Lewis for part of his fieldwork, thought the formation slightly older, having been deposited "near the very close of the glacial period" (Wright 1881a:144). Deglaciation, Wright estimated based on peat accumulation in a New England bog and the cutting of Niagara gorge, had occurred roughly 10,000 years ago (Wright 1881b, 1885).

Importantly, the "rude" implements were rarely found on the surface associated with the readily distinguishable "relics of the indians" (Abbott 1877:32, 1878:252–253; also Haynes 1882:385; Hoffman 1879:115; Wilson 1889:239). And on this basis rested the conclusion that the Paleolithic groups were a separate race, certainly descended from European Paleolithic peoples, and possibly either ancestral to the Eskimo or wholly unrelated to later native American groups (Abbott 1881b:517; Haynes 1882:389; Putnam 1890:700; Wilson 1897:1041). The historically known native Americans had not lived "in a paleolithic stage" (Abbott 1881a:125).

Abbott's discoveries were soon replicated by others. In the spring of 1883 G. F. Wright predicted that "When observers become familiar with the rude form of these paleolithic implements they will doubtless find them in abundance" (Wright 1883; see Abbott 1883). He was correct (Holmes 1893d:161). At the AAAS meeting that summer there came a report of Paleolithic remains from Little Falls, Minnesota (Babbitt 1883, 1884; Upham 1888), and by decade's end Paleolithic artifacts had been recorded from a number of sites including Madisonville (Putnam 1888a) and Newcomerstown (Mills 1890; Wright 1890b, 1893c), Ohio; Claymont, Delaware (Cresson 1889a); Medora, Indiana (Cresson 1889b); and around Washington, D. C. (Hoffman 1879; McGee 1889:232–233; Wilson 1889, 1890). Reports even came in from unglaciated areas, notably McGee's (1887) discovery of an obsidian implement in Quaternary lake sediments in the Great Basin.

Cresson's discovery of the Claymont paleolith in the Philadelphia Brick Clay and Red Gravel was particularly striking since this formation was older than the Trenton gravels and equivalent to McGee's Potomac Valley Columbian formation (McGee 1888a:452–453; Wright 1889a:553,1889b:154–155). That formation, at least to adherents of multiple glaciations, was "from 30,000 to 150,000 years old" (McGee 1888a:463; Wright 1889b:155). Those who, like Wright, steadfastly maintained there had been only one glacial advance during the Pleistocene suggested that the Claymont paleolith was only older than the Trenton forms "perhaps by many thousand years" (Wright 1889b:156). He admitted to McGee privately that it would "greatly relieve the archaeologists if we can get along without the two glacial periods this side of the Alleghenies" (Wright to McGee, Jan 14, 1889, WJM/LC). But far more than that halfhearted effort would be required to bring McGee around, for the idea of multiple glaciations was becoming firmly embedded in glacial geology, and Wright's view was not.

Thousands of paleoliths were "found principally on the surface" (Wilson 1889:237), but Thomas Wilson (1832–1902), Curator at the United States National Museum (USNM), showed no hesitancy about their age. His long experience in Europe where many paleoliths were found on the surface taught him they could be correctly identified by comparison with those found in the Pleistocene gravels (Wilson 1890:694).

Putnam, no stranger to such comparisons (Putnam 1888b), was a bit more cautious. Proudfit's (1889) account of the quarry debris at the Piney Branch site had reminded Putnam of his own experiences at New England quarry sites, where he too had seen "paleolithic forms" associated with "the highest type of chipped implements" (Putnam 1889:267). Form alone, Putnam cautioned, "can tell us but little of the time when an implement was made," and so he placed responsibility for determining age in the willing hands of geologists, like WJ McGee, to ascertain which came "unquestionably from the glacial gravels" (Putnam 1889:267–268). This would prove no mean feat.

But if there was skepticism about the American Paleolithic, it was well hidden. After all, Boyd Dawkins himself had said that the American "implements are of the same type, and occur under exactly the same conditions, as the river-drift implements of Europe" (1883:347). The last years of the 1880s saw the publication of McGee's (1888b) synthesis of the American Paleolithic, and the first of Wright's popular compendia, *The Ice Age in North America* (1889a).

Wright's volume was mostly about glacial geology, but included two chapters on evidence for human artifacts from glacial deposits, and in neither these chapters nor the earlier ones was Wright breaking any ground. The book was, rather, a synthesis for a popular audience. McGee had been invited to contribute a few pages on the Columbian formation, but graciously declined (Wright to/from McGee January 14 and 22, 1889, WJM/LC). The book's first press run of 1500 copies sold out within the year (Morison 1971:228), and it was widely hailed (Anonymous [probably J. D. Dana] 1889; Upham 1889; Winchell 1889).

Wright received a negative response, privately, from Thomas C. Chamberlin (1843–1928), then Chief of the USGS Glacial Division. Chamberlin wrote that a volume that "purported to instruct the general unscientific" reader on matters such as glacial geology and human antiquity was "premature and unfortunate both for science and the public," since it implied that the "truth" of such matters were known. In Chamberlin's view this was not the case and its publication would become a barrier to the "reception of the truth when it shall be ascertained" (Chamberlin to Wright, January 24, 1889; quoted in Chamberlin 1893:8). Regarding human antiquity, Chamberlin wrote, matters were not even to the point where one could specify the problem, much less a solution. This was not the first instance when Chamberlin and Wright had disagreed (Morison 1971:271); their differences had surfaced soon after Wright was appointed (1884) a part-time assistant in Chamberlin's USGS Glacial Division and had steadily deteriorated in the course of Wright's work and reports (e.g., Chamberlin 1890; Wright 1890a). They would only worsen in the years to come.

The Great Paleolithic War

With the new decade there would be a full assault on Wright, Abbott, and the American Paleolithic, largely from archaeologists at the Bureau of American Ethnology (BAE). Under its founder, John Wesley Powell (1834–1902), the BAE aimed to create a new kind of holistic anthropology" of final, positive knowledge to explain and justify the wide disparities in human conditions, past, present and future" (Hinsley 1981:151). Its centerpiece was an evolutionary vision of a universal, progressive history of humankind.

BAE archaeologists adopted the spirit, if not the details, of Powell's grand vision (Meltzer 1983:12–13). Theirs was a uniformitarian archaeology that began with the known material remains of historic tribes and traced them backward "gradually and without sensible break" to their prehistoric ancestors (Powell 1890:500). But not so far back as an American Paleolithic; to accept an unrelated Paleolithic race who were non-Indian and left no descendants would rupture the Bureau's methodological link from present to past, and deny their theory of historical evolutionary progress (Powell 1890:500; Thomas 1898). After all, if American Indian prehistory began, as prehistory did in Europe, in Pleistocene times, why had the Indians not transcended savagery and just passed from savagery "into barbarism when the good queen sold her jewels" (Powell 1890:503)?

Powell directed BAE archaeologist William Henry Holmes (1846–1933) to turn his attention to the American Paleolithic. Holmes began with fieldwork at the Piney Branch quartzite quarries in what was then the Washington, D. C. suburbs (Holmes 1890). Holmes realized, quite early in his Piney Branch work, that an artifact might appear "rude" merely because it was unfinished, and not because it was ancient. The resemblance to European Paleoliths had no "chronologic significance whatever" (Holmes 1890:25), and only showed that in the process of making an individual stone tool one passed through each of the steps in the long evolution of stone-tool-making (Holmes 1894). This was ontogeny recapitulating phylogeny, applied to stone tools.

Indeed, the history of flaked stone implements, as discerned from the quarries of Algonquian groups at Piney Branch, "is their history everywhere" (Holmes 1897:15), and to separate a "single specimen from the main body of flaked stone art in America, save upon purely geological evidence, is wholly unwarranted" (Holmes 1892:296). Given the many agencies known to disturb the soil to considerable depths, which could move artifacts from the surface into deeper, older deposits, that geological evidence would have to be unimpeachable (Holmes 1892:297).

From Piney Branch, Holmes embarked on a systematic, critical examination of the Paleolithic sites at Little Falls (Holmes 1893f), Ohio (Holmes 1893d), and Trenton (Holmes 1893b). In each case he believed the finds had been "prematurely announced and unduly paraded" (Holmes 1893d:163).

Among the problems he saw were that "typical rejects of the modern blade maker" were being mistakenly identified as evidence of Paleolithic culture when it was "safest to assign all to the historic Indian (Holmes 1893b:18,27; 1893d:154, 163). Many of these had fallen by chance into otherwise intact Pleistocene deposits (Holmes 1893d:161, 1893f:236–239). Others had been collected from redeposited gravels or other, recent formations, such as talus deposits, that had not been recognized as redeposited (Holmes 1893b:24–25, 1893d:149):

> Talus deposits form exceedingly treacherous records for the would be chronologist. They are the reef upon which more than one paleolithic adventurer has been wrecked (Holmes 1893b:27).

Such mistakes were virtually guaranteed when finds were made by mere "relic hunters" who "lacked adequate knowledge," had "preconceived notions," and practiced an "unscientific method" (e.g., Holmes 1893b:21,29,34–35, 1893d:147,150,160, 1893f:240). None of the finds could be verified (Holmes 1893d:149), which only exacerbated the situation since when Holmes visited these sites he never found any artifacts in such Pleistocene formations, leading him to suspect those deposits "are and always were wholly barren of art" (Holmes 1893b:23). Far more confidence might be placed in his work, aided as it was by "some of the foremost geologists and anthropologists of the country" (Holmes 1892:297). As to Abbott's Trenton Paleolithic/Eskimo/Indian sequence, Holmes thought that "had William Penn paused in his arduous traffic with the tawny Delawares," for just a few moments and watched "an uncouth savage" making a stone tool he would have "gleaned the story of the ages" (Holmes 1893b:34). As it was:

> Two hundred years of aboriginal misfortune and Quaker inattention and neglect have resulted in so mixing up the simple evidence of a day's work, that it has taken twenty-five years to collect the scattered fragments, separate and classify them, and to assign them to theoretic places in a scheme of culture evolution that spans ten thousand years (Holmes 1893b:34). (Abbott was the Quaker in reference. See Holmes to I.J. Wistar, April 8, 1893, WHH/SIA.)

Paleolithic proponents immediately mounted a counterattack and the serious debate began (e.g., Abbott 1892a, 1892b, 1893a, 1893b; Brinton 1892a; Haynes 1893a, 1893b, 1893c, 1893d; Holmes 1893c, 1893e; Wright 1893a, 1893d). That there would be a vigorous dispute was certain, but what gave it more heat and bitterness than it might otherwise have had was the appearance of Wright's *Man and the Glacial Period* (1892).

This new book was condensed from his earlier work (Wright 1889a), with some new evidence, and also aimed at a lay audience. Like its predecessor, it received favorable reviews (Winchell 1892; Youmans 1892), but these were far outweighed by a battery of highly critical, often vicious ones (e.g., Brinton 1892b; Chamberlin 1892; McGee 1892, 1893a, 1893b; Salisbury 1892, 1893). The critics, following Holmes, attacked Wright's defense of the American Paleolithic, and his insistence on but a single glacial advance. But what riled them most was the issue Chamberlin had privately raised three years before: the Reverend Wright, a "betinseled charlatan" in their eyes (McGee 1893a:95), was not "entitled to speak on behalf of science" to the general public (Chamberlin 1892:303).

The searing attack on Wright's book triggered a caustic explosion, but it was only nominally about the American Paleolithic and whether Wright's view of glacial history was correct (Meltzer 1983, 1991). This was really a proprietary dispute, where BAE and USGS scientists sought to revolutionize the field, and overthrow the "old archaeology" (Holmes 1893c:29). Laced as it was with the poisonous undertones of a federally-funded attack on non-federal science, the dispute quickly transcended the scientific issues at hand (e.g., Baldwin 1893, Claypole 1893a, 1893b, 1893c; Cope 1893; Youmans 1893a, 1893b; cf. Powell 1893).

In this cauldron positions quickly hardened and became irreconcilable (Meltzer 1983:18–23). Until the turn of the century, proponents and opponents of the Paleolithic talked past one another. Abbott could no more see similarities between Holmes' "quarry rejects" and his Paleolithic artifacts (Abbott 1890:8), than Holmes or McGee could agree with Abbott that those alleged paleoliths had been found in primary Pleistocene contexts (Holmes 1893b:24–25; McGee 1891:73). Accusations of shoddy fieldwork, poor science, and preconceived bias flew in all directions. Even when all sides agreed that the key in sorting unfinished rejects from finished Paleoliths was to look for signs of use, they disagreed completely over whether usewear was present even when looking at the very same artifacts (Abbott 1892a:271; Haynes 1893a:66; Wright 1893b:66; cf. Holmes 1893c:29).

By 1900 the American Paleolithic dispute had stalled; neither party obtained a decided victory, neither acknowledged defeat (Fowke 1902; McGee and Thomas 1905:50). Yet in one significant respect Paleolithic proponents had suffered a major setback. Sir John Evans, at the 1897 meeting of the BAAS (in Toronto), examined a sample of the Trenton paleoliths and concluded:

> Clearly and emphatically ... that whatsoever the Trenton material may mean, it has absolutely nothing to do with that which in Europe is called paleolithic and assigned considerable antiquity (McGee to Holmes, September 2, 1897, BAE/NAA).

Not surprisingly, few discoveries of paleoliths were subsequently made (cf. Winchell 1913).

Skeletons Adrift?

Over the next two decades the dispute over human antiquity in the New World took a different course, triggered by the discovery by Ernest Volk (1845–1919) on December 1, 1899, of a human femur deep in the deposits at Trenton (Volk 1911:115). Volk, who with Putnam's support had spent the previous ten years doggedly searching for Paleoliths in the Trenton gravels, thought that this new discovery was "the key to it all" (Volk to Putnam, December 1, 1899, PMP/HU). Putnam agreed this was "the most important thing yet brought to light in connection with age of man in the Valley," but added anxiously, "We must not make any blunder about it" (Putnam to Volk, December 13, 1899, PMP/HU). He was appropriately cautious, for the Washington critics heard of it almost immediately, and reacted "with scorn and contumely":

> It will be the old fight against Abbott over again. What evidence, they do say and will say, have we that Volk in his naturally ardent desire to do something, to find something, to show something, all this to justify his continuance in employment, should not have planted this bone to the end that he should afterwards find it with his camera. And they enquire—"Who is Volk, anyhow?" Can we, simply on the faith, the say-so of this man ... accept such an unheard of and unbelievable proposition as the genuine discovery of this bone? (Wilson to Putnam, January 3, 1900, PMP/HU).

Putnam turned the specimens over to Aleš Hrdlička (1869–1943), a young physical anthropologist then in Putnam's employ. Hrdlička did not think the specimen was "especially remarkable," either in its condition or in comparison with historically documented skeletal material. Its age "must be based principally on [its] location with regard to geological formation" (Hrdlička in Volk 1911:247). And that, as Wright believed, pointed unmistakably to the Pleistocene: the gravels overlying the fine sands in which the femur was found had been "laid down by the glacial floods at Trenton" and with no "possibility of accidental or fraudulent burial" (Wright in Volk 1911:243). Volk had "done his work well," a satisfied Abbott wrote, and

> If he has not demonstrated Glacial—Pre-Indian—and Indian clearly, then evidence such as we have hoped for, is unattainable (Abbott to Putnam, December 27, 1900, PMP/HU).

Yet, the "strong story" of human antiquity told by the Trenton gravels femur (Putnam to Mason, March 7, 1900, USNM/SIA), would not accomplish what either Abbott or Putnam had hoped it would—a silencing of the critics. Only McGee would be shaken by it:

> This osteologic material ... seems to me to warrant reopening the Trenton case for Glacial man, with so strong a presumption in his favor that the burden of proof must fall on the opposition (McGee to Fairchild, April 27, 1903, BAE/NAA).

And even McGee's change of faith (if not demeanor) was not because he was overwhelmed by irrefutable fact, but from a more mundane cause: just as his 1889–1890 conversion to Paleolithic critic came as he ingratiated himself into the inner circles of power in Washington geology and anthropology (Meltzer 1983:26), this latest conversion came as he was being rejected from the inner circle, and was fighting a desperate, bitter and losing battle with Holmes and the Washington scientific elite to succeed Powell as Director of the BAE.

From 1900 to 1926 some three dozen human skeletons in apparently ancient localities across North and South America were discovered or reported. (The significant North American sites include Lansing, Kansas [Upham 1902; Williston 1902a; Winchell 1902], Gilder Mound near Omaha, Nebraska [Barbour and Ward 1906a, 1906b], Vero and Melbourne, Florida [Loomis 1924, 1925; Sellards 1916a, 1916b]. These sites are listed in Hrdlička [1907, 1918]; the South American sites are in Hrdlička [1912a]). Without exception, they proved no less vulnerable to critical examination than the discoveries of Paleoliths, and none escaped the watchful eyes of Hrdlička, who in 1903 moved to the Smithsonian. This move was engineered by Holmes (who drew up the civil service exam for Hrdlička and the other two candidates using questions based on Hrdlička's published research). The hiring was protested by McGee and, I suspect, long regretted by Putnam, for Holmes and Hrdlička proved a highly potent critical force (Holmes WHH/RR 8:110–112; McGee to Boas, December 21, 1902, FB/APS).

Soon thereafter, Hrdlička's approach to purportedly ancient human skeletal material subtly but significantly changed. Skeletons of purported antiquity had to occur in indisputable stratigraphic context, show fossilization, and display "marked serial somatological distinctions in the more important osseous parts" (Hrdlička 1907:13; also 1912a:2–3). In practice, the last criterion became more important to Hrdlička than the first two (Hrdlička 1907:98, 1912a:3; Meltzer 1983:29–30), for he well appreciated the potential problems in relying on geological evidence, to the occasional distress of his geologist colleagues (Chamberlin 1919:320).

Hrdlička's developing distrust of geological evidence came from many sources. He came to appreciate effects of human burial. Humans had been burying their dead since Neanderthal times, and even a moderate estimate of the number of burials made within the last 4000 years of pre-Columbian America reached two billion (Hrdlička, unpublished manuscript ca. 1916, AH/NAA). He therefore argued (as had Holmes before him) that it was better to begin by assuming that all skeletal material in purportedly ancient deposits was intrusive—and then try to disprove that assumption (Hrdlička 1907:11–12, 1912b:551, 1917:48).

He knew as well that in some localities fossilization occurred rapidly, or not at all, regardless of age (Hrdlička 1907:12). Thus, the Nebraska finds should have been fossilized, but weren't (Hrdlička 1907:90), while many of the Florida discoveries were fossilized, but should not have been (Hrdlička 1907:64). As Ameghino's *Homo pampaeus* showed, fossilization is far more a question of environment than of time (Hrdlička 1912a:297). Moreover, the circumstances of these discoveries were often less than optimal. The Lansing skeletons were found by the Concannon brothers, "excavating a tunnel for storing fruit, vegetables, milk, butter, etc." (Upham 1902:135):

> The men are farmers and did not appreciate the significance of the discovery, breaking the skull with the pick and scattering the pieces with the rest of the skeleton, hardly taking pains to throw the fragments into a place by themselves (Winchell 1902:189).

Robert Gilder (1856–1940), a journalist for the Omaha *World Herald* who found the original specimens of the Nebraska "Loess Man" had no clue the bones could be of great antiquity, and his servant—afraid of human bones in the house—buried the skeletal parts in the rubbish pile in the yard. Only after Gilder learned of their possible age were they re-excavated from his rubbish pile, scattered and broken (Barbour to Hrdlička, January 25, 1906 AH/NAA). The refrain was the same elsewhere (e.g., Sellards 1916c:131).

Even after competent observers became involved, circumstances might not improve. As often as not, the most important discoveries had already been made, and later visitors could only hope for the odd bone or artifact to corroborate statements on stratigraphic position and geological context made by untrained and (perhaps) dishonest observers. Proponents and skeptics were acutely aware of the vulnerability of this kind of testimony (Winchell 1902:194). Speaking of the Trenton femur, Wilson trenchantly remarked:

> The whole affair depends upon the faith and credit given to Volk, and that depends largely upon his reputation and character for truth and honesty.... It would have been wise for us to have given expression to our belief in Volk's honesty and integrity, and thus our acceptance of this discovery as genuine (Wilson to Putnam, January 3, 1900, PMP/HU).

But as Robert Gilder admitted in a moment of remarkable (and unintentional?) candor, truth was relative, or at least fleeting:

> We of the press can make a statement and deny it the next day if necessary, but an *honest* investigator could not afford so haphazard a method (Gilder to Hrdlička, December 15, 1907, AH/NAA, emphasis added).

This Gilder would later illustrate fully: four years after the appearance of Hrdlička's critical comments on the Nebraska discovery, he claimed

> in reading Dr. Hrdlička's report the writer's attention was at once attracted to the many and persistent "inaccuracies" in its pages and I wrote the doctor calling his attention to one of the most glaring (Gilder 1911:157–158).

Gilder did, in fact, write Hrdlička (December 15, 1907, AH/NAA), but what he said was "There is only *one* matter that I can find in a critical reading of the paper that is not strictly accurate," which he then explained (see Gilder 1911:158 in response to Hrdlička 1907:69). He concluded that

> with this single error I believe your paper could not be improved upon with the knowledge we all had at the time you were here (Gilder to Hrdlička, December 15, 1907, AH/NAA).

Of course, if further discoveries of skeletal materials were made in unimpeachable context, or if the context of the original discoveries proved acceptable (Chamberlin 1902:763; Holmes 1902:744), there was still the problem of determining the age of the enclosing deposits. In those pre-Libby days, this was no easy task, for such questions rapidly became entangled in contentious geological disputes. The Lansing and Nebraska specimens, for example, were found in or associated with a formation described as "loess." At Lansing, the human remains were in unstratified debris below "loess" (Winchell 1902:190); at Nebraska, in "original undisturbed loess" (Barbour and Ward 1906b:327). Yet, the various geologists visiting these sites were irreconcilably split over whether these deposits rightly deserved to be designated as "loess" (cf. Chamberlin 1902; Upham 1903; Winchell 1903).

There was also a dispute centered around whether loess was laid down by water or wind. Loess as an "aqueous" deposit was the more traditional view, held by George Frederick Wright (1904, 1905) who again found himself at odds with Chamberlin, McGee, and Salisbury. Each of them had once supported an aqueous origin for loess, but by the early 1900s believed it was aeolian (cf. Chamberlin and Salisbury 1885 vs. Chamberlin and Salisbury 1906:409; also Shimek 1903).

Not surprisingly, proponents of human antiquity maintained that the Lansing and Nebraska skeletons came from true loess, derived from glacial waters—which confirmed its Pleistocene age:

> The finer portion of the drift, swept down from the icefields by the abundant waters of their melting and of rains, was spread on the lower lands and along valleys in front of the departing ice, as the loess of the Missouri.... In or just beneath the basal beds of the Missouri loess was the Lansing fossil man.... (Upham 1902:143).

The loess at Lansing was attributed to the "Iowan" glacial stage (immediately pre-Wisconsin), which implied an age on the order of 12,000 to 35,000 yr B.P. (Upham 1902:147; Upham 1903:33 later bracketed the age to between 12,000 and 15,000 years; see also Winchell 1903:290). The Lansing skeleton was in deposits thought to be "not much older than the loess" (Winchell 1902:190).

Critics would accept none of that, arguing instead that the Lansing deposit was not a true loess, but instead a "secondary deposit, in part, and only in part, derived from loess" (Chamberlin 1902:775; Shimek 1903:358, 1908:244):

> Loess-like silt [that] was probably derived in the main by wash from the loess mantle of the adjacent hills, but in part also by winds from the Missouri bottoms; possibly also brought in by creep (Chamberlin 1902:769).

Not only was the formation not Iowan (Shimek 1903:362), it was doubtful there was *any* true Iowan loess present in the Lansing area (Chamberlin 1902:772; Shimek 1903:364; cf. Wright 1905:237–238). The age of the Lansing skeletons, consequently, was "much short of the close of the glacial invasion" (Chamberlin 1902:773).

The "original undisturbed loess" of the Gilder Mound (Barbour and Ward 1906b:327) was no less disputable. Critics claimed the skeletons were found in a "recently disturbed soil," and "certainly not undisturbed loess" (Shimek 1908:249–250; cf. Gilder 1911:169), but which was underlain by a loess in which only few fragments of human bone were found, and easily explained as intrusive (Shimek 1908:251). Even if those fragments in the true loess were in primary context, there was still no proof that the loess itself was a glacial-age deposit (Shimek 1908:254).

The Lansing and Nebraska specimens were either Pleistocene or Modern, depending on which geologist one chose to follow. Under these circumstances, it comes as no particular surprise that Hrdlička and others sought to bypass the geologists altogether, and infer the age of the specimens directly from their morphology.

The Nebraska specimen was argued to be similar to (though somewhat advanced over) "the Neanderthal type," with skulls possessing "thick protruding brows, low forehead devoid of frontal eminences, narrow temples, thick skull walls, and small brain capacity" (Barbour 1907:346). This was "radically" different from those of the historically known native Americans, more "primitive," and therefore older (Ward 1907:412).

Critics, Hrdlička foremost among them (also Holmes 1902:744), responded that the Nebraska skeletons, and every other find where enough of the bone was preserved for comparison, looked no different from "the average skeleton of the present-day Indian of the Central states" (Hrdlička 1907:49). And yet, were those specimens of the great antiquity claimed, they should be like the "geologically ancient crania of Europe," and show anatomical differences "pronounced enough to be easily apprehended" (Hrdlička 1907:13). It is important to bear in mind that this "acid test" of antiquity (Hooton 1937:112) was based on Hrdlička's belief that *Homo sapiens sapiens* had appeared in the relatively recent past, following a Neanderthal phase. Thus, any purportedly "early" specimen—one belonging to the "Pleistocene and older geological periods" (at least 20,000 years old [Hrdlička 1907:10])—must show "primitive" anatomical features.

In turn, some proponents shifted ground and responded that a modern appearance in geologically ancient skeletons was insignificant, since *Homo sapiens sapiens* appeared at least "100,000 years" ago (Upham 1903:34). Thus, the similarity between ancient and modern only showed that

> the culture and therefore the ancestry, of the historic Indian extend backward far beyond the Wisconsin glacial epoch, and it is not unreasonable to expect to find the skeleton and skull of the Indian, in all important respects, not dissimilar to those of his ancestors (Winchell 1913:174).

Hrdlička's claim of Neanderthals as human ancestors was obviously not shared by many of his peers (Spencer and Smith 1981:436). Even Ernst Hooton, in a book dedicated to Hrdlička, would disagree:

> I cannot admit that a requisite of the geological antiquity of human remains found in the Americas would be an inferior morphological status comparable to that exhibited by Neanderthal man. The fact that human skeletons, supposedly of Pleistocene date, have been invariably those of Indians differing in no significant aspect from recent Indian skeletons does not refute the claims of their antiquity. I should expect a late glacial or third interglacial type of man in America to display "Indian" characteristics (Hooton 1930:351). [Hrdlička's copy of the volume bears no margin notes that register his reaction.]

Other proponents, like Wright, adopted a slightly different tactic. Wright believed that the Pleistocene ended more recently than Upham or Winchell had it, and thus the age of the Lansing and Nebraska material on the order of ten to twelve thousand years old, and so even by Hrdlička's standards their modern appearance was reasonable (Wright 1912:236; see Meltzer 1991). Had Hrdlička used Wright's estimates of Pleistocene chronology (and not the higher ones given in Chamberlin and Salisbury 1906), and had he accepted the geological context of the specimen, then he *might* have been willing to accept these specimens as "Pleistocene" for they would not then fall into his category of "geological antiquity" and hence not require possession of "primitive" traits. But, of course, he did not.

Discussion stalled once again, the victim of irreconcilable theoretical differences over human evolutionary history exacerbated by incompatible scales of relative and absolute chronology—not to mention ambiguity in matters of geology and geological context.

One might also add, parenthetically, that Hrdlička's behavior as recorded by his contemporaries belies the apocryphal tales that now surround his role in this dispute. Henry Ward (1865–1945), who had quite a different interpretation of the Nebraska skeletons, wrote of Hrdlička's (1907) discussion "I feel that your treatment of the subject is very fair, even though your conclusions are apparently radically opposed to those which we advanced" (Ward to Hrdlička, December 10, 1907, AH/NAA).

Achieving Resolution

In late August of 1908, a torrential storm dumped 13 inches of rain over Johnson Mesa, near the town of Folsom, New Mexico (Hillerman 1971:26–27). The subsequent flooding exposed the deeply buried remains of bison in Dead Horse (or Wild Horse) arroyo (Agogino 1971; Hewett 1971). An obscure but remarkable New Mexico ranch foreman by the name of George McJunkin (ca. 1856–1922) spotted the bones, although whether he also found artifacts is unknown (Agogino 1971:42–43).

McJunkin did, however, tell the townspeople of the bones, but only in 1926 would an outsider—Harold J. Cook (1887–1962), rancher and (after 1925) part-time paleontologist for the Denver Museum of Natural History—visit the site (Hewett 1971:23). And only in 1926 would crews from the Denver Museum begin excavations at the site—prompted by the urgings of Folsom locals such as cattle inspector Fred Howarth and blacksmith Carl Schwacheim.

The fieldwork was overseen by the Denver Museum's Director, Jesse Figgins (1867–1944), and he instructed his crew to excavate the bones carefully, to obtain an unbroken skeleton suitable for museum display. Unexpectedly, two projectile points also came out with the bison bones. Unfortunately, the points were not found in situ.

Figgins was well aware of the importance of this discovery (Figgins 1927), and in early 1927 he travelled to Washington, bringing with him the Folsom projectile points. Owing (perhaps) to regular agitating on the part of paleontologist Oliver Hay (1846–1940), Figgins had worked himself into a lather anticipating his reception from Holmes and Hrdlička, who by then were as formidable in demeanor as they were intimidating in appearance. Figgins feared the worst (Figgins to Hay, February 23, 1927, OPH/SIA). But much to his surprise both were quite courteous and pleasant, and Figgins left their meeting with "nothing other than respect for Dr. Hrdlička" (Figgins to Hay, September 29, 1927, OPH/SIA). In fact, Hrdlička's chief statement was of regret that:

> I had not called in scientists from other institutions to study the artifacts in situ, together with all the contributory evidence. That is perfectly reasonable and meets my fullest agreement. Only, as you know, the artifacts had been displaced before they were discovered (Figgins to Hay, September 29, 1927 OPH/SIA).

Hrdlička had given Figgins very good advice (Meltzer 1989). For Figgins himself admitted that:

> I know nothing whatever, about archaeology and allied subjects, and but a smattering of palaeontology and geology; certainly not enough to make my views of value or importance (Figgins to Hay, December 21, 1926, OPH/SIA).

Therefore, when fieldwork in late August 1927 uncovered more points, this time in situ, telegrams were sent to various institutions announcing "another arrowhead found in position with bison remains," and inviting interested parties to examine the finds (J. Figgins to O. Hay, August 30, 1927, OPH/SIA; Meltzer 1983:35).

Frank Roberts (1897–1966) and A.V. Kidder (1885–1963) travelled up from the Pecos Conference near Santa Fe, and were joined by American Museum of Natural History paleontologist Barnum Brown (1873–1963). All agreed that the remarkably fashioned fluted projectile points found embedded in the ribs of the extinct species of bison had entered the formation "at the same time the bones did" (Roberts to Fewkes, September 13, 1927, BAE/NAA). Of that, there was not the slightest doubt (Brown 1928; Kidder 1927).

Demonstrating the contemporaneity of the artifacts and the extinct bison was necessary, if any arguments were to be made about the age of the site. And by virtue of the fact that Folsom was a kill site, where 19 fluted points were found in unimpeachable association with nearly two dozen extinct bison, it was possible for waves of visiting scientist to each witness a point in situ, reinforcing the fact of contemporaneity.

The contemporaneity of the artifacts and the bison, however, was not sufficient evidence of the site's Pleistocene age. That awaited detailed studies by Barnum Brown and the other scientists attracted to the site. Among the most important was Alexander Wetmore, who as Assistant Secretary of the Smithsonian Institution supported fieldwork at Folsom by USGS geologist Kirk Bryan (1888–1951). Together Brown and Bryan confirmed the association of the points with the bison, and inferred an "antiquity as great but not earlier than *late Pleistocene*" (Bryan to Wetmore, August 3, 1928, USNM/SIA; also Brown 1928, 1929). Humans had been in North America since at least the latest Pleistocene.

There was a great sense of "relief" that greeted the Folsom finds (Bryan 1937; Kidder 1936), for the forty years of controversy was settled. And, although nobody had accurately predicted what a Pleistocene human presence would look like, after all that discussion they certainly knew one when they saw it. The rapid acceptance of Folsom, by advocates and skeptics alike, is testimony to that (Meltzer 1991 deals with the spurious claim that Folsom was unacceptable until the advent of radiocarbon dating.)

Recently, Rogers and Martin have wondered why the Lone Wolf Creek site, a Paleoindian bison kill discovered just two years earlier than Folsom, had not been accepted while Folsom was (Rogers and Martin 1986:44, 1987:82). The answer is twofold: Lone Wolf Creek was discovered by Charles N. Vaughan, whom Figgins described as "an ignorant rancher" who had not paid any attention to the bones of associated artifacts at the time of his excavation (Figgins to Hay, December 21, 1926, OPH/SIA). Then there was the matter of the telegrams. Telegrams were sent from Folsom in 1927, but not from Lone Wolf Creek in 1925. Recall why telegrams were sent in 1927.

Hrdlička usually plays the villain in accounts of this dispute (e.g., Alsoszatai-Petheo 1986; Lorenzo 1978; MacNeish 1982), but I think unfairly. I have previously argued he quite knowingly advanced the cause of human antiquity in America by his rigorous standards and his insistence on unimpeachable field evidence (Meltzer 1983:37; also Krieger 1964:25). Now I take great pleasure in the irony that he deserves an even larger share of the credit for Folsom, since it was he who convinced Figgins that the best strategy to resolve the problem was to leave the evidence in place. Hrdlička responded to Figgins not as legend suggests he should have, but as any objective scientist would have. We must shun cardboard stereotypes of Hrdlička, and critics generally, in this dispute.

THE LESSONS OF HISTORY

Buddy, Can You Spare a Paradigm?

There has been much clamoring in recent years for a new "paradigm" in the study of the earliest Americans. One is necessary it is said because the old one blinds us from seeing genuine sites pre-12,000 yr B.P. (Alsoszatai-Petheo 1986:18–20; Bryan 1986:1–5), just as, it is claimed, Holmes and Hrdlička were blind to genuine Pleistocene sites (Alsoszatai-Petheo 1986:18). Only with a new paradigm will we make "real progress" (Alsoszatai-Petheo 1986:23).

In another paper I explore whether this dispute was historically driven by "paradigms" and "paradigm bias" (Meltzer 1991). Let me summarize here the salient points of that discussion. First, while there were conceptual differences between proponents and opponents of deep human antiquity, those occurred at so many levels—institutional, methodological, theoretical—as to defy ready grouping under the simple term "paradigm." George Frederick Wright and John Wesley Powell were more alike than different in their evolutionary theory, for example, and yet from that same theoretical base they came to quite distinct interpretations of American prehistory. There was no single "paradigm" that drove critics (or proponents) to do what they did.

Not only was there no "paradigm," there is no evidence for "paradigm" bias. Among the scores of artifacts or human remains discovered before 1927 for which *explicit* claims were made of Pleistocene antiquity, only one proved to be that old. The remainder were recent. The exception, Lone Wolf Creek, was not rejected because of "paradigm" bias but because the evidence was unreliable. Figgins knew that, which is why he so readily heeded Hrdlička's advice and was so careful at Folsom several years later.

Parenthetically, it is also claimed that 12 Mile Creek (Williston 1902b) and Meserve (Meserve and Barbour 1932), two apparently Late Pleistocene sites, were rejected in the years before Folsom because of "paradigm" bias (Rogers and Martin 1986, 1987). Yet, neither 12 Mile Creek nor Meserve was claimed to be of Pleistocene age at the time of their discovery (Meltzer 1991) and had not been rejected as such. They were just bison kills, whose age was unknown.

One is on equally shaky ground claiming a new "paradigm" is necessary in order to make "real progress." Folsom was not the result of a new "paradigm"; it was confirmed because Figgins sent telegrams, and for the first time legitimate evidence that met longstanding criteria was exposed and viewed by a competent team of elite scientists. Those who would argue a new "paradigm" comes first have it backwards (Grayson 1988:111): only after Folsom was a new paradigm created, which goes some distance toward explaining why, in the following decade, there was a sudden proliferation of Paleoindian site discoveries (Meltzer 1988).

Moreover, history bears witness to the fact that creating a new "paradigm" of expectation based on, at best, doubtful and controversial evidence, can be rather useless. For over 40 years there was a compelling "paradigm" that anticipated what a Pleistocene human occupation had to look like. Operating under this "paradigm" many such occupations were found. But, of course, none of them were what they claimed to be, and when Folsom was discovered it looked nothing what it was supposed to look like although it was still Late Pleistocene in age.

I believe we gain little and risk much by forcing evidence into a new "paradigm" based on our current *speculation* about what the pre-12,000 yr B.P. record *ought* to look like. The chances are very good that our current speculations will prove to be completely wrong.

Folsom was acceptable not because it was predicted (because it wasn't), or because a new "paradigm" had replaced the old (because it hadn't), but simply because the set of fundamental criteria for any ancient human site—explicitly spelled out very early on in the dispute (e.g., Chamberlin 1903)—had finally been met. If there is a pre-12,000 yr B.P. site out there, it can and should meet the same requirements met by Folsom—which brings up the matter of judgement.

Site Visits and Blue-ribbon Panels

Three months after the high drama at Folsom, Hrdlička was asked by Roland Dixon to participate in a symposium on "Early man in America" at the American Anthropological Association that December. Hrdlička had previous plans and could not attend, but he did observe that Folsom highlighted:

> The need of a joint committee ... of representatives of the sciences most closely involved, and commanding some means, which I think, with the help of the National Research Council could be found for this important object. To such a committee would be reported or referred every serious discovery seeming to show ancient man, as soon as possible after the find was made and before the remains were removed from situ. The Committee would then send its representatives to the site and these would investigate the conditions on the spot, to the limit of possibilities.
>
> I believe that in some such way only can we arrive at conclusions that will command the confidence of every worker. Unless something of this nature is done, there will accumulate in the course of time many more or less ambiguous cases and claims, which will impede progress in American anthropology (Hrdlička to Dixon, December 2, 1927, AH/NAA).

Just a few years ago, Haynes made a virtually identical suggestion. As he wrote:

> The implications of Monte Verde for American archaeology are so important that I think a panel of objective conservatives should be formed and funded by NSF to visit the site, examine it, take samples, etc. If a positive consensus results we can then accept the interpretation and formulate new hypotheses for peopling of the New World. If not Monte Verde will have to be relegated to the bin of possible pre-Clovis sites awaiting further data.... (Haynes to Meltzer, September 12, 1986).

I give this quote not to make the claim that Haynes is Hrdlička incarnate (however much that might be believed by some), but to show that in the 1980s, as in the 1920s, two highly esteemed skeptics see site visits as a valuable means of determining the fate of a purportedly ancient site (see also Adovasio et al. 1980:589; Dincauze 1984:295; Haynes 1969:714; Martin 1987:13).

History sends mixed signals on this score. Site visits were common between 1890 and 1927, but not always welcome. As Abbott remarked after everyone had left Trenton in late June 1897:

> I cannot say, looking back on the past four days, that I have enjoyed it. There is too much assumption of extra-carefulness, as they call it, which is simply alot of childish twaddle. They cannot grasp the subject in its entirety and see the facts and their interrelations.... They may all be very eminent men, but it took me a good deal less time

to learn that we had here evidences of man's antiquity; all of which they had been denying for ten years but can't anymore (Abbott to Robins, June 28, 1897, CCA/ANS)

These visits were often exercises in incompatibility (Meltzer 1983, 1985). At Lansing, for example, parties of proponents and skeptics visited the site on August 9 and September 20, 1909, looked at the very same physical evidence, and came away with radically different interpretations.

All the same, they often worked: a Pleistocene age at Trenton, Lansing and Vero could not be proven, and that much was apparent from the site visits. At Folsom, the results were different, and there the site visit was crucial. As Bryan remarked, the Folsom finds were *"discovered"* by Figgins and Cook, but they were *"confirmed* by the masterly excavation of the site by Barnum Brown" (Bryan 1937:139-140).

Site visits led, appropriately, to the rejection of some sites, and the acceptance of others. But is this a viable strategy today? One must be mindful of the fact that site visits in those days were a response to very specific problems: the lack of agreed-upon field techniques, the preponderance of discoveries made by rank amateurs, the necessity of determining the age of a site solely on field evidence. While we still must pay careful attention to context, association, and stratigraphy, the means by which we today ascertain age are far different. With the advent of radiometric methods, age determination takes place in the laboratory, not in the field.

There is an asymmetry here. Site visits can be sufficient to *reject* a claim of great antiquity, but are insufficient to *prove* a case, since that must be accomplished partly in the laboratory where we cannot realistically expect the oversight of a blue-ribbon panel of judges.

There is an added matter: the role of the judges. American archaeology in the late 1920s had far fewer practitioners, and there was a readily identifiable core of elite scientists whose opinions mattered very much. When A.V. Kidder publicly accepted the evidence from Folsom, that had a tremendous impact on the archaeological community. I suspect that today there are few figures whose influence is as far-reaching as Kidder's was in 1927.

Just How Much Can We Learn from Non-archaeological Sources?

In recent years, as in times past, evidence from physical anthropology and linguistics has been brought to bear on the number and timing of migrations to America. The diversity among modern native Americans suggests in rather vague terms a relatively deep antiquity, as Holmes himself admitted:

I have always taken the view that the [prehistoric American] race must have occupied this continent for a very long time. Great antiquity is clearly proved by the facts derived from other than archaeologic or geologic sources. It does not require argument to show that the development of many well differentiated nations and tongues means a prolonged occupation. It does not take argument to demonstrate the proposition that...a thousand distinct cultures could not spring up in a day (Holmes 1898:364)

But how much more precise can we be? Perhaps not that much. The problem is that diversity within our linguistic or physical groupings of modern native Americans is not necessarily a product of long differentiation from a single ancestral group. Such variability could equally result from the amalgamation of a series of distinct migratory groups, and thus, "Until the character of the incoming people with respect to homogeneity is determined, it is practically unavailing to attempt an estimate of the chronologic significance of present similarities and differences" (Holmes 1919:55; also Sapir 1949:454).

What, then, to make of our modern efforts? Some of these models, especially those in which linguistic and physical results converge (e.g., Greenberg et al. 1986:494), are so elegant that many of us would like to believe they are true. But before we succumb to these sirens, we must consider that all of these models are based largely on evidence from modern populations, the ones who succeeded in colonizing the Americas, and not the ones who failed.

Moreover, while these modern groups (Amerind) are assumed to be descendants of a discrete (Clovis?) migration involving a single, genetically and linguistically homogeneous founding population, can we disprove the possibility they are the product of multiple migratory "dribbles" (Hrdlička 1926:9), perhaps dispersed from spatially and temporally distinct sources that were physically or linguistically unrelated (Meltzer 1989)? Both Sapir and Greenberg would suggest not (Greenberg 1987:42; Sapir 1949:454–455). In effect, there is no compelling linguistic evidence, and I believe this holds true of the physical and genetic data as well, to believe that each modern group must represent the descendants of a single migratory pulse (Meltzer 1989:25–26).

If the earliest migration was not a single episode but a multiple series, and if some of those may have failed without issue, this nicely explains why Clovis looks so different from the contemporary Northeast Asian archaeological record, and it has had profound implications for why the pre-12,000 yr B.P. record may not be a pre-Clovis record, why a pre-12,000 yr B.P. presence may be difficult to detect, and why it may look radically different from Clovis if it is (Meltzer 1989).

Meanwhile, we should not saddle ourselves with the belief that there cannot have been more than three separate migrations to America, and that the earliest was necessarily Clovis, merely because that is inferred from linguistic and physical evidence (cf. Ruhlen 1987). Only archaeological data has the answer to when and how often migratory groups came to America, for there is no other means of calibrating rates of linguistic, dental, or genetic change (Turner 1985:8).

Are Old Sites Worth Another Look?

The archaeological acceptance of a pre-12,000 yr B.P. claim has, in the view of some, certain entailments, one of which is that afterward it is worthwhile to reexamine the previously rejected sites to see if any become acceptable. Bryan, for example, has argued that the "acceptance of Monte Verde requires that the evidence from all other sites be examined with a new framework so that the abundantly available evidence can be seen to make sense" (Bryan 1986:5,10). But more than make sense, it should "break the log jam that has held back acceptance of dozens of other sites now floating in the "equivocal" pool" (Bryan 1986:7). This is an argument that also reaches back to the earlier dispute (also Krieger 1964; Nelson 1933:100). In 1927, Pliny Earle Goddard, having read Cook's report on Lone Wolf Creek and believing that it showed "man was here in Pleistocene times," accordingly calibrated some previous finds:

> The petrified human femur, with cuttings on it, taken from the Trenton gravels may now be accepted as of the origin indicated. The Argillite culture described by Skinner and Spier is now referable to the Pleistocene (Goddard 1927:264).

The belief that previously equivocal or rejected sites "cannot all be set aside as insignificant" (Krieger 1964:44) and warrant reexamination stems from the belief that a highly conservative "paradigm" led to the rejection of legitimate evidence of a Pleistocene human occupation (Alsoszatai-Petheo 1986), and that under a new "paradigm" such evidence would be recognized and accepted. I disagree with this argument, for reasons already detailed.

Some 60 years ago Holmes considered this matter, and wrote to Henry Fairfield Osborn that:

> If when fully examined the California evidence seems to favor great antiquity, you may find it advisable some day to send one of your best men down into New Jersey, accompanied by a glacial geologist, to reexamine some of the sites worked by Abbott and others. However, there seems little chance that traces of very early man have been found there or elsewhere in America (Holmes to Osborn, March 28, 1924, WHH/SIA).

No matter how we view the record today, whatever the "paradigm" we bring to the evidence, we cannot change the fact that if a site is not old then it is not old. Spinden was right: "It seems unlikely that the battle can ever be refought" (Spinden 1937:105).

Setting the Odds

From 1890 to 1927, scores of purportedly ancient sites were put forward, and virtually all were rejected. Optimists drew from this the hope that since there were so many different sites believed by so many, then the American Paleolithic must be real (Winchell 1913:175). Pessimistic critics, naturally, carped that since so many sites had failed to be as old as advertised, then there probably was no Pleistocene human occupation of the Americas. In 1927 Folsom proved that both of those conclusions were wrong.

Today, optimists and pessimists still draw these judgements (e.g., Alsoszatai-Petheo 1986; Carter 1980:235; Martin 1987:13), yet both are logically unsupportable, and may still be proven wrong. However many purported pre-12,000 yr B.P. sites we have, they cannot be the basis for setting odds that the likelihood the first Americans arrived before 12,000 yr B.P. is high or low (Meltzer 1989:31). They provide no more than an incentive to search, and a warrant for skepticism.

The final lesson, then, is that whether people were or were not here more 12,000 years ago is wholly independent of what we may currently think about the archaeological record. No amount of weak evidence can prove—or disprove—the case for a pre-12,000 yr B.P. human occupation in America.

Hrdlička well understood this. After observing that no evidence to date had been found of "human bones of undisputed geological antiquity," he closed his 1907 monograph with the remark that "this must not be regarded as equivalent to a declaration that there was no early man in this country" (Hrdlička 1907:98).

ACKNOWLEDGMENTS

I would like to thank Rob Bonnichsen for his kind invitation to participate in the 1989 World Summit Conference in Orono, at which this paper was given. It was a memorable occasion. Site visits, as I just argued, may not work very well in resolving today's controversy over human antiquity in the Americas, but it sure was useful, educational, and a helluva lot of fun to get all the site proponents and skeptics together on one campus to hash over data and differences.

After writing this chapter, I undertook extensive archival and historical research on the pre-Folsom human antiquity controversy. The results were too many to try incorporating here, so I didn't. They will appear in a book, now in preparation. Thus, the chapter as it stands here reflects my thinking on the subject in the spring of 1989. Caveat emptor.

A NOTE ON ARCHIVAL SOURCES

Unpublished archival materials were cited in this chapter using the following abbreviations:

AH/NAA	Aleš Hrdlička papers, National Anthropological Archives, Washington, D.C.
BAE/NAA	Bureau of American Ethnology papers, National Anthropological Archives, Washington, D.C.
CCA/ANS	Charles Conrad Abbott, Abbott-Robins Correspondence, Academy of Natural Sciences, Philadelphia, PA.
FB/APS	Franz Boas papers, American Philosophical Society, Philadelphia, PA.
OPH/SIA	Oliver P. Hay papers, Smithsonian Institution Archives, Washington, D.C.
PMP/HU	Peabody Museum papers, Harvard University Library, Cambridge, MA.
USNM/SIA	United States National Museum, Administrative Files, Smithsonian Institution Archives, Washington, D.C.
WHH/RR	William Henry Holmes, *Random Records of a Lifetime*, National Anthropological Archives, Washington, D.C.
WHH/SIA	William Henry Holmes papers, Smithsonian Institution Archives, Washington, D.C.
WJM/LC	WJ McGee papers, Library of Congress, Washington, D.C.

REFERENCES CITED

Abbott, C. C.
   1872 The Stone Age in New Jersey. *American Naturalist* 6:144–160, 199–229.
   1873 Occurrence of Implements in the River Drift of Trenton, New Jersey. *American Naturalist* 7:204–209.
   1876 Indications of the Antiquity of the Indians of North America, Derived from a Study of Their Relics. *American Naturalist* 10:65–72.
   1877 On the Discovery of Supposed Paleolithic Implements from the Glacial Drift in the Valley of the Delaware River, Near Trenton, New Jersey. *Peabody Museum Annual Report* 10:30–43. Cambridge, MA.
   1878 Second Report on the Paleolithic Implements from the Glacial Drift in the Valley of the Delaware River, Near Trenton, New Jersey. *Peabody Museum Annual Report* 11:225–257. Cambridge, MA.
   1881a Historical Sketch of Their Discovery. *Proceedings of the Boston Society of Natural History* 21:124–132. Boston.
   1881b *Primitive Industry*. G. Bates, Salem, MA.
   1883 Evidences of Glacial Man. *Science* 2:437–438.
   1890 Report of the Curator of the Museum of American Archaeology, University of Pennsylvania. *Annual Report* 1:1–54.
   1892a Paleolithic Man in America. *Science* 20:270–271.
   1892b Paleolithic Man: A Last Word. *Science* 20:344–345.
   1893a Are There Relics of Man in the Trenton Gravels? *The Archaeologist* 1:81–82.
   1893b The So-called "Cache Implements." *Science* 21:122–123.

Adovasio, J., J. Gunn, J. Donahue, R. Stuckenrath, J. E. Guilday, and K. Volman
   1980 Yes Virginia, It Really Is That Old: A Reply to Haynes and Mead. *American Antiquity* 45:588–595.

Agogino, G.
   1971 The McJunkin Controversy. *New Mexico Magazine* 49(5-6):41–47.

Alsoszatai-Petheo, J.
   1986 An Alternative Paradigm for the Study of Early Man in the New World. In *New Evidence for the Pleistocene Peopling of the Americas*, edited by A. Bryan, pp. 15–23. Center for the Study of Early Man, University of Maine, Orono.

Anonymous
   1889 Review of *The Ice Age in North America and Its Bearing upon the Antiquity of Man*, by G. F. Wright. *American Journal of Science* 38:412–413.

Babbitt, F.
   1883 Vestiges of Glacial Man in Central Minnesota. *Science* 2:369–370.
   1884 Vestiges of Glacial Man in Central Minnesota. *Proceedings American Association Advancement Science* 32:385–390.

Baldwin, C. C.
   1893 Review extraordinary of *Man and the Glacial Period* by a member of the United States Geological Survey, with annotations and remarks thereon. Privately printed.

Barbour, E.
   1907 Evidence of Loess Man in Nebraska. *Nebraska Geological Survey* 2 (6):331–346.

Barbour, E., and H. Ward
   1906a Discovery of an Early Type Man in Nebraska. *Science* 24:628–629.

1906b Preliminary Report on the Primitive Man of Nebraska. *Nebraska Geological Survey* 2(5):219–237.

Brinton, D.
1892a Relics of Glacial Man. *Science* 19:317.
1892b Review of "Man and the Glacial Period." *Science* 20:249.

Brown, B.
1928 Recent Finds Relating to Prehistoric Man in America. Discussion of *The Origin and Antiquity of Man in America*, by A. Hrdlička. *New York Academy of Medicine Bulletin* 4(7):824–828.
1929 Folsom Culture and Its Age. With Discussion by K. Bryan. *Geological Society of America Bulletin* 40:128–129.

Bryan, A.
1986 Paleoamerican Prehistory as Seen from South America. In *New Evidence for the Pleistocene Peopling of the Americas*, edited by A. Bryan, pp. 1–14. Center for the Study of Early Man, University of Maine, Orono.

Bryan, K.
1937 Geology of the Folsom Deposits in New Mexico and Colorado. In *Early Man*, edited by G. G. MacCurdy, pp. 139–152. Lippincott, Pennsylvania.

Carter, G.
1980 *Earlier Than You Think*. Texas A&M University Press, College Station.

Chamberlin, T. C.
1890 Introduction. In *The Glacial Boundary in Western Pennsylvania, Ohio, Kentucky, Indiana and Illinois*, by G. F. Wright. *USGS Bulletin* 58:13–38.
1892 Geology and Archaeology Mistaught. *The Dial* 13:303–306.
1893 Professor Wright and the Geological Survey. *The Dial* 14:7–9.
1902 The Geologic Relations of the Human Relics of Lansing, Kansas. *Journal of Geology* 10:745–779.
1903 The Criteria Requisite for the Reference of Relics to a Glacial Age. *Journal of Geology* 11:64–85.
1919 Investigation Versus Propagandism. *Journal of Geology* 27:305–338.

Chamberlin, T. C., and R. D. Salisbury
1885 Preliminary Report on the Driftless Area of the Upper Mississippi Valley. *USGS Annual Report* 6:199–322.
1906 *Geology*. 3 vols. Henry Holt and Company, New York.

Claypole, E.
1893a Preglacial Man not Improbable. *American Geologist* 11:191–194.
1893b Professor G. F. Wright and His Critics. *Popular Science Monthly* 42:764–781.
1893c Major Powell on "Are There Evidences of Man in the Glacial Gravels?" *Popular Science Monthly* 43:696–699.

Cope, E. D.
1893 Wright's Man and the Glacial Period. *American Naturalist* 27:550–553.

Cresson, H. T.
1889a Early Man in the Delaware Valley. *Proceedings of the Boston Society of Natural History* 24:141–150. Boston.
1889b Remarks on a Chipped Implement, Found in Modified Drift, on the East Fork of the White River, Jackson County, Indiana. *Proceedings of the Boston Society of Natural History* 24:150–152. Boston.

Dawkins, W. B.
1883 Early Man in America. *North American Review* 137:338–349.

Dincauze, D.
1984 An Archaeological Evaluation of the Case for Pre-Clovis Occupations. In *Advances in World Archaeology*, vol. 3, edited by F. Wendorf and A. Close, pp. 275–323. Academic Press, New York.

Evans, J.
1872 *The Ancient Stone Implements, Weapons and Ornaments of Great Britain*. Appleton, New York.

Figgins, J. D.
1927 The Antiquity of Man in America. *Natural History* 27:229–239.

Fowke, G.
1902 *Archaeological History of Ohio*. Ohio State Archaeological and Historical Society, Columbus.

Gilder, R.
1911 Scientific "Inaccuracies" in Reports Against Probability of Geological Antiquity of Remains of Nebraska Loess Man Considered by its Discoverer. *Recent Past* 10:157–169.

Goddard, P. E.
1927 Facts and Theories Concerning Pleistocene Man in America. *American Anthropologist* 29:262–266.

Gossip, W.
1869 On the Antiquity of Man in America. *Transactions of the Nova Scotia Institute of Natural Science* III:35–78.

Gould, S. J.
   1987 *Time's Arrow, Time's Cycle. Myth and Metaphor in the Discovery of Geological Time.* Harvard University Press, Cambridge.

Grayson, D. K.
   1983 *The Establishment of Human Antiquity.* Academic Press, New York.
   1988 Perspectives on the Archaeology of the First Americans. In *Americans Before Columbus: Ice Age Origins*, edited by R. Carlisle. Ethnology Monographs 12:107–123.

Greenberg, J. H.
   1987 *Language in the Americas.* Stanford University Press, Stanford.

Greenberg, J. H., C. Turner, and S. Zegura
   1986 The Settlement of the Americas: A Comparison of the Linguistic, Dental, and Genetic Evidence. *Current Anthropology* 27:477–497.

Gruber, J.
   1965 Brixham Cave and the Antiquity of Man. In *Context and Meaning in Cultural Anthropology*, edited by M. Spiro, pp. 373–402. Free Press, New York.

Hallowell, A. I.
   1960 The Beginnings of Anthropology in America. In *Selected Papers from the American Anthropologist, 1888–1920*, edited by F. de Laguna, pp. 1–90. American Anthropological Association, Washington, D.C.

Haven, S.
   1856 The Archaeology of the United States. *Smithsonian Contributions to Knowledge* 8:1–168.

Haynes, C. V.
   1969 The Earliest Americans. *Science* 166:709–715.

Haynes, H. W.
   1881 Their Comparison with Paleolithic Implements from Europe. *Proceedings Boston Society of Natural History* 21:132–137. Boston.
   1882 Some Indications of an Early Race of Men in New England. *Proceedings Boston Society of Natural History* 21:382–390. Boston.
   1893a Palaeolithic Man in North America. *Science* 21:66–67.
   1893b The Paleolithic Man Once More. *Science* 21:208–209.
   1893c The Paleolithic Man in Ohio. *Science* 21:291.
   1893d Early Man in Minnesota. *Science* 21:318–319.

Hewett, J.
   1971 The Bookish Black at Wild Horse Arroyo. How the Folsom Man Came to Light. *New Mexico Magazine* 49(1–2):20–24.

Hillerman, T.
   1971 Or: How Folsom Was Saved to History. *New Mexico Magazine* 49 (1–2):25–27.

Hinsley, C. M.
   1981 *Savages and Scientists: The Smithsonian Institution and the Development of American Anthropology, 1846–1910.* Smithsonian Institution Press.
   1985 From Shell-Heaps to Stellae. Early Anthropology at the Peabody Museum. *History of Anthropology* 3:49–74.

Hoffman, W. J.
   1879 The Discovery of "Turtle-back" Celts in the District of Columbia. *American Naturalist* 13:109–115.

Holmes, W. H.
   1890 A Quarry Workshop of the Flaked Stone Implement Makers in the District of Columbia. *American Anthropologist* 3:1–26.
   1892 Modern Quarry Refuse and the Palaeolithic Theory. *Science* 20:295–297.
   1893a Distribution of Stone Implements in the Tidewater Country. *American Anthropologist* 6:1–14.
   1893b Are There Traces of Man in the Trenton Gravels? *Journal of Geology* 1:15–37.
   1893c Gravel Man and Palaeolithic Culture: A Preliminary Word. *Science* 21:29–30.
   1893d Traces of Glacial Man in Ohio. *Journal of Geology* 1:147–163.
   1893e A Question of Evidence. *Science* 21:135–136.
   1893f Vestiges of Early Man in Minnesota. *American Geologist* 11:219–240.
   1894 A Natural History of Flaked Stone Implements. In *Memoirs of the International Congress of Anthropology*, edited by C. Wake, pp. 120–139. Chicago.
   1897 Stone Implements of the Potomac-Chesapeake Tidewater Province. *BAE Annual Report* 15:3–152.
   1898 Primitive Man in the Delaware Valley. *Proceedings of the American Association Advancement Science* 46:364–370.
   1902 Fossil Human Remains Found Near Lansing, Kansas. *American Anthropologist* 4:743–752.
   1919 Handbook of Aboriginal American Antiquities. Part I. *BAE Bulletin* 60.

Hooton, E.
   1930 *Indians of Pecos Pueblo.* Yale University Press, New Haven.
   1937 *Apes, Men and Morons.* G. P. Putnam's, New York.

Hrdlička, A.
1907 Skeletal Remains Suggesting or Attributed to Early Man in North America. *BAE Bulletin* 33.

1912a Early Man in South America. (In collaboration with W. Holmes, B. Willis, F. Wright and C. Fenner.) *BAE Bulletin* 52.

1912b Early Man in America. *American Journal Science* 34:543–554.

1917 Preliminary Report on Finds of Supposedly Ancient Human Remains at Vero, Florida. *Journal of Geology* 43–51.

1918 Recent Discoveries Attributed to Early Man in America. *BAE Bulletin* 66.

1926 The Race and Antiquity of the American Indian. *Scientific American* 135:7–9.

Jarcho, S.
1959 Origin of the American Indian as Suggested by Fray Joseph de Acosta. *ISIS* 50:430–438.

Jefferson, T.
1975 Notes on the State of Virginia (original 1787). In *The Portable Thomas Jefferson*, edited by M. Peterson, pp. 23–232. Penguin Books, New York.

Kidder, A. V.
1927 Early Man in America. *The Masterkey* 1(5):5–13.

1936 Speculations on New World Prehistory. In *Essays in Anthropology*, edited by R. Lowie, pp. 143–151. University of California Press, Berkeley.

Krieger, A.
1964 Early Man in the New World. In *Prehistoric Man in the New World*, edited by J. Jennings and E. Norbeck, pp. 23–81. University of Chicago Press, Chicago.

Lewis, H. C.
1880 The Trenton Gravel and Its Relation to the Antiquity of Man. *Proceedings of the Academy of Natural Sciences of Philadelphia* 32:296–309.

1884 The Terminal Moraine of Pennsylvania. *Second Geology Survey of Pennsylvania* Report Z.

Loomis, F. B.
1924 Artifacts Associated with the Remains of a Columbian Elephant at Melbourne, Florida. *American Journal of Science* 8:503–508.

1925 The Florida Man. *Science* 62:436.

Lorenzo, J.
1978 Early Man Research in the American Hemisphere: Appraisal and Perspectives. In *Early Man in America*, edited by A. L. Bryan, pp. 1–9. Archaeological Researches International, Edmonton.

McGee, WJ
1887 On the Finding of a Spear Head in the Quaternary Beds of Nevada. *Scientific American Supplement* 23:9221–9222.

1888a Three Formations in the Middle Atlantic Slope. *American Journal of Science* 35:120–143, 328–330, 367–387, 448–466.

1888b Paleolithic Man in America: His Antiquity and His Environment. *Popular Science Monthly* 34:20–36.

1889 The Geologic Antecedents of Man in the Potomac Valley. *American Anthropologist* 2:227–234.

1891 Some Principles of Evidence Relating to the Antiquity of Man. *American Antiquity* 13:69–79.

1892 Man and the Glacial Period. (Letters to the Editor) *Science* 20:317.

1893a Man and the Glacial Period. *American Anthropologist* 6:85–95.

1893b A Geologic Palimpsest. *Literary Northwest* 2:274–276.

McGee, WJ, and C. Thomas
1905 *Prehistoric North America*. G. Barrie and Sons, Philadelphia.

MacNeish, R.
1982 A Late Commentary on an Early Subject. In *Peopling of the New World*, edited by J. Ericson, R. Taylor and R. Berger, pp. 311–315. Ballena Press, Los Altos, California.

Martin, P.
1987 Clovisia the Beautiful. *Natural History* 96(10):10–13.

Meltzer, D.
1983 The Antiquity of Man and the Development of American Archaeology. *Advances in Archaeological Method and Theory* 6:1–51.

1985 North American Archaeology and Archaeologists. *American Antiquity* 50:249–260.

1988 Late Pleistocene Human Adaptations in Eastern North America. *Journal of World Prehistory* 2:1–52.

1989 Why Don't We Know When the First People Came to North America? *American Antiquity* 54(3).

1991 On "Paradigms" and "Paradigm Bias" in Controversies over Human Antiquity in America. In *The First Americans: Search and Research*, edited by T. D. Dillehay and D. J. Meltzer, pp. 13–49. CRC Press, Boca Raton, FLA.

Meserve, F. and E. Barbour
 1932 Association of an Arrow Point with *Bison occidentalis* in Nebraska. *The Nebraska State Museum Bulletin* 27:239–242.

Mills, W. C.
 1890 Account of Discovery. In *Discovery of a Paleolithic Implement at New Comerstown, Ohio*, by W. C. Mills and G. F. Wright, pp. 3–4. Western Reserve Historical Society Tract 75.

Morison, W.
 1971 George Frederick Wright: In Defense of Darwinism and Fundamentalism, 1838–1921. Unpublished Ph.D. dissertation, Department of History, Vanderbilt University.

Nelson, N. C.
 1933 The Antiquity of Man in America in the Light of Archaeology. In *The American Aborigines: Their Origin and Antiquity*, pp. 87–130. University of Toronto Press, Toronto.

Powell, J. W.
 1890 Prehistoric Man in America. *The Forum* 8:489–503.
 1893 Are There Evidences of Man in the Glacial Gravels? *Popular Science Monthly* 43:316–326.

Proudfit, S. V.
 1889 Ancient Village Sites and Aboriginal Workshops in the District of Columbia. *American Anthropologist* 2:241–246.

Putnam, F. W.
 1881 Concluding Remarks. *Proceedings of the Boston Society of Natural History* 21:147–149. Boston.
 1888a Untitled Remarks on Madisonville Paleolith. *Proceedings of the Boston Society of Natural History* 23:242. Boston.
 1888b Comparison of Paleolithic Implements. *Proceedings of the Boston Society of Natural History* 23:421–424. Boston.
 1889 Discussion of *The Aborigines of the District of Columbia and the Lower Potomac*. *American Anthropologist* 2:266–268.
 1890 Prehistoric Remains in the Ohio Valley. *The Century Magazine* 39:698–703.

Rogers, R., and L. Martin
 1986 Replication and the History of Paleoindian Studies. *Current Research in the Pleistocene* 3:43–44.
 1987 The Folsom Discovery and the Concept of Breakthrough Sites in Paleoindian Studies. *Current Research in the Pleistocene* 4:81–82.

Ruhlen, M.
 1987 Voices from the Past. *Natural History* 96(3):6–10.

Salisbury, R.
 1892 Review of Wright's *Man and the Glacial Period* by G. F. Wright. *The Nation* 55:496–497.
 1893 Man and the Glacial Period. *American Geologist* 11:13–20.

Sapir, E.
 1949 Time Perspective in Aboriginal American Culture: A Study in Method. In *Selected Writings of Edward Sapir in Language, Culture and Personality*, edited by D. Mandlebaum, pp. 389–462. (Originally published 1916) University of California Press, Berkeley.

Sellards, E. H.
 1916a Discovery of Fossil Human Remains in Florida in Association with Extinct Vertebrates. *American Journal Science* 42:1–18.
 1916b Human Remains from the Pleistocene of Florida. *Science* 44:615–617.
 1916c Human Remains and Associated Fossils from the Pleistocene of Florida. *Annual Report of the Florida Geological Survey* 8:122–160.

Shaler, N.
 1889 The Geology of Nantucket. *USGS Bulletin* 53.

Shimek, B.
 1903 The Loess and the Lansing Man. *American Geologist* 32:353–369.
 1908 Nebraska 'Loess' Man. *Bulletin Geological Society of America* 19:243–254.

Spencer, F., and F. Smith
 1981 The Significance of Ales Hrdlička's "Neanderthal Phase of Man": A Historical and Current Assessment. *American Journal of Physical Anthropology* 56:435–459.

Spinden, H.
 1937 First Peopling of America as a Chronological Problem. In *Early Man*, edited by G. G. MacCurdy, pp. 105–114. Lippincott, Pennsylvania.

Steward, J.
 1973 *Alfred Kroeber*. Columbia University Press, New York.

Thomas, C.
 1898 *Introduction to the Study of North American Archaeology*. Robert Clarke, Cincinatti.

Turner, C.
 1985 The Modern Human Dispersal Event: The Eastern Frontier. *The Quarterly Review of Archaeology* 6:8–9, 13.

Upham, W.
 1888 The Recession of the Ice-sheet in Minnesota in Its Relation to the Gravel Deposits Overlying

the Quartz Implements Found by Miss Babbitt at Little Falls, Minnesota. *Proceedings of the Boston Society of Natural History* 23:436–447. Boston.

1889 Review of *The Ice Age in North America and Its Bearing Upon the Antiquity of Man*, by G. F. Wright. *Popular Science Monthly* 35:557.

1902 Man and the Ice Age at Lansing, Kansas and Little Falls, Minnesota. *American Geologist* 30:135–150.

1903 Valley Loess and the Fossil Man of Lansing, Kansas. *American Geologist* 31:25–34.

Volk, E.
1911 *The Archaeology of the Delaware Valley*. Papers of the Peabody Museum No. 5. Cambridge, MA.

Wadsworth, M.
1881 On the Lithological Character of the Implements. *Proceedings Boston Society of Natural History* 21:146–147.

Wallace, A. R.
1887 The Antiquity of Man in North America. *Nineteenth Century* 22:667–679.

Ward, H.
1907 Peculiarities of the "Nebraska Man." *Putnam's Magazine* January pp. 410–413.

Wauchope, R.
1962 *Lost Tribes and Sunken Continents. Myth and Method in the Study of the American Indians*. The University of Chicago Press, Chicago.

Whittlesey, C.
1869 On the Evidences of the Antiquity of Man in the United States. *Proceedings of the American Association for the Advancement of Science* 16:268–288.

Williston, S.
1902a A Fossil Man from Kansas. *Science* 16:195–196.
1902b An Arrow-Head Found with the Bones of *Bison occidentalis*, Lucas, in Western Kansas. *American Geologist* 30:313–315.

Wilson, T.
1897 The Antiquity of the Red Race in America. *The United States National Museum Annual Report* 1895:1039–1045.

1889 The Paleolithic Period in the District of Columbia. *American Anthropologist* 2:235–241.

1890 Results of an Inquiry as to the Existence of Man in North America During the Paleolithic Period. *United States National Museum Annual Report* 1888:677–702.

Winchell, N.
1889 Review of *The Ice Age in North America and Its Bearing Upon the Antiquity of Man*, by G. F. Wright. *American Geologist* 2:51–54.

1892 Review of *Man and the Glacial Period*, by G. F. Wright. *American Geologist* 10:387–389.

1902 The Lansing Skeleton. *American Geologist* 30:189–194.

1903 The Pleistocene Geology of the Concannon Farm Near Lansing, Kansas. *American Geologist* 31:263–308.

1913 *The Weathering of Aboriginal Stone Artifacts*. Minnesota Historical Society Collections No. 16.

Wright, G. F.
1881a On the Age of the Trenton Gravel. *Proceedings of the Boston Society of Natural History* 21:137–145. Boston.

1881b An Attempt to Calculate Approximately the Date of the Glacial Era in North America. *American Journal of Science* 21:120–123.

1883 Glacial Phenomena in Ohio. *Science* 1:269–271.

1885 The Niagara Gorge as a Chronometer. *Science* 5:399–401.

1889a *The Ice Age in North America and Its Bearing Upon the Antiquity of Man*. D. Appleton, New York.

1889b The Age of the Philadelphia Red Gravel. *Proceedings of the Boston Society of Natural History* 24:152–157. Boston.

1890a The Glacial Boundary in Western Pennsylvania, Ohio, Kentucky, Indiana and Illinois. *USGS Bulletin* 58:39–100.

1890b Report. In *Discovery of a Paleolithic Implement at New Comerstown, Ohio*, by W. C. Mills and G. F. Wright, pp. 5–14. Western Reserve Historical Society Tract No. 75. Cleveland.

1892 *Man and the Glacial Period*. D. Appleton, New York.

1893a Some of Professor Salisbury's Criticisms on *Man and the Glacial Period*. *American Geologist* 11:121–126.

1893b Some Detailed Evidence of an Ice-Age Man in Eastern America. *Science* 21:65–66.

1893c Evidences of Glacial Man in Ohio. *Popular Science Monthly* 43:29–39.

1893d Mr. Holmes's Criticisms Upon the Evidence of Glacial Man. *Science* 21:267–268.

1904 Evidence of the Agency of Water in Distributing the Loess in the Mississippi Valley. *American Geologist* 33:205–222.

1905 Professor Shimek's Criticism of the Aqueous Origin of Loess. *American Geologist* 35:236–240.

1912 *Origin and Antiquity of Man*. Bibliotheca Sacra, Oberlin.

Youmans, W. J.
  1892 Review of *Man and the Glacial Period*, by G. F. Wright. *Popular Science Monthly* 42:258–262.
  1893a The Insolence of Office. *Popular Science Monthly* 42:841–842.
  1893b The Attack on Professor Wright. *Popular Science Monthly* 43:412–413.

Radiocarbon Dating of Bone Using Accelerator Mass Spectrometry: Current Discussions and Future Directions

R. E. TAYLOR
Radiocarbon Laboratory
Department of Anthropology
Institute of Geophysics and Planetary Physics
University of California, Riverside
Riverside, California

More than a decade of operational experience with accelerator (or atomic) mass spectrometry (AMS) as applied to the measurement of ^{14}C has demonstrated its ability to achieve two of the three capabilities initially proposed as possible with this technology: first, reduction by several orders of magnitude in sample size requirements; and second, similar reductions in counting times from that previously required with conventional decay counting. The third initially projected capability—a significant increase in ^{14}C time range—has not been demonstrated, primarily due to the inability of current techniques used to produce graphitic solids currently required in the ion sources of most AMS systems to produce sample background blanks with equivalent ages exceeding about 50,000 years. The further development of various sample pretreatment strategies combined with improvements in AMS ion source technology may, in the future, reduce background attributable to sample pretreatment and measurement techniques and further extend the ^{14}C dating range.

Current AMS technology now permits the ^{14}C dating of a range of molecular fractions isolated from fossil bone. Data obtained from AMS-based studies indicate that although accurate ^{14}C age estimates can generally be obtained on bone samples retaining significant amounts of intact collagen, in cases where bones are seriously depleted in their original protein (mostly collagen) content, seriously anomalous ^{14}C values can be obtained. Current efforts to address this problem include investigations aimed at determining if noncollagen proteins of bone such as osteocalcin will retain isotopic integrity in collagen-depleted bone samples.

INTRODUCTION

One of the best-known, most bitter, and long-standing debates in American archaeology concerns the nature and timing of the peopling of the Western Hemisphere (Wilmsen 1965). Historically, this debate has centered on two issues: (1) the scientific validity of data offered as evidence for human presence; and (2) the accuracy of the age estimates associated with this data. More recently, discussions have centered on the validity of purported Paleoindian materials with ages in excess of the well-documented Clovis period occupation of North America (Dincauze 1984; Irving 1985; Owen 1984; Payen 1982; Stanford 1982; Taylor 1991; Taylor and Payen 1979). It is generally accepted that debates concerning the validity of dating frameworks associated with Paleoindian materials—and, particularly, purported pre-Clovis materials—were substantively transformed with the introduction of the ^{14}C method some four decades ago. For most investigators, the ^{14}C method acquired the status as the final arbiter of the accuracy of chronological inferences for materials associated with actual or purported Paleoindian contexts (Bonnichsen et al. 1987). However, there was the recognition that there was some variability in the validity of ^{14}C-inferred ages depending on the type of sample material employed. One of the suspected sample types was bone.

This chapter will provide a brief overview of the current issues and problems of obtaining accurate ^{14}C determinations on bone in the context of the development over the last decade of ^{14}C measurements by accelerator (or atomic) mass spectrometry (AMS). The purpose of this discussion is to clarify some possible misconceptions concerning the validity of ^{14}C determinations on bone and the role of AMS technology in these studies. The immediate context of this review is the question of the validity of ^{14}C age determinations on human bone samples—specifically human skeletal samples from New World archaeological contexts of purported late Pleistocene age. The overall context of accuracy and precision of ^{14}C values along with a history of work on the ^{14}C dating of bone will be briefly reviewed, in order to put in context why bone began as a suspected sample type and review the role of AMS technology in studies concerned with the ^{14}C dating of bone over the last decade.

ACCURACY AND PRECISION OF RADIOCARBON VALUES

A comprehensive listing of the factors influencing accuracy and precision of ^{14}C-based age inferences in general would include: (1) *sample provenance factors*, the degree to which the sample on which the ^{14}C determination has been obtained can be unambiguously associated with the event for which temporal placement is being sought; (2) *sample composition factors*, primarily relating to contamination and fractionation effects; (3) *experimental factors*, which include constraints imposed by the nature of means by which natural ^{14}C concentrations are measured, along with the implications of the statistical nature of ^{14}C counting data; and finally, (4) *systemic factors* involving such considerations as reservoir and secular variation effects (Taylor 1987b:105–146). A critical analysis of a set of ^{14}C determinations involves attention to how these factors— separately and in combination—might influence a given ^{14}C value and how correction and calibration procedures might appropriately be applied.

Table 1 presents a listing of some of the major causes of anomalous age estimates associated with the presentation of ^{14}C evidence, divided into factors that would cause "younger than expected" and "older than expected" ^{14}C age determinations. While obviously not exhaustive, these factors probably explain a significant percentage of problematical ^{14}C data. Heading both lists are problems with either misinterpretation of sample context and/or unidentified disturbance of depositional conditions. A second set of causes involves insufficient laboratory sample pretreatment efforts. A third grouping would involve reporting errors (e.g., mislabelled samples in the field or laboratory). It appears that relatively few seriously erroneous ^{14}C values can be traced to analytical or instrumental errors, i.e., errors in the actual measurement of the ^{14}C content of a sample in the laboratory.

It is the view of the writer that the most frequent cause of anomalous ^{14}C values is a misassociation or misidentification of sample material with archaeological and/or geological context. This explanation is particularly relevant as a generalization about the corpus of ^{14}C age estimates associated with the prehistory of the Western Hemisphere and particularly ^{14}C values associated with actual or purported Paleoindian sites. The basic issue was framed in simple and straightforward terms more than two decades ago by Frederick Johnson (1965:776) when he suggested that a ^{14}C age estimate "does not date a site . . . or a grave or a level. The date is that of the sample and it is the task of the archaeologist to discover the true relationship between the sample and the area or place it came from."

This problem is exemplified in the first ^{14}C age determination on charcoal from the Folsom site. The first printed listing of ^{14}C values issued by the Chicago laboratory included a sample (C-377) described as charcoal from a fire pit at the Folsom site, New Mexico, located *below* bison bones and artifacts collected by H. J. Cook in 1933. The ^{14}C age of this sample, based on an average of two analysis, was 4283 ± 250 yr B.P. This result generated the comment "surprisingly young" (Arnold and Libby 1950:10). Cook revisited the Folsom site in June 1950 and determined that the "sample had been taken from a hearth in the fill of a secondary channel which

Table 1. Major Sources of Apparently Anomalous ^{14}C Values for Typical Archaeological Contexts (Taken from Taylor 1987b:107).

I. Apparent Age Significantly Younger Than Expected
1. Misidentification of sample with stratigraphic level or purported context.
2. Reworked or eroded deposits, mixing of deposits by bioturbation or geoturbation.
3. Insufficient removal of rootlets (from charcoal and bone).
4. Insufficient removal of organic decay products (humics) from stratigraphically higher levels.
5. Inappropriate application of reservoir correction values.
6. Careless sample storage or inappropriate sample containers (paper bags, cloth bags, cardboard boxes).
7. Unreported application of preservative produced from modern carbon source.
8. Mislabeled samples in field or in laboratory.

II. Apparent Age Significantly Older Than Expected
1. Misidentification of sample with stratigraphic level or purported context.
2. Reworked or eroded deposits, mixing of deposits by bioturbation or geoturbation.
3. Insufficient removal of rootlets (from charcoal and bone).
4. Insufficient removal of organic decay products (humics) from older deposits.
5. Insufficient removal of groundwater carbonates.
6. Inappropriate application of reservoir correction values.
7. Unreported application of preservative produced from fossil carbon source.
8. Mislabeled samples in field or in laboratory.

had cut through the original deposit of bison bone and artifacts" (Roberts 1951:116).

In the first formal publication of the results (Arnold and Libby 1951:116), C-377 was listed as "charcoal from a hearth in secondary channel of later date than bison and artifact deposit." A ^{14}C date of 9883 ± 350 yr B.P. (C-558) was subsequently obtained on burned bison (*Bison antiquus*) bone from what was interpreted as the Folsom horizon at Lubbock Lake, Texas (Libby 1952:293). This value, according to Roberts, "more closely approximates the magnitude estimated for Folsom on geologic evidence" (Roberts 1951:20–21; cf. Haynes 1982:384). In the 1980s, geological evidence combined with additional ^{14}C determinations led to the suggestion that the burned bone sample used for C-558 did not, in fact, come from the Folsom levels at the Lubbock Lake site (Holliday and Johnson 1986; cf. Haas et al. 1986). If this is correct, the first ^{14}C age determination actually associated with Folsom materials was obtained on charcoal (I-141, 10,780 ± 375 ^{14}C yr B.P.) collected at Lindenmeier (Haynes and Agogino 1960).

Table 2 contrasts the "essential certainty" of association of sample with archaeological context accomplished by the use of human bone with the lower levels of confidence associated with other sample materials. When ^{14}C age determinations are obtained directly on a bone sample clearly identified on widely-accepted morphological criteria as being genus *Homo*, any question of human involvement or instrumentality is, by definition, rendered moot and one can evaluate the accuracy of a ^{14}C date on physiochemical grounds alone.

RADIOCARBON DATING OF BONE

From the very inception of ^{14}C studies, essentially on the basis of *a priori* considerations, bone acquired a reputation as an unreliable sample type. This view of bone as a problematical material for ^{14}C analysis continues down to the present (e.g., Brown 1988). The initial experience of the Chicago laboratory yielded a hierarchy of reliable sample materials which began with charcoal and wood, followed by grasses, cloth and peat, well-preserved antler, and, at the bottom of the list, well-preserved shell. Surprisingly, "heavily burned bone" was listed along with charcoal at the top of this list. However, the organic material was not primarily the bone fabric itself but carbonized skin, hair and other residual fatty tissues. As such, bone was excluded from the Libby listing. His initial view was that bone would be a "very poor prospect" because of its relatively low, largely inorganic, carbon content, its very porous structure and the "potential for alteration"—i.e., isotopic exchange of the carbonates in the bone with ground water and soil carbonates. While he conceded that it was "barely conceivable" that bone measurements might yield accurate results, in his view the quantities required were so large that, as there usually were other acceptable sample materials associated in a site with bone, "it [did] not seem to be an urgent matter to pursue" (Libby 1952:45).

Other laboratories, however, did undertake the measurement of bone samples and confirmed Libby's view that bone would yield inconsistent results when compared with the results from other sample types. In reviewing the literature in the early 1960s, Olson (1963) documented that ^{14}C measurements on bone were often rejected when compared with charcoal, wood, peat, antler, and shell (Table 3). The problem with bone was

Table 2. Definition of Confidence Levels Denoting Reliability of Association of Sample Materials with Archaeological/Human Skeletal Feature. Taken from Taylor 1987b:115.

Confidence level	Definition	Example
Essential certainty	Age estimate on object for which temporal placement sought	^{14}C analysis on human bone to obtain age estimate on human burial
High probability	Age estimate on material in direct functional relationship with object/event for which temporal placement sought	^{14}C analysis of textile used to wrap burial to obtain age estimate on burial
Reasonable possibility	Age estimate on enclosing deposits of assumed similar age to the object/event for which temporal placement sought	^{14}C analysis of charcoal in sediments adjacent to burial to obtain age estimate on burial
Possibility	Age estimate on component of deposit correlated with deposits containing object/event for which temporal placement sought	^{14}C analysis of charcoal in sediments associated stratigraphically/geomorphologically or cross-dated on the basis of some cultural feature with the burial to obtain age estimate on burial

traced to the fact that the ^{14}C measurements were being carried out on the total or whole-bone matrix, which is composed largely of inorganic constituents (Sinex and Faris 1959). Inorganic carbonates in a bone that has been buried in an active soil profile can be derived from either primary carbonates associated with the indigenous apatite structure (calcium carbonate incorporated in calcium phosphate crystals and other amorphous, carbon-containing inorganic materials) or secondary or diagenetic carbonates which had been transported into the bone matrix from the groundwater and soil environment by chemical exchange and/or through dissolution and reprecipitation processes. Without detailed information concerning the geochemistry of a given burial environment, it is difficult to generalize concerning the age relationships of the organic and inorganic fractions in a given bone, since it has been determined that ^{14}C values obtained on a total carbonate fraction can be significantly older, essentially the same age, or younger than an organic fraction from the same bone (Taylor 1982).

Table 4 illustrates the lack of concordance in the ^{14}C ages exhibited by the total inorganic and organic fractions in the same bone samples. An example of a significantly inflated age of an inorganic fraction is exemplified in the age initially assigned to a tool made from a caribou tibia recovered from the Old Crow Basin, Yukon Territory, Canada. The original ^{14}C determination was made on a sample of CO_2 released from the bone by treatment with acid (Irving and Harrington 1973). Although this fraction was characterized as "bone mineral apatite," a more accurate designation would probably be "total inorganic carbon fraction." A ^{14}C analysis on an organic fraction of this bone more than one decade later yielded a late Holocene age (Nelson et al. 1986). An example of concordant inorganic/organic

Table 3. Radiocarbon Sample Type Reliability: First Decade of Experience (Based on Olson 1963).

	Charcoal	Wood	Peat	Antler	Shells	Bone
	n = 13	15	14	11	20	27
	percentage					
Acceptable	46	80	28	9	5	11
Acceptable with reservations	31	20	50	36	35	22
Rejected with reservations	15	0	22	46	40	45
Rejected	8	0	0	9	20	22

Table 4. Comparisons of ^{14}C Determinations on Inorganic and Organic Components of Bone Samples.

Source	Inorganic Fraction	Organic Fraction
Old Crow, Yukon	27,000 $^{+3000}/_{-2000}$ [a]	1,350 ± 150 [b]
12-Mile Creek, Kansas	10,435 ± 260 [c]	10,245 ± 335 [d]
CA-SJo-112, California	880 ± 90 [e]	2,875 ± 70 [f]

[a] GX-1640, Irving and Harrington 1973.
[b] RIDDL-145, Nelson et al. 1986.
[c] GX-5812A, Rogers and Martin, 1984.
[d] GX-5812, Rogers and Martin, 1984.
[e] Average of two analysis, UCR-449A and UCR-450A, Taylor and Slota, 1979.
[f] Average of four analysis, UCR-449B, UCR-449C, UCR-450B and UCR-450C, Taylor and Slota, 1979.

fraction results is exemplified in the ^{14}C analysis of a bison tibia from the 12-Mile Creek site in Kansas (Rogers and Martin 1984), while significantly younger ^{14}C values are exhibited on the inorganic fractions of two bones from the same burial from a late Holocene California archaeological site (Taylor and Slota 1979).

In fossil bone, a significant amount of the ^{14}C contained in the inorganic carbon components can be introduced through isotopic exchange. Thus, the ^{14}C activity of the total inorganic fraction generally reflects the environmental source(s) of the carbonates in the soils to which the bone was exposed and the degree of isotopic exchange between the bone and ground water carbonates and soils—not the actual age of the bone specimen. Studies to develop techniques which would isolate the in situ apatite fraction in bone continue to be pursued (e.g., Haas and Banewics 1980; H. Haas, personal communication). However, difficulties in accomplishing this on a consistent basis have led the majority of researchers to focus their attention on the isolation of one or more organic fractions.

Between 60%–70% of the organics in fresh, fat-free mammalian bone is the protein collagen. *In vivo* mammalian collagen can be distinguished by a number of biogeochemical indices, e.g., characteristic amounts of nitrogen (both total and amino acid derived), a distinctive nitrogen/carbon ratio, and a pattern in the relative concentrations of the approximately 20 amino acids which make up mammalian collagen. The presence of significant quantatives of hydroxyproline, an amino acid found almost exclusively in collagen, represents another characteristic of collagen. Table 5 illustrates several of these parameters to characterize modern and fossil bone. Modern or nondiagenetically effected bone is illustrated by both total and amino acid nitrogen concentration of 4% (the typical range is 3–4%), a C/N ratio of 3.2, hydroxyproline concentration over 8%, a glycine/glutamic (Gly/Glu) ratio of over 4, and a glycine/aspartic ratio of about 7. Values obtained on three diagenetically effected fossil bones illustrate how the indices change as the collagen denatures and is removed from the bone. As the collagen concentration decreases in a bone (or any other sample type), the potential age dilution effects attributable to the introduction of more recent or even modern contamination increase significantly and, even with the use of chromatographic methods, it can be sometimes difficult in seriously diagenetically affected bones to distinguish denaturation products of the indigenous organic compounds from, for example, the various types of humic and fulvic compounds present in most soils.

The problem is greatly exacerbated when an organic preservative has been applied to the bone by excavators or curators or when segments of the bone have been repaired by the application of a collagen-based glue. Incomplete—or in some cases totally erroneous—information concerning the substance(s) applied to a bone in the field and during its curatorial history is often encountered with bone obtained from museum depositories. It is often not possible to determine simply by visual appearance whether a preservative has been applied to the surface of a bone. Until positive evidence based on specific tests confirms that such has not been the case, pretreatment approaches should begin with the assumption that bone will be contaminated with a preservative.

Once the absence of a preservative has been confirmed or, if present, the preservative has been removed by the application of appropriate solvent extraction techniques, the chemical separation of an indigenous organic fraction can be attempted. In ^{14}C studies on bone, a wide spectrum of organic substances has been extracted and labeled with a variety of terms—including collagen, gelatin, purified proteins, acid soluble, acid insoluble, base soluble, base insoluble, total amino acids, and one or more amino acids. In some reports, "collagen" has been used as a generic label to designate the organic residue of a bone which remains following the destruction of all carbonates by treatment with an acid (Berger et al. 1971). Depending on the diagenetic history of the bone, this designation may or may not correctly characterize the physical nature of the extracted organic residue. In the absence of specific biochemical data (e.g., amino acid composition), a more accurate reference for such an organic fraction would be "total acid insoluble fraction."

Two related strategies have been employed in working with bone samples undergoing ^{14}C analysis. The goal of the first approach is to develop a technique that can be generally applied to all bones and will exclude contami-

Table 5. Example of Variations in Biogeochemical Data on Modern and Fossil Bone. Data Taken from Hare and von Endt 1990, Taylor 1987c, and Ajie et al. 1990.

	N_t^1 (%)	N_a^2 (%)	C/N^3	Hyp^4 (%)	Gly/Glu^5	Gly/Asp^6
Modern	4.0	4.0	3.2	8.6	4.7	7.1
Fossil	–	–	11.1	5.9	3.4	4.7
Fossil	–	–	18.3	5.0	3.8	5.8
Fossil	0.1	0.02	50	–	2.2	–

[1] N_t = total nitrogen content.
[2] N_a = total amino acid nitrogen.
[3] C/N = elemental carbon/nitrogen ratio.
[4] Hyp = hydroxyproline content.
[5] Gly/Glu = glycine/glutamic acid ratio.
[6] Gly/Asp = glycine/aspartic acid ratio.

nants and yield a product composed exclusively of organics indigenous to the sample bone. A widely employed method of bone pretreatment in this tradition is based in whole or in part on a technique first described by Longin in the early 1970s. Following the elimination of the inorganic carbonates by acid treatment, this approach extracts the insoluble residue with water at 90°C at a controlled pH to produce a gelatinous residue. In the original study, it was assumed that only collagen would be present in the insoluble gelatin product because the impurities would be removed in the liquid fraction (Longin 1971).

The second strategy utilizes similar preparative techniques but focuses on the isolation and separate ^{14}C analysis of different organic fractions from the same bone. This approach evaluates the accuracy of the ^{14}C values on the basis of the degree of concordance among the these fractions. For example, one recent discussion has suggested that when "critical" bone samples are analyzed, a protocol which includes the ^{14}C analysis of multiple organic fractions be carried out (Taylor 1987c). Critical samples are defined as those in which ^{14}C data are central to the support for or refutation of some inference of major archaeological or paleoanthropological significance. By this definition, all human bones—or bones with clear evidence of having been modified by human behavior (e.g., artifacts fabricated from bone or bone with unambiguous artifact associations)—of suspected late-Pleistocene age from sites in the Western Hemisphere would be classed as "critical" samples.

Various types of studies have undertaken multiple ^{14}C measurements on different fractions of the same bone. Table 6 summarizes ^{14}C data obtained on a series of bone samples from European cave sites (Horvatincic et al. 1983). In this study, three different fractions were obtained on each bone. It should be emphasized that in the preparation of two fractions—the total organic and total inorganic fractions—*no attempt was made to remove actual or suspected contamination by chemical means*. The only pretreatment involved surface mechanical cleaning followed by crushing, grinding, and sifting to eliminate fine dust. The total organic fraction was obtained by combustion at 550°C in oxygen in a closed system. A total inorganic fraction was collected by then raising the temperature to 800°C, which results in the decomposition of the carbonates in the bone. The ^{14}C age of the total inorganic fraction would reflect both the age of the indigenous apatite structure as well as any diagenetic secondary carbonates obtained through exchange. The total organic fraction would reflect the age of the indigenous organics along with any organic contaminant(s). The gelatin fraction, prepared using the Longin procedures summarized above, would presumably reflect more closely the actual age of the bone.

The first three of the bones listed in Table 6 are of Holocene age. In the first two cases, there is reasonable agreement between the ^{14}C age of the gelatin and total organics fractions. In the case of the third sample (Briord), the organic fraction is slightly younger than the corresponding gelatin fraction. As expected, the ^{14}C ages exhibited by the total inorganic fractions in these bones are inconsistent—younger (Bezdanjaca Cave), older (Briord), and essentially the same (Brina Cave) as those of the corresponding organic fractions. The last two bones listed in Table 6 are of Pleistocene age. The ^{14}C age of the gelatin fraction of the Grotte Patrone bone was about 30,000 yr B.P. In this case, the finite ^{14}C age may represent a minimum age; it may, in fact, be of infinite ^{14}C age, i.e., >40,000 yr B.P. The Vindija Cave sample is thought to be in excess of 50,000 yr B.P. The ^{14}C activity in both of the nonchemically pretreated total organic fractions clearly reflects the presence of significantly younger organics.

There is a view that most organics isolated from bone samples by conventional acid and base solubility

Table 6. Radiocarbon Ages of Different Fractions of Bone Samples Prepared with No Chemical Pretreatment. Data Taken from Table 1 in Horvatincic et al. 1983.[1]

SITE	TOTAL INORGANICS[2]	TOTAL ORGANICS	GELATIN FRACTION[3]
Bezdanjaca Cave, Yugoslavia	590 ± 126	3008 ± 100[4]	2970 ± 100
Brina Cave, Yugoslavia	5365 ± 117	5456 ± 130	5341 ± 122
Briord, France	1858 ± 94	1652 ± 91	1875 ± 100
Grotte Patrone, France	17252 ± 400	15500 ± 250	29600 ± 1100
Vindija Cave, Yugoslavia[5]	3600 ± 97	2480 ± 97	–[6]

[1] All ^{14}C values were calculated with a half life of 5730 years.
[2] Described as "thermally released CO_2." Inorganic carbonates would represent the bulk of the sample.
[3] Pretreatment by method outlined in Longin (1971).
[4] Age of associated charcoal sample, 3150 ± 90 years.
[5] Report states that age of bones are "beyond the limits of the radiocarbon method (60,000 to 100,000 years old)."
[6] Report states that sample contained "no collagen."

approaches will tend to exhibit ^{14}C ages somewhat younger than the actual age of bone. This generalization derives from the reasonable assumptions that: (1) soil humic compounds would be the most likely contaminant and the most difficult to completely remove in diagenetically effected bone without the use of chromatographic techniques; and (2) the ^{14}C activity in these compounds would reflect the presence of younger organics. There indeed does seem to be a general trend in which ^{14}C analysis on organic fractions of bone tends to indicate ages somewhat younger than expected. However, the important issue is the *magnitude* of these differences.

In bone where the collagen is still retained intact in sufficient amounts, it appears that with proper chemical pretreatment, which involves the purification of the extracted protein residue, the ^{14}C activity of most organic fractions can be used to infer an accurate age to within ± 1000–2000 yr B.P. *if* no preservatives were applied or if the nature of the preservative is such that it can be totally removed. However, there are occasions, even in Holocene-age bone exhibiting a collagen amino acid profile and where preservatives have not been applied, in which serious age anomalies have been encountered. For example, a 6000- to 8000-year discordance among the ages of organic fractions has been observed in a Holocene-age bone (Taylor 1987c). Three organic fractions extracted from a single bone sample exhibited ^{14}C ages that averaged about 8500 years; while three duplicate preparations of a fourth organic product, a gelatin fraction prepared according to the Longin technique (including a base extraction step to solubilize humic compounds), exhibited ages ranging from modern (<150 years) to about 2700 ^{14}C yr B.P. It appears that a very recent or modern organic fraction contained in the bone was not being removed by a standard method.

Since the preservation of the collagen in this sample was excellent as measured by the amino acid composition and nitrogen content, the difficulty experienced in this experiment could not be attributed to diagenetic effects. Other laboratories obtained ages ranging from 7977 ± 155 to 8450 ± 77 ^{14}C yr B.P. on organic fractions of this bone. The exact source of the discrepancy is still unclear, but the fact that the bone came from a marine rather than a terrestrial mammal—a whale—has led to the suggestion that some organic product associated with a marine environment or some aspect of the variant biological architecture of marine mammal bone may be involved.

A major problem in the examination of validity of ^{14}C determinations on bone has been that the yields of organic product in many bones—especially those of Pleistocene age—are relatively low. With conventional ^{14}C decay counting technology, these low yields raised difficulties in that they sometimes required adjustments in the pretreatment procedures. The sample size requirement in some cases impeded an intensive investigation of the biogeochemistry of a bone sample to insure that indigenous bone fractions were identified and extracted. The advent of accelerator (or atomic) mass spectrometry (AMS) has permitted meaningful analysis to be obtained on sample sizes several orders of magnitude below that possible with conventional decay counting. To put the nature of this method of ^{14}C analysis in perspective, the basis of this technology will be briefly reviewed.

ACCELERATOR/ATOMIC MASS SPECTROMETRY

Until the early 1980s, all ^{14}C age determinations were obtained using decay counting technology involving gas or liquid scintillation systems. As the term denotes, decay counting infers ^{14}C concentrations by counting decay events in some type of ionization or scintillation detector and comparing the ^{14}C count rate observed in an unknown age sample to that which is exhibited in appropriate standards under a common set of experimental conditions. For ^{14}C, this involves the counting of beta particle emissions.

At least since the late 1960s, it was recognized that the significantly higher efficiencies of atom-by-atom detection employed in conventional mass spectrometers would permit the use of sample sizes several orders of magnitude below those typically possible with decay counting (e.g., Oeschger et al. 1970:487–488). Mass spectrometers take advantage of the differences in mass of different isotopes to detect and measure their concentrations. The process of measurement requires that the sample atoms be ionized by stripping off or adding to the electrons on the outer "shells" of the atoms. The atom in ion form can then be influenced by magnetic fields. This property of ions permits them to be accelerated in a vacuum. When such acceleration occurs, the trajectories of these particles can be deflected by passing the particles through a magnetic field of appropriate strength. The degree of deflection of the pathway of a monoenergetic ionized beam largely depends on the difference in mass of the different isotopes comprising it.

Figure 1 illustrates, in simplified form, the essential components of a conventional mass spectrometer: an ion source where the sample either in the form of a solid or gas is ionized and accelerated, a high-vacuum pathway, an analyzing magnet, and a detector. The ions of the isotope selected for analysis reach the collector in greatest concentration. Ions of greater mass are insufficiently deflected (because of their greater inertia) for a given magnetic field strength, whereas ions of lesser mass are excessively deflected. These ions lose energy and are removed from the spectrometer by pumping. By varying the strength of the magnet or the energy imparted to the ions, relative concentration of different isotopes can be measured. Using an isotope of known concentration as a standard, quantitative measurements of isotope ratios can be obtained.

If the amount of a given isotope is sufficient and the differences in mass are large enough, the isotopic composition of a sample can be obtained with a conventional mass spectrometer. This is the method routinely used to obtain stable carbon isotope ratios ($^{12}C/^{13}C$). However, attempts to make direct counting measurements of ^{14}C using conventional mass spectrometers were frustrated because of the extremely low natural ^{14}C concentrations ($^{14}C/^{12}C$ = ca. 10^{-12}) and because ^{14}N and stable molecular ions with similar charge-to-mass ratios as ^{14}C, e.g., ^{13}CH or $^{12}CH_2$, could not be sufficiently eliminated from the mass spectra. Because of this, there were significant problems in suppressing relatively high backgrounds (Anbar 1978; Wilson 1979).

In the late 1970s, successful direct counting of ^{14}C was accomplished by accelerating sample atoms in the form of ions to much higher energies than were employed in conventional mass spectrometers. As illustrated in Figure 2, this was accomplished by inserting some type of particle accelerator between the ion source and the analyzing magnet. To obtain AMS-based isotopic measurements, initial investigators employed both a cyclotron (Muller 1977) and, as illustrated in Figure 2, tandem particle accelerators (Bennett et al. 1977; Nelson et al. 1977). At first, the term high-energy mass spectrometry (HEMS) was used to designate this approach. Accelerator (or atomic) mass spectrometry (AMS) is now more commonly used, while tandem accelerator mass spectrometry (TAMS) refers to the use of a tandem accelerator for AMS measurements.

The term "tandem" refers to the fact that particle acceleration in these systems is accomplished in a two-step "pull-push" process. Negative ions are accelerated through a voltage to a positive terminal ("pull") and then "stripped" to produce a positive ion which is accelerated away from the terminal ("push"). Although research on the use of a cyclotron for AMS measurement continues (Bertsche et al. 1987), currently all operational AMS systems employ TAMS-type instruments. The great advantage of TAMS instruments is that ^{14}N does not form negative ions or does not form negative ions that live long enough to pass through the accelerator to the detector. In addition, the stripping that takes place in a tandem accelerator system insures that no molecules survive in their transit through the accelerator. These two factors account for a significant portion of the sources of background experienced in the earlier conventional mass spectrometry experiments with ^{14}C.

While Figure 2 illustrates the required components of an AMS system, the actual configuration of operating AMS instruments is somewhat varied. For example, Figure 3 is a simplified schematic of the arrangement of the

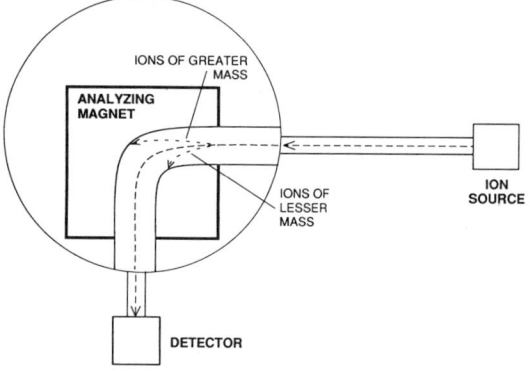

Figure 1. Elements of conventional mass spectrometry instrumentation. For additional discussion, please see Taylor 1987c:73–74.

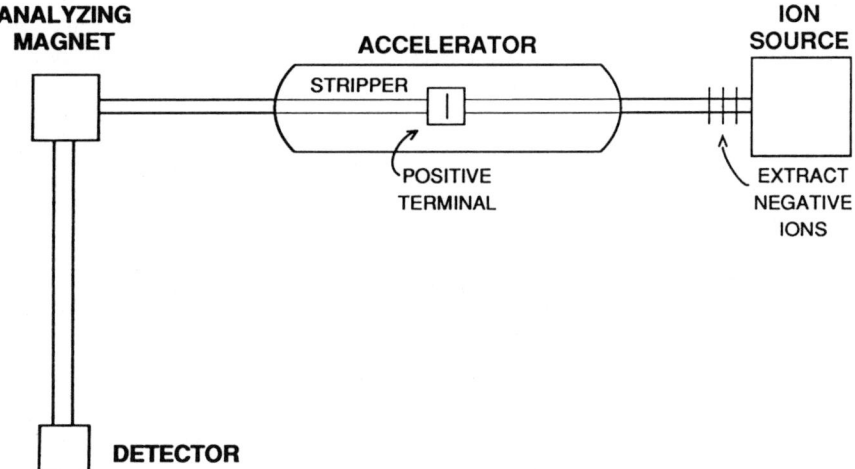

Figure 2. Elements of TAMS type of accelerator (or atomic) mass spectrometry instrumentation. For additional discussion, please see Taylor 1987c:90–95.

major elements of the University of California AMS system operating at the Lawrence Livermore National Laboratory. In this system, which is one of more than twenty TAMS instruments now being used to obtain AMS ^{14}C measurements, an injection magnet directs the ion beam into the accelerator and there are two analyzing magnets. Stable carbon isotope measurements (^{13}C and ^{12}C) are obtained using detectors measuring ion current located between the two analyzing magnets. The technical features of the various types of AMS systems have been extensively reviewed (e.g., Kutschera 1983; Litherland 1984). Taylor (1987b:94) has listed earlier general literature references along with early comments on the implications and results of the use of AMS ^{14}C technology in the measurement of archaeologically related samples.

Three advantages of AMS technology in the measurement of cosmogenic isotopes such as ^{14}C were anticipated as a result of the greatly enhanced efficiency (Muller 1977). These were: (1) major reductions in sample sizes—from gram amounts of carbon to 1–5 milligrams and, with additional efforts, to the level of several hundred micrograms); (2) major reductions in counting times—to achieve ± 1% counting statistics, reductions from several days for conventional systems and even weeks and months with micro- and mini-counting systems (e.g., Harbottle et al. 1979) to minutes and hours for AMS systems; and (3) significant increase in the ^{14}C time frame—from the currently routine 40,000/50,000 years out to as much as 100,000 years (Muller 1977; Taylor 1987a). The third projected advance possible with AMS technology was anticipated due to a consideration of the data summarized in Table 7.

In a gram of modern carbon, there are approximately 5.9×10^{10} atoms of ^{14}C. However, on the average, over a one-minute period, fewer than 14 of these atoms will decay and be available for detection. In a sample 100,000 years old, the decay rate of ^{14}C will have dropped to a level far below the detection limit of any decay-counting instrument. However, in one gram of such a sample,

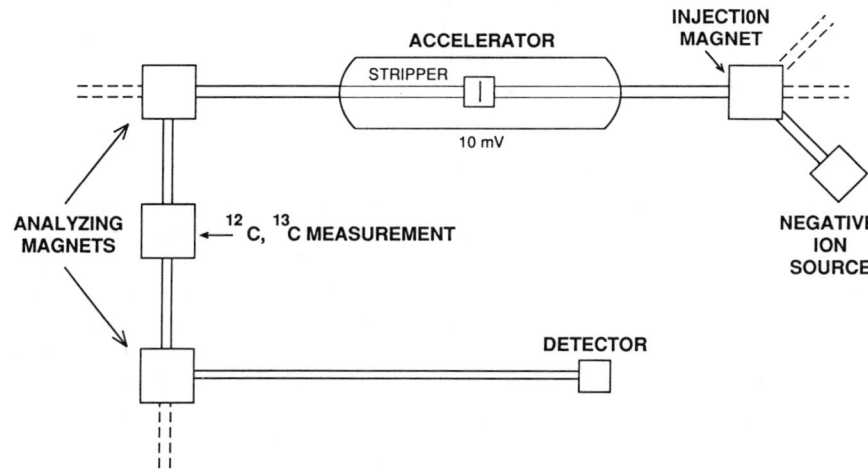

Figure 3. Simplified representation of AMS system at the University of California, Lawrence Livermore National Laboratory (LLNL), Van de Graaff Tandem-Accelerator Laboratory.

Table 7. Comparison of ^{14}C Decay (Beta) and Direct (Ion) Counting.

	^{14}C DECAY COUNTING	DIRECT COUNTING
	dpm/gm carbon	atoms ^{14}C/gm carbon
modern	13.5	5.9×10^{10}
50,000	0.03	1.4×10^{8}
100,000	0.00007	3.2×10^{5}

there are still over 10^5 atoms of ^{14}C available for detection. It has been suggested that the ultimate upper limit for ^{14}C using AMS technology would be a function of neutron flux in soils into which samples are deposited. Very low levels of ^{14}C would be produced in situ. However, additional studies are necessary to determine the degree to which even this effect could be detected even in samples approaching 10^5 years in age (Wand 1981:254–270).

The first two of the three anticipated benefits of AMS technology have been fully realized over the last decade (Haynes et al. 1984; Hedges and Gowlett 1986; Taylor et al. 1984). However, the projected third advance has been frustrated due to general inability at present to exclude microcontamination of samples primarily with modern carbon introduced during sample preparation. The source of a significant portion of this contamination results from the current requirement that samples must be converted to graphite for use in the ion source of all but one AMS system. Parts per million of modern carbon contamination translates into background levels which generally limit the maximum ages that can be resolved to between 40,000 and 50,000 years. In a study of this problem carried out by the University of Washington AMS group, an AMS ^{14}C measurement of $69,030 \pm 1,700$ was obtained on a specially prepared sample of geological graphite. However, graphite prepared from CO_2 obtained from a sample of marble—which, like geologic graphite, should exhibit no ^{14}C activity due to its great geologic age—yielded an apparent age of $47,960 \pm 670$ (Schmidt et al. 1987). For several years, the development of a CO_2 gas source for use on AMS systems has been underway by the Oxford AMS group. Such a source eliminates the requirement that samples be converted to graphite. However, backgrounds currently are comparable to that of graphite systems (Hedges et al. 1992).

The development of AMS technology has now provided the technical means by which very low carbon content sample types, such as organic extracts from bone, can be effectively and efficiently dated by ^{14}C. This technology has been employed to obtain ^{14}C measurements on a series of human bone samples and a bone artifact from New World sites which had previously been dated from 17,000 to 70,000 years on the basis of several criteria, including decay counting ^{14}C, uranium series and amino acid racemization-inferred ages. As a consequence of these AMS-based ^{14}C determinations, which are summarized in Table 8, all of the previous age assignments were reduced to less than 7000 ^{14}C years (Taylor 1983; Taylor et al. 1985).

RADIOCARBON DATING OF BONE: USE OF AMS TECHNOLOGY

Table 9 compares the steps required to obtain a ^{14}C age determination using decay and direct counting. At the present time, the principle contribution of AMS ^{14}C analysis lies in its ability to obtain ^{14}C measurements on sample sizes measured in units of milligrams of carbon—and with additional efforts, even several hundred microgram amounts—along with the ability to obtain meaningful analysis with counting times measured in minutes and hours rather than days and weeks. As illustrated in Figure 4, the use of AMS ^{14}C technology permits several orders of magnitude reduction in sample sizes along with a significant decrease in counting times. Table 9 and Figure 4 highlight the fact that AMS-based ^{14}C age determinations are not inherently more—or less—accurate than decay counting. There simply now exists the routine capability to obtain suites of ^{14}C measurements on microsize samples.

Over the last decade, the use of AMS technology, combined with the use of a wide spectrum of analytical and preparative chemical techniques, has resulted in an examination of the distribution of ^{14}C ages exhibited in various organic products contained in fossil bone. Studies carried out by several laboratories have provided a foundation on which to build a framework for understanding the interrelationship of various biogeochemical diagenetic processes, the sources and characteristics of contamination, and the pattern of ^{14}C ages found in fossil bones.

Several reviews of the AMS ^{14}C data obtained on fossil bone have attempted to quantify the potential sources and effects of contamination in bone samples. They have proposed, in the context of the AMS-derived data, various criteria to evaluate the likelihood that a given ^{14}C analysis would yield an accurate age estimate. For example, Taylor (1987c) proposed a protocol which, in addition to tests to positively detect, and, if present, remove organic preservative(s) on bone, suggested, as a minimum requirement, the isolation of: (1) a total HCl-insoluble; (2) a total amino acid; and (3) a humic/fulvic-acid fraction. The basis of this suggestion was that the ^{14}C analysis on a total HCl-insoluble fraction would provide an age estimate on the "generic organics" in the bone

Table 8. Revisions in Age Estimates on Bone from Purported New World Late Pleistocene Contexts Based on AMS ^{14}C Determinations (Data taken from Taylor 1992:Table 25.5 and Taylor et al. 1992). Except for the Old Crow Sample, All Bones were Identified as Human Skeletal Material.

SKELETON/ARTIFACT	ORIGINAL ESTIMATE		REVISED ESTIMATE	
	BASIS	AGE	^{14}C AGE	LABORATORIES
Sunnyvale	AAR	70,000	3600–4850	UCR/Arizona AMS
	U-series	8300/9000	6300[1]	UCSD(Scripps)/ Oxford AMS
Haverty (Angeles Mesa)	AAR	>50,000	4050–13,500	UCR/LLNL-CAMS AMS DSIR, New Zealand
Del Mar	AAR	41,000–48,000	4900[1]	UCSD(Scripps)/ Oxford AMS
	U-series	11,000/11,300		
Los Angeles (Baldwin Hills)	^{14}C	>23,000[1]	3560	UCR/Arizona AMS
	AAR	26,000		
Taber	geologic	22,000–60,000	3550	Chalk River AMS
Yuha	^{14}C	22,000[2]	1650–3850	Arizona AMS
	AAR	23,000		
	U-series	5800		
Old Crow[3]	^{14}C	27,000	1350	Simon Frazer/ McMaster AMS
Laguna	^{14}C	7100–17,150	5100[1]	UCSD(Scripps)/ Oxford AMS
Natchez	geologic	Pleistocene	5580	Arizona AMS
Tepexan	geologic	late Pleistocene	1980	Arizona AMS
Calaveras	geologic	Pliocene	740	UCR/Arizona AMS

[1] Amino acid fraction.
[2] Diagenetic carbonates.
[3] Artifact fabricated from bone.

Table 9. Comparison of Procedures for Decay and Direct Counting Technologies in Radiocarbon Measurements. Pretreatment: Isolation of *in situ*/Indigenous Fraction of Sample.

DECAY COUNTING	DIRECT COUNTING
Preparation: conversion of sample to form required by method of measurement (gas/LS)	Preparation: conversion of sample to form required by method of measurement (solid or CO_2)
	Production of ions from sample
	Acceleration of ions
	Separation of ^{14}C from all other isotopes and molecules
Count decay events of ^{14}C	Count individual ^{14}C ions
Infer ^{14}C concentration by comparison with standards	Infer ^{14}C concentration by comparison with standards

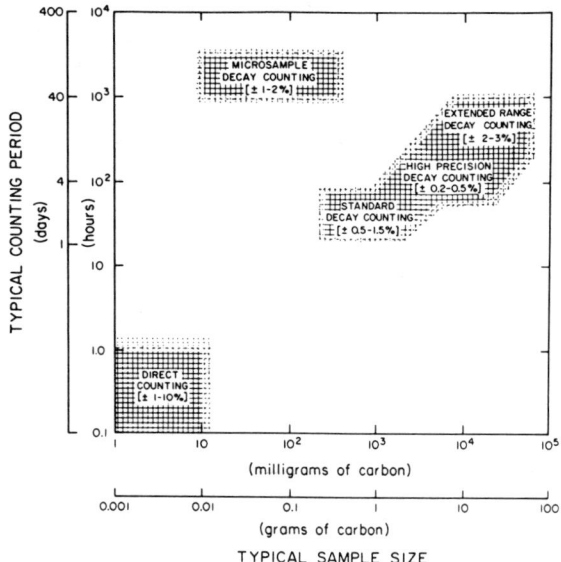

Figure 4. Relationship between sample size and typical counting periods for different types of conventional decay counting system as compared with direct counting by AMS technology. Taken from Figure 3.4 in Taylor 1987c.

while the humic- or fulvic-acid fraction ^{14}C value would permit a positive determination of the age of what is typically the principle organic contaminant. The degree of concordance of the total HCl-insoluble and total amino-acid fractions and the age separation between these two fractions (if any) and the humic/fulvic-fraction would provide a quantitative basis on which to evaluate the distribution of ^{14}C activities in the major organic constituents of a bone.

It was also proposed that additional consideration should be given to the separation of one or more individual amino acids. Because the amino acid hydroxyproline had been thought to have a very limited distribution other than as a constituent of collagen, it had been suggested as an optimum fraction for bone ^{14}C dating. (Stafford et al. 1982; Wand 1981; cf. Taylor 1987b:56). However, from a practical point of view, the use of hydroxyproline is severely limited even with the use of AMS technology due to the fact that it is present in very low concentrations in many fossil bones. In addition, this amino acid, along with several others, has been detected in natural waters, sometimes in significant amounts (Long et al. 1989; Thurman 1985:151–155).

The increasing number of ^{14}C determinations on bone using AMS technology has suggested to several research groups a pattern with important implications for procedures developed to guide the processing of bone samples for ^{14}C analysis. Based on the experiences of the Oxford AMS laboratory, the issues and problems associated with sample pretreatment protocols for bone depend primarily on the amount of recoverable collagen contained in a bone specimen (Hedges and Law 1989). For bone samples containing significant quantities of well-preserved collagen, it is now generally agreed that appropriate physical and chemical pretreatment can, in most cases, effectively isolate and purify the residual collagen.

For such bone samples, various types of chromatographic methods have been used to remove humate compounds (e.g., Gillespie et al. 1986; Stafford et al. 1987; Stafford et al. 1988) and isolate a total amino acid fraction (Long et al. 1989:234). The Longin method of collagen extraction has been modified by adding an ultrafiltration step designed to exclude low molecular weight species. Brown et al. (1988) assumed that most of the exogenous contamination will be contained in this fraction. Another approach developed to purify collagen for stable isotope analyses involves the use of collagenase which preferentially isolates peptides of known length from the surviving collagen fragments (DeNiro and Weiner 1988a, 1988b; van Klinken and Hedges 1992).

In contrast to several techniques currently employed to purify collagen, one of the most serious challenges currently confronting investigators is that of obtaining reliable ^{14}C determinations on chemically and microbiologically degraded bone—those samples where intact collagen has been almost entirely removed from the bone matrix.

Although studies are currently underway by several groups, there is currently no consensus as to biogeochemical methods that can be routinely used in bones exhibiting very low or trace amounts of collagen to distinguish indigenous non-collagen proteins, amino acids, peptides, and other products of collagen diagenesis from external contamination.

Recent measurements undertaken by Stafford et al. (1987, 1990, 1991) examining the range of ^{14}C values exhibited in bones of varying degrees of preservation and denaturation of the collagen component have highlighted problems in the ^{14}C dating of collagen-deficient bone. Using a relatively well-preserved bone of a mammoth (Domebo *Mammuthus* sp) associated with a wood sample dated at 11,490 ± 450 ^{14}C years, these researchers obtained ^{14}C measurements on a wide spectrum of organic fractions prepared by a variety of preparative methods (Figure 5). These fractions ranged from untreated gelatin, HCl-insoluble residues with and without gelatinization, ion exchange purified components, individual and combined amino acids, and fulvic acids. In the Stafford et al. (1987) report, nine fractions yielded ^{14}C ages within 2 sigma of the wood value, whereas five fractions exhibited still younger ages. With the exception of one organic fraction which was prepared using a solvent extraction technique and fulvic acids, the youngest organic fraction was about 2000 (± 500) years younger than the actual age of the bone. The principal contaminant in the bone was identified as

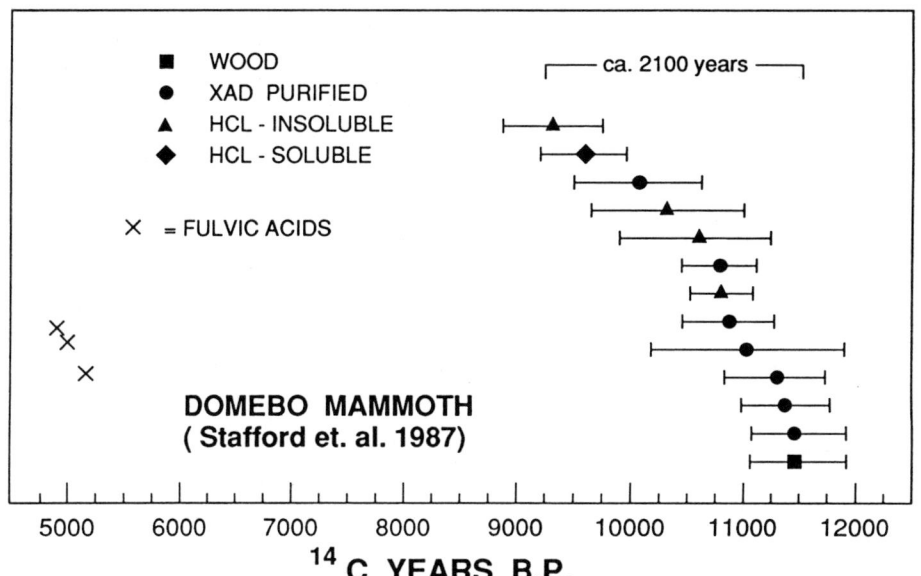

Figure 5. Distribution of ^{14}C values on wood associated with the Domebo Mammoth and various organics extracts from Domebo Mammoth bone. Data taken from Stafford et al. 1987.

humic compounds (fulvic acids), which yielded ^{14}C ages of about 5000 ^{14}C years.

Stafford et al. (1990) also obtained AMS ^{14}C measurements on a comparable series of fractions—25 analyses on 14 different chemical fractions—from another mammoth (Escapule *Mammuthus sp*) bone exhibiting a non-collagen amino acid composition pattern. The actual age of the mammoth was inferred to be approximately 11,000 yr B.P. on several lines of evidence. The ^{14}C age of individual amino acids extracted from the Escapule mammoth ranged from about 3000 to 4500 yr B.P. The youngest ^{14}C value—2270 ± 360 yr B.P.—was obtained on a combined aliquot containing four amino acids: aspartic acid, glutamic acid, serine, and threonine. Extracted fulvic acid yielded ages ranging from about 7200-8800 yr B.P. The oldest ^{14}C value obtained on the Escapule mammoth—12,280 ± 110 yr B.P. (AA-2972)—was obtained on a fraction described as "nonhydrolyzable organic matter (humins)."

Based on data from these and three other bone samples, including human bones from two portions of the Del Mar skeleton, Stafford et al. (1990:114–118) suggested that ^{14}C analyses on organic fractions of non-collagenous bone samples—including total and individual amino acids—will significantly underestimate the actual age of the bone. In their view, these ages "will be a measure of the bones mean ^{14}C activity, not its true geologic age." They argue that the only means of evaluating ^{14}C dates on samples of trace amounts of protein material and a noncollagenous amino-acid pattern is to obtain ^{14}C determinations on the "fulvic, humic acid, and humin fractions" and compare them with ^{14}C measurements on individual and total amino acids. According to them, even if the fulvic/humic acid fraction(s) and amino acid extract ages are concordant, the concordant age should still be considered as a minimum age which still could be thousands of years too young.

There now appears to be a general consensus among investigators concerning the reliability of bone ^{14}C values: (1) that where appropriate biochemical purification procedures are employed, accurate ^{14}C age estimates can be obtained on bones retaining significant amounts of intact collagen; and (2) that bones seriously depleted in their original protein (mostly collagen) content can yield seriously anomalous ^{14}C values. The recognition that anomalous ^{14}C values were being reported for usually reliable fractions isolated from seriously collagen-degraded bone has prompted several groups of investigators to begin to examine the potential usefulness of employing various non-collagen proteins contained in bone. The first non-collagen protein on which ^{14}C values have been obtained is osteocalcin (Ajie et al. 1990)

AMS technology also permits a practical means of examining the range in ^{14}C activities exhibited in microsections of bone samples. Optimally, this characterization process would involve a series of ^{14}C values obtained along the axis of a microcore or microsection that would physically sample the ^{14}C activities of organics in increments of a few millimeters beginning at the surface of the bone and proceeding to a center point. The basis of this approach is the assumption that in a bone where the physical matrix is intact, diagenetic contamination would typically be more pronounced at the surface of a sample and would decrease as one proceeds towards the interior.

The characteristics of the ^{14}C profile obtained from such a 5–10 mm microcore or microsection might provide one basis on which to quantitatively evaluate the levels of diagenetic contamination exhibited in a bone sample. Figure 6 illustrates four ideal types of profile "signatures" that might be observed on different samples. The diffusion-type ("J-shaped") profile would be one in which higher ^{14}C activities (i.e., younger ^{14}C ages) would be registered on the sample near surface while ^{14}C activities would decrease and then plateau, remaining constant in two or more interior samples. Such a distribution of values might be interpreted to indicate that the higher ^{14}C values reflect contamination processes and the plateau values represent the indigenous ^{14}C activity of the sample. Minze Stuiver (personal communication, 1987) has observed this type of profile in a series of samples taken from a 2- to 3-millimeter section of a Pleistocene arctic marine shell.

In contrast to the J-shaped curve, a continuously decreasing profile which lacks any interior plateau might be interpreted to indicate that contamination has moved far into the matrix of the sample and that further profiling would be required to determine if any interior plateau exists. The variable ("W-shaped") profile may indicate that contamination has diffused throughout the sample in an erratic manner. Finally, the constant level profile in which there is no significant change from surface to interior may indicate either that the surface contamination has been physically eroded off the sample before processing so that the ^{14}C levels observed represent the indigenous ^{14}C, or it may also indicate that contamination has uniformly been distributed throughout the profile, i.e., the diffusion species has reached steady state.

With microscale profile data, an investigator would have an independent, objective basis on which to characterize and rank samples with regard to level of difficulty of dealing with diagenetic contamination. One could initially assume that samples exhibiting J-shaped profiles would constitute a preferred class of samples. Two clear zones of ^{14}C activity would be exhibited with an initial hypothesis that, in each case, the plateau ^{14}C values represent the indigenous ^{14}C activity in the sample. It would be interesting, in as many cases as possible, to obtain ^{14}C data from two sets of microsample. One set would be subjected to appropriate pretreatment; the other set would be analyzed without pretreatment. One would then be able to evaluate the precise effect of a specific pretreatment on a given sample.

SUMMARY

Clearly, bone can be a very difficult sample type with which to work—requiring great care and attention to detail in sample pretreatment and preparation. However, the capabilities of AMS technology have provided researchers with a very powerful tool which has the capability to providing a detailed "temporal map" of carbon-containing compounds contained in a bone sample. Not only can the range of ^{14}C ages exhibited in various organic compounds be documented, but the spatial relationship of the ages exhibited by these compounds can be identified.

The goal of all such studies is, of course, to develop a preparative methodology which would accurately identify organics indigenous to a bone irrespective of its diagenetic history. Currently, there is a general consensus on the ability to obtain relatively accurate ^{14}C age

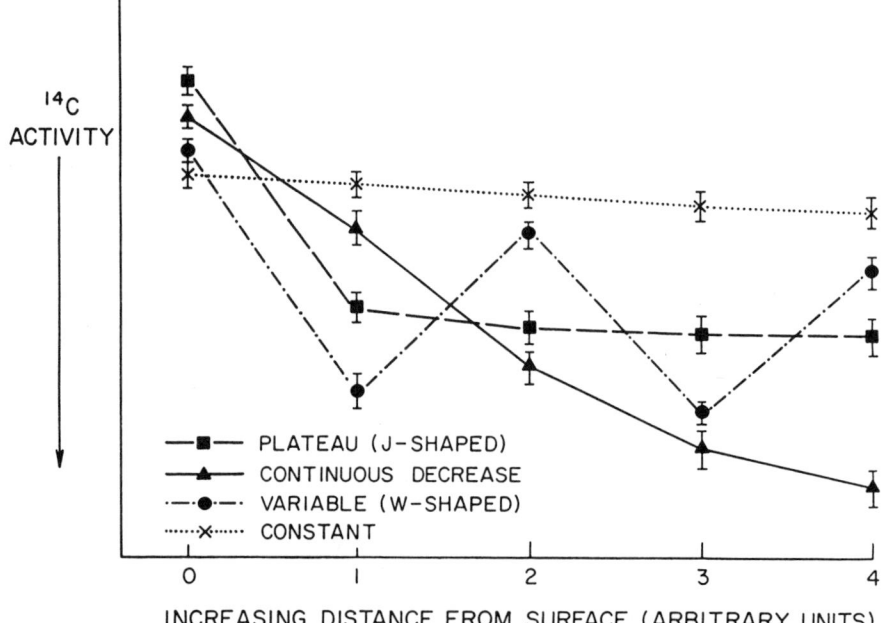

Figure 6. Hypothetical distribution of ^{14}C ages as a function of increasing distance from sample surfaces.

estimates on bone that still retains a significant amount of intact collagen. The future of bone ^{14}C research will be to be demonstrate the routine ability to obtain accurate ^{14}C age determinations on bone that has undergone significant biogeochemical alteration.

ACKNOWLEDGMENTS

The research reported in this paper undertaken by the UCR Radiocarbon Laboratory was supported by the National Science Foundation (Anthropology Program; BNS-9119958) and the Department of Energy, Lawrence Livermore National Laboratory, with additional funds supplied by UCR Chancellor Rosemary S. J. Schraer. This is contribution 89-9 of the Institute of Geophysics and Planetary Physics, University of California, Riverside.

REFERENCES CITED

Ajie, H. O., I. R. Kaplan, P. J. Slota, Jr., and R. E. Taylor
   1990 AMS Radiocarbon Dating of Bone Osteocalcin. *Nuclear Instruments and Methods* B52:433–437.

Anbar, M.
   1978 The Limitations of Mass Spectrometric Radiocarbon Dating Using CN⁻ Ions. In *Proceedings of the First Conference on Radiocarbon Dating with Accelerators*, edited by H. E. Gove, pp. 152–155. University of Rochester, Rochester.

Arnold, J. R., and W. F. Libby
   1950 *Radiocarbon Dates*. Institute for Nuclear Studies, University of Chicago, Chicago.
   1951 Radiocarbon dates. *Science* 113:111-120.

Bennett, C. L., R. P. Beukens, M. R. Clover, H. E. Gove, R. B. Liebert, A. E. Litherland, K. K. Purser, and W. E. Sondheim
   1977 Radiocarbon Dating Using Accelerators; Negative Ions Provide the Key. *Science* 198:508–509.

Berger, R., R. Protsch, R. Reynolds, R. Rozaire, and J. R. Sackett
   1971 New Radiocarbon Dates Based on Bone Collagen of California Paleoindians. *Contributions of the University of California Archaeological Research Facility* 12:43–49.

Bertsche, K. J., P. G. Friedman, D. E. Morris, R. A. Muller, and J. J. Welch
   1987 Status of the Berkeley Small Cyclotron AMS Project. *Nuclear Instruments and Methods in Physics Research* B29:105–109.

Bonnichsen, R., D. Stanford, and J. L. Fastook
   1987 Environmental Change and Development History of Human Adaptive Patterns: The Paleoindian Case. In *North America and Adjacent Oceans during the Last Deglaciation*, edited by W. F. Ruddiman and H. E. Wright Jr., pp. 403–424. Geological Society of America, Boulder.

Brown, F. H.
   1988 Geochronometry. In *Encyclopedia of Human Evolution and Prehistory*, edited by I. Tattersall, E. Delson and J. Van Couvering, pp. 222–225. Garland Publishing, New York.

Brown, T. A., D. E. Nelson, S. J. Vogel, and J. R. Southon
   1988 Improved Collagen Extraction by Modified Longin Method. *Radiocarbon* 30:171–177.

DeNiro, M. J., and S. Weiner
   1988a Chemical, Enzymatic and Spectroscopic Characterization of "Collagen" and Teeth Organic Fraction from Prehistoric Bones. *Geochemica et Cosmochemica Acta* 52:2197–2206.
   1988b Use of Collagenase to Purify Collagen from Prehistoric Bones for Stable Isotope Analysis. *Geochimica et Cosmochimica Acta* 52:2425–2432.

Dincauze, D. F.
   1984 An Archaeo-logical Evaluation of the Case of Pre-Clovis Occupations. In *Advances in World Archaeology*, vol. 3, pp. 275–323. Academic Press, New York.

Gillespie, R., R. E. M. Hedges, and M. J. Humm
   1986 Routine AMS Dating of Bone and Shell Proteins. *Radiocarbon* 28:451–456.

Haas, H., and J. J. Banewics
   1980 Radiocarbon Dating of Bone Apatite Using Thermal Release of CO_2. *Radiocarbon* 22:537–544.

Haas, H., V. Holliday, and R. Stuckenrath
   1986 Dating of Holocene Stratigraphy with Soluble and Insoluble Organic Fractions at the Lubbock Lake Archaeological Site, Texas: An Ideal Case Study. *Radiocarbon* 28:473–485.

Harbottle, G., E. V. Sayre, and R. W. Stoenner
   1979 Carbon 14 Dating of Small Samples by Proportional Counting. *Science* 206:683–685.

Hare, P. E., and D. von Endt
   1990 Variable Preservation of Organic Matter in Fossil Bone. In *1989 Yearbook of the Carnegie Institution of Washington*. Carnegie Institution of Washington, Washington, D.C.

Haynes, C. V., Jr.
   1982 Were Clovis Progenitors in Beringia? In *Paleoecology of Beringia*, edited by D. M. Hopkin, J. B.

Matthews, Jr., C. E. Schweeger, and S. B. Young, pp. 383–398. Academic Press, New York.

Haynes, C. V., Jr., and G. Agogino
1960 *Geological Significance of a New Radiocarbon Date from the Lindenmeir Site*. The Denver Museum of Natural History, Proceedings No. 9. Denver Museum of Natural History, Denver.

Haynes, C. V., D. J. Donahue, A. J. T. Jull, and T. H. Zabel
1984 Application of Accelerator Dating to Fluted Point Paleoindian Sites. *Archaeology of Eastern North America* 12:184–191.

Hedges, R. E. M., M. J. Humm, J. Foreman, G. J. van Klinken, and C. R. Bronk
1992 Developments in Sample Combustion to Carbon Dioxide and in the Oxford AMS Carbon Dioxide Ion Source System. *Radiocarbon* 34:306–311.

Hedges, R. E. M., and J. A. J. Gowlett
1986 Radiocarbon Dating by Accelerator Mass Spectrometry. *Scientific American* 254:100–107.

Hedges, R. E. M., and I. A. Law
1989 The Radiocarbon Dating of Bone. *Applied Geochemistry* 4:249–253.

Holliday, V. T., and E. Johnson
1986 Re-evaluation of the First Radiocarbon Age for the Folsom Culture. *American Antiquity* 51:332–338.

Horvatincic, N. D., D. Srdoc, B. Obelic, and A. Sliepcevic
1983 Radiocarbon Dating of Fossil Bones: Development of a New Technique for Sample Processing. In *Proceedings of the First International Symposium ^{14}C and Archaeology*, edited by W. G. Mook and H. T. Waterbolk, pp. 377–384. Council of Europe, Strasbourg.

Irving, W. N.
1985 Context and Chronology of Early Man in the Americas. *Annual Review of Anthropology* 14:529–555.

Irving, W. N., and C. R. Harrington
1973 Upper Pleistocene Radiocarbon-Dated Artifacts from the Northern Yukon. *Science* 179:335–340.

Johnson, F.
1965 The Impact of Radiocarbon Dating upon Archaeology. In *Proceedings of the Sixth International Conference Radiocarbon and Tritium Dating*, compiled by R. M. Chatters and E. A. Olson, pp. 762–780. Clearinghouse for Federal Scientific and Technical Information, Springfield, Virginia.

Kutschera, W.
1983 Accelerator Mass Spectrometry: From Nuclear Physics to Dating. *Radiocarbon* 25:677–691.

Libby, W. F.
1952 *Radiocarbon Dating*. University of Chicago Press, Chicago.

Litherland, A. E.
1984 Accelerator Mass Spectrometry. *Nuclear Instruments and Methods in Physics Research* 233(B5):100–108.

Long, A., A. T. Wilson, R. D. Ernst, B. H. Gore, P. E. Hare, and N. Tuross
1989 AMS Radiocarbon Dating of Bones at Arizona. *Radiocarbon* 31:231–238.

Longin, R.
1971 New Method of Collagen Extraction for Radiocarbon Dating. *Nature* 230:241–242.

Muller, R. A.
1977 Radioisotope Dating with a Cyclotron. *Science* 196:489–494.

Nelson, D. E., R. G. Korteling, and W. R. Scott
1977 Carbon-14: Direct Detection at Natural Concentrations. *Science* 198:507–508.

Nelson, D. E., R. E. Moreland, J. S. Vogel, J. R. Southern, and C. R. Harington
1986 New Radiocarbon Dates on Artifacts from the Northern Yukon Territory: Holocene Not Upper Pleistocene in Age. *Science* 232:749–751.

Oeschger, H., J. Houtermans, H. Loosli, and M. Wahlen
1970 The Constancy of Cosmic Radiation from Isotope Studies in Meteorites and on the Earth. In *Radiocarbon Variations and Absolute Chronology*, edited by I. U. Olsson, pp. 471–498. Almqvist and Wiksell, Stockholm.

Olson, E. A.
1963 The Problem of Sample Contamination in Radiocarbon Dating. Unpublished Ph.D. dissertation, Department of Geology, Columbia University.

Owen, R. C.
1984 The Americas: The Case Against an Ice-age Human Population. In *The Origins of Modern Humans: A World Survey of the Fossil Evidence*, edited by F. H. Smith and F. Spencer, pp. 517–563. Alan R. Liss, Inc, New York.

Payen, L. A.
1982 The Pre-Clovis of North America: Temporal and Artifactual Evidence. Unpublished Ph.D. dissertation, Department of Anthropology, University of California, Riverside.

Roberts, F. H. H.
1951 Radiocarbon Dates and Early Man. In *Radiocarbon dating*, compiled by F. Johnson, pp. 20–21. Society for American Archaeology, Memoirs No. 8.

Rogers, R. A., and L. D. Martin
1984 The 12 Mile Creek Site: A Reinvestigation. *American Antiquity* 49:757–764.

Schmidt, F. H., D. R. Balsley, and D. D. Leach
1987 Early Expectations of AMS: Greater Ages and Tiny Fractions. One Failure?—One Success. *Nuclear Instruments and Methods in Physics Research* B29:97–99.

Sinex, F. B., and B. Faris
1959 Isolation of Gelatin from Ancient Bones. *Science* 129:969.

Stafford, T. W. Jr., D. Brendel, and R. C. Duhamel
1988 Radiocarbon, C-13, and N-15 Analysis of Fossil Bone: Removal of Humates with XAD-2 Resin. *Geochimica et Cosmochimica Acta* 52:2257–2267.

Stafford, T. W., Jr., R. C. Duhamel, Haynes, C. V., and K. Brendel
1982 Isolation of Proline and Hydroxyproline from Fossil Bone. *Life Science* 31:931–938.

Stafford, T. W., Jr., A. J. T. Jull, K. Brendel, R. C. Duhamel, and D. Donahue
1987 Study of Bone Radiocarbon Dating Accuracy at the University of Arizona NSF Accelerator Facility for Radioisotope Analysis. *Radiocarbon* 29:24–44.

Stafford, T. W., Jr., P. E. Hare, L. Currie, A. J. T. Jull, and D. Donahue
1990 Accuracy of North American Human Skeleton Ages. *Quaternary Research* 34:111–120.

1991 Accelerator Radiocarbon Dating at the Molecular Level. *Journal of Archaeological Science* 18:35–72.

Stanford, D. J.
1982 A Critical Review of Archaeological Evidence Relating to the Antiquity of Human Occupation of the New World. *Smithsonian Contributions to Anthropology* 30:202–218.

Taylor, R. E.
1982 Problems in the Radiocarbon Dating of Bone. In *Nuclear and Chemical Dating Techniques: Interpreting the Environmental Record*, edited by L. A. Currie, pp. 453–473. American Chemical Society, Washington, D.C.

1983 Non-concordance of Radiocarbon and Amino Acid Racemization Age Estimates on Human Bone: Implications for the Dating of the Earliest Homo sapiens in the New World. *Radiocarbon* 25:647–654.

1987a Dating Techniques in Archaeology and Paleoanthropology. *Analytical Chemistry* 59:317A–331A.

1987b *Radiocarbon Dating, An Archaeological Perspective*. Academic Press, New York.

1987c AMS ^{14}C Dating of Critical Bone Samples: Proposed Protocol and Criteria for Evaluation. *Nuclear Instruments and Methods in Physics Research* B29:159–163.

1991 Frameworks for Dating the Late Pleistocene Peopling of the Americas. In *The First Americans: Search and Research*, edited by T. D. Dillehay and D. J. Meltzer, pp. 77–112. CRC Press, Boca Raton.

1992 Radiocarbon Dating of Bone: To Collagen and Beyond. In *Radiocarbon After Four Decades, An Interdisciplinary Perspective*, edited by R. E. Taylor, A. Long, and R. S. Kra, pp. 375–492, Springer-Verlag, New York.

Taylor, R. E., D. J. Donahue, T. H. Zabel, P. E. Damon, and A. J. T. Jull
1984 Radiocarbon Dating by Particle Accelerators: An Archaeological Perspective. In *Archaeological Chemistry III*, edited by G. B. Lambert, pp. 333–356. American Chemical Society, Washington, D.C.

Taylor, R. E., and L. A. Payen
1979 The Role of Archaeometry in American Archaeology: Approaches to the Evaluation of the Antiquity of Homo sapiens in California. In *Advances in Archaeological Method and Theory*, vol. 2, edited by M. Schieffer, pp.239–283. Academic Press, New York.

Taylor, R. E., L. A. Payen, C. A. Prior, P. J. Slota Jr.,R. Gillespie, J. A. J. Gowlett, R. E. B. Hedges, A. J. T. Jull, T. H. Zabel, D. J. Donahue, and R. Berger.
1985 Major Revisions in the Pleistocene Age Assignments for North American Human Skeletons by ^{14}C Accelerator Mass Spectrometry: None Older Than 11,000 ^{14}C Years B.P. *American Antiquity* 50:136–140.

Taylor, R. E., L. A. Payen, and P. J. Slota, Jr.
1992 The Age of the Calaveras Skull: Dating the "Piltdown Man" of the New World. *American Antiquity* 57:269–275.

Taylor, R. E., and P. J. Slota, Jr.
1979 Fraction Studies on Marine Shell and Bone Samples for Radiocarbon Analysis. In *Radiocarbon Dating*, edited by R. Berger and H. E. Suess, pp 422–431. University of California Press, Berkeley.

Thurman, E. M.
  1985 *Organic Geochemistry of Natural Waters*. Kluwer, Boston.

van Klinken, G. J., and R. E. M. Hedges
  1992 Experiments on ^{14}C Dating of Contaminated Bone Using Pepides Resulting from Enzymatic Cleavage of Collagen. *Radiocarbon* 34:292–295.

Wand, J. O.
  1981 Microsample Preparation for Radiocarbon Dating. Unpublished dissertation, Department of Physics, Oxford University.

Wilmsen, E. N.
  1965 An Outline of Early Man Studies in the United States. *American Antiquity* 31:172–192.

Wilson, H. W.
  1979 Possibility of Measurement of ^{14}C by Mass Spectrometer Techniques. In *Radiocarbon Dating*, edited by R. Berger and H. E. Suess, pp. 238–245. University of California Press, Berkeley.

Accelerator C-14 Dating of Human Fossil Skeletons: Assessing Accuracy and Results on New World Specimens

THOMAS W. STAFFORD, JR.
Center for Geochronological Research
INSTAAR, University of Colorado
Boulder, Colorado 80309-0450

The geologic age of human skeletal material in the New World must be based on the direct dating of the human skeletons. Dating skeletons by stratigraphic correlation is never definitive, because many skeletons are isolated discoveries and now reside in museums, or the burials could be stratigraphically intrusive but are not identified as such. Dating should be by accelerator mass spectrometry because only a few grams of bone are needed and several chemical fractions can be dated from one specimen.

Accurate bone dates can be obtained if the fossil contains >0.1-0.2% N *and* the bone has a collagenous amino acid composition. Bones that are poorly preserved and have non-collagenous compositions cannot be dated accurately; they provide only a minimum age for the fossil. If the chemical condition of the bone is known well and its geologic provenance is documented, the correct dating procedures can be used for AMS C-14 dating and the accuracy of the resulting date can be assessed.

Three fossils that were purportedly Pleistocene-age were established to be Holocene, based on the dating of total bone protein and individual amino acids. The Del Mar, California, human fossil dated 5000 yr B.P. and was found to contain human material from two geologic localities. The Anzick, Montana, burial comprised individuals that were 8600 years old and 10,680 years old. The ocher-stained, 10,680-year-old skull fragment is the best dated Clovis Indian-age skeleton presently known. The 11,000–12,000-year-old Tepexpan, Mexico, skeleton dated <2000 yr B.P. and was associated secondarily with mammoth fossils.

INTRODUCTION

The definitive chronology for New World human fossils should be based on the direct dating of fossil human bone. In practice, establishing when humans first entered the New World is difficult because sites are rare, stratigraphic proof of age frequently is missing, and absolute dating methods often fail to give accurate, concordant ages for sediments and associated artifacts. The validity of many Late Pleistocene archaeological sites remains questionable because: (1) experts disagree whether or not humans were involved in the deposition and manufacture of the living features or artifacts; or (2) experts question the veracity of ages determined by geochronologists. Sites remain controversial for decades because scientists accept either great antiquity *or* human presence, but never both conditions.

Whether or not a site is Paleoindian or older (>11,500 yr B.P.) is tested rigorously only if unquestionable artifacts are dated. Examples are human skeletal fossils and bone, wood, or ivory artifacts. The use of human fossils eliminates misinterpretations of stratigraphy and artifact association. The negative aspect of dating human fossils directly is that bone has the lowest credibility of any organic matter used for C-14 dating.

The critical need to date bone, especially human skeletons directly, was the incentive to study the C-14 dating of bone in detail. Our ability to date bone accurately or to assess whether or not bone dates were valid would have a major impact on the chronology of humans in the New World. The following sections present problems and solutions of dating human skeletons, how C-14 dates can be measured accurately, and the results of dating three human fossil localities in the New World.

Dating Controversies for Human Bone

Dating of human skeletal material from North America is the best case study of problems in determining the antiquity of New World humans. The controversy has continued over several decades and opinions have fluctuated from estimates of <12,000–70,000 yr B.P., and now back to <11,000 yr B.P. for these skeletons.

The consensus before 1970 was that human occupation of the New World was no older than 12,000 yr B.P. (Haynes 1967; Martin 1967) and dated predominately to the Holocene epoch (<11,000–11,500 yr B.P.). In 1971, substantially older C-14 dates were obtained on the Laguna (17,150 ± 1470 yr B.P.) and Los Angeles (>23,600 yr B.P.) human fossils (Berger et al. 1971). Using the Laguna fossil to calibrate aspartic acid racemization (AAR) dating of human bone, AAR ages were determined on several human skeletons: Los Angeles Man dated as 26,000 yr B.P. (Bada and Helfman 1975), the Del Mar skeletons as 41,000–48,000 yr B.P. (Bada and Helfman 1975; Bada, et al. 1974), La Jolla Shores Man (W-2) as 44,000 yr B.P. (Bada and Helfman 1975), and the Sunnyvale fossil as 70,000 yr B.P. (Bada and Helfman 1975).

Several of these human fossils were redated in the 1980s by C-14, which revised the ages from 20,000–70,000 yr B.P. to within the Holocene Epoch (<11,000 yr B.P.). Radiocarbon dating by Taylor (1983) yielded ages of 1800–8000 yr B.P. on human fossils dated originally as 28,000–70,000 yr B.P. The advent of accelerator mass spectrometer (AMS) C-14 dating and its ability to date 1 mg of carbon enabled additional human fossils to be measured for C-14: the Sunnyvale fossil's age changed from 70,000 to <5000 yr B.P. (Taylor et al. 1983), and that on Yuha from 23,600 to <4000 yr B.P. (Stafford et al. 1984). Five additional human skeletons previously assigned Pleistocene ages dated to <8470 ± 140 yr B.P. (Bada et al. 1984). Although these Holocene ages were accepted as proof that no human skeletons in the New World were older than ca. 11,000 yr B.P. (Bada 1985; Bada et al. 1984; Gowlett 1986; Taylor et al. 1985), there is experimental evidence that many of the dated human fossils would have yielded Holocene dates even if the fossils had been Pleistocene-age (Stafford et al. 1990).

RADIOCARBON DATING OF FOSSIL BONE

Historically, bone has been the least preferred material for radiocarbon dating. Beginning in 1952 (Libby 1955) and continuing virtually to the present (De Vries and Barendsen 1954; Meltzer and Mead 1983; Münnich 1957; Stafford et al. 1988; Tamers and Pearson 1965), bone has ranked poorly as a datable fossil. It was not until the advent of accelerator mass spectrometer (AMS) C-14 dating that the problems of dating bone became understandable (Stafford et al. 1991).

The difficulty in working with fossil bone is that it is a complex matrix that becomes increasingly more heterogeneous over geologic time. The inorganic or mineral phase of bone, carbonate hydroxyapatite (dahllite), contains natural CO_3^{-2} that exchanges with groundwater, soil and sediment-derived carbonate, thereby contaminating bone apatite's C-14 content. The remaining 20% by weight of bone is organic matter, predominately the protein collagen (Table 1), plus minor amounts of other proteins (e.g., osteonectin and osteocalcin), lipids, and peptides. Over geologic time, these organic constituents lose chemical properties that make them easily separable, and the proteins denature, hydrolyze, and are leached from the bone. In addition, substantial amounts of foreign humates and peptides enter the bone from surrounding sediments and soils. The result is an extremely complex and heterogenous bone chemistry.

Accelerator C-14 dating (Elmore and Phillips 1987; Gove et al. 1987; Hedges and Gowlett 1986) enables most fossil bones to be dated accurately because milligram amounts of highly purified organic fractions can be isolated from the fossil. This approach was impossible by conventional (β-decay counting) C-14 dating, which requires 1000 times more mass of bone. With AMS dating, elaborate chemical separations are used to remove specific contaminants and to isolate well-defined molecular fragments from the original bone collagen.

Chemical Pretreatment of Fossil Bone

Details of the chemical pretreatment of fossil bone have been given previously (Stafford et al. 1988, 1990, 1991). Briefly, bone is first assayed for its carbon, hydrogen, and nitrogen (CHN) content and its quantitative amino acid composition is determined on less ~100 mg of bone powder. Modern bone contains 4 to 4.5% N and has the composition of the protein collagen (Table 1). A fossil bone is dated only if it has >0.1-0.2% N *and* a collagenous amino acid composition. After physical cleaning to remove sediment and soil-derived organic matter, the fossil is decalcified in weak HCl. The insoluble residue contains collagen, sediment, and modern cellulose contaminants. The residue is extracted with hot (90°C) water, which dissolves the collagen, but not plant cellulose or foreign proteins, which are precipitated. After filtering and freeze drying of the gelatin solution, the gelatinized collagen is hydrolyzed into its individual amino acids by heating with $6N$ HCl at 110°C for 24 hours. The supernatant is passed through an adsorption resin (XAD-2) that removes fulvic acids, the major contaminant in fossil bone (Stafford et al. 1988). This fraction, the XAD-purified gelatin hydrolyzate, is used either for AMS C-14 dating, or it is resolved further into specific amino acids. The isolation of individual amino acids is performed by using liquid chromatography and requires HCl to elute the amino acids from cation exchange resins. The amino acids are detected by their UV absorbance as they elute (Macko et al 1987; Stafford et al. 1988). Each amino acid is collected in a glass tube and dried under vacuum to a crystalline solid. The amino acid is combusted to CO_2, which is purified and converted to a graphite target (Verkouteren et al. 1987) for AMS C-14 measurement (Donahue et al. 1983, 1987). Present capabilities of AMS enable 0.5-1.0 mg of carbon to be dated routinely. Present precisions are approximately ± 1%; i.e., ± 90–110 years for samples 11,000 years old.

The size limitations and dating accuracy for fossil bones are controlled not by the accelerator technique but by the chemical and geological condition of the fossil bone. AMS C-14 dates can be measured on as little as 50 µg (0.05 mg) of carbon (Verkouteren et al. 1987). The optimal amount of carbon is 1 mg for the dating of human fossils. One gram of modern bone yields 200 mg of collagen protein or 90 mg of carbon (collagen is 45% C by weight). A fossil bone that contains only 10% of its original protein will have approximately 0.4% N and will yield approximately 20 mg of protein (~9 mg carbon). Considering the losses that occur during the numerous pretreatment steps, one gram of bone is the minimum amount that should be submitted for an AMS C-14 date. This is especially true for bones that are suspected to be older than 20,000 yr B.P., because at this and older ages, contamination with modern carbon must be kept to a minimum, which is done by using as "large" a sample as possible.

Radiocarbon Experiments of Known-Age Fossil Bone

Understanding the chemical problems of dating fossil bone required the measurement of C-14 on bones having a known geologic age (Stafford et al. 1987). Only by using known-age material can contaminants be identified conclusively. The known-age fossils (mammoths) were from four North American Clovis sites—Domebo, Oklahoma (Leonhardy 1966), Dent, Colorado (Haynes 1974), Escapule, Arizona (Hemmings and Haynes 1969) and the BLM mammoth site, which is near the Escapule locality and in the same geologic stratum as Escapule. Clovis-age mammoth bones were used for two reasons: (1) the fossils were dated independently to 11,000–11,500 yr B.P. (Haynes 1984, 1987); and (2) the bones were old enough that trace-levels of modern-carbon contamination would significantly affect the C-14 age. Because diagenesis substantially affects dating accuracy, fossils with different degrees of preservation and contamination were selected: the Domebo and Dent mammoths had collagenous compositions, whereas the Escapule and BLM mammoths had a non-collagenous composition (Table 1).

Figures 1–3 and Table 2 summarize dating results for the known-age mammoths. The data show the accuracy achieved by dating individual amino acids and explain why Pleistocene-age fossils often yield Holocene ages. The most important aspect about the C-14 dates on each of the three specimens is that each has a different pattern of C-14 ages. In common among the fossils is that the collagenous bones were dated accurately, whereas the non-collagenous bones dated inaccurately. The Domebo and Dent fossils have nearly identical percent N and amino acid compositions, yet the same chemical fractions that dated accurately for one fossil dated inaccurately for the other. The C-14 dates did not become consistently accurate until the XAD-purified phases were used. Fractions such as total collagen, base-leached collagen, and gelatin are the chemical phases that have been and continue to be used for C-14 dating of bone. Dates on these fractions should be considered questionable and their use discontinued for C-14 dating.

The dates for the Escapule and BLM mammoth bones contrast markedly with those for the collagenous bones.

Table 1. Amino Acid and Percent Nitrogen Analyses for Fossil Bones. Analyses Compare Bones with Collagenous Amino Acid Compositions.

SAMPLE	MODERN BONE	SIGMA BOVINE COLLAGEN	DENT	DOMEBO	ESCAPULE	BLM MAMMOTH	MURRAY SPRINGS MAMMOTH	DEL MAR SPHENOID
Percent N	4.5	15.64	0.83	0.69	0.03	0.01	0.03	0.69
Amino Acid Residues ‰								
Hydroxyproline	90	90	91	84	0	0	0	95
Aspartic Acid	53	47	48	54	293	218	223	47
Threonine	19	17	19	23	29	45	32	17
Serine	35	31	36	37	0	50	42	29
Glutamic Acid	71	73	71	73	131	150	174	78
Proline	124	114	124	123	41	0	0	121
Glycine	322	338	327	322	279	236	189	342
Alanine	89	113	123	124	84	97	89	118
Valine	27	26	27	30	12	30	38	31
Methionine	7	7	5	7	0	29	14	5
Isoleucine	14	12	11	12	28	32	19	10
Leucine	32	26	27	33	29	44	36	24
Tyrosine	6	4	1	5	5	0	0	0
Phenylalanine	16	20	14	17	13	0	15	7
Histidine	5	4	2	4	0	0	17	2
Hydroxylysine	5	16	0	0	4	0	0	13
Lysine	28	21	28	29	51	68	54	30
Arginine	56	39	44	22	0	0	58	30
Total	999	998	998	999	999	999	1000	999

Even at the molecular level, the Escapule and BLM bone were found to be contaminated with recent C-14. The significance is that there is a dichotomy in bone radiocarbon dating—collagenous bones can be dated accurately, but non-collagenous fossils are contaminated at the molecular level. Regardless of the chemical pretreatment used and how advanced the C-14 measurement methods, these poorly preserved fossils will yield C-14 ages that are hundreds to several thousand of years too young.

AMS C-14 Dating of Human Fossils

The geologic ages were evaluated on four purportedly Pleistocene-age human skeletons from North and Central America. These human skeletons were analyzed by using AMS C-14 dating of total protein and individual amino acids. The four skeletons were considered to have considerable probability to be Clovis-age or older. The specimens were from the Del Mar site, California (Stafford and Tyson 1988), the Anzick site, Montana (Taylor 1969), and the Tepexpan site, Mexico (de Terra 1951; Martinez 1947). The AMS C-14 ages are summarized in Figures 4–6 and Table 5.

Del Mar, California, Human Fossil

The Del Mar fossil was believed to be 11,000–48,000 yr B.P. based on dating by aspartic acid racemization (Bada and Helfman 1975; Bada et al. 1974) and uranium series disequilibrium (Bischoff and Rosenbauer 1981). Subsequent C-14 dating by accelerator mass spectrometry revised the age to 5270–5400 yr B.P. (Bada et al. 1984).

Additional inquiry revealed that more than one human skeleton had been curated as the "Del Mar Man" and the bones were not only from different individuals, but probably were from different geological environments. The skull on display in the San Diego Museum of Man was well preserved, had a collagenous amino acid composition, and contained 0.69% N. The tibia (frequently misidentified in publications as a femur) was non-collagenous and contained 0.06% N (Stafford and Tyson 1989).

Seven additional AMS C-14 dates were measured on the Del Mar tibia and a sphenoid fragment from the skull on display (Table 3, Figure 4) (Stafford and Tyson 1989). The results were that the two tibia C-14 dates were different by 4000 years (5380 ± 390 and 1150 ± 410 yr B.P.), whereas five dates on the sphenoid collagen and individual amino acids were concordant at two

Del Mar Tibia	Tepexpan	Gelatin Anzick White	Gelatin Anzick Fe
0.06	0.06	–	–
0	0	97	89
132	244	46	45
32	38	17	18
49	36	29	35
111	81	75	76
74	0	117	113
276	359	334	326
126	53	114	112
37	0	24	28
0	40	21	10
37	36	11	11
46	40	26	26
2	10	0	3
26	19	18	17
1	0	2	5
5	5	8	9
13	26	27	30
32	13	33	47
999	1000	999	100

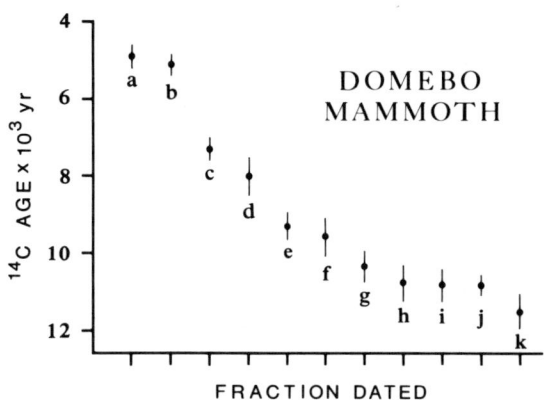

Figure 1. Domebo mammoth AMS radiocarbon dates arranged in order of increasing geologic age. Sample descriptions including Arizona Accelerator laboratory numbers: a) fulvic acids (AA-812); b) fulvic acids (AA-819); c) untreated bone hydroxyapatite (AA-818); d) total carbon, untreated bone (AA-801); e) HAc-treated-bone apatite (AA-815); f) weak-acid soluble carbon (AA-802); g) unpurified gelatin (AA-803); h) total carbon, HAc-treated bone (AA-804); i) XAD-purified gelatin hydrolyzate (AA-805); j) weak-acid insoluble collagen (AA-824); k) XAD-purified collagen hydrolyzate (AA-825). Error bars are one standard deviation of the measurement of counting error.

standard deviations. The average age for the five sphenoid dates was 4900 ± 40 yr B.P.

The significance of the last set of AMS C-14 measurements is that the Del Mar skull is unquestionably Holocene in age; however, this conclusion is based on dates from the sphenoid fragment, *not* the tibia. The age concordance between the skull and tibia fossils is considered fortuitous because the tibia is very poorly preserved, has a non-collagenous composition, and is unsuitable for absolute C-14 dating. The 4000-year difference between the two tibia C-14 dates is a dating characteristic identical to the Escapule mammoth bone, which dated 5000 years too young. Due to the non-collagenous composition of the Del Mar tibia, it would have yielded a Holocene C-14 age even had it been >11,000 years old.

Anzick Human Calvaria, Montana

The Anzick collection comprised two juvenile, human cranial fragments that had been collected ex situ from a Montana rock shelter (Lahren and Bonnichsen 1974; Taylor 1969). One calvarium was stained with hematite and the second was bleached white. Both were believed

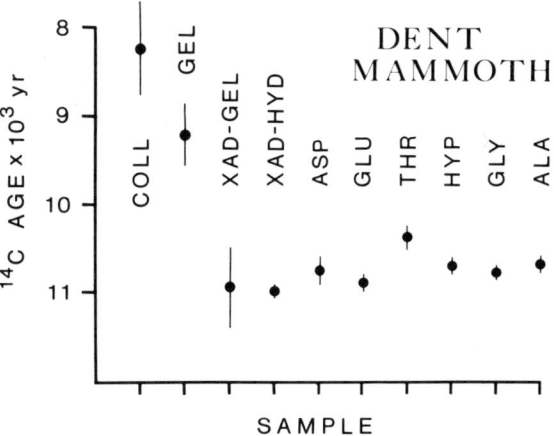

Figure 2. Dent mammoth AMS radiocarbon dates arranged in order of increasingly more pure chemical fractions. COLL = collagen; GEL = gelatin; XAD-GEL = XAD-2-purified gelatin hydrolyzate; XAD-HYD = XAD-2-purified collagen hydrolyzate; ASP = aspartic acid; GLU = glutamic acid; SER = serine; THR = threonine; HYP = hydroxyproline; GLY = glycine. Error bars are one standard deviation of the measurement of counting error.

to have been contemporaneous with hematite-stained lithic and bone artifacts that were attributed stylistically to a Clovis-culture tool assemblage. Each specimen was dated by using gelatin, hydrolyzed gelatin, and indi-

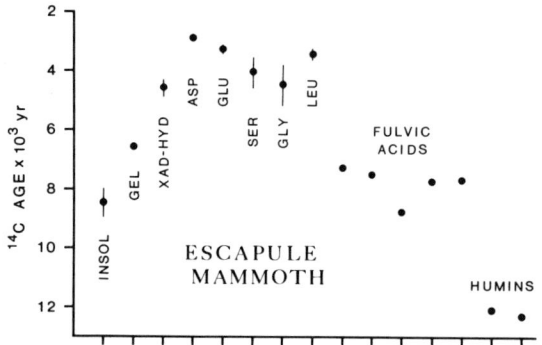

Figure 3. Escapule mammoth AMS radiocarbon dates. INSOL = weak HCl insoluble residue; GEL = gelatin; XAD-HYD = XAD-2-purified collagen hydrolyzate; ASP = aspartic acid; GLU = glutamic acid; SER = serine; GLY = glycine; ALA = alanine; LEU = leucine. Error bars are one standard deviation of the measurement of counting error.

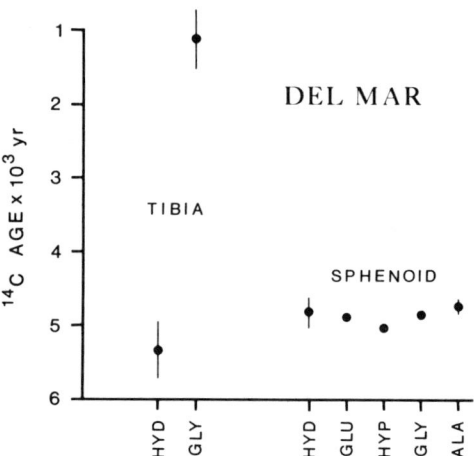

Figure 4. Del Mar, California human skeleton AMS radiocarbon dates, San Diego Museum collection SDM-16709. Sphenoid fragment is from displayed skull; tibia is remainder of sample previously dated by uranium series (Bischoff and Rosenbauer 1981) and aspartic acid racemization (Bada and Helfman 1975; Bada et al. 1974). HYP = hydroxyproline; GLY = glycine; GLU = glutamic acid; ALA = alanine. Error bars are one standard deviation of the measurement of counting error.

Table 2. AMS Radiocarbon Dates on Two Poorly Preserved, Non–Collagenous-Composition, Known-Age Fossil Mammoths

AMS Lab No. Target	Sample Description	C-14 Date, yr b.p.	
Escapule Mammoth (.03% N)	Known Age = 11,000 yr B.P.		
AA-2653	0.6N HCl insoluble residue	8460 ± 270	Fe-C
AA-2964	"Gelatin" fraction	6610 ± 90	Graphite
AA-2655	XAD-purified hydrolyzate of AA-2653	4750 ± 370	Fe-C
AA-2958	Aspartic acid, HCl insoluble phase	3100 ± 110	Fe-C
AA-2959	Aspartic acid; "gelatin" phase	2080 ± 170	Fe-C
AA-2961	Glutamic acid; HCl insoluble phase	3470 ± 160	Fe-C
AA-2658	Serine; HCl insoluble phase	4070 ± 490	Fe-C
AA-2660	Aspartic and glutamic acids, serine; HCl insoluble phase	2270 ± 360	Fe-C
AA-2661	Glycine; HCl insoluble phase	4540 ± 710	Fe-C
AA-2962	Leucine, isoleucine, lysine, histidine, and arginine; HCl insoluble phase	3460 ± 210	Fe-C
AA-2968	Fulvic acids; HCl insoluble phase, acetone eluted from XAD-2 resin	7260 ± 80	Graphite
AA-2970	Fulvic acids; HCl insoluble phase, NaOH-eluted from XAD-2 resin	8780 ± 80	Graphite
AA-2965	Hot water insoluble phase from weak HCl insoluble fraction	9340 ± 90	Graphite
AA-2972	6N HCl insoluble residue from hydrolysis of weak HCl insoluble residue	12,280 ± 110	Graphite
BLM Mammoth (0.01% N)	Known Age = 11,000 yr		
AA-4937	XAD-2-purified protein hydrolyzate	6030 ± 250	Graphite

vidual amino acids. The AMS C-14 dates on each skull fragment were evidence that only one of the human skeletons was Clovis-age. The bleached specimen had an average date of 8600 ± 90 yr B.P., whereas the ocher-stained calvarium dated at 10,680 ± 50 yr B.P. The younger skeleton was apparently derived from an overlying Archaic site and had become associated secondarily with the Clovis artifacts. Had bone not been dated directly, both skeletons would have been attributed to the Clovis time period.

The dates are considered valid for these reasons: (1) both fossils had collagenous compositions (Table 1); and (2) ages on XAD-purified hydrolyzates were concordant with dates on individual amino acids (Table 4, Figure 5). Without dates on individual amino acids, the 2000-year age difference between the two skulls could not have been recognized.

These results indicate why an age determination on a single chemical fraction is not absolute proof of age.

Tepexpan, Mexico, Human Skeleton

The Tepexpan site, near Mexico City, Mexico, yielded a human skull and postcranial bones that were associated with a fossil mammoth, itself being associated with an obsidian artifact (Martinez 1947). The burial was dated by stratigraphic association based on C-14 as 11,000–12,000 years old (de Terra 1951). The human skeleton

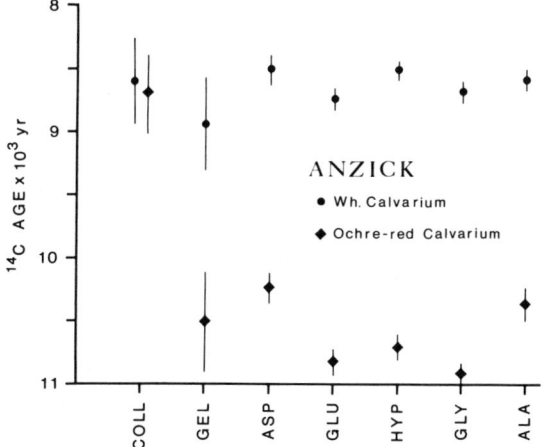

Figure 5. Anzick, Montana, human skeleton AMS radiocarbon dates on a bleached white calvarium (dots) and ocher-stained calvarium (diamonds). COLL = untreated, weak-acid insoluble collagen; GEL = untreated gelatin; ASP = aspartic acid; GLU = glutamic acid; HYP = hydroxyproline; GLY = glycine; ALA = alanine. Error bars are one standard deviation of the measurement of counting error.

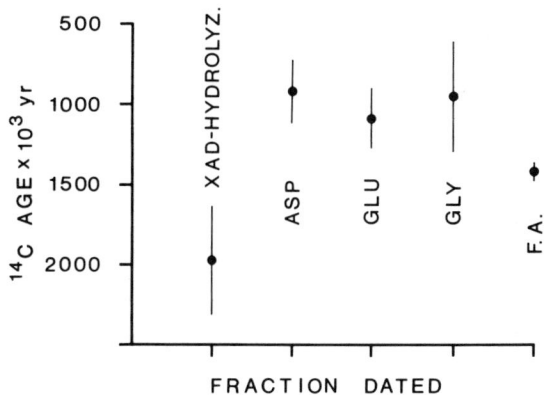

Figure 6. Tepexpan, Mexico, human skeleton AMS radiocarbon dates. XAD-HYD = XAD-purified hydrolyzate; ASP = Aspartic Acid; GLU = glutamic acid; GLY = glycine; F.A. = fulvic acids. Error bars are one standard deviation of the measurement of counting error.

Table 3. Del Mar Skeleton AMS Radiocarbon Dates. Samples Are Tibia and Sphenoid Fragments of the Human Burial.

AMS Lab No. Target	Sample Description	C-14 Date, Yr B.P.	
(Sphenoid)			
AA-2665	XAD-2-purified collagen hydrolyzate	4830 ± 200	Fe-C
AA-2948	Glutamic acid	4900 ± 70	Graphite
AA-2949	Hydroxyproline	5060 ± 80	Graphite
AA-2950	Glycine	4870 ± 60	Graphite
AA-2951	Alanine	4750 ± 100	Graphite
(Tibia)			
AA-2666	XAD-2-purified hydrolyzate of insoluble residue 0.6N HCl	5380 ± 390	Fe-C
AA-2952	Glycine	1150 ± 410	Fe-C

had particular importance because Tepexpan is only a few kilometers north of the Paleoindian site Santa Isabel Iztapan (Aveleyera 1956).

It was difficult to date the Tepexpan skeleton because it was very poorly preserved chemically, despite being well preserved physically. The bone contained 0.1–0.06% N and had a non-collagenous amino acid composition (Table 1). Had dates existed only on the amino acids from the Tepexpan bone, its age would have been indeterminate because the fossil's poor preservation would have precluded accurate dating. The additional data were a date on fulvic acids from the bone and stratigraphic work at the Tepexpan site.

All C-14 dates on the Tepexpan fossil were <2000 yr B.P., including the fulvic acids (Table 5, Figure 6). The fulvic acids are contaminants that enter the bone during burial and will have a mean C-14 age; i.e., contain carbon derived over the duration of the bone's burial. Fossils with a known age of 11,000 yr B.P. (Table 2, Figure 1) have fulvic acids dating around 5000 yr B.P. The geologically recent age for the Tepexpan fulvic acids is evidence that the fossil could have been buried <4000–5000 yr B.P., but not 11,000 yr B.P.

The *maximum* age for the Tepexpan skeleton was based conclusively on stratigraphic evidence collected by the author during the summer of 1986, when Diana Santamaria of Instituto Nacional de Anthropologia Arqueologia E Historia of Mexico City directed excavations near the original Tepexpan site. The sediments containing the Tepexpan skeleton were found to overly disconformably the Pleistocene sediments that contained mammoth bones. The sediments containing the human bones also contained pottery, thus dating the burial as no older than 3500 yr B.P.

CONCLUSIONS

The preceding results are an illustration that specific fossil bones can be dated accurately and that AMS C-14 dating can resolve controversies regarding the antiquity of human skeletons in the New World. The antiquity of humans will continue to be obscured by endless debates over artifacts vs. geofacts and over whether an artifact-bearing stratum dates as Holocene or Pleistocene. Only by combining rigorous geologic studies with C-14 dating of charcoal and bone can these problematic sites and human remains be dated properly.

Accurate bone C-14 dates can be obtained if the fossils are selected properly and if the preservation of the fossil is characterized chemically. Bone can be dated accurately if: (1) the bone has >0.1-0.2% N *and* a collagenous amino acid composition; (2) the chemical pretreatment is rigorous and allows for the removal of humic and fulvic acids; (3) individual amino acids are isolated for the verification of dates on total collagen hydrolyzates; and (4) if non-collagenous bones are identified as such and *not* used for absolute C-14 dating. Poorly preserved bone does have value, but only if certain chemical fractions (humins) are dated and it is

Table 4. Anzick Site AMS Radiocarbon Dates on Two Human Skulls

AMS LAB NO. TARGET	SAMPLE DESCRIPTION	C-14 DATE, YR B.P.	
(White Calvarium)			
AA-313C	0.6N HCl insoluble collagen	8620 ± 340	Fe-C
AA-313D	Untreated gelatin	8940 ± 370	Fe-C
AA-2973	Aspartic acid from hydrolyzed gelatin	8510 ± 120*	Graphite
AA-2974	Glutamic acid from hydrolyzed gelatin	8740 ± 90*	Graphite
AA-2975	Hydroxyproline from hydrolyzed gelatin	8520 ± 80*	Graphite
AA-2976	Glycine from hydrolyzed gelatin	8680 ± 90*	Graphite
AA-2977	Alanine from hydrolyzed gelatin	8590 ± 90*	Graphite
Average C-14 age based on fractions designated with *		8610 ± 90	
(FE-Stained Calvarium)			
AA-313A	0.6N HCl insoluble collagen	8690 ± 310	Fe-C
AA-313B	Untreated gelatin	10,500 ± 400	Fe-C
AA-2978	Aspartic acid from hydrolyzed gelatin	10,240 ± 120*	Graphite
AA-2979	Glutamic acid from hydrolyzed gelatin	10,820 ± 100*	Graphite
AA-2980	Hydroxyproline from hydrolyzed gelatin	10,710 ± 100*	Graphite
AA-2981	Glycine from hydrolyzed gelatin	10,940 ± 90*	Graphite
AA-2982	Alanine from hydrolyzed gelatin	10,370 ± 130*	Graphite
Average C-14 age based on fractions designated with *		10,680 ± 50	

Table 5. Tepexpan Human Skeleton AMS Radiocarbon Dates

AMS Lab No. Target	Sample Description	C-14 Date, Yr B.P.	
AA-2667	XAD-2-purified weak HCl insoluble collagen hydrolyzate	1980 ± 330	Fe-C
AA-2953	Aspartic acid	920 ± 190	Fe-C
AA-2954	Glutamic acid	1090 ± 180	Fe-C
AA-2955	Glycine	960 ± 340	Fe-C
AA-2956	Fulvic acids	1430 ± 60	Graphite

recognized that the dates are minimum ages for the fossil. Future controversies can be avoided if the geologic context of the fossil is known accurately and if the most detailed AMS C-14 dating is applied to the fossil materials.

ACKNOWLEDGMENTS

Funding for this research was provided by National Science Foundation Grant BNS 86-16891, the Leakey Foundation, the American Philosophical Society, and postdoctoral fellowships from the Carnegie Institution of Washington, D.C. and the National Research Council.

REFERENCES CITED

Aveleyra A. de Anda, L.
  1956 The Second Mammoth and Associated Artifacts and Santa Isabel Iztapan, Mexico. *American Antiquity* 22:12–28.

Bada, J. L.
  1985 Aspartic Acid Racemization Ages of California Paleoindian Skeletons. *American Antiquity* 50:645–647.

Bada, J. L., and P. M. Helfman
  1975 Amino Acid Racemization Dating of Fossil Bones. *World Archaeology* 7:160–173.

Bada, J. L., R. Gillespie, J. A. J. Gowlett, and R. E. M. Hedges
  1984 Accelerator Mass Spectrometry Radiocarbon Ages of Amino Acid Extracts from Californian Palaeoindian Skeletons. *Nature* (London) 312:442–444.

Bada, J. L., R. A. Schroeder, and G. F. Carter
  1974 New Evidence for the Antiquity of Man in North America Deduced from Aspartic Acid Racemization. *Science* 184:791–793.

Berger, R., R. Protsch, R. Reynolds, C. Rozaire, and J. R. Sackett
  1971 New Radiocarbon Dates Based on Bone Collagen of California Paleoindians. *Contributions of University of California Archaeological Research Facility* 12:43–49.

Bischoff, J. L., and J. R. Rosenbauer
  1981 Uranium Series Dating of Human Skeletal Remains from the Del Mar and Sunnyvale Sites, California. *Science* 213:1003–1005.

de Terra, H.
  1951 Radiocarbon Age Measurements and Fossil Man in Mexico. *Science* 113:124–125.

De Vries, H., and G. W. Barendsen
  1954 Measurements of Age by the Carbon-14 Technique. *Nature* (London) 174:1138–1141.

Donahue, D. J., A. J. T. Jull, T. W. Linick, A. Hatheway, L. Toolin, B. Gore, and P. Damon
  1987 Some Results from the Arizona TAMS Facility: AMS Ages of Athletic, Artistic, and Animal Artifacts. *Nuclear Instruments and Methods in Physics Research.* B29:169–172.

Donahue, D. J., A. J. T. Jull, T. H. Zabel, and P. E. Damon
  1983 The Use of Accelerators for Archaeological Dating. *Nuclear Instruments and Methods in Physics Research* 218:425–429.

Elmore, D., and F. M. Phillips
  1987 Accelerator Mass Spectrometry for Measurement of Long-Lived Radioisotopes. *Science* 236:543–550.

Gove, H. E., A. E. Litherland, and D. Elmore
  1987 Accelerator Mass Spectrometry. *Nuclear Instruments and Methods in Physics Research* B29:1–445.

Gowlett, J. A. J.
  1986 Problems in Dating Early Human Settlement of the Americas. In *Archaeological Results from Accelerator Dating*, edited by J. A. J. Gowlett and R. E. M. Hedges, pp. 51–62. Oxford University Press, Oxford.

Haynes, C. V., Jr.
  1967 Carbon-14 Dates and Early Man in the New

World. In *Pleistocene Extinctions: The Search for a Cause*, edited by P. S. Martin and H. E. Wright, pp. 267–286. Yale University Press, New Haven.

1974 Archaeological Geology of Some Selected Paleo-Indian Sites. In *History and Prehistory of the Lubbock Lake Site*, edited by C. Black, pp. 133–139. The Museum Journal, vol. 15. West Texas Museum Association, Lubbock.

1984 Stratigraphy and Late Pleistocene Extinction in the United States. In *Quaternary Extinctions: A Prehistoric Revolution*, edited by P. S. Martin and R. G. Klein, pp. 345–353. The University of Arizona Press, Tucson.

1987 Clovis Origin Update. *Kiva* 52:83–93.

Hedges, R. E. M., and J. A. J. Gowlett
1986 Radiocarbon Dating by Accelerator Mass Spectrometry. *Scientific American* 254:100–107.

Hemmings, E. T., and C. V. Haynes, Jr.
1969 The Escapule Mammoth and Associated Projectile Points, San Pedro Valley, Arizona. *Journal of the Arizona Academy of Sciences* 5:184–188.

Lahren, L., and R. Bonnichsen
1974 Bone Foreshafts from a Clovis Burial in Southwestern Montana. *Science* 186:147–150.

Leonhardy, F. C., editor
1966 *Domebo: A Paleo-Indian Mammoth Kill in the Prairie-Plains*. Contributions of the Museum of the Great Plains No. 1. Great Plains Historical Association, Lawton.

Libby, W. F.
1955 *Radiocarbon Dating*. The University of Chicago Press, Chicago.

Macko, S. A., M. L. Fogel, P. E. Hare, and T. C. Hoering
1987 Isotopic Fractionation of Nitrogen and Carbon in the Synthesis of Amino Acids by Microorganisms. *Chemical Geology* 65:79–92.

Martin, P. S.
1967 Prehistoric Overkill. In *Pleistocene Extinctions: The Search for a Cause*, edited by P. S. Martin and H. E. Wright, pp. 75–120. Yale University Press, New Haven.

Martinez del Rio, P.
1947 El Hombre de Tepexpam. *Cuadernos Americanos* 34:139–150.

Meltzer, D. J., and J. I. Mead
1983 The Timing of Late Pleistocene Mammalian Extinctions in North America. *Quaternary Research* 19:130–135.

Münnich, K. O.
1957 Heidelberg Natural Radiocarbon Measurements I. *Science* 126:194–199.

Stafford, T. W., Jr., K. Brendel, and R. C. Duhamel
1988 Radiocarbon, ^{13}C and ^{15}N Analysis of Fossil Bone: Removal of Humates with XAD-2 Resin. *Geochimica et Cosmochimica Acta* 52:2257–2267.

Stafford, T. W., Jr., P. E. Hare, L. Currie, A. J. T. Jull, and D. Donahue
1990 Accuracy of North American Human Skeleton Ages. *Quaternary Research* 34:111–120.

1991 Accelerator Radiocarbon Dating at the Molecular Level. *Journal of Archaeological Science* 18:35–72.

Stafford, T. W. Jr., A. J. T. Jull, K. Brendel, R. C. Duhamel, R. C., and D. Donahue
1987 Study of Bone Radiocarbon Dating Accuracy at the University of Arizona NSF Accelerator Facility for Radioisotope Analysis. *Radiocarbon* 29:24–44.

Stafford, T. W., Jr., A. J. T. Jull, T. H. Zabel, D. J. Donahue, R. C. Duhamel, K. Brendel, C. V. Haynes, Jr., J. L. Bischoff, L. A. Payen, and R. E. Taylor
1984 Holocene Age of the Yuha Burial: Direct Radiocarbon Determinations by Accelerator Mass Spectrometry. *Nature* (London) 308:446–447.

Stafford, T. W., Jr., and R. A. Tyson
1989 Accelerator Radiocarbon Dates on Charcoal, Shell and Human Bone from the Del Mar Site, California. *American Antiquity* 54:389–395.

Tamers, M. A., and F. J. Pearson, Jr.
1965 Validity of Radiocarbon Dates on Bone. *Nature* (London) 208:1053–1055.

Taylor, D.
1969 The Wilsall Excavations: An Exercise in Frustration. *Montana Academy of Science Proceedings* 29:147–150.

Taylor, R. E.
1983 Non-Concordance of Radiocarbon and Amino Acid Racemization Deduced Age Estimates on Human Bone. *Radiocarbon* 25:647–654.

Taylor, R. E., L. A. Payen, B. Gerow, D. J. Donahue, T. H. Zabel, A. J. T. Jull, and P. E. Damon
1983 Middle Holocene Age of the Sunnyvale Human Skeleton. *Science* 220:1271–1273.

Taylor, R. E., L. A. Payen, C. A. Prior, P. Slota, Jr., R. Gillespie, J. A. J. Gowlett, R. E. M. Hedges, A. J. T. Jull, T. H. Zabel, D. J. Donahue, and R. Berger
1985 Major Revisions in the Pleistocene Age Assignments for North American Human Skeletons by C-14 Accelerator Mass Spectrometry: None Older Than 11,000 C-14 Years B.P. *American Antiquity* 50:136–140.

Verkouteren, R. M., G. A. Klouda, L. A. Currie, D. Donahue, A. J. T. Jull, and T. W. Linick
   1987 Preparation of Microgram Samples on Iron Wool for Radiocarbon Analysis via Accelerator Mass Spectrometry: A Closed System Approach. *Nuclear Instruments and Methods in Physics Research* B29:41–44.

The Role of Geoarchaeology in Paleoindian Research

C. REID FERRING
*Institute of Applied Sciences
University of North Texas,
Denton, TX 76203*

INTRODUCTION

To varying degrees, North American archaeologists have almost always borrowed concepts and/or methods from the earth sciences as components of their research. Formal, or at least explicit, application of geological methods to archaeological problems is known as geoarchaeology or archaeological geology. These are close to subdisciplines in the opinion of some archaeologists and many geologists; others consider such borrowing as mere multidisciplinary research. Regardless, the volume of literature devoted to geoarchaeology and the formal integration of geology into archaeological research (especially in Cultural Resources Management projects) have increased substantially in recent years.

My objective in this paper is to briefly describe several key aspects of Paleoindian archaeology that entail substantial application of geological concepts and methods. The focus is on those concepts and methods. These discussions will be illustrated with reference to broadly distributed Paleoindian research, and with specific examples from my own research in the Upper Trinity River Drainage Basin in Texas. This paper does not include a "model" for research strategies, but simply a discussion of some important and recurrent research issues associated with Paleoindian archaeology.

From a historical perspective, it is significant that geology and geologists have been integral components of Paleoindian archaeology from its inception (Ferring 1990a; Haynes 1990). Recent literature shows that this association persists. However, I believe that the prominent role of geology in Paleoindian archaeology is more than a historical coincidence, and is explained by (1) the geological character and contexts of many Paleoindian sites; and (2) by the distinctive archaeological, paleoenvironmental, and evolutionary problems that are addressed by students of the Paleoindian period. Clearly, many of the problems and research methods I consider here are germane to other time periods and archaeological contexts. However, both environmental and cultural conditions in North America at the close of the Pleistocene were unique.

Late Quaternary environmental changes in North America, particularly changes about the Pleistocene-Holocene boundary, were profound (Bryant and Holloway 1985; Martin and Klein 1984; Porter 1983; Ruddiman and Wright 1987). Within a relatively brief period there were significant changes in climate, sea level, fluvial processes, glacial ice volume, and biotic communities. With respect to the North American archaeological record, Paleoindian occupations occurred at a time of environmental and geologic changes on a scale that has not been repeated in the Holocene. Geoarchaeological investigations of the Paleoindian period thus entail consideration of patterns of geologic change at the high end of the scale of "steady state equilibrium" as defined by Schumm (1977). Changes at the Pleistocene-Holocene boundary were qualitatively distinct compared to Holocene patterns of geologic responses to climate change.

Also, Paleoindian archaeology focuses on the initial peopling of the New World and the rapid patterns of adaptive change that followed. This cultural scenario is radically different from the subsequent culture history of North America, and requires different assumptions concerning fundamental issues of culture change and cultural ecology. Indeed, when the unique cultural setting for the peopling of an uninhabited continent is superposed on the rapid and dramatic changes in landscapes and biotic communities of North America during that period, one must conclude that Paleoindian archaeology, and geoarchaeology, present unique research challenges.

The following discussions draw from a broad range of papers on Paleoindian geoarchaeology. In later parts of the paper, I also provide brief descriptions of our work in the Upper Trinity River Drainage Basin, Texas, and particularly at the Aubrey Clovis Site (Ferring 1990b; Figure 1). Quaternary geology in the Upper Trinity Basin has been renewed in recent years, following a long period when no Quaternary Geology was conducted (Ferring 1986, 1987). Rather than add a short "report" on these investigations, which are still in progress, it seemed more economical to allude to this research along with discussion of similar kinds of research at other localities in other regions.

GEOARCHAEOLOGY AND PALEOINDIAN RESEARCH

In the broadest sense, geoarchaeology is the application of methods and concepts from the earth sciences to archaeological problems. While the specific framework for this integration of methods (and specialists) is debated (Butzer 1982), the results of this interdisciplinary approach are usually the same and are almost always beneficial to archaeological research.

The potential advantages of geological methods and concepts for archaeological research are wide-ranging. Here, I emphasize geoarchaeological research strategies that are implemented in the field. Certainly geological concepts and methods are used in the laboratory, for analysis of sediments, soils, and interpretation of geoarchaeological records. But as in most geology, fieldwork is the most critical phase of investigation. It is during fieldwork that descriptions of intact sediments and soils are made, that sampling strategies are defined and implemented, and where geological information is integrated into archaeological research strategies involving site survey, testing, excavation, and analysis. There are few situations where lab work can atone for inadequate fieldwork. This is equally true for geology and archaeology. In my opinion, one of the major differences between academic training in geology and archae-

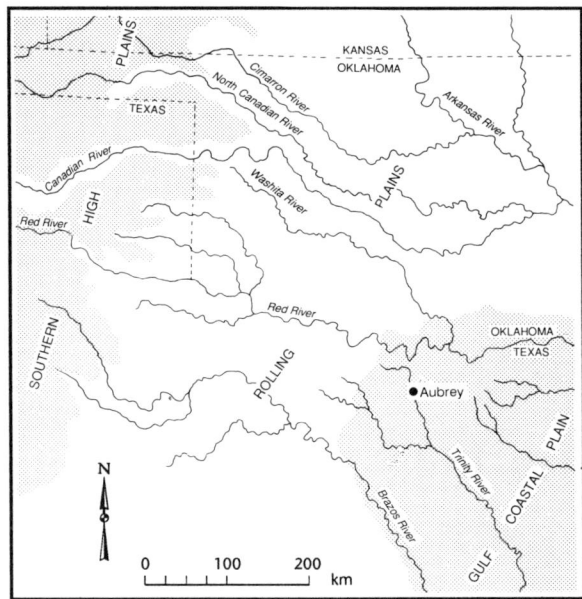

Figure 1. Map of the Southern Plains with Aubrey Clovis Site Location.

ology is the strong emphasis on fieldwork in most geology curricula contrasted with minimal emphasis in most archaeology programs.

In the following discussions, I will stress several areas of fieldwork that pertain to Paleoindian archaeology: site prediction and discovery, stratigraphy and dating, reconstruction of past environments, and site formation histories. These are areas of concern to archaeologists working in any temporal frame; here I will simply discuss them with reference to Paleoindian contexts and illustrate approaches to these problems with examples from the Paleoindian literature.

I must emphasize that the focus here on *geoarchaeological* concepts and methods is explicit. Broader theoretical and substantive issues concerning Paleoindian populations, patterns of adaptation, and processes of culture change are critical aspects of Paleoindian research. Archaeologists are ultimately concerned with the behavioral and evolutionary dynamics of Paleoindian populations. Geoarchaeology is only one research strategy that plays a role in Paleoindian archaeology. While I allude to kinds of problems that geoarchaeology can address, it is not my intent to discuss general theoretical aspects of archaeology. Without such discussions, this paper may appear overly empirical or to register ignorance of important broader archaeological issues such as espoused by Binford (1981, 1982, 1986).

Geology and archaeology are practiced at a range of scales, from large regional surveys to microstratigraphic analysis of individual sites to analysis of artifact or fossil attributes and taphonomy. Here I discuss geoarchaeological research at scales ranging from large regional or basin investigations to within-site investigations of stratigraphy, past environments, and site formation processes. The temporal scale of discussions is limited to the Paleoindian period in North America, which is late Pleistocene to early Holocene (ca. 11,500–8500 yr B.P.).

REGIONAL GEOARCHAEOLOGY: FRAMEWORKS FOR PALEOINDIAN SITE ANALYSIS

At the scale of physiographic regions or depositional basins, geoarchaeological strategies are useful for studying multiple Paleoindian sites. Specific objectives of research at this scale include: (1) delineation of site associations with extensive (i.e., mappable) geomorphic features or stratigraphic units; (2) definition of region-scale past environments; and (3) use of geologic data to develop strategies for site detection and settlement pattern analysis. These goals and the methods used to achieve them are comparable to those discussed by Butzer (1982:43–66) as part of establishing the landscape contexts of archaeological sites.

BASIN-LANDSCAPE SETTINGS: MULTISITE ANALYSES

Depositional basins are geomorphically defined areas that constitute logical areal units for geoarchaeological investigation of Paleoindian sites. In general there are broad associations between basin type, geologic processes, and resultant sedimentary-geomorphic features. Examples include alluvial drainage basins, lacustrine basins, and marine coastlines. Periglacial regions and interior eolian landscapes (e.g., Stanford et al. 1990; Thorson 1990) are also landscapes that are often studied as units. The following discussions focus on geoarchaeological strategies for site detection and on evaluation of regional patterns of Paleoindian site locations. The first level of analysis for basin or region-scale investigations is usually geomorphic; then regional stratigraphic frameworks are considered.

Perhaps the most obvious, albeit logistical reason for regional geologic studies associated with Paleoindian archaeology is simply to assist in finding sites. Although other important data are generated in this cause, the discovery of Paleoindian sites is not only essential, but also is one of the more difficult challenges because of complex late Quaternary geologic records and patterns of site destruction by Holocene geologic agents. A signal study in this respect is Hoffecker's (1988) work in central Alaska. Although his analysis also addressed site formation processes, Hoffecker used detailed historical geomorphology for reconstructing landscape evolution. From that record he developed an explicit strategy for site survey that included detection of surface sites as well as those potentially buried in different sedimentary environments (e.g., in glacial outwash, alluvium, loess, and colluvium).

The rationale for geoarchaeological approaches to regional investigations of multiple Paleoindian sites is straightforward when the archaeological objectives of such research are considered. Synchronic studies of sites vis à vis paleolandscapes, settlement patterns, and subsistence strategies require that site locational analysis focus on regional reconstructions of paleoenvironments. Mapping of landforms, coupled with vegetation and faunal reconstructions, is integral to this objective. Similarly, diachronic analysis of culture change relative to changing environments necessitates regional data on site associations with geomorphic and stratigraphic units.

Archaeologists commonly examine the regional distributions of Paleoindian sites and artifacts with respect to past environments and the geographic areas occupied by culture groups (Brosten and Norton 1990; Hofman 1987; Johnson 1989; Judge 1973; Largent and Waters 1990; Meltzer 1987, 1988; Tankersley et al. 1990; Wendorf and Hester 1962). When the simple geographic distributions of sites or artifacts are partitioned with data on geomorphology, soils and sedimentary environments, the archaeological value of such studies is vastly increased. Applications of this kind have been conducted in different kinds of basins that exhibit distinct late Quaternary geologic records.

Research in coastal settings, for example, is conditioned by the records of terminal Pleistocene rise in sea level. The geomorphic-stratigraphic position of Paleoindian sites in coastal settings is closely tied to the sedimentary-geomorphic results of rapid late glacial transgressions (Kraft 1985; Meighan 1983). A major problem in this regard is that many Paleoindian sites may occur in now-submerged portions of the continental shelf. Pearson et al. (1986) reconstructed late Quaternary coastal geologic history and then used the geologic data to predict the position of submerged Paleoindian sites. Their project was along the lower Sabine River (Texas and Louisiana) and on adjacent portions of the inundated continental shelf. A barge-mounted coring rig was used to sample submerged Late Pleistocene and early Holocene marine, littoral, and fluvial deposits. These data, along with seismic profiles, were used to define the stratigraphy and past sedimentary environments. Detailed mapping of late Quaternary sediments and environmental reconstructions were used to develop a sophisticated predictive model for Paleoindian site locations.

Late Pleistocene lacustrine geologic records also reflect profound climate change and varied settings for Paleoindian sites. The Pleistocene lakes of interior basins in the western United States have left complex records of lake level changes and associated geomorphic-stratigraphic contexts for Paleoindian sites (Haynes et al. 1987; Waters 1989; Willig 1988). Perhaps the most complex lacustrine records are associated with glacial lakes and periglacial features in the Great Lakes region. There, late Pleistocene changes in the ice margin positions, lake levels, and drainage patterns have been defined. That these were coupled with rapid biotic successions means that Paleoindian occupations of that region were conditioned by remarkably varied environments and short term patterns of environmental change.

Studies of Paleoindian sites in the Great Lakes region have exploited geoarchaeological strategies. Larsen (1985) developed a model for predicting Paleoindian site contexts along Great Lakes coasts. His research included reconstruction of lake level fluctuations and resulting stratigraphic positioning of Paleoindian sites. Buchner and Pettipas (1990) studied the geologic history of glacial Lake Agassiz as it bears on Paleoindian site distributions and stratigraphic settings. Muller and Calkin (1988) provide an excellent regional geological framework for study of the Hiscock Site in New York State (Laub et al. 1988).

Jackson's (1983) study of Paleoindian site distributions in Ontario is an excellent example of how site locations may be usefully interpreted when they are placed into geomorphic or physiographic frameworks indicative of past environments. This work was followed by further integration of site physiographic contexts with reconstruction of ecological zones, resource availability, settlement patterns, and Paleoindian adaptive strategies (Jackson and McKillop 1991). These approaches are, in my opinion, truly geoarchaeological, in that the geologic data are used explicitly in gaining strengthened interpretations of archaeological records relative to specific problems such as settlement-subsistence systems.

Despite the fact that many Paleoindian sites occur in alluvial basins, examples of region-scale investigations of site contexts are not common. Sites may occur on terrace surfaces or as buried sites within terrace alluvium or below flood plains (Gardner and Donahue 1985). In the central Mississippi valley, Bettis and Benn (1989) defined the geomorphic position of Paleoindian sites and also determined that erosion has removed the majority of pre-10.5ka landforms in their study area. Holliday (1987) combined geomorphic, sedimentary, and soils data to evaluate Paleoindian site contexts on the South Platte River in Colorado. On the Southern High Plains Stafford (1981) and Holliday (1990) have addressed region-scale positions of Paleoindian sites that occur in "draws," the local term for shallow drainages that are usually filled with eolian, lacustrine, and some alluvial sediments. In the Central Plains, studies of alluvial geomorphology and stratigraphy pertinent to Paleoindian site prediction have been undertaken (Johnson and Logan 1990; Johnson and Martin 1987; May and Holen 1985).

In the Upper Trinity River Basin, Texas, geoarchaeological research has centered about the Elm Fork Trinity and West Fork Trinity valleys (Figure 2). In a context of regional geologic analysis, emphasis was placed on alluvial landforms and sediments (Ferring 1986, 1987, 1990a, 1990c). In addition to field investigations of terrace and flood plain exposures of alluvium, numerous borehole logs were inspected (Figure 3). Field and borehole data, including radiocarbon ages, were used to develop a geomorphic and stratigraphic framework for the alluvial valleys (Figure 4). Conclusions concerning the potential position of Paleoindian sites were quite different from those presented earlier (Crook and Harris 1957, 1958). It was proposed that virtually all terraces are at least 20,000 years old and that no Clovis or younger sites should be expected in situ in terrace alluvium. Terminal Pleistocene sediments, on the other hand, are buried deeply beneath the flood plain, and Paleoindian sites should be deeply buried at the contact with early Holocene alluvium (Ferring 1986, 1987). Subsequent work, including the fortuitous discovery of the Aubrey Clovis Site, has supported the overall stratigraphic framework. It seems likely that Late Pleistocene valley trenching, followed by early Holocene alluviation, has led to the deep burial of Paleoindian sites over a much larger part of the Southern Plains.

REGIONAL STRATIGRAPHY

Stratigraphic analysis of late Quaternary deposits on a regional scale is integral to the discovery and correlation of Paleoindian sites. While stratigraphic study of individual localities or sites is the basis for regional correlations, the regional objectives are different from the specific ones. Stratigraphic analysis of deposits is first a means of establishing chronological relations among stratigraphic units at different localities. Of principal concern here, obviously, are deposits that contain archaeological or environmental data of Paleoindian age. Stratigraphic analysis is conducted on a variety of different kinds of geologic deposits and materials including sediments, soils, fossils, and isotopes. Even volcanic ashes are used to define the age and stratigraphic position of Paleoindian sites in the Northwest (Mehringer and Foit 1990).

Here the focus is on sediments that contain or have the potential to contain Paleoindian archaeological materials; this focus is therefore on established and potential contexts for Paleoindian sites and associated paleoenvironmental evidence. In addition to establishing relative geochronologic frameworks, stratigraphic analysis can assist directly in developing site discovery strategies (e.g., Bettis and Benn 1989; Hoffecker 1988). While stratigraphic research is done in a variety of dif-

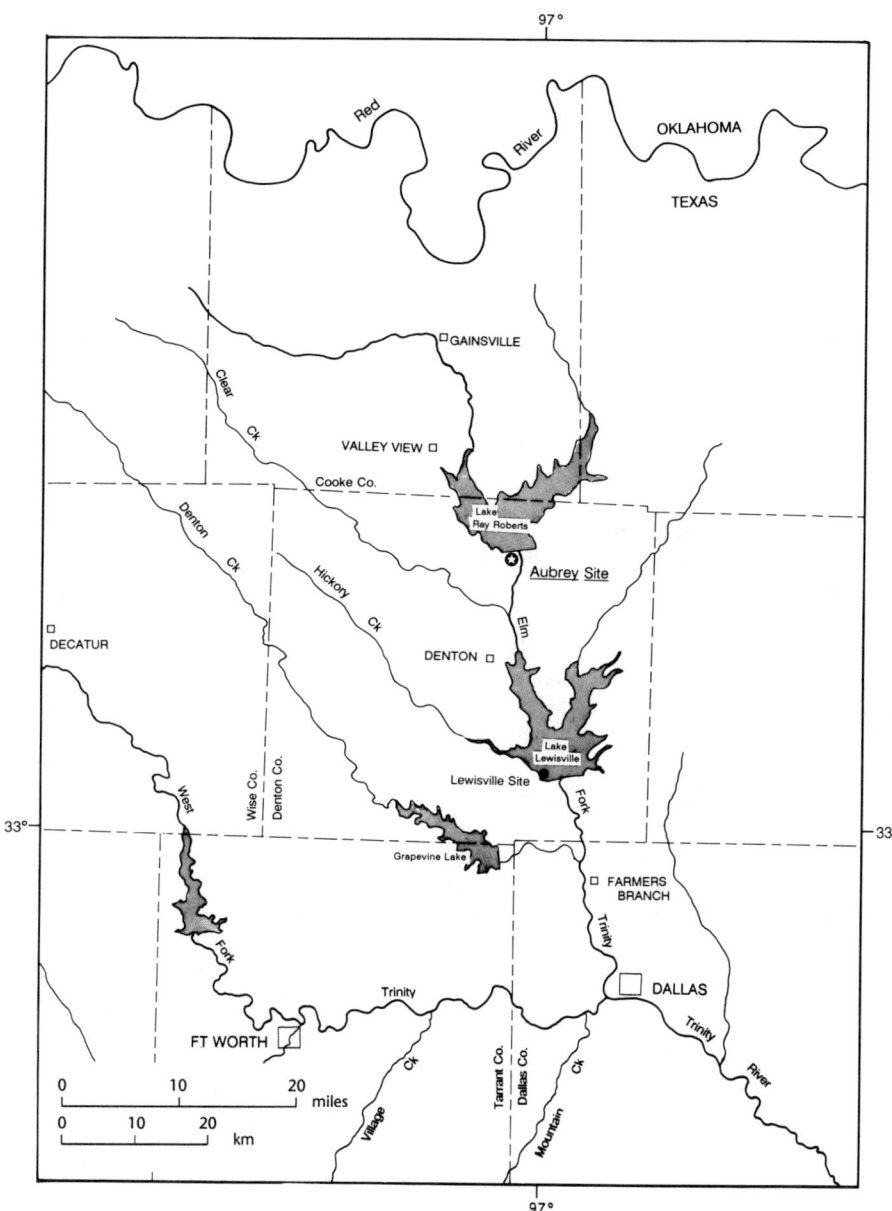

Figure 2. Map of North Central Texas and Upper Trinity River Valley, with Aubrey Clovis Site Location.

ferent geologic contexts (see above), alluvial settings are emphasized in the following discussion.

Alluvial stratigraphy has been important to Quaternary geology because alluvial records register stream response to climate change (Knox 1983), and because alluvial sediments frequently contain evidence of past environments such as soils, pollen, vertebrates, and invertebrates. Alluvial sediments are probably the most common context for in situ Paleoindian sites as well. The emphasis given to stratigraphic study of buried Paleoindian sites extends back to early phases of research (Haynes 1990), when dating was accomplished by stratigraphic analysis of artifacts associated with fossils and other evidence for the age of the deposits and the environments of deposition (Albritton and Bryan 1939; Antevs 1937; Bryan 1937, 1938, 1941; Howard 1935). This early emphasis on stratigraphy of Paleoindian sites has persisted as an important component of research.

Important stratigraphic correlations of sediments containing Paleoindian sites have been conducted by Haynes (1970, 1975, 1985). Haynes' work has focused on alluvial stratigraphy and radiocarbon dating of alluvium and Paleoindian sites. Beyond establishing the lithostratigraphic position of Paleoindian sites in western localities, this research has also related alluvial histories to climate change (Haynes 1968) and has evaluated the stratigraphy of Late Pleistocene deposits vis à vis mammalian extinctions (Haynes 1984).

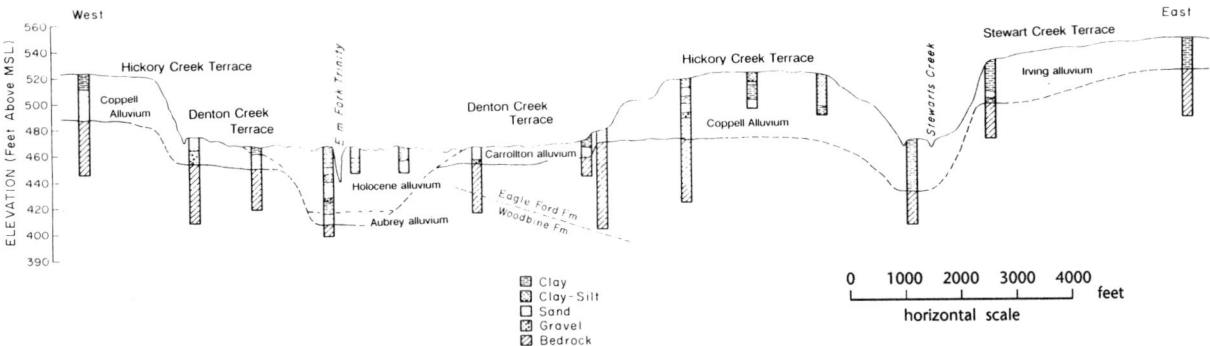

Figure 3. Geologic Cross Section of the Elm Fork Trinity River Near Lewisville, Texas.

Efforts to establish the age of Paleoindian cultural complexes through radiocarbon dating have implications that surpass simple chronometry. Increased efforts to define the age and distribution of traditionally recognized "cultures" such as Clovis, Folsom, or Goshen suggest, that far greater techno-stylistic and spatial-temporal complexity exists than had been assumed when fewer data were available (Haynes et al. 1984). It is clear that processes of culture change as well as the nature of synchronic cultural-adaptive variation during Paleoindian times must be studied within the framework of a precise geochronology; older, simplistic developmental schemes may not apply, and only dating of individual archaeological components at multiple sites will allow testing of temporal-spatial hypotheses that concern culture process and cultural affiliations of "groups" defined through stylistic and technological analyses of lithic assemblages (Frison 1988).

Significant applications of stratigraphy to Paleoindian studies have been made on the Southern High Plains, where research has been done since the landmark documentation of Folsom artifacts with extinct bison (Figgins 1927). In this region E. H. Sellards (1938, 1952, 1955) made important contributions to the stratigraphy of several Paleoindian sites, not to mention the archaeological analyses he conducted at the same time. He collaborated with other geologists who were busy establishing paleoenvironmental and geologic background for archaeological studies (e.g., Sellards et al. 1947). During the same interval, stratigraphic work was being conducted at a number of sites (Evans and Meade 1945; Roberts 1942). Interest in this region's geologic and archaeological records led to the interdisciplinary work headed by Wendorf (Wendorf 1961; Wendorf and Hester 1975), with stratigraphic contributions from Harbour (1975) and Haynes (1975). Recent study of Paleoindian sites and late Quaternary stratigraphy has been actively pursued by Holliday (1984, 1985a, 1990). His work has emphasized stratigraphic correlations over broad areas, identification of local controls on sedimentary environments, such as springs, and most notably, application of soils science to stratigraphic and paleoenvironmental investigations.

GEOARCHAEOLOGY AT PALEOINDIAN LOCALITIES

Geoarchaeological research at a locality (a site *and* its immediate geologic context) narrows the scope of inves-

Figure 4. Diagrammatic Cross Section of the Upper Trinity River Drainage Basin. Note that all terraces are Pleistocene, the youngest dated to ca. 20 ka. In situ Paleoindian sites in alluvium are at the Pleistocene-Holocene stratigraphic contact below flood plains, and in deeply buried early Holocene sediments.

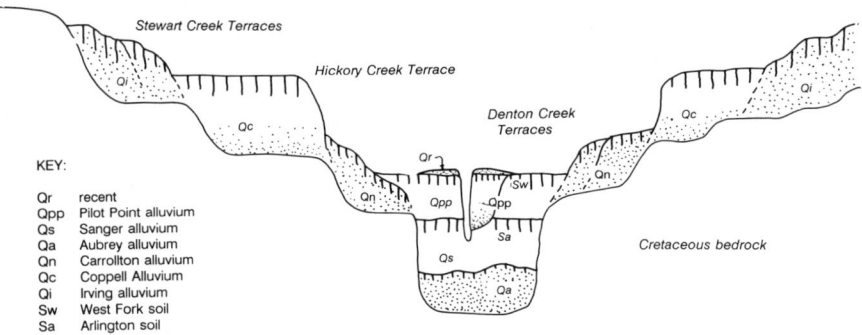

tigations from the broader regional context, including a paleoenvironmental framework, to the locality-specific scale. Obviously the research done at localities contributes to regional studies. Indeed, geologic research at Paleoindian localities often forms a significant portion of total regional data bases concerning late Quaternary geology and environments. Discovery of in-place Paleoindian materials frequently draws Quaternary scientists from many disciplines; this is because Paleoindian sites give an immediate temporal frame to the locality, because terminal Pleistocene paleoecological studies enjoy broad interest, and because archaeologists have been successful in finding money for interdisciplinary research teams. In the best of circumstances geoarchaeology at localities should be but one research perspective among those being applied by a diverse team of interdisciplinary scientists. The need for interdisciplinary research at localities is evident when the goals of geoarchaeological research are considered.

The objectives of geoarchaeology at a locality include definition of the age of the deposits containing Paleoindian materials and definition of the *local* paleoenvironmental context (i.e., habitat-scale, not regional-scale paleoenvironments or paleoclimates). These objectives are met through studying different aspects of the geology of the locality, hopefully with contributions from specialists in other disciplines. A seminal application of this perspective is the interdisciplinary project led by Leonhardy (1966) at the Domebo Clovis site in Oklahoma. Leonhardy's team studied geology, pollen, vertebrates, and invertebrates allowing reconstruction of local habitats for the mammoth kill as well as inferences concerning regional paleoenvironments.

It is important to note that from a perspective of scale, both the temporal and environmental studies should bracket the Paleoindian occupations as much as possible. By expanding the temporal scale of investigation, a record of geologic processes before, during, and after the Paleoindian occupations can be established. This not only improves contributions to broader studies, but is often essential for understanding the physical and biotic conditions during occupations. Similarly, post-occupational geologic histories may bear strongly on-site formation analyses, as described later. On a spatial level, it is important to document geologic evidence of landforms, hydrology, and biotic habitats around the occupation site. Nearby landforms may indicate sediment sources or controls on deposition that are pertinent to understanding the geology within site. Establishing the broader site context enhances analysis of site-location selection and reconstruction of resource availabilities in the site area.

Investigations at the Aubrey Clovis Site included geomorphic study of the entire site area, including bedrock slopes, alluvial terraces, and sediments below the flood plain that contained the site (Ferring 1989, 1990b, 1990c; Figure 5). Seventeen boreholes were drilled around the site from the flood plain to the Late Pleistocene sediments, enabling a reconstruction of the paleogeography of the locality. These efforts focused on the position and size of the pond that existed before and during Clovis occupations, and also on the position of the river during that interval. Sediments in the terrace

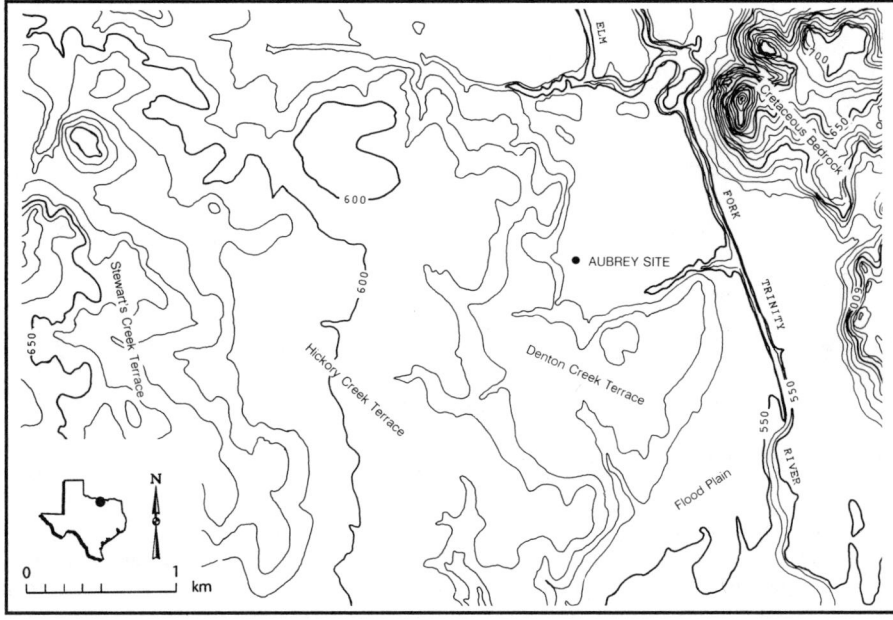

Figure 5. Topographic Map of the Aubrey Clovis Site Area. The Clovis occupation surface is ca. 8–9 m below the flood plain. Note Pleistocene terraces above and to the west of the site area.

above the site were studied in detail, since this was a source area for colluvial deposition in the western part of the site area (Figure 6). Numerous backhoe trenches were excavated along the slope of the artificial channel that exposed the site ca. 8–9 m below the flood plain. These trench profiles enabled detailed descriptions and sampling of sediment for subsequent laboratory analysis. They were also where samples were collected for pollen, mollusc, insect, vertebrate, and radiocarbon analyses.

STRATIGRAPHY AND GEOCHRONOLOGY

As mentioned above, there are different kinds of stratigraphic frameworks based on different kinds of data. Focusing on fieldwork, stratigraphic sections based on sediments and soils are most pertinent to this discussion. Comprehensive stratigraphic work should include available physical and biotic data, and of course artifact assemblages and features to establish cultural stratigraphy.

Stratigraphic units are essentially the sediments between boundaries. In practice the most common kinds of boundaries seen in Quaternary sediments are erosional unconformities, distinct changes in sediment lithology (but see discussion of facies below), and soil horizons. Boundaries between stratigraphic units may represent intervals of time that vary significantly. Independent dating methods are required to determine the intervals of time represented, although some relative inferences can be made in the field when time-dependent processes such as weathering are involved. Stratigraphic units defined through fieldwork define the structure for description and sampling. After laboratory work and radiometric dating, the refined stratigraphic framework may be used in correlation with other sections. In all cases, however, locality-specific designations are used prior to any correlations. Describing the stratigraphy of a site with a "template" of regional stratigraphic scope in mind is sometimes done at the beginning of good careers but only in the middle of bad ones—it is risky, poor science.

Because geologists were involved in the earliest stages of Paleoindian research, stratigraphic studies of sites have been part of this geoarchaeological tradition. This is well illustrated by work done at Southern High Plains localities by Sellards (1952, 1955), Haynes (1975), Holliday (1985b, 1985c), and Johnson (1974) and Stafford (1981). Several of the Southern High Plains localities' stratigraphic units may be correlated quite well owing to apparent climatic controls on patterns of sedimentation (Holliday 1985c, 1990). In several draws, late Pleistocene alluvial deposits are overlain by early Holocene spring and lacustrine marls while the middle and late Holocene sediments are mostly eolian sands. Thus at specific sites, such as Lubbock Lake, the major stratigraphic units are distinct types of sediments reflecting local depositional environments (Holliday 1985b; Holliday and Allen 1987).

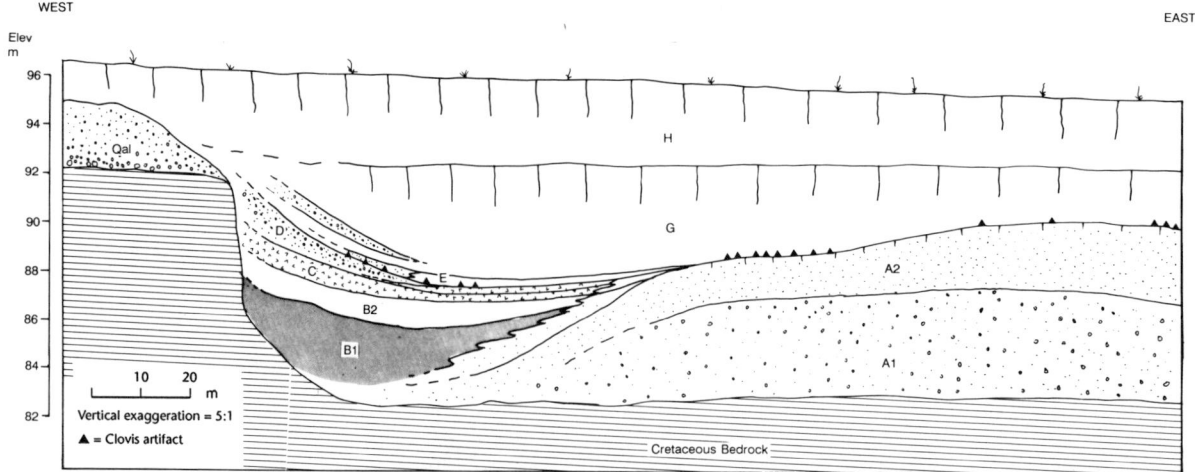

Figure 6. Stratigraphic Cross Section of the Aubrey Clovis Site. See Table 1 for description of geologic history. Note cutoff Pleistocene channel in western part of locality. This became a spring-fed pool during the late Pleistocene and early Holocene. Clovis-age artifacts and vertebrates were found at the disconformity in the pond area, where a probable bison kill was excavated, and on the alluvial remnant at the eastern edge of the pond where a Clovis camp was excavated.

Because of regional climate changes, similar sequences of sediments are present at other High Plains localities. Meltzer (1991), for example, compares the stratigraphy of the Mustang Springs locality with others in the region. Another good example of stratigraphic analysis of a Paleoindian site on the Plains is from the Colby Site in Wyoming by Albanese (1986). At the Kimmswick Site in Missouri, stratigraphic units ranging in age from Late Pleistocene through Holocene were defined as part of the study of the Clovis occupations there (Graham et al. 1981; Graham and Kay 1988). In Arizona, Haynes has conducted stratigraphic studies at two well-known Clovis Sites: Murray Springs (Haynes 1981) and the nearby Lehner Site (Haynes 1982).

The stratigraphy of the Aubrey Clovis Site was defined following lengthy study of data from trenches and boreholes (Figures 6, 7). Geomorphic controls on sedimentation included the terrace above the site and the cut-off channel that became a spring pool (pond). Spring activity and climatic controls on fluvial deposition were also key aspects of the geologic history of the locality (Table 1). Radiocarbon ages were obtained for most of the stratigraphic units (Figure 7). These not only established the ages of the stratigraphic units, but also were used to determine rates of sedimentation and intervals of soil formation.

SEDIMENTARY ENVIRONMENTS AND SOILS

Reconstruction of the local site environment is integral to any geoarchaeological study. This is accomplished using a variety of geologic data and ancillary investigations including palynology, malacology, vertebrate paleontology, and isotopic analysis. Geoarchaeological fieldwork focuses on environmental (in this context meaning landscapes and habitats) reconstruction using geomorphology, reconstruction of sedimentary environments, and pedology. Usually (or hopefully) these studies are conducted as part of a unified research strategy, since the data are generally derived from the same exposures or sections (e.g., Johnson 1987; Wendorf and Hester 1975). In concert with stratigraphic work, the geologic studies not only provide direct evidence of the site environment, but also provide the framework for collection of samples for the other investigators. Geologic context is critical for assessment of the sources and associations of assemblages of pollen, snails, insects, and other biotic data that are used in environmental reconstruction. This role of geologic analysis of Paleoindian sites, and geoarchaeological research strategies in general, are crisply explicated by Dillehay (1989:27–43). Dillehay's orchestration of interdisciplinary study of the setting and microenvironments of the Monte Verde Site (Chile) is probably singular with respect to the variety of data collected, analyzed, and integrated into a comprehensive interpretation.

Analysis of sedimentary environments enables reconstruction of the depositional processes associated with streams, springs, and ponds/lakes, as well as depositional or erosional processes on slopes. Holliday's (1985b) work at the Lubbock Lake Site (Texas) described alluvial, lacustrine, eolian, and slope deposits all in a rather small area of Yellowhouse Draw. These sedimentary environments were the context for other data such as snails and vertebrates used in environmental reconstruction. Syntheses of these data were used to define the microenvironments surrounding Paleoindian activity areas at this intensively studied locality (Johnson 1987).

Soils analyses complement study of sediments at sites. The sediments are the parent material for the soils. Soil formation thus post-dates deposition of the sediments containing artifacts and biotic remains. Soil profile characteristics can be used to define post-deposi-

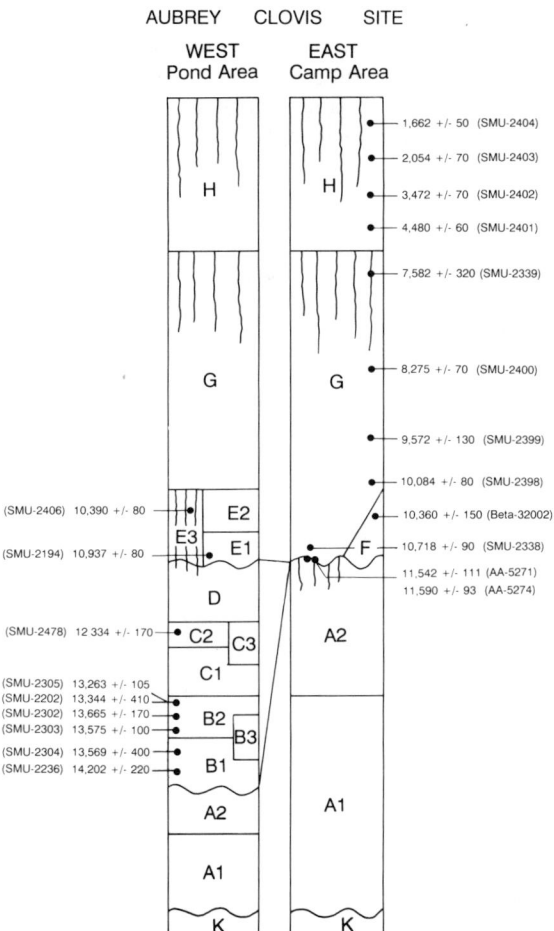

Figure 7. Stratigraphic Columns and Radiocarbon Ages for the Aubrey Clovis Site. Note the more complex late Pleistocene stratigraphy of the pond area, compared to the camp section where late Pleistocene sands (Unit A) were stable or eroding from ca. 14–11 ka.

tional histories of sites, as well as pre-occupational landform histories (Albanese 1986; Holliday 1985d, 1990; Reider 1980, 1990). Soils data are especially useful in assessing groundwater histories at sites, as done by Reider (1982) at the Agate Basin Site (Wyoming).

At the Aubrey Clovis Site, environments were reconstructed using facies analysis of sediments (Table 1). Still in progress are studies of vertebrates, molluscs, pollen, insects, and also stable isotopes from organic sediments and inorganic carbonates.

WITHIN SITE GEOARCHAEOLOGY: SITE FORMATION ANALYSIS

Study of site formation processes (Butzer 1982:77–122; Schiffer 1983, 1987) perhaps epitomizes geoarchaeology as an interdisciplinary approach to archaeological problem solving. Conducted within archaeological sites, formation studies address the cultural and natural processes that operated during site construction, as well as the post-occupational processes that effected modification of the archaeological materials and their sedimentary context (Ferring and Peter 1987). The ultimate objective of these studies is better understanding of the processes that shaped the archaeological record of human activities (Binford 1981, 1982). Formation analysis addresses records of spatial patterning of artifacts and faunas, the taphonomy of vertebrate remains, patterns of vertical and horizontal displacement of artifacts, and differential exposure of materials to physical and geochemical weathering. Because formation analysis addresses the mix of cultural and natural agents involved in the "genesis and diagenesis" of archaeological records, both archaeological and geologic approaches must be applied *in the field*, and concepts from both disciplines must be employed during analysis and interpretation of field data (see Dillehay 1989).

Formation analysis is as pertinent to Paleoindian archaeology as to any setting. Unfortunately, few specific applications in Paleoindian research contexts are published, although a good part of this apparent deficiency is attributable to the lack of contemporary jargon in otherwise solid, perceptive studies of Paleoindian sites. Notable applications include the studies in progress at Monte Verde (Dillehay 1989), at the Kimmswick Site (Graham and Kay 1988), and at Lubbock Lake (Holliday 1985b, 1990).

At the Aubrey Clovis Site, formation analyses are still in progress. Our strategy included integration of field geology, excavation methods, and laboratory analyses. All artifacts that could be found during excavations were mapped in place (all excavations were done slowly, with careful trowelling). Raw material differences permit refitting of many pieces. The refit data will be used to assess vertical and horizontal displacement of artifacts during or after occupation. Orientations of larger bones were also recorded for the same purpose. Each excavator made notes on evidence of bioturbation or pedoturbation in each of the 50 x 50 cm excavation units. Soil samples were collected from each unit. Magnetic susceptibility analyses have been done (by Dr. Brooks Ellwood, University of Texas at Arlington) to assess the concentrations of burned bone found in the camp areas.

Spatial patterning of artifacts and faunas in the camp areas are indicative of cultural patterning with little evidence of post-occupational disturbance (Figure 8). These patterns will be tested further with refit data. Over 11,000 lithic artifacts and ca. 3,500 bone fragments were recovered in excavations of two camp areas totalling ca. 200 square meters in area. Additional lithic artifacts and ca. 15,000 bone fragments were recovered in the pond area at the western part of the locality (Figure 6). Comparisons of bone taphonomy in these two areas and in the colluvial "red wedge" are in progress to assess bone deposition and modification in different sedimentary environments. Both cultural and natural processes of bone modification are being evaluated (by Bonnie Yates

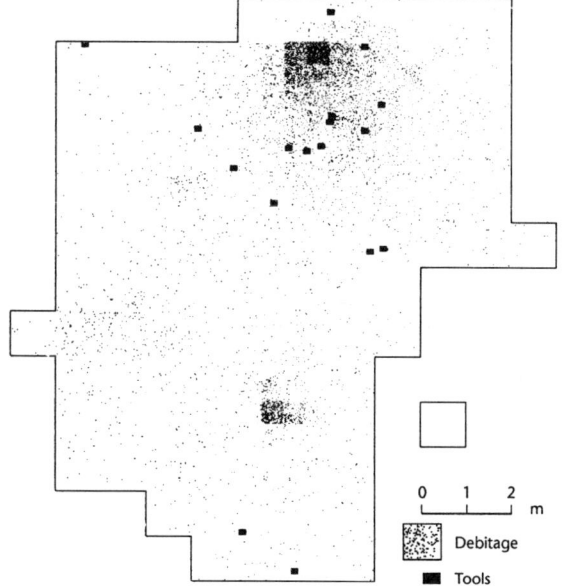

Figure 8. Spatial Distribution of ca. 8,000 lithic artifacts from "Camp B" at the Aubrey Clovis Site. This camp area excavation is at the eastern margin of the pond in Figure 6. Artifact positions include ca. 800 mapped pieces; the remainder are chips that were recovered in fine screening. Their mapped positions were randomized within the 50 x 50 cm excavation units with a computer program.

Table 1. Summary of Geologic History of the Aubrey Clovis Site

1.	>15 ka (ca. 25ka?)	Deposition of coarse alluvium on bedrock bench by large bedload or braided stream. These sediments (Carrollton alluvium) are now below the Denton Creek terrace surface above the Aubrey locality. A moderately developed soil has formed at the terrace surface. Molluscs from the lower part of the terrace fill suggest a braided stream environment.
2.	>15 ka (between 25?–15 ka)	Incision into bedrock. Unit A sand, gravel left as lag channel/bar deposits. These sediments were stable or eroding during deposition of pond sediments (Units B,C), and formed the surface that Clovis folk used for camps near the pond and river channel.
3.	ca. 15–13.8 ka	Unit B1 silts, clays, and peats deposited in spring pool. This was a period of low spring discharge and limited if any alluvial deposition.
4.	ca. 13.8–13.3 ka	Unit B2 peats, spring travertines, and tufas deposited in spring pool, with no apparent alluvium. This was a period of increased spring activity, compared to B1. The spring was a groundwater spring, with major conduits and feeders at the western edge of the pond. Peat deposits, probably related to floating sedge mats, were present near the spring, and periodically spread over much of the pond. There is no evidence for fluvial deposition.
5.	ca. 13.3–12.3 ka	Unit C crossbedded tufas and marls deposited in spring pool by seep spring. Gradual change to silty, sandy marl at western margin of pond as colluvium began to wash in from terrace above pond.
6.	ca. 12.3–11.5 ka	Unit D colluvium prograded over western margin of spring pool, forming the "red wedge". The colluvium is sand and gravel, derived from the terrace above the western margin of the pond. This was followed by stability of the "red wedge" and probable deflation of pond marls in the pond axis. Clovis occupation debris and vertebrates occur on the surface of the "red wedge" and on the deflated surface of the marls in the pond axis.
7.	ca. 11.5–10,950 ka	Clovis occupation of locality. Artifacts and faunas occur on the surface of the "red wedge", on the deflated disconformity in the pond axis, and on the surface of Unit A sands at the eastern margin of the pond and about 125 m farther east near the Clovis paleochannel of the Elm Fork Trinity River.
8.	ca. 10,950–10,500(?) ka	Unit E alluvial clay, interstratified with thin marl beds, deposited in pond above Clovis age faunas and artifacts. This is also period when alluvial fill (Unit F) continued to aggrade in paleochannel at eastern part of locality. This is the first evidence of fluvial activity since ca. 15 ka.—a major change in environments.
9.	ca. 10,900–7,600 ka	Unit G alluvium (overbank clays-silts) aggrades, continuing burial of Clovis site. This documents an early Holocene phase of rapid alluvial deposition.
10.	ca. 7,600–4,500 ka	Slow aggradation, with soil formation. This middle Holocene period is characterized by diminished flooding and probable diminished precipitation.
11.	ca. 4,500–present	Unit H alluvium (overbank clays-silts) aggrades. This late Holocene period is characterized by increased flood frequency-magnitude, probably the result of increased precipitation.

and Pegi Jodry). Overall, our site formation analyses are directed towards gaining better understanding of the taphonomic, spatial, and stratigraphic character of the lithic and bone assemblages, relative to the patterns of Clovis occupation at the site.

CONCLUSIONS

This paper is a brief review of geoarchaeological approaches to Paleoindian archaeology. At scales ranging from regional analysis of site distributions and paleoenvironmental reconstruction to within-site study of stratigraphy and site formation processes, methods and concepts from the earth sciences can be integrated with archaeological research strategies to improve and expand the scope of archaeological investigations. While geologists and paleontologists have devoted much of their own independent research to the close of the Pleistocene and problems of extinctions, the Paleoindian period has been a focus for collaborative research among archaeologists and geologists for many years. These interactions have not only improved the quality of Paleoindian research but also they have noticeably spilled over into broader archaeological programs, including academic curricula. For some, the integration of geology and archaeology into a unified set of methods is logical enough to warrant expectations that eventually geoarchaeology will simply be considered sound archaeology.

ACKNOWLEDGMENTS

I wish to thank the U.S. Army Corps of Engineers, Fort Worth District, for support of research at the Aubrey Clovis Site. I also acknowledge the valuable discussions with Vance Holliday, David Meltzer and Vance Haynes.

REFERENCES CITED

Albanese, J.
   1986 The Geology and Soils at the Colby Site. In *The Colby Mammoth Site*, edited by G. C. Frison and L. C. Todd, pp. 143–163. University of New Mexico Press, Albuquerque.

Albritton, C. C. Jr., and K. Bryan
   1939 Quaternary Stratigraphy in the Davis Mountains, Trans-Pecos, Texas. *Geological Society of America Bulletin* 50:1423–1474.

Antevs, E.
   1937 Climate and Early Man in North America. In *Early Man*, edited by G. G. MacCurdy, pp. 125–132. J.B. Lippencott, Philadelphia.

Bettis, E. A. III, and D. W. Benn
   1989 Geologic Contexts of Paleoindian and Archaic Occupations in a Portion of the Mississippi Valley, Iowa and Illinois. *Current Research in the Pleistocene* 6:85–86.

Binford, L. R.
   1981 *Bones: Ancient Men and Modern Myths*. Academic Press, New York.
   1982 The Archaeology of Place. *Journal of Anthropological Archaeology* 1(1):5–31.
   1986 In Pursuit of the Future. In *American Archaeology Past and Future*, edited by D. J. Meltzer, D. D. Fowler and J. A. Sabloff, pp. 459–479. Smithsonian Institution Press, Washington.

Broster, J. B., and M. R. Norton
   1990 Paleoindian Fluted Point and Site Survey in Tennessee the 1989 Season. *Current Research in the Pleistocene* 7:5–7.

Bryan, K.
   1937 Geology of the Folsom Deposits in New Mexico and Colorado. In *Early Man*, edited by G. G. MacCurely, pp. 139–152. J. B. Lippencott, Philadelphia.
   1938 Deep Sites Near Abilene Texas. *Bulletin of the Texas Archeological and Paleontological Society* 10:248–262.
   1941 Geologic Antiquity of Man in America. *Science* 93(2422):505–514.

Bryant, V. M. Jr., and R. G. Holloway (editors)
   1985 *Pollen Records of Late Quaternary North American Sediments*. American Association of Stratigraphic Palynologists, Dallas.

Buchner, A. P., and L. F. Pettipas
   1990 The Early Occupations of the Glacial Lake Agassiz Basin in Manitoba; 11,500 to 7700 BP. In *Archaeological Geology of North America*, edited by N. P. Lasca and J. Donahue, pp. 51–59. Geological Society of America, Centennial Special Volume No. 4. Boulder.

Butzer, K.
   1982 *Archaeology as Human Ecology*. Cambridge University Press, Cambridge.

Crook, W. W. Jr., and R. K. Harris
   1957 Hearths and Artifacts of Early Man Near Lewisville, Texas and Associated Fauna. *Bulletin of the Texas Archeological Society* 28:7–97.
   1958 A Pleistocene Campsite Near Lewisville, Texas. *American Antiquity* 23(3):233–246.

Dillehay, T. D. (editor)
   1989 *Monte Verde, A Late Pleistocene Settlement in Chile. Volume 1, Paleoenvironment and Site Context*. Smithsonian Institution Press, Washington, D.C.

Evans, G. L., and G. E. Meade
   1945 Quaternary of the Texas High Plains. *University of Texas Bulletin* 4401:485–507.

Ferring, C. R.
   1986 Late Quaternary Geology and Environments of the Upper Trinity Basin, in *An Assessment of the Cultural Resources in the Trinity Basin, Dallas, Tarrant and Denton Counties, Texas*, edited by B. C. Yates and C. R. Ferring, pp. 32–112. North Texas State University, Institute of Applied Sciences, Denton.

1987 Archaeological Geology of the Upper Trinity River Basin, North Central Texas. *Geological Society of America Abstracts with Programs* 19(7):661.

1989 The Aubrey Clovis Site: A Paleoindian Locality in the Upper Trinity River Basin, Texas. *Current Research in the Pleistocene* 6:9–11.

1990a Archaeological Geology of the Southern Plains. In *Archaeological Geology of North America*, edited by N. P. Lasca and J. Donahue, pp. 253–266. Geological Society of America, Centennial Special Volume 4. Boulder.

1990b The 1989 Investigations at the Aubrey Clovis Site, Texas. *Current Research in the Pleistocene* 7:10–12.

1990c Late Quaternary Geology and Geoarchaeology of the Upper Trinity River Drainage Basin, Texas. GSA Guidebook No. 11. Dallas Geological Society, Dallas.

1991 Upper Trinity River Drainage Basin, Texas. In *Quaternary Non-Glacial Geology: Conterminous United States*, edited by R. Morrison. Decade of North American Geology, vol. K-2. Geological Society America, Boulder. In press.

Ferring, C. R., and D. E. Peter
1987 Geoarchaeology of the Dyer Site, A Prehistoric Occupation in the Western Ouachitas, Oklahoma. *Plains Anthropolgist* 32(118):351–366.

Figgins, J. D.
1927 The Antiquity of Man in America. *Natural History* 27:229–239.

Frison, G. C.
1988 Paleoindian Subsistence and Settlement During Post-Clovis Times on the Northwestern Plains, the Adjacent Mountain Ranges, and Intermontane Basins. In *Americans Before Columbus: Ice-Age Origins*, edited by R. C. Carlisle, pp. 83–106. Ethnology Monographs No. 12. Department of Anthropology, University of Pittsburgh.

Gardner, G. D., and J. Donahue
1985 The Little Platte Drainage, Missouri: A Model for Locating Temporal Surfaces in a Fluvial Environment. In *Archaeological Sediments in Context*, edited by J. K. Stein and W. R. Farrand, pp. 69–89. Center for the Study of Early Man, University of Maine, Orono.

Graham, R. W., C. V. Haynes, D. L. Johnson, and M. Kay
1981 Kimmswick: A Clovis-Mastodon Association in Eastern Missouri. *Science* 213:1115–1117.

Graham, R. W., and M. Kay
1988 Taphonomic Comparisons of Cultural and Noncultural Faunal Deposits at the Kimmswick and Barnhart Sites, Jefferson County Missouri. In *Late Pleistocene and Early Holocene Paleoecology and Archaeology of the Eastern Great Lakes Region*, edited by R. S. Laub, N. G. Miller and D. W. Steadman. Bulletin of the Buffalo Society of Natural Sciences 33:227–240.

Harbour, J.
1975 General Stratigraphy. In *Late Pleistocene Environments of the Southern High Plains*, edited by F. Wendorf and J. J. Hester, pp. 33–55. Fort Burgwin Research Center, Southern Methodist University, Dallas.

Haynes, C. V. Jr.
1968 Geochronology of Late-Quaternary Alluvium. In *Means of Correlation of Quaternary Successions*, edited by R. B. Morrison and H. E. Wright, pp. 591–631. University of Utah Press, Salt Lake City.

1970 Geochronology of Man-Mammoth Sites and Their Bearing Upon the Origin of the Llano Complex. In *Pleistocene and Recent Environments of the Central Great Plains*, edited by W. Dort Jr. and J. K. Jones Jr., pp. 77–92. University of Kansas Special Publication No. 3. University of Kansas Press, Lawrence.

1975 Pleistocene and Recent Stratigraphy. In *Late Pleistocene Environments of the Southern High Plains*, edited by F. Wendorf and J. J. Hester, pp. 591–631. Fort Burgwin Research Center, Southern Methodist University, Dallas.

1981 Geochronology and Paleoenvironments of the Murray Springs Clovis Site, Arizona. *National Geographic Research Reports* 14:243–251.

1982 Archaeological Investigations at the Lehner Site, Arizona, 1974–1975. *National Geographic Research Reports* 14:325–334.

1984 Stratigraphy and Late Pleistocene Extinction in the United States. In *Quaternary Extinctions, A Prehistoric Revolution*, edited by P. S. Martin and R. G. Klein, pp. 345–353. The University of Arizona Press, Tucson.

1985 *Mastodon-Bearing Springs and Late Quaternary Geochronology of the Lower Pomme de Terre Valley, Missouri*. Geological Society of America Special Paper No. 204. Boulder.

1990 The Antevs-Bryan Years and the Legacy for Paleoindian Geochronology. In *Establishment of a Geologic Framework for Paleoanthropology*, edited by L. F. Laporte, pp. 55–68. Geological Society of America Special Paper No. 242. Boulder.

Haynes, C. V. Jr., D. J. Donahue, A. J. T. Jull, and T. H. Zabel
1984 Application of Accelerator Dating to Fluted

Point Paleoindian Sites. *Archaeology of Eastern North America* 12:184–191.

Haynes, C. V. Jr., A. Long, and A. J. T. Jull
  1987 Radiocarbon Dates at Willcox Playa, Arizona, Bracket the Clovis Occupation Surface. *Current Research in the Pleistocene* 4:124–126.

Hoffecker, J. F.
  1988 Applied Geomorphology and Archaeological Survey Strategy for Sites of Pleistocene Age: An Example from Central Alaska. *Journal of Archaeological Science* 15:683–713.

Hofman, J. L.
  1987 The Occurrence of Folsom Points in Oklahoma. *Current Research in the Pleistocene* 4:57–59.

  1988 Dating the Lower Member of the Domebo Formation in Western Oklahoma. *Current Research in the Pleistocene* 5:86–88.

Holliday, V. T.
  1984 Observations on the Geologic Setting of Paleoindian Sites on the Southern High Plains. *Current Research in the Pleistocene* 1:88–99.

  1985a Holocene Soil-Geomorphological Relations in a Semiarid Environment: The Southern High Plains of Texas, In *Soils and Quaternary Landscape Evolution*, edited by J. Boardman, pp. 325–357. John Wiley and Sons, Chichester, UK.

  1985b Archaeological Geology of the Lubbock Lake Site, Southern High Plains of Texas. *Geological Society of America Bulletin* 96:1483–1492.

  1985c New Data on the Stratigraphy and Pedology of the Clovis and Plainview Sites, Southern High Plains. *Quaternary Research* 23:388–402.

  1985d Early and Middle Holocene Soils at the Lubbock Lake Archaeological Site, Texas. *Catena* 12:61–78.

  1987 Geoarchaeology and Late Quaternary Geomorphology of the Middle South Platte River, Northeastern Colorado. *Geoarchaeology* 2(4):317–319.

  1990 Pedology in Archaeology. In *Archaeological Geology of North America*, edited by N. P. Lasca and J. Donahue, pp. 525–540. Geological Society of America, Centennial Special Volume No. 4. Boulder.

Holliday, V. T., and B. L. Allen
  1987 Geology and Soils, In *Lubbock Lake, Late Quaternary Studies on the Southern High Plains*, edited by E. Johnson, pp. 14–21. Texas A & M University Press, College Station.

Howard, E. B.
  1935 Evidence of Early Man in North America, Based on Geological and Archaeological Work in New Mexico. *University of Pennsylvania Museum Journal* 24(2-3):55–171.

Jackson, L. J.
  1983 Geochronology and Settlement Disposition in the Early Paleo-Indian Occupation of Southern Ontario, Canada. *Quaternary Research* 19:388–399.

Jackson, L., and H. McKillop
  1991 Approaches to Paleo-Indian Economy: An Ontario and Great Lakes Perspective. *Midcontinental Journal of Archaeology* 16(1):34–68.

Johnson, C.
  1974 Geologic Investigations at the Lubbock Lake Site, In *History and Prehistory of the Lubbock Lake Site*, edited by C. C. Black, pp. 79–106. The Museum Journal, vol. 15. West Texas Museum Association, Texas Tech University.

Johnson, E. (editor)
  1987 *Lubbock Lake, Late Quaternary Studies on the Southern High Plains.* Texas A&M University Press, College Station.

Johnson, L. Jr.
  1989 *Great Plains Interlopers in the Eastern Woodlands During Late Paleo-Indian Times: The Evidence from Oklahoma, Texas and Areas Close By.* Office of the State Archaeologist, Report No. 36. Texas Historical Commission, Austin.

Johnson, W. C., and B. Logan
  1990 Geoarchaeology of the Kansas River Basin, Central Great Plains. In *Archaeological Geology of North America*, edited by N. P. Lasca and J. Donahue, pp. 267–300. Geological Society of America, Centennial Special Volume No. 4. Boulder.

Johnson, W. C., and C. W. Martin
  1987 Holocene Alluvial-Stratigraphic Studies from Kansas and Adjoining States of the East-Central Plains. In *Quaternary Environments of Kansas*, edited by W. C. Johnson, pp. 109–122. Guidebook Series No. 5. Kansas Geological Survey, Lawrence.

Judge, W. J.
  1973 *Paleoindian Occupation of the Central Rio Grande Valley in New Mexico.* University of New Mexico Press, Albuquerque.

Julig, P. J., J. H. Andrews, and W. C. Mahaney
  1990 Geoarchaeology of the Cummins Site on the Beach of Proglacial Lake Minong, Lake Superior Basin, Canada. In *Archaeological Geology of North America*, edited by N. P. Lasca and J. Donahue,

pp. 21–50. Geological Society of America, Centennial Special Volume No. 4. Boulder.

Knox, J. C.
  1983 Responses of River Systems to Holocene Climates. In *The Holocene*, edited by H. E. Wright, Jr., pp. 26–41. Late Quaternary Environments of the United States, vol. II. University of Minnesota Press, Minneapolis.

Kraft, J. C.
  1985 Marine Environments: Paleogeographic Reconstructions in the Littoral Region. In *Archaeological Sediments in Context*, edited by J. K. Stein and W. R. Farrand, pp. 11–125. Peopling of the Americas Series, vol. 1. Center for the Study of Early Man, University of Maine, Orono.

Largent, F. B., and M. R. Waters
  1990 The Distribution of Folsom Points in Texas. *Current Research in the Pleistocene* 7:27–28.

Larsen, C. E.
  1985 Geoarchaeological Interpretation of Great Lakes Coastal Environments. In *Archaeological Sediments in Context*, edited by J. K. Stein and W. R. Farrand, pp. 91–110. Peopling of the Americas Series, vol. 1. Center for the Study Early Man, University of Maine, Orono.

Laub, R. S., M. F. DeRemer, C. A. Dufort, and W. L. Parsons
  1988 The Hiscock Site: A Rich Late Quaternary Locality in Western New York State. In *Late Pleistocene and Early Holocene Paleoecology and Archaeology of the Eastern Great Lakes Region*, edited by R. S. Laub, N. G. Miller, and D. W. Steadman, pp. 67–81. Bulletin of the Buffalo Society of Natural Sciences No. 33.

Leonhardy, F. C. (editor)
  1966 *Domebo, A Paleo-Indian Mammoth Kill in the Prairie Plains*. Museum of the Great Plains, Lawton, Oklahoma.

Martin, P. S., and R. G. Klein (editors)
  1984 *Quaternary Extinctions, a Prehistoric Revolution*. University of Arizona Press, Tucson.

May, D. W., and S. R. Holen
  1985 A Chronology of Holocene Erosion and Sedimentation in the South Loup Valley, Nebraska. *Geographical Perspectives* 56:8–12.

Mehringer, P. J. Jr., and F. F. Foit Jr.
  1990 Volcanic Ash Dating of the Clovis Cache at East Wenatchee, Washington. *National Geographic Research* 6(4):495–503.

Meighan, C. W.
  1983 Early Man in the New World. In *Quaternary Coastlines and Marine Archaeology*, edited by P. M. Masters and N. C. Fleming, pp. 441–461. Academic Press, New York.

Meltzer, D. J.
  1987 The Clovis Paleoindian Occupation of Texas: Results of the Texas Clovis Fluted Point Survey. *Bulletin of the Texas Archeological Society* 57:27–68.
  1988 Late Pleistocene Human Adaptations in Eastern North America. *Journal of World Prehistory* 2(1):1–52.
  1991 Altithermal Archaeology and Paleoecology at Mustang Springs, on the Southern High Plains of Texas. *American Antiquity* 56(2):236–267.

Muller, E. H., and P. E. Calkin
  1988 Late Pleistocene and Holocene Geology of the Eastern Great Lakes Region: Geologic Setting of the Hiscock Paleontological Site, Western New York. In *Late Pleistocene and Early Holocene Paleoecology and Archaeology of the Eastern Great Lakes Region*, edited by R. S. Laub, N. G. Miller, and D. W. Steadman. Bulletin of the Buffalo Society of Natural Sciences 33:53–63.

Pearson, C. E., D. B. Kelley, R. A. Weinstein, and S. M. Gagliano
  1986 *Archaeological Investigations on the Outer Continental Shelf: A Study within the Sabine River Valley, Offshore Louisiana and Texas*. Coastal Environments Inc., Baton Rouge.

Porter, S. C. (editor)
  1983 *The Pleistocene*. Late Quaternary Environments of the United States, vol. I. University of Minnesota Press, Minneapolis.

Reider, R. G.
  1980 Late Pleistocene and Holocene Soils of the Carter/Kerr-McGee Archaeological Site, Powder River Basin, Wyoming. *Catena* 7:301–315.
  1982 Soil Development and Paleoenvironments. In *The Agate Basin Site*, edited by G. C. Frison and D. J. Stanford, pp. 331–344. Academic Press, Inc., New York.
  1990 Late Pleistocene and Holocene Pedogenic and Environmental Trends at Archaeological Sites in Plains and Mountain Areas of Colorado and Wyoming. In *Archaeological Geology of North America*, edited by N. P. Lasca and J. Donahue, pp. 335–360. Geological Society of America, Centennial Special Volume No. 4. Boulder.

Roberts, F. H. H. Jr.
  1942 *Archaeological and Geological Investigations in the San Jon District, Eastern New Mexico*. Smithsonian Miscellaneous Collection 103(4).

Ruddiman, W. F., and H. E. Wright Jr. (editors)
  1987 *The Geology of North America, vol. K-3. North America and Adjacent Oceans During the Last Deglaciation*. Geological Society of America, Boulder.

Schiffer, M. B.
  1983 Toward the Identification of Formation Processes. *American Antiquity* 48:675–706.
  1987 *Formation Processes of the Archaeological Record*. University of New Mexico Press, Albuquerque.

Schumm, S.
  1977 *The Fluvial System*. John Wiley and Sons, New York.

Sellards, E.
  1938 Artifacts Associated with Fossil Elephant. *Geological Society of America Bulletin* 49:999–1009.
  1952 *Early Man in America*. University of Texas Press, Austin.
  1955 Fossil Bison and Associated Artifacts from Milnesand, New Mexico. *American Antiquity* 20(4):336–344.

Sellards, E., Evans, G. L., and G. E. Meade
  1947 Fossil Bison and Associated Artifacts from Plainview, Texas. *Geological Society of America Bulletin* 58:927–954.

Stafford, T. W.
  1981 Alluvial Geology and Archaeological Potential of the Texas High Plains. *American Antiquity* 46:548–565.

Stanford, D. J., J. W. Jordan, E. J. Dixon, and M. A. Jodry
  1990 Archaeological Reconnaissance in the Great Kobuk Sand Dunes, Northwest Alaska. *Current Research in the Pleistocene* 7:44–47.

Tankersly, K. B., E. E. Smith, and D. R. Cochran
  1990 The Distribution of Fluted Points in Indiana: An Update. *Current Research in the Pleistocene* 7:47–49.

Thorson, R. M.
  1990 Geologic Contexts of Archaeological Sites in Beringia. In *Archaeological Geology of North America*, edited by N. P. Lasca and J. Donahue, pp. 399–420. Geological Society of America, Centennial Special Volume No. 4. Boulder.

Waters, M. R.
  1989 Late Quaternary Lacustrine History and Paleoclimatic Significance of Pluvial Lake Cochise, Southeastern Arizona. *Quaternary Research* 32:1–11.

Wendorf, F. (editor)
  1961 *Paleoecology of the Llano Estacado*. Fort Burgwin Research Center, Southern Methodist University, Dallas.

Wendorf, F., and J. J. Hester
  1962 Early Man's Utilization of the Great Plains Environment. *American Antiquity* 28(2):159–171.

Wendorf, F., and J. J. Hester (editors)
  1975 *Late Pleistocene Environments of the Southern High Plains*. Fort Burgwin Research Center, Southern Methodist University, Dallas.

Willig, J. A.
  1988 Paleo-Archaic Adaptations and Lakeside Settlement Patterns in the Northern Alkali Basin, In *Early Human Occupation in Far Western North America: The Clovis-Archaic Interface*, edited by J. A. Willig, C. M. Aikens, and J. L. Fagan, pp. 417–482. Nevada State Museum Anthropology Papers No. 21. Carson City.

Pleistocene Peoples of China and the Peopling of the Americas

Wu Xinzhi

A brief introduction to the morphology and chronology of Pleistocene hominid fossils found in China is given. It is reasonable to infer that Pleistocene humans in China experienced a gradual evolutionary change in morphology. Common morphological features are identified, many of which differ from the features of European contemporaries in shape and frequency of occurrence. This indicates that human evolution in China has been a continuous lineage since at least one million years ago. Morphological evidence also indicates gene exchange between the human populations of China and those of the other parts of the world, especially the West Pacific region and the Americas.

Pleistocene human fossils have been found at many localities in China. The number of localities at which Paleolithic artifacts have been found, however, are much more numerous than the sites that have yielded human fossils. According to the current taxonomy, Chinese human fossils can be divided into three groups: *Homo erectus*, early *Homo sapiens* and late *Homo sapiens*, or anatomically modern *Homo sapiens*. The following discussion provides an introduction to some of the more important specimens from the three groups.

HOMO ERECTUS

Yuanmou

The Yuanmou incisors are usually said to be the earliest human remains found in China. They consist of two upper median incisors found at an open-air site in the southwestern part of China. The incisors are similar in size and morphology to those found at Zoukoudian. They are shovel-shaped with prominent basal tubercles and finger-like projections. In lateral view, the longitudinal axis of the crown lies in the same direction as that of the root. Based on faunal correlation, the Yuanmou specimens are of early Pleistocene age. Paleomagnetic dating of this locality has yielded conflicting results. Some scholars insist that this locality is about 1.7 million years old; others consider an age of 600,000 to 700,000 years to be a better estimate of the locality's antiquity (Wu and Wang 1985).

Lantian

Lantian is a county situated to the southeast of Xian, one of the famous ancient capitals of China. In this county there are two sites that have yielded human fossils. Both were covered with loess dated to the time of the formation of the fourth terrace of the Bahe River, which flows from the north slope of the Qingling Range.

Gongwangling is the earlier of the two sites. Several fragments of a skull recovered from this site are believed to belong to a woman over 30 years of age. The supraorbital ridges on the frontal bone appear to form a continuous, transverse bar which is 17 mm thick along its medial segment. The bones of the cranial vault are also very thick. For example, the thickness of the frontal bone at its center, the parietal bone at the intersection of the coronal and sagittal sutures (i.e., in the bregma region) and the temporal bone at the center of the squamous are 15.0 mm, 16.0 mm, and 11.5 mm, respectively. The frontal bone is rather flat. The postorbital constriction is very prominent. The cranial capacity is probably around 780 cc. No frontal sinus exists. The fronto-nasal and fronto-maxillary sutures combine to form a line that is slightly convex. The midline contour of the anterior surface of alveolar process of the maxilla is convex. The distance is rather short between the root of the maxillary zygomatic process and the alveolar border (Wu 1966).

Chenjiawe, the second of the two sites, has yielded the mandible of an old woman. In terms of robustness, the form of the alveolar arch, and other features, the mandible is close to that of a female *Homo erectus* from Zhoukoudian. It possesses two and four mental foramina on the left and right sides, respectively. There is no sign of the germ of a third molar on the X-ray film of the mandible.

Gongwangling and Chenjiawo are dated palaeomagnetically to about one million years and to one-half million years, respectively (Wu and Wang 1985).

Zhoukoudian, Locality 1

Locality 1 of Zhoukoudian (ZKD) has yielded numerous human fossils including six skull-caps, fourteen cranial fragments, fifteen mandibular fragments, one hundred fifty-three teeth, seven femoral fragments, three fragments of humerus and fragments of a solitary clavicle, a lunar bone and a tibia. Collectively, the fossils represented about forty individuals.

The supraorbital torus on most of the crania and calvariae resembles a transverse bar when viewed from above. The frontal visor is thicker medially (13.0–19.6 mm) than laterally (11.2–14.5 mm). The bones of the skulls are very thick. The mean thickness at different parts of the skull is as follows: the center of the frontal squamous, 9.3 mm (range: 7.0–13.0 mm); the parietal bone near bregma, 8.8 mm (range: 7.0–10.0 mm); and the parietal eminence, 10.8 mm (range: 5.0–10.0 mm). A sagittal ridge exists on the frontal and parietal bones. The occipital ridge and angular torus are prominent.

The fronto-nasal and fronto-maxillary sutures form a more or less horizontal curve. The infraorbital region is rounded. The distance is relatively large between the inferior border of the maxillary zygomatic process and the maxillary alveolar border. A deep maxillary notch is present in this region of the splanchocranium. Auditory exostoses appear on the lateral surface of the maxillary alveolar process and on the wall of the auditory meatus. The midline profile of the anterior surface of the maxillary alveolar process is convex (Weidenreich 1943).

Generally the frontal sinus is small or absent. The average adult cranial capacity is 1088 cc.

Variation in the Zhoukoudian mandibles attributable to sexual dimorphism is very marked. The symphysial region of the mandible inclines downward and backward. No mental protuberances exist. Multiple mental foramina however do occur with high regularity. About half of the mandibles possess mandibular tori.

Limb bones of *Homo erectus* from Zhoukoudian are basically similar to those of modern humans except that they have thicker walls and narrower medullary canals.

On the basis of the length of a portion of a male femur, the stature of Peking Man is estimated to be around 156 cm.

Homo erectus fossils found at ZKD Locality 1 span a long period of time (i.e., from 230,000 to 500,000 years ago) according to various dating methods such as fission track, amino acid racemization, uranium series, thermoluminescence, etc. (Wu and Wang 1985). Their morphology changed slightly and gradually through time. The thickness of the walls of and the prominence of the ridges on the frontal bones and the occipital bones diminished through time. The distance between inion and the internal occipital protuberance became shorter. The cranial capacity became larger (Qiu et al. 1973).

Hexian

In addition to several fossil fragments, the Hexian cave site has yielded a rather complete skull-cap of a man about 20 years old. The thickness of the brow ridge toward the lateral end approaches the upper limit of the ZKD specimens. The inclination and the degree of bulging of the outer surface of the frontal squama are close to that of the ZKD specimens. However, the supratoral sulcus is shallower than that of the latter and closer to the Trinil specimens of Java. The supraorbital process and supraorbital notch are more weakly developed than those of Peking Man. A sagittal ridge extends from the level of the frontal tubercle toward bregma where it gradually diminishes. The occipital torus is well developed and is most prominent at the midline. The upper border of the temporal squamous is curved. There is an angular torus. The external auditory aperture is deep and is 14–15 mm in the medial to auriculare dimension.

The thickness of the walls of the cranium is varied. The thickness of the frontal bone corresponds to the lower limit of the range of variation of the ZKD specimens; the thicknesses of the parietal and temporal bones on the other hand are greater than the averages of the ZKD specimens.

Three mental foramina occur on the left side of mandible. As in the case of the ZKD specimens, the third molar is the smallest of the three molars (Wu and Dong 1982).

On the basis of uranium series dating, the age of this skull is estimated to be about 200,000-300,000 yr B.P. (Chen et al. 1987).

EARLY *HOMO SAPIENS*
Dali

Dali is located near Lantian. The solitary skull from the site is large and robust. It belonged to a male less than 30 years of age. The skull possesses two supraorbital ridges which converge anteriorly instead of forming a transverse bar. Each supraorbital ridge is as thick as the continuous supraorbital visor of Peking Man. However, the thickest part occurs at the middle of each brow ridge. A keel extends along the midline of the frontal bone and continues along the sagittal suture between the parietals. The occipital torus forms an angulate juncture between the occipital and the nuchal surfaces of the occipital bone. A triangular Inca bone is probably present. The superior border of the temporal squamous is curved. The pterion region is of an I-type. A small exostosis is present on the posterior wall of the right auditory meatus.

The fronto-maxillary and fronto-nasal sutures form a fundamentally horizontal curve. The profile angle of the nasal bones approaches 90 degrees. A narrow longitudinal ridge occurs along the midline of the nasal bones. The infero-lateral section of the orbital margin is rounded. The antero-lateral surface of the fronto-sphenoidal process of the zygomatic bone faces more forward than it does on Neanderthal skulls. The zygomatic arch is very slender and is parallel to and slightly lower than the Frankfurt Plane. The upper part of lower margin of the maxillary zygomatic process runs more horizontally than it does on Neanderthals. Also the lower margin of zygomatic process forms a deeply concave profile. The juncture between the lower margin of this process and the maxillary body is farther from the alveolar border than in the case of Neanderthals.

The major branching pattern of the middle meningeal artery is very similar to that of the latest Peking Man skull, although the small branches are much more complicated. In addition, the fronto-parietal branch of this artery is slightly thicker and shorter than the superior temporal branch. Significantly, the ratio of the size of the cerebral to that of the cerebrallar fossae is around 3:2, while the distance between inion and endion is 11 mm. The cranial capacity is 1120 cc (Wu 1981).

Based on the results of the uranium series dating, the Dali skull is thought to be around 200,000 years old (Chen et al. 1984).

Jinniushan

Jinniushan is a small hill in the northeastern part of China. A rather complete skull probably belonging to a male around 30 years of age was found at the site. Comparative studies reveal that the thickness of the brow ridge falls within the range of variation of Peking Man. On the other hand, the supraorbital sulcus is shallower than that of the Dali skull. The angular torus is rather weak. The general configuration of the sutures between maxilla, nasal, and frontal bones is similar to that of Dali skull. The zygomatic arch is slender and dips at an angle around 10 degrees below the Frankfurt Plane.

An occipital torus that marks the juncture of the occipital and the nachal surfaces extends over the middle two-thirds of the width of the occipital squamous. In posterior view, the lateral cranial walls are as steep as those of the Dali skull although the vault is generally narrower than that of Dali skull. The cranial capacity is estimated to be about 1390 cc (Wu 1988).

Based on the results of uranium series dating, the site is estimated to be about 200,000-300,000 yr B.P. (Chen et al. 1984).

The Maba calotte was discovered in a limestone cave in the southern part of China. The skull-cap is rather large and probably belonged to a middle-aged individual (Wu and Wu 1985). Its vault seems slightly wider than that of the Jinniushan skull. The frontal bone is more bulging that those of the Dali and Jinniushan skulls. There is a faint keel along the middle portion of the frontal bone. The supraorbital torus is divided and each ridge is curved following the supraorbital margin. The medial end of each ridge is positioned more forward and is slightly thicker than the lateral extremity. The supratoral groove, or sulcus, is rather deep. As evident also in the top view of the Dali skull, the Maba glabella recedes slightly behind the brow ridges. However, the postorbital constriction is even more exaggerated than that of the Dali skull. The frontal sinus, partitioned by a septum, is enormous.

The sutures that connect the maxilla and the nasal bones with the frontal bone are basically colinear. From portions of the facial bones that survive, the nasomalar angle was probably large. The lateral surface of the fronto-sphenoidal process of the zygomatic bone reveals that the upper portion of the face was flat. The orbit is rather high and circular in shape. However, the infero-lateral margin of the orbit is not rounded. A narrow ridge exists along the midline of the nasal bones.

According to uranium series dating of the faunal remains from the cave, the Maba hominid lived about 130 thousand years ago (Yuan et al. 1986).

LATE *HOMO SAPIENS* (ANATOMICALLY MODERN *HOMO SAPIENS*)

Zhoukoudian, Upper Cave

The Zhoukoudian Upper Cave is located geologically above the Zhoukoudian Lower Cave which yielded the 40-odd *Homo erectus* individuals. At least eight individuals have been found in the Upper Cave. Among the human fossils are three complete skulls that share several features. These features include (1) a relatively low cranial index; (2) a maximum skull breadth close to temporal squama; (3) poorly developed frontal and parietal eminences; (4) well-developed superciliary arches; (5) mesene facial shapes according to the upper facial indices; (6) a large interorbital breadth; (7) a low orbital (chaemaconchic) index; (8) a shallow lacrimal fossa; (9) a premaxillary index indicating only slight protrusion of the middle facial region; (10) a wide pyriform aperture; (11) a prenasal fossa; (12) a rounded transition from the temporal to the infratemporal surfaces of the sphenoid bone; and (13) a foramen magnum that faces slightly backward. By focusing on the dissimilarities (rather than the similarities) of the three skulls, Franz Weidenreich has attributed the three skulls to different racial types.

Some other distinctive features deserve mention. For example, on skull No. 101 a narrow ridge exists along midline of the nasal bones. On the same skull, the profile of the anterior surface of the alveolar process along the midline of the maxilla is convex. A maxillary torus exists on the lateral surface of the alveolar process of maxilla No. 110, and a mandibular torus occurs on the medial surface of mandible No. 101 near the second molar. The existence of a transverse furrow on the forehead of skull No. 102 suggests probable artificial deformation. On average, the index of the height of the mental foramen is 44.5, which indicates that the mental foramen is located slightly below the midpoint of the mandibular body height (Wu and Zhang 1985).

According to C-14 dating, the Upper Cave was occupied by humans between 11,000 and 18,000 years ago.

Liujiang

Liujiang is a county in southern China. A human skull, vertebrae, and pelvic and lower limb bones were unearthed from a cave site in the county. In top view, the skull is ovid. A bun-like eminence, reminiscent of those seen on Neanderthal skulls, occurs on the superior portion of the occipital squama. The hard palate and teeth are moderate in size for a male individual. The third molars had not yet erupted.

The suture joining the frontal bone with the nasal and maxilla bones forms a horizontal curve. The face is low and broad and the pyriform aperture is wide. Interestingly, the nasomalar angle and the orientation of the fronto-sphenoidal process of the zygomatic bone indicate Mongoloid affinity. In addition, the preserved right medial maxillary incisor is shovel-shaped. The vertebrae and pelvic bones are small and, by modern Chinese morphological standards, probably belonged to a male individual. Two thick-walled, femoral shaft fragments reveal a relatively short individual (Wu 1959; Wu and Zhang 1985). Based on the length of one of the femoral fragments, the individual's stature was probably around 157 cm.

The uranium series dating of the associated faunal remains indicates the cave was occupied around 67,000 years ago (Yuan et al. 1986).

OTHER FOSSIL LOCALITIES

In addition to the important sites mentioned above, China possesses a series of sites that have yielded human fossils. For example, Yunnxian, Yunxi, Nanzhao, Xichuan, Jianshi, and Xiyuan have all yielded *Homo erectus* fossils. The first five localities have produced teeth only, while the last site has yielded teeth and fragments of a skull. Temporally later early-*Homo sapiens* fossils have also been found at Changyang, Dingcun, Xujiayao, and Chaoxian. Interestingly, the parietal bones from Dingcun and Xujiayao indicate the probable presence of Inca bone (Wu 1980). The nasal cavities of the Changyang and Chaoxian crania appear comparatively wide, while the midline contour of the anterior surface of maxillary alveolar process of both specimens is convex (Xu et al. 1986). Anatomically modern fossil skulls of probable Pleistocene age have been found at Ziyang, Chuandong, and Lijiang in southern China. Among the skulls we find median sagittal ridges, weak bun-like eminences on the occipital bones, and large nasomalar angles. A cruciate eminence and an angular torus appear on the Ziyang skull. The preceding list of fossil localities is far from exhaustive; bone fragments and isolated teeth of anatomically modern humans have been discovered at many other Pleistocene localities.

SUMMARY AND CONCLUSION

From the available fossil evidence it is reasonable to infer that Pleistocene people in China had experienced a gradual evolutionary change in their morphology. For example, the cranial vault became lower. The frontal bone became less flat. The distance between inion and endion became shorter. The ratio of the size of cerebellar fossa to the size of the cerebral fossa became larger. The supraorbital torus was transformed from a continuous transverse bar to two separated superciliary arches. The occipital ridge evolved from a transverse bar of near uniform breadth into a rhomboidal eminence. The upper border of the temporal squamous changed from a straight line to an arch. The mandibular fossa became broader and shallower. The zygomatic arch migrated upward toward the Frankfurt Plane, and the cranial walls became thinner. Morphological changes in the preceding features were not synchronous with similar changes in the human fossil record from other regions of the world. It is noted, for example, that very thick cranial walls persisted in the Chinese fossil record long after the feature had disappeared elsewhere. Xujiayao Man, who lived around 100 to 125 thousand years ago, possessed cranial walls just as thick as those of Peking Man.

Despite the gradual evolutionary changes mentioned above, some morphological traits continued as commonly shared features throughout the different stages of human evolution in China. The shared features include (1) the shortness and flatness of the upper facial region of the skull, including the nasal saddle; (2) the Mongoloid characteristics of the cheek region; (3) the generally horizontal orientation of the fronto-nasal and fronto-maxillary sutures; (4) the convex profile of the midline anterior surface of the maxillary alveolar process; (5) the rounded infero-lateral orbital margin; and (6) the shovel-shaped upper incisors. Although these features occur elsewhere besides China, they fail to rival the frequencies or the duration of their appearance in China. In addition to the six features mentioned above, there are others that appear in China that are equally distinctive although perhaps less persistent. These include (7) the sagittal ridge on the skull vault; (8) Inca bones; and (9) exostoses on maxilla, mandible, and walls of the auditory meatus. The frequencies of the last three traits are generally higher in China than in other regions of the world (Wu and Zhang 1978).

Early *Homo sapiens* of China also possessed several features which distinguished them from their European contemporaries. The most significant include (1) a sagittal eminence, or keel, along the top of the cranial vault; (2) Inca bones; (3) a forward-facing antero-lateral surface of the frontosphenoidal process of the zygomatic bone; (4) with the exception of the Jinniushan skull, a concave glabella region; (5) a generally horizontal configuration of the sutures between the nasal, maxilla and frontal bones; (6) an angle of the nasal bone profile approaching a right angle; (7) with the exception of the Maba skull, a rounded infero-lateral segment of the orbital margin; (8) a zygomatic process that extends from the lowest point on the maxilla first obliquely and then horizontally, instead of in the uniformly olique manner observed on Neanderthal skulls; (9) a greater distance between the alveolar border and the juncture of the lower margin of the maxillary zygomatic process and the maxillary body; and (10) shovel-shaped upper incisors. Several of the preceding features can be traced back without interruption from anatomically modern humans to *Homo erectus* in China. Such continuity supports the argument that human evolution in China has created a continuous lineage.

According to the most recent fossil and archaeological evidence, tool-using humans appear to have originated in Africa about two to three million years ago. Descendents of these earliest hominids spread to China about one to two million years ago. Some primitive features of the colonizing population, such as flatness of the face and shovel-shaped incisors, appear to have been retained for a much longer time and in much higher frequencies in China than in Europe. The marked difference between human fossils from China and those from Europe indicates that the former had flourished in relative isolation from other regions of the world for a considerable period of time.

Other evidence indicates that gene flow was not totally interrupted but continued at a low level between the two regions of the Old World. For example, the bulge between the supero-lateral border of the pyriform aperture and the infero-medial section of the orbital margin of Neanderthal skulls also exists on the Dali and the Jinniushan skulls. In addition, the height, the spherical shape, and sharpness of the infero-lateral margin of the Maba orbit are common within European Pleistocene human populations. Lastly, the large size of the Maba frontal sinus as well as the chignon-like structure existing on the skulls from Liujiang, Lijiang, and Ziyang may be the results of gene exchange with European populations. Overall, however, the extent of gene flow was so small that it could not obliterate the evolving differences between humans in China and Europe.

During the late *Homo sapiens* stage, evidence exists for human migration between China and islands in the Pacific Ocean. Comparative studies reveal that the coefficient of divergence (CD) between the Liujiang and the Niah skulls (i.e., 0.00) is remarkably close to that between the Liujiang and the Minatogawa No. 1 (male) skulls (i.e., 0.029). These figures are indistinguishable from the CD values reflecting intrapopulation divergence between two female skulls from Upper Cave (0.030) and between two female skulls from Miantogawa (0.037). Furthermore, the estimated stature of Liujiang Man (157 ± 3.59 cm) is close to that of the Minatogawa male individual (156.1 cm). The cranial index of the Niah skull (77.8) is virtually identical to that of the Liujiang (75.1) and the Ziyang (77.8) skulls, but it is markedly different from Australian Pleistocene skulls, which have a cranial index generally of less than 74. In addition, the size of the palate of the Niah skull more closely approaches that of the Liujian skull than that of Australian skulls. In short, the affinity between the Liujian and the Niah skulls appears to be stronger than it is between the Niah and Australian Pleistocene skulls. Further afield, the agenesis of the third molar on the Tabon mandible and the existence of a narrow longitudinal ridge on the Tabon nasal bone may be evidence of genetic affinity between the Tabon and the Chinese fossils. Based on the preceding evidence, it seems that the anatomically modern human populations spread both southward and southeastward from southern China.

Of significance to the problem of the initial peopling of the Americas, it is noted that the frequency of Inca bones in the ZKD *Homo erectus* population is 50%. The same high frequency of Inca bones persists during the early *Homo sapiens* stage of China as exemplified by the Dali, the Xujiayao, and the Dingcun skulls. The trait all but disappears among later populations of China. On the other hand, the American Indians continue to manifest a high frequency of Inca bones. It seems reasonable to infer that the founding population possessing the high frequency of the genes responsible for the expression of Inca bones moved into the Americas sometime after the early *Homo sapiens* stage.

Concerning later migrations into the New World, the cranial index, the upper facial index and the maxilloalveolar index of the Upper Cave humans most closely approximate those of modern Eskimos. Upper Cave skull No. 103 in particular possesses several Eskimo traits; namely, dolichocephaly, acrocephaly, a large transverse craniofacial index, and a sagittal keel. On the other hand, the total facial index and the breadth-height index of Upper Cave Man are closer to those of American Indians than of Eskimos. In conclusion, the late *Homo sapiens* populations of northern China were probably responsible for the peopling of the Arctic and southern regions of the Americas.

REFERENCES CITED

Chen, T., S. Yuan, and S. J. Gao
1984 The Study on Uranium Dating of Fossil Bones and an Absolute Age Sequence for the Main Paleolithic Sites of North China. *Acta Anthropologica Sinica* 3:259–269.

Chen, T., S. Yuan, S. J. Gao, and Y. Hu
1987 Uranium Series of Dating of Fossil Bones from Hexan and Chaoxian Fossil Human. *Acta Anthropologica Sinica* 6:249–254.

Qui, Z., Y. Gu, Y. Zhang, and S. Zhang
1973 Newly Discovered *Sinanthropus* Remains and Stone Artifacts at Choukoutien. *Vertebrata PalAsiatica* 11:109–131.

Wiedenreich, F.
1943 The Skull of *Sinanthropus pekinensis*: A Comparative Study on a Primitive Hominid Skull. *Palaeontologica Sinica* New Series D, 10:1–485.

Wu, M.
1980 Human Fossils Discovered at Xuijiayao Site in 1977. *Verebrata PalAsiatica* 18:229–238.

Wu, R.
1959 Human Fossils Found in Liujiang, Kwangsi, China. *Palaeovertebrata et Palaeoanthropologica* 1:97–104.

1966 The Hominid Skull of Lantian, Shensi. *Vertebrata PalAsiatica* 10:1–22.

1988 The Reconstruction of the Fossil Human Skull from Jinniushan, Yinkou, Liaoning Province and Its Main Features. *Acta Anthropologica Sinica* 7:97–101.

Wu, R., and X. Dong
1982 Preliminary Study of *Homo erectus* Remains from Hexian, Anhui. *Acta Anthropologica Sinica* 1:2–13.

Wu, X.
1981 The Well Preserved Cranium of an Early *Homo sapiens* from Dali, Shaanxi. *Scientia Sinica* 24(4):200–206.

Wu, X., and L. Wang
1985 Chronology in Chinese Paleaoanthropology. In *Palaeoanthropogy and Palaeolithic Archaeology in the People's Republic of China*, edited by Rukang Wu and J. W. Olsen, pp. 29–52. Academic Press, Orlando.

Wu, X., and M. Wu
1985 Early *Homo sapiens* in China. In *Palaeoanthropogy and Palaeolithic Archaeology in the People's Republic of China*, edited by Rukang Wu and J. W. Olsen, pp. 91–106. Academic Press, Orlando.

Wu, X., and Y. Zhang
1978 Chinese Palaeoanthropological Multidisciplinary Studies. In *Collected Papers of Palaeoanthropology*, edited by Institute of Vertebrate Paleontology and Paleoanthropology, pp. 28–42. Science Press, Beijing.

Wu, X., and Z. Zhang
1985 *Homo sapiens* Remains from Late Palaeolithic and Neolithic China. In *Palaeoanthropogy and Palaeolithic Archaeology in the People's Republic of China*, edited by R. Wu and J. W. Olsen, pp. 107–133. Academic Press, Orlando.

Xu, C., Y. Zhang, and D. Fang
1986 Human Fossils Newly Discovered at Chaoxian, Anhui. *Acta Anthropologica Sinica* 5:310–312.

Yuan, S., T. Chen, and S. J. Gao
1986 Uranium Series Chronological Sequence of Some Palaeolithic Sites in South China. *Acta Anthropologica Sinica* 5:189–196.

Origins and Affinities of the Native Peoples of Northwestern North America: The Evidence of Cranial Nonmetric Traits[1]

NANCY S. OSSENBERG
Department of Anatomy
Queen's University
Canada

Mean Measures of Divergence (MMDs) based on 25 nonmetric cranial traits were computed for 50 recent and prehistoric skeletal samples from northwest North America and Northeast Asia (N=2800 individuals). A novel method introduced in this study, plots of MMD versus Spearman's r_s for pairwise population comparisons, proved to be a useful adjunct to cluster analysis for two-dimensional depiction of group relationships.

Patterns of affinity among the Amerinds were interpreted to reflect differences in timing and amount of gene flow between (1) groups derived from a 10,000 yr B.P. population stratum (named Paleoarctic Amerind) associated with the American Paleoarctic tradition and most strongly represented in the ancestry of Aleut and Na-Dene; and (2) 4500–2500 yr B.P. immigrants (named Neoarctic Amerind) associated with Neolithic Asian cultural elements leading to Norton and Thule traditions, hence to historic Eskimo.

The findings for Aleuts, contrary to the prevailing view of their monophyletic origin with Eskimos, were reinforced by additional analyses based on a subset of the 15 cranial traits most powerful for Eskimo-Indian discrimination. These placed Athapaskans intermediate between Aleuts and Eskimos, both on a trait-by-trait basis as well as in multivariate comparisons. This pattern suggested that Athapaskan ancestry involved mixture between Paleoarctic and Neoarctic people; Aleut, isolated in their archipelago, represented a relict Paleoarctic population. Historic tribes of the northern Plains and their Late Woodland ancestors appeared to be influenced by the Paleoarctic branch, harking back to a long-discredited view of the peopling of North America, that of G. K. Neumann. Remains from Namu (5000–2000 yr B.P.) on the central British Columbia

---

[1] This paper is a version of one prepared in connection with the Circum-Pacific Prehistory Conference, Seattle 1989, expanded by the inclusion of three early samples (Illinois Hopewell, Old Punuk, and Namu) and by additional analyses focused on the affinities of the Aleut.

coast, not unexpectedly, also clustered with Aleut–Na-Dene. Diachronic comparisons of crania from the Uyak site, Kodiak Island (3500–500 yr B.P.) revealed microevolutionary divergence away from Aleut–Na-Dene and toward Eskimos, interpreted to result from assimilation of Eskimos from the Bering Sea area by Paleoarctic indigenes of Kodiak, as consistent with the archaeological record. MMDs indicated that these Americans were derived more directly from the Arctic Mongoloid stock which evolved in Northeast Asia during the last glaciation (whose Asian descendants were represented in this study by Chukchi and Siberian Eskimo) than from the Classic Mongoloid stock (represented by Japanese and Tungus). A Proto-Mongoloid stock with roots in Southeast Asia (represented here by Jomon and Ainu) was apparently not involved in the ancestry of these particular Americans. Though many more populations need to be surveyed, the findings based on nonmetric cranial traits generally were in agreement with those based on genetics, craniometric data, and dental morphology.

INTRODUCTION

Nonmetric Skeletal Traits

Nonmetric discrete traits are those which in an individual can be denoted by presence or absence, hence in a population by percentage frequency. Interest in this class of skeletal variants goes back to the very earliest anatomists, who tended to see them as curiosities. By the first decade of this century they had been inventoried in the classics of descriptive skeletal morphology, and by the 1930s a few anthropologists had suggested that frequency differences of a trait among various human groups possibly reflect their divergent historical paths. However, the landmark study, which first actually demonstrated that by mustering the evidence of a number of such features simultaneously one can address a specific ethnohistorical question, was that of Laughlin and Jørgensen (1956). Using eight discrete cranial traits and seven measurements, they derived two sets of coefficients of divergence, found them congruent, and on the evidence of both data sets confirmed their hypothesis about the direction of movements and contacts of Eskimo isolates around the coast of Greenland. They concluded that discontinuous morphological variants are eminently suitable for problems of biological distance between human groups even though gene frequency ratios cannot be computed, nor the effect of various evolutionary agencies such as selection, mixture, mutation, and drift.

The theoretical basis of any such investigation is a biological population model that assumes that the traits used are primarily under genetic control. Unlike polymorphisms in the blood, however, nonmetric skeletal traits are not inherited in a simple Mendelian pattern. Rather, as elucidated by studies of analogous variants in inbred strains of laboratory mice (initiated by Grüneberg 1952), such a trait is inherited according to the "quasi-continuous" model, in which presence or absence results from an intrinsic threshold mechanism superimposing discontinuity on an underlying continuous variable. The example most often given is absence of the third molar in mice: the underlying continuous variable in this case is size of the tooth rudiment. It is controlled by multiple genes with additive effects. If, at a certain stage of development (about five days after birth) the tooth rudiment has not reached a critical size, it simply fails to develop further so that phenotypic expression of the trait becomes *third molar absent*. Besides the genetic constitution of the individual, any generalized or localized factor which influences size (mother's genetic constitution, age, parity, litter size, postnatal environment) can affect liability for the trait. Thus, in its dependence on an underlying continuously distributed trait liability, and with the multiple genes involved being remote from their phenotypic effects, a quasi-continuous trait has more in common with a measurement attribute such as cranial breadth than with the ABO blood groups.

Since the pioneer work of Laughlin and Jørgensen, many ethnohistorical studies based on nonmetric traits of the skull have been reported worldwide. Recently, however, this stream of research has slowed to a trickle, possibly because spurious outcomes in some cases have led to skepticism concerning the validity of the features. As with any category of attribute, so with nonmetric traits there are problems and limitations involved in their use. Appropriately, in the last twenty years or so research has tended to focus on the theoretical assumptions and techniques of biological distance analysis (Bocquet-Appel 1984; Buikstra et al. 1990; Finnegan and Rubison 1984; Sjøvold 1984). Building on the traditions of classical morphology, anthropologists also are making renewed efforts now to meticulously describe individual features, standardize criteria for scoring them (e.g., Dodo 1980, 1987; Hauser and De Stefano 1989; Kozintsev 1988) and probe their etiology and significance in the light of modern physiological concepts. (For a recent critical review see Saunders 1989.)

Nonmetric skeletal traits have demonstrated their validity in several ethnohistorical cases, especially when

Objectives of the Study

It is now generally accepted that the ancestors of Native Americans originated in Asia and entered the New World via Beringia. Still in question are the number of founding groups, the specific regions of Asia whence they dispersed, the dates of their migrations, and the correspondence between archaeological complexes and particular founding groups. Multivariate distance analyses based on morphology of the bones and teeth provide comparisons of extinct American and Asian populations with which we can address these questions.

Based on a one-observer survey of nonmetric features of the dental crown and roots in a large number of Asian, American and other Circum-Pacific skeletal samples (Greenberg et al. 1986; Turner 1976, 1983, 1985, 1986, 1989; Turner and Bird 1981), two distinct dental complexes are defined: "Sinodonty" and "Sundadonty." All native peoples of North and South America, including the very earliest remains that have been found, are Sinodonts. This strongly differentiated Mongoloid dental pattern, which characterizes Northeast Asians as well as all Amerinds, provides evidence tracing Amerind ancestry ultimately to North China. Here Sinodonty apparently evolved during the last glaciation, and was present by about 20,000 yr B.P. On the other hand, Sundadonty, a less differentiated Proto-Mongoloid dental complex that characterizes Southeast Asians as well as Japan's Ainu and Neolithic Jomonese, is not expressed prehistorically in the New World.

Focusing on microevolutionary dental variation in the fundamentally Sinodont New World, Turner discerns, in a large number of Amerind skeletal samples (N=9,000 individuals), three major clusters: Eskimo-Aleut, Greater Northwest Coast (Na-Dene), and all other North and South American Indians (Macro-Indian). Congruities in regional distributions of dental morphology, genetic data, archaeological complexes, and languages are interpreted to reflect three founding migrations in late Pleistocene times, each apparently from a different region of Northeast Asia (Greenberg et al. 1986; Turner 1983, 1985, 1986). While this reconstruction is novel, it agrees with those of other anthropologists (e.g., Dumond 1965, 1977; Harper and Laughlin 1982; Laughlin 1963, 1975, 1980; Laughlin and Harper 1988; McGhee 1976) in at least one important respect: the presumption of Eskimo-Aleut *biological* as well as cultural and linguistic affinity which distinguishes them from all other Amerinds.

Disputing this assumption are two diachronic and independent data sets, serological genetic traits in contemporary populations and skeletal epigenetic traits in 500–100 yr B.P. populations, both demonstrating an unexpectedly close Eskimo–Na-Dene relationship, and one (skeletal) demonstrating an even closer Aleut–Na-Dene relationship. This is interpreted to reflect either a common Eskimo–Aleut–Na-Dene ancestry at the 10,000 yr B.P. level or two founding groups biologically convergent due to early and extensive gene flow (Szathmary and Ossenberg 1978). This and other physical anthropological reports are, in part, what prompted revision of an earlier model of Eskimo-Aleut prehistory (Dumond 1965, 1977) to one which recognizes stronger affiliations, ca. 10,000 yr B.P. of these with Na-Dene and possibly other Indians, and postulates a decreased time-depth, ca. 4000 yr B.P. for Eskimo-Aleut appearance and beginning divergence in Alaska (Dumond 1987a).

A one-observer survey of nonmetric cranial traits begun in 1960 provided data for previous reports focused in part on ethnohistorical questions, in part on the description of the bony features and on the theory and methodology pertaining to their use in population studies (Ossenberg 1969, 1970, 1974a, 1974b, 1976, 1977, 1981a, 1981b, 1986a, 1986b, 1987; Szathmary and Ossenberg 1978). The previously reported cranial data set (Szathmary and Ossenberg 1978), expanded to include Asian and additional North American samples, allowed two main objectives concerning the peopling of the New World to be addressed in this paper: the first was to aid in the search for Asian roots of native Americans by assessing their affinities to Proto-Mongoloids (Jomon and Ainu), Classic Mongoloids (Japanese and Tungus), and Arctic Mongoloids (Siberian Eskimo and Chukchi). The second objective was to help reconstruct a prehistoric scenario for northwestern North America which best accounts for the observed pattern and degree of biological divergence within and between the Eskimo-Aleut and Na-Dene linguistic phyla. In examining different models of New World prehistory, evidence from tooth morphology and cranial measurements was reviewed and compared with findings based on cranial nonmetric traits.

MATERIALS AND METHODS

Population Samples

The samples (Figure 1) represented various time depths ranging from about 5000 yr B.P. for the skeletons from Namu, Coastal British Columbia, 4000 yr B.P. for remains from the deepest layers in the Chaluka midden on Umnak Island, to late nineteenth century for Plains tribes, and even more recent for Black Americans (not shown in Figure 1) included as a non-Mongoloid comparison. Certain samples spanned only a few generations, others possibly more than a hundred generations. Their temporal/geographic provenience provided the

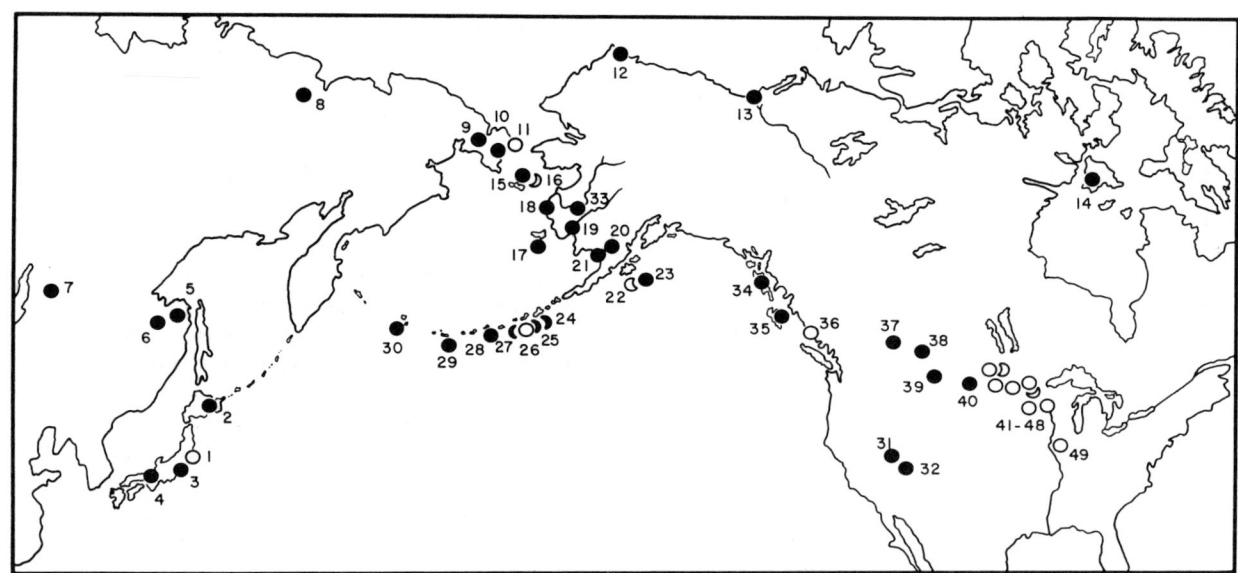

Figure 1. Geographic distribution of populations sampled in the study. Open circles indicate early time periods. Closed circles indicate recent ones, or those in the Aleutians of uncertain temporal provenience.

Japan: 1: Jomon (N 56), late phase ca. 5000–2500 yr B.P., mainly from the Tsukumo site in Western Honshu. 2: Ainu (N 119), nineteenth century. 3 and 4: skeletons of recent Japanese dissecting-room subjects from the Kanto and Kinki districts, respectively.

Siberia: 5, 6 and 7: Tungus tribes, respectively, Ulchi (N 30), Negidal (N 26) and Evenki (N 27). 8: Yukaghir (N 27). 9: Coastal Chukchi (N 39). 10: Siberian Eskimo (N 41). 11: Ekven Cemetery Eskimo (N 77), Old Bering Sea phase, 2000–1800 yr B.P. approximately (Alexseev 1979b:75).

Inupiaq Eskimo: 12, 13 and 14: seventeenth- to nineteenth-century samples from Pt. Barrow (N 86), Mackenzie Delta (N 52) and Southampton Island (Sadlermiut) (N 52).

Alaskan Yupik Eskimo: 15: St. Lawrence Is., seventeenth to nineteenth century (N 76). 16: St. Lawrence Is., Old Punuk phase (N 26), ca. 1200–900 yr B.P. (Ackerman 1984:110). 17: Nunivak Is. (N102). 18–21: South Mainland Alaska, respectively, Hooper's Bay (N 28), Kuskokwim R. (N 69), Nushagak R. (N 41), Bristol Bay (N 35).

Kodiak Island: samples from the stratified Uyak Bay site, 22: Kodiak Early (N 59), 3500–2000 yr B.P. 23: Kodiak Late (Koniag Eskimo) (N 100), 1000–400 yr B.P. (Clark 1984:Figure 2). Kodiak Middle (N 109) 2000–1000 yr B.P., not shown on the map, was also included in the study. The possibility exists that skeletal remains from the three levels were, to some extent, commingled by Hrdlicka's excavation and sorting methods. Nevertheless, it is judged that the three skeletal series do provide useful information about the temporal sequence at Kodiak (Clark 1974:175). In Heizer's (1956) view, intermingling of remains from successive strata during or subsequent to their retrieval was minimal, at least as far as the artifacts are concerned.

Aleutian Islands: 24–26: Eastern Aleut, respectively, Amchitka Is. (N 48), Shiprock Is. (N 46), Umnak Is. (N 64). 27–29: Central Aleut, respectively, Kagamil Is. (N 111), Andreanov group (N 51), Rat group (N 35). 30: Western Aleut, or Near group (N 26). Remains from the Chaluka midden, Umnak Is. are dated ca. 4000–1000 yr B.P. Kagamil Is. mummy caves were late prehistoric, 500–300 yr B.P. (McCartney 1984:130, 131). Temporal provenience of other Aleut samples is unknown.

Na-Dene: 31 and 32: Southern Athapaskans respectively, Navajo (N 27) and Apache (N 33). 33: Northern Athapaskans, a series comprised of Ingalik (possibly including Koyukon and Holikachuk (N 72) from the Yukon R. above Holy Cross; Tanaina (N 7); Kutchin, Hare, Dogrib (N 4). 34: Tlingit (N 17). 35: Haida (N 144). 36: Namu (N 25), skeletons dating approximately 5000–2000 yr B.P. from a stratified site on the British Colulmbia coast (Curtin 1984; Carlson 1989).

Northern Plains: 37–40: nineteenth century tribes, respectively, Blackfoot (N 81), Assiniboin (N 31), Cheyenne (N 29), Dakota (N 146).

Northeastern Plains Periphery: 41–48: Late Woodland burial mound complexes dated ca. 1500–300 yr B.P., respectively, Melita (N 49), Manitoba (N 86), Devil's Lake (N 36), Red River Arvilla (N 83), Red River South (N 75), Blackduck North (N 51), Blackduck South (N 43), Mille Lacs (N 48). These were shown to be ancestral to the Northern Plains tribes (Ossenberg 1974b).

Illinois Hopewell: 49: a sample (N 63) of undeformed crania from the Pete Klunk Mound 2 and the Wilson site. These are Middle Woodland, 2100-1900 yr B.P. approximately.

necessary framework within which the distance measures were interpreted. Problems inherent in the use of archaeological skeletal samples (Burke 1981; Cadien et al. 1976) may have serious implications for attempts to identify ancestor-descendant relationships in a narrow regional and temporal context. However, for analyses such as the present one which seek to outline broader populational or intercontinental patterns, the samples were judged to be satisfactory.

Pooling of samples was done when (1) prior analysis had demonstrated a close affinity among them; and (2) no additional ethnohistorical information pertinent to the problem at hand would be derived from their individual consideration. Thus, for example, at different stages of analysis data for eight Late Woodland mound complexes were aggregated, three Tungus samples formed a second aggregate, two or more Athapaskan a third, and so on. An advantage of regional pooling is that it averages out frequency oscillations due to strong genetic drift in small populations (Cavalli-Sforza et al. 1988) and also ameliorates the effect of a particular sample being non-random; i.e., rather in the nature of a total universe from the cemetery of a single family or small community of related individuals.

Sample sizes ranged from N 17 for Tlingit to N 505 for the Late Woodland aggregate, indicating the number of individuals represented. However, when remains were fragmentary, the number of observations that could be made for any trait was smaller than N suggests.

Traits

All data on nonmetric cranial variants in this report were collected by one observer. The 25 traits used in the study were selected from a much larger potential list by screening out those found to be simply too invariant in the populations under consideration to be informative, too ambiguous for scoring presence or absence (i.e., sutural configurations at pterion and lambda), or suspected of a strongly mechanical or functional cause (i.e., mandibular torus) (Ossenberg 1981b; Wright 1987). Previous work indicates that this battery yields valid taxonomical information: population distance estimates significantly correlated with known historical relationships (Ossenberg 1976), with rankings of Eskimo samples based on linguistic and geographic criteria (Ossenberg 1977), with craniometric distance measures in East Asians (Ossenberg 1986a), and with genetic distances based on serological data in North Americans and Siberians (Szathmary and Ossenberg 1978).

The traits and their criteria for scoring have been described previously. They are listed in Table 1 in rank order of their power in discriminating between Indian and Eskimo samples, along with frequencies in eight Eskimo, Indian, and Aleut samples and aggregates.

Statistical Methods

The distance measure used is a modification of Smith's Mean Measure of Divergence (MMD), using the Freeman-Tukey inverse sine transformation of trait frequencies (Sjøvold 1977). Cluster analysis produced a series of dendrographs, in which measures along both axes contain information about sample linkages: within-group linkages distances along the x axis, and between-group along the y (McCammon and Wenninger 1970). Because the affinities of Aleut were a particular focus of this study, MMDs were also calculated and the corresponding dendrograph plotted based on a subset of the 15 traits most powerful in Eskimo-Indian discrimination.

A novel approach to distance analysis attempted here was the use of Spearman's r_s to test correlation between the ranks of MMDs of population A versus all other populations, and the ranks of MMDs of population B versus those populations. The rationale was that if A and B were closely related as members of a single lineage descended from a common ancestor then they should show significant positive correlation in addition to having a small A-B MMD. Two-dimensional plots of r_s versus MMD were made to illustrate this approach.

Spearman's r_s was also used to test rank correlation between MMDs based on cranial traits and those based on dental traits. The non-parametric test was appropriate in all cases owing to the fact that distance measures were not normally distributed.

RESULTS AND DISCUSSION

Table 1 lists the 25 features and gives their frequencies in eight aggregates and key samples. Table 2 lists MMDs in rank order, along with values of Spearman's r_s, for each of 24 samples and aggregates[2]. Table 3 presents MMDs and r_s values for Aleutian and Kodiak samples based on a subset of 15 traits. Table 4 is Aleut summary data, and Table 5 a summary of Asian-Amerind MMDs. Figures 2, 3, 4 and 8, 9 are dendrographs; Figures 5, 6, 7 and 10 are other graphic depictions of relationships.

Relationships are discussed cumulatively, from within to between groups, in the following order: Aleuts; Eskimos; Indians; Aleuts, Eskimos, and Indians; North Americans versus Northeast Asians.

---

[2] The triangular matrix of all pairwise comparisons of 48 samples (all those in the present report except Old Punuk, Namu, and Hopewell) is not reproduced here, but is given in Ossenberg 1989.

Table 1. Incidence of Cranial Traits in Aleuts, Indians, North American Eskimos and Chukotkans. Traits are listed in rank order of their contribution to the mean of 100 Mean Measures of Divergence (MMDs) for 10 Eskimo *vs* 10 Indian samples. Incidence of bilateral traits is in total left plus right sides.

TRAIT	PALEO-ALEUT (UMNAK)		ALEUT (EASTERN AND CENTRAL)		NA-DENE (HAIDA, TLINGIT, ATHAPASKANS)	
	N	%	N	%	N	%
1 Supraorbital foramen	109	65.2	533	75.2	557	75.4
2 Wormian bones	81	56.8	472	46.0	528	56.4
3 Mylohyoid bridge	87	27.6	355	29.6	414	19.8
4 Marginal foramen, tympanic plate	98	33.7	506	26.7	549	17.9
5 Frontal grooves	91	36.3	511	32.3	556	39.0
6 Pharyngeal fossa	47	8.5	276	10.5	294	14.6
7 Tympanic dehiscence	103	41.8	518	49.2	566	37.6
8 Infraorbital suture	75	40.0	423	45.2	516	32.8
9 Clinoid bridge	89	9.2	539	20.4	593	17.7
10 Lateral pterygoid plate foramen	69	8.7	408	9.3	527	10.4
11 Parietal process of temporal squama	82	3.7	474	1.7	568	7.9
12 Trochlear spur	85	2.4	513	3.9	557	2.5
13 Pterygobasal bridge	90	4.5	498	2.4	560	7.1
14 Intermediate condylar canal	81	24.7	400	23.5	503	35.0
15 Foramen spinosum open	86	7.0	445	12.8	559	11.3
16 Paracondylar process	78	15.4	513	13.6	560	12.3
17 Os Japonicum trace	70	10.0	376	21.0	453	18.5
18 Upper third molar suppressed	74	10.8	470	7.0	503	6.0
19 Accessory optic canal	69	8.7	474	6.1	551	3.8
20 Squamo-parietal fusion	82	3.7	484	2.7	587	1.7
21 Postcondylar canal absent	94	13.8	562	21.4	583	13.7
22 Accessory mental foramen	103	17.5	458	9.8	483	6.8
23 Hypoglossal canal bridged	96	33.3	528	23.7	581	21.7
24 Pterygospinous bridge	101	5.9	583	4.6	590	8.0
25 Odonto-occipital articulation	58	1.7	294	0.68	292	0.0

[a] Owing to age-regression in expression, the subsample for scoring many of the features is restricted to individuals in certain age categories. Traits 1, 2, 13 and 16 are assigned weighted scores based on degree of expression. Descriptions of individual features, age categories and criteria for scoring are given in previous reports.

Aleuts

Aleuts were in the upper cluster of Figure 2, where the linkage of six samples followed a gradient of affinities from east to west. This pattern was wholly consistent with the "directional configuration of the geographic domain, a longitudinal and linear distribution of islands that directed gene flow and the diffusion of cultural traits along an east-west axis and promoted a relatively high degree of isolation" (Laughlin 1980:1–2).

The samples, though temporal provenience was generally poor, varied greatly in time depth, with Umnak being earliest and remains from the Kagamil mummy caves probably most recent. Thus, temporal and geographical effects were confounded in the observed cline. Nevertheless, the pattern was strikingly consistent with what one would expect according to Laughlin's reconstruction for the Aleutians. Tightest dendrographic linkages formed in the eastern sector of highest population density, Paleo-Aleut from the deep, stratified Chaluka village site on Umnak Island fitting comfortably with the presumably more recent samples from Amaknak and Shiprock. Thus the nonmetric cranial traits agreed with the archaeological evidence of an uninterrupted occupation of the islands by Aleuts and only Aleuts, for at least four millenia (Dumond 1987b; McCartney 1984). They did not support Hrdlička's

LATE WOODLAND		KODIAK EARLY		KODIAK LATE		ESKIMO (YUPIK, INUPIAQ)		CHUKOTKANS (EKVEN, ESKIMO CHUKCHI)	
N	%	N	%	N	%	N	%	N	%
615	57.7	101	90.1	136	86.0	1081	78.6	303	74.6
438	33.6	73	76.8	119	80.7	1033	67.1	286	72.4
565	29.6	104	19.2	140	12.9	753	8.1	197	11.2
581	39.4	78	24.4	142	19.7	1057	13.3	306	6.9
567	27.7	92	34.8	151	21.9	944	23.3	272	21.0
255	11.8	45	2.2	96	1.0	591	5.2	147	8.8
673	39.8	78	53.8	110	38.2	1057	24.9	307	29.7
359	36.2	57	35.1	101	39.6	884	50.2	282	57.1
485	24.9	68	7.4	194	5.7	1167	10.7	288	11.8
299	11.4	54	7.4	114	6.1	770	5.5	205	7.8
482	10.4	102	0.0	162	2.5	1073	3.3	300	0.33
558	10.8	81	2.5	199	3.0	1037	3.3	294	1.36
527	7.2	82	7.3	195	6.2	1187	4.1	285	4.6
366	42.9	69	29.0	100	37.0	890	29.9	265	27.5
482	15.4	70	14.3	136	15.4	1062	15.6	283	24.7
452	21.2	72	25.0	175	25.7	950	15.9	218	15.6
396	13.1	72	19.4	112	17.0	835	24.6	279	19.0
461	5.4	88	8.0	129	10.9	905	12.4	244	15.6
386	4.7	74	6.8	187	1.6	1121	3.5	289	2.8
514	2.5	102	1.9	175	1.7	1131	0.62	299	1.0
525	11.8	92	12.0	196	20.9	1158	17.8	289	18.7
680	8.2	141	17.7	196	8.2	915	8.7	198	6.6
550	22.9	95	13.7	137	16.8	1135	18.9	296	20.6
550	6.0	102	6.9	193	8.8	1192	8.1	288	5.6
265	4.5	45	0.0	96	0.0	584	0.68	150	0.0

theory of racial discontinuity whereby an earlier longheaded population was replaced by late prehistoric brachycephals.

In situ microevolutionary change is thought to be responsible for observed physical changes over time and distance. For example, the trend to brachycephaly was most rapid in the large eastern population and spread westward (Laughlin 1963, 1980). Likewise, dental trait frequencies in these skeletal samples show an east-west gradient, but no significant differences between Paleo- and Neo-Aleut crania, indicating population continuity in this region (Turner 1967).

The Near Island group (Attu, Agattu) was outside the Aleut subcluster. Instead, it joined the Yupik Eskimo at a low level of affinity. Small sample size, N 26, may have been partly responsible for this, but it was also possible that its relationships in Figure 2 and Table 2 reflected a real difference from other Aleuts. Dental features in living Aleuts (Moorrees 1957), as well as blood group allele frequencies for ABO and MN loci (Laughlin 1951), and somatic and head measurements (Laughlin 1951, 1966; Harper 1975) reveal differences between Eastern and Western isolates. Because brachycephalization in its east-west trend apparently had not reached it, the Western isolate was more similar to Paleo- than to Neo-Aleut with respect to cranial shape. Table 2 did show Western Aleut closer to Paleo-Aleut (Umnak MMD 152) than to recent Aleut (Kagamil MMD 181). However, little importance could be attached to this difference considering the low position of the Kagamil-Near and Umnak-Near MMD in the ranked lists of MMDs for each of these three groups.

Eskimos

The lower cluster in Figure 2 accommodated six groups of recent (possibly seventeenth- to nineteenth-century) Yupik-speaking Eskimo, and a 1000–400 yr B.P. sample from the Uyak Bay site on Kodiak Island (Kodiak Late) thought to represent Koniag Eskimo. Two earlier samples from the same site (Kodiak Early and Kodiak Middle) formed with Koniags the tightest linkage in the dendrograph. A comparison of the affinities of the three Kodiak samples, crucial for ethnohistorical reconstruction in Alaska, is included in the section "Aleuts, Eskimos, and Indians."

Nearly as closely related to each other were the samples from Bristol Bay and Nushagak River. Again, the factor of population density seemed to be reflected among these geographically close groups in southwestern Alaska as in the eastern Aleutians.

On the other hand, Nunivak and St. Lawrence were rather loosely joined to the Yupik subcluster, possibly reflecting genetic drift or founder effects maintained through isolation on these islands. The close linguistic and historical ties of St. Lawrence with Siberian rather than Alaskan Eskimos (Krauss 1973; Oswalt 1967; Woodbury 1984) were suggested earlier as the reason for the apparent genetic divergence of St. Lawrence from Alaska (Szathmary and Ossenberg 1978). Now, with Asian samples included in the analysis, that explanation no longer fit because St. Lawrence was divergent also from Siberian Eskimo.

The three Inupiaq groups formed a subcluster which, instead of joining the Yupik clusters, joined Aleut in Figure 2. This linkage, deriving from the close affinity of Inupiaq to Amaknak and Andreanov, appeared on the

Table 2a. Ranked Mean Measures of Divergence (MMDs) Based on 25 Nonmetric Cranial Traits in 24 Asian and American Population Samples. Rank Correlation for Each Population Pair is Tested by Spearman's r_s.

JOMON (SAMPLES 1, N 56)		AINU (SAMPLES 1, N 119)		JAPANESE (SAMPLES 2, N 95)	
49 (.928)	Ainu[1]	49 (.928)	Jomon	42 (.754)	Tungus
141 (.595)	Japanese	79 (.607)	Japanese	65 (.680)	Inupiaq
166 (.294)	Inupiaq Eskimo	82 (.356)	Inupiaq	67 (.455)	Chukchi
186 (-.159)	Tlingit	114 (.089)	Siberian Eskimo	67 (.508)	Siberian Eskimo
191 (-.071)	Chukchi	130 (-.088)	Chukchi	68 (.560)	Ekven
193 (-.201)	Haida	136 (.051)	Ekven	79 (.607)	Ainu
205 (.020)	Ekven	136 (.106)	Hopewell	91 (.187)	Hopewell
223 (.098)	Siberian Eskimo	141 (-.143)	Haida	95 (.187)	Yupik SMA
226 (.069)	Nunivak Eskimo	143 (-.158)	Tlingit	102 (.487)	Nunivak
227 (.231)	Tungus	144 (.086)	Nunivak	103 (.321)	Kodiak Late
230 (.163)	Illinois Hopewell	145 (.208)	Tungus	114 (-.087)	Athapaskans
234 (-.278)	Umnak Aleut	154 (-.278)	Umnak	114 (-.295)	Umnak
237 (-.255)	Yupik SMA Eskimo	170 (-.222)	Athapaskans	122 (-.176)	Haida
245 (-.182)	Athapaskans	173 (-.051)	Plains	126 (-.061)	Tlingit
253 (-.176)	Kagamil Aleut	174 (-.068)	Late Woodland	126 (.484)	St. Lawrence
264 (-.025)	Plains	184 (-.024)	Kodiak Late	127 (.172)	Kodiak Early
266 (-.008)	Kodiak Late	189 (-.205)	Yupik SMA	141 (.595)	Jomon
270 (-.091)	Kodiak Early	204 (-.155)	Kodiak Early	146 (-.199)	Namu
273 (.005)	Late Woodland	216 (-.285)	Namu	153 (-.199)	Kagamil
282 (-.215)	Namu	229 (-.152)	Kagamil	153 (.552)	Western Aleut
317 (.050)	St. Lawrence Eskimo	251 (.032)	St. Lawrence	157 (-.146)	Late Woodland
317 (.129)	Western Aleut	264 (.174)	Western Aleut	158 (-.132)	Plains
450 (-.051)	Old Punuk	315 (-.052)	Old Punuk	193 (.444)	Old Punuk

[1] Two numbers are listed for each population pair; for example, for Jomon-Ainu the first number is the MMD x 10^3, the second (in parentheses) is Spearman's r_s measuring the correlation between the ranks of 23 populations vs. Jomon and the ranks of those 23 vs. Ainu. Values of r_s are significant at the 5% and 1% level when equal or greater than ± .35 and ± .497, respectively. All values of MMD are significant except those marked by an asterisk.

* Non-significant values of MMD; i.e., less than twice their standard deviation.

Table 2b. Ranked Mean Measures of Divergence (MMDs).

TUNGUS			CHUKCHI, COASTAL			SIBERIAN ESKIMO		
(SAMPLES 3, N 83)			(SAMPLES 1, N 39)			(SAMPLES 1, N 41)		
42	(.754)	Japanese	6*	(.902)	Siberian Eskimo	*6	(.902)	Chukchi
68	(.667)	Chukchi	22	(.818)	Ekven	19	(.861)	Ekven
83	(.578)	Inupiaq	28	(.797)	Yupik SMA	22	(.860)	Inupiaq
88	(.599)	Siberian Eskimo	34	(.470)	Athapaskans	30	(.513)	Athapaskans
88	(.503)	Yupik SMA	34	(.726)	Kodiak Early	34	(.858)	Kodiak Late
102	(.764)	Ekven	36	(.708)	Inupiaq	44	(.736)	Yupik SMA
103	(.662)	St. Lawrence	38	(.869)	Kodiak Recent	49	(.702)	Kodiak Early
110	(.500)	Kodiak Late	55	(.852)	St. Lawrence	51	(.283)	Umnak
119	(.625)	Nunivak	57	(.189)	Umnak	52	(.514)	Hopewell
122	(.628)	Western Aleut	60	(.307)	Kagamil	60	(.615)	Nunivak
124	(.033)	Athapaskans	64	(.589)	Nunivak	62	(.771)	St. Lawrence
129	(-.248)	Umnak	67	(.455)	Japanese	65	(.274)	Haida
132	(.183)	Hopewell	67	(.371)	Namu	67	(.508)	Japanese
137	(-.067)	Namu	68	(.667)	Tungus	73	(.728)	Old Punuk
138	(.379)	Kodiak Early	71	(.429)	Hopewell	77	(.521)	Namu
142	(-.078)	Kagamil	76	(.234)	Tlingit	82	(.227)	Late Woodland
145	(.208)	Ainu	81	(.789)	Old Punuk	82	(.392)	Kagamil
149	(-.065)	Tlingit	84	(.236)	Haida	88	(.599)	Tungus
157	(-.109)	Haida	109	(.487)	Western Aleut	90	(.486)	Tlingit
165	(.675)	Old Punuk	125	(.176)	Late Woodland	98	(.269)	Plains
190	(-.147)	Late Woodland	130	(-.088)	Ainu	114	(.089)	Ainu
191	(-.177)	Plains	138	(.191)	Plains	143	(.649)	Western Aleut
227	(.231)	Jomon	191	(-.071)	Jomon	223	(.098)	Jomon

Table 2c. Ranked Mean Measures of Divergence (MMDs).

EKVEN			INUPIAQ ESKIMO			ST. LAWRENCE ESKIMO		
(SAMPLES 1, N 77)			(SAMPLES 3, N 190)			(SAMPLE 1, N 76)		
19	(.861)	Siberian Eskimo	22	(.860)	Siberian Eskimo	36	(.866)	Yupik SMA
22	(.818)	Chukchi	32	(.782)	Ekven	50	(.867)	Old Punuk
24	(.828)	Kodiak Late	36	(.708)	Chukchi	55	(.852)	Chukchi
26	(.765)	Yupik SMA	46	(.374)	Athapaskans	62	(.771)	Siberian Eskimo
29	(.841)	Nunivak	50	(.534)	Yupik SMA	70	(.809)	Kodiak Late
32	(.782)	Inupiaq	53	(.696)	Kodiak Late	73	(.392)	Namu
45	(.827)	Old Punuk	58	(.613)	Nunivak	74	(.744)	Ekven
49	(.333)	Athapaskans	61	(.217)	Haida	75	(.565)	Athapaskans
51	(.444)	Hopewell	65	(.680)	Japanese	83	(.779)	Kodiak Early
57	(.597)	Kodiak Early	67	(.173)	Umnak	92	(.704)	Inupiaq
60	(.762)	Western Aleut	68	(.619)	Hopewell	103	(.662)	Tungus
68	(.560)	Japanese	68	(.256)	Namu	113	(.196)	Haida
74	(.744)	St. Lawrence	82	(.356)	Ainu	117	(.266)	Umnak
75	(.113)	Umnak	82	(.597)	Kodiak Early	119	(.441)	Kagamil
75	(.246)	Namu	83	(.578)	Tungus	125	(.583)	Nunivak
76	(.056)	Haida	89	(.221)	Late Woodland	126	(.484)	Japanese
87	(.226)	Tlingit	90	(.383)	Tlingit	141	(.419)	Hopewell
102	(.764)	Tungus	91	(.211)	Plains	158	(.762)	Western Aleut
113	(.205)	Kagamil	92	(.704)	St. Lawrence	175	(.240)	Late Woodland
133	(.063)	Late Woodland	96	(.602)	Old Punuk	178	(.379)	Tlingit
136	(.051)	Ainu	104	(.309)	Kagamil	199	(.256)	Plains
140	(.050)	Plains	131	(.593)	Western Aleut	251	(.032)	Ainu
205	(.020)	Jomon	166	(.294)	Jomon	317	(.050)	Jomon

Table 2d. Ranked Mean Measures of Divergence (MMDs).

OLD PUNUK	NUNIVAK ESKIMO	YUPIK, SOUTH MAINLAND ALASKA ESKIMO
(SAMPLES 1, N 26)	(SAMPLES 1, N 102)	(SAMPLES 4, N 173)
45 (.827) Ekven	29 (.841) Ekven	17 (.909) Kodiak Late
47 (.879) Yupik SMA	47 (.581) Hopewell	*20 (.440) Namu
50 (.867) St. Lawrence	52 (.836) Western Aleut	26 (.765) Ekven
52 (.844) Kodiak Late	53 (.615) Yupik SMA	28 (.797) Chukchi
73 (.728) Siberian Eskimo	58 (.613) Inupiaq	30 (.835) Kodiak Early
75 (.335) Athapaskans	60 (.615) Siberian Eskimo	33 (.577) Athapaskans
80 (.708) Nunivak	62 (.695) Kodiak Late	36 (.866) St. Lawrence
81 (.789) Chukchi	64 (.589) Chukchi	44 (.736) Siberian Eskimo
83 (.674) Kodiak Early	79 (.206) Athapaskans	47 (.879) Old Punuk
86 (.287) Namu	80 (.708) Old Punuk	50 (.534) Inupiaq
96 (.602) Inupiaq	81 (.206) Tlingit	51 (.720) Western Aleut
102 (.756) Western Aleut	87 (.169) Namu	53 (.615) Nunivak
123 (.393) Hopewell	93 (.117) Umnak	66 (.310) Umnak
140 (.117) Haida	97 (.532) Kodiak Early	67 (.392) Kagamil
143 (.153) Umnak	102 (.487) Japanese	70 (.191) Haida
165 (.675) Tungus	119 (.157) Haida	70 (.392) Hopewell
168 (.198) Tlingit	119 (.625) Tungus	85 (.328) Tlingit
176 (.280) Kagamil	125 (.583) St. Lawrence	89 (.503) Tungus
193 (.444) Japanese	143 (.186) Kagamil	95 (.187) Japanese
202 (.129) Late Woodland	144 (.086) Ainu	125 (.182) Late Woodland
215 (.063) Plains	149 (.097) Late Woodland	136 (.138) Plains
315 (-.052) Ainu	149 (.087) Plains	189 (-.205) Ainu
450 (-.051) Jomon	226 (.069) Jomon	237 (-.255) Jomon

Table 2e. Ranked Mean Measures of Divergence (MMDs).

WESTERN ALEUT	KAGAMIL ALEUT	UMNAK ALEUT
(SAMPLES 1, N 26)	(SAMPLES 1, N 111)	(SAMPLES 1, N 64)
51 (.720) Yupik SMA	35 (.851) Namu	*13 (.844) Namu
52 (.836) Nunivak	35 (.861) Athapaskans	19 (.842) Athapaskans
60 (.762) Ekven	36 (.899) Umnak	31 (.630) Kodiak Early
83 (.694) Kodiak Late	51 (.793) Tlingit	33 (.885) Late Woodland
102 (.756) Old Punuk	58 (.746) Kodiak Early	34 (.576) Hopewell
109 (.487) Chukchi	60 (.307) Chukchi	35 (.827) Tlingit
112 (.111) Namu	64 (.802) Late Woodland	36 (.899) Kagamil
113 (.510) Kodiak Early	69 (.392) Yupik SMA	40 (.868) Haida
122 (.628) Tungus	71 (.850) Haida	44 (.879) Plains
127 (.404) Hopewell	75 (.809) Plains	51 (.420) Kodiak Late
131 (.593) Inupiaq	82 (.392) Siberian Eskimo	51 (.283) Siberian Eskimo
143 (.649) Siberian Eskimo	92 (.555) Kodiak Recent	57 (.189) Chukchi
145 (.308) Athapaskans	94 (.617) Hopewell	66 (.310) Yupik SMA
149 (.239) Tlingit	104 (.309) Inupiaq	67 (.173) Inupiaq
152 (.115) Umnak	113 (.205) Ekven	75 (.113) Ekven
153 (.552) Japanese	119 (.441) St. Lawrence	93 (.117) Nunivak
158 (.762) St. Lawrence	142 (-.078) Tungus	114 (-.295) Japanese
181 (.232) Kagamil	143 (.186) Nunivak	117 (.266) St. Lawrence
201 (.080) Haida	153 (-.199) Japanese	129 (-.248) Tungus
264 (.174) Ainu	176 (.280) Old Punuk	143 (.153) Old Punuk
266 (.009) Late Woodland	181 (.232) Western Aleut	152 (.115) Western Aleut
270 (.027) Plains	229 (-.152) Ainu	154 (-.278) Ainu
317 (.129) Jomon	253 (-.176) Jomon	234 (-.278) Jomon

Table 2f. Ranked Mean Measures of Divergence (MMDs).

KODIAK LATE	KODIAK EARLY	TLINGIT
(SAMPLES 1, N 100)	(SAMPLES 1, N 59)	(SAMPLES 1, N 17)
*5 (.892) Kodiak Early	*5 (.892) Kodiak Late	35 (.827) Umnak
17 (.909) Yupik SMA	17 (.890) Athapaskans	40 (.707) Athapaskans
24 (.828) Ekven	*25 (.760) Namu	41 (.699) Hopewell
25 (.678) Athapaskans	30 (.835) Yupik SMA	51 (.793) Kagamil
34 (.858) Siberian Eskimo	31 (.630) Umnak	55 (.750) Haida
38 (.869) Chukchi	34 (.726) Chukchi	68 (.633) Kodiak Early
42 (.547) Namu	49 (.702) Siberian Eskimo	72 (.805) Namu
51 (.420) Umnak	57 (.597) Ekven	76 (.234) Chukchi
52 (.844) Old Punuk	58 (.746) Kagamil	81 (.470) Kodiak Late
53 (.696) Inupiaq	68 (.633) Tlingit	81 (.206) Nunivak
62 (.695) Nunivak	74 (.585) Haida	82 (.775) Plains
68 (.581) Hopewell	82 (.597) Inupiaq	85 (.328) Yupik SMA
70 (.809) St. Lawrence	83 (.779) St. Lawrence	87 (.226) Ekven
76 (.385) Haida	83 (.674) Old Punuk	88 (.798) Late Woodland
81 (.470) Tlingit	84 (.665) Hopewell	90 (.486) Siberian Eskimo
83 (.694) Western Aleut	97 (.532) Nunivak	90 (.383) Inupiaq
92 (.555) Kagamil	99 (.544) Late Woodland	126 (-.061) Japanese
103 (.321) Japanese	113 (.510) Western Aleut	143 (-.158) Ainu
106 (.310) Late Woodland	119 (.536) Plains	149 (-.065) Tungus
110 (.500) Tungus	127 (.172) Japanese	149 (.239) Western Aleut
124 (.300) Plains	138 (.379) Tungus	168 (.198) Old Punuk
184 (-.024) Ainu	204 (-.155) Ainu	178 (.379) St. Lawrence
266 (-.008) Jomon	270 (-.091) Jomon	186 (-.159) Jomon

Table 2g. Ranked Mean Measures of Divergence (MMDs).

HAIDA	NAMU	ATHAPASKANS
(SAMPLES 1, N 144)	(SAMPLES 1, N 25)	(SAMPLES 5, N 143)
25 (.766) Namu	*13 (.844) Umnak	*13 (.879) Namu
25 (.739) Athapaskans	*13 (.879) Athapaskans	17 (.890) Kodiak Early
40 (.868) Umnak	*20 (.440) Yupik SMA	19 (.842) Umnak
55 (.750) Tlingit	*25 (.760) Kodiak Early	25 (.739) Haida
55 (.931) Plains	25 (.766) Haida	25 (.678) Kodiak Late
56 (.934) Late Woodland	35 (.851) Kagamil	30 (.513) Siberian Eskimo
57 (.681) Hopewell	42 (.547) Kodiak Late	33 (.577) Yupik SMA
61 (.217) Inupiaq	54 (.758) Late Woodland	34 (.470) Chukchi
65 (.274) Siberian Eskimo	54 (.464) Hopewell	35 (.861) Kagamil
70 (.191) Yupik SMA	57 (.772) Plains	40 (.707) Tlingit
71 (.850) Kagamil	67 (.371) Chukchi	41 (.705) Late Woodland
74 (.585) Kodiak Early	68 (.256) Inupiaq	46 (.374) Inupiaq
76 (.385) Kodiak Late	72 (.805) Tlingit	48 (.690) Plains
76 (.056) Ekven	73 (.392) St. Lawrence	48 (.528) Hopewell
84 (.236) Chukchi	75 (.246) Ekven	49 (.333) Ekven
113 (.196) St. Lawrence	77 (.521) Siberian Eskimo	75 (.565) St. Lawrence
119 (.157) Nunivak	86 (.287) Old Punuk	75 (.335) Old Punuk
122 (-.176) Japanese	87 (.169) Nunivak	70 (.206) Nunivak
140 (.117) Old Punuk	112 (.111) Western Aleut	114 (-.087) Japanese
141 (-.143) Ainu	137 (-.067) Tungus	124 (.033) Tungus
157 (-.109) Tungus	146 (-.199) Japanese	145 (.308) Western Aleut
193 (-.201) Jomon	216 (-.285) Ainu	170 (-.222) Ainu
201 (.080) Western Aleut	282 (-.215) Jomon	245 (-.182) Jomon

Table 2h. Ranked Mean Measures of Divergence (MMDs).

PLAINS		LATE WOODLAND		HOPEWELL, ILLINOIS	
(SAMPLES 4, N 289)		(SAMPLES 8, N 505)		(SAMPLES 2, N 63)	
7 (.993)	Late Woodland	7 (.993)	Plains	34 (.576)	Umnak
44 (.879)	Umnak	33 (.885)	Umnak	41 (.699)	Tlingit
48 (.690)	Athapaskans	41 (.705)	Athapaskans	47 (.097)	Nunivak
55 (.931)	Haida	54 (.758)	Namu	48 (.528)	Athapaskans
57 (.772)	Namu	56 (.934)	Haida	51 (.444)	Ekven
75 (.809)	Kagamil	64 (.802)	Kagamil	52 (.514)	Siberian Eskimo
80 (.599)	Hopewell	72 (.595)	Hopewell	54 (.464)	Namu
82 (.775)	Tlingit	82 (.227)	Siberian Eskimo	57 (.681)	Haida
91 (.211)	Inupiaq	88 (.798)	Tlingit	68 (.581)	Kodiak Late
98 (.269)	Siberian Eskimo	89 (.221)	Inupiaq	68 (.619)	Inupiaq
119 (.536)	Kodiak Early	99 (.544)	Kodiak Early	70 (.392)	Yupik SMA
124 (.300)	Kodiak Late	106 (.310)	Kodiak Late	71 (.429)	Chukchi
136 (.138)	Yupik SMA	125 (.182)	Yupik SMA	72 (.595)	Late Woodland
138 (.191)	Chukchi	125 (.176)	Chukchi	80 (.599)	Plains
140 (.050)	Ekven	133 (.063)	Ekven	84 (.665)	Kodiak Early
149 (.087)	Nunivak	149 (.097)	Nunivak	91 (.187)	Japanese
158 (-.132)	Japanese	157 (-.146)	Japanese	94 (.617)	Kagamil
173 (-.051)	Ainu	174 (-.068)	Ainu	123 (.393)	Old Punuk
191 (-.177)	Tungus	175 (.240)	St. Lawrence	127 (.404)	Western Aleut
199 (.256)	St. Lawrence	190 (-.147)	Tungus	132 (.183)	Tungus
215 (.063)	Old Punuk	202 (.129)	Old Punuk	136 (.106)	Ainu
264 (-.025)	Jomon	266 (.009)	Western Aleut	141 (.419)	St. Lawrence
270 (.027)	Western Aleut	273 (.005)	Jomon	230 (.163)	Jomon

whole to be anomalous. Data for the three samples (not listed separately in Table 2) are summarized below. Note that the Point Barrow–Mackenzie MMD, 9.5, was insignificantly different from zero despite the nearly 1,000 miles separating the sites.

	Pt. Barrow	Mackenzie	Southampton
Mackenzie	9.5	-	52.7
Southampton	59.0	52.7	-
Yupik range	44.5–127.9	51.6–116.1	70.4–105.6
mean (8 samples)	80.0	71.8	88.0
Kodiak (3-sample aggreg)	67.2	76.7	94.3
Aleut range	39.6–164.3	66.7–146.8	53.8–131.5
mean (6 samples excluding Near)	75.3	88.9	96.0

Indians

The Plains tribes Blackfoot, Dakota, Cheyenne, and Assiniboin clustered together (Figure 3). Increased contacts among these tribes during the protohistoric and historic periods presumably resulted in genetic mixture and convergence (Blakeslee 1975; Jantz 1973) in spite of language differences between the tribes. Fitting into this subcluster, and related especially closely to Cheyenne and Assiniboin, was Late Woodland, a large aggregate of eight samples from archaeologically defined burial-mound complexes in the upper Mississippi Valley dated from ca. 1500–300 yr B.P. An earlier report (Ossenberg 1974b) demonstrates close affinities between these early and historic samples, strongly suggestive in certain cases of an ancestral lineage even though no continuity is evident in material culture. As in the Aleutians, a temporal trend to brachycephalization and increased low-vaultedness is apparent in the Northern Plains and northeastern Plains periphery.

Four Na-Dene[3] samples also were closely joined in one subcluster. That these data revealed an historic relationship between peoples presumably diverged from a common ancestral stock as long as nine millenia ago (Greenberg et al. 1986:479), and subject to environmental forces as dramatically different as those of

---

[3] The status of Na-Dene as a language phylum is disputed. Krauss, having reviewed recent analyses, now ranks Haida as a language isolate. Also, the genetic relationship of Tlingit to Athapaskan is said to be not demonstrable (Krauss 1979).

Aleuts, Eskimos, and Indians

With the addition of Indian samples to the cluster analysis (Figure 3) it is noteworthy that Aleut, Yupik, and Inupiaq maintained their integrity as well-defined subclusters. Even the pattern within each was fairly stable; i.e., among Aleut the east-west gradient in descending order of affinity persisted. As in the previous dendrograph Inupiaq linked preferentially to Aleut rather than to Yupik.

The most remarkable feature of Figure 3, however, was that Aleut were linked most closely to Na-Dene, and next most closely to the Woodland-Plains subcluster. Six Aleut and twelve Indian samples ultimately were linked at a level comparable to that at which nine Yupik Eskimo and Kodiak samples joined each other. The apparent affinity of Aleut to Na-Dene and other Indians was contrary to their language differences and totally at odds with the present widely accepted view that Aleut and

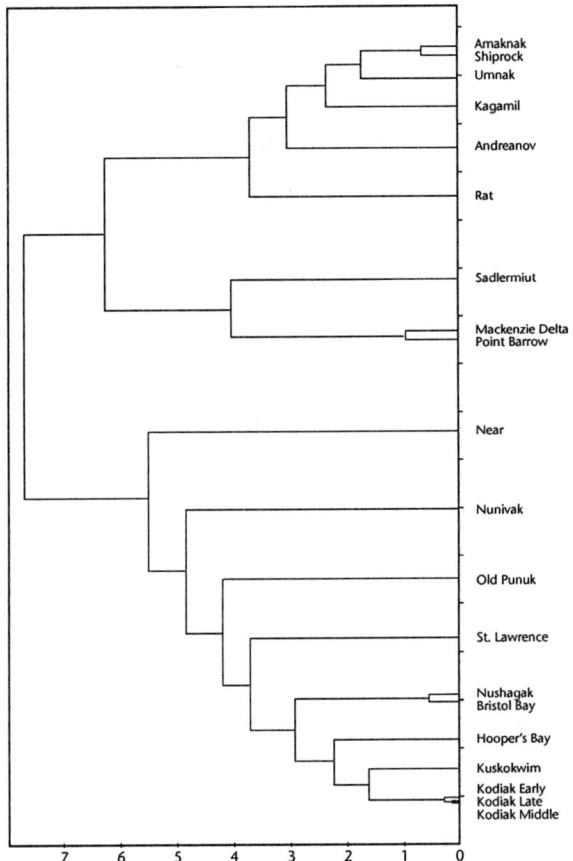

Figure 2. Dendrograph of 20 Aleut and Eskimo population. Prehistoric samples were Umnak (Paleo-Aleut), Old Punuk, and three time levels from Kodiak Island.

the North Pacific coast (Tlingit, Haida) and desert Southwest (Apache, Navajo), was good evidence of the stability and conservatism of nonmetric cranial traits.

Linguistically, Na-Dene has deeper internal divisions than Aleut-Eskimo (Greenberg et al. 1986), yet the dendrographs did not reflect this, nor were Haida the outlier group in the dendrographs as the deepest cleavage within Na-Dene might predict. Tlingit were more loosely joined, but sample size (N 17) was probably a factor in this. The outlier was the Northern Athapaskan sample, comprised mainly of Ingalik from the Yukon River. Nonmetric cranial traits consistently placed this sample (Figures 3, 4, 8, 9) with Aleut, and particularly Eastern Aleut.

Namu, the very early British Columbia coastal sample, fits in this subcluster tightly linked to Apache. Last to join the Na-Dene was an apparent misfit—Illinois Hopewell. Relationships of Namu and Hopewell are discussed in a later section of this paper.

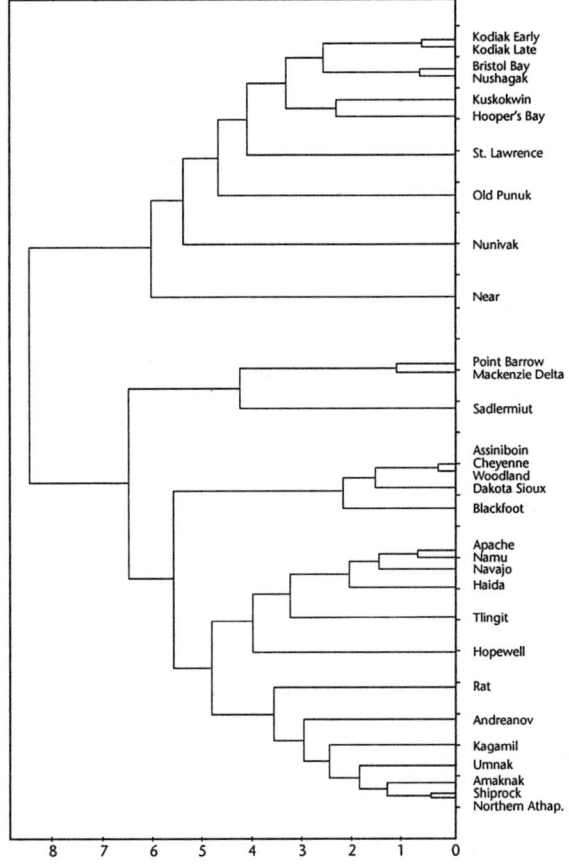

Figure 3. Dendrograph of 19 Aleut and Eskimo populations (omitting Kodiak Middle) and 12 Indian populations. Prehistoric Indian samples were Namu, Hopewell, and Late Woodland from the northeastern Plains periphery.

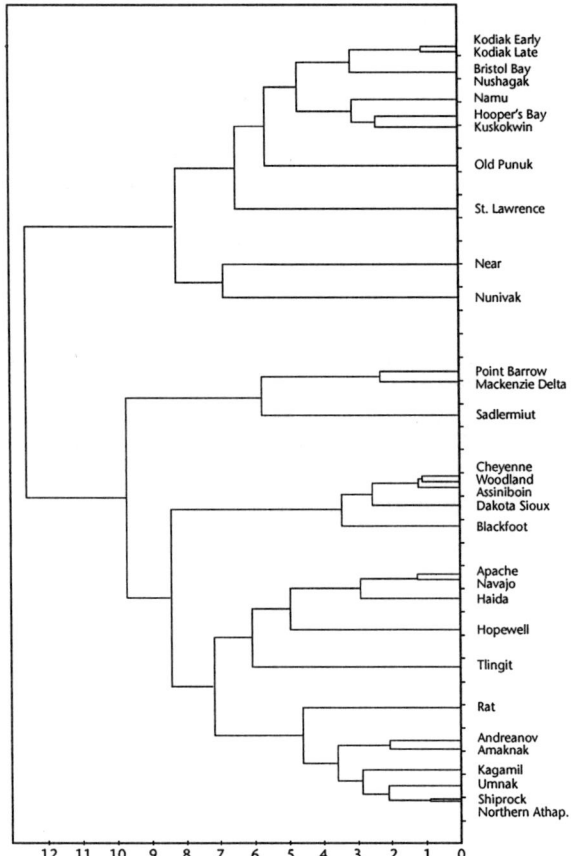

Figure 4. Dendrograph of 31 Aleut, Eskimo and Indian populations (same as Figure 3) based on a subset of the 15 highest-ranking traits for Eskimo-Indian discrimination.

Eskimo diverged from a common stem distinct from all Amerinds.

Aleuts versus Indians and Eskimos

To focus more precisely on this problem Aleuts were compared to the other two groups with respect to the features most powerful for discriminating between them. Looking at univariate comparisons (Table 1) I noted that Aleuts (Eastern and Central aggregate) were closer to Na-Dene than to Eskimo for nine of the ten highest ranking traits, the exception being *infraorbital suture*. Aleut frequencies were also closer to Late Woodland than to Eskimo for eight of ten traits. In particular, high Aleut frequencies of *mylohyoid bridge*, *tympanic dehiscence*, and *clinoid bridge* conspicuously allied them with Indians rather than Eskimo. The Paleo-Aleut (Umnak) sample, critical for assessing temporal depth of relationships, was closer to Na-Dene than to Eskimo for eight of the ten, and to Late Woodland for seven of the ten.

MMDs were calculated for a subset of the 15 traits contributing most to the mean of 100 MMDs for 10 Eskimo versus 10 Indian samples (Table 1). The dendrograph based on this analysis is Figure 4. The 15-trait subset maximized MMDs for all Indian versus Eskimo comparisons such that if Figure 4 were on the same scale as Figure 3, the second dendrograph would be approximately one-third larger. Aside from the scale difference, the configuration of samples in this dendrograph was very similar to the previous one. Namu has abandoned Na-Dene for the Yupik subcluster. Otherwise the membership in each subcluster and the order of higher linkages were exactly the same.

Table 3 lists MMDs for Aleuts based on the 15-trait subset along with values of Spearman's r_s. Figure 5 is a graphic depiction of Aleut relationships according to these data. The plots nicely illustrated a linear pattern between MMD and r_s: a population to which an Aleut sample was closely related also tended to have a closely similar ranking of MMDs versus other populations. In the plot for Western Aleut these two measures strongly clustered four Eskimo samples (three Yupik plus Ekven, an early Chukotkan sample) in the lower left quadrant. Straggling out in the upper right quadrant were five Indian samples (Northern Athapaskans, Tlingit, Haida, Late Woodland, and Plains). In contrast, values for Indians (especially Northern Athapaskans and Namu) dominated the lower left quadrants of the plots for Central and Eastern Aleut. Here, the exclusively Indian clusters of points were invaded only by Andreanov's and Amaknak's values for Inupiaq, Siberian Eskimo, and Chukchi. On the whole, then, these subsidiary analyses underscored the findings based on the full suite of traits.

Nevertheless, there are additional points that should be noted. Contrary to the dichotomy between the Near sample and all other Aleut in terms of their outside relationships as depicted in the dendrographs (Figures 2–4), there were in fact more subtle patterns which could be discerned only in the MMDs. These were hinted at in Figure 5, where Indian and Eskimo samples were segregated better in the Eastern than in the Central plots; that is, in the latter, the dispersion of points tended to lie closer to the middle of the graph indicating less difference between Aleut-Indian and Aleut-Eskimo affinities.

East-west trending patterns were revealed in Table 4, a summary of Aleut MMDs. In comparisons both of variously computed mean MMDs as well as MMDs for aggregates, the following trends for Eastern, Central, and Western sectors were noted:

(1) Indian MMDs increased
(2) Eskimo MMDs increased
(3) the ratio of Indian/Yupik MMDs increased
(4) the ratio of Inupiaq/Yupik MMDs increased

The sole irregularity in the Eastern-Central-Western clines was the small Near-Yupik MMD.

Of all seven Aleut samples, Umnak (Paleo-Aleut) was closest to Indians, second-closest to Yupik (only Near being closer), and third-closest to Inupiaq (Amaknak and Andreanov being closer). Umnak had the smallest Indian/Eskimo MMD ratio.

To summarize these findings: Just as Aleut populations showed a gradient of affinities among themselves (Figures 2–4), so they showed an east-west gradient of decreasing affinities, both to Indians and to Eskimos. While affinities to both outside groups decreased with geographic distance from the Alaska peninsula, the gradient of Eskimo MMDs was less steep than that of Indian—culminating in the extreme (reversed) case: Near-Yupik MMD smaller than Near-Indian MMD. That these clines were ancient was evidenced by MMDs for Umnak, 4000–1000 yr B.P., which placed this Paleo-Aleut sample at or near the eastern extreme of the gradients. These patterns proved to be critically important for reconstructing population history in the Aleutians.

Eskimos versus Indians and Aleuts

In univariate comparisons in Table 1, where Aleut were closer to Na-Dene than to Eskimo for nine of the ten highest ranking traits, an additional observation was that Eskimo also tended to be more like Na-Dene. Athapaskan frequencies (excluding Haida and Tlingit) were even more often intermediate, so that Eskimo were closer to Athapaskans than to Aleut for eight of the ten highest ranking traits (excluding only *frontal grooves* and *infraorbital suture*.

Eskimo and Athapaskan MMDs based on the top 15 traits (Table 1) in aggregated samples are ranked below. Chukotkan MMDs (each based on the mean of Ekven, Siberian Eskimo, and Chukchi MMDs) are also listed.

Table 3a. Ranked Mean Measures of Divergence (MMDs) of Aleut and Kodiak Islanders Based on 15 Cranial Traits Most Powerful for Eskimo-Indian Discrimination (Table 1). Rank Correlation of Each Population Pair is Tested by Spearman's r_s.

KODIAK ISLAND		WESTERN ALEUT
EARLY	LATE	NEAR (N 26)
* 4 (.685) Kod Late	* 4 (.685) Kod Early	61 (.766) SMA[1]
32 (.665) N Athap	16 (.919) SMA	62 (.820) Nunivak
34 (.523) SMA	36 (.725) Ekven	75 (.759) Ekven
40 (.404) Umnak	48 (.450) Sib Eskimo	85 (.755) Kod Late
49 (.697) Namu	48 (.229) N Athap	90 (.300) Old Punuk
53 (.703) S Athap	55 (.497) S Athap	106 (.284) Namu
53 (.407) Shiprock	58 (.293) Namu	118 (.349) Kod Early
61 (.675) Rat	60 (-.034) Umnak	138 (.210) Hopewell
64 (.502) Chukchi	61 (.626) Chukchi	160 (.168) S Athap
65 (.234) Ekven	66 (.701) Old Punuk	165 (.363) Chukchi
71 (.381) Sib Eskimo	81 (.276) Hopewell	177 (.380) Sib Eskimo
76 (.491) Kagamil	82 (.528) Inupiaq	185 (-.389) Umnak
80 (.353) Amaknak	85 (.755) Near	191 (.308) Inupiaq
90 (.416) Andreanov	88 (.671) Nunivak	212 (-.147) N Athap
91 (.414) Haida	90 (-.105) Shiprock	226 (-.114) Rat
101 (.311) Hopewell	98 (.192) Andreanov	232 (.621) St. Lawrence
107 (.354) Old Punuk	102 (.094) Haida	239 (-.114) Amaknak
114 (.356) Tlingit	103 (.683) St. Lawrence	251 (-.337) Kagamil
118 (.349) Near	111 (.183) Amaknak	251 (-.156) Andreanov
123 (.461) Inupiaq	118 (.148) Rat	251 (-.111) Tlingit
125 (.589) St. Lawrence	125 (-.033) Kagamil	279 (-.218) Haida
151 (.232) Nunivak	138 (.050) Tlingit	290 (-.322) Shiprock
152 (.258) Late Woodland	161 (-.218) Late Wood	353 (-.483) Late Wood
197 (.248) Plains	196 (-.200) Plains	370 (-.429) Plains

[1] Two numbers are listed for each population pair; for example, for Near-SMA (South Mainland Alaska). The first number is MMD x 10^3, the second (in parentheses) is Spearman's r_s measuring the correlation between the ranks of 24 populations versus Near and the ranks of those 24 versus SMA. Values of r_s are significant at the 5% and 1% level when equal or greater than ± .343 and .485, respectively.

* Non-significant values of MMD; i.e., less than twice their standard deviaiton.

Table 3b. Ranked Mean Measures of Divergence (MMDs) of Aleut and Kodiak Islanders.

CENTRAL ALEUT		
RAT (N 35)	ANDREANOV (N 51)	KAGAMIL (N 111)
30 (.861) Kagamil	*14 (.897) Amaknak	*17 (.927) Shiprock
43 (.799) Shiprock	21 (.721) N Athap	25 (.790) Umnak
58 (.718) Namu	26 (.600) Chukchi	30 (.861) Rat
61 (.675) Kod Early	27 (.661) Shiprock	47 (.681) Amaknak
62 (.755) N Athap	32 (.563) Sib Esk	49 (.730) N Athap
75 (.468) S Athap	49 (.440) Umnak	53 (.619) Namu
82 (.487) Amaknak	50 (.609) Inupiaq	62 (.583) Andreanov
84 (.738) Umnak	62 (.583) Kagamil	71 (.429) S Athap
85 (.476) Andreanov	77 (.213) Ekven	76 (.491) Kod Early
109 (.046) SMA	85 (.476) Rat	78 (.770) Late Wood
118 (.148) Kod Late	88 (.499) Late Wood	88 (.558) Tlingit
119 (.583) Late Wood	89 (.393) Haida	94 (.073) Chukchi
134 (.220) Chukchi	90 (.416) Kod Early	100 (.699) Haida
141 (.570) Haida	95 (.186) Hopewell	102 (.706) Plains
144 (-.126) Old Punuk	96 (-.083) SMA	106 (-.267) SMA
155 (.562) Plains	97 (.393) Namu	116 (.241) Hopewell
157 (.159) Sib Eskimo	98 (.353) S Athap	119 (.070) Sib Eskimo
168 (-.196) Ekven	98 (.192) Kod Late	125 (-.033) Kod Late
169 (.599) Tlingit	119 (.491) Plains	144 (.164) Inupiaq
178 (.117) Hopewell	154 (.246) St. Lawrence	149 (-.375) Ekven
200 (.349) St. Lawrence	161 (-.189) Old Punuk	176 (-.077) St. Lawrence
203 (.200) Inupiaq	170 (-.097) Nunivak	219 (-.423) Old Punuk
226 (-.114) Near	175 (.454) Tlingit	228 (-.424) Nunivak
255 (-.250) Nunivak	251 (-.156) Near	251 (-.337) Near

Table 3c. Ranked Mean Measures of Divergence (MMDs) of Aleut and Kodiak Islanders.

EASTERN ALEUT		
UMNAK (N 64)	SHIPROCK (N 46)	AMAKNAK (N 48)
*15 (.856) Shiprock	*3 (.806) N Athap	*13 (.777) Shiprock
25 (.790) Kagamil	*13 (.777) Amaknak	*14 (.897) Andreanov
26 (.741) N Athap	*15 (.856) Umnak	33 (.770) N Athap
*29 (.688) Namu	*17 (.927) Kagamil	38 (.666) Umnak
37 (.833) Haida	*36 (.547) Namu	38 (.416) Sib Eskimo
38 (.666) Amaknak	27 (.661) Andreanov	41 (.413) Chukchi
39 (.630) S Athap	30 (.842) Late Wood	47 (.681) Kagamil
40 (.404) Kod Early	43 (.799) Rat	58 (.642) Haida
40 (.325) Hopewell	47 (.716) Haida	59 (.230) Hopewell
45 (.803) Late Woodland	53 (.407) Kod Early	62 (.685) Late Wood
49 (.440) Andreanov	66 (.469) S Athap	64 (.321) S Athap
50 (.803) Tlingit	67 (.764) Plains	67 (.534) Inupiaq
60 (-.034) Kod Late	86 (.077) Sib Eskimo	80 (.353) Kod Early
60 (.802) Plains	87 (.110) Chukchi	80 (-.070) Ekven
73 (.026) Sib Eskimo	88 (.192) Hopewell	82 (.487) Rat
74 (-.240) SMA	90 (-.105) Kod Late	83 (.441) Namu
75 (.150) Inupiaq	100 (.589) Tlingit	87 (.668) Plains
84 (.738) Rat	102 (-.257) SMA	101 (.518) Tlingit
88 (-.348) Ekven	103 (-.245) Inupiaq	109 (-.151) SMA
89 (.072) Chukchi	138 (-.354) Ekven	111 (.183) Kod Late
145 (-.403) Nunivak	164 (-.072) St. Lawrence	156 (-.194) Nunivak
185 (-.389) Near	218 (-.446) Nunivak	198 (.111) St. Lawrence
186 (-.051) St. Lawrence	224 (-.414) Old Punuk	219 (-.321) Old Punuk
206 (-.442) Old Punuk	229 (-.322) Near	239 (-.114) Near

	Inupiaq	Chukotkan	Yupik	Athapaskan
Inupiaq	-	37.8	59.2	62.7
Chukotkan	37.8	-	31.7	51.9
Yupik	59.2	31.7	-	38.7
Athapaskan	62.7	51.9	38.7	-
Aleut	88.9	78.0	83.4	19.4

In these rankings Athapaskans, though certainly closest to Aleut, were nevertheless intermediate between Aleut and Eskimo. Except for Athapaskan-Aleut, positive regression of MMD against geographic distance also is apparent in these data. In sum, then, these analyses strengthened the case for biological affinity between North American Eskimos and Athapaskans (Szathmary 1979a, 1979b, 1984, 1985; Szathmary and Ossenberg 1978).

Kodiak

In the dendrographs (Figures 2–4) the time-sequenced samples for Kodiak Island linked most closely to each other, joining next to South Mainland Alaskan Yupik samples. Dendrographs, however, obscured certain important relationships that must be sought in trait frequencies and MMDs.

For seven of the ten highest ranking traits (Table 1) Eskimo frequencies were closer to Kodiak Late than to Kodiak Early, Kodiak Late being intermediate in six of the ten. Table 3 giving ranked MMDs with their corresponding values of r_s indicated that, even though the Kodiak Early-Late MMD was not significantly different from zero, the two populations had somewhat different patterns of affinities with other groups. According to all MMDs and r_s values Eskimos were more like Late than Early Kodiak, while for Indians and Aleuts the relationship was reversed.

Temporal trends on Kodiak are summarized below in 15-trait MMDs for Early, Middle, and Late. MMDs are for aggregates except where noted.

[4] Though three sequenced Kodiak MMDs versus aggregates indicated a regular change over time, those for certain individual samples were erratic. This was especially true for Athapaskans: Apache and Navajo were closest to, Northern Athapaskans most unlike, Kodiak Middle. Bristol Bay Eskimo (just across the Alaska Peninsula from Kodiak) was most unlike Middle. I noted an excess of female skeletons in this sample (Hrdlička's "Red" series), a discrepant sex ratio commented on also by others (Clark 1974:175), suggesting that this may have been a period of volatile population structure, and that separate male-female analyses might be particularly helpful in this case.

[5] The Old Punuk phase skeletal series was excavated in the 1930s by Henry Collins from sites on St. Lawrence and Punuk Islands. A few of the remains, very dark and brittle,

	Kodiak MMDs		
	Early	Middle	Late
North Pacific Coast (mean of Namu, Haida, Tlingit)	84.3	89.6	99.2
Aleut	53.3	92.0	88.0
Athapaskan	28.7	31.6	38.9
Yupik	37.6	22.4	10.8
Chukotkans (mean of 3)	66.6	64.2	48.1
Inupiaq	122.6	108.4	82.1

These data showed Kodiak's divergence away from Aleut and Na-Dene and towards Eskimo. As well as temporal trends (rows), the MMDs showed clines (columns) of decreasing affinity with geographic distance from Kodiak. These MMDs and the data from Table 3 plotted in Figure 6 dramatically illustrated microevolutionary change on Kodiak and hinted at the pivotal role of this region for reconstructing events in the peopling of the Northwest[4].

Old Punuk, Namu, and Hopewell

According to the three-migration model proposed by Greenberg and colleagues (1986), each of these early samples would represent descendents of one of the immigrant stocks, from youngest to oldest: Punuk–Aleut-Eskimo, Namu–Na-Dene, Hopewell–Macro-Indian. The nonmetric cranial traits of these samples had not previously been analyzed in a broad regional context. Therefore, in this study the position of each in the ranked MMDs and dendrographs was of particular interest.

Archaeologically, the Neo-Eskimo tradition (also named Northern Maritime and Thule tradition), of which Punuk is one phase, was first manifest on St. Lawrence and neighbouring islands as well as on the Chukotkan coast of Bering Strait at about 2000 yr B.P. On St. Lawrence, Punuk, 1200–900 yr B.P., underwent a gradual transition, with only minor intrusive Thule phase influence, to late prehistoric–protohistoric Eskimo (Ackerman 1984). Table 2 showed the small Punuk sample (N 26) most closely related to Ekven (Old Bering Sea phase 2000–1800 yr B.P. from Chukotka), South Mainland Alaska, St. Lawrence, Kodiak Late, and Siberian Eskimo. Spearman's r_s values for these were high. In the dendrographs, Old Punuk was linked most closely to St. Lawrence. These data all showed, as expected, that Punuk fit in the Yupik rather than Inupiaq biological lineage[5].

Namu, a deeply stratified site on the central coast date to the preceding Old Bering Sea phase (the late L. Oschisky, personal communication). With such a long interval between my study of this series (1963) and the crania

Table 4. Aleut Summary Data: Indian versus Eskimo MMDs Based on the 15 Most Discriminatory Traits

	EASTERN		
	AMAKNAK	SHIPROCK	UMNAK
Mean of 9 Indian MMDs[a]	69.7	54.4	40.7
Mean of 7 Yupik MMDs[b]	135.2	131.4	102.8
Mean of 3 Inupiaq MMDs	82.0	113.1	90.4
Ratio of mean Indian/Yupik MMDs	(0.52)	(0.41)	(0.40)
Ratio of mean Yupik/Inupiaq MMDs	(1.65)	(1.16)	(1.14)
Overall mean MMD by sector			
Indian		54.9 (mean of 27)	
Yupik		123.1 (mean of 21)	
Inupiaq		95.2 (mean of 9)	
Ratio Indian/Yupik		(0.45)	
Ratio Yupik/Inupiaq		(1.29)	
Athapaskan aggregate	31.0	17.1	17.6
Yupik aggregate	97.1	99.4	69.6
Inupiaq aggregate	66.9	102.6	75.0
Ratio Athapaskan/Yupik	(0.32	(0.17)	(0.25
Ratio Yupik/Inupiaq	(1.45)	(0.97)	(0.93)
Overall mean MMD by sector			
Athapaskan		21.9 (mean of 3)	
Yupik		88.7 mean of 3)	
Inupiaq		59.0 (mean of 3)	
Ratio Athapaskan/Yupik		(0.25)	
Ratio Yupik/Inupiaq		(1.50)	
	EASTERN AGGREGATE		
Athapaskan aggregate	14.8		
Yupik aggregate	78.7		
Inupiaq aggregate	71.5		
Ratio Athapaskan/Yupik	(0.19)		
Ratio Yupik/Inupiaq	(1.10)		

[a] The Indian series are: Late Woodland, Plains, Haida, Tlingit, Apache, Navajo, Northern Athapaskans, Namu, Kodiak Early.

of British Columbia, dated from about 9000 yr B.P. and is classed in the Paleoarctic tradition. This tradition, whose hallmark is microblades, has clear earlier connections to Northeast Asia. Sites occur near the zone that was left unglaciated during the late Pleistocene, and include Anangula in the eastern Aleutians, several in east-central Alaska, and others distributed down the North Pacific Coast (Carlson 1983; Dumond 1987b). The human skeletal remains from Namu, which are described in a detailed report by Curtin (1984), were found in the upper levels of the site and, dating from about 5000–2000 yr B.P., were the earli-

from the Ekven cemetery (1981), with no check on intraobserver error, it was reassuring to find a close multivariate relationship between them.

In comparisons of Old Punuk to Yupik and Inupiaq Eskimo, Punuk was on the whole closer to the former. Nevertheless, Punuk and Southampton were unexpectedly close to each other given the geographic distance, 5,500 miles, separating them. In accordance with geographic distance, the overwhelming majority of samples in the study were closest to Point Barrow of the three Inupiaq groups, and least closely related to Southampton. The Punuk-Southampton MMD, 64.7, would rank fifth (Table 2) for Old Punuk; for Sadlermiut, this value ranked close to those for Point Barrow, Siberian Eskimo and Chukchi

	CENTRAL		WESTERN
KAGAMIL	ANDREANOV	RAT	NEAR
81.4	96.9	113.1	220.7
140.3	122.2	150.7	99.1
151.7	60.2	204.7	206.3
(0.58)	(0.79)	(0.75)	(2.23)
(0.92)	(2.03)	(0.74	(0.48)
	97.1 (mean of 27)		220.7 (mean of 9)
	137.7 (mean of 21)		99.1 (mean of 7)
	138.9 (mean of 9)		206.3 (mean of 3)
	(0.71)		(2.23)
	(0.99)		(0.48)
43.5	41.2	54.5	177.3
113.9	86.6	124.8	67.3
143.5	50.0	203.2	191.2
(0.38)	(0.48)	(0.44)	(2.63)
(0.79)	(1.74)	(0.61)	(0.35)
	46.4 (mean of 3)		177.3
	108.4 (mean of 3)		67.3
	132.2 (mean of 3)		191.2
	(0.43)		(2.63)
	(0.82)		(0.35)
	CENTRAL AGGREGATE		WESTERN
	28.1		177.3
	93.3		67.3
	110.8		191.2
	(0.30)		(2.63)
	(0.84)		(0.35)

[b] The Yupik series are: Kodiak Late, Bristol Bay, Nushagak, Kuskokwim, Hooper's Bay, Nunivak, St. Lawrence.

est included in this study. Table 2 indicated that this small series (N 25) was insignificantly different from Umnak, Athapaskans, Kodiak Early, and South Mainland Alaska. Haida, Kagamil, and Kodiak Late followed closely in the list of ranked MMDs. All except South Mainland Alaska had high positive values of r_s. In

the dendrographs, Namu linked with Na-Dene and Aleut, except in Figure 4, where 15 top ranking traits moved it into the Yupik subcluster. On the whole, then, nonmetric cranial traits placed Namu in the lineage which included Aleut, Kodiak Islanders, and Na-Dene[6].

(59.0, 59.0, and 66.1, respectively). The reciprocally close Punak-Southampton relationship (if, indeed, it was not simply a vagary of sampling) might be explained if the peopling of the eastern Arctic resulted more directly than did that of North Alaska from the Old Bering Sea tradition-Thule tradition continuum; i.e., with less influence from South Alaska. This explanation, however, was

not supported by the Inupiaq affinities of Ekven which, like those of virtually every other sample, place Point Barrow first.

[6] Though MMDs aligned Namu with Aleut and Na-Dene, this did not mean that the people interred at Namu were specifically ancestral to any group represented here. In fact, the Namu crania seemed to have unique morphological

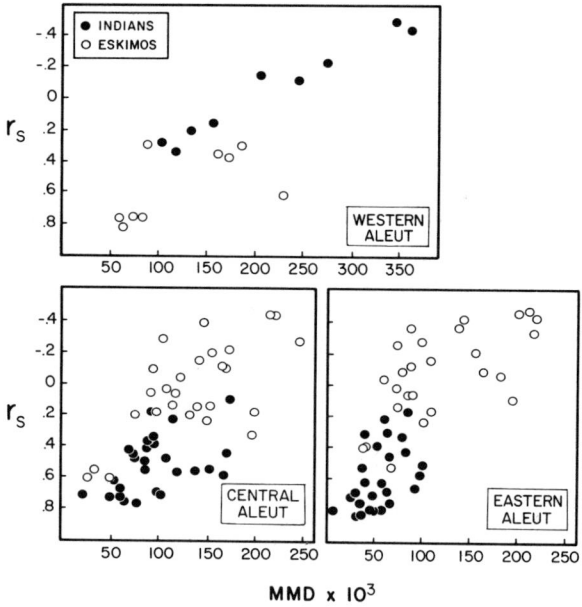

Figure 5. Aleut relationships depicted in three plots of Spearman's r_s against MMD. Values were based on a subset of the 15 highest-ranking traits for Eskimo-Indian discrimination (Table 3).

The Illinois Hopewell skeletal sample (N 63) derived from 2100–1900 yr B.P. burial mounds of a Middle Woodland period culture in eastern North America (Hopewell), characterized by incipient agriculture, sedentary population, wide trade networks, and elaborate ceremonialism. A previous report (Ossenberg 1974b), according to evidence mainly from discrete cranial morphology but also from craniometrics, rejected the hypothesis that Illinois Hopewell was biologically ancestral to Late Woodland mound-building populations of the northeastern Plains periphery, hence to the historic northern Plains tribes. In the present study, as expected, Hopewell did not join the Late Woodland-Plains subcluster (Figures 3, 4). But because the clustering procedure continued until all taxonomic units were joined, willy nilly, Hopewell, having been rejected by Plains-Woodland, had only one Indian alternative—the Na-Dene subcluster—and this seemed to be incorrect.

It was difficult to interpret the ranked MMDs for Hopewell in Table 2. Unlike those for Old Punuk and Namu, Hopewell's were not coherent. They did not link the sample unequivocally to any lineage represented by other samples in the study. The upper third of the list included Umnak, Tlingit, Nunivak,

characteristics, such as pronounced external occipital protuberance in certain adults, unlike any other northwestern groups I had examined previously. Certainly, they did not remind me of Haida, Kodiak, or Aleut.

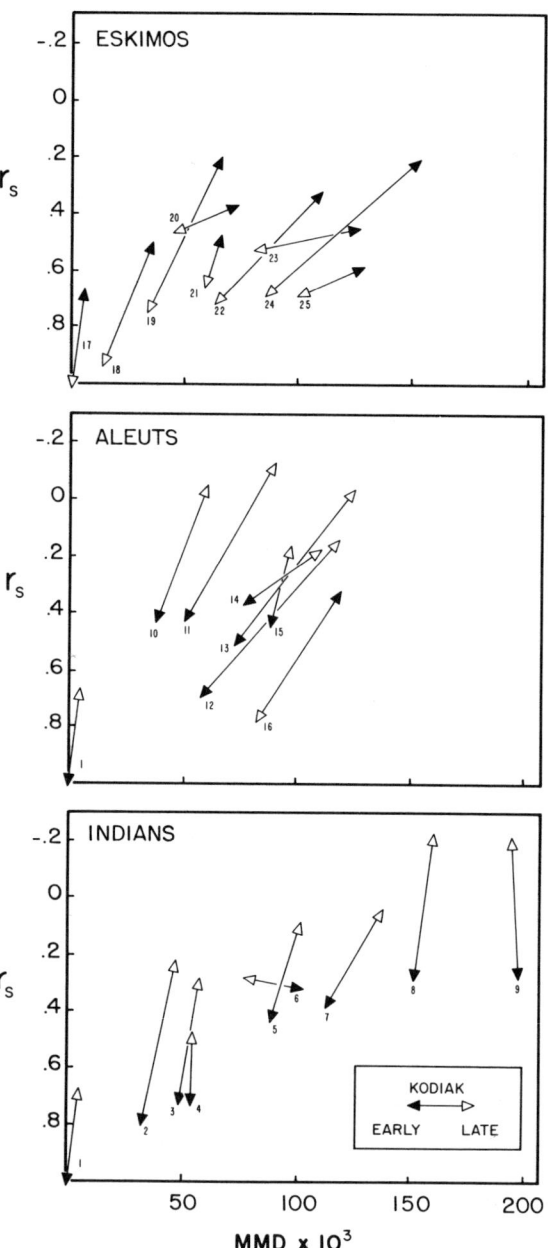

Figure 6. Microevolutionary divergence on Kodiak Island depicted in MMD versus r_s plots for Indians, Aleuts, and Eskimos. The affinity of each sample to Kodiak is represented by a double-headed arrow: black is Kodiak Early (3500–2000 yr B.P.), white is Kodiak Late (1000–400 yr B.P.). Values are from Table 3. Samples: *Indians*—1 Kodiak Early, 2 N. Athapaskans, 3 Namu, 4 S. Athapaskans, 5 Haida, 6 Hopewell, 7 Tlingit, 8 Late Woodland, 9 Plains; *Aleuts*—10 Umnak, 11 Shiprock, 12 Rat, 13 Kagamil, 14 Amaknak, 15 Andreanov, 16 Near; *Eskimos*—17 Kodiak Late, 18 South Mainland Alaska, 19 Ekven, 20 Siberian Eskimo, 21 Chukchi, 22 Old Punuk, 23 Inupiaq, 24 Nunivak, 25 St. Lawrence.

Athapaskans, Ekven, Siberian Eskimo, and Namu. The only generalization that sprang to mind here was that three of these were early: Umnak, Ekven, and Namu. The dispersion of r_s values was narrow compared to that of other samples. The highest positive values, 0.70 for Tlingit and 0.68 for Haida, while statistically significant, nevertheless were lower than, say, Namu-Umnak 0.84, Punuk-St. Lawrence 0.87, or Late Woodland-Plains 0.99. And at the other extreme, the lowest values, for Ainu 0.11, and Jomon 0.16, were higher than those for any American sample except Inupiaq.

Figure 7 plots data from Table 2, MMD versus r_s, for Old Punuk, Namu, and Hopewell. To compare with these, St. Lawrence, Umnak, and Late Woodland also were plotted. These patterns were most revealing. The similarity of Punuk to St. Lawrence was immediately apparent. Namu, Umnak, and Late Woodland were strikingly similar but not at all like the two Eskimo plots. In contrast, Hopewell was not like any of these. Its Indian, Aleut, and Eskimo values were interspersed in a desultory clump in the lower left quadrant, indicating affinity of Hopewell to everyone in general, but no one in particular. If indeed Hopewell was the only sample in this analysis representing a people wholly descended from the Macro-Indian founding migration, then, ideally, once data are available to include additional representatives, together they will have sufficient weight to form their own distinct subcluster in the dendrographs and other diagrams.

Northwest North America–Northeast Asia

Figures 8 and 9 are dendrographs depicting American-Asian relationships. Two Black samples were included in these cluster analyses as out-group comparisons with the Mongoloids.

To a remarkable degree the two major Amerind clusters identified in previous dendrographs maintained their integrity with the addition of Asians and Blacks. An improvement was that the Inupiaq subcluster had detached from Aleut–Na-Dene–Plains (Figures 3, 4) and now properly joined Eskimo. Thus reconstituted, the larger Eskimo cluster contained two subclusters: one formed by Inupiaq closely tied to three Chukotkan samples, the second containing South Mainland Alaska and Kodiak Islanders. These Eskimo subclusters, having

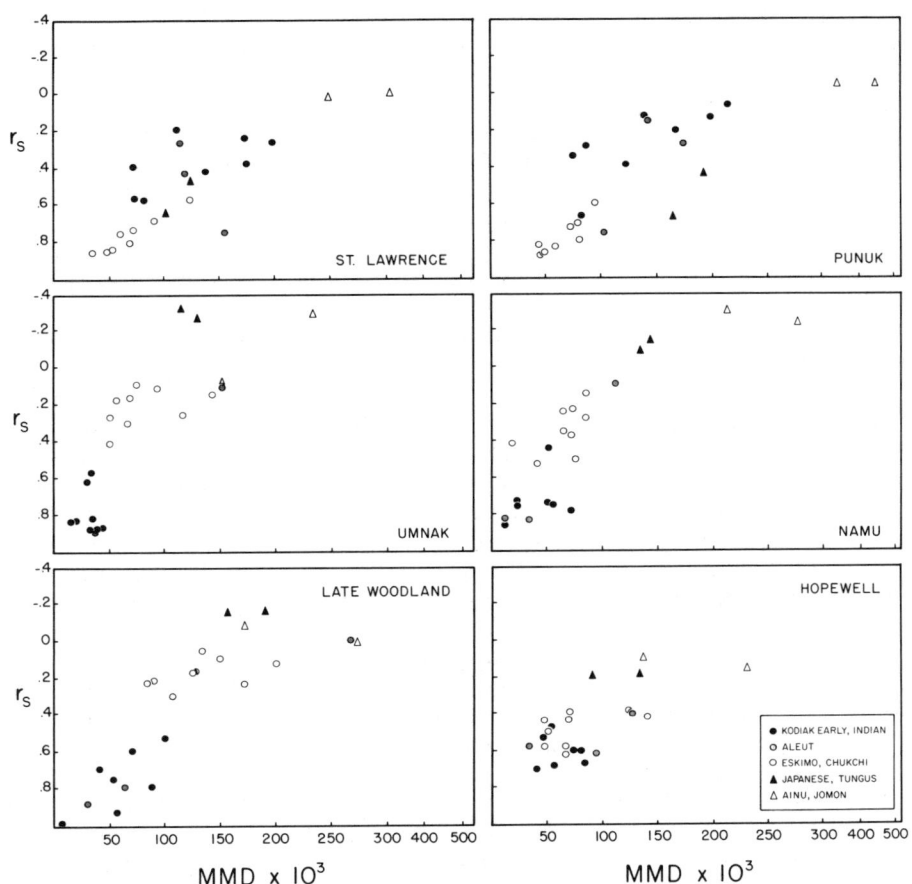

Figure 7. Relationships of Old Punuk, Namu, and Hopewell—each hypothesized to represent a separate migration in peopling of the New World—are depicted in plots of 25-trait MMDs versus r_s (values from Table 2). For comparison with these, plots for St. Lawrence (recent), Umnak and Late Woodland also are shown. Note change in scale on the right side of the X axis.

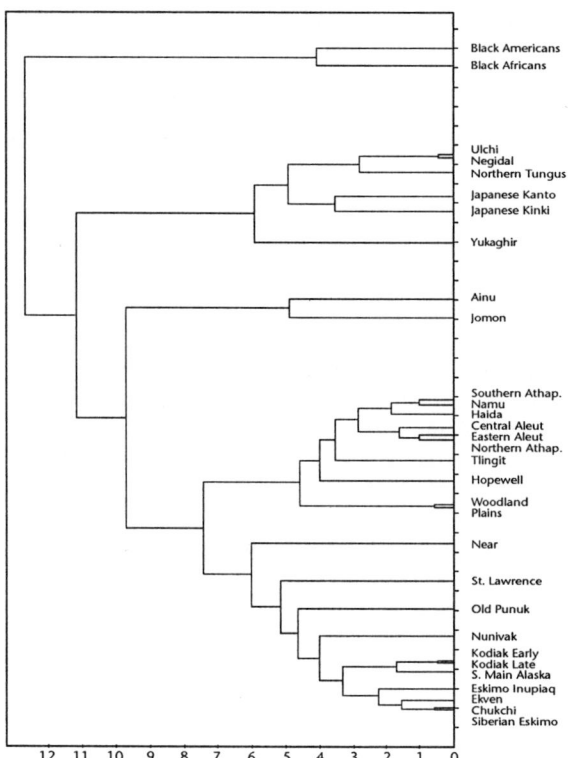

Figure 8. Dendrograph showing Amerind-Asian relationships. Americans were represented by 18 samples and aggregates, Asians by 11. Black samples were included as out-group comparisons. Note that Ainu-Jomon joined the Americans and northeast Siberians before Japanese-Tungus did.

joined, collected in stepwise fashion Nunivak, Old Punuk, St. Lawrence and finally, as in the previous dendrographs, Western Aleut (Near). Again it was remarkable that relationships within the Eskimo cluster were not any closer than those within the linguistically disparate one containing Eastern Aleut, Central Aleut, Na-Dene and Plains.

Of the other Asian samples, two distinct clusters were seen: Ainu with Jomon, and Japanese with Tungus and Yukaghir. Thus, the three Asian clusters were the same as previously described (Ossenberg 1986a), except that with the addition of the American samples the Siberian Eskimo and Chukchi now make their home with Inupiaq.

As for the highest level linkages, Ainu-Jomon joined the Amerinds before Japanese-Tungus. The pair of Black samples joined last, as expected.

Figure 9 is a summary cluster analysis for which Asian samples were pooled. It conformed best to the MMD rankings in that Japanese-Tungus joined the Americans before Ainu-Jomon. The American clusters and subclusters were the same with aggregates as with individual samples.

American-Asian MMDs for aggregates and key samples are in Table 5, from which the ranking of MMDs from the American point of view can be summarized as

1	Chukotkans
2	Japanese
3 (4,2)	Tungus
4 (3,5)	Ainu
5	Yukaghir
6	Jomon

Specifically, each of 19 Amerind samples was closer by far to Chukotkans than to any other Asian sample. At the other extreme, all but four were most distant from Jomon. Tungus and Ainu were the most inconsistently ranked. That Tungus in several instances changed places with Japanese was understandable considering that these were closely related to each other (Table 2); but Tungus as often changed places with Ainu, and Ainu with Yukaghir, even though relationships among those three were *not* close.

Notable differences from the general pattern summarized above: Nunivak, St. Lawrence, Punuk, and Near Aleut (all Yupik speakers or closely related to them) were more like Yukaghir than Ainu. Plains and Late-Woodland were more like Ainu than like Tungus. For two Inupiaq (Point Barrow, Mackenzie) and two North Pacific samples (Haida and Tlingit), both Ainu and Jomon were shifted up in the ranking.

American-Asian relationships can perhaps best be appreciated as four Asian MMD profiles (Figure 10). For simplicity's sake Yukaghir were omitted, and Japanese-Tungus represented by a single profile (on which each point was a mean of two MMDs). The ranking given above was clearly seen. Two other important features were noted.

First, the Chukotkan profile followed a gradient: the greater the geographic distance a North American sample was from Bering Strait, the weaker its affinity to northeast Siberians. Positive regression of MMD against geographic distance was noted also in a previous section which listed 15-trait MMDs for Chukotkans, Inupiaq, Yupik, and Athapaskans. The southwestern Athapaskans (Apache and Navajo) were not out of order in view of their recent northern origin. Similarly, the affinity of Mackenzie Delta and Southampton Island samples to Chukotkans was not inconsistent with the vast distances separating them, considering that prior to the Thule migrations at about 1000 yr B.P. the Birnirk ancestors of these Inupiaq Eskimos were somewhere in the close vicinity of Bering Strait (McGhee 1984; Utermohle 1984). The gradient was weak at its northern end because MMDs for Inupiaq, South Mainland Alaska, and Athapaskans were quite close (range 29.6–37.9). Reciprocally, those Amerind aggregates had MMDs versus

Chukotkans similar to their MMDs with each other (range 33.3–50.0, Table 2)[7].

The second notable feature in Figure 10 was that Ainu and Jomon profiles were parallel even though widely separated. Compared to the smooth slope of the Chukotkan profile, those of Ainu and Jomon were erratic, owing to their relatively close affinity to Eastern Aleut and Haida-Tlingit. For their part, Haida and Tlingit were closer to Ainu than to Tungus and to Jomon than to Yukaghir (Table 5).

Comparison of Craniometric and Nonmetric Trait Affinities

Worldwide

New ideas about the origin and dispersals of Homo sapiens emerging from mitochondrial DNA studies have sparked enthusiastic comparisons of worldwide reconstructions based on other categories of data. Thus, it is interesting to compare findings in the present study, even though these are not as universally representative, with reconstruction based on recent comprehensive craniometric surveys.

In a survey of present-day regional skull shape (Howells 1989), 57 craniofacial measurements were made on 28 cranial series. Cluster analysis based on intergroup correlations (C-scores) of the male data construct six clusters corresponding to broad geographic regions, though with outliers in each. Eskimo fall into the Polynesian cluster along with Guam and Ainu; in turn, this cluster links most closely to the Asian one. On the other hand, three Amerind series (Arikara, Santa Cruz, Peru) are in the same cluster as Buriat and Berg Norwegians; in turn, this is linked most closely with one containing Norse, Zalavar Hungarians, and Egyptians.

The corresponding dendrogram for 26 female series differs, installing Peru in the European cluster, while the other two Amerind samples are with the Asians along with Buriat, Guam, and Ainu. Again, Eskimo are with Polynesians, separated from American Indians.

Better results, in terms of geographically coherent clusters containing no odd members, were obtained with analysis based on Mahalanobis' D. Nevertheless, New World Mongoloids still do not link preferentially to Asia rather than to Europe.

Mid-sex C-scores derived from 21 craniofacial measurements were used to construct Euclidean distance dendrograms of 41 circum-Pacific population samples (Brace et al. 1989). The groups sort into five distinct regional clusters composed and linked as follows:

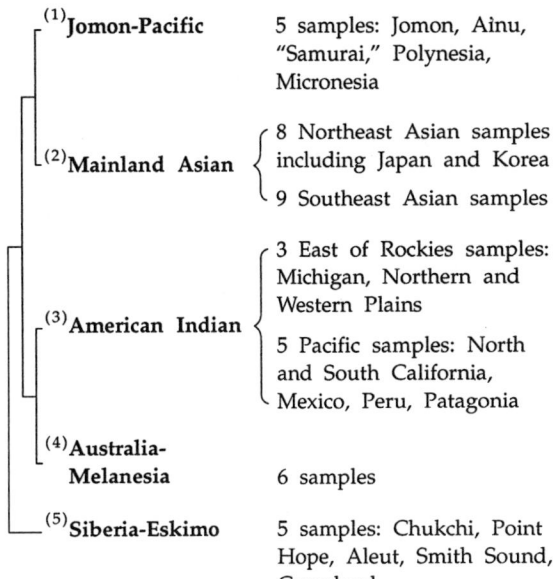

In this analysis as in Howells', contrary to that based on nonmetric traits, Indians and Eskimos do not link preferentially to each other or to Asians. A summary dendrogram based on 24 measurements in the 5 regional aggregate samples shows a stepwise linkage from closest to most removed: (1), (2), (3), (5), (4). When the analysis is expanded to eight major geographic samples, American Indians join Europe and India, an historically incorrect relationship interpreted as the possible result of parallel selection acting on the nasofacial complex.

Brace et al. (1989) note that the separation between the Eskimo-Siberian cluster (which includes the Aleuts) and the American Indian cluster is consistent with the model of Greenberg and colleagues. In Brace's view, the two subclusters formed by the Indians, one east of the Rockies and one Pacific coastal, do not fit the picture of an ancient Macro-Indian–Na-Dene linguistic split. Owing to meagre sample size and representative coverage, they offer this only as a preliminary suggestion to be tested by future research. Nevertheless, considering the linkage of Plains in the nonmetric trait dendrographs, I wonder whether

---

[7] Six of the seven Yupik Eskimo samples (the exception being St. Lawrence) were closer to at least one Athapaskan sample than to Chukchi and/or Siberian Eskimo. Inupiaq (pooled) was closer to Navajo (30.5) than to Chukchi (35.6). Thus, the picture of Siberian-American relationships emerging from the analysis of nonmetric cranial traits with the inclusion of additional samples was substantially the same as described previously (Szathmary and Ossenberg 1978). Note that the pattern of MMDs suggested only that North American Eskimo, (especially Yupik speakers) were about as closely related to Athapaskans as to Chukotkans, not more closely.

Table 5. Amerind-Asian MMDs Based on 25 Traits. Value are x10³.

	CHUKOTKANS (MEAN OF 3 MMDS)	JAPANESE	TUNGUS	AINU	YUKAGHIR	JOMON
Inupiaq (aggregate)	29.6	65.3	82.6	81.7	158.5	165.9
Southampton Is.	61.5	109.3	113.0	168.4	207.9	284.6
Mackenzie	47.9	92.8	91.9	85.4	173.8	150.1
Point Barrow	22.7	55.2	87.2	56.6	155.1	134.2
Yupik (aggregate)	20.8	81.5	81.5	163.3	150.4	230.7
Yupik and related samples						
South Mainland Alaska	32.7	94.8	89.4	189.2	157.8	237.1
Nunivak	51.0	101.7	119.3	144.0	124.8	225.7
St. Lawrence	63.4	126.2	102.5	251.0	219.5	316.6
Old Punuk	66.4	192.7	165.1	315.0	244.7	450.2
Kodiak, Late	31.8	102.8	110.3	183.6	204.3	265.6
Kodiak, Early	47.0	126.7	138.3	204.0	234.5	270.3
Athapaskans	37.9	113.7	123.8	170.1	206.2	245.4
Aleut, Eastern	48.1	92.7	115.2	135.9	190.4	207.6
Aleut, Central	62.1	139.8	140.7	216.3	233.0	259.7
Aleut, Western	104.2	152.7	122.3	263.5	126.4	317.3
Namu	73.0	146.0	136.8	216.0	231.3	282.0
Tlingit	84.2	125.5	149.1	142.7	211.3	185.8
Haida	74.9	122.1	156.9	141.2	231.6	193.4
Late Woodland	113.4	157.3	190.1	174.0	241.5	272.6
Plains	125.4	157.7	191.3	173.2	223.5	263.5
Hopewell	58.0	91.3	132.1	136.4	150.0	230.4

Summary of MMD rank distribution of Asian samples[a]

Number of times ranked						
first	19	-	-	-	-	-
second	-	13	5	-	-	-
third	-	4	9	5	1	-
fourth	-	2	5	9	3	-
fifth	-	-	-	4	11	2
sixth	-	-	-	-	4	15

[a] Ranks for individual Inupiaq and Yupik samples were counted, not aggregates.

their "east of the Rockies" subcluster might have some Na-Dene affinity, albeit not a linguistic one.

North America, Siberia

Based on principal component scores for 9 measurements on 80 North American and Asian cranial series (measurements made by Hrdlička and reported in the *Catalogs of Human Crania in the United States National Museum*), Brennan and Howells (1976) delineated five groups. Three of these encompass, with various other cranial series, representatives of virtually all the American and Siberian regions represented in my study[8].

Group I: Siberians (except Siberian Eskimo and Chukchi), "pre-Aleuts" (mainly the Umnak sample and some crania from Shiprock), Dakota Sioux, Cheyenne, Arikara, and some groups from New York and California.

Group II: Aleuts (Kagamil and other), Late Kodiak, Northwest Coast Indians, Tlingit, Navajo, Apache.

Group V: Eskimo of Alaska, Canada, Greenland,

---

[8] Series not reported in Hrdlička's *Catalog of Crania* were those in Canadian and other U.S. museums: Blackfoot, Assiniboin, Haida, Late Woodland, Illinois Hopewell, Namu, and Southampton.

Siberia; Yukon River Indians (i.e., Ingalik, Koyukon, and other Northern Athapaskans); Early Kodiak; Chukchi.

These groups show similarities to the pattern seen in the nonmetric MMDs, notably that the Aleuts are placed with the Athapaskans and Plains tribes, separate from Eskimos.

Strangely, the Ingalik, whose nonmetric traits would not permit them to disconnect from the Eastern Aleuts in the dendrographs, have cranial measurements more similar to their Eskimo neighbours in Alaska. A craniometric analysis of Eskaleutian relationships in northwestern North America based on a large battery of measurements (Heathcote 1986) likewise aligned Ingalik with Eskimo[9].

Univariate comparisons indicate that certain metric traits have considerable utility for revealing ethnogenetic relationships among Mongoloid peoples. In particular, nasiomalar angle, zygomaxillary angle (Alexseev 1979a), other measures of facial flatness (Dodo 1986), and dimensions of the mandibular ramus (Laughlin et al. 1976) appear to class Eskimos and Aleuts together and distinct from American Indians. While not disputing the taxonomic value of univariate or bivariate comparisons, Heathcote (1981) reports original data for northwestern Indians showing some overlap between their facial angle values and those of Eskimo-Aleut. Certain components of the facial skeleton also are influenced by masticatory or other functions through genetic selection, plasticity, or both; hence are possibly less reliable for ethnohistocial reconstruction than more "trivial" features (Brace et al. 1989).

Head shape shows a linear progression from lowest cephalic index values (long narrow heads) in Greenland to highest in the Aleutians. The clinal distribution of cephalic index and discontinuities in the cline at the boundaries between major linguistic-geographic divisions are interpreted as a reflection of the ancestral unity and migratory history of the Eskimo-Aleut stock (Laughlin et al. 1979).

In contrast to the importance placed on the geographic distribution of cranial index, clines seem to figure less prominently in interpretations based on multivariate analyses. Rather, independent investigators using different trait batteries and multivariate techniques (Brennan and Howells 1976; Heathcote 1986; Utermohle 1984; Zegura 1975) consistently stress that Inupiaq Eskimo, though thinly dispersed across an enormous expanse of Arctic coast, form a remarkably homogeneous morphological group in contrast to the southwestern Alaskans. There is an important disagreement between metric and nonmetric data with respect to

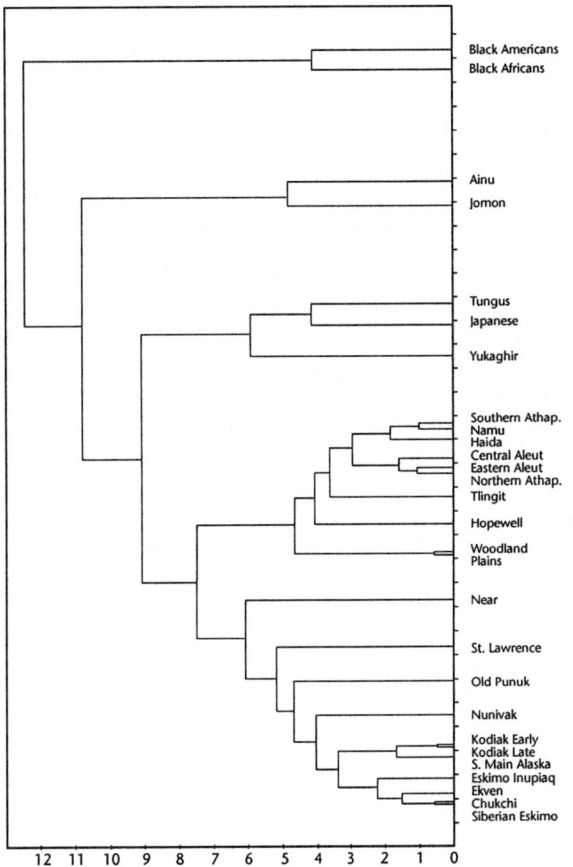

Figure 9. Dendrograph of Amerinds and Asians. Same samples as in Figure 8, but two Japanese samples were aggregated, as were three Tungus samples. With this change, Japanese-Tungus joined the Amerind cluster before Ainu-Jomon.

affinities among the latter: craniometrics place the brachycephalic Koniag and recent Aleut closer to each other than either group is to other Alaskan Eskimo, while nonmetric data were more concordant with linguistics in that Koniag were closer to other Yupik-speakers than to recent Aleut (Table 2: MMDs for Kodiak Late and Kagamil Aleut).

Brachycephalization

An evolutionary trend to brachycephalization occurring worldwide but asynchronously in different populations seems to have greatly muddled the ethnohistorical picture in Alaska. On the one hand, change over time

---

[9] Paleo-Aleut from Amaknak compared craniometrically with a wide range of groups from Siberia to New England were found to have a close resemblance only to an "early Athapaskan group" (Richards 1946, Master's thesis from the University of Chicago, cited by Utermohle 1984:128).

coincidentally manifest in the skeletal series from Kodiak Island and the Aleutians, and clinal variation in headform within the Eskimo-Aleut territory, are interpreted as a valuable record of this phenomenon (Laughlin 1963:6; Laughlin et al. 1979:95–97) "caught in the act" as it were. Others, focusing on the dolichocranic high-vaulted prototypical Inupiaq Eskimo skull, interpret deviation from this type through space and time in Alaska as mixture with, or replacement by, non-Eskimo. Having reviewed these writings, Szathmary (1979a:24–27) concludes that it is not possible to distinguish objectively between craniometric similarity caused by admixture between Indians and Eskimos and similarity produced either by common ancestry or by adaptive evolutionary convergence.

It is precisely situations such as this that call for help from nonmetric skeletal traits. Thus, the grouping together of recent Aleut and Koniag in independent craniometric analyses of Brennan and Howells (1976), Utermohle (1984:350), Zegura (1975), and others, probably reflects both common ancestry and convergence due to brachycephalization rather than mixture with Indians. Similarly, the separation of Paleo- from Neo-Aleut, and Early from Late Kodiak, by craniometric analysis likely gives an incorrect historical picture. Findings in the present study suggested within-region continuity and between-region isolation for Aleutian and Kodiak populations, at least since 4000 yr B.P., in support of the reconstruction of Laughlin and his co-workers. Brachycephalization on Kodiak could not have been due to swamping of that densely populated area by Indians: such a scenario is impossible to reconcile with the linguistic reconstruction according to which, during the same period, the population exchanged its Indian language for the Pacific Eskimo speech imposed by immigrants from the Alaska Peninsula (Dumond 1987a). Distance measures provided by the minor cranial variants showed divergence of Kodiak away from Na-Dene and a shift of affinity towards Eskimo, which was altogether consistent with the reconstruction based on language and archaeology.

Resurrection of an Old Hypothesis

The clustering apart from Eskimo of Aleut–Na-Dene–Plains in the analysis of Brennan and Howells is more difficult to dismiss as spurious: MMDs showed the same thing. Brennan and Howells point out that their groups correspond quite well with the varieties discerned by G. K. Neumann (1952), whose old-fashioned typological approach is discredited today. Neumann, however, was an experienced craniologist who examined thousands of skulls before offering a reconstruction of New World ethnohistory. In his view, the Aleut represent a specialized form of his "Deneid" variety. He proposes that this variety arrived in one of the last major migrations to the New World, exerting profound influences on both North Pacific Coast and Southwest populations. Further, it contributed to the differentiation of a hybrid "Lakotid" variety which by historic times was represented in all the northern Plains tribes. The "Inuid" variety to which all Eskimo belong, and the "Lenapid" (or "Lenapid-Walcolid" hybrid) to which Illinois Hopewell belongs, contrast strongly with the Deneid and Lakotid.

Like Neumann, Hrdlička consistently disclaims the Eskimo affinity of the Aleuts. He is the first to draw attention to the remarkable similarity between the "pre-Aleut" (i.e., Umnak) and Dakota Sioux skull. He concludes that the two groups must have had a common and not very far back ancestry, and anticipates that early Sioux bones if ever recovered would trace the origins of this tribe to a common ancestry with "pre-Aleuts" (Hrdlička 1945:555, 582–584). This hypothesis is little more than a hunch based on what he sees as the remarkable similarities between the skulls, and backed up by no archaeological or linguistic evidence. Yet, nonmetric cranial MMDs seemed to make good his prediction.

In summary, the cranial evidence concerning Aleuts, Eskimo, and Indian affinities from several independent observers does not come down solidly in support of the assertion that "in no other part of the New World is there as profound a dichotomy in physical characteristics between groups as that between Aleuts and Eskimos on the one hand, and Indians on the other hand" (Laughlin et al. 1979:98).

Comparison of Cranial and Dental Distance Measures

At the outset it is fair to acknowledge that the assumption fundamental to the use of morphology in this type of historical research, namely, that the traits are predominantly genetic, may be more secure in the case of individual crown and root traits: they can be more readily examined in living relatives. Moreover, once fully developed, teeth do not respond to intrinsic physiological processes to the same extent as bone tissue does. On the down side, however, for archaeologically retrieved remains, the portion of the total N in which dental traits can be recorded is more restricted (because of incomplete development in children, pathology, attrition, trauma, and loss) so that data from several sites more often must be aggregated. Thus, fewer within-group diachronic and geographical comparisons are available for fine-tuned ethnohistorical interpretation; for example, for Aleuts, Kodiak Islanders, and Eskimos 3 dental MMDs are reported (Greenberg et al. 1986) compared to 210 cranial MMDs. Each category of feature, then, complements the other by its own particular strengths.

Trait-by-trait analysis of dental variation in the Aleutians shows, on the whole, no difference between teeth of Paleo- and Neo-Aleut skulls; however, it is recognized that because "Paleo" and "Neo" classes were set up according to cranial index (with pan-Aleutian site representation in each) and because the samples were small, this result is not conclusive (Turner 1967:174). For comparison, the Paleo-Neo (Umnak-Kagamil) cranial MMD .036 is significantly different from zero, but still relatively small. Based on univariate comparisons, Turner (1967) reports greater geographic differences (Eastern, Central, and Western aggregates) than temporal ones, in agreement with the cranial MMDs.

Multivariate distance analysis based on 23 key traits in an Eastern aggregate (including Kagamil) and a Western (west of Amukta Pass) gives an MMD .003, insignificantly different from zero (Turner et al. 1982) (though the 1967 East-Central-West comparisons do show regular frequency gradients for 15 of the traits). Dental MMDs for Eastern and Western aggregates versus Kodiak (Uyak site, all levels) are .054 and .064, respectively (Turner et al. 1982), very similar to cranial MMDs, .051 and .066 for Eastern and Central aggregates versus Kodiak.

Nonmetric traits of the skull agreed with those of the teeth that Kodiak was more like Na-Dene than like Arctic Coast Eskimo. So closely, in fact, do dental traits align Kodiak (Uyak site all-levels aggregate) with Na-Dene (Northern Maritime, Central Maritime, Gulf of Georgia/Puget Sound, Athapaskans) that, of the ten MMDs for this group ranging from .003–.043, only two are significantly different from zero, prompting Turner to conclude "there is no odontological support for the assumption that the prehistoric Kodiak was Eskimo rather than Na-Dene" (1983:152). While essentially agreeing with that conclusion, the findings in the present study (which included three Uyak levels and six Bering Sea Yupik-speaking Eskimo samples not separately represented by dental MMDs) suggested a somewhat more complex scenario for Kodiak, involving gene flow from Eskimo to an indigenous Na-Dene population.

The same report based on 23 dental features also shows: teeth from Namu statistically indistinguishable from those of Kodiak (MMD .005) and other people of the North Pacific Coast; Aleut most closely related to Namu (.037) and Athapaskans (.045); Aleut and Eskimo both more like Kodiak and three other North Pacific Na-Dene populations (range of eight MMDs .055–.105) than like each other (.108). This pattern is very similar to that seen in the cranial data.

Subsequent analyses use a larger suite of 28 traits in a greatly expanded data base to examine hypotheses of Native American origins in the relevant context of circum-Pacific and Eurasian dental variation (Greenberg et al. 1986; Turner 1985, 1986, 1989). Some of the Amerind samples previously reported (Turner 1983) are increased and/or reorganized. With the changes noted, the Eskimo-Aleut MMD formerly .108 is now .040. Even so, Eskimo remain closer (.032) to Kodiak, which in Turner's view is Na-Dene, than to Aleuts. As do cranial MMDs, dental data show Aleuts closer to Athapaskans (.031) than to Eskimo (.040). Correlation between dental and cranial MMDs for eight samples common to both data sets was tested (Ossenberg 1989). Spearman's r_s corrected for tied ranks was 0.69 (.01>p).

Cranial evidence for Amerind relationships was limited in the present study to data from northwestern North America, whereas Turner's three-migration model is based on the total pattern of dental relationships for samples broadly representative of North and South America. Dental data do, indeed, show Aleut and Eskimo closer to each other than to *most* other Amerinds; but not all. Along with Dumond (1987a:41–42, 52), I question whether that relationship is sufficiently strong and unambiguous to provide unqualified support for a model that reconstructs an Eskimo-Aleut founding group distinct from the one which gave rise to Na-Dene and perhaps other Indians of the Pacific Northwest.

As do the teeth, cranial variants distinguished Northeast Asians and Amerinds from Jomon and Ainu. Further, both data sets concurred that, among Northeast Asians, Amerinds were more closely related to Chukotkans than to Tungus or Japanese.

The taxonomic value of minor morphological traits of the teeth is amply demonstrated by Turner in his series of contributions entitled *Peopling of the Pacific Basin and Adjoining Areas*. A remarkably coherent ethnohistorical picture is emerging, based on population affinities determined by these strongly heritable and evolutionarily conservative traits. Whether or not cranial traits prove to be as powerful as those of the teeth for discriminating between major geographic populations worldwide is a question remaining for future investigations. But in any case, since each category of trait presumably samples a large and to a major extent different portion of the genome, the statistically significant rank correlation between dental and cranial MMDs is also *biologically* significant because it underscores the enormous potential of skeletal remains for historical reconstruction.

ETHNOHISTORICAL RECONSTRUCTION

Circum-Pacific Affinities

Cranial MMDs showing reciprocally close affinity between Chukotkans and northwestern North Americans suggested that both derived from the stock ancestral to Arctic Mongoloids, rather than from the Classic Mongoloid stock of the North Asian interior ancestral to Tungus and Japanese. Similarly, skull measurements, anthropometry of living peoples, as well as observations of hair/skin colour and shape of facial features lead to the interpretation that the Siberian Arctic Mongoloid morphological complex resembles the North American more closely than do any of the other five Siberian complexes; further, that the ancestral population differentiated in the coastal regions of North Asia rather than in the interior (Alexseev 1979b:67,85).

In keeping with the archaeological record showing that Neolithic Japan exerted no influence on the New World (Chard 1974), the American samples including the earliest (Umnak, Kodiak Early, and Namu) were unanimous with respect to their great nonmetric cranial trait distance from Jomon. Next in order of distance was Ainu. Ainu and Jomon (Proto-Mongoloids) are thought to have their ancestral roots in Southeast Asia, and this is reflected in the craniometric characteristics of Ainu affiliating them with Pacific peoples such as Maori, Hawaiians, and inhabitants of Guam (Brace et al. 1989; Howells 1976, 1989).

Ainu, Jomon, Southeast Asians and South Pacific peoples share a common Sundadont dental pattern. On the other hand, the Sinodont dental complex affiliates Northeast Asians (i.e., Japanese, Tungus, Chukchi, Eskimo) with all New World indigenous peoples including the earliest for which remains have been studied (Turner and Bird 1981). Likewise, a genetic tree based on all available classical marker data (120 alleles) in 42 populations representing the world aborigines links Eskimos and American Indians to Northeast Asians (Cavalli-Sforza et al. 1988).

Yet some physical anthropological data do suggest similarities between American Indians and/or Eskimos to Ainu, Southeast Asians, or Pacific Islanders (Hanihara 1977; Howells 1976, 1989; Kirk 1979; Kozintsev 1988:166; Nei and Roychoudhury 1982; Salzano 1985; Yamaguchi 1977). In my dendrographs (Figures 8, 9 and 1989: Figures 4–6) Ainu-Jomon and Japanese-Tungus were indecisive as to which linked first to Americans. Though earlier Pacific samples (Namu, Kodiak Early, Umnak) notably were not, Haida and Tlingit were ambivalent about their affinity to Ainu versus Japanese-Tungus, and were also somewhat closer to Jomon than were other Amerinds (Tables 2 and 5, Figure 10). These findings seemed particularly tantalizing in view of circum-Pacific cultural parallels (Chard 1974; Levin 1963); the evidence of a partly unglaciated littoral, together with linguistic diversity in the North Pacific, pointing to this region of the New World as a possible Pleistocene refugium and initial route of entry (Fladmark 1983; Gruhn 1988; Rogers 1985); and the regional archaeological record, which suggests that Tlingit and Haida ancestry involved amalgamation of an immigrant microblade tradition at about 9000 yr B.P. with a remnant pebble tool tradition which had occupied the area for some time previously (Carlson 1979, 1983). The major center of Upper Pleistocene pebble-tool industries was Southeast Asia (Jennings 1983:42), and although the antiquity of the pebble-tool industries in the New World apparently has not been fully demonstrated, they still may be indicative of very early movements into the New World. The point is that although Jomon itself was not significantly involved, if at all, in peopling of the New World, nevertheless the present archaeological and physical anthropological evidence seems too ambivalent and certainly too incomplete to rule out the possibility of Proto-Mongoloid movements from Southeast Asia around the Pacific littoral and into the New World.

Northwestern North America

The two distinct clusters seen in the dendrographs, Aleut–Na-Dene–Plains and Eskimo, were interpreted to reflect two migrations from northeast Siberia. The earlier of the two brought people of an old Arctic Mongoloid stock whose artifactual remains in Alaska dating from about 10,000 yr B.P. are classed by Dumond (1987b), following Anderson (1968), as the American Paleoarctic tradition. This physical stock, which I have named *Paleoarctic Amerind*, formed the deepest underlying stratum of genetic heritage common to speakers of Eskimo-Aleut, Na-Dene and perhaps other North Pacific languages. The differences between the Anangula blade site in the eastern Aleutians and other Paleoarctic assemblages of the Alaskan interior perhaps represented Aleuts and Na-Dene speakers differentiating with respect to language and culture. However, the hypothetical reconstruction presented here required that, for whatever reason, genetic divergence within the Paleoarctic Amerind stock remained small. During a time level perhaps 9000–5000 yr B.P., groups dispersed from southwestern Alaska. Paleoarctic navigators who settled the Aleutian Islands found no inhabitants except the Steller sea lion and other creatures of an abundant maritime ecozone. Some groups moved down the North Pacific Coast where microblades follow a north-south gradient as far as the Columbia River (Carlson 1983, 1989), others wandered east to the Plains and northeastern Plains periphery. As suggested by Neumann (1952) in his reconstruction for the "Deneid" variety such movements would have involved mixture with, and in some cases language capture by, people encountered in these regions.

With respect to movements to and from the Plains: during the Thermal Maximum, 7000–5000 yr B.P., people advanced into the Alaskan interior, possibly from somewhat farther south, and possibly following the spread of the boreal forest. Here, as suggested by the conjunction of side-notched points with microblades and microcores in artifact assemblages of the Northern Archaic tradition (Dumond 1987b:47–54) the newcomers may have assimilated Paleoarctic people. It was tempting to speculate that some southern movement of resulting Alaskan peoples onto the Plains carried in its gene pool a preponderant contribution from

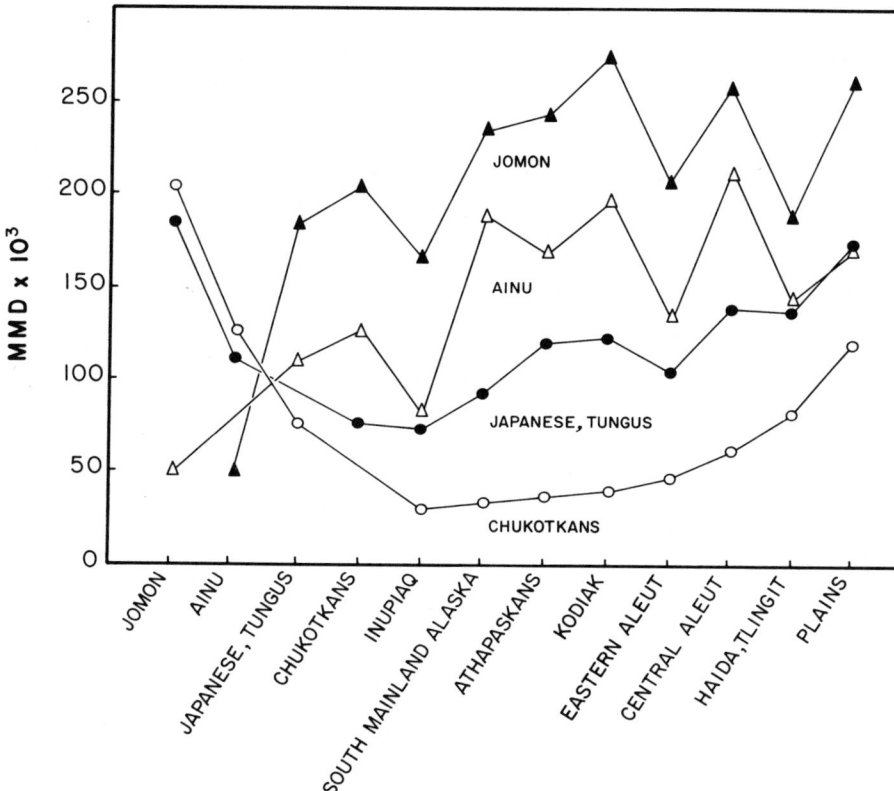

Figure 10. Four profiles showing affinities of northeast Asians to each other and to Amerinds. Values plotted were MMDs (Table 2) for single samples or aggregates, except the following which were mean MMDs: Japanese, Tungus (mean of MMDs for two aggregates); Chukotkans (mean of three); Haida, Tlingit (mean of two). Kodiak was represented by the aggregated sample: Early, Middle, Late.

the Paleoarctic stock; hence the affinity of the Paleo-Aleut (Umnak) to the Late Woodland ancestors of the Dakota, Assiniboin, Blackfoot, and Cheyenne.

The most recent migration or series of movements from Siberia was of a physical stock that I have named *Neoarctic Amerind*. Though these people and Paleoarctic Amerinds may have originated in the same late Pleistocene ancestral stock at about 14,000 yr B.P., now after eight or nine millenia of separation the new immigrants had a pattern of minor skeletal variants and other traits (possibly including those which define Neumann's "Inuid" variety) that distinguished them from their relatives already in Alaska. Neoarctic people may have brought Neolithic Asian cultural elements, manifest by 4500 yr B.P. in the Arctic Small Tool tradition (AST_t), later arrivals brought elements leading by 3000 yr B.P. to Norton, thence to Thule who were the immediate ancestors of historic Eskimo.

These movements would have resulted in gene flow between the newcomers and Paleoarctic descendent peoples whom they encountered. For example, the Norton tradition of Alaska, 3000–1000 yr B.P., is thought to have received its impetus from Asian immigrants originating perhaps in the Sea of Okhotsk area, who brought new elements such as pottery-making which coalesced with AST_t (Dumond 1982, 1987b), and probably also with traits originating in the North Pacific region (Clark 1982, 1984; Workman 1982, 1988). It was reasonable to infer that such cultural amalgamation was accompanied by genetic mixture.

Eskimo population history would have been especially complex in Alaska, a region presumably more densely populated by Paleoarctic descendents and impacted by more episodes of demic diffusion (AST_t, Norton, Thule) than were the Arctic shores east of Mackenzie River which, according to Dumond (1982), was the terminus of Norton. By cluster analysis Eskimo MMDs clearly reflected the Yupik-Inupiaq language division. Their ranking followed a linguistic-geographic gradient that traced affinities from the Bering Strait region northeastwards through Inupiaq territory (Point Barrow, Mackenzie, Southampton); and southwards along the path of differentiation of the five Yupik languages (not all represented among my samples) from simplest in Siberia (Yupik) to most phonologically complex in the Gulf of Alaska (Suk language of Koniag and Chugach). Dialect distribution in the Bering Sea region (Central Alaskan Yupik language) suggests an expansion that left Nunivak and Hooper's Bay in geographically isolated pockets (Woodbury 1984). The greater diversity in Yupik may be interpreted as the outcome of Thule encounter with fairly densely populated speech communities that had been differentiating during Norton times (Dumond 1987a).

Substantial cultural continuities are seen in the earlier Ocean Bay archaeological sequences on Kodiak dated from about 6000–4000 yr B.P., followed by changes during the later stage of the Kodiak tradition (Kachemak stage 3500–1000 yr B.P.) suggestive of a gradual assimilation of cultural elements from the Bering Sea region rather than wholesale population displacement (Clark 1984; Dumond 1977, 1987b; Workman 1980). Likewise, the nonmetric cranial traits did not indicate a massive influx of newcomers to Kodiak over the time span of the three samples perhaps 3500–400 yr B.P.; i.e., from near the beginning of the Kachemak stage through the time of the Thule expansion beginning around 1000 yr B.P. Rather, the slight shift of affinity away from Na-Dene and Aleut and towards Eskimo clearly supported the reconstruction based on archaeology.

The gradient of Chukotkan-Amerind MMDs overall (Table 5, Figure 10) revealed that Siberian Arctic Mongoloids were most closely related to Eskimo, and that affinity weakened with geographic distance in the order: Athapaskans, Aleut, Na-Dene and Plains. This gradient was interpreted to have resulted from differential intensity of gene flow between Neo- and Paleoarctic at the northern end, and at the southern end between Paleoarctic and other Amerinds (those presumably already in North America before the later two migrations). At the northern end, the remarkably close relationship between Athapaskans and Yupik Eskimo would presumably reflect not only their common Paleoarctic ancestry, but also to some extent shared gene flow from the more recent Asian immigrants; there was hybridization in the ancestry of both, but the Paleoarctic predominated in Athapaskans, and the Neoarctic in Eskimo. Even when considered trait by trait, the frequencies for Eskimo, Athapaskans, and Aleut strongly supported the reconstruction that Koniag and Athapaskan ancestry involved hybridization between an Eskimo-related (Neoarctic) and Aleut-related (Paleoarctic) genetic stock.

What reconstruction best accounts for the cranial MMDs of the Aleut? According to Laughlin the very first migrants to the Aleutians, evidenced by 8000 yr B.P. at the Anangula core and blade site, not only survived but flourished in their isolated thousand-mile-long archipelago, and were directly ancestral to the historic Aleut. Other archaeologists, however, are not convinced by evidence of continuity between Anangula and the later midden cultures (McCartney 1984).

According to Dumond (1987a) people represented in Norton-like assemblages of the Aleutian tradition, dating from 4500 yr B.P. at Port Moller on the Alaska Peninsula and some centuries later in base Chaluka, amalgamated with people already resident on the Peninsula and in the eastern Aleutians. It is likely that bearers of the Aleutian tradition were the earliest speakers of ancestral Eskimo-Aleut to appear in Alaska; their arrival foreshadowing a second wave of immigrants from Siberia at about 3000 yr B.P., bringing the Eskimo language and cultural elements that led to the full-fledged Norton tradition on the Bering Sea coast. A few skeletal remains retrieved with the Port Moller Aleutian tradition materials are said to be Paleo-Aleut (Laughlin 1966). On the other hand, statistical treatment of both craniometric and nonmetric data align Port Moller with Bering Sea Eskimo rather than Aleut (Okada and Yamaguchi 1976).

MMDs for the Aleutians did support the reconstruction of genetic continuity from Paleo-Aleut (base Chaluka) to recent Aleut. Moreover, all evidence in this analysis pointed overwhelmingly to a preponderant Paleoarctic component in the genetic substrate of the archipelago, which could push continuity back in time to Anangula. However, the picture seemed more complex than that.

Whatever the population history between Anangula and the beginning of the Aleutian tradition, the reconstruction that best fit the available data was that the latter was launched from the Alaska Peninsula at about 4500 yr B.P. by an Eskaleut-speaking people of Neoarctic genetic stock, as inferred from the Eskimo ascription of the Port Moller skulls. Even as the founding group was colonizing the Aleutians, it was followed by Paleoarctic people sufficiently early and in large enough numbers to give the Umnak Paleo-Aleut sample its unequivocally closer affinity to Indians than to Eskimo. Here, as in the case of Alaskan Eskimo, the model of demic diffusion (Weiss 1988) was invoked, whereby an immigrant population expands into occupied territory assimilating the inhabitants so that a gradient of genetic traits is set up due to differential mixture: the communities closest to the point of origin of the expanding front having the largest contribution of immigrant genes, those at the periphery preserving the largest contribution from the earlier inhabitants. However, while Bering Sea and Kodiak prehistory apparently involved Neoarctic immigrants assimilating a Paleoarctic indigenous population, MMDs for the Aleutians suggested the reverse, in that the strongest Paleoarctic (Na-Dene) affinities were manifest in the Eastern sector, whereas the Near Islands sample at the western periphery apparently preserved the strongest trace of the Neoarctic (Eskimo) characteristics of the Aleutian tradition founding group.[10] While Aleut affinities to both groups decreased with geo-

---

[10] Here I was proposing that a group of Neoarctic physical stock bearing the Aleutian tradition was able to establish itself as a small local "host" population prior to being inundated genetically, before 4000 yr B.P. (base Chaluka), through assimilation by Paleoarctic immigrants from the eastern Aleutians, North Pacific Coast, or even the Alaskan interior. This reconstruction supposed that the Paleoarctic immigrants though more numerous and, perhaps, if they

graphic distance from the Alaska Peninsula as would be consistent with a simple isolation by distance model, closer analysis revealed that the gradient of Aleut-Indian MMDs was steeper than that of Aleut-Eskimo MMDs, a pattern that seemed to fit better to the model of population structure suggested here.

Another difference seen between demic diffusion in the Aleutians and that in the Bering Sea and Kodiak regions was that the latter was apparently accompanied by language capture but the former was not. Were the Paleoarctic people, moving into the archipelago in the wake of the Aleutian tradition, speakers of a related Eskaleut language? If so, their assimilation would have been easier. Alternatively, they may have been Na-Dene from the North Pacific coast, a possibility for which there is no acceptable linguistic evidence considering that Aleut has no loan words from Athapaskan or other Na-Dene. Yet, there is an intriguing hint of such a connection in that Aleut is distinguished from other Eskimoan languages by loss of a labial stop phoneme ("p" sound). This peculiarity "may reflect earlier proximity to Tlingit or Athapaskan, which both lack labial consonants almost entirely" (Woodbury 1984:62).

Considering the important role credited to demic diffusion in this reconstruction, some further points were worth mention. In the case of maritime-adapted Arctic populations, migration and gene flow always have been configured by the coasts in a linear fashion (Laughlin et al. 1979). Simulations demonstrate that *linear* gradients of gene frequency generated by demic expansion are remarkably stable and not easily dissolved by subsequent gene flow between neighbours (Cavalli-Sforza 1986:25). The inherent conservatism of gradients of population affinity structured by gene flow has been demonstrated, as far as bone nonmetric traits are concerned, in the case of Greenland (Laughlin and Jørgensen 1956), Japan (Ossenberg 1986a), and, most dramatically, Tasmania, where affinities structured during the time those areas were connected by land persisted 8000 years after communication totally ceased (Pardoe 1991).

It may be that skeletal analysis can never resolve the issue of continuity versus population replacement in the Aleutians. Nevertheless, based on available evidence from remains dated 4000–300 yr B.P., my reconstruction for the archipelago was that it represented, as do other isolated marginal areas of the world, a true refugium. Regardless of culture and linguistic changes that may have occurred there during the eight millenia preceding contact, and regardless of the reinforcements that may have arrived at various times—perhaps when pressure built up elsewhere in Alaska as a result of culture change and dislocations related to the Neoarctic movements (especially Thule)—Neoarctic impact on the Aleutians was not sufficient to obscure the Paleoarctic genetic heritage of the population. Thus, except for the Near Islanders, the Aleuts encountered by the Russians in the eighteenth century were, essentially, a relic Paleoarctic population, much as eighteenth-century Ainu prior to extensive Wajin mixture represented a relic group descended from the Jomonese.

To summarize: The reconstruction of ethnohistory in the American Northwest presented here agreed in important respects with previous models, notably those of Neumann (1952) and Dumond. In agreement with Turner, I saw the Northwest peopled by two migrations. But contrary to his model the earlier of the two was most strongly represented in Aleut and Na-Dene (not Aleut

came from the North Pacific where sea-mammal hunting had been established two millenia earlier, bearing a technology just as sophisticated, nevertheless exchanged their language (Na-Dene?) for that of the Aleut host population. The scenario gains better credibility if, alternatively, the Paleoarctic immigrants came from the Alaskan interior, particularly in view of the coincidence in timing of this hypothetical movement with the appearance of the AST_t in the hinterland adjacent to the Alaskan coasts. Later dislocations associated with Norton and Thule also may have reinforced the Aleutian population with Paleoarctic genes. In any case, most of the Archipelago became a refugium for a relic Paleoarctic population apparently insulated to a greater degree than some other non-Eskimo populations (i.e., Athapaskans) from Neoarctic gene flow.

That the MMD pattern of Western Aleut was different from that of other Aleut was consistent with other physical anthropological data for this isolate. Moreover, ethnological and archaeological evidence underscores the uniqueness of Western Aleut (Black 1983; Dumond 1987b; McCartney 1984). The cranial MMD affinity of the Near Island skeletal sample to Bering Sea Eskimo rather than to the Paleoarctic stock (Na-Dene and other Aleut) might be explained if the western islands were settled by descendants of a segment of my postulated Neoarctic Aleut founding group which split off before mixing with Paleoarctic people. Unfortunately, because the earliest assemblages from Attu and Agattu dating from about 2600 yr B.P. are apparently reminiscent less of the Aleutian tradition than of the preceding Ocean Bay tradition of 6000–4500 yr B.P. with its widespread affinities through the Kodiak and Alaska Peninsula regions and perhaps the eastern Aleutians (Dumond 1987b:59, 75–77), my explanation for the Near Island cranial relationships raised as many questions as it answered. Alternatively, according to Soviet research (reviewed by Black 1983) the possibility should not be ruled out that Attu and Agattu were settled in part by people navigating eastward from Kamchatka or the Southern Okhotsk Sea area (but see McCartney 1984:135). Urgently needed now to answer these questions is analysis of nonmetric cranial traits of early skeletons from those regions of the Soviet primore and, particularly considering the small N of the Near Island series in the present study, more data for Western Aleut.

and Eskimo), and the most recent one contributed predominantly to Eskimo. Fitting the reconstruction of Laughlin and his co-workers, mine recognized additional evidence of the east-west cline of morphological features along the Aleutian chain, supported the hypothesis of an ancient biological divergence between Aleuts and Eskimos, and underscored the unique importance of the Aleuts as survivors of the Bering Land Bridge.

ACKNOWLEDGMENTS

Financial support for study of the North American collections derived from the following sources: National Research Council of Canada (doctoral fellowship, 1963–64), Boreal Institute of the University of Alberta (1970), Canada Council (1975–77), Advisory Research Council, Queen's University (1973–74) and Faculty of Medicine 1989. Support for study of collections in Japan and the USSR was provided by a 1980–81 leave fellowship from the Social Sciences and Humanities Research Council of Canada. Data analysis was funded during 1981–82 and 1990–91 by the Advisory Research Council of Queen's University.

Institutions and individuals that made this research possible include: University of Toronto, J. E. Anderson; Archaeological Survey of Canada, L. Oschinsky, D. Hughes, J. S. Cybulski; Royal Ontario Museum, W. A. Kenyon; University of Manitoba; University of Alberta, G. Nicks; Simon Fraser University, M. Skinner; U.S. Museum of Natural History, J. L. Angel, D. Ortner, L. St. Hoyme; American Museum, H. Shapiro, I. Tattersall, P. Ward; Field Museum, G. Cole; University of Minnesota, E. Johnson; University of Indiana, G. Neumann; W. H. Over Museum, J. Howard; Tokyo University, K. Hanihara; National Science Museum, Tokyo, B. Yamaguchi; Kyoto University, J. Ikeda; USSR Institute of Ethnography, T. Kuzmina, A. Pestriakov, A. Zubov, V. Alexseev, and A. Kozintsev.

I am grateful to Don Dumond for reading an earlier version of this paper. On his suggestion I changed the term "Inupik," now outmoded, to "Inupiaq," and revised certain references in the ethnohistorical reconstruction to more faithfully reflect the statements and views expressed in the current literature.

REFERENCES CITED

Ackerman, R. E.
  1984 Prehistory of the Asian Eskimo Zone. In *Arctic*, edited by D. Damas, pp. 106–118. Handbook of North American Indians vol. 5, W. G. Sturtevant, general editor. Smithsonian Institution, Washington, D.C.

Alexseev, V. P.
  1979a On Eskimo Origins. *Current Anthropology* 20:158–161.
  1979b Anthropometry of Siberian Peoples. In *The First Americans: Origins, Affinities, and Adaptations*, edited by W. S. Laughlin and A. B. Harper, pp. 57–90. Gustav Fischer, New York.

Anderson, D.
  1968 A Stone Age Campsite at the Gateway to America. *Scientific American* 218(6):24–33.

Black, L.T.
  1983 Some Problems in Interpretation of Aleut Prehistory. *Arctic Anthropology* 29(1):49–78.

Blakeslee, D. J.
  1975 *The Plains Interband Trade System: An Ethnohistoric and Archaeological Investigation*. Ph.D. dissertation, University of Wisconsin, Milwaukee. University Microfilms, Ann Arbor.

Bocquet-Appel, J. P.
  1984 Biological Evolution and History in 19th Century Portugal. In *Multivariate Statistical Methods in Physical Anthropology*, edited by G. N. Van Vark and W. W. Howells, pp. 289–321. Reidel, Dordrecht.

Brace, C. L., L. Yongyi, S. L. Smith, K. D. Hunt, and Z. Zhenbiao
  1989 A Craniofacial Comparison of Circum-Pacific Peoples. Paper presented at the Circum-Pacific Prehistory Conference, Seattle.

Brennan, M. J., and W. W. Howells
  1976 A Craniometric and Linguistic Grouping of Selected North American and Asian Peoples. Manuscript prepared for Handbook of North American Indians, vol. 2.

Buikstra, J. E., S. R. Frankenberg, and L. W. Konigsberg
  1990 Skeletal Biological Distance Studies in American Physical Anthropology. *American Journal of Physical Anthropology* 82:1–7.

Burke, T. D.
  1981 *A Comparative Analysis of Synchronic and Diachronic Variation in Modern Homo Sapiens*. Ph.D. dissertation, University of Colorado, Boulder. University Microfilms, Ann Arbor.

Cadien, J. D., E. F. Harris, W. P. Jones, and L. J. Mandarino
  1976 Biologic Lineages, Skeletal Populations, and Microevolution. *Yearbook of Physical Anthropology* 18:194–201.

Cavalli-Sforza, L. L.
  1986 Population Structure. In *Evolutionary Perspectives and the New Genetics*, edited by

H. Gershowitz, D. L. Rucknagel, and R. E. Tashian, pp. 13–30. Liss, New York.

Cavalli-Sforza, L. L., A. Piazza, P. Menozzi, and J. Mountain
1988 Reconstruction of Human Evolution: Bringing Together Genetic, Archaeological and Linguistic Data. *Proceedings of the National Academy of Science U.S.A.* 85:6002–6006.

Carlson, R. L.
1979 The Early Period on the Central Coast of British Columbia. *Canadian Journal of Archaeology* 3:211–222.
1983 The Far West. In *Early Man in the New World*, edited by R. Shutler, Jr., pp. 73–96. Sage Publications, Beverly Hills.
1989 Circum-Pacific Drift and Coastal British Columbia. Paper prepared for the Circum-Pacific Prehistory Conference, Seattle.

Chard, C. S.
1974 *Northeast Asia in Prehistory*. The University of Wisconsin Press, Madison.

Clark, D. W.
1974 *Koniag Prehistory: Archaeological Investigations at Late Prehistoric Sites on Kodiak Island, Alaska*. Tübinger Monographien Zur Urgeschichte, Bd. 1, Kohlhammer, Stuttgart.
1982 From Just Beyond the Southern Fringe: A Comparison of Norton Culture and the Contemporary Kachemak Tradition of Kodiak Island. *Arctic Anthropology* 19(2):123–132.
1984 Prehistory of the Pacific Eskimo Region. In *Arctic*, edited by D. Damas, pp. 136–148. Handbook of North American Indians, vol. 5, W. G. Sturtevant, general editor. Smithsonian Institution, Washington, D.C.

Curtin, A. J.
1984 *Human Skeletal Remains from Namu (ElSx1): A Descriptive Analysis*. Unpublished master's thesis, Department of Archaeology, Simon Fraser University, Burnaby, B.C.

Dodo, Y.
1980 Appearance of Bony Bridging of the Hypoglossal Canal During the Fetal Period. *Journal of the Anthropological Society of Nippon* 88:229–238.
1986 A Study of the Facial Flatness in Several Cranial Series from East Asia and North America. *Journal of the Anthropological Society of Nippon* 94:81–93.
1987 Supraorbital Foramen and Hypoglossal Canal Bridging: The Two Most Suggestive Nonmetric Traits in Discriminating Major Racial Groupings of Man. *Journal of the Anthropological Society of Nippon* 95:19–35.

Dumond, D. E.
1965 On Eskaleutian Linguistics, Archaeology, and Prehistory. *American Anthropologist* 67:1231–1257.
1977 *The Eskimos and Aleuts*. Thames and Hudson, London.
1982 Trends and Traditions in Alaskan Prehistory: the Place of Norton Culture. *Arctic Anthropology* 19(2):39–51.
1987a A Reexamination of Eskimo-Aleut Prehistory. *American Anthropologist* 89:32–56.
1987b *The Eskimos and Aleuts*. Revised edition. Thames and Hudson, London.

Finnegan, M., and R. M. Rubison
1984 Multivariate Distances and Multivariate Classification Systems Using Non-Metric Traits in Biological Studies. In *Multivariate Statistical Methods in Physical Anthropology*, edited by G. N. Van Vark and W. W. Howells, pp. 169–80. Reidel, Dordrecht.

Fladmark, K. R.
1983 Times and Places: Environmental Correlates of Mid-to-Late Wisconsinan Human Population Expansion in North America. In *Early Man in the New World*, edited by R. Shutler, Jr., pp. 13–41. Sage Publications, Beverly Hills.

Greenberg, J. H., C. G. Turner II, and S. L. Zegura
1986 The Settlement of the Americas: A Comparison of the Linguistic, Dental and Genetic Evidence. *Current Anthropology* 27:477–497.

Grüneberg, H.
1952 Genetical Studies on the Skeleton of the Mouse IV. Quasi-Continuous Variations. *Journal of Genetics* 51:95–114.

Gruhn, R.
1988 Linguistic Evidence in Support of the Coastal Route of Earliest Entry into the New World. *Man* (N.S.) 23:77–100.

Hanihara, K.
1977 Dentition of the Ainu and the Australian Aborigines. In *Orofacial Growth and Development*, edited by A. A. Dahlberg and T. M. Graber, pp. 195–200. Mouton, The Hague.

Harper, A. B.
1975 *Secular Change and Isolate Divergence in the Aleutian Population System*. Ph.D. dissertation, University of Connecticut, Storrs. University Microfilms, Ann Arbor.

Harper, A. B., and W. S. Laughlin
1982 Inquiries into the Peopling of the New World:

Development of Ideas and Recent Advances. In *A History of American Physical Anthropology 1930-1980*, edited by F. Spencer, pp. 281-304. Academic Press, New York.

Hauser, G., and G. F. De Stefano
1989 *Epigenetic Variants of the Human Skull*. E. Schweizerbart'sche Verlagsbuchhandlung, Stuttgart.

Heathcote, G. M.
1981 On Alekseyev on Eskimo Origins. *Current Anthropology* 22(5):582-584.

1986 *Exploratory Human Craniometry of Recent Eskaleutian Regional Groups from the Western Arctic and Subarctic of North America*. BAR International Series 301. Oxford.

Heizer, R. F.
1956 Archaeology of the Uyak Site, Kodiak Island, Alaska. *Anthropological Records* 17(1). University of California Press, Berkeley.

Howells, W. W.
1976 Metrical Analysis in the Problem of Australian Origins. In *The Origin of the Australians*, edited by R. L. Kirk and A. G. Thorne, pp. 141-160. Australian Institute of Aboriginal Studies, Canberra.

1989 *Skull Shapes and the Map: Craniometric Analyses in the Dispersion of Modern Homo*. Papers of the Peabody Museum of Archaeology and Ethnology, Harvard University vol. 79. Harvard University, Cambridge, MA.

Hrdlička, A.
1945 *The Aleutian and Commander Islands and Their Inhabitants*. Wistar Institute, Philadelphia.

Jantz, R. L.
1973 Microevolutionary Change in Arikara Crania: A Multivariate Analysis. *American Journal of Physical Anthropology* 47:467-472.

Jennings, J. D.
1983 Origins. In *Ancient North Americans*, edited by J. D. Jennings, pp. 25-68. W. H. Freeman, San Francisco.

Kirk, R. L.
1979 Genetic Differentiation in Australia and the Western Pacific and Its Bearing on the Origin of the First Americans. In *The First Americans: Origins, Affinities, and Adaptations*, edited by W. S. Laughlin and A. B. Harper, pp. 221-237. Gustav Fischer, New York.

Kozintsev, A. G.
1988 *Ethnographic Cranioscopy: Racial Variations in the Sutures of the Skulls of Modern Man*. Scientific Academy of the U.S.S.R., Nauka, Leningrad. (In Russian, with English summary).

Krauss, M. E.
1973 Eskimo-Aleut. In *Linguistics in North America*, edited by T. A. Sebeok, pp. 796-902. Current Trends in Linguistics, vol. 10, Mouton, The Hague.

1979 Na-Dene and Eskimo-Aleut. In *The Languages of Native America: Historical and Comparative Assessment*, edited by L. Campbell and M. Mithun, pp. 803-901. University of Texas Press, Austin.

Laughlin, W. S.
1951 The Alaska Gateway Viewed from the Aleutian Islands. In *The Physical Anthropology of the American Indian*, edited by W. S. Laughlin, pp. 98-126. Viking Fund, New York.

1963 Eskimos and Aleuts: Their Origin and Evolution. *Science* 142:633-645.

1966 Paleo-Aleut Crania from Port Möller, Alaska Peninsula. *Arctic Anthropology* 3(2):154.

1975 Aleuts: Ecosystem, Holocene History and Siberian Origin. *Science* 189:507-515.

1980 *Aleuts: Survivors of the Bering Land Bridge*. Holt, New York.

Laughlin, W. S., and A. B. Harper
1988 Peopling of the Continents: Australia and America. In *Biological Aspects of Human Migration*, edited by C. G. N. Mascie-Taylor and G. W. Lasker, pp. 14-40. Cambridge Studies in Biological Anthropology No. 2. Cambridge University Press, Cambridge, England.

Laughlin, W. S., and J. B. Jørgensen
1956 Isolate Variation in Greenlandic Eskimo Crania. *Acta Genetica et Statistica Medica* 6:3-12.

Laughlin, W. S., J. B. Jørgensen, and B. Frøhlich
1979 Aleuts and Eskimos: Survivors of the Bering Land Bridge Coast. In *The First Americans: Origins, Affinities, and Adaptations*, edited by W. S. Laughlin and A. B. Harper, pp. 91-104. Gustav Fischer, New York.

Laughlin, W. S., A. P. Okladnikov, A. P. Derevyanko, A. B. Harper, and I. V. Atseev
1976 Early Siberians from Lake Baikal and Alaskan Population Affinities. *American Journal of Physical Anthropology* 45:651-660.

Levin, M. G.
1963 *Ethnic Origins of the Peoples of Northeastern Asia*. Arctic Institute of North America, Anthropology of the North, Translations from Russian Sources vol. 3, edited by H. N. Michael. University of Toronto Press, Toronto.

McCammon, R. B., and G. Wenninger
  1970 *The Dendrograph*. Computer Contribution No. 48. State Geological Survey, University of Kansas, Lawrence.

McCartney, A. P.
  1984 Prehistory of the Aleutian Region. In *Arctic*, edited by D. Damas, pp. 119-135. Handbook of North American Indians vol. 5, W. G. Sturtevant, general editor. Smithsonian Institution, Washington, D.C.

McGhee, R.
  1976 Parsimony Isn't Everything: An Alternative View of Eskaleutian Linguistics and Prehistory. *Canadian Archaeological Association Bulletin* 8:62-81.
  1984 Thule Prehistory of Canada. In *Arctic*, edited by D. Damas, pp. 369-376. Handbook of North American Indians vol. 5, W. G. Sturtevant, general editor. Smithsonian Institution, Washington, D.C.

Moorrees, C. F. A.
  1957 *The Aleut Dentition*. Harvard University Press, Cambridge, MA.

Nei, M. and A. K. Roychoudhury
  1982 Genetic Relationship and Evolution of Human Races. *Evolutionary Biology* 14:1-60.

Neumann, G. K.
  1952 Archeology and Race in the American Indian. In *Archeology of Eastern United States*, edited by J. B. Griffin, pp. 13-34. University of Chicago Press, Chicago.

Okada, H., and B. Yamaguchi
  1976 Further Human Cranial Remains Excavated in 1974 at the Hot Springs Village Site, Port Moller, Alaska Peninsula. *Bulletin of the National Science Museum, Tokyo, Series D (Anthropology)* 2:25-35.

Ossenberg, N. S.
  1969 *Discontinuous Morphological Variation in the Human Cranium*. Unpublished Ph.D. dissertation, Department of Anatomy, University of Toronto, Toronto.
  1970 The Influence of Artificial Cranial Deformation on Discontinuous Morphological Traits. *American Journal of Physical Anthropology* 33:357-372.
  1974a The Mylohyoid Bridge: An Anomalous Derivative of Meckel's Cartilage. *Journal of Dental Research* 53:77-82.
  1974b Origin and Relationships of Woodland Peoples: the Evidence of Cranial Morphology. In *Aspects of Upper Great Lakes Anthropology: Papers in Honor of Lloyd A. Wilford*, edited by E. Johnson, pp. 15-39. Minnesota Prehistoric Archaeology Series No. 11. Minnesota Historical Society, St. Paul.
  1976 Within Race and Between Race Distances in Population Studies Based on Discrete Traits of the Human Skull. *American Journal of Physical Anthropology* 45:701-716.
  1977 Congruence of Distance Matrices Based on Cranial Discrete Traits, Cranial Measurements and Linguistic-Geographic Criteria in Five Alaskan Populations. *American Journal of Physical Anthropology* 47:93-98.
  1981a An Argument for the Use of Total Side Frequencies of Bilateral Nonmetric Skeletal Traits in Population Distance Analysis: the Regression of Symmetry on Incidence. *American Journal of Physical Anthropology* 54:471-479.
  1981b Mandibular Torus: A Synthesis of New and Previously Reported Data and a Discussion of Its Cause. In *Contributions to Physical Anthropology 1978-80*, edited by J. S. Cybulski, pp. 1-52. National Museum of Man Mercury Series. Archaeological Survey of Canada, Ottawa.
  1986a Isolate Conservatism and Hybridization in the Population History of Japan: the Evidence of Nonmetric Cranial Traits. In *Prehistoric Hunter-Gatherers in Japan: New Research Methods*, edited by T. Akazawa and C. M. Aikens, pp. 199-215. The University Museum, The University of Tokyo, Bulletin No. 27. University of Tokyo Press, Tokyo.
  1986b Temporal Crest Canal: Case Report and Statistics on a Rare Mandibular Variant. *Oral Surgery, Oral Medicine, Oral Pathology* 62:10-12.
  1987 Retromolar Foramen of the Human Mandible. *American Journal of Physical Anthropology* 73:119-128.
  1989 Nonmetric Traits of the Skull Help Reconstruct Prehistory in Northwest North America. Paper presented at the Circum-Pacific Prehistory Conference, Seattle, WA.

Oswalt, W. H.
  1967 *Alaskan Eskimos*. Chandler, San Francisco.

Pardoe, C.
  1991 Evolution and Isolation in Tasmania. *Current Anthropology* 32:1-21.

Rogers, R. A.
  1985 Glacial Geography and Native North American Languages. *Quaternary Research* 23:130-137.

Salzano, F. M.
  1985 The Peopling of the Americas as Viewed from South America. In *Out of Asia: Peopling the Americas and the Pacific*, edited by R. Kirk and

E. Szathmary, pp. 19–29. The Journal of Pacific History, Canberra.

Saunders, S. R.
1989 Nonmetric Skeletal Variation. In *Reconstruction of Life from the Skeleton*, edited by Y. Iscan and K. Kennedy, pp. 95–108. Alan R. Liss, New York.

Sjøvold, T.
1977 *Non-Metrical Divergence Between Skeletal Populations; the Theoretical Foundation and Biological Importance of C. A. B. Smith's Mean Measure of Divergence*. OSSA International Journal of Skeletal Research No. 4, Supplement 1. University of Stockholm Osteological Research Laboratory, Solna.
1984 A Report on the Heritability of Some Cranial Measurements and Non-Metric Traits. In *Multivariate Statistical Methods in Physical Anthropology*, edited by G. N. Van Vark and W. W. Howells, pp. 223–245. Reidel, Dordrecht.

Szathmary, E. J. E.
1979a Eskimo and Indian Contact: Examination of Craniometric, Anthropometric and Genetic Evidence. *Arctic Anthropology* 16(2):23–48.
1979b Blood Groups of Siberians, Eskimos, and Subarctic and Northwest Coast Indians: The Problem of Origins and Genetic Relationships. In *The First Americans: Origins, Affinities, and Adaptations*, edited by W. S. Laughlin and A. B. Harper, pp. 185–209. Gustav Fischer, New York.
1984 Human Biology of the Arctic. In *Arctic*, edited by D. Damas, pp. 64–71. Handbook of North American Indians, vol. 5, W. G. Sturtevant, general editor. Smithsonian Institution, Washington, D.C.
1985 Peopling of North America: Clues from Genetic Studies. In *Out of Asia: Peopling the Americas and the Pacific*, edited by R. Kirk, and E. Szathmary, pp. 79–104. The Journal of Pacific History, Canberra.

Szathmary, E. J. E., and N. S. Ossenberg
1978 Are the Biological Differences Between North American Indians and Eskimos Truly Profound? *Current Anthropology* 19:673–701.

Turner, C. G. II
1967 *The Dentition of Arctic Peoples*. Ph.D. dissertation, University of Wisconsin, Madison. University Microfilms, Ann Arbor.
1976 Dental Evidence on the Origins of the Ainu and Japanese. *Science* 193:911–913.
1983 Dental Evidence for the Peopling of the Americas. In *Early Man in the New World*, edited by R. Shutler, Jr., pp. 147–157. Sage Publications, Beverly Hills.
1985 The Dental Search for Native American Origins. In *Out of Asia: Peopling the Americas and the Pacific*, edited by R. Kirk and E. Szathmary, pp. 31–78. The Journal of Pacific History, Canberra.
1986 The First Americans: The Dental Evidence. *National Geographic Research* 2:37–46.
1989 Teeth and Prehistory in Asia. *Scientific American* 260(2):88–96.

Turner, C. G. II, and J. Bird
1981 Dentition of Chilean Paleo-Indians and Peopling of the Americas. *Science* 212:1053–1055.

Turner, C. G. II, P. Mamula, and C. J. Utermohle
1982 New Anthropological Evidence Bearing on the Issue of Neo-Aleut Origins. *Arctic Anthropology* 19:127–140.

Utermohle, C. J.
1984 *From Barrow Eastward: Cranial Variation of the Eastern Eskimo*. Ph.D. dissertation, Arizona State University. University Microfilms, Ann Arbor.

Weiss, K. M.
1988 In Search of Times Past: Gene Flow and Invasion in the Generation of Human Diversity. In *Biological Aspects of Human Migration*, edited by C. G. N. Mascie-Taylor and G. W. Lasker, pp. 130–166. Cambridge University Press, Cambridge, MA.

Woodbury, A. C.
1984 Eskimo and Aleut Languages. In *Arctic*, edited by D. Damas, pp. 49–63. Handbook of North American Indians vol. 5, W. G. Sturtevant, general editor. Smithsonian Institution, Washington, D.C.

Workman, W. B.
1980 Continuity and Change in the Prehistoric Record from Southern Alaska. In *Alaska Native Culture and History*, edited by Y. Kotani and W. B. Workman, pp. 49–101. Senri Ethnological Studies No. 4. National Museum of Ethnology, Osaka.
1982 Beyond the Southern Frontier: The Norton Culture and the Western Kenai Peninsula. *Arctic Anthropology* 19(2):101–122.
1988 The Development of Sea Mammal Hunting Among Prehistoric North Pacific Cultures. Paper presented at the Symposium on Human-Animal Relationships, Abashiri, Hokkaido.

Wright, T. L.
1987 *The Association Between Mandibular Torus and the*

Transverse Component of Masticatory Force: A Biomechanical Analysis Based on Eskimo Skulls. Unpublished master's thesis, Department of Anatomy, Queen's University, Kingston.

Yamaguchi, B.
 1977 A Comparative Study of the Skulls of the Ontario Iroquoians and of Asiatic Populations. *Bulletin of the National Science Museum, Tokyo, Series D (Anthropology)* 3:23-35.

Zegura, S. L.
 1975 Taxonomic Congruence in Eskimoid Populations. *American Journal of Physical Anthropology* 43:271–284.

Modelling Ancient Population Relationships from Modern Population Genetics

EMŐKE J. E. SZATHMARY
Dean
Faculty of Social Science
The University of Western Ontario
London, Ontario N6A 5C2
Canada

On the basis of dental evidence, Turner (1983) suggested that there have been three waves of migration of peoples from Asia to North America. One occurred between 40,000 to 16,000 years ago ("Paleoindian" wave), another 14,000 to 12,000 years ago ("Na-Dene" wave) and the last some 9000 years ago ("Eskimo-Aleut" wave). Geneticists using highly informative genetic systems such as Immunoglobulin Gm (Williams et al. 1985) concur with this tripartite division, and have provided scenarios whereby current patterns of gene distribution could have come about in the descendants of the claimed three founding groups. Others (Szathmary 1984) suggest that the available evidence permits the deduction only that there may have been populations, south of the Wisconsin ice sheets as well as northwest of them, which underwent genetic differentiation separately. However, this evidence does not permit conclusions about the number of "waves of migration" into North America.

To test whether the Gm distribution supports the "three-migration" model, Gm haplotype frequencies were used to derive genetic distances among populations, and these have been displayed in dendrograms. There are clear problems with the approach, stemming mainly from the fact that a single locus cannot provide conclusive evidence about biological history. The results show that Ojibwa and Cree groups of the Subarctic culture area and Haida of the Queen Charlotte Islands cluster with American Indians resident in the Southwest culture area (Hopi, Papago, Pima, Walapai, Zuni). However, Athapaskan-speaking groups, whether in the Southwest or the Subarctic (Apache, Chipewyan, Dogrib, Navajo) are interspersed in clusters that include Eskimos. This distribution is consistent with a southern versus northwestern derivation of different groups of Indians. The pattern, however, is not consistent with Turner's model of the occupation of the Americas or Szathmary's model of intracontinental genetic relationships regarding the affinities of the Haida (classed in the Na-Dene phylum). Information from multiple loci is required to resolve these issues.

Until 1976, none of the models of Eskimo origins had been tested with genetic data. In that year, genetic distance analyses, based on 8 polymorphic blood group loci (24 genes), were undertaken on data from north Asiatics (Mongoloids), Eskimos, Siberians, and Indian peoples of the Northwest Coast, and the eastern and western Subarctic. Pooled genetic data from Eskimos and from northern Indians were also compared with aggregate data available in Cavalli-Sforza and Bodmer (1971) for "Mongoloids," "Caucasoids," and "Negroids." The results did not support any of the origin models. They showed, rather, that Eskimos and Indians were more closely related to each other than either was to any of the three major races (Szathmary 1979). Examined at a more local level, it was clear that Eskimos in particular were close to speakers of the following languages: Haida, Tlingit and Northern Athapaskan—that is, people who have been categorized linguistically as members of the Na-Dene phylum (Voegelin and Voegelin, 1966). Northern Algonkians were more remote, as were the Nootka, a sea-faring people of Vancouver Island (Szathmary, 1979).

Subsequent work with the anatomist Nancy Ossenberg showed that the closeness between Eskimos and peoples of the Na-Dene phylum was also demonstrable with discreet traits of the skull (Szathmary and Ossenberg 1978). Further independent study, with better data from Siberian groups (see criticism in Ferrell et al. 1981), and an increase in the number of genetic systems in the test battery (now 14 loci) confirmed that some Indians (Northern Athapaskans) were genetically closer to Eskimos than were other Indians (Algonkians) (Szathmary 1981). The linking of this information with archaeological evidence suggested that Algonkian-speakers could be the descendants of populations south of the Wisconsin ice sheets, while Athapaskans were of a northwestern derivation, perhaps of populations that inhabited Beringia during Wisconsin times (Szathmary 1984).

While I was pursuing my own interest in the origins and affinities of northern peoples, others were looking at the broader issue of the peopling of the Americas. An origin model that has received much attention recently is the "three waves of migration" hypothesis (Greenberg et al. 1986). This model derives from Turner's (1983, 1985) extensive studies of dental morphology in North and South America, which showed three broad patterns of dental variation, each being a slightly altered form of a widely distributed dental pattern in North Asia ("Sinodonty"). Turner argued that the variability in the Americas reflected population ancestry. In his view, three distinct populations entered North America from Asia at three different points in time. In his (1983) original formulation the earliest were the "Paleoindians," a group he believed to have moved into the New World between 40,000 to 16,000 years ago. The "Na-Dene" entered next, some 12,000 to 14,000 years ago, and the Eskimo-Aleut ancestors arrived last, approximately 9000 years ago. Greenberg's tripartite classification of Native American languages fits with this schema, but the genetic evidence is less conclusive (Greenberg et al. 1986). The strongest support cited by Greenberg et al. (1986) is based on the distribution of Immunoglobulin Gm haplotypes in Eskimos and Amerindians (Williams et al. 1985).

The latter study detailed the immunoglobulin Gm and Km gene frequencies of over 5000 southwestern Amerindians, representing four different cultural groups. Comparison of this material with published data from other Indians and Eskimos led Williams et al. (1985) to conclude that the three-migration hypothesis into America was plausible. The argument hinged on the presence and claimed absence of specific Immunoglobulin Gm haplotypes from the ancestral groups of Paleoindians, the Na-Dene, and the Eskimo-Aleuts. Williams et al. (1985) suggested that the ancestral Paleoindians likely had two Gm haplotypes ($Gm^{1;21}$ and $Gm^{1;2;21}$). These were also present in the ancestors of the Na-Dene, along with a third haplotype ($Gm^{1;11;13}$). This latter haplotype was retained by the ancestors of the Eskimo-Aleuts, but the cluster $Gm^{1;2;21}$ had been lost. In their opinion, this evidence did not support the conclusions of Szathmary and Ossenberg (1978) "that the Na-Dene are closer to the Eskimo than to other Native Americans" (Williams et al. 1985:17). On the other hand, they also felt that "one would not want to make one genetic system the definitive statement about Native American origins and relations" (Williams et al. 1985:17).

The purpose of this paper is to consider the reconstruction of ancient population relationships from modern genetic data. That such reconstruction is possible has been amply demonstrated in many studies that have addressed the phylogeny of related species (e.g., Nei 1987). Within-species determinations of biologic history are more problematic (Nei and Roychoudhury 1982:3), but this does not mean that good results cannot be obtained through careful selection and handling of the data (Cavalli-Sforza et al. 1988). My emphasis here will be on the problems and pitfalls associated with data selection, and the subsequent impact of different kinds of data on genetic distances and the dendrograms that display these distances in two-dimensional space. The data I employ are the Immunoglobulins Gm and Km, given the importance the former system has had among proponents of the "three-migration" model of the occupation of the Americas.

METHODS

Selection of the Genetic Distance Statistic

In the study of human population relationships, two kinds of genetic distance statistics have been widely employed. Cavalli-Sforza and Edwards' genetic distance (1967) has different forms, as does Nei's (1972). There is an extensive literature comparing these and other genetic distance approaches (e.g., Crow and Denniston 1974; Goodman 1974; Weiner and Huizinga 1972). The advantages of the standard distance D have been widely described (Nei 1975; Nei 1987), so that even Cavalli-Sforza et al. (1988) employ D in their work. Interestingly, in the study of within-species variation, it does not seem to matter much which statistic is used, in spite of the fact that the process through which evolutionary divergence occurs is modelled differently in the two approaches. For example, Cavalli-Sforza et al. (1988) found a significant and high correlation (r = 0.86) between their chord distance and Nei's standard distance D. Similar findings were observed by Szathmary (1979).

Nei's standard distance D (1972) is the statistic used in this paper. To calculate D, all that is required are gene frequencies for alleles at the same locus in two different populations. Gene frequencies range in value between 0.0 (gene absent) and 1.0 (gene is fixed in everyone). Thus the restriction is not that a gene is absent from a population, but that the locus in question has been tested for a given variant. The derivation of D depends on the probability that two alleles at the same locus in two different populations are identical. Thus, if X and Y are different populations, the normalized probability that two genes, one from each group, are identical at locus N is

$$I_n = \Sigma x_i y_i / \sqrt{(\Sigma x_i^2 y_i^2)}$$

where x_i and y_i are the frequencies of the ith allele in populations X and Y, respectively. The value of I is 0.0 if no alleles are held in common between populations X and Y. Its value is 1.0 if the alleles in X and Y occur in identical frequencies. When several loci are considered, the mean genetic identity is

$$I = J_{XY} / \sqrt{(J_X J_Y)}$$

where J_{XY}, J_X, and J_Y are the arithmetic means over all loci of $\Sigma x_i y_i$, Σx_i^2, and Σy_i^2. The probability of having different alleles over all loci is given by $D_X = 1 - J_X$, $D_Y = 1 - J_Y$, and $D_{XY} = 1 - J_{XY}$, respectively. The mean genetic distance is given by $D = -\log_e I$.

Clearly, the standard genetic distance D depends only upon gene frequencies. D also has a specific genetic meaning when the data used in its derivation are frequencies of protein and enzyme alleles. This meaning (the number of gene substitutions since the split of an ancestral group into its daughter populations) does not apply, for example, when blood group genes, or HLA antigen genes are considered. However, because D is based on probabilities, it always has a statistical meaning, and is thus a convenient statistical measure of accumulated genetic differences between pairs of populations.

The logic behind the genetic distance approach is an evolutionary one. It is assumed in Nei's (1972) model that at some point in time an ancestral group split into two daughter populations. Mutations accumulated within each daughter group over time, and random genetic drift also altered allele frequencies within each daughter group. Eventually, each daughter population also split, and mutation and genetic drift again accumulated between the separated descendant groups. Genetic distances measure these accumulated genetic differences between groups at one particular point in time. It is worth emphasizing that the rate of evolutionary change is assumed to be constant over time in this model, and it is also assumed that once a population splits, the daughter groups do not have any genetic exchange between them. Gene frequency change because of admixture, then, is precluded in the model, as is the operation of natural selection (Nei 1975, 1987). Assumptions inherent in the model have been tested, with results summarized in Nei (1987).

Construction of Dendrograms

Once a set of pairwise genetic distances has been determined for a set of populations, the distances can be clustered to obtain a two-dimensional "tree" diagram. Such dendrograms at minimum permit a visual display of the genetic distances, although in the ideal situation they display the path of evolution that led to the extant relationships among the populations (i.e., the trees display phylogeny). Because genetic differentiation of human populations does not fit all of the assumptions of the evolutionary models (e.g., gene flow *does occur* between daughter populations), it is not possible to be certain that the branchings of a tree reflect the actual paths of evolution. Although there is disagreement among population geneticists on this issue (e.g., Cavalli-Sforza et al. 1988), Nei thinks it is inappropriate to refer to dendrograms derived for human groups as phylogenetic trees (Nei and Roychoudhury 1982).

Several methods are available for dendrogram construction (Cavalli-Sforza and Edwards 1967; Cavalli-Sforza and Piazza 1963; Kidd and Cavalli-Sforza 1971; Sokal and Sneath 1973), and numerous technical papers have undertaken assessment of the accuracy of computed trees (e.g., Chakraborty 1977; Chakraborty et al. 1980; Nei et al. 1983; Nei et al. 1985; Sourdis and Nei 1988). Sokal and Sneath's (1963) unweighted pair group method (UPGMA) yields trees with correct branch lengths, provides a root without requiring an external referent, and is not costly in computer time. This method (Szathmary 1981, 1984) was used to derive the dendrograms in this paper.

Immunoglobulin Data and the Populations Selected for Analysis

Nine different genetic distance analyses were undertaken with the following data:

1. The first batch consisted of Gm haplotype frequencies uncorrected for European admixture for all samples in Table 18 of Williams et al. (1985), excluding those in which the sample size was less than 100. The sole exception to this criterion were the Mescalero Apaches (N=82). The groups included six samples of Athapaskan-speaking peoples: two Navajo (Gallup and Keams Canyon), two Apache (San Carlos and Mescalero), and two northern Athapaskan tribes (Dogrib and Chipewyan). Seven samples were obtained from the following Eskimos: Siberian (New Chaplino), St. Lawrence Island (Bering Sea), Igloolik (Canada), Thule (northwest Greenland), Augpilagtok Island (west Greenland), southwest Greenland, and Angmagssalik (east Greenland). The Asiatics included two groups of Chukchi (Reindeer and Coast) from the Kamchatka and Chukotka peninsulas, respectively, and two Uralic-speaking peoples, the forest Nenets (distributed north of the Ob river and southwest of the Taz river on the West Siberian plain), and the Nganasan (Taymyr peninsula).

    To increase North American Indian representation, Gm data from the following populations were added to this data set. Algonkian-speakers: Ojibwa (Szathmary et al. 1974), Cree (Schanfield, cited in Sukernik and Osipova 1982); Uto-Aztecan–speakers: Pima, Papago, and Walapai in Table 13 of Williams et al. (1985); Zuni and Hopi from the same table. Of these added samples, all but the Hopi exceeded a sample size of 100.

2. The second batch of data included all the samples named in (1), but with the Gm haplotype frequencies corrected for European admixture (Williams et al. 1985). The correction of non-Athapaskan gene frequencies followed the methods described in Williams et al. (1985).

3. The number of samples compared was reduced by restricting the samples to those that provided information on the Gm and Km systems. Frequencies at both loci were left uncorrected for non-Indian admixture. In addition the Keams Navajo and the Mescalero Apache samples were deleted, leaving in the data set only the two larger samples of Navajos and Apaches, respectively. Km frequencies were obtained from Williams et al. (1985), Szathmary et al. (1974), Schanfield (cited in Sukernik and Osipova 1982), and Steinberg et al. (1974). The imposition of the Km requirement on the data meant that three Eskimo groups were lost from the population array. Fortunately, two Eskimo samples unavailable to Williams et al. (1985) had been tested for Gm and Km antigens, and these were added to the data set: North Alaskan (Matsumoto et al. 1982) and South Alaskan Eskimo (Peterson et al. 1986). Km data for North Alaska were obtained from Mackenzie delta Eskimos (Schanfield, personal communication 1986), a Canadian group that has been shown to be closely related to North Alaskans (Szathmary and Ossenberg 1978).

4. Data set (3) was also analyzed with Km data deleted.

5. To see how inclusion of Gm data affects conclusions based on earlier studies, the 11 populations for which information on 14 loci was available (Szathmary 1981) were analyzed with Gm (15 loci) and then Gm and Km (16 loci) data added. The following samples were examined. Eskimos: Siberian, St. Lawrence Island, South Alaskan, North Alaskan, and Central Arctic; Indian: Northern Athapaskan, Northern Algonkian; Asiatic: "Mongoloid" (Steinberg and Kageyama 1970), Ainu, and Nenets (Nentzi: Sukernik et al. 1980). The Gm frequencies of Northern Athapaskans were based on Kutchin (villages of Ft. Yukon, Arctic Village, and Beaver, Alaska (Matsumoto et al. 1982), Chipewyan (Schanfield, cited in Sukernik and Osipova 1982), and Dogrib (Szathmary et al. 1983). Where possible, gene frequencies were recalculated from the literature with MAXLIK (Reed and Schull 1968). Km frequencies were available for Chipewyan and Dogrib only. Northern Algonkian Gm and Km frequencies are those of the Pikangikum Ojibwa (Szathmary et al. 1974) and the Cree (Schanfield, cited in Sukernik and Osipova 1982).

6. Because pooling of data can sometimes obscure details of population affinities, the data in (5) were run exactly as described, but with the Northern Athapaskan frequencies replaced by the two tribes for which information is available for 15 loci (Kutchin and Dogrib). The 16-locus analysis was not undertaken because the Km data for the Kutchin are unknown.

7. Field et al.'s (1988) data on Haida Gm frequencies came to attention after all original calculations had been completed, and resultant figures were drawn. Nevertheless, calculations (2) and (4) were repeated with this data, with the correction for admixture employing the gene frequencies employed by Williams et al. (1985) rather than those used by Field et al. (1988).

RESULTS

The three-migration model predicts the clustering of Eskimos, then Na-Dene (Haida, Tlingit, Athapaskan), then all other Indians, and lastly, Asiatics. Szathmary's (1984) model predicts the grouping of Athapaskans with Eskimos rather than with other Amerindians. Members

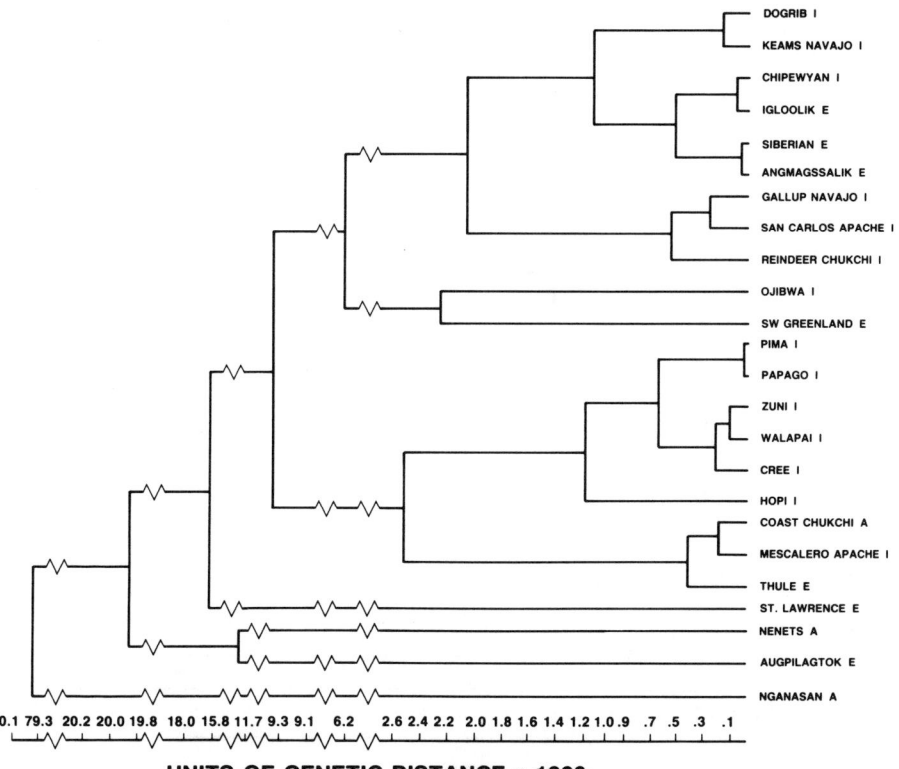

Figure 1. Dendrogram of genetic distances among 24 populations. Nei's standard distance, D, is based on the Immunoglobulin Gm system. The haplotype frequencies are not corrected for European gene flow. Distances are read along the horizontal axis. Vertical positioning of populations is irrelevant. The genetic distance between any two populations is the sum of the lengths of the horizontal lines that connect the two groups. I=Indian, E=Eskimo, A=Asiatic.

of the Na-Dene phylum (e.g., Haida) are also predicted to cluster with Athapaskans and Eskimos. In the interpretation of the dendrograms, detail at the first-order clustering level is ignored, and only larger aggregations (i.e., clusters within clusters) are considered.

Figure 1 shows the tree derived from genetic distances based on Gm frequencies in 24 populations. Contrary to the tripartite model, the Eskimos do not form a distinct unit; rather, their largest aggregate includes only four samples (Siberian Eskimo, Igloolik, Angmagssalik, and southwest Greenland Eskimo), and these are interspersed in a cluster that includes the Ojibwa and all Athapaskans except the Mescalero Apache. The other three Eskimo groups are scattered throughout the dendrogram. The only cluster that includes no Eskimos or Athapaskans is the unit that includes Pima, Papago, Zuni, Walapai, and Hopi, all from the American Southwest, and the Cree from Canada. The Ojibwa who should be in this latter cluster according to the tripartite model are, as noted above, linked instead to the southwest Greenland Eskimos.

Figure 2, based on genetic distances derived from Gm frequencies corrected for European gene flow, again does not fit the three-migration model. Although the Ojibwa now cluster with the southwestern Indian group, three Eskimo populations are now misclassified, and the Mescalero Apache are still separated from other Athapaskans. Neither of the Chukchi groups links with an Asian population.

Figure 3, the dendrogram based on distances derived from Gm frequencies in 21 populations, shows a bipartite division. One large cluster includes all Athapaskans, six of the seven Eskimo groups, and all Chukchi. Another cluster unites all other Indians. These two aggregates are linked, and to them is added the anomalous grouping of the western Siberian Nenets and the west Greenland Augpilagtok Eskimos. The Nganasan do not link with the Nenets. Although this tree does not fit the three-migration model, it corresponds more closely with expectations arising from Szathmary's work (1981, 1984), which predicts a closer linking of Athapaskans and Eskimos (and Chukchi) with each other than with any other Indian group. Indeed, only one population (Augpilagtok Eskimo) of the twenty-one here is misclassified under her expectation.

Figure 4 is based on genetic distances derived from Gm and Km frequencies of 21 populations. This tree is more anomalous than that shown in Figure 3. Several populations are now misclassified, whether under the three-migration model or Szathmary's model.

Figure 5 is based on genetic distances derived from frequencies at 15 loci: ABO, RH, MNSs, Diego, Duffy,

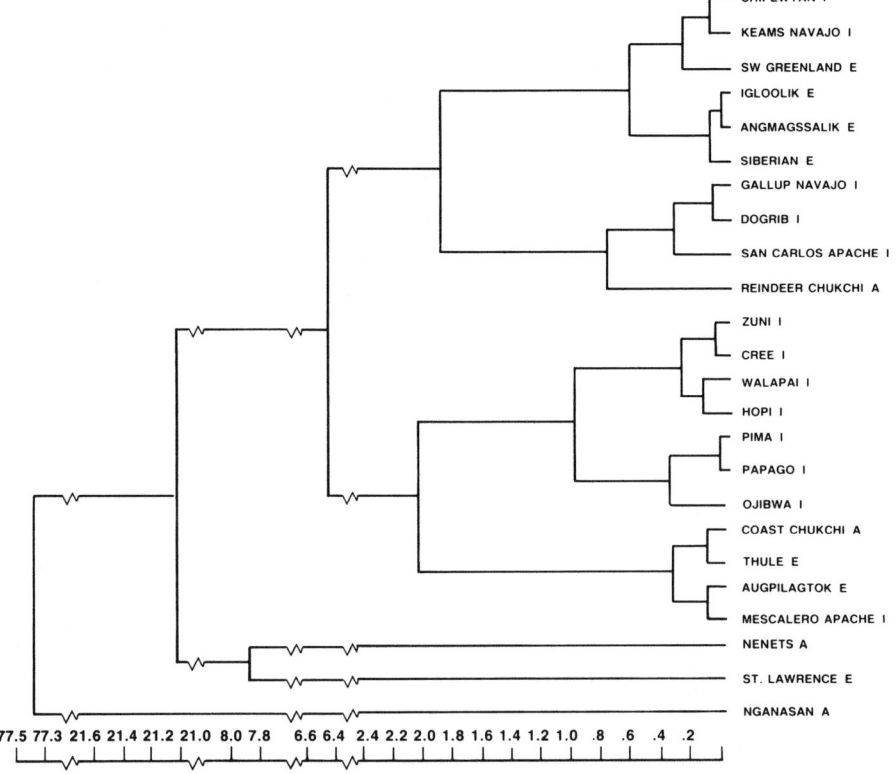

Figure 2. Dendrogram of genetic distances among 24 populations. Nei's standard distance, D, is based on the Immunoglobulin Gm system. The haplotype frequencies are corrected for European gene flow. I = Indian, E = Eskimo, A = Asiatic.

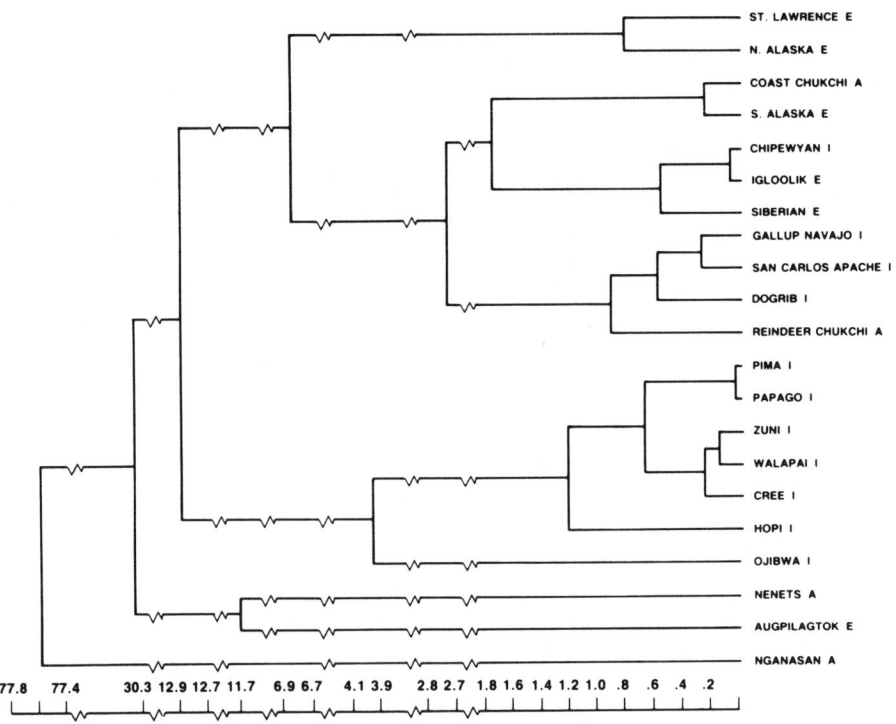

Figure 3. Dendrogram depicting genetic distances (Nei's standard distance D) among 21 populations; data are uncorrected for gene flow. D is based on Gm frequencies only, but the populations shown have been tested for Gm and Km allotypes. I = Indian, E = Eskimo, A = Asiatic.

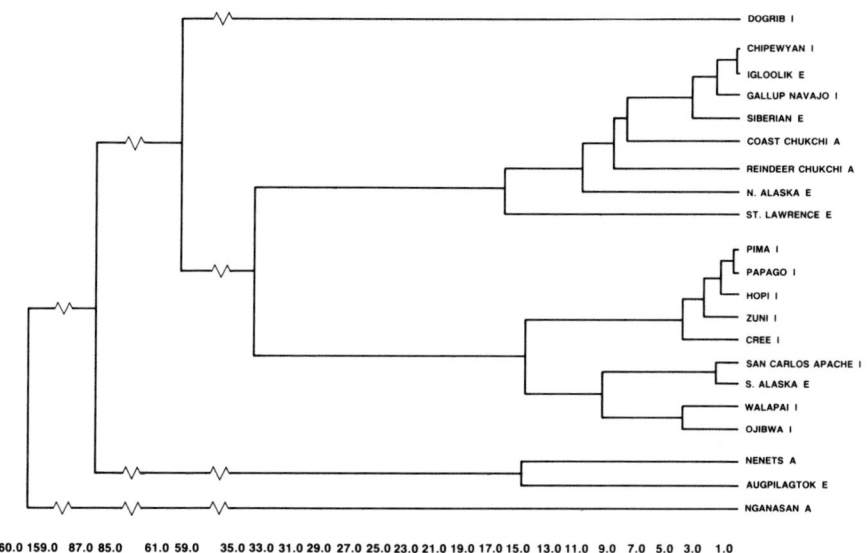

Figure 4. Dendrogram showing genetic distances (Nei's standard distance D) among populations. Genetic distances are based on Gm and Km frequencies. I = Indian, E = Eskimo, A = Asiatic.

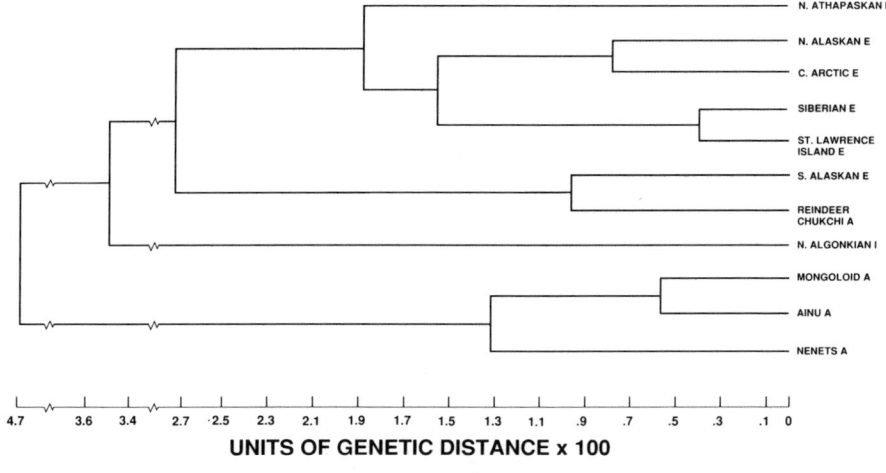

Figure 5. Dendrogram of genetic distances (Nei's standard distance D) between 11 populations. The distances are based on gene frequencies at 15 loci: ABO, RH, MNSs, Diego, Duffy, Kell, Kidd, P, Gc, Hp, ACP, AK, PGD, PGM_1, and Gm. I=Indian, E=Eskimo, A=Asiatic.

Kell, Kidd, P, Gc, Hp, ACP, AK, PGD, PGM_1, and Gm. Northern Athapaskans are part of the cluster that includes all Eskimos and the Reindeer Chukchi. Northern Algonkians are more distant, but closer to the Americans than is the cluster comprised of "Mongoloids," Ainu, and Siberian Nenets. The tree does not fit with the three-migration model, but does show that Athapaskans are closer to Eskimos than to other Indians.

Figure 6 contains the same populations as Figure 5, but is based on distances derived from the 15 loci named above plus Km. The addition of this one genetic system removes the Northern Athapaskans from the Eskimo cluster and groups them with the Northern Algonkians. This dendrogram does not fit either of the models considered in this paper, but accords with the well-known textbook descriptions of Eskimos (and Chukchi) being distinct from Indians.

Figure 7 is based on the 15 loci enumerated for Figure 5, and includes tribal Indian groups rather than pooled Northern Athapaskan and Northern Algonkian samples. This dendrogram does show a tripartite separation of populations: an Eskimo (and Chukchi) cluster linked at a higher level to an Athapaskan (Dogrib and Kutchin) cluster, and these then linked to an Algonkian (Cree and Northern Ojibwa) cluster. More remote are the three remaining Asian populations.

Figure 8 is the dendrogram based on calculations that involve the Haida of the Queen Charlotte Islands. All Gm frequencies of the 25 populations displayed in this dendrogram have been corrected for gene flow. Contrary to the three-migration model, contrary to Szathmary's (1979) finding based on 8 blood group systems, and contrary to Szathmary and Ossenberg's observations based on 11 blood group and serum protein

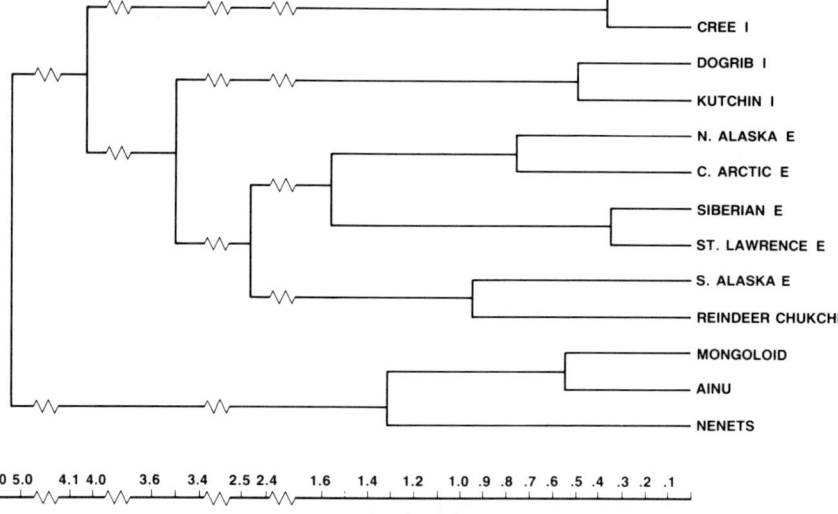

Figure 6. Dendrogram of genetic distances (Nei's standard distance D) between 11 populations. The distances are based on gene frequencies at 16 loci: ABO, Rh, MNSs, Diego, Duffy, Kell, Kidd, P, Gc, Hp, ACP, AK, PGD, PGM_1, Gm, and Km. I=Indian, E=Eskimo, A=Asiatic.

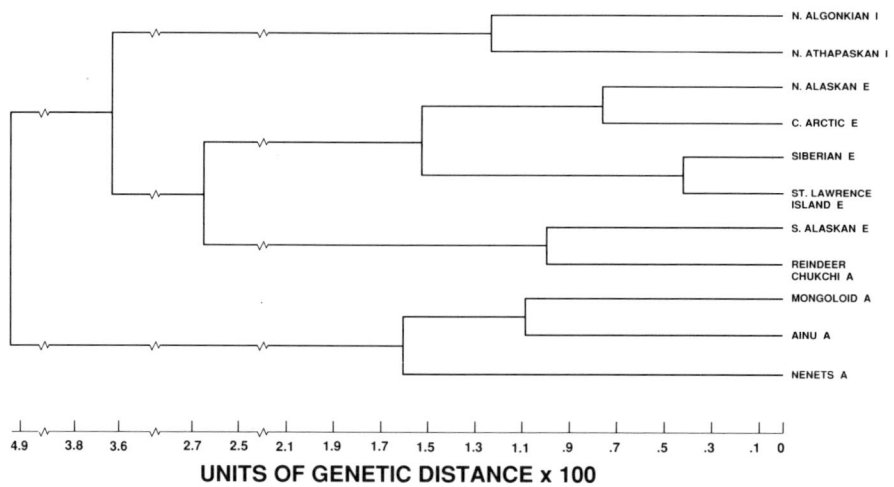

Figure 7. Dendrogram of genetic distances (Nei's standard distance D) between 13 populations. The distances are based on gene frequencies at 15 loci: ABO, RH, MNSs, Diego, Duffy, Kell, Kidd, P, Gc, Hp, ACP, AK, PGD, PGM_1, and Gm. I=Indian, E=Eskimo, other=Asiatic.

systems, the Haida do not form a cluster with Athapaskans, nor with Athapaskans and Eskimos, when only their Gm frequencies are examined.

Haida data were also included in a repeat of calculation (4) (only those populations for which Gm and Km data are available). The resultant dendrogram is not displayed here, but the Haida's position remains unchanged: they still cluster with Ojibwa and the southwestern Amerindian group (plus Cree) as in Figure 8. In this dendrogram the St. Lawrence Island Eskimos and the North Alaskan Eskimos are also displaced from their northern position (see Figure 3) and are relocated outside the large cluster that links the two groups of Native Americans.

DISCUSSION

Population Affinities and the Reliability of Genetic Distance Approaches

The findings in this paper show clearly the need for caution when attempting to determine population affinities with genetic data. The reliability of deductions is dependent on the statistics used to make decisions, but the statistics are dependent on the amounts of information available.

The analyses carried out in this paper demonstrate that the use of a single genetic system to classify populations is not particularly desirable. As the differences

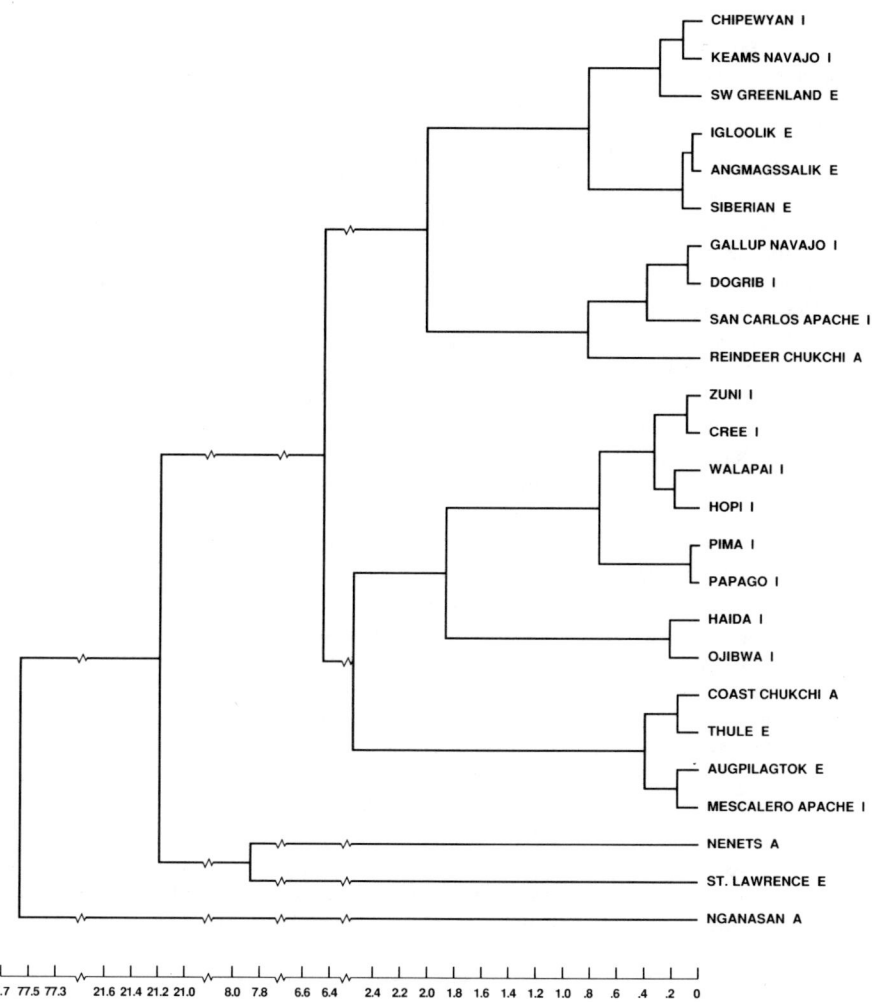

Figure 8. Dendrogram of genetic distances based on Gm haplotype frequencies. The tree connects 25 populations, including Haida of the Northwest Coast. See text for discussion. I=Indian, E=Eskimo, A=Asiatic.

between Figure 1 and Figure 2 indicate, when a dendrogram is based on only one locus, correction of its gene frequencies for the effects of European admixture can cause major changes in the configuration of the tree. This is not the case when many loci (gene frequencies corrected for admixture) go into the derivation of genetic distances. In such instances the changes that are seen influence branch lengths only. Modest amounts of admixture tend to make branch lengths shorter in multiple-locus–based trees, indicating that gene flow is increasing genetic similarity among Native Americans (Spuhler 1979; Szathmary and Auger 1983), and is counteracting the genetic diversification brought about by genetic drift.

On the basis of tribal data, rather than pooled population aggregates, Williams et al. (1985) have stated that the Gm data concur with the "three waves of migration" model of the peopling of the Americas, and that the data do not support Szathmary and Ossenberg's (1978) conclusion that the Na-Dene are closer to Eskimos than are other Amerindians. The findings here show that when these data are subjected to distance analysis and then the distances are clustered to elucidate patterns of genetic similarity, *no tripartite* division of New World peoples is seen.

With respect to the claimed lack of closeness of Eskimos to Na-Dene, an important issue is whether Athapaskans can be considered to "stand in" for the Na-Dene, when Gm frequencies of Haida and Tlingit are unavailable (Williams et al. published their paper in 1985, before the Gm haplotypes were determined in the Haida). Although Szathmary and Ossenberg (1978) have shown that genetic distances derived from eight blood groups, and three serumprotein systems cluster Haida, Tlingit, Navajo and Northern Athapaskans (but not the Apache), it does not necessarily follow that they will be aggregated this way on the basis of distances derived from Gm frequencies only. Figure 8 demonstrates unambiguously that when only Gm haplotypes are considered, Haida do not cluster with the populations to which 11 other genetic systems have assigned them. One can speculate why such differences arise, but the most likely explanation is that one genetic system cannot reflect accurately the totality of genetic differentiation between populations. It is worth noting that the St. Lawrence Island Eskimos and the Siberian Eskimos have been found to be very similar to each other genetically on the basis of multiple loci (Crawford et al. 1981; Ferrell et al. 1981), but this closeness is not reflected when analysis is confined (in this paper) to only one (Gm) or two (Gm and Km) systems.

On the other hand, the Gm data do show that Athapaskan-speaking peoples and Eskimos have similar haplotype frequencies. Accordingly, in clusters that include Eskimos, Indians and Chukchi, whether these are the first order clusters (Figure 2) or even a fourth order cluster (Figure 3), the Indians are always Athapaskan-speakers.

When populations are highly dispersed geographically, and separation among them is of very long duration, genetic distances based on a single system may not be able to show the affinities that are present. This, for example, may be the problem with the failure of all Eskimo groups to cluster together in Figures 1 and 2. The criterion for choosing data set (3) was samples that had been tested with Gm *and* Km antisera. Because this removed all Greenlandic Eskimos but one (Augpilagtok Island retained; three others deleted), two other Eskimo samples were added. It was happenstance (although useful) that both samples were from different Eskimo groups (Yupik and Inupik speakers) in Alaska. Figure 3, based on the Gm system only, is in keeping with the bipartite model of Native American affinities that groups Chukchi, Eskimos, and Athapaskans, and sets them apart from other Amerindians. Figure 4, however, shows that any satisfaction Szathmary might have about the pattern in Figure 3 is premature. The addition of Km data distorts the "bipartite" pattern considerably, by moving the Dogrib, the San Carlos Apache, and the South Alaskan Eskimos out of "their" cluster (i.e., as in Figure 3).

While one highly specific genetic marker system such as Gm can provide a great deal of information about population affinities, the most reliable evidence is based on genetic distances from multiple genetic systems. For this reason, further calculations were undertaken to see whether there is evidence in support of either the tripartite model of Native American origins or the bipartite genetic difference model under consideration in this paper. The dendrograms in Figures 5 and 6 are based on genetic distances derived from gene frequencies at 15 and 16 loci, respectively, in 11 populations. In these calculations pooled frequencies for Northern Athapaskans and Northern Algonkians were used (Szathmary 1981). Such pooling allows input from many tribal groups, even if individually each has not been tested from the full array of loci used in calculation of genetic distances. Pooling of populations in itself is considered to be desirable (Cavalli-Sforza et al. 1988), as this tends to eliminate the vagaries that drift can bring about within loci within single tribal groups.

The explanation for the shift in the placement of the Indians in the two dendrograms is connected with the quality of the Km gene frequency data available for Northern Athapaskans and Northern Algonkians. Although other gene frequencies of the Athapaskans are pooled from *more* than two tribes, the Km pooled frequencies are dependent on only two: the Dogrib and the Chipewyan. Km^1 in the Dogrib has a frequency of 0.561 (Szathmary et al. 1983, plus new unpublished data), while in the Chipewyan it is 0.280 (Schanfield cited in Sukernik and Osipova 1982). Km^1 frequencies known for four other Athapaskans are all under 0.39 (Williams et al. 1985), and Eskimo frequencies range between 0.192 and 0.334. In the 13 non-Athapaskan North American Indian samples examined for Km, the frequency of Km^1 is above 0.355 in all but two: the Walapai (Williams et al. 1985) and the Pikangikum Ojibwa (Szathmary et al. 1974). Because Nei's (1972) standard distance is based on multiplication of input gene frequencies, the exceptionally high average Km^1 frequency in the Northern Athapaskans has to be responsible for the shift in their position in the 16 locus dendrogram. This high frequency, however, may well be an artifact. We will not know whether it is until Km^1 frequencies of other Northern Athapaskans are available. On the other hand, if Km^1 frequencies of all known Athapaskans are pooled and used in the genetic distance calculations, the Northern Athapaskans remain in the Chukchi-Eskimo cluster (dendrogram is not shown). The need to maximize gene loci for genetic distance calculation by the pooling of populations clearly has a price: if insufficient populations have been studied, an average based on only two may yield distorted gene frequency values. This can then cause distortions in the genetic patterns revealed by distance analysis.

Although the Immunoglobulin Gm system has great discriminatory power, addition of Gm data to the calculation of genetic distances does not necessarily bring about changes in tree topology. The dendrogram in Figure 7 is based on 15 loci, including Gm. With the exception of the Diego frequencies in the Nenets and the Kidd frequencies of the Siberian Eskimo (these estimates did not affect the positions of the Nenets and Siberian Eskimo: see Szathmary 1981), all gene frequencies are those observed in the given groups. The pattern of population affinities is unchanged from that observed for 14 locus genetic distances (Szathmary 1984).

Clearly, the study of population affinities from genetic markers has its pitfalls. Although some have claimed that highly polymorphic systems may yield as much information as several different loci (Piazza and

Viganotti 1973), this has been disputed. Ryman et al. (1983), for example, found considerable differences between dendrograms constructed with HLA gene frequencies compared to one based on electrophoretically detectable genes that conformed to externally known criteria of relationship. One genetic system may not reflect accurately the evolutionary pathways that produced extant populations, hence genetic relationships should be based on many loci rather than one (Nei 1975, 1981).

Reliable patterns of affinity (i.e., stable dendrograms that do not change when new data are added) can be elucidated only when many genetic systems are used in the calculation of genetic distances. Although Nei and his associates thought initially that 20 loci yielded stable trees, in fact more than 30 loci are required (Nei et al. 1983), and no more than eight populations should be compared. Estimates of missing gene frequencies for any member of the population array that is being compared are undesirable, unless other calculations show that the estimates have validity.

The most reliable dendrograms in this study are those shown in Figures 5 and 7. These are based on 15 loci, including Gm. The pattern of the populations shows at minimum that there are differences among the Indian people of North America in their relationship to Eskimos. Northern Athapaskans, either as a group or at the tribal level, are closer to Eskimos and Chukchi than are the Algonkians.

Genetic Diversity in North America, and Native American Origins

Szathmary (1984) has argued that the closeness of Athapaskans to Eskimos rather than to other Amerindians is explicable if there is truth in the claims that humans were present south of the Wisconsin and Laurentide ice sheets some 21,000 years ago (Adovasio et al. 1983). Given the evidence that the corridor between the two ice sheets was probably impenetrable between latitudes 55° and 60° N between 15,000 and 18,000 years ago (Fladmark 1983), then some degree of genetic differentiation is expected among the descendants of people south and northwest of the glaciers. Szathmary (1984) suggested that the Athapaskans may be the descendants of ancient northwestern Americans who roamed over and presumably along the margins of Beringia, and who also may have given rise to the ancestors of the Aleuts and Eskimos. The Chukchi may be the descendants of the peoples who roamed along the Siberian edges of Beringia (Szathmary 1981). The Algonkians currently in the Subarctic are thought by some to have moved into the Subarctic from the Plains area as the Laurentide glaciation receded (Wright 1972). Implicitly then, they would be descendants of people south of the Laurentide ice sheet.

The known genetic diversity in Native populations of North America is considerable. Whether this reflects a diversity extant before entry of ancestral groups into North America or is a diversity that came into existence after the occupation of the continent is a question that needs to be answered. That there is a concordance between language and genes in North America north of Mexico (Spuhler 1972, 1979) suggests that the in situ model may be more correct. To date no American Indian language family has been linked conclusively to an Asiatic language family, and, furthermore, intracontinental genetic distances are always smaller than inter-continental genetic distances (Szathmary 1979, 1981). It is worth noting that Szathmary's explanations for the observed genetic differences between northwestern and other Amerindians does not have to presume a great time depth for Amerindian presence in North America. It hinges on *separation* of people on the continent for a geologically short time period, as would have been the case if movement from the northwest was blocked by coalescence of glaciers, and other routes southward (e.g., Fladmark 1978; Gruhn 1988) were technologically impossible.

Szathmary's arguments notwithstanding, the fact is that her deductions regarding genetic differentiation south of the glaciers and northwest of the glaciers rest on information obtained from only 15 genetic systems in a restricted set of populations. The number of loci studied are far short of the maximum needed for the confident reconstruction of the biological history of even northern Native Americans.

The broader issue of the peopling of the Americas has not been systematically addressed by anyone using genetic data, since few populations have been studied for an appreciable number of loci (i.e., more than 10 loci). The most detailed studies on genetic variation in North America have been undertaken by Spuhler (1972, 1979), but he refrained from addressing the issue of origins.

New work on mitochondrial DNA in North American peoples has been published (Wallace et al. 1985). For an assessment of post 1985 data see Szathmary 1993, but the data were derived mainly from Pima Indians and cannot be representative of all of Native North America. Nevertheless, the results are exciting, because they do show the likelihood of multiple founder populations in the ancestry of modern Native Americans. Time depths for occupation of the continent can be derived from mtDNA data, but the veracity of these time depths would be compromised as much as time depths derived from genetic distances based on conventional genetic markers. The problem to be overcome is that of admixture, not just with Europeans and Africans (women from these groups have married into the Native American gene pool), but also among different populations of Native Americans. Existing models of evolution on which genetic distances are based preclude gene flow after population fission. Derivation of time elapsed since splitting will be biased, since human groups do have genetic contact with each other even after group fissions take place.

A new and promising approach that can amplify DNA products in sera through techniques of DNA polymerization is being pursued by a few labs (e.g., Ward, personal communication 1989). The goal is to obtain large amounts of genetic information from sera collected decades ago, but left languishing in deep freezes until new technological developments made their assays feasible. The only risk with these newer approaches is that much of the available information we do have on the so-called "classical genetic markers" (Cavalli-Sforza et al. 1988) will not be used in newer reconstructions of population history, and it will take some time to collect sufficient information on a wide array of populations.

The genetic investigation of the biological history of the Americas therefore remains open for further debate and exploration, until we have sufficiently large gene frequency arrays from a sufficiently large number of tribal populations to resolve existing controversies.

ACKNOWLEDGMENTS

An abbreviated and less complete version of this paper was given in April 1986 in the symposium "Genetic Approaches to Physical Anthropology: Symposium in Honor of James N. Spuhler," held during the American Association of Physical Anthropologists annual meeting. This paper is dedicated to Dr. Spuhler.

REFERENCES CITED

Adovasio, J. M., J. Donahue, K. Cushman, R. C. Carlisle, R. Stuckenrath, J. D. Gunn, and W. C. Johnson
   1983 Evidence from Meadowcroft Rock Shelter. In *Early Man in the New World*, edited by R. Shutler Jr., pp. 163–190. Sage Publications, Beverly Hills.

Cavalli-Sforza, L. L., and A. W. F. Edwards
   1967 Phylogenetic Analysis: Models and Estimation Procedures. *American Journal of Human Genetics* 19:233–257.

Cavalli-Sforza, L. L., and W. F. Bodmer
   1971 *The Genetics of Human Populations*. W. H. Freeman, San Francisco.

Cavalli-Sforza, L. L., and A. Piazza
   1975 Analysis of Evolution: Evolutionary Rates, Independence, and Treeness. *Theoretical Population Biology* 8:127–165.

Cavalli-Sforza, L. L., A. Piazza, P. Menozzi, and J. Mountain
   1988 Reconstruction of Human Evolution: Bringing Together Genetic, Archaeological and Linguistic Data. *Proceedings of the National Academy of Science U.S.A.* 85:60002–60006.

Chakraborty, R.
   1977 Estimation of Time of Divergence from Phylogenetic Studies. *Canadian Journal of of Genetics and Cytology* 19:217–223.

Chakraborty, R., P. Fuerst, and M. Nei
   1980 Statistical Studies on Protein Polymorphism in Natural Populations. III Distribution of Allele Frequencies and the Number of Alleles per Locus. *Genetics* 94:1039–1063.

Crawford, M. H., J. H. Mielke, E. J. Devor, D. D. Dykes, and H. F. Polesky
   1981 Populations Structure of Alaskan and Siberian Indigenous Communities *American Journal of Physical Anthropology* 55:167–186.

Crow, J. F., and C. Denniston (editors)
   1974 *Genetic Distance*. Plenum, New York.

Ferrell, R. E., R. Chakraborty, H. Gershowitz, W. S. Laughlin, and W. J. Schull
   1981 The St. Lawrence Island Eskimos: Genetic Variation and Genetic Distance. *American Journal of Physical Anthropology* 55:351–358. Corrections to published data provided by R. E. Ferrell, personal communication.

Field, L. L., J. P. Gofton, and T. D. Kinsella
   1988 Immunoglobulin (Gm and Km) Allotypes and Relation to Population History in Native Peoples of British Columbia: Haida and Bella Coola. *American Journal of Physical Anthropology* 76:155–164.

Fladmark, K. R.
   1978 The Feasibility of the Northwest Coast as a Migration Route for Early Man. In *Early Man in America from a Circum-Pacific Perspective*, edited by A. L. Bryan. Occasional Papers No. 1. University of Alberta, Edmonton.

   1983 Times and Places: Environmental Correlates of Mid-to-Late Wisconsinan Human Populations Expansion in North America. In *Early Man in the New World*, edited by R. Shutler Jr., pp. 13–42. Sage Publications, Beverly Hills.

Goodman, M. M.
   1974 Genetic Distances: Measuring Dissimilarity Among Populations. *Yearbook of Physical Anthropology* 17:1–38.

Greenberg, J. H., C. H. Turner II, and S. L. Zegura
   1986 The Settlement of the Americas: A Comparison of the Linguistic, Dental and Genetic Evidence. *Current Anthropology* 27:477–498.

Gruhn, R.
1988 Linguistic Evidence in Support of the Coastal Route of Earliest Entry into the New World. *Man* 23:77–100.

Kidd, K. K., and L. L. Cavalli-Sforza
1971 Number of Characters Examined and Error in Reconstruction of Evolutionary Trees. In *Mathematics in the Archaeological and Historical Sciences*, edited by F. R. Hodson, D. G. Kendall, and P. Tautu, pp. 335–346. Edinburgh University Press, Edinburgh.

Matsumoto, H., T. Miyazaki, N. Ishida, and K. Katayama
1982 Mongoloid Populations from the Viewpoints of Gm Patterns. *Japanese Journal of Human Genetics* 27:271–282.

Nei, M.
1972 Genetic Distance Between Populations. *American Naturalist* 106:283–292.

1975 *Molecular Population Genetics and Evolution*. North-Holland/American Elsevier, New York.

1981 Genetic Distance and Molecular Taxonomy. In *Proceedings of the XIV International Congress of Genetics, Moscow 1978*, vol. 2, pp. 7–21. MIR Publisher, Moscow.

1987 *Molecular Evolutionary Genetics*. Columbia University Press, New York.

Nei, M, and A. K. Roychoudhury
1982 Genetic Relationship and Evolution of Human Races. *Evolutionary Biology* 14:1–60.

Nei, M., F. Tajima, and Y. Tateno
1983 Accuracy of Estimated Phylogenetic Trees from Molecular Data. II Gene Frequency Data. *Journal of Molecular Evolution* 19:153–170.

Nei, M., J. C. Stephens, and N. Saitou
1985 Methods for Computing the Standard Errors of Branching Points in an Evolutionary Tree and Their Application to Molecular Data from Humans and Apes. *Molecular Biological Evolution* 2:66–85.

Peterson, G. M., J. I. Ward, T. I. Terasaki, M. S. Schanfield, M. S. Park, J. I. Rotter, and D. R. Silimperi
1986 Genetic Markers in Southwest Alaskan Eskimos: Estimates of HLA Haplotype Frequencies. Manuscript in possession of authors.

Piazza, A., and C. Viganotti
1973 Evolutionary Trees and HL-A Polymorphism. *Histocompatibility Testing 1972*, pp. 731–738. Munksgaard, Copenhagen.

Reed, T. E., and W. J. Schull
1968 A General Maximum Likelihood Estimation Program. *American Journal of Human Genetics* 20:579–580.

Ryman, N., R. Chakraborty, and M. Nei
1983 Differences in the Relative Distribution of Human Gene Diversity Between Electrophoretic and Red and White Cell Antigen Loci. *Human Heredity* 33:93–102.

Sokal, R. R., and P. H. A. Sneath
1963 *Principles of Numerical Taxonomy*. W. H. Freeman, San Francisco.

Sourdis, J., and M. Nei
1988 Relative Efficiencies of the Maximum Parsimony and Distance-Matrix Methods in Obtaining the Correct Phylogenetic Tree. *Molecular Biological Evolution* 5:298-311.

Spuhler, J. N.
1972 Genetic, Linguistic and Geographical Distances in Native North America. In *The Assessment of Population Affinities in Man*, edited by J. S. Weiner and J. Huizinga, pp. 72–95. Clarendon Press, Oxford.

1979 Genetic Distances, Trees, and Maps of North American Indians. In *The First Americans: Origins, Affinities and Adaptations*, edited by W. S. Laughlin and A. B. Harper, pp. 135–184. Gustav Fischer, New York.

Steinberg, A. G., and S. Kageyama
1970 Further Data on the Gm and Inv Allotypes of the Ainu: Confirmation of the Presence of a $Gm^{2,17,21}$ Phenogroup. *American Journal of Human Genetics* 22:319–325.

Steinberg, A. G., A. Tiilikainen, M. R. Eskola, and A. W. Eriksson
1974 Gammaglobulin Allotypes in Finnish Lapps, Finns, Åland Islanders, Maris (Cheremis), and Greenland Eskimos. *American Journal of Human Genetics*. 26:223–243.

Sukernik, R. I., and L. P. Osipova
1982 Gm and Km Immunoglobulin Allotypes in Reindeer Chukchi and Siberian Eskimos. *Human Genetics* 61:148–153.

Sukernik, R. I., L. P. Osipova, T. M. Karaphet, and T. A. Abanina
1980 Studies on Blood Groups and Other Genetic Markers in Forest Nentzi: Variation Among Subpopulations. *Human Genetics* 55:397–404.

Szathmary, E. J. E.
1979 Blood Groups of Siberians, Eskimos, Subarctic and Northwest Coast Indians: The Problem of Origins and Genetic Relationship. In *The First Americans: Origins, Affinities and Adaptations*,

edited by L. S. Laughlin and A. B. Harper, pp. 185–210. Gustav Fischer, New York.

1981 Genetic Markers in Siberian and Northern North American Populations. *Yearbook of Physical Anthropology* 24:37–74.

1984 Peopling of Northern North America: Clues from Genetic Studies. *Acta Anthropogenetica* 8:79–110.

1993 Genetics of Aboriginal North Americans. *Evolutionary Anthropology* 1(6):202–220.

Szathmary, E. J. E., and F. Auger
1983 Biological History: Genetic Distance and Admixture. In *Boreal Forest Adaptations: Algonkians of Northern Ontario*, edited by A. T. Steegmann, Jr., pp. 289–316. Plenum, New York.

Szathmary, E. J. E., and N. S. Ossenberg
1978 Are the Biological Differences Between North American Indians and Eskimos Truly Profound? *Current Anthropology* 19:673–685.

Szathmary, E. J. E., D. W. Cox, H. Gershowitz, D. L. Rucknagel, and M. S. Schanfield
1974 The Northern and Southeastern Ojibwa: Serum Proteins and Red Cell Enzyme Systems. *American Journal of Physical Anthropology* 44:49–65.

Szathmary, E. J. E., R. E. Ferrell, and H. Gershowitz
1983 Genetic Differentiation in Dogrib Indians: Serum Protein and Erythrocyte Enzyme Variation. *American Journal of Physical Anthropology* 62:249–254.

Turner, C. G. II
1983 Dental Evidence for the Peopling of the Americas. In *Early Man in the New World*, edited by R. Shutler Jr., pp. 147–158. Sage Publications, Beverly Hills.

1985 The Dental Search for Native American Origins. In *Out of Asia*, edited by R. Kirk and E. Szathmary, pp. 31–78. Journal of Pacific History, Canberra.

Voegelin, C. F., and F. M. Voegelin
1966 *Map of North American Indian Languages*. Publications of the American Ethnological Society No. 20. Seattle.

Wallace, D. C., K. Garrison, and W. C. Knowler
1985 Dramatic Founder Effects in Amerindian Mitochondrial DNAs. *American Journal of Physical Anthropology* 68:149–157.

Weiner, J. S., and J. Huizinga (editors)
1972 *The Assessment of Population Affinities in Man*. Clarendon Press, Oxford.

Williams, R. C., A. G. Steinberg, H. Gershowitz, P. H. Bennett, W. C. Knowler, D. J. Pettitt, W. Butler, R. Baird, L. Dowda-Rea, T. A. Burch, H. G. Morse, and C. G. Smith
1985 Gm Allotypes in Native Americans: Evidence for Three Distinct Migrations Across the Bering Land Bridge. *American Journal of Physical Anthropology* 66:1–20.

Wright, J. V.
1972 *The Shield Archaic*. National Museums of Canada Publications in Archaeology No. 3. Ottawa.

Relating Eurasian and Native American Populations Through Dental Morphology

CHRISTY G. TURNER II
Department of Anthropology
Arizona State University
Tempe, Arizona 85287-2402 U.S.A.

Statistical analyses of 29 dental traits in more than 15,000 Native American, Old World, and Pacific Basin crania show that teeth of Native Americans are more like those of Northeast Asians than of other major world populations. Native Americans and Northeast Asians form one of two major world clusters. The second cluster contains Africans, Europeans, Southeast Asians, and Oceanic peoples. The origin of Native Americans is in Northeast Asia.

This pattern of dental relationships does not match the findings of Cavalli-Sforza et al. (1988) based on many monogenic traits of living peoples. These workers found Europeans clustered with Northeast Asians and Native Americans. Their north Eurasian-American cluster could be used to argue that Paleoindians originated out of an old European stock, a possibility having some archaeological support. As the dental data are largely from prehistoric samples, collected by a single observer, and most traits seem to have a polygenic mode of inheritance, it is proposed that the dental data provide better estimates of Eurasian-American relationships than do the monogenic traits. Also, there is much less chance of dental admixture, no inter-observer error, and less opportunity for selection or drift to cause evolutionary convergence in northern Eurasia. Diachronic dental studies of northern Eurasians show marked dissimilarities between Europeans and Asians until about Neolithic times, when admixture becomes evident.

Teeth have been an important if not the major means for reconstructing phylogenetic relationships for the taxonomy and classification of all living and extinct mammals and some other vertebrates. Teeth have been used to distinguish between and characterize mammalian orders, such as primates and carnivores; to identify groups within an order, such as apes and humans; and to define populations within a species, such as Indians and Aleuts. The dentition have this power for direct diachronic and synchronic affinity measurement and classification because dental traits are genetically determined; there are scores of traits, with probably hundreds of genes involved; the traits are largely independent, permitting polythetic classification; there is direct diachronic evidence that teeth evolve very slowly; they have behavioral correlates; they can be studied easily and compared directly in both ancient and living populations; and they preserve on the average better than any other tissue because of their extreme hardness. Where there is an environmental component to trait expression, it can often be recognized. No other biological system provides as much evidence for evolutionary research at such a low unit cost.

Over the last twenty years, I have assembled a very large single-observer database on the dentition of prehistoric populations in the Americas and the Old World, a series containing more than 15,000 variously complete individuals. Most of the teeth attributed to Paleoindians have been studied, as have large series of Archaic and later populations in both North and South America. Nearly all of these thousands of Indians and Aleut-Eskimos are prehistoric, so there is no meaningful European or African admixture problem. In the Old World I have examined numerous skeletal samples, and, especially relevant to this conference, thousands of individuals from throughout the USSR, including almost all of the Soviet dentitions dating to late Pleistocene and early Holocene times.

MATERIALS AND METHODS

My observation and recording methods are highly standardized, even to the extent that the angle and amount of light used for inspection are maintained as constant as possible. All observations are made with rigid definitions for scoring, even when a standardized reference plaque is not needed (Turner et al. 1991). This system keeps intra-observer error to a minimum, and there is no inter-observer error whatsoever in the data used for this paper.

There are 29 key morphological features that are used here. These include both crown and root traits. Upper jaw: I1 winging, I1 shovel (Figure 1), I1 double-shovel (Figure 1), I2 interruption grooves, I2 tuberculum dentale (Figure 1), C mesial ridge, C distal accessary ridge, Uto-Aztecan P1 (Figure 1), M2 hypocone, M1 cusp 5, M1 Carabelli, M3 parastyle, M1 enamel extension, P1 root number, M2 root number, M3 reduction. Lower jaw: P2 lingual cusps, M2 groove pattern, M1 cusp number, M2 cusp number, M1 deflecting wrinkle, M1 distal trigonid crest, M1 protostylid, M1 cusp 7, Tome's root

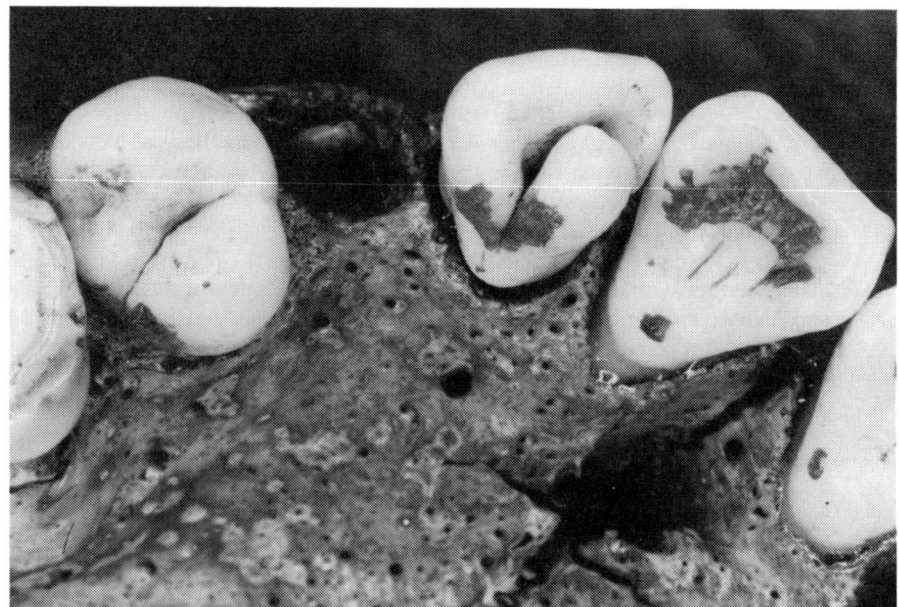

Figure 1. Occlusal view of upper anterior teeth belonging to a ten-year-old child from the prehistoric central Arizona Mogollon culture site called Grasshopper. Whole tooth at left has the Uto-Aztecan first premolar polymorphism (Morris et al. 1978); space is the unerupted canine; tooth in middle is lateral incisor with large tuberculum dentale and lingual surface shoveling; right whole tooth is central incisor with lingual surface shoveling and labial surface (towards top) double-shoveling. Excavated by the University of Arizona Archaeological Field School (CGT neg. no. 11-23-79/23). These features are rarely seen in Europeans but are common in Northeast Asians and Native Americans. The Uto-Aztecan premolar occurs mainly in American Indians.

P1, C root number, M1 root number, M2 root number, odontome upper and lower P1 and P2. Information on provenience, sample sizes, and sources of these teeth is given in Turner (1987a, 1989, 1990a, 1990b), and additional information is available from the author.

Most of the 29 traits are believed to be inherited in a quasi-continuous autosome threshold fashion with environmental influence less than that for metric features such as tooth size (Harris 1977; Nichol 1989, 1990; Perzigian 1984; Scott 1973). (Other aspects of dental genetics and microevolution are reviewed in Scott and Turner 1988.) Most have a non-occurrence grade, and several grades of expression when present. This suggests that there are a minimum of three or four genes for each, perhaps even more. Thus, some 100 or more genes are likely involved. For affinity assessment there is an obvious advantage of using one relatively stable biological system whose function is known over a mix of genetic traits whose functions are unknown and/or whose relative evolutionary stability cannot be determined by direct paleontological means. Elsewhere, I have shown just how stable human teeth have been since late Pleistocene times (Turner 1986).

My large dental anthropology database of more than 15,000 individuals is being analyzed in several ways. One way is on a trait-by-trait basis, that is, univariately. Figure 2 shows an example of such a univariate comparison. This figure shows that the mean occurrence and range of sample frequencies of three-rooted lower first molars in Europeans more closely resemble those of Africans than those of Asians or Native Americans. Many other dental traits show this African-European/Asian-American relationship. While univariant comparisons are perfectly reasonable, there is an inherent danger in their use, namely, traits can be subconsciously selected to prove a particular point. This potential bias can be circumvented by examining many traits simultaneously, that is, multivariantly. In this way no trait is favored or given any weight over any other trait. Possible biases are swamped out by the weight of many considerations done at the same time.

Should some traits in a multivariate matrix be given more importance than others? This long-standing taxonomic problem is not an issue here because all the traits belong to one morphological and developmental complex. In addition, each is a secondary trait of the dentition; that is, each is of very little significance in the development of the primary dental characters (crown, root, tooth type, tooth number). Finally, human secondary dental-trait-weighting would be senseless in view of the buffering of selection by stone tools and other technology which served as substitutes for food processing, defense, and other dental functions for tens of thousands of years.

One multivariant statistic that works especially well with rank-scaled and discontinuous dental morphological variation, developed by C. A. B. Smith, is the mean

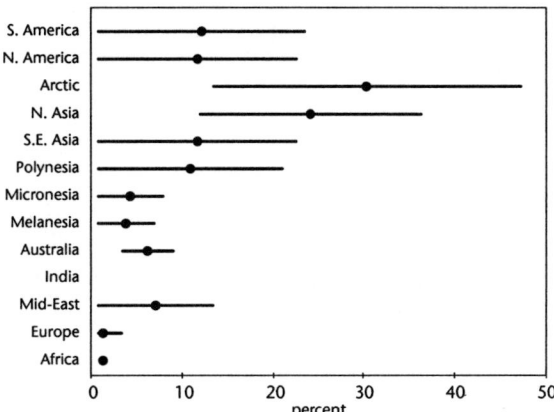

Figure 2. World distribution of three-rooted lower first permanent molars. Mean (●) and range of sample frequencies; n = 11,318 crania. From Turner and Benjamin (1989).

measure of divergence (MMD) (Berry and Berry 1967). When the mean measure of divergence formula is adjusted for the possible effects of small sample size (Green and Suchey 1976) and further modified to determine if a resulting value is statistically significant (Sjøvold 1973), very powerful estimates of affinity can be obtained. Table 1 shows the statistically significant results of a recent large-scale computer analysis performed to evaluate the multivariant dental similarity between New and Old World populations. For those unfamiliar with the mean measure of divergence statistic, a small value indicates greater similarity than does a large value.

FINDINGS

In the left column we see that a series of English teeth are most similar to a series from Denmark (MMD = 0.01), and least similar to the Brazilian series (0.688). Note also that the English teeth are more like those from West Africa (0.322) than like any series from Northeast Asia or the Americas (0.412 to 0.688).

The middle column shows that the West Africans are most like Egyptians of North Africa, and least like Brazilians. The West Africans are more like the Europeans than like the Northeast Asians or Native Americans. Finally, the right column reveals that the Mongolians are most like the Japanese, and least like the West Africans. The Mongolians are more like Native Americans than like Africans or Europeans. These relationships make good sense on geographic, ethnographic, historic, other biological, and archaeological grounds. Africa is nearer Europe than it is to east Asia. Human populations in Africa and Europe share a long, complex evolutionary

Table 1. Mean Measures of Divergence (29 dental traits).

ENGLAND		WEST AFRICA		MONGOLIA	
Denmark	.010	Egypt	.011	Japan	.028
Egypt	.032	S. Australia	.096	Maryland	.102
Thailand	.140	New Britain	.159	Kodiak	.111
Hawaii	.158	Thailand	.219	Hawaii	.162
New Britain	.274	Hawaii	.269	Thailand	.171
S. Australia	.285	Denmark	.280	Arizona	.183
West Africa	.322	England	.322	Brazil	.211
Japan	.412	Japan	.455	S. Australia	.275
Mongolia	.453	Mongolia	.514	New Britain	.292
Arizona	.489	Maryland	.542	Egypt	.348
Maryland	.524	Arizona	.615	England	.453
Kodiak	.536	Kodiak	.654	Denmark	.454
Brazil	.688	Brazil	.769	West Africa	.514

Computer reference: World 13.

history (Brauer 1984). Mongolia and Japan are much closer geographically than either is to Europe, and like Eurafrica they have an inter-related evolutionary history (Turner 1985). Groups that live near each other are often commonly derived or share common ancestors.

These mean measures of divergence can be mathematically transformed into graphic trees called dendrograms. In Figure 3 a different set of MMD comparisons was calculated for several large dental series to learn about dental relationships in the Old World. One inspects a dendrogram beginning at the far left or at the base of the tree, which here is lying on its side. As can be seen, the trunk splits very quickly into a China-Mongol branch and a branch containing all the other dental series. The Africans branch off next from the other members of the upper cluster, but it is evident, as was the case with the numerical data, that Africans are more like Europeans than like the Northeast Asians. Said another way, the Old World contains two major dental divisions—Northeast Asians and non-Northeast Asians.

The dendrogram in Figure 4 shows the MMD relationships for representative samples of Native Americans, Northeast Asians, and Europeans. Again, inspecting from left to right, we see that the Europeans branch away quickly from the Northeast Asian Amur, China-Mongol, and American series. This indicates that European teeth are very dissimilar from those of Mongoloids. The Northeast Asian Mongoloids and Native Americans are very similar, so much so that I have named them both Sinodonts—in reference to the type series from China where I first recognized this dental pattern (Turner 1983). Clearly, the genetic homeland for all Native Americans must have been in eastern Asia.

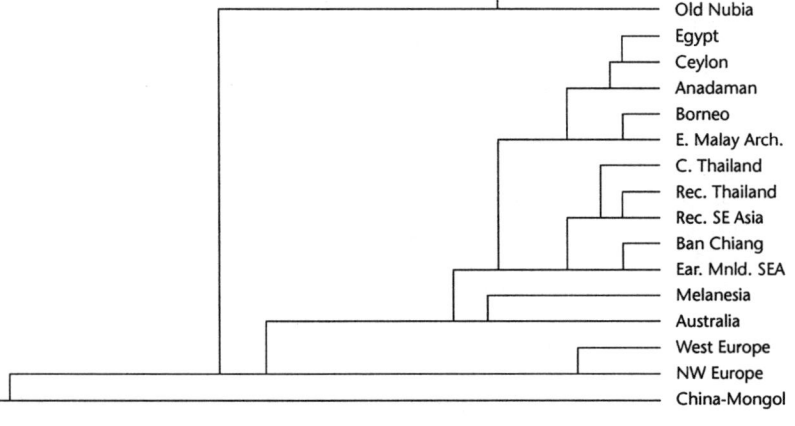

Figure 3. Dendrogram of Old World odontological relationships. Computer reference: Eurafrica/SE Asia #3, 28 traits (Uto-Aztec P1 deleted since rare outside New World). E=East, C=Central, Rec=Recent, Ear Mnld SEA=Early Mainland SE Asia.

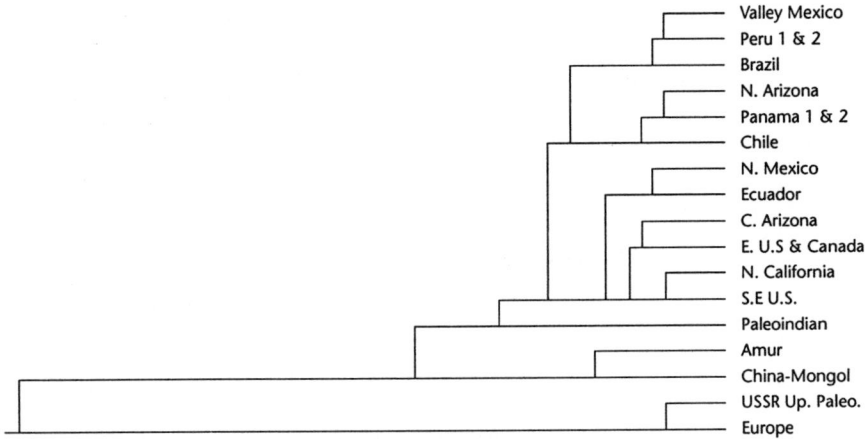

Figure 4. Dendrogram of Old and New World odontological relationships. Computer reference: American Indian origins #2, 29 traits.

The Soviet Upper Paleolithic series, made up of Kostienki, Mal'ta, Samarkand, Sunghir, and other Cro-Magnon remains (Turner 1985) were obviously early Caucasoids, and could not have been the primary ancestors of Native American Mongoloids.

We have seen that Native Americans are odontologically more like Northeast Asians than like Europeans, Africans, or other major world populations. The origin of Paleoindians was in the late Pleistocene gene pool of North China, Mongolia, and eastern Siberia. Dentally, the world has two major dental divisions—Northeast Asian-Americans, and all other populations. There is nothing novel in these findings. The archaeological record is highly concordant. But this clear-cut dental classification does not match perfectly the world racial classification by Cavalli-Sforza and his colleagues (1988) based on published accounts of many genetic traits studied in scores of living populations. This is not especially disturbing, since different biological systems sometimes give different affinity assessments. However, it is always useful where possible to try to determine why such differences occur.

As previously, we inspect the Cavalli-Sforza et al. genetic tree (Figure 5) first from the left. We find that Africans quickly branch away from all other populations. Like the dental tree, this dendrogram also reveals that the world is divided into two major divisions of humans, but it is an African/non-African dichotomy instead of the dental dichotomy of Northeast Asian-American/all others. The next genetic branchpoint links Caucasoids, Northeast Asians, and Native Americans.

DISCUSSION

Both the genetic and dental trees have a great deal of internal consistency. There is but little short-branch sample disagreement or misclassification based on expectations of geographic, archaeologic, ethnographic, and linguistic distances. But the genetic and dental trees differ at the lower and phylogenetically more important branchpoints, assuming that dendrograms are reasonable estimates of phylogeny. Cavalli-Sforza et al. (1988) interpret their genetic tree to mean that the great divergence of Africans from other groups indicates that modern populations arose first in Africa. If we accept this idea that maximum divergence pinpoints the Garden of Eden location, then the dental tree would have to be interpreted as indicating that eastern Asia was where Adam and Eve fell from grace.

As there are fossil remains in both Africa and Austroasia that could be candidates for the earliest modern humans, the fossil record does not help us decide whether the genetic or dental tree is wrong (Brauer 1984; Rightmire 1984; Wolpoff et al. 1984). Nor is mitochondrial DNA information decisive. While R. Cann and associates pick Africa as the genetic homeland of modern humans, D. Wallace can point to southeast China (Tierney et al. 1988). The mtDNA work by Saitou and Harihara (1989) could be read both ways. Indeed, there seems to be as strong an argument for genetic continuity to the present day in eastern Asia as there is for Africa (Lu 1989; Pope 1989a, 1989b; Simons 1989; Wolpoff 1989; Wolpoff et al. 1984; Xue 1989). Logically, both the dental and genetic trees cannot be correct, unless one believes that modern humans arose in more than one location, although neither the genetic nor dental data seem to point to this.

The fact that Europeans link up with Asians in the genetic tree opens the door to the possibility that Paleoindians originated partly in the European Cro-Magnon gene pool of 25,000 years ago. This possibility has been advocated by very competent and reasonable scholars, including archaeologists H. Müller-Beck (1982), C. V. Haynes (1987), and B. Fagen (1987). If the genetic tree is correct, then their views would have physical anthropological support not available from the dental evidence. So let us take a closer look at the genetic and dental

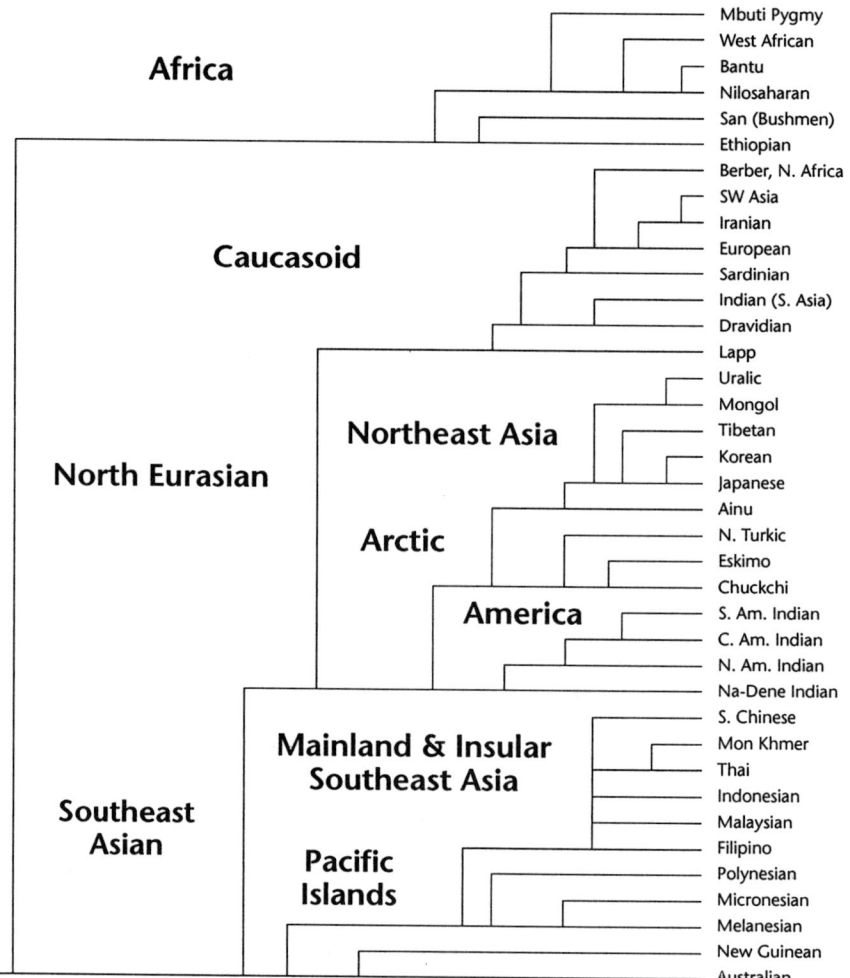

Figure 5. Dendrogram of Old and New World genetic relationships (redrawn and used with permission from Cavalli-Sforza et al. 1988).

findings. We can ignore the differences in the respective statistical methods, as both involve similar procedures and mathematical assumptions. Where the resulting trees differ most is in three other methodological areas.

There are three possible sources for the dental and monogenic differences—data collection, data source, and data type. First, the genetic data are drawn from many published investigations of serological and other genetic polymorphisms collected by many researchers over a considerable number of years, possibly as many as 50 years, using various techniques to identify the genes involved. Older studies on blood antigens were done using glass slides, test tubes or capillary tubes—each with its own technical problems. Gene-detecting antisera and electrophoresis gels can differ considerably from batch to batch. Not surprisingly, given the costs involved, there are very few genetic studies on the same individuals using different batches of reagents to test for technical reliability. Faulty antisera are believed to be the cause of unusual blood type find-

ings for some southwestern U.S. Indians (Merbs 1992). Zegura (Greenberg et al. 1986) prudently suggests caution in the taxonomic use of literature-based genetic information, at least for the Americas. The published genetic data must have some amount of inter-observer error, but how much can never be determined. On the other hand, all the dental data were collected by a single observer over a shorter span of time using only one method of observation, so there cannot be any inter-observer error. Thus with respect to data collection the dental information has to be better.

Second, with respect to data source, the genetic information was obtained from living populations. Although Cavalli-Sforza et al. (1988:6003) assert that little or no admixture is present in their samples, one has to ask, how can they be certain? What is their prehistoric baseline? The answer, of course, is that there is none. This is the fundamental weakness of studies tethered to living populations where their biological prehistory cannot be directly checked. Moreover, if, as the prehistoric Siberian archaeological and physical anthropological record seems to indicate, Europeans and Asians were meeting in western Siberia and interbreeding during and shortly before Neolithic times (Alexseev and Gokhman 1983; Martynov 1981), then prehistoric admixture would be the underlying cause of the Eurasian linkage in the genetic tree, not phylogeny. Morphometrically and genetically their Lapp and Uralic series are Eurasian hybrids (Kozintsev 1988; Zubov 1981) (see Turner 1987b, 1987c for extensive bibliography of Soviet physical anthropological research on these and related populations), and these series might well be the underlying cause of the linkage between Europe and Northeast Asia. Interestingly, L. Heapost's (1981) blood group study of Estonians did not show the expected link with Lapps despite the strong linguistic tie, whereas K. Mark's (1975) craniological study did. My unpublished work on Estonian teeth also links these people with the Lapp-Ob Finno-Ugrian community.

The Southeast Indians (Dravidian languages) used by Cavalli-Sforza et al. (1988) could also be pulling Europe and Asia together because there is considerable evidence of prehistoric admixture between India and Southeast Asia; i.e., through Assam before 4000 yr B.P., and across Tibet (Bowles 1977). Finally, thousands if not millions of Central and West Asians must have received East Asian genes as a result of the massive westward Mongol population expansion beginning in the early 1200s, that of the Khan-led Golden Horde (Maclean 1978). Even such a simple feature as the east-west Eurasian gradient for allele B of the ABO system shows that the Mongol empire probably had a marked genetic effect on western populations. Obviously, historic and archaeological evidence indicates that admixture was likely, and therefore the dental findings are preferable over the monogenic data source which, among other problems, cannot be evaluated by direct diachronic means.

As for data type, the genetic traits are single-gene or monogenic characters, whereas the inheritance of the dental traits follows a polygenic pattern. It is now fairly well accepted that monogenic traits are more susceptible to the evolutionary forces of random genetic drift and natural selection than are polygenic characters. This effect is illustrated in all American Indians by their lack of the monogenic B gene which is common in Asia, while the polygenic shovel trait of the incisors occurs about equally in Northeast Asians and Native Americans, even allowing for more environmental influence on polygenic than monogenic character expression and occurrence.

The apparent phylogenetic linkage of Europeans and Northeast Asians produced by the genetic analysis of Cavalli-Sforza et al. (1988) could also be the result of parallel evolution or convergence by disease or other selective forces operating in the similar latitudes and climates of Europe and Northeast Asia. As there is no known adaptive value for the dental traits, and some are worn off by, or during, reproductive age, the possibility of selection for these minor crown and root variants is low at best. The fact that Europeans and Northeast Asians have such dissimilar dental patterns, despite a similar northern environment, suggests that selection probably has had but a minor role in shaping the various dental trait frequencies of northern Eurasia. With respect to data type, there is reason to believe that the dental data are as good as that produced by the monogenic traits, although with both sets we are largely in the dark with respect to adaptive values, especially shifting values that could have accompanied changes in population size, density, structure and related technological advances.

Finally, I can report that my examinations of Siberian and other Soviet dentitions show no evidence of a link between European and Northeast Asian populations until Holocene times (Turner 1992). All the late Pleistocene teeth in the CIS as far east as Lake Baikal fit the Europoid (Caucasoid) dental pattern. Even the seemingly Neandertal teeth, more than 35,000 years old, excavated by A. P. Derevyanko and associates from Okladnikov and Denisova caves in the Altai Mountains of central Siberia, have no suggestion of Asian affiliation or Asian admixture despite the proximity of the Altai region with Mongolia (Turner 1990c). It is not until Neolithic and subsequent Bronze and Iron Ages that admixture can be recognized dentally, and also by heterogeneous artifact assemblages of nomadic steppe and taiga herding groups.

This can be especially appreciated in the teeth of several hundred burials excavated by V. I. Molodin at the west Siberian Neolithic-Bronze Age site called Sopka (Turner 1991). Cluster analysis of the Sopka population shows that it links up only remotely with Northeast Asians, suggesting perhaps one-third European admixture. Soviet physical anthropologist Tatyana Chickasheva (personal communication 1987) finds that the Sopka people are craniologically intermediate also. Neither teeth nor crania are similar to those of ancient or recent Native Americans and Northeast Asians. The Sopka artifact assemblage also shows mixing of east and west elements (V. I. Molodin, personal communication 1987).

In sum, I propose that the dental data provide a cleaner and better approximation of the true phylogeny and population history of northern Eurasia and the Americas than do genetic data collected so far. Dental morphology indicates that the Americas were colonized by small bands of Siberians whose genetic ancestry was with the evolving late Pleistocene Mongoloid population that culturally adapted to the Arctic frontier north of China, Mongolia, and southeastern Siberia. If there was any European contribution to the first American gene pool, it was too small to be detected in the teeth of Paleoindians and all subsequent prehistoric Native Americans.

The proximate homeland of Paleoindians was in northeastern Siberia, where several specialized stone tool traditions emerged for slightly differing lifeways, on the Arctic steppe with socially gregarious herd animals, in the fish-rich patchy wooded river valleys, and along the ice-packed sea mammal-rich Okhotsk-Beringian coastal shelf. As Siberian archaeologist Y. Mochanov (1977) has observed, these technological specializations evolved out of the generalized small tool or microlithic tradition that had existed in the ultimate paleo-Siberian homeland of North China and Mongolia for at least 20,000 years. Chun Chen (1993) shows how part of this 24,000-year-old microblade tradition of North China corresponds to the growing number of Alaskan microblade sites. A. P. Derevyanko (1989) recently reported on a similar site called Selemgda in the middle Amur River basin, dating around 20,000 years ago. On Asian archaeological and dental grounds, the origin of Paleoindians need not be sought in Europe. The Pleistocene people and cultures of China and Mongolia had plenty of biocultural variation and marked resemblances to the first Americans and their cultural inventory.

ACKNOWLEDGMENTS

I am very grateful for the assistance that Robson Bonnichsen, Director of the Center for the Study of the First Americans, and his staff provided, which made my participation at the conference possible. L. L. Cavalli-Sforza generously provided many helpful comments on this paper. However, any errors are mine. The data used herein were collected with financial and other assistance from the National Geographic Society, the National Science Foundation, the U.S. Academy of Science, the U.S.S.R. Academy of Science, IREX, and Arizona State University. A large number of individuals and institutions in several countries are deeply thanked for their generosity, time, help, and willingness to permit examination of their respective skeletal and archeological collections. Jacqueline A. and Korri Dee Turner helped with the collection of much of the Eurasian data. This is contribution No. 39 to Peopling of the Pacific Basin and Adjoining Areas series.

REFERENCES CITED

Alexeev, V. P., and I. I. Gokhman
1983 *Physical Anthropology of Soviet Asia*. Rassengeschichte der Menscheit. 9. Lieferung. Asien II. Edited by I. Schwidetzky. R. Oldenbourg Verlag, Muchen.

Berry, A. C., and R. J. Berry
1967 Epigenetic Variation in the Human Cranium. *Journal of Anatomy* 101(2):361–379.

Bowles, G. T.
1977 *The People of Asia*. Scribner's Sons, New York.

Brauer, G.
1984 A Craniological Approach to the Origin of Anatomically Modern *Homo sapiens* in Africa and Implications for the appearance of Modern Europeans. In *The Origins of Modern Humans: A World Survey of the Fossil Evidence*, edited by F. H. Smith, and F. Spencer, pp. 327–410. A. R. Liss, Inc., New York.

Cavalli-Sforza, L. L, A. Piazza, P. Menozzi, and J. Mountain
1988 Reconstruction of Human Evolution: Bringing Together Genetic, Archaeological, and Linguistic Data. *Proceedings of the National Academy of Sciences U.S.A.* 85:6002–6006.

Chen, Chun
1993 A Preliminary Comparison of Microblade Cores Between North China and North America. Paper presented at the First World Summit Conference on the Peopling of the Americas, Center for the Study of the First Americans, Orono, Maine.

Derevyanko, A. P.
1989 The Late Pleistocene Sites in the Slendia River Basin and Their Significance for Correlation with Upper Paleolithic Assemblages of the Pacific. In *Circum-Pacific Prehistory Conference Program and Abstracts*, p. 36. Seattle.

Fagen, B. M.
1987 *The Great Journey: The Peopling of the Ancient Americas*. Thames and Hudson, London.

Green, R., and J. Suchey
1976 The Use of the Inverse Sine Transformation in the Analysis of Non-Metric Cranial Data. *American Journal of Physical Anthropology* 45(1):61-68.

Greenberg, J. H., C. G. Turner II, and S. L. Zegura
1986 The Settlement of the Americas: A Comparison of Linguistic, Dental, and Genetic Evidence. *Current Anthropology* 27:477–497.

Harris, E. F.
1977 *Anthropologic and Genetic Aspects of the Dentition of Solomon Islanders, Melanesia*. Ph.D. dissertation, Department of Anthropology, Arizona State University, Tempe.

Haynes, V. C.
1987 Clovis Origin Update. *Kiva* 52(2):83–93.

Heapost, L.
1981 Distribution of Blood Groups Among the Estonians. In *Congressus Quintus Internationalis*

Kozintsev, A. G.
1988 *Ethnic Cranioscopy. Racial Variation of Cranial Sutures in Modern Man*. Nauka Press, Leningrad. In Russian.

Lu, Zun E.
1989 Mosaic Evolution of Jinniushan Archaic *Homo sapiens*. In *Circum-Pacific Prehistory Conference Program and Abstracts*, p. 46. Seattle.

Maclean, F.
1978 *Holy Russia*. Century Publishing Co., London.

Mark, K.
1975 *Anthropology of the Pre-Baltic and Finnish People*. Institute of History, Academy of Sciences of Estonia SSR. Valgus, Tallinn. In Russian.

Martynov, A. I.
1981 Siberia Before the Mongols: New Findings and Problems. *Journal of the Stewart Anthropological Society* 12(2):441–506.

Merbs, C. F.
1991 ABO, MN and Rh Frequencies Among the Havasupai and Other Southwest Indian Groups. *Kiva* 58:67–88.

Mochanov Y. A.
1977 *The Most Ancient Stages of the Human Settlement of Northeast Asia*. Nauka Press Siberian Division, Novosibirsk. In Russian.

Morris, D. H., S. Glasstone Hughes, and A. A. Dahlberg
1978 Uto-Aztecan Premolar: The Anthropology of a Dental Trait. In *Development, Function and Evolution of Teeth*, edited by P. M. Butler and K. A. Joysey, pp. 69–79. Academic Press, London.

Müller-Beck, H.
1982 Late Pleistocene Man in Northern Alaska and the Mammoth-Steppe Biome. In *Paleoecology of Beringia*, edited by D. M. Hopkins, J. V. Matthews, Jr., C. E. Schweger, and S. B. Young, pp. 329–352. Academic Press, New York.

Nichol, C. R.
1989 Genetic and Environmental Influences on Tooth Crown Dimensions: A Path Analysis. *American Journal of Physical Anthropology* 78(2):280.

1990 *Dental Genetics and Biological Relationships of the Pima Indians of Arizona*. Ph.D. dissertation, Department of Anthropology, Arizona State University, Tempe.

Perzigian, A. J.
1984 Human Odontometric Variation: An Evolutionary and Taxonomic Assessment. *Anthropologie* 22:193–198.

Pope, G. G.
1989a New Paleoanthropological Evidence from the Far East. In *Circum-Pacific Prehistory Conference Program and Abstracts*, p. 50. Seattle.

1989b Hominid Evolution in China and Indonesia. *American Journal of Physical Anthropology* 78(2):330.

Rightmire, G. P.
1984 *Homo sapiens* in Sub-Saharan Africa. In *The Origins of Modern Humans: A World Survey of the Fossil Evidence*, edited by F. H. Smith and F. Spencer, pp. 295–325. Alan R. Liss, Inc., New York.

Saitou, N., and S. Harihara
1989 Phylogenetic Analysis of Human Mitochondrial DNA Types. In *Circum-Pacific Prehistory Conference Program and Abstracts*, p. 52. Seattle.

Scott, G. R.
1973 *Dental Morphology: A Genetic Study of American White Families and Variation in Living Southwest Indians*. Ph.D. dissertation, Department of Anthropology, Arizona State University, Tempe.

Scott, G. R., and C. G. Turner II
1988 Dental Anthropology. *Annual Review of Anthropology* 17:99–126.

Simons, E. L.
1989 Human Origins. *Science* 245:1343–1350.

Sjøvold, T.
1973 The Occurrence of Minor Non-metrical Variants in the Skeleton and Their Quantitative Treatment for Population Comparisons. *Homo* 24:204–233.

Tierney, J., L. Wright, and K. Springen
1988 The Search for Adam and Eve. *Newsweek*. January 11:46–52.

Turner, C. G. II
1983 Sinodonty and Sundadonty: A Dental Anthropological View of Mongoloid Microevolution, Origin, and Dispersal into the Pacific Basin, Siberia, and the Americas. In *Late Pleistocene and Early Holocene Cultural Connections of Asia and America*, edited by R. S. Vasilievsky, pp. 72–76. U.S.S.R. Academy of Sciences, Siberian Branch, Novosibirsk. In Russian.

1985 The Dental Search for Native American Origins. In *Out of Asia. Peopling the Americas and the Pacific*, edited by R. Kirk and E. Szathmary, pp. 31–78. The Journal of Pacific History, Inc., Canberra.

Fenno-Ugristarum Turku 20–27. VIII. 1980. Pars VIII, edited by O. Ikola, pp. 364–370. Suomen Kielen Seura, Turku, Finland.

1986 Dentochronological Separation Estimates for Pacific Rim Populations. *Science* 232:1140–1142.

1987a Late Pleistocene and Holocene Population History of East Asia Based on Dental Variation. *American Journal of Physical Anthropology* 73:305–321.

1987b Physical Anthropology in the U.S.S.R. Today, Part I. *Quarterly Review of Archaeology* 8(2):11–14.

1987c Physical Anthropology in the U.S.S.R. Today, Part II. *Quarterly Review of Archaeology* 8(3):4–6.

1989 *Out of Southeast Asia: Dentition and the Peopling of the Pacific Basin and Adjoining Areas.* Paper presented at the Circum-Pacific Prehistory Conference, Seattle. (Submitted to Washington State University Press, Pullman).

1990a Origin and Affinity of the Prehistoric People of Guam: A Dental Anthropological Assessment. In *Recent Advances in Micronesian Archaeology*, edited by R. L. Hunter-Anderson, pp. 403–416. Micronesica, Supplement No. 2, University of Guam Press, Mangilao.

1990b The Major Features of Sundadonty and Sinodonty, Including Suggestions About East Asian Microevolution, Population History, and Late Pleistocene Relationships with Australian Aboriginals. *American Journal of Physical Anthropology* 83:295–317.

1990c Paleolithic Teeth of the Central Siberian Altai Mountains. Paper presented at the International Symposium on the Chronostratigraphy of Paleolithic North, Central, and East Asia, and America: The Paleoecological Aspect, Novosibirsk, USSR.

1991 *The Sopka Dentition. A Comparative Study of West Siberian Dental Characteristics.* USSR Academy of Sciences, Siberian Branch. In press.

1992 New World Origins: New Research from the Americas and Soviet Union. In *Ice Age Hunters of the Rockies*, edited by D. J. Stanford and J. S. Day, pp. 7–50. University Press of Colorado, Niwot.

Turner, C. G., and O. Benjamin
 1989 World Variation in Three-Rooted Lower First Permanent Molars. Paper presented at the International Conference on Dental Morphology, Jerusalem.

Turner, C. G. II, C. R. Nichol, and G. R. Scott
 1991 Scoring Procedure for Key Morphological Traits of the Permanent Dentition: The Arizona State University Dental Anthropology System. In *Advances in Dental Anthropology*, edited by M. A. Kelly and C. S. Larsen, pp. 13–31. Wiley-Liss, New York.

Wolpoff, M. H.
 1989 East Asian Human Fossils and the Origin of Races. In *Circum-Pacific Prehistory Conference Program and Abstracts*, p. 60. Seattle.

Wolpoff, M. H., X. Z. Wu, and A. G. Thorne
 1984 Modern *Homo sapiens* Origins: A General Theory of Hominid Evolution Involving the Fossil Evidence From East Asia. In *The Origins of Modern Humans: A World Survey of the Fossil Evidence*, edited by F. H. Smith and F. Spencer, pp. 411–483. A.R. Liss, Inc., New York.

Xue, X-x.
 1989 The Geological Age and Evolution of Fossil Human of Erectus and Neanderthal Stage in China. In *Circum-Pacific Prehistory Conference Program and Abstracts*, p. 60. Seattle.

Zubov, A. A.
 1981 Comparative Analysis of Dental Materials in the Modern Population of Finland and the Problems of Ethnogenesis of the Finno-Ugric Peoples. In *Congressus Quintus Internationalis Fenno-Ugristarum Turku 20–27. VIII. 1980.* Pars VIII, edited by O. Ikola, pp. 444–449. Suomen Kielen Seura, Turku, Finland.

Paleobiological Evidence of the Peopling of the Americas: A Morphometric View

D. GENTRY STEELE AND JOSEPH F. POWELL
Department of Anthropology
Texas A&M University
College Station, Texas, 77843

A metrical analysis of 8,500- to 10,000 year old human skeletal remains from North America substantiates that their closest affinities are with Asian populations. Earlier (Paleoindian and Early Archaic) North American skeletal samples are distinguished by their relatively long and narrow crania and small, narrow faces. Later populations tended to be more brachycranic and exhibited larger, broader faces. Where Paleoindian specimens differed from modern northern Asians, they tended to structurally resemble southern Asian and European populations. These assessments generally support the inference that populations entered the Americas from northern Asia, but before the cranial features of modern northern Asians and Native Americans were fully developed. Based on the data examined, no date can be specified for time of entrance of the first populations, but the lack of any archaic *Homo sapiens* features supports the contention that entrance into the Americas was a relatively recent event. The number of founding populations cannot be established on the basis of these metric data.

Currently, few biological anthropologists wishing to reconstruct the origins and evolution of American populations rely on the oldest skeletal remains recovered from the Americas. Rather, they have turned to the comparative analyses of Late Holocene or extant American Indian, Asian, and other world populations, typically relying on biological data other than osteometrics. As examples of this approach, Turner (1971, 1983a,b, 1985a,b, 1986a,b, 1987) has compared relatively recent world populations on the basis of discrete characters of the dentition; Brace and colleagues (Brace and Nagai 1982; Brace et al. 1984; Brace and Hunt 1990) have compared Asian populations on the basis of linear dimensions of the face; and Ossenberg (1969, 1974, 1976, 1977, 1986) has compared Asians and American Indians on the basis of discrete traits of the skeleton. With the exception of Turner (1983b) and Turner and Bird (1981), these researchers have compared samples with little consideration given to their relative antiquity.

There are a variety of reasons underlying the reliance on the comparative analyses of recent populations. Most significant is the meager and fragmented nature of the skeletal remains of the early populations. There are fewer than 50 North American sites that contain human skeletal remains older than 5,000 years B.P., and probably no more than 25 of these sites are older than 8,000 B.P. (Table 1). More frustrating is the fact that the earliest sites are represented by one or two very incomplete and fragmented skeletons. Only five of the Paleoindians are represented by crania free of distortion and complete enough for a detailed osteometric analysis.

This reliance on comparative analyses of recent populations, however, dictates that two assumptions be accepted. The first is that little or no evolutionary change has occurred in the populations during the past 10,000 years. Unfortunately, if all descendent populations have altered the ancestral condition, then none can be used as a valid model of the ancestor. The second assumption is that gene flow between populations has not occurred. If any gene flow did occur, then the relative dissimilarities between the populations are no longer solely a reflection of how long ago these groups separated from their common ancestor. Because these assumptions may not always be correct, it is necessary to verify them against the fossil record. Steele and Powell (1992), and Neves and Pucciarelli (1989, 1991) have evaluated the evolutionary history of the American populations based upon the fossil record, and found the earlier populations to differ structurally from more recent indigenous populations of the Americas. The present study is an elaboration of Steele and Powell's (1992) study, comparing the craniofacial structure of the earliest recovered North American and Northern Asian samples with more recent samples from Eurasia and the Pacific rim region.

MATERIALS AND METHODS

The emphasis in this paper is a morphometric evaluation of the craniofacial dimensions of the earliest human remains recovered from North America. Skeletal remains from 16 sites are currently considered by us to be verifiably the oldest North American remains (Steele and

Table 1. Probable and Affirmed Paleoindian Specimens in North America. (Those above the line used in this study.)

LOCALITY	N	REMAINS	DATES (YR B.P.)
Whitewater Draw, AZ (1)	2	skeletons	8,000–10,000
Gordon Creek, CO (2)	1	skeleton	9,700 ± 250
Browns Valley, MN (3)	1	skeleton	8,700 ± 110
Pelican Rapids, MN (4)	1	skeleton	—
Sauk Valley, MN (5)	1	skeleton	—
Wilson-Leonard, TX (6)	1	skeleton	9,000–11,000
Horn Shelter, TX (7)	2	skeletons	9,000–10,000
Shifting Sands, TX (8)	1	T fragments	—
Arlington Springs, CA (9)	12	femora	10,000 ± 310
La Brea, CA (10)	1	skeleton	9,000 ± 80
Mostin, CA (11)	1	fragments	10,000–11,000
Marmes, WA (12)	3	C fragments	10,000–11,000
Fishbone Cave, NV (13)	1	PC fragments	10,900–11,200
Anzick (Wilsal), MT (14)	2	C fragments	8,620–10,500
Vero Beach, FL (15)	1	C fragments	—
Warm Mineral Springs, FL (16)	1	PC fragments	10,260 ± 190

C = cranial, PC = post cranial, T = tooth.

(1) Waters 1986
(2) Breternitz et al. 1971
(3) Jenks 1937
(4) Jenks 1936
(5) Jenks and Wilford 1938
(6) Steele 1989; Weir 1985
(7) Young 1986, 1988
(8) Owsley, personal communication
(9) Orr 1962
(10) Berger 1975, Kroeber 1962
(11) Kaufman 1980, Taylor et al. 1985
(12) Fryxell et al. 1968
(13) Orr 1956, 1974
(14) Taylor 1969; Stafford et al. 1987
(15) Stewart 1946
(16) Clausen et al. 1975.

Powell, 1992), and are identified as Paleoindians (Table 1). Following a variety of scholars (Roberts 1940; Steele and Powell 1992; Young 1985, 1986, 1988; Young et al. 1987) we are using the term "Paleoindian" to refer to the oldest known inhabitants of the Americas, rather than using the term to refer to a distinct subsistence economy based on hunting now-extinct megafauna (Griffin 1979; Shafer 1977; Suhm et al. 1954).

Because the sites are so widely scattered within North America, and because the associated artifacts at some sites indicate different subsistence patterns, we do not presume that these individuals represent a single lifestyle. As examples, Horn Shelter (Redder 1985) and Whitewater Draw (Sayles and Antevs 1941; Sayles 1983; Waters 1985, 1986) are associated with a generalized hunting and gathering mode of subsistence, and Anzick (Taylor 1969) and Shifting Sands (Daniel S. Amick, personal communication), appear to have been associated with big-game hunting economies. Similarly, we realize that these samples do not represent a single local breeding population. In fact, the analyzed material has been recovered from localities as disparate as the American Southwest and the upper Midwest. In spite of the geographical distribution of the sample, the combined Paleoindian sample which we are using has a range of variation for the individual measurements that does not differ significantly from the ranges present in larger and more recent comparative samples. Therefore, we believe that this assemblage of late Pleistocene/early Holocene human remains (Table 1) is collectively the best representation of the earliest Americans currently available.

We have not included skeletal remains more recent than 8,500 years B.P. in our Paleoindian sample, following Steele and Powell (1992), Young (1986, 1988), and Young et al. (1987). This date coincides with the last of the Great Plains fluted-point traditions and their derivatives, such as Firstview, Cody, Eden and Scottsbluff (Jennings 1983), but is more recent than the 10,000 B.P. date assigned for the Early Archaic east of the Mississippi (Fagan 1991; Jennings 1983). This overlap in time between the sites which we have identified as Paleoindian and eastern samples which have been identified as Archaic reflects the confusion created by using these terms to indicate either antiquity or adaptation type. It also is a reflection of the different times in various regions of the Americas when the megafauna became extinct or lost their significance as a resource base for humans.

The sample in Table 1 includes skeletal remains of 21 individuals from 16 sites. Remains from the first eight sites are the most securely dated, and represent the sample used in the morphometric analysis. This portion of the sample also represents the primary evidence used in the subjective assessment of the sample, although in some instances (as indicated in the discussion) the other specimens were also considered. In addition to the remains in Table 1 there are other sites which may ultimately prove to be of great antiquity, but for the present the age of these sites is not secure. For example, the Midland specimen (Wendorf et al. 1955; Wendorf and Krieger 1959) was not included because of the wide range of dates which have been proposed for it, even though in all probability it is mid-Holocene or even older in age. Similarly, the Bonner Springs specimens were excluded because this channel bar assemblage, which includes mineralized remains, is currently undergoing evaluation (Dort and Martin 1988; Steele et al. 1991). Other specimens, previously considered to be of great antiquity, have been excluded because more recent assessments have failed to substantiate their antiquity (Cotter 1991; Taylor et al. 1985).

We conducted both a subjective assessment of the skeletal remains and metric analyses. The subjective analysis focuses on trying to determine if any characters indicative of an affinity with Old World Archaic *Homo sapiens* or *Homo erectus* are present in the Paleoindian assemblage. The metric analyses complement the subjective analysis and focus on a more detailed comparison of the Paleoindians with 33 male and 31 female late-Holocene human populations from North America, northern Asia, the southern Pacific and Australia, and Europe. Additionally, the Paleoindians were compared with the late Pleistocene/early Holocene material from the Jomon culture of Japan, the Minatogawa site on Okinawa Island, and the site of Upper Cave in China. The names, localities, and antiquity the sites as well as the published sources for the measurements used are presented in Table 2.

We used craniometric data to more objectively determine the relationship between Paleoindians and more recent human populations from Europe, Asia, and the Americas. Metric data offer the advantage of being easily standardized, relatively objective, and easy to analyze. In addition, metric data have been collected for virtually every living population and for many prehistoric groups. Cranial dimensions were recorded for each individual in the Paleoindian sample following the techniques described in Howells (1973). These data are presented in Table 3. Because of the fragmentary nature of the Paleoindian crania, only a limited number of cranial and facial dimensions were available for morphometric analysis. The dimensions used in this study included maximum cranial length (GOL), maximum cranial breadth (XCB), upper facial height (NPH), bizygomatic diameter (ZYB), nasal height (NLH), nasal breadth (NLB), orbital height (OBH), and orbital breadth (OBB). Falk and Corruccini (1982) found that five of these eight "traditional" dimensions were more useful in discriminating between modern human populations than less traditional basicranial and nonlinear measurements of the skull. In order to compare the Paleoindian cranial dimensions to those of modern human populations, we compiled the means for the eight cranial dimensions from published sources (Tables 4 and 5). These data form the basis of all univariate and multivariate analyses presented here.

Table 2: Age and Location of Populations used in Univariate Comparisons

POPULATION NAME	LOCATION	AGE	REFERENCE
European			
Armenian	Gagra and Akhalkalak, Armenia (CIS)	Modern	Abdushelishvili 1960
Berg	Carinthia, Austria	Modern	Howells 1973
Georgian	Rustavi, Georgia (CIS)	Modern	Abdushelishvili 1960
Lombards	Austria, Germany, Hungary, Italy	Medieval	Kiszely 1979
Norse	Oslo, Norway	Medieval	Howells 1973
Zalavar	Zalavar, Hungary	Medieval	Howells 1973
African			
Bushman	Kalahari Desert, South Africa	Modern	Howells 1973
Dogon	Bandiagara Plateau, Mali	Modern	Howells 1973
Egypt	Gizeh, Egypt	Prehistoric	Howells 1973
Teita	Teita, Kenya	Modern	Howells 1973
Zulu	Wits, South Africa	Modern	Howells 1973
Australian/Melanesian			
Andaman	Andaman Islands (South Pacific)	Modern	Howells 1973
Mokapu (Polynesian)	Oahu, Hawaii	Prehistoric-Modern	Howells 1973
South Australia	Lake Alexdrina, Australia	Modern	Howells 1973
Tasmania	Tasmania, Australia	Modern	Howells 1973
Tolai (Melanesian)	Ralûm, Papua New Guinea	Modern	Howells 1973
East Asian			
Buriats	Lake Baikal, Siberia, CIS	Modern	Howells 1973
Chinese (Peking)	Peking, China	Modern	Black 1928[a]
Chukchi	Chukchi Peninsula, CIS	Modern	Hrdlička 1944
Japanese (Kanto)	Japan	Modern	Morita 1950[a]
Jomon (Kanto)	Japan	Neolithic	Suzuki 1969[a]
Minatogawa	Naha City, Okinawa	Upper Pleistocene	Suzuki 1982
Ostiak	Little Ob River, CIS	Modern	Hrdlička 1944
Upper Cave	Zhoukoudien (Peking), China	Upper Pleistocene	Weidenreich 1938[a]
Native American			
Pre-Aleut	Aleutian Islands, Alaska	Prehistoric	Hrdlička 1944
Aleut	Aleutian Islands, Alaska	Modern	Hrdlička 1944
Arikara	Sully Site, South Dakota	Protohistoric	Howells 1973
Eskimo (Inugsuk)	Southeastern Greenland	Modern	Howells 1973
Indian Knoll	Ohio Co., western Kentucky	Prehistoric	Snow 1948
Northwest Coast	British Columbia, Canada	Modern	Hrdlička 1944
Pecos Pueblo	Northcentral New Mexico	Prehistoric	Hooton 1930
Peru	Huarochiri and Yauyos Provinces, Peru	Prehistoric	Howells 1973
Texas Archaic	Oso and Palm Harbor Sites, Texas	Prehistoric	Comuzzie et al. 1986; Woodbury & Woodbury 1935
Tennessee Archaic	4 middle and west Tennessee sites	Prehistoric	Boyd 1988
Tennessee Woodland	6 east Tennessee sites	Prehistoric	Boyd 1988
Tennessee Mississippian	6 middle and east Tennessee sites	Prehistoric	Boyd 1988

[a] As cited in Suzuki 1982

Modern: 300 yr B.P. to Present
Protohistoric: 450–150 yr B.P.
Prehistoric: 450–10,000 yr B.P.
Upper Pleistocene: 10,000–18,000 yr B.P.

Table 3: Cranial Dimensions of Female and Male Paleoindian Specimens

	FEMALES		MALES		
	Pelican Rapids[1]	Gordon Creek[2]	Browns Valley[3]	Sauk Valley	Horn Shelter[4]
Maximum Cranial Length	179	173*	193	186	187
Maximum Cranial Breadth	138	138*	142	137	140
Basion-bregma Height	127	—	142	138	—
Auricular Height	116*	100*	124*	—	138*
Minimum Frontal Breadth	93*	—	92*	—	95*
Basion-alveolar Length	(94)	—	—	—	—
Basion-nasion Length	102	—	—	102	—
Bizygomatic Breadth	127	—	140	135	—
Upper Facial Height	67*	57*	66*	—	—
Total Facial Height	114*	108*	110*	—	—
Nasal Height	47*	47*	51*	—	—
Nasal Breadth	21	—	24	28	24
Orbital Height	34*	29*	36*	—	—
Orbital Breadth	38*	37*	38*	—	—

( ) = estimated or reconstructed
*data drawn from original source; all other data recorded by authors

1 Jenks 1936
2 Breternitz et al. 1971
3 Jenks 1937
4 Young 1986

Univariate and bivariate examinations of the data were conducted to determine whether the Paleoindian sample differed significantly from more recent Holocene populations. T-tests for differences in mean craniofacial dimensions between the Paleoindian and other populations were conducted using Bonferroni's experiment-wise alpha protection. The Bonferroni alpha protection for each variable was obtained by dividing the typical 0.05 level of significance by the number of pairwise t-tests conducted. In some cases, the sample size of either the Paleoindians or the comparative population was one. In these situations, a point t-test, which allows a single observation to be compared to a population, was performed (Sokal and Rohlf 1969). In addition to univariate tests of significance, selected data were plotted in bivariate scattergrams (Figures 1–3) showing the position of Paleoindians relative to other groups.

Multivariate analyses offer an advantage over univariate comparisons between populations because they can present a simultaneous picture of population relationships (Howells 1969). In most cases, we did not have access to the original data for the comparative samples. Distance measures typically used to display relationships among populations, such as Mahalanobis' generalized distance (Mahalanobis 1936), could not be computed without the covariation matrix of the original data. Rao (1952) and Penrose (1954) have suggested approximations of generalized distance, but these measures require the acceptance of assumptions which cannot be met by most anthropometric data.

We chose a principal components analysis (PCA) as an alternative to an analysis of the generalized distances between populations (Goodman 1972; Reyment et al. 1984). In the case of PCA, there is no *a priori* grouping of the data; in other words, the relationship between populations is not affected by their geographic proximity or other factors, and is strictly a proximity based on morphological similarity. Other researchers (Kamminga and Wright 1990; Neves and Pucciarelli 1991) have had success in analyzing vectors of population means with PCA to determine relationships between modern and fossil human populations. All statistics and plots for the principal components analysis were generated using the PROC PRIN procedure in SAS (SAS Institute, 1985).

One problem in assessing morphological similarities derived from metric data is the effect of similarities in size compared to similarities derived from shape alone. Some researchers have elected to eliminate size through log-scaling of the data (Reyment et al. 1984; Simmons et al. 1991) or by dividing each measurement by the geometric mean of variables in that case (Darroch and Mosimann 1985; Simmons et al. 1991). We have eliminated size effects by using a Q-mode correction of the data following Corruccini (1973) and Neves and Pucciarelli (1991).

Table 4: Male Means and T-test Results for Selected Craniometric Dimensions in Paleoindians, Prehistoric, and Modern Populations throughout the World[1].

POPULATION	CRANIAL LENGTH (GOL)	CRANIAL BREADTH (XCB)	BIZYGOMATIC BREADTH (ZYB)	UPPER FACIAL HEIGHT (NPH)	NASAL HEIGHT (NLH)	NASAL BREADTH (NLB)	ORBITAL HEIGHT (OBH)	ORBITAL BREADTH (OBB)
Paleoindian	188.67	139.67	137.50	66.00	51.00	25.33	36.00	38.00
Norse	188.47	141.87	134.44	68.93	51.96	25.42	33.74	40.38
Berg	180.32	147.61	135.55	67.89	51.71	25.46	33.75	40.14
Zalavar	185.22	141.39	133.06	68.50	51.41	25.37	32.65	39.98
Lombards	188.21	136.79	132.03	70.00	50.99	23.94	32.44	—
Georgians	175.50*	150.54*	135.44	70.59	52.71	24.57	34.17	42.03
Armenians	172.44*	144.23	133.27	73.50	54.11	25.41	34.70	42.11
Egypt	185.62	139.22	128.83*	68.43	51.74	24.83	32.95	39.50
Teita	183.88	129.85*	131.00	66.00	50.09	27.91	33.29	39.65
Dogon	177.85*	137.29	129.56*	64.85	47.83	28.35	33.79	39.71
Zulu	185.13	134.11	129.94*	67.33	50.00	28.65	33.76	40.44
Bushman	178.37*	133.58	123.56*	57.51	43.76	27.17	30.83	39.27
Andaman	167.81	135.38	123.69*	60.69	46.54	24.50	32.58	37.54
Tolai	183.53	130.36*	136.00	66.07	48.44	27.82	32.24	41.18
Mokapu	186.31	143.72	138.82	68.61	53.31	27.39	35.06	40.69
S. Australian	190.31	131.94*	136.77	64.77	49.69	27.88	33.46	41.86
Tasmanian	185.29	138.18	135.73	62.41	48.70	28.86	31.04	40.70
Upper Cave	206.00*	144.00	143.00	76.00	58.00	33.00	34.00	45.00
Chinese	178.50	138.20	132.70	75.30	55.30	25.00	35.50	44.00
Minatogawa	182.00	148.00	144.00	63.00	49.00	26.00	30.00	46.00
Jomon	181.90	144.10	144.60	66.00	49.60	27.10	33.00	43.20
Japanese	178.90	140.30	132.90	70.70	52.00	25.00	34.30	42.70
Buriat	181.83	154.96*	144.43	74.50	56.89	28.48	35.87	41.52
Chukchi	185.70	142.70	142.50	79.60	55.10	24.40	—	—
Ostiak	183.10	142.80	141.10	75.70	54.00	25.70	—	—
Pre-Aleut	186.90	142.60	144.10	76.40	52.80	25.60	36.20	39.70
Aleut	180.40*	150.80*	144.20	74.30	51.60	25.40	—	—
Eskimo	188.30	133.94	139.59	71.70	54.11	23.68	36.18	41.96
NW Coast	177.40*	144.00	142.80	76.00	51.90	24.50	36.00	—
Pecos Pueblo	175.74*	137.84	138.56	72.85	50.96	25.80	34.90	39.49
Arikara	179.48*	141.55	140.88	71.69	54.45	27.09	34.95	40.55
TX Archaic	185.00	130.80	142.00	—	—	.25.00	34.00	41.00
Indian Knoll	178.80*	135.40	136.00	70.00	51.00	24.40	33.30	42.70
TN Archaic	179.08*	136.08	136.14	69.48	—	—	—	—
TN Woodland	173.83*	143.33	136.17	69.16	—	—	—	—
TN Missisippian	165.78*	147.83	139.71	73.57	—	—	—	—
Peru	177.96	*137.94	134.93	67.78	50.34	25.24	34.27	38.25

* Significant at p= 0.05 using Bonferroni's alpha protection.

[1]T-test for upper facial height, nasal height, nasal breadth, orbital height, and orbital breadth were conducted using a point t-test for comparison of a single Paleoindian observation to a population mean (Sokal and Rohlf 1969:224). All other tests utilzed a standard Student's t. Sample sizes and standard deviations available upon request.

Table 5: Female Means and T-test Results for Selected Craniometric Dimensions in Paleoindians, Prehistoric, and Modern Populations throughout the World[1].

POPULATION	CRANIAL LENGTH (GOL)	CRANIAL BREADTH (XCB)	BIZYGOMATIC BREADTH (ZYB)	UPPER FACIAL HEIGHT (NPH)	NASAL HEIGHT (NLH)	NASAL BREADTH (NLB)	ORBITAL HEIGHT (OBH)	ORBITAL BREADTH (OBB)
Paleoindian	176.00	138.00	127.00	62.00	47.00	21.00	31.50	37.50
Norse	179.98	136.29	124.44	64.25	49.16	24.18	33.22	39.20
Berg	170.53	140.36	126.38	63.49	48.23	24.89	32.75	38.38
Zalavar	176.44	136.89	125.44	63.18	48.49	24.67	32.09	38.67
Lombards	179.88	136.95	126.56	67.80	48.45	23.12	32.57	—
Georgians	167.81	139.62	124.93	64.28	48.41	23.68	32.68	40.09
Armenians	166.19*	140.92	124.30	69.06*	51.02	24.00	34.09	40.52
Egypt	175.58	135.57	120.06	64.06	48.96	24.02	32.83	37.87
Teita	174.61	126.37*	124.14	60.98	46.43	27.18	32.18	37.75
Dogon	169.83	132.21	121.09	61.43	46.09	27.70*	32.75	38.07
Zulu	179.38	131.91	122.89	63.40	47.34	27.98*	32.91	39.25
Bushman	171.71	128.37*	116.53	56.12	42.86	25.92	30.96	37.67
Andaman	160.61*	131.61	118.18	56.68	43.79	24.07	32.39	36.61
Tolai	174.74	128.11*	126.40	62.80	46.65	26.67	32.29	39.07
Mokapu	175.39	138.67	126.88	63.75	49.39	26.02	34.12	39.43
S Australian	181.10	127.51	125.78	61.14	46.51	26.24	33.10	39.96
Tasmanian	177.90	133.02	125.62	58.36	45.36	27.64*	30.74	39.59
Upper Cave [2]	190.00	133.50	134.00	68.75	48.75	25.75	30.15	42.95
Minatogawa [2]	171.00*	136.00	136.00	58.00	46.00	24.00	—	31.00
Buriat	171.82	148.42*	134.45	69.45	53.42*	26.82	34.91	39.78
Chukchi	177.50	136.80	132.00	73.90*	51.00	23.80	35.70*	39.00
Ostiak	174.10	139.60	131.10	69.90*	50.60	24.90	34.50	37.90
Pre-Aleut	178.80	138.20	133.5	71.40*	49.50	24.40	35.10	38.70
Aleut	171.90	144.20	133.80	70.20*	49.20	24.20	35.40	38.60
Eskimo	180.81	131.02	130.17	67.06	50.39	23.31	35.13	40.46
NW Coast	170.10	138.50	131.20	68.90	49.60	24.00	35.30	37.70
Pecos Pueblo	163.65*	138.04	129.87	69.04*	48.20	25.33	34.49	38.14
Arikara	171.11	136.48	130.67	67.63	50.52	25.81	34.63	39.22
TX Archaic	181.50	130.00	—	57.00	—	25.00	38.00	—
Indian Knoll	172.10	131.50	127.40	65.40	47.60	23.80	32.80	40.40
TN Archaic	176.29	135.10	—	64.44	—	—	—	—
TN Woodland	163.00	143.00	—	67.80	—	—	—	—
TN Missisippian	159.35*	144.92	—	70.82*	—	—	—	—
Peru	169.00	134.93	125.60	63.65	47.65	23.96	34.14	36.82

*Significant at p = 0.05 using Bonferroni's alpha protection.

[1] T-test for upper facial height, nasal height, nasal breadth, orbital height, and orbital breadth were conducted using a point t-test for comparison of a single Paleoindian observation to a population mean (Sokal and Rohlf 1969:224). All other tests utilized a standard Student's t. Sample sizes and standard deviations available upon request.

[2] Single individual compared to the Paleoindian sample using a point t-test (Sokal and Rohlf 1969:224).

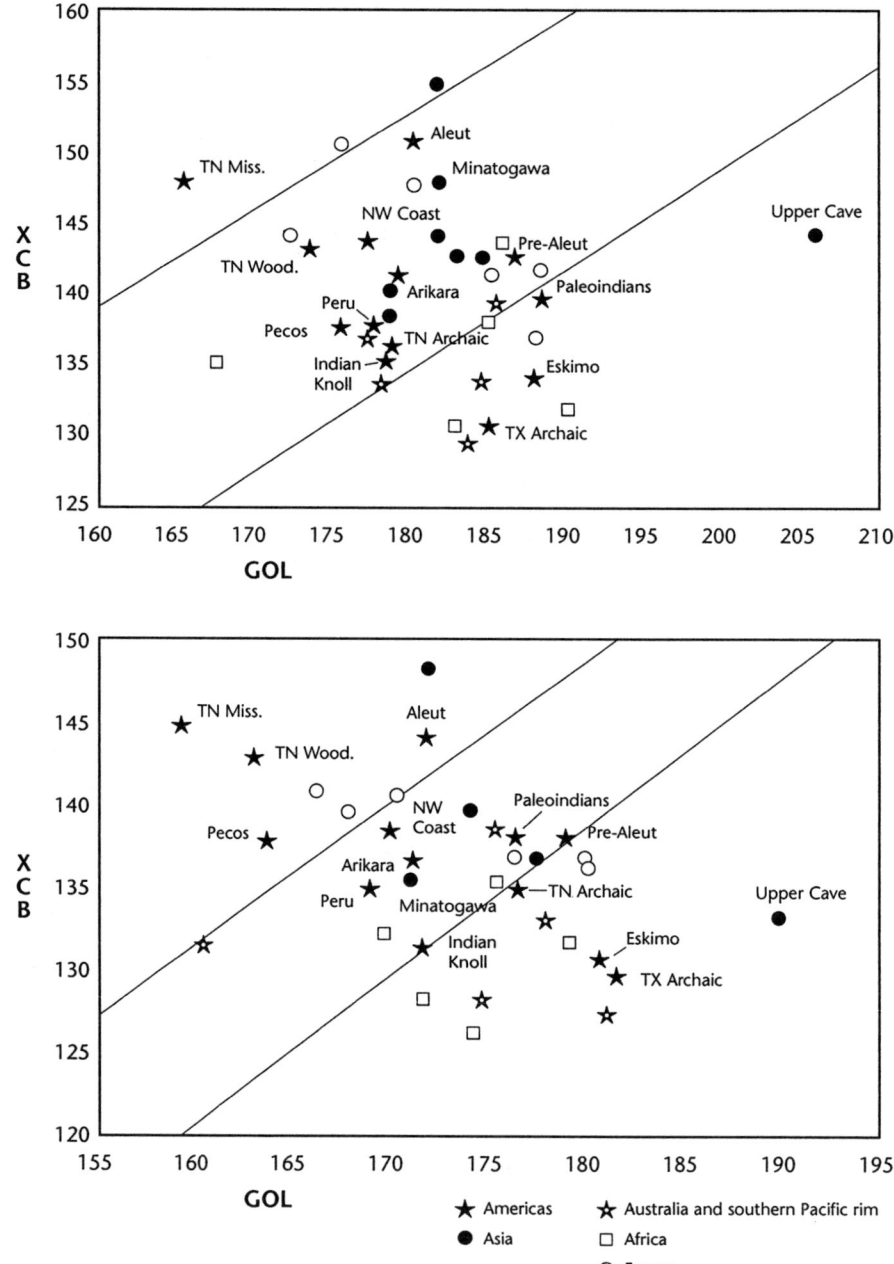

Figure 1. Plot of mean cranial length (GOL) vs. mean cranial breadth (XCB) for males (upper portion) and females (lower portion) in modern and prehistoric world populations. Lines (top to bottom) separate brachycranic, mesocranic, and dolicocranic groups.

The Q-mode correction involves dividing each measurement in a case by the arithmetic average across all measurements for that particular case. This type of correction is similar to that of Darroch and Mosimann (1985), but uses the arithmetic average rather than the geometric mean. The Q-mode correction eliminates size differences by giving each population "the same average character state or magnitude over all the measurements taken on it" (Corruccini 1973:747).

The results of the PCA for the uncorrected vector of population means (i.e., size-and-shape data) are presented in Figures 4 and 5, and in Tables 6 and 7. The Q-mode corrected PCA (i.e., shape only), presented in Figures 6 and 7 and Tables 8 and 9, can be contrasted with the size-and-shape results to determine the effects of size on relationships between the populations examined.

We also analyzed the population means using a canonical discriminant function analysis generated by PROC CANDISC in SAS (SAS Institute, 1985). Each population was assigned to one of five major geographic

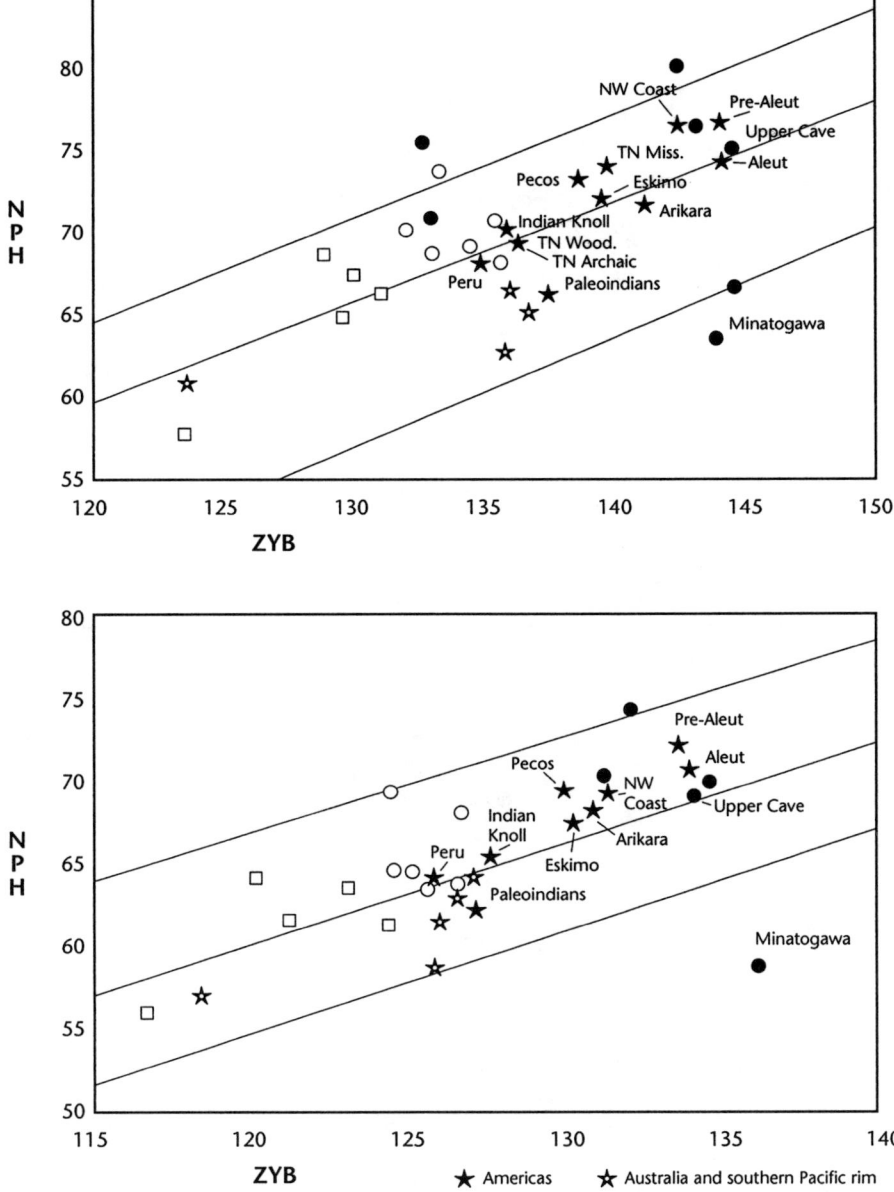

Figure 2. Plot of mean bizygomatic breadth (ZYB) vs. mean upper facial height (NPH) for males (upper) and females (lower) in modern and prehistoric world populations. Lines (top to bottom) separate leptene, mesene, Euryene, and hypereuryene.

groups based on a presumably common cultural and biological history: Europeans, northeast Asians, southern Pacific populations (including Australians, Tasmanians, and Melanesians), and American Indians. These *a priori* classes were entered into the canonical discriminant analysis, where the algorithm attempts to best summarize the differences between classes and partition them through a linear combination of the variables. The Paleoindian, Upper Cave, Minatogawa, and Jomon populations were not assigned to a particular geographic group, so that their positions among the classes could be better assessed. The results of this analysis are presented in Figures 8 and 9 and Table 10.

RESULTS

Because the model depicting the makers of Clovis projectile points as the first colonizers of the Americas is not universally accepted (Carter 1978; Gruhn 1987; Simpson

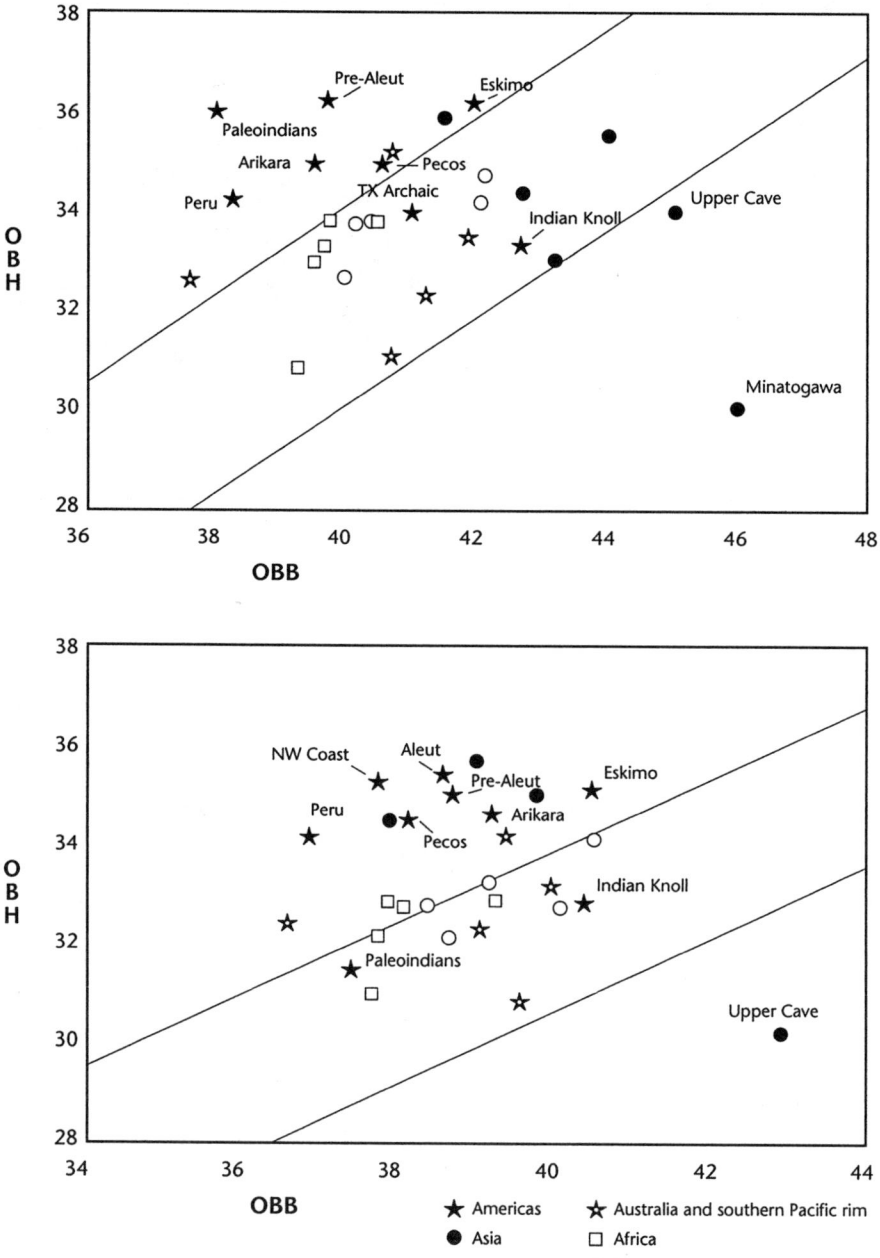

Figure 3. Plot of mean orbital breadth (OBB) vs. mean orbital height (OBH) for males (upper) and females (lower) in modern and prehistoric world populations. Lines (top to bottom) separate hypsiconch, mesoconch, and chamaeconch groups.

1978; Simpson et al. 1986), proposed early human remains are typically examined for "primitive" features which would link them to earlier human populations such as *Homo erectus* or archaic forms of *Homo sapiens* (Givens 1968a,b; Bryan 1978; Davis et al. 1980). Primitive features usually considered diagnostic of earlier populations are massive and protruding browridges, a low rising frontal, marked postorbital constriction of the frontal, thick cranial elements, a prominent and protruding occipital, small mastoid processes, and a massive face.

Of the Paleoindians specimens listed in Table 1, the Browns Valley, Gordon Creek, Horn Shelter, La Brea, Pelican Rapids, Sauk Valley, Whitewater Draw, and Wilson-Leonard remains are represented by cranic complete enough to evaluate one or more of the primitive features. Browns Valley, Sauk Valley and the Horn Shelter adult are the most robust, and all three are considered to be male based on the features of the *os coxae* and the robustness of the skeleton. Gordon Creek, Pelican Rapids, La Brea, and Wilson-Leonard are considered adolescent or

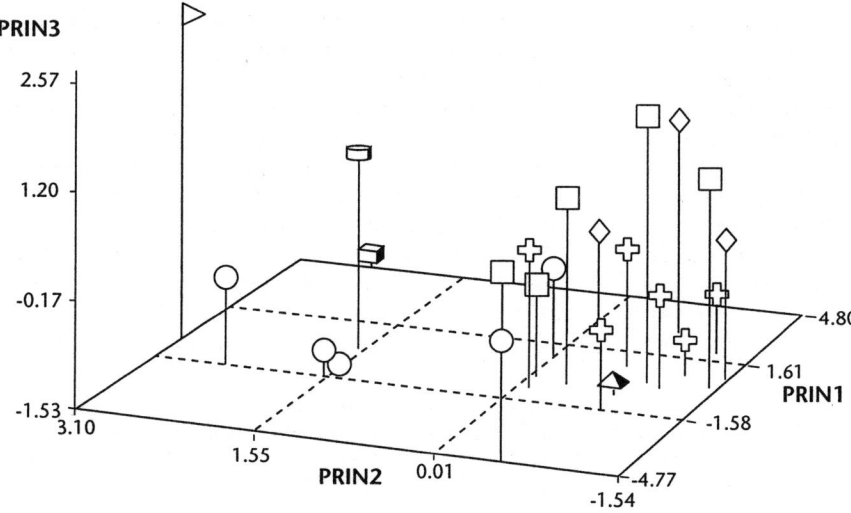

Figure 4. Principal Component Analysis of size and shape data for males showing the first, second, and third principal components.

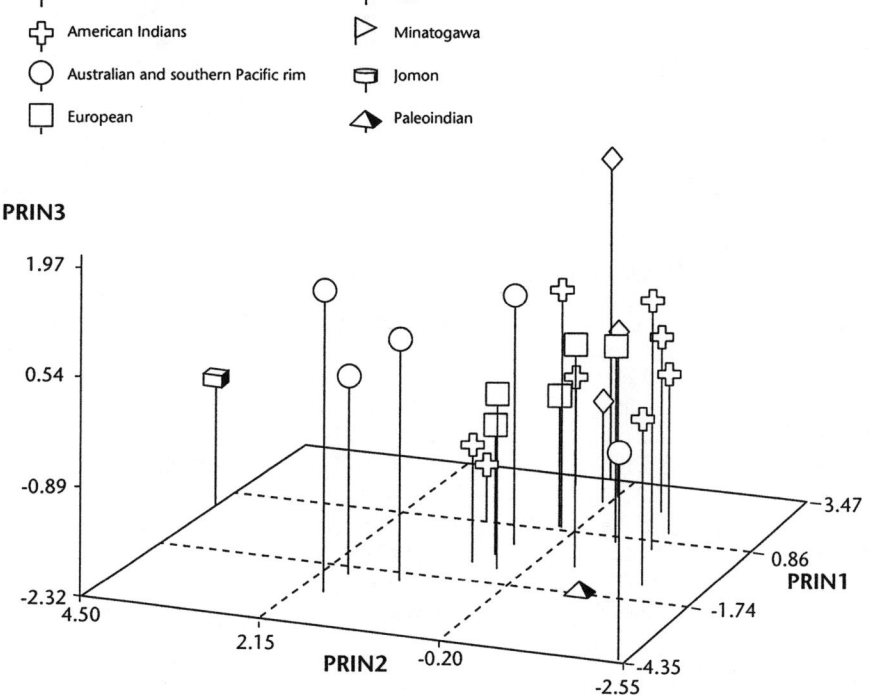

Figure 5. Principal Component Analysis of size and shape data for females showing the first, second, and third principal components.

adult females and are distinguished by their gracile skeleton. The browridges of Browns Valley and Sauk Valley have been characterized as robust and prominent (Jenks 1936; Jenks and Wilford 1938; Smith 1976), but in both of these specimens it is the supracilliary arches near glabella which are prominent (here we follow the browridge terminology established by Schwalbe 1909, as cited in Russell 1985). In contrast, the supraorbital sulcus is present in both specimens and the lateral extension of the supraorbital arches are reduced. This browridge configuration is typical of robust anatomically modern male crania. The Horn Shelter male differs from these two only in its slightly more prominent development of the supraorbital arch. In the Horn Shelter male, the lateral aspect of the supraorbital arch approximates the size of the arch seen in Middle and Upper Paleolithic specimens such as the Middle Paleolithic Skhul V, Israel, and the Upper Paleolithic Predmost 3, Czechoslovakia (Day 1986). Although uncommon, we have also seen supraorbital arches this prominent in Late Archaic and Late Prehistoric specimens from the Texas coast, and in other anatomically modern assemblages.

None of the Paleoindian specimens exhibit particularly thick frontals, parietals or occipitals indicative of archaic *Homo* populations. The Sulphur Springs Woman I (Sayles and Antevs 1941) has notably thick parietal elements near the sagittal suture, but upon examination, this thickness is due to an expansion of the diplöe with concomitant reduction of the cortical bone, a pattern that suggests the presence of porotic hyperostosis. An examination of the Paleoindian specimens in *norma lateralis* also confirms that the general height of the braincase, the development of the frontal expansion, and the prominence of the occipital protuberance are well within the range of variation of anatomically modern humans, and does not provide evidence for an archaic *Homo* linkage.

The bivariate plots of eight measurements of the braincase (cranial length and breadth) and face (bizygomatic breadth, upper facial height, nasal height and breadth, orbital height and breadth) were used to evaluate the

Table 6: Eigenvalues and Eigenvectors for the First Four Principal Components Using Male Data for Size and Shape.

	COMPONENT I	COMPONENT II	COMPONENT III	COMPONENT IV
Eigenvectors				
GOL	0.32604	0.34876	-0.50657	0.05489
XCB	0.27958	-0.03302	0.67064	0.51308
ZYB	0.39590	0.22737	0.09055	0.30035
NPH	0.43065	-0.36316	-0.02930	-0.26264
NLH	0.49337	-0.22759	0.00117	-0.13806
OBH	0.26983	-0.56044	-0.27832	0.10458
OBB	0.27071	0.34015	0.37800	-0.70460
NLB	0.28952	0.46054	-0.25342	0.21929
Cumulative Eigenvalues:	3.31918	1.92560	1.09902	0.71837
% of Variance:	0.41490	0.65560	0.79297	0.88277

Table 7: Eigenvalues and Eigenvectors for the First Four Principal Components Using Female Data for Size and Shape.

	COMPONENT I	COMPONENT II	COMPONENT III	COMPONENT IV
Eigenvectors				
GOL	0.06214	0.58662	-0.34700	0.12826
XCB	0.36045	-0.25992	0.24775	-0.66163
ZYB	0.45140	0.21475	-0.03007	0.19284
NPH	0.50236	0.02326	-0.14410	0.13017
NLH	0.49695	0.02989	0.04821	-0.17099
OBH	0.38875	-0.31248	0.03625	0.52931
OBB	0.10752	0.57813	-0.01065	-0.34949
NLB	-0.02097	0.32997	0.89039	0.24519
Cumulative Eigenvalues:	3.49486	2.10726	0.91528	0.63651
% of Variance:	0.43686	0.70026	0.81467	0.89424

cranial structure of Paleoindians compared to a selection of anatomically modern human populations. Cranial length and breadth can be used to describe the overall shape of the braincase. The male Paleoindian sample has one of the longest cranial lengths of the 36 samples evaluated (Table 4). Of these 36, only six average 188.0 mm or more, and only two of the samples, South Australians and Upper Cave, exceed the Paleoindian mean of 188.67. Thirteen of the 36 samples possess cranial lengths significantly shorter than those of the Paleoindian males, eight of which are American Indian populations. Nineteen of the 36 samples exceed the Paleoindian sample in cranial breadth, and four of these are significantly broader. The relationship between cranial length and breadth is traditionally presented as the Cranial Index or in a bivariate plot (upper portion, Figure 1). Considering both dimensions simultaneously, the Paleoindians were one of only 10 male samples which are identified as dolichocranic (long-headed). The female Paleoindian sample, on the other hand, is not as long-headed relative to the other female samples, nor as narrow. Even though the female Paleoindians are among the larger of the female samples (mean cranial length = 176.00 mm), 12 of the 33 modern female populations exceed the Paleoindian mean for cranial length. None of these 12, however, are significantly larger; in fact, five female samples are significantly shorter than Paleoindians. In cranial breadth, the Paleoindian females are again among the larger samples (mean cranial breadth = 138.00 mm). Twelve have a greater cranial breadth and one is significantly broader. Three of the 33 samples that have a narrower cranial breadth are significantly smaller. When cranial length and breadth are plotted for the females (lower portion, Figure 1), the female Paleoindian sample is more typical

Table 8: Eigenvalues and Eigenvectors for the First Four Principal Components Using Q-mode Corrected Male Data for Shape Only.

	COMPONENT I	COMPONENT II	COMPONENT III	COMPONENT IV
Eigenvectors				
GOL	-0.34082	0.53975	-0.10066	-0.02548
XCB	0.08922	-0.64265	0.00491	-0.52723
ZYB	-0.28302	-0.27582	-0.45899	0.47804
NPH	0.48987	0.13656	0.12877	0.26803
NLH	0.47608	0.17835	0.32778	-0.05342
OBH	0.42963	0.16579	-0.44034	0.07273
OBB	-0.16648	-0.23854	0.62546	0.52911
NLB	-0.34184	0.29111	0.26465	-0.36456
Cumulative Eigenvalues:	3.11201	1.69382	1.22250	0.95492
% of Variance:	0.38900	0.60073	0.75354	0.87291

Table 9: Eigenvalues and Eigenvectors for the First Four Principal Components Using Q-mode Corrected Female Data for Shape Only.

	COMPONENT I	COMPONENT II	COMPONENT III	COMPONENT IV
Eigenvectors				
GOL	-0.47486	-0.15067	-0.20776	-0.20043
XCB	0.28024	0.51112	0.36498	-0.41138
ZYB	0.10497	-0.67942	0.39145	0.02879
NPH	0.39884	-0.34262	-0.34306	0.20263
NLH	0.38847	0.25861	-0.41720	0.27684
OBH	0.38930	0.03657	0.15341	0.33980
OBB	-0.38796	0.18100	-0.33542	0.31025
NLB	-0.27000	0.18995	0.49254	0.67848
Cumulative Eigenvalues:	3.43595	1.49556	1.11126	0.81009
% of Variance:	0.42949	0.61644	0.75535	0.85661

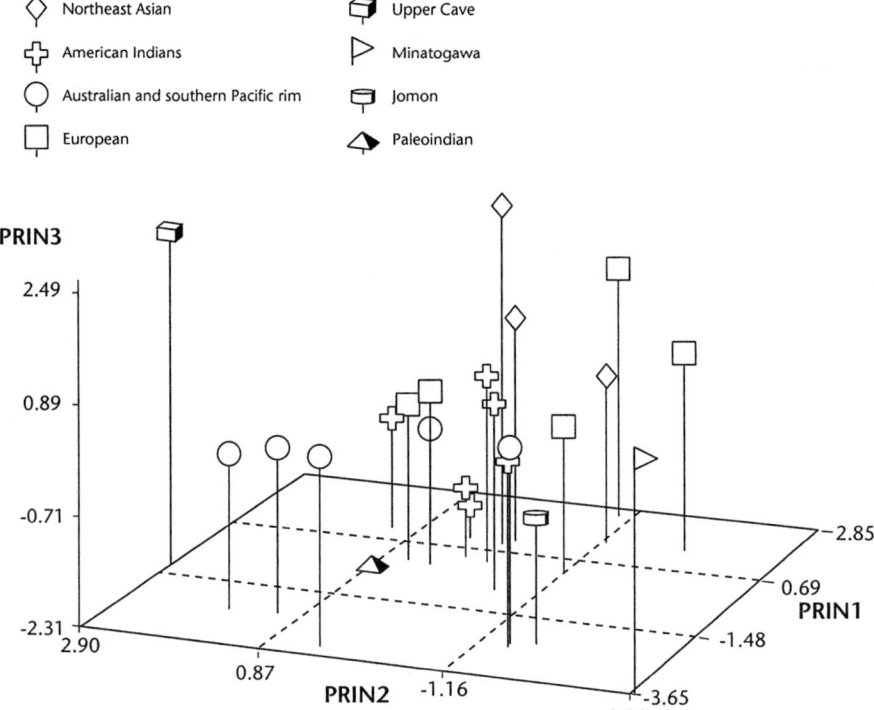

Figure 6. Principal Component Analysis of size-corrected data for males showing the first, second, and third principal components.

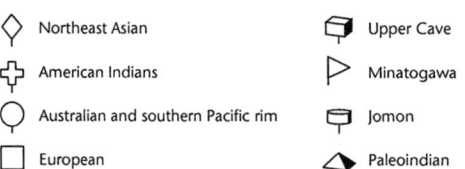

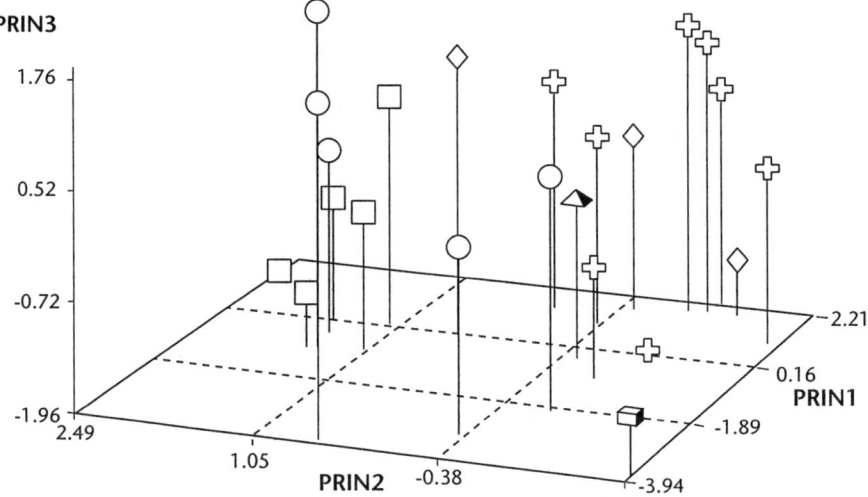

Figure 7. Principal Component Analysis of size-corrected data for females showing the first, second, and third principal components.

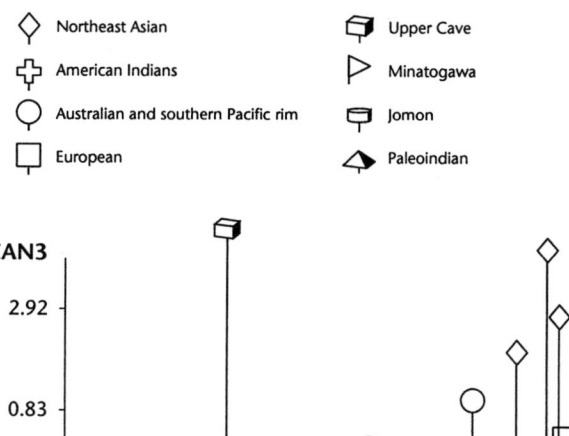

Figure 8. Canonical Discriminant Function Analysis of size and shape data for males showing the first, second, and third variates.

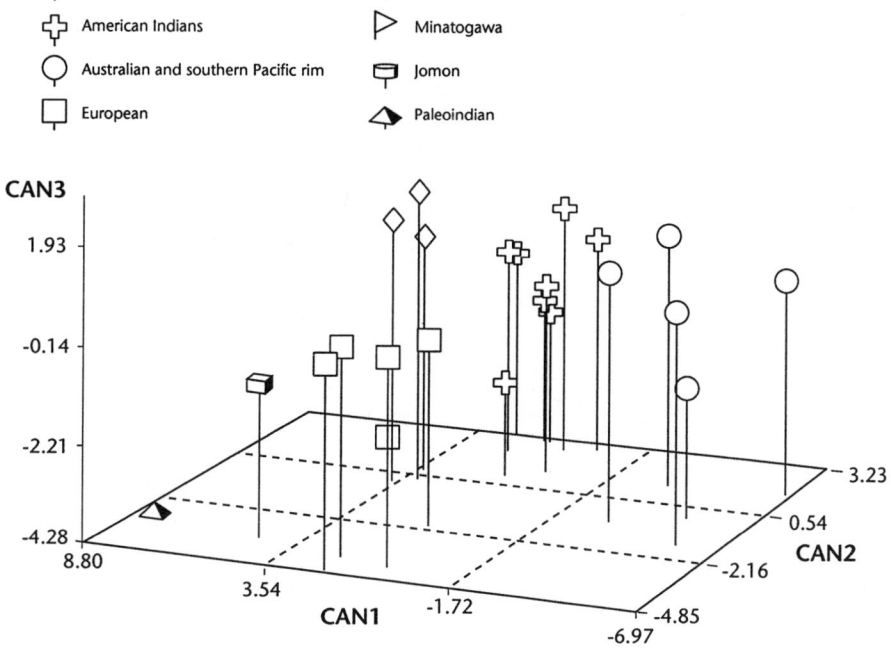

Figure 9. Canonical Discriminant Function Analysis of size and shape data for females showing the first, second, and third variates.

Table 10: Canonical Discriminant Analysis of Male and Female Craniometric Data.

	MALE			FEMALE		
	Canonical Axis I	Canonical Axis II	Canonical Axis III	Canonical Axis I	Canonical Axis II	Canonical Axis III
Variable						
GOL	-0.0384	-0.2072	-0.0628	-0.1192	0.0438	0.1305
XCB	0.0895	0.7795	-0.2081	0.5493	-0.5730	0.0977
ZYB	0.6818	0.2311	-0.0308	0.8612	-0.0009	0.2890
NPH	0.4751	0.6561	0.4456	0.7539	-0.3087	0.4851
NLH	0.3529	0.6946	0.1616	0.6313	-0.4977	0.3323
OBH	0.4739	0.4380	0.5025	0.7702	-0.0141	0.4564
OBB	0.0803	0.5516	-0.1101	0.1880	-0.2170	-0.3626
NLB	-0.4327	-0.4530	-0.1429	-0.5846	0.3229	0.2390
Eigenvalue:	10.6377	2.9819	0.5534	9.7883	1.8753	0.9761
% Variance: (Cumulative)	0.7389	0.9332	0.9711	0.7646	0.9111	0.9873

of other populations and falls within the mesocranic range.

While the bivariate analysis of cranial length and breadth documents relatively similar positions for males and females of the same population, five populations (in addition to the Paleoindians) exhibit marked sexual dimorphism in cranial shape. Three of these populations are American Indian (Tennessee Woodland, Aleut, and Pecos Pueblo) and two are European (Lombard and Georgian). Of the five populations that show sexual dimorphism in cranial shape, only two (Tennessee Woodland and Pecos Pueblo) also exhibit sexual dimorphism in cranial length.

Six measurements were used to describe the shape of the face: facial height and breadth, nasal height and breadth, and orbit height and breadth. When we consider all populations tested, both the male and the female Paleoindians have a relatively broad face, their facial breadth being exceeded by only 15 of 36 male and 12 of 29 female populations. Of these, five of the male samples have significantly narrower faces, while none of the females populations differ significantly. A different perspective is obtained when comparing Paleoindians to northern Asians and American Indians. While not significantly different, the majority of the modern northern Asian and American Indian populations have a broader face.

In contrast, the upper facial height of Paleoindians compared to all populations is shorter than 29 of the male samples and 25 of the female samples, with five of the female samples being significantly longer. When considering just northern Asian and American Indian populations, all of the American Indian populations exhibit longer faces, while the faces of northern Asian populations are approximately the same height. What is particularly noteworthy is that of the five female samples which exhibit significantly longer faces, two of them are North American Indians, and two are modern northern Asian populations. When facial length and breadth are considered simultaneously (Figure 2), however, the relatively short and broad euryene face of the Paleoindian face is apparent. Only four of the male and two of the female populations have relatively broader faces. Considering the relative effects of upper facial height and bizygomatic breadth in determining facial shape, it is apparent that the marked shorter face of the Paleoindians contributes to the euryene (broad) upper facial index.

Examination of the nasal dimensions reveals that the Paleoindians have relatively short and narrow nasal apertures, but only three female samples (Dogon, Zulu, and Tasmania) have significantly broader nasal apertures than the Paleoindians. While not differing significantly, the majority of the northern Asians and American Indians have longer and broader nasal apertures.

Orbit dimensions exhibit a different pattern (Figure 3). The American Indian populations consistently exhibit high orbits, but orbit width is not as diagnostic. The Paleoindian males follow this pattern, exhibiting one of the largest means for orbit height. Paleoindian females, however, do no follow this trend, having one of the smallest orbit heights. Both Paleoindian males and females exhibit narrower orbits than all but a few samples, but there is no clear pattern of orbit breadth in any of the geographical regions.

We have used univariate and bivariate analyses to support the distinctiveness of specific structural features of Paleoindians. To statistically summarize the relationship of the Paleoindians to the other populations using all measurements simultaneously we have used two principal components analyses and one canonical discriminant analysis. The principal-components analysis of the uncorrected size-and-shape data (Tables 6 and 7, and Figures 4 and 5) aligns both the male and female

Paleoindians with the American Indians and northern Asians on the basis of the first two principal components, but separates them slightly along the third component. No discernible relationship among the fossil samples (Paleoindian, Jomon, Upper cave and Minatogawa) can be seen in this analysis. The first three components account for 79.29% and 81.86% of the variance seen in the male and female samples, respectively.

When the data are corrected following Corruccini (1973) so that PCA distinguishes populations on the basis of shape alone, the Paleoindian male sample aligns between the American Indians and southern Pacific populations, and away from modern northern Asians (Tables 8 and 9, Figures 6 and 7). The female Paleoindian sample follows this same pattern, with the American Indian and northern Asian samples forming a loose group along the second component. The fossil samples, while still widely dispersed on the basis of the second and third principal components, are aligned more with the southern Pacific and European samples, rather than with American Indians and northern Asians. For the shape data, the first three principal components account for 75.35% and 75.54% of the male and female variance, respectively.

When the canonical discriminant analysis is examined (Table 10, Figures 8 and 9), the Paleoindian males are separated from the American Indians and move towards southern Pacific and Australian groups. However, the pattern for female samples is more dispersed, with Paleoindians somewhat isolated, but closer to the European populations than with any other group. When the fossil samples are considered, the close similarity of Paleoindians and Jomon is apparent in the males (Figure 8). For Paleoindian females, the closest fossil assemblage is the Upper Cave sample.

DISCUSSION

As noted above, the subjective analysis clearly aligns the 8,500–10,000 year B.P. sample of Paleoindian remains with anatomically modern humans, and there is no anatomical evidence of a morphological linkage to an earlier, isolated Archaic American *Homo* population. If we assume that similarities in craniofacial morphology to some degree reflect genetic relationships between populations, rather than parallel evolution in craniofacial shape, we can make some interpretive statements about the results presented above. Our data suggest that the Paleoindian samples, which currently represent the oldest North American human remains, are genetically derived from the anatomically modern human population which evolved in the Old World before colonizing the Americas. This viewpoint is held by most, if not all, physical anthropologists who have examined the American fossil record (Hrdlička 1923, 1937; Neumann 1956; Protsch 1978; Smith 1976; Steele and Powell 1992; Stewart 1960, 1981; Young 1986, 1988).

The above statement, however, does not preclude the possibility that the North American Paleoindian population differs from later Holocene populations in both the Americas and other populations along the Pacific rim. One of the longest-held views concerning the peopling of the Americas is that the earliest populations entering from the Bering Strait region differed from more recent northern Asian and American Indian populations in several respects. Typically, these early peoples, while still falling within the range of anatomically modern populations, were characterized as dolichocranic (long-headed) with a low rising frontal and commonly with a prominent occipital protuberance.

Dixon (1923), one of the first researchers to describe this suite of features for the first colonizers, proposed that by more recent times these populations had been replaced in the central portions of the Americas by later-arriving brachycranic populations with more typical mongoloid features. This hypothesis is remarkably similar to models of ancestor displacement derived from vicariance biogeography (Rosen 1978). Other researchers expressing this view include Birdsell (1951), Hooton (1930, 1933), Hrdlička (1923), Newman (1962), Rivet (1925), and Stewart (1949, 1973). Neumann (1952), one of the few physical anthropologists to attempt a comprehensive summarization of the structural variation of North American Indians, identified the remnants of these early populations as the "Otamid variety." He based his description of the variety on a Texas central coastal sample of 18 specimens, and identified the Browns Valley Paleoindian male as an early example of an "Otamid." Neumann felt that these "Otamid" descendants of the earliest colonizers were relict populations restricted to marginal environments.

Since both European and southern Pacific populations have a more long-headed cranial shape, many researchers have proposed that these populations were possibly more closely related to Paleoindians by a common ancestor. Neves and Pucciarelli (1991), Neumann (1962), Protsch (1978), and Stringer and Andrews (1988) have all proposed that the Asian ancestors to the American Indians lacked the markedly broad face and cranium associated with modern northern Asians, and in this respect were more European or southern Asian in appearance. Generally, those espousing this view have identified the Asian ancestor as "proto-mongoloid," "archaic-mongoloid," "proto-caucasoid," or "pre-mongoloid" (Kamminga and Wright 1990; Neves and Pucciarelli 1991, Neumann 1962, Protsch 1978). Typically, the Upper Cave male is used as an Asian fossil example of such a dolichocranic ancestor to the American Indians (Kamminga and Wright 1990; Neves and Pucciarelli 1989, 1991; Neumann 1956).

In general, our results and those published elsewhere (Steele and Powell 1992) substantiate the distinctiveness of the Paleoindians. In many of the univariate analyses presented, the Paleoindians are found to fall at one extreme end of the American Indian range, away from northern Asians and nearer to southern Asians and Europeans. The features distinguishing the Paleoindians from the more recent American Indians are the narrower and longer braincase and the smaller and slightly narrower face and nasal aperture. The multivariate morphometric pattern that emerges is one where later Holocene northern Asians, and to a slightly lesser extent the American Indians, fall on one extreme in a suite of craniofacial features, while southern Pacific and European populations fall on the other. Paleoindians, when they differ from more recent American Indians, fall between these two extremes. These assessments are summarized in the principal components analyses and are most markedly illustrated in the canonical discriminant analysis. This more central position of the earliest North American populations among those of the Pacific rim also has been confirmed for early South American populations (Neves and Pucciarelli 1989, 1991).

Turner and colleagues (Greenberg et al. 1986; Turner 1971, 1983a,b, 1985a,b, 1986a,b, 1987; Turner and Bird 1981) have provided the most comprehensive evaluation of the peopling of the Americas, their views being based principally upon dental similarities of populations. Their data, particularly Turner (1985b), verify the distinctiveness of Paleoindians from more recent American Indians and northern Asians.

While there seems to be a long historical record of the recognition of the distinctiveness of the earliest American populations from later populations in the New World, and an apparent consensus among recent scholars on the more moderate structural features of the Paleoindians, we are still cautious in modeling universal American trends towards the simultaneous brachycephalization of the braincase and enlargement of the face in all American populations. In our analyzed sample, two temporal sequences within specific regions permit us to evaluate these changes in late-Holocene North American populations: the Tennessee populations examined by Boyd (1988) and the pre-Aleut and Aleut samples reported by Hrdlička (1944). While both of these sequences depict a consistent increase in the relative width of the braincase through time, the Tennessee samples as reported by Boyd (1988) exhibit a slight reduction in the face over time.

The last point we would like to make concerns the relationship of the Paleoindian sample to the other early Holocene/Late Pleistocene samples of the Pacific rim. As mentioned previously, the Paleoindian population is commonly considered similar to the Upper Cave remains from northern Asia. Further, these latter remains are commonly considered evidence of the presence of a population in China which lacks the typical broad features of later norther Asians (Kamminga and Wright 1990). While this view can be held when considering individual features, the Upper Cave remains (both male and female) appear as aberrant outliers in all of our multivariate analyses. An examination of the two Principal Components analyses reveals that the fossil remains of the Paleoindians, the Upper Cave specimens, and the Jomon sample from Japan are all aligned with southern Pacific and Australian populations on the basis of the first principal component. However, the second and third principal components of each analysis tend to separate these fossil groups from one another. Considering the univariate analyses and the eigenvectors presented in Tables 6–9, it is apparent that in part these components are being influenced by the dolichocranic shape of the braincase. In the canonical discriminant analysis the alignment of Paleoindians with Jomon is apparent in the males, as is the uniqueness of the Upper Cave male. We also feel that it is important to recognize that while the fossil samples differ from one another to a lesser or greater degree, they all differ to a marked degree from modern northern Asians.

In conclusion, we believe that our analysis provides the most careful consideration of the Paleoindian remains to date, and that this analysis supports the distinctiveness of the Paleoindian sample from the more recent Holocene American Indians. Our analysis also supports the previous work describing the structural similarities between Paleoindians, and southern Pacific and European populations. At the present time, it is our opinion that the late Pleistocene and early Holocene populations of northern Asia and the Americas differed morphologically, but we are unsure of the cause of these differences. One view is that these differences substantiate that the earliest colonizing populations entering Beringia had a different genetic structure than later northern Asians and their North and South American descendants. The second view is that these differences reflect an adaptation of later populations to a different environment or lifestyle, possibly associated with the origins of agriculture, and that these adaptations were accomplished by the general plasticity of a common genome. At the present time we cannot resolve this last issue.

REFERENCES CITED

Abdushelishvili, M. G.
  1960 Craniology of the Caucasus. In *Contributions to the Physical Anthropology of the Soviet Union*, edited by V. V. Bunak, G. F. Debets, and M. G. Levin. Russian Translation Series of the Peabody Museum of Archaeology and Ethnology, vol. 1, No. 2. Peabody Museum, Cambridge.

Berger, R.
  1975 Advances and Results in Radiocarbon Dating: Early Man in America. *World Archaeology* 7:174–184.

Birdsell, J. B.
  1951 The Problem of the Early Peopling of the Ameri-

cas as Viewed from Asia. In *The Physical Anthropology of the American Indian*, edited by W. S. Laughlin, pp. 1–68. Edwards Brothers, Ann Arbor.

Black, D.
1928 A Study of Kansu and Honan Aeneolithic Skulls and Specimens from Later Kansu Prehistoric Sites in Comparison with North China and Other Recent Crania. *Paleontologica Sinica* 6:1–83.

Boyd, D. C. M.
1988 *A Functional Model for Masticatory-Related Mandibular, Dental, and Craniofacial Microevolutionary Change Derived from a Selected Southeastern Indian Skeletal Temporal Series.* Unpublished Ph.D. dissertation, Department of Anthropology, University of Tennessee, Knoxville.

Brace, C. L., and K. D. Hunt
1990 A Nonracial Craniofacial Perspective on Human Variation: A(ustralia) to Z(uni). *American Journal of Physical Anthropology* 82:341–360.

Brace, C. L., and M. Nagai
1982 Japanese Tooth Size: Past and Present. *American Journal of Physical Anthropology* 59:399–411.

Brace, C. L. X. Shao, and Z. Zhang
1984 Prehistoric and Modern Tooth Size in China. In *The Origins of Modern Humans: A World Survey of the Fossil Evidence*, edited by F. H. Smith and F. Spencer, pp. 485-516. Alan R. Liss, New York.

Breternitz, D. A., A. C. Swedlund, and D. C. Anderson
1971 An Early Burial from Gordon Creek, Colorado. *American Antiquity* 36:170–182.

Bryan, A. L.
1978 An Overview of Paleo-American Prehistory from a Circum-Pacific Perspective. In *Early Man in America from a Circum-Pacific Perspective*, edited by A. L. Bryan, pp. 306–327. Archaeological Researches International, Edmonton, Alberta.

Carter, G. F.
1978 The American Paleolithic. In *Early Man in America from a Circum-Pacific Perspective*, edited by A. L. Bryan, pp. 10–18. Archaeological Researches International, Edmonton, Alberta.

Clausen, C. J., H. K. Brooks, and A. B. Wesollowsky
1975 The Early Man Site at Warm Mineral Springs, Florida. *Journal of Field Archeology* 2:191–213.

Comuzzie, A. G., M. Marek, and D. G. Steele
1986 Analysis of Human Skeletal Remains from the Palm Harbor Site (41AS80), A Mortuary Site on the Central Gulf Coast of Texas. *Bulletin of the Texas Archeological Society* 55:213–249.

Corruccini, R. S.
1973 Size and Shape in Similarity Coefficients Based on Metric Characters. *American Journal of Physical Anthropology* 38:743–754.

Cotter, J. L.
1991 Update of Natchez Man. *American Antiquity* 56:36–39.

Darroch, J. N., and J. E. Mosimann
1985 Canonical and Principal Components of Shape. *Biometrika* 72:241–252.

Davis, E. L., K. H. Brown, and J. Nichols
1980 *Evaluation of Early Human Activities and Remains in the California Desert.* Great Basin Foundation, Riverside, California.

Day, M. H.
1986 *Guide to Fossil Man.* 4th ed. Cassell, London.

Dixon, R. B.
1923 *The Racial History of Man.* Charles Scribner's Sons, New York.

Dort, W. Jr., and L. D. Martin
1988 Geological Setting of Ancient Human Bones at Bonner Springs, Northeastern Kansas. *American Journal of Physical Anthropology* 75:204–205.

Fagan, B. M.
1991 *Ancient North America: The Archaeology of a Continent.* Thames and Hudson, London.

Falk, D., and R. Corruccini
1982 Efficacy of Cranial Versus Dental Measurements for Separating Human Populations. *American Journal of Physical Anthropology* 57:123–127.

Fryxell, R., T. Bielicki, R. D. Daugherty, C. E. Gustafson, H. T. Irwin, and B. C. Keel
1968 A Human Skeleton from Sediments of Mid-Pinedale Age in Southeastern Washington. *American Antiquity* 33:511–514.

Givens, D. H.
1968a A Preliminary Report on Excavations at Hitzfelder Cave. *Bulletin of the Texas Archeological Society* 38:47–50.

1968b On the Peopling of America. *Current Anthropology* 9:120.

Greenberg, J. H., C. G. Turner, and S. L. Zegura
1986 The Settlement of the Americas: A Comparison of the Linguistive, Dental, and Genetic Evidence. *Current Anthropology* 27:477–497.

Goodman, M. M.
1972 Distance Analysis in Biology. *Systematic Zoology* 21:174–186.

Griffin, J. B.
1979 The Origin and Dispersion of American Indians in North America. In *The First Americans: Origin, Affinities, and Adaptations*, edited by W. S.

Laughlin and A. B. Harper, pp. 1–12. Gustav Fischer, New York.

Gruhn, R.
1987 On the Settlement of the Americas: South American Evidence for an Expanded Time Frame. *Current Anthropology* 28:363–365.

Hooton, E. A.
1930 *The Indians of Pecos Pueblo.* Yale University Press, New Haven, Connecticut.
1933 Racial Types in America and Their Relation to Old World Types. In *The American Aborigines,* edited by D. Jenness, pp. 131–163. Russell and Russell, New York.

Howells, W. W.
1969 The Use of Multivariate Techniques in the Study of Skeletal Populations. *American Journal of Physical Anthropology* 31:311–314.
1973 *Cranial Variation in Man: A Study by Multivariate Analysis of Patterns of Differences Among Recent Human Populations.* Papers of the Peabody Museum No. 67. Harvard University, Cambridge.

Hrdlička, A.
1923 The Origin and Antiquity of the American Indian. In *Annual Report of the Board of Regents of the Smithsonian Institution,* pp. 481–493. U. S. Government Printing Office, Washington, D.C.
1937 Early Man in America: What Have the Bones to Say? In *Early Man as Depicted by Leading Authorities at the International Symposium at the Academy of Natural Sciences, Philadelphia, March 1937,* edited by G. G. MacCurdy, pp. 93–104. J. B. Lippincott Co., Philadelphia.
1944 Catalog of Human Crania in the United States National Museum Collections: Non-Eskimo People of the Northwest Coast, Alaska, and Siberia. *Proceedings of the United States National Museum* 94:1–172.

Jenks, A. E.
1936 *Pleistocene Man in Minnesota: A Fossil Homo sapiens.* University of Minnesota Press, Minneapolis.
1937 *Minnesota's Browns Valley Man and Associated Burial Artifacts.* Memoirs of the American Anthropological Association No. 49. Menasha, Wisconsin.

Jenks, A. E., and L. A. Wilford
1938 Sauk Valley Skeleton. *Bulletin of the Texas Archaeological and Paleontological Society* 10:162–163.

Jennings, J. D.
1983 Origins. In *Ancient North Americans,* edited by J. D. Jennings, pp. 1–41. W. H. Freeman, San Francisco.

Kamminga, J., and R. S. V. Wright
1988 The Upper Cave at Zhoukoudian and the Origins of the Mongoloids. *Journal of Human Evolution* 17:739–767.

Kaufman, T. S.
1980 *Early Prehistory of the Clear Lake Area, Lake County, California.* Unpublished Ph.D. dissertation, Department of Anthropology, University of California, Los Angeles.

Kiszely, I.
1979 *The Anthropology of the Lombards, Part I.* B.A.R. International Series 61(i). British Archaeological Review, Oxford.

Kroeber, A. L.
1962 The Rancho La Brea Skull. *American Antiquity* 27:416–419.

Mahalanobis, P. C.
1936 On the Generalized Distance in Statistics. *Proceedings of the National Institute of Science, India* 2:49–55.

Morita, S.
1950 *Anthropological Studies on the Skull of the Recent Japanese in Kanto District.* Memoirs of the Department of Anatomy. Tokyo Jikeikai Medical College, Tokyo.

Neumann, G. K.
1952 Archeology and Race in the American Indian. In *Archeology of Eastern United States,* edited by J. B. Griffin, pp. 13–43. University of Chicago Press, Chicago.
1956 The Upper Cave Skulls from Choukoutien in Light of Paleo-Amerind Material. *American Journal of Physical Anthropology* 14:380.

Neves, W. A., and H. M. Pucciarelli
1989 Extra-continental Biological Relationships of Early South American Human Remains: A Multivariate Analysis. *Ciência e Cultura* 41:566–575.
1991 Morphological Affinities of the First Americans: An Exploratory Analysis Based on Early South American Human Remains. *Journal of Human Evolution* 21:261-273.

Newman, M. T.
1962 Evolutionary Changes in Body Size and Head Form in American Indians. *American Anthropologist* 64:237–257.

Orr, P. C.
1956 Pleistocene Man in Fishbone Cave, Pershing County, Nevada. *Nevada State Museum Bulletin* 2:1–20.
1962 The Arlington Springs Site, Santa Rosa Island. *American Antiquity* 27:417–419.
1974 *Notes on the Archaeology of the Winnemucca Lake*

Caves, 1952–1958. Nevada State Museum Anthropological Papers No. 16. Carson City.

Ossenberg, N. S.
1969 *Discontinuous Morphological Variation in the Human Cranium*. Ph.D. dissertation, University of Toronto. University Microfilms, Ann Arbor, Michigan.
1974 Origin and Relationships of Woodland Peoples: The Evidence of Cranial Morphology. In *Aspects of Upper Great Lakes Anthropology: Papers in Honor of Lloyd A. Wilford*, edited by E. Johnson, pp. 15–39. Minnesota Prehistoric Archaeology Series No. 11. Minnesota Historical Society, St. Paul.
1976 Within and Between Race Differences in Population Studies Based on Discrete Traits of the Human Skull. *American Journal of Physical Anthropology* 45:701–716.
1977 Congruence of Distance Matrices Based on Cranial Discrete Traits, Cranial Measurements, and Linguistic-Georgraphic Criteria in Five Alaskan Populations. *American Journal of Physical Anthropology* 47:93–98.
1986 Isolate Conservatism and Hybridisation in the Population History of Japan: The Evidence of Nonmetric Cranial Traits. In *Prehistoric Hunter-Gatherers in Japan*, edited by T. Akazawa and C. M. Aikens, pp. 149–215. University of Tokyo Press, Tokyo.

Penrose, L. S.
1954 Distance, Size and Shape. *Annals of Eugenics* 18:337–343.

Protsch, R. R.
1978 *Catalog of Fossil Hominids of North America*. Gustav Fischer, New York.

Rao, C. R.
1952 *Advanced Statistical Methods in Biometric Research*. Wiley, New York.

Redder, A. J.
1985 Horn Shelter No. 2: The South End, A Preliminary Report. *Journal of the Central Texas Archaeological Society* 10:37–65.

Reyment, R. A., R. E. Blackith, and N. A. Campbell
1984 *Multivariate Morphometrics*. 2nd ed. Academic Press, London.

Rivet, P.
1925 Les Origines de L'homme Americain. *L'Anthropologie* 35:293-319.

Roberts, F. H. H.
1940 Developments in the Problem of the North American Paleo-Indian. *Smithsonian Miscellaneous Collections* 100:51–116.

Rosen, D. E.
1978 Vicariant Patterns and Historical Explanation in Biogeography. *Systematic Zoology* 24:431–464.

Russell, M. D.
1985 The Supraorbital Torus: "A Most Remarkable Peculiarity." *Current Anthropology* 26:337–360.

SAS Institute, Inc.
1985 *SAS User's Guide, 1985 Edition*. SAS Institute, Raleigh, N.C.

Sayles, E. B.
1983 *The Cochise Cultural Sequence in Southeastern Arizona*. The University of Arizona Press, Tucson.

Sayles, E. B., and E. Antevs
1941 *The Cochise Culture*. Medallion Papers No. 29. Gila Pueblo, Globe, Arizona.

Schwalbe, G.
1906 Das Schadelfragment von Brux und Verwandte Shadelframen. *Zeitschrift fur Morphologie und Anthropologie*. Special issue.

Sciulli, P. W.
1990 Deciduous Dentition of a Late Archaic Population of Ohio. *Human Biology* 62:221–245.

Sellards, E. H.
1952 *Early Man in America*. University of Texas Press, Austin.

Shafer, H. J.
1977 Early Lithic Assemblages in Eastern Texas. In *Paleoindian Lifeways*, edited by E. Johnson, pp. 187–197. The Museum Journal XVIII. West Texas Museum Association, Lubbock.

Simmons, T., A. B. Falsetti, and F. H. Smith
1991 Frontal Bone Morphometrics of Southwest Asian Pleistocene Hominids. *Journal of Human Evolution* 20:249–269.

Simpson, R. D.
1978 The Calico Mountains Archaeological Site. In *Early Man in America from a Circum-Pacific Perspective*, edited by A. L. Bryan, pp. 218–220. Occasional Papers No. 1 of the Department of Anthropology, University of Alberta. Archaeological Researches International, Edmonton.

Simpson, R. D., L. W. Patterson, and J. W. Smith
1986 Lithic Technology of the Calico Mountains Site, Southern California. In *New Evidence for the Peopling of the Americas*, edited by A. L. Bryan, pp. 89–107. Peopling of the Americas Symposia Series. Center for the Study of Early Man, University of Maine, Orono.

Smith, F. H.
1976 The Skeletal Remains of the Earliest Americans: A Survey. *Tennessee Anthropologist* 1:116–147.

Snow, C. E.
　1948　Indian Knoll Skeletons of Size OH2, Ohio County, Kentucky. University of Kentucky Reports in Anthropology No. 3, Pt. 2. 4:371–355.

Sokal, R. R., and R. J. Rohlf
　1969　Biometry. W. H. Freeman, San Francisco.

Stafford, T. W. Jr., A. J. T. Hull, K. Brendel, R. C. Duhamel, and D. Donahue
　1987　Study of Bone Radiocarbon Dating Accuracy at the University of Arizona NSF Accelerator Facility for Radioisotope Analysis. Radiocarbon 29:24–44.

Steele, D. G.
　1989　Recently Recovered Paleoindian Skeletal Remains from Texas and the Southwest (Abstract). American Journal of Physical Anthropology 78:307.

Steele, D. G., and J. F. Powell
　1992　Peopling of the Americas: Paleobiological Evidence. Human Biology 64:303–336.

Steele, D. G., L. D. Martin, W. Dort Jr., and J. F. Powell
　1991　Human Remains from Bonner Springs, Kansas: A Late Pleistocene/Holocene Locality. Paper presented at the 56th annual meeting of the Society for American Archaeology, New Orleans.

Steward, T. D.
　1946　A Reexamination of the Fossil Human Skeletal Remains from Melbourne, Florida. Smithsonian Miscellaneous Collections 106:1–28.
　1949　The Development of the Concept of Morphological Dating in Connection with Early Man in America. Southwest Journal of Anthropology 5:1–16.
　1960　A Physical Anthropologist's View of the Peopling of the New World. Southwest Journal of Anthropology 16:259–273.
　1973　The People of America. Charles Scribner's Sons, New York.
　1981　The Evolutionary Status of the First Americans. American Journal of Physical Anthropology 56:461–466.

Stringer, C. B., and P. Andrews
　1988　Genetic and Fossil Evidence for the Origin of Modern Humans. Science 239:1263–1268.

Suhm, D. A., A. D. Krieger, and E. B. Jelks
　1954　An Introductory Handbook of Texas Archeology. Bulletin of the Texas Archeological Society 25:1–582.

Suzuki, H.
　1969　Microevolutional Changes in the Japanese Population from the Prehistoric Age to the Present-day. Journal of the Faculty of Sciences, University of Tokyo Section V 3:279–308.
　1982　Skulls of the Minatogawa Man. In The Minatogawa Man: The Upper Pleistocene Man from the Island of Okinawa, edited by H. Suzuki and K. Hanihara, pp. 7–49. Bulletin of the University of Tokyo Museum No. 19. University of Tokyo.

Taylor, D. C.
　1969　The Wilsall Excavations: An Exercise in Frustration. Proceedings of the Montana Academy of Sciences 29:147–150.

Taylor, R. E., L. A. Payen, C. A. Prior, P. J. Slota Jr., R. Gillespie, F. A. Gowlett, R. M. C. Hedges, A. J. T. Jull, T. H. Zabel, D. J. Donahue, and R. Berger
　1985　Major Revisions in the Pleistocene Age Assignments for North American Human Skeletons by C-14 Accelerator Mass Spectrometry: None Older than 11,000 C-14 Years B.P. American Antiquity 50:136–140.

Turner, C. G.
　1971　Three-rooted Mandibular First Permanent Molars and the Question of American Indian Origins. American Journal of Physical Anthropology 34:229–241.
　1983a　Sinodonty and Sundadonty: A Dental Anthropological View of Mongoloid Microevolution, Origin, and Dispersal into the Pacific Basin, Siberia, and the Americas. In Late Pleistocene and Early Holocene Cultural Connections of Asia and America, edited by R. S. Vasilievsky, pp. 72–76. U.S.S.R. Academy of Sciences, Siberian Branch, Novosibirsk, Siberia.
　1983b　Dental Evidence for the Peopling of the Americas. In Early Man in the New World, edited by R. Shutler, pp. 147–157. Sage Publications, Beverly Hills.
　1985a　Dental Evidence for the Peopling of the Americas. National Geographic Society Research Reports 19:573–596.
　1985b　The Dental Search for Native American Origins. In Out of Asia, edited by R. Kirk and E. Szathmary, pp. 31–78. Journal of Pacific History Inc., Australian National University, Canberra, Australia.
　1986a　Dentochronological Separation Estimates for Pacific Rim Populations. Science 23:1140–1142.
　1986b　The First Americans: The Dental Evidence. National Geographic Research 2:37–46.
　1987　Late Pleistocene and Holocene Population History of East Asia Based on Dental Variation. American Journal of Physical Anthropology 73:305–321.

Turner, C. G., and J. Bird
1981 Dentition of Chilean Paleo-Indians and the Peopling of the Americas. *Science* 212:1053–1054.

Wallenstein, S., C. Zucker, and J. Fleiss
1980 Some Statistical Methods Useful in Circulation Research. *Circulation Research* 47:1–9.

Waters, M. R.
1985 Early Man in the New World: An Evaluation of the Radiocarbon Dated Pre-Clovis Sites in the Americas. In *Environments and Extinctions: Man in Late Glacial North America*, edited by J. I. Mead and D. J. Meltzer, pp. 125–142. Center for the Study of Early Man, University of Maine, Orono.

1986 Sulphur Springs Woman: An Early Human Skeleton from South-Eastern Arizona. *American Antiquity* 51:361–365.

Weidenreich, F.
1938 On the Earliest Representatives of Modern Mankind Recovered on the Soil of East Asia. Peking Natural history Bulletin 133.

Weir, F. A.
1985 An Early Holocene Burial at the Wilson-Leonard Site in Central Texas. *Mammoth Trumpet* 2:1–3.

Wendorf, F. and A. D. Krieger
1959 New Light on the Midland Discovery. *American Antiquity* 25:66–78.

Wendorf, F., A. D. Krieger, and C. C. Albritton
1955 *The Midland Discovery: A Report on the Pleistocene Human Remains from Midland, Texas with a Description of the Skull by T. D. Stewart.* University of Texas Press, Austin.

Woodbury, G., and E. Woodbury
1935 *Prehistoric Skeletal Remains from the Texas Coast.* The Medallion, Globe, Arizona.

Young, D. E.
1985 The Paleoindian Skeletal Material from Horn Rock Shelter in Central Texas. *Current Research in the Pleistocene* 2:39–40.

1986 *The Paleoindian Skeletal Material from Horn Shelter, Number 2 in Central Texas: An Analysis and Perspective.* Unpublished Master's thesis, Department of Anthropology, Texas A&M University, College Station, Texas.

1988 The Double Burial at Horn Shelter: An Osteological Analysis. *Central Texas Archaeologist* 11:11–115.

Young, D., S. Patrick, and D. G. Steele
1987 An Analysis of the Paleoindian Double Burial from Horn Shelter No. 2, in Central Texas. *Plains Anthropologist* 32:275–299.

Molecular Approaches to the Isolation and Analysis of Ancient Nucleic Acids

DAVID L. ANDREWS
*Department of Biochemistry and Biophysics and Department of Horticultural Sciences**
Texas A&M University
College Station, Texas 77843-2133

The use of molecular methods to retrieve nucleic acids from ancient tissue samples and the analysis of them have almost become commonplace events due to advancements in analytical techniques. To date, data from DNA estimated to be in excess of 15 million yr B.P. have been published (Golenberg et al. 1990). Both nuclear and organellar sequences have been characterized, and this research has enabled the collaboration of anthropologists, biochemists, molecular biologists, and geneticists to answer common questions with a different and powerful approach.

In this chapter we will examine this phenomenon by focusing on some of the landmark publications from this area of research with respect to the basic techniques, the variety of samples to which they have been applied, the specific methods used by the individual investigators, some of the data obtained and the conclusions drawn from these results. Further details regarding standard methods and terminology will be provided in the cited references. Specific examples of sequence data from the genes examined and oligonucleotides mentioned can also be found in their respective references.

This newest area of DNA technology gives another quantitative way to answer questions concerning the peopling of our planet, the evolution of prokaryotic and eukaryotic organisms and also to assay the effect of disease and pathogens on the genetic material of those affected.

CLONING

Under usual conditions, when researching the biochemical aspects of an extant organism, there are two basic goals of the molecular cloning process. First, the nucleic acid sequence of interest must be isolated from among the total DNA and RNA contained in each cell. The amount of nuclear DNA in eukaryotes ranges from about 7.0×10^7 base pairs (bp) in *Arabadopsis thaliana* to 8.8×10^{10} bp in various Broadbean species, with human

---

* Direct correspondence to Dept. of Horticultural Sciences

beings in between with 3.9 x 10^9 bp per diploid genome. The sizes of DNA molecules in cellular organelles are somewhat less, being about 1.6 x 10^5 bp for chloroplast DNA (*Zea mays*) and similar amounts for mitochondrial DNA (*Homo sapiens*) (Kochert 1989).

Since the average size of a specific sequence to be investigated is probably much smaller, at most several thousand bases in length, than the genomic DNA, it must first be sheared into small enough segments (15,000–20,000 bases) to be conveniently examined individually. Several methods exist whereby this can be accomplished without losing any portion of sequence during the process. After identification of an important sequence has been done by hybridization with radioactive probe sequences, or by translation into protein and subsequent enzymatic or immunologic methods, isolation proceeds by using techniques previously described (Maniatis et al. 1982).

Once the DNA fragment of importance has been isolated from the total cellular nucleic acids, it must be replicated in order to provide large quantities of material identical to the original isolate for analysis. This is accomplished by cloning, the replacement of a nonessential region of a bacterial or viral expression vector with the sequence of interest. The advantage with these systems is their rapid growth rate, enabling large quantities of foreign DNA to be produced *in vitro* in a very short time.

When working with ancient DNA the first step has been found to be unnecessary, in as much as the oxidative damage which has occurred over the course of time has already reduced the nucleic acids to short segments. This damage usually consists of a loss of purine and pyrimidine bases (Pääbo 1985a), single- and double-strand breakage (Pääbo 1989) and other modifications of bases by reaction with hydroxyl radicals (Scholer et al. 1960).

Cloning was used to obtain DNA from the quagga (*Equus quagga*), a zebra-like species extinct since 1883 (Higuchi et al. 1984). After isolation, the DNA was cloned into a bacterial virus (bacteriophage) for further study. The sample from which the DNA was isolated came from the preserved skin of a museum specimen which had died some 140 years ago. The majority of fragments of DNA obtained were smaller than 500 bp and, after cloning into Lambda GT 10 phage and subsequent screening with radiolabeled mitochondrial DNA from the mountain zebra (*Equus zebra*), yielded about 25,000 positive quagga sequences which had some homology to the mountain zebra probe. Nuclear DNA was also present in this sample as was shown by using mountain Zebra satellite DNA as the probe.

A bacterial plasmid (pUC 8) (Vieira and Messing 1982), an extra-chromosomal, circular DNA molecule, was employed to clone and amplify DNA isolated from an artificially mummified Egyptian child (Pääbo 1985b). The sample was estimated to be about 2,400 years old and the products of the isolation were less than 500 bp, although some appeared to be near 15,000 bases (kb). The fragments were ligated into the plasmid DNA molecules and transformed into *E. coli*. In this case, about a thousand clones were obtained and some 700 were screened by hybridization with human Alu repeat sequences. The family of Alu repeats is nuclear in origin and exists at greater than 300,000 copies per genome. One plasmid isolate that contained an insert of 3.4 kb was analyzed by DNA sequencing and then compared with Alu consensus sequences.

REVIEW OF MOLECULAR TECHNIQUES

The sequencing of DNA fragments is accomplished by either an enzymatic or a chemical method. The enzymatic method developed by Sanger and Coulson (Sanger et al. 1975) used sequential synthesis, with DNA polymerase I, and degradation, with DNA exonuclease, to produce a population of DNA fragments of varying lengths. The alternate method developed by Maxam and Gilbert (Maxam and Gilbert 1977) employs chemical modifications to cleave the fragments of single-stranded DNA selectively, also resulting in a mixed-length population. The enzymatic sequencing of nucleic acids has been much improved with the introduction of the chain-termination method (Tabor and Richardson 1989). This protocol utilizes 2' or 3' dideoxy analogues of the nucleotide triphosphates (NTP) to terminate extension whenever one is incorporated. Four reactions are run simultaneously, each with a different dideoxy analogue at proper concentrations to terminate the chain at each position possible, thereby giving the complete sequence. All of these methods employ radiolabeled nucleotides, acrylamide gel electrophoresis and autoradiography to separate the DNA fragments and allow determination of the order of individual nucleotides. Once sequence information has been obtained from ancient DNA from an organism of interest, comparisons can be made with sequences of modern, related species as was done with the quagga/zebra/cow comparison and the modern Alu sequences with respect to homologous sequences obtained from the mummified child, as referenced above.

Certain problems can arise when ancient DNA is cloned directly into bacterial plasmids and amplified *in vivo*. This DNA has been extensively damaged over time and therefore will be difficult to clone, which could result in poor uptake by bacteria and thus low cloning efficiency. Damaged molecules that are incorporated will be repaired by the bacterial systems, which can result in incorrect base substitution and mutagenized, error-rich sequences (Pääbo et al. 1989).

The development of the polymerase chain reaction

(PCR) protocol for DNA amplification circumvents this problem (Saiki et al. 1985). PCR is an *in vitro* process which enzymatically amplifies very small quantities of pre-selected segments of DNA with copies originating from specific oligonucleotides added to the reaction mixture. The resulting DNA can then be used for cloning, sequencing or other forms of genetic analysis. PCR was developed for the most part by workers at Cetus Corporation (Perkin Elmer Cetus, Norwalk, CT), who should be contacted for the latest developments, materials and reagent systems.

The PCR amplification is made possible by the use of a DNA polymerase enzyme which was isolated from the thermophilic bacterium *Thermus aquaticus* (Taq) (Saiki et al. 1988). The Taq polymerase enzyme has a thermal stability that allows polymerization to occur at temperatures which would inactivate enzymes isolated from bacteria (e.g., *E. coli*) that grow at 37° C. The PCR protocol consists of the repetition of individual cycles composed of three major steps, denaturation, annealing and extension.

The first step denatures (melts) the double-stranded DNA molecules, yielding the single-stranded form that is required as the template for Taq polymerase. Temperatures for denaturation range from 91–94° C for about 1-1.5 minutes. Enzyme efficiency is reduced by lower temperatures that leave some molecules double-stranded and unable to hybridize with the specific primers. Elevated temperatures can cause inactivation of the enzyme prematurely in the series of reaction cycles.

After the strands have separated, the temperature is lowered to allow annealing of the single-stranded oligonucleotides (20–30 bases) to their respective regions of homology in the sample DNA. Random annealing will take place if the temperature is too low, and no annealing will take place if the temperature is too high. The proper temperature to insure specific annealing should be determined empirically. Generally, annealing temperature will be in the range of 50 to 60° C, but lower temperatures will work in certain applications; e.g., for shorter oligonucleotides. Again, 1–1.5 minutes is sufficient for this step.

The Taq enzyme functions optimally at temperatures of 72–74° C, so this range is used for the polymerization of nucleotides. In the elongation step nucleotide triphosphates are added to the 3' end of the oligonucleotides, two of which have hybridized, during the annealing step, to opposite ends of the opposite strands so that their 3' ends face each other. The single-stranded DNA of the sample serves as the template and determines the complementary bases added to the oligonucleotides in the formation of the second strand. The time for this step depends on the length of the sequence to be copied, one minute for 500 bases or less, two minutes for about 1000 bases and three minutes for 2000–3000 bases. These three steps are repeated 30–50 times, and the number of target molecules doubles with each cycle.

Several variations on this basic theme exist. Lesions in ancient DNA can sometimes be repaired by an initial elongation step with the Klenow fragment of DNA polymerase I (Clark and Beardsly 1987). Since this enzyme comes from the *E. coli* bacterium it would be inactivated in the first denaturation step. Some investigators begin the series with an extended denaturation time (four to five minutes) to insure complete conversion to the single-stranded form (Lawlor et al. 1991); this would also serve to denature any proteases that survived the isolation process (Golenberg et al. 1990). An extended final elongation step of five to seven minutes will complete polymerization of any molecules with remaining single-stranded regions (Perkin Elmer Cetus).

The fidelity of synthesis was examined for the Taq enzyme, and it was found that errors as single-base substitutions occurred at a rate of 1 for each 9000 bases polymerized (Tindall and Kunkel 1988). Frameshift errors were less abundant and were introduced at a rate of 1 per 41,000. These authors found that Taq polymerase lacks the 3'–5' exonuclease (proofreading) activity which removes mismatched bases after an incorporation error has been made. This may account for the loss of accuracy seen when this enzyme was compared to the Klenow fragment from *E. coli*. It is interesting to take note of the findings of these investigators with respect to the nature of the base-pair changes that were most common in this research for comparison to the ancient DNA results. For example, 78% of the observed misincorporations were T to C transitions resulting from the replacement of original C residues with a G. In addition, ten of the forty-two frame shift mutations observed involved AT to GC transitions, which follows from the previously mentioned observations. Repeated denaturation and heating steps are an important part of the PCR protocol, but the previous data resulted from analysis after only one cycle, so actual error rates after repeated cycles would be higher. Also, merely heating DNA to temperatures used in the PCR reaction has been shown to be mutagenic, causing transitions (Baltz et al. 1976) and transversions (Battula and Loeb 1976) to occur.

While the power of the PCR technique is obvious, its extreme sensitivity cannot be overemphasized, especially when analyzing human sequences. False positives resulting from the amplification of DNA from nonsterile labware, reagents or contaminants in the sample are extremely likely if conditions are not rigorously controlled. Only several molecules of DNA are required to give a visible product, and if the investigator is not careful it will be his/her own DNA which has been amplified and sequenced.

Four control reactions should be run with the samples of interest to insure contamination-free results: A positive control which gives the expected product, a negative control which gives no product similar in size, an isolation control in which an empty tube is subjected to the isolation process to verify that the reagents used in the extraction were DNA-free, and a "no DNA" control to show a lack of contamination in the PCR reagents. Without these types of data, conclusions made from PCR results may be fallacious.

SAMPLES FOR ANCIENT DNA EXTRACTION

Keeping in mind the likelihood of amplifying sequences other than those from the ancient sample, as much care as possible should be taken when preparing samples for DNA extraction. Whenever possible, material to be analyzed should be taken from an interior portion of the sample to eliminate contamination with DNA deposited in the unavoidable handling of the tissue during its discovery, handling, and preparation for exhibition. In most cases, less than one gram of sample is sufficient for DNA isolation, and several aliquots of the same sample should be subjected to the isolation procedure on different occasions and amplified separately to verify that the same banding patterns are evident in each.

For the most part, samples used for the isolation of ancient DNA have been dried remains. Mummified remains have been sampled and analyzed on several occasions and can be divided into specimens which have naturally dried following death, both of animal (Pääbo 1989) and plant origin (Rogers and Bendich 1976), and those dried artificially, either in relatively recent times for display purposes (Pääbo 1989) or mummified in ancient times as part of a ritualistic protocol (Pääbo 1985b). Wet remains include frozen tissue (Johnson et al. 1985), chemically preserved museum specimens (Pääbo 1989) and naturally preserved tissue of plants (Golenberg et al. 1990) and animals (Lawlor et al. 1991; Pääbo et al. 1988) from an anaerobic, acid environment. Several published cases of DNA isolations from ancient teeth and bones exist, (Hagelberg et al. 1989; Hanni et al. 1990; Williams et al. 1990) as well as the use of insects enclosed in amber as starting material (Hansen and Gurtler 1983). So it appears that the potential exists for extracting DNA from tissues preserved by most common methods.

EXTRACTION METHODS

The techniques used for ancient DNA extraction are modifications of standard protocols for isolating DNA from fresh samples (Maniatis et al. 1982). Mitochondrial DNA was isolated from the dried museum specimen of quagga skin and muscle (Higuchi et al. 1984) by first treating the sample with proteinase K and detergent. DNA was purified by phenol extraction and precipitated with ethanol. Yield in this case was about 5 µg DNA per gram of tissue, approximately 1% of the amount which could be expected if the isolation was done on fresh tissue.

Nuclear DNA was isolated from an Egyptian mummy with sodium perchlorate and detergent (Pääbo 1985b) also followed by phenol extraction and precipitation. These investigators were able to retrieve 20 µg DNA per gram of tissue. A portion of this sample of tissue was rehydrated and treated with a variety of nuclear stains, including ethidium bromide, in order to visually detect nucleic acids remaining in intact nuclei. In several samples it was found that peripheral tissues contained a larger number of what appeared to be nuclei, but most of the samples of tissue examined in this manner appeared to lack nucleic acids entirely. The author speculated that the rapidity of the drying process was of primary importance to nucleic acid preservation, with peripheral tissues drying at a faster rate and thus retaining nucleic integrity. This observation has also been made by other investigators (Chapel at al. 1981; Daniels and Post 1970). Rapid drying would rapidly decrease the time of degradation by making conditions unfavorable for nucleolytic enzymes.

The protocol above was modified and applied to samples of dried tissue (Pääbo 1989) and also to human brain tissue preserved in the Little Salt Spring (North Port, Fla.) (Pääbo et al. 1988). Samples were placed into a solution of 10 mM Tris-HCl (pH 8.0), 2 mM EDTA, and 10 mM NaCl and broken into small sections, after which collagenase was added. Following a three-hour incubation, sodium dodecyl sulfate (SDS) was added to 1% and 80 mg of dithiothreitol also included. Incubation was then continued for about 20 hours. When most of the solid tissue had been solublized, the sample was phenol extracted and concentrated by centrifugation in Centricon 30 filter apparatus (Amicon, Inc., Danvers, MA). Frequently, after extraction a brown contaminant was noted which was identified as products of Maillard degradation of reducing sugars (Reynolds 1965). This contaminating substance was removed by ultracentrifugation through 10–40% sucrose gradients at 15°C, for 24 hours at 100,000 x g.

The DNA yield in this case was determined by measuring ethidium bromide fluorescence and varied between samples from 1 to 200 µg per gram of tissue for the 0.1 to 0.5 g of dried tissues extracted and similar amounts from 0.5 to 1.0 g of brain tissue. Quantization of ancient DNA samples is sometimes impossible by UV spectroscopy due to an unknown contaminant which absorbs near 260 nm and obscures the nucleic acid peak.

Nuclear DNA was isolated and amplified from similar brain tissue by other investigators using a similar protocol (Lawlor et al. 1981). Their initial buffer was 0.3 M NaCl, 0.03 M Na citrate (pH 7.4), and 2% SDS. The incubation time was 1 hour, and the collagenase step and subsequent 20-hour incubation was omitted.

The oldest material to be extracted has been from plant tissue (Golenberg et al. 1990). Using a method based on standard cetyltrimethylammonium bromide (CTAB) extraction procedures (Murray and Thompson 1980; Taylor and Powell 1982), chloroplast DNA was isolated from a compression fossil of the genus Magnolia that was 17–20 million years old. When this method was used on samples of mummified plant material (Rogers and Bendich 1976), it also gave good yields and the DNA was shown to be of high molecular weight. In the previous examples, DNA fragment length was rarely greater than 500 bp, while the magnolia fossil DNA was reported to be about 4,200 bp long. The other investigators using this same method have extracted DNA from eight different plant species with an average length of 3,400 bp (Rogers and Bendich 1976). These samples ranged in age from 1,200 to greater than 45,000 years old, as determined by radiocarbon dating, and yielded an average of 24 µg per gram of tissue. An advantage of this protocol is the small amounts of tissue required for good yield, usually less than 100 milligrams. DNA has also been isolated from individual maize kernels by simply rinsing them in a detergent mixture and, after overnight soaking in the same solution, grinding them to a fine powder in liquid nitrogen (Rollo et al. 1988).

As documented so far, isolation of DNA is possible from preserved soft-tissue samples of varied origin. However, the isolation of nucleic acids from bone is also of interest because of the number of specimens of skeletal material which exist. Several groups have reported isolation of DNA from bone (Hagelberg et al. 1989; Williams et al. 1990; Hanni et al. 1990), but of all the different branches of the newly emerging science of paleomolecular biology, this source of material has been examined the least. DNA extraction was accomplished using methods similar to those applied to soft tissue with minor modifications. Mitochondrial DNA fragments were isolated by first removing the outer surface of the sample mechanically and then reducing the sample to a fine powder with a low-temperature mill (Hagelberg et al. 1989). Two grams of powdered bone were decalcified with 0.5 M EDTA, and DNA was extracted and concentrated by using methods previously described (Maniatis et al. 1982). This protocol yielded 5–10 µg of DNA per 2 g of bone in several different samples.

In our lab, we have developed a rapid protocol not requiring ultracentrifugation. With this method we have successfully isolated DNA from bone samples ranging in age from 150 to 15,000 years. PCR has demonstrated amplifiable sequences with several probes, and we are presently involved in sequencing these fragments. Starting with 0.5 g of the interior portion of the bone, the sample is coarsely broken and transferred to a 1.5-ml eppendorf tube. Approximately 1 ml of a solution containing 0.25 M EDTA and 1.0 M sodium phosphate (pH 8.0) is added and the sample is subjected to repeated freeze/thaw cycles (-80 to 37°C) until the sample is reduced to a fine powder. After phenol extraction and ethanol precipitation (from sodium acetate) the brown pigment, seen with soft tissue samples, was still present. This was removed by adding 0.6 volumes of 20% polyethylene glycol (m.w. 8000), 2.5 M NaCl and incubating for one hour at 37°C followed by centrifuging at 13,000 x g for 15 minutes. After vacuum drying, DNA was obtained which ranged from several hundred to several thousand base pairs with amounts from 2–5 µg per gram of human bone. While a portion of the high molecular weight DNA isolated is undoubtedly due to contamination, PCR results do give the correct product length and sequencing will further verify this method.

Several modifications of the standard PCR protocol were made by researchers working with ancient biological samples. An overview of these changes can provide alternative strategies for amplification of sequences not amenable to the standard protocols. PCR standard assay conditions follow (for a 100-µl reaction). The reaction mixture contains purified water, reaction buffer, 200 µM in each NTP, 1 µM in each primer, 1 ng of template DNA and 2.5 units of Taq enzyme. The reaction buffer includes 0.1% Triton X-100, 50 mM KCl, 10 mM Tris-HCl (pH 8.3), 1.5 mM $MgCl_2$ and 0.01 % gelatin. For a 500-bp fragment of undamaged DNA, reaction steps are as follows; initially, 1.5 minutes at 94°C, 2 minutes at 37°C, 3 minutes at 72°C and 1 minutes at 94°C. The last three steps are repeated 25 times, and after cycle 25 has been completed the extension temperature is maintained for seven minutes. These standard conditions are included for comparison purposes with the forthcoming modifications.

The amplification of regions of ancient DNA from dried tissue samples was accomplished with slightly different reaction conditions and an excess of Taq enzyme. This was deemed necessary to overcome an inhibitory effect on enzyme function by some unknown contaminant (Pääbo 1989). Successful reaction conditions were found to be: 67 mM Tris-HCl (pH 8.8), 2.0 mM $MgCl_2$, 10 mM β-mercaptoethanol, 250 µM in each NTP, 2.0 µg/ml bovine serum albumen (BSA) and 12.5 units of enzyme (Pääbo 1989). Apparently the increased amount of enzyme added was not the deciding factor in overcoming the inhibition; in a subsequent article the same author reports the makeup of the reaction mix with the same amount of added BSA, but the amount of enzyme was returned to its normal level (Pääbo 1990). Generally, authors report using 2–5% of total extracts for an amplification which has been estimated as containing 100–300 fg (Pääbo et al. 1988).

Some of the oxidative damage incurred by ancient DNA has been found to be repaired by the inclusion of a DNA repair reaction with either Klenow fragment or reverse transcriptase as the initial step of amplification (Kornberg 1980; Feinberg and Vogelstein 1983). Investigators also have suggested that DNA molecules with varying degrees of damage are the inhibiting factor rather than an external contaminant (Pääbo et al. 1989).

The size of the amplifiable fragment possible was also proposed to be an intrinsic property of ancient DNA samples. An inverse relationship has been drawn between the age of a sample and the size of the largest amplifiable sequence from it (Pääbo et al. 1988). For example, in modern extracts, both 100-bp and 500-bp segments will amplify equally well. However, the larger fragment would allegedly not be obtainable from ancient isolates. This anomalous behavior was hypothesized as one criterion for determining the authenticity of amplified products. It was further proposed that the maximum length of fragment associated with archaeological discoveries was 150 bp, while the maximum length obtainable from chemically preserved museum specimens was 500 bp (Pääbo et al. 1989). However, other investigators have been able to generate fragments larger than the limits hypothesized above. Some of these include: 179 bp from human brain tissue (Lawlor et al. 1991), 205 bp from human bone (Hagelberg et al. 1989), 250 bp from South American, pre-Columbian mummies (Rogan and Salvo 1990a; Rogan and Salvo 1990b) and 820 bp from the fossilized Magnolia leaf (Golenberg et al. 1990). While the limits previously proposed are not actually a maximum, the concept does hold in that modern analogues of these samples would give products thousands of bases in length.

RESULTS

The most important application of molecular techniques to anthropology and genetics is the ability to verify relationships derived with other methods by direct comparison of the genetic material of the organisms in question. These comparisons have been done with antibodies raised to albumens from frozen mammoth muscle tissue and have shown a close relationship between the mammoth albumen protein and its counterpart in both African and Indian elephants, while it was much less related to albumens from other mammals (Benjamin et al. 1984). Radioimmunoassay, which also exploits antibody/antigen reactions, has been used to confirm this result as well as providing genealogical data on the Tasmanian wolf (Lowenstein et al. 1981) and Stellers sea cow (Rainey et al. 1984).

The improvement of molecular methods has now made it possible to examine ancient nucleic acids even though they have been heavily modified over millenia and still provide usable evidence for establishing evolutionary and biological relationships.

Two sequences were analyzed when the DNA isolated from the quagga museum specimen was compared to the modern mountain zebra (Higuchi et al. 1984). One of these sequences comprised an open reading frame of 117 bp that encoded an unidentified mitochondrial protein. The other sequence examined was a 112-bp fragment of the mitochondrial cytochrome oxidase I gene. The two sequences differed from those of the mountain zebra at 12 sites, 2 of which caused changes in the amino acid sequence of the resulting protein with no additions or deletions found. Analysis of sequences from the modern, domestic cow showed a closer relationship with the zebra than with the quagga but that the cow was more closely related to both than was man. Phylogenetic analysis of the sequence data showed that the quagga/zebra divergence occurred some three to four million years ago. However, the two base changes that caused the amino acid differences were later interpreted as having occurred during the period following the death of the organism, during the degradation of the tissue, and were not evolutionary in origin (Higuchi et al. 1987).

The initial cloning of mummy DNA (Pääbo 1985b) reported two members of the set of Alu repeated sequences seen in modern human DNA. Sequence data showed a 77% homology with contemporary human repeat sequences. The majority of the base changes were transitions with only 30% transversion; this ratio has been reported to be similar to divergences previously noted (Deininger et al. 1981). The region sequenced was flanked by 9-bp direct repeats and contained a 3-bp addition and several deletions of 1 or 2 bp. The effect of changes in sequence which seemed to be due to post-mortem modifications did not seem to cause significant changes in the data with respect to the Alu repeats.

The previous reports showed that DNA could be obtained from dried, preserved samples and could provide accurate data, especially in the second report. That the same could be done with samples preserved in a moist environment is shown in the mitochondrial sequences amplified using PCR from human brain tissue preserved in salt springs (Pääbo et al. 1988). Several sets of oligonucleotide primers were used to amplify sequences of 97, 121 and 471 bp. The 121-bp product is from the intergenic spacer region located between the genes coding for lysyl tRNA and cytochrome oxidase II. This small region contains two interesting features: a 9-bp repeat is usually present in most human lineages but has been eliminated in a certain proportion of racial groups which originated from Asian ancestors (Horai and Matsunaga 1986; Wrischnik et al. 1987), these groups include North American Indians (Pääbo et al. 1988) and natives of New Guinea (Stoneking and Wilson 1988). Also, in this sequence is an A-to-G transition which causes the elimination of one restriction site (Hae III) and the creation of another (Ava II). This change has been shown to occur in 3 out of 241 individuals representing diverse locations throughout the world (Cann et al. 1987; Stoneking 1986). The transition occurs at base 8251 (Anderson et al. 1981) and the restriction site replacement occurs in 5 mitochondrial DNA variants comprising one clade in the phylogeny of the 62 total mitochondrial varieties of the Japanese people (Deininger et al. 1981). Interestingly, an identical transition and restriction site change is evident in all five types. Another important diagnostic site (Hinc II) begins at nucleotide 13259. This site is not present in two out of five American Indians (Wallace et al. 1985) and is missing in one of fifty-five Orientals surveyed (Blanc et al. 1985). This region was examined in the ancient brain tissue and the site was present; however, sequence data here were confounded by the possibility of contamination, so no conclusions could be made (Pääbo et al. 1988). When attempts were made to amplify the 471-bp fragment, no product was visible. This satisfied the criterion, as stated earlier, that large fragments are not amplifiable from authentic ancient samples. From these data it was hypothesized that this individual, because of the retention of the Hinc II site and the 9-bp repeat, belonged to a previously unknown ancient founding group.

Other investigators have also isolated DNA from brain tissue preserved in the Windover group, determined to be 6000–8000 years old by radiocarbon dating (Lawlor et al. 1991), and examined six genes, encoded in the nucleus. One of these represented the β2-microglobulin gene, and five were from the class I HLA heavy-chain gene family. Primers specific for segments of these genes were used for amplification, and it was found that 11 of 35 independent isolates gave the same insert with respect to contemporary β2-microglobulin and 9 of 14 clones corresponded to members of the HLA family. Of particular interest was a clone which appeared to be a previously undiscovered member of this family, and corroborating evidence was later published which supported this finding. Clones that did not correspond to any single extant sequence were assumed to be composed of sequence motifs from several genes that had been assembled into a chimeric sequence during the PCR reaction. This phenomenon, sometimes referred to as "jumping PCR" (Pääbo et al. 1989), has been reported by several other authors as well. These mosaic sequences are caused by the large number of damaged molecules with respect to full-length sequences in ancient DNA samples. For example, if two primers will amplify a 400-bp fragment in modern DNA, the chances of their binding to shorter, incomplete sequences are increased in ancient damaged DNA. The primers will elongate minimally, but not to completion. Because the 3' ends are now different, they can then serve to prime different regions that have homology to the newly added portion of the primer. The process will continue to the point where the ends of the two chimeric primers will overlap and extension will continue to completion, forming an artifactual product. If the process occurs early in the PCR cycle, this product can represent a major proportion of the final output. The products of "jumping PCR" are generally longer than the expected sequence. When a large proportion of damaged molecules are present they can quickly cause the amplification of these chimeric sequences.

Interestingly, other researchers working with Windover remains have noted that although the peat-bog environment promoted remarkable preservation of tissue, it can also contribute to the level of contamination in those samples. It has been found that a large proportion of nucleic acids isolated from samples preserved in this manner are actually plant sequences (Doran et al. 1986). This illustrates the profound influence that the surrounding matrix can have on the final isolation products. In some cases it may even be advisable to include a sample of this material as an additional control when the DNA is isolated.

By far, the oldest and least damaged nucleic acids isolated have come from ancient plant material. Leaves preserved as compression fossils, in an anaerobic, acidic environment, are found to be virtually intact with minimal damage to their infrastructures. Using a modification of a standard protocol, large fragments of DNA were obtained from leaf tissue later identified as *Magnolia latahensis* (Berry) Brown, commonly found in the Miocene (17- to 20-million-year-old) Clarkia deposit. Similar to mitochondrial DNA found in ancient mammalian tissue, which survived because of the large number of molecules per cell, chloroplasts from plant leaves would also be preserved because of their abundance in these organs. Ribulose bisphosphate Carboxylase Oxygenase (Rubisco) is an enzyme with multiple subunits which is found in the chloroplast with its largest subunit (Rbc L) encoded there. This enzyme has been proposed as being the most abundant protein on earth and as such would provide a good source for comparison with other plant species. Rubisco specific oligonucleotides enabled the amplification of an 820-bp sequence which was compared with Rbc L sequences from 16 other plant types. This analysis showed the greatest homology with an extant Magnolia species (*M. macrophylla*) and the least with the monocot *Zea mays*. Surprisingly, there were only 17 nucleotide substitutions (2% compared with 23% reported in human tissue documented in Pääbo 1985b), twelve of which were transitions.

Dried plant samples from a Peruvian tomb (Rollo et al. 1988), did not produce sequences as long as those obtained from the compression fossil. The amplification of mitochondrial cytochrome C oxidase sequences from 1000-year-old maize ears produced bands of 100 and 130 bp but failed to give products of 149 and 150 bp. However, restriction digests of the 130 bp fragment did show the presence of a diagnostic Hae III site in this maize sequence.

A variety of dried plant tissues were subjected to an isolation method capable of obtaining high DNA yields from minimal amounts of starting material (Rogers and Bendich 1976). The plant tissues (leaves, seeds, embryos and ovules) in this investigation ranged in age from recent times to greater than 45,000 years old. DNA isolated from these samples was reported to be sensitive to Eco RI restriction as well as being sensitive to DNase I degradation. Large fragments were obtained, with even the oldest tissues exhibiting sequences from 4–30 kb. These last three reports illustrate the controversy surrounding the observation that only short DNA fragments are to be found in ancient tissues.

There are several reports of DNA extraction and amplification from teeth and bone tissue (Hagelberg et al. 1989; Hanni et al. 1990; Williams et al. 1990). The age of the samples used in these experiments ranged from 200–5500 years old (Hagelberg et al. 1989), and electrophoretic separation showed DNA fragments generally below 500 bp in length, although some high molecular weight DNA was evident from several of the human samples. Whether this DNA was an ancient sequence or a contaminant is not known. PCR amplification was used to amplify two portions of the gene for human mitochondrial NADH dehydrogenase, subunit 4, from two separate samples and the products were found to correspond to the published sequence (Anderson et al. 1981). The only change noted was a T-to-C transition in the 205-bp region, and complete correspondence in a 121-bp sequence. These authors reported the successful amplification of a 600-bp segment from 750-year-old bone, but were unable to amplify longer segments in older extracts.

Ancient human teeth recovered from the south of France ranging from 150 to 5000 years old were also extracted and the isolates amplified for an unspecified 121-bp region of the mitochondrial genome (Hanni et al. 1990). The results mentioned were from the 150-year-old sample, which was cloned and sequenced. This region was found to be identical to the published sequence.

A slightly different approach was used with DNA isolated from human skeletal remains from a site in southern Peru (Williams et al. 1990). These authors radiolabeled a sample of the ancient DNA and hybridized it to modern human DNA in a slot blot format. The DNA obtained was of high molecular weight, but this was attributed to a high degree of cross-linking and the size was judged to be artifactual. However, the hybridization data do suggest the presence of human DNA in the isolation product despite the chemical modification and/or microbiological contamination.

Clearly, the isolation of DNA from bone tissue is important because of the abundance of skeletal samples available. However, there have been few instances where the evidence presented has been unequivocal. DNA isolated from human remains is very difficult to authenticate when it is (and is expected to be) 100% homologous to modern human sequences. For this reason, many researchers have reserved judgment until more data is available from this tissue source.

The analyses described so far all used detection techniques designed for the identification and characterization of DNA. However, it has been proposed that the nucleic acids remaining in ancient samples consist primarily of RNA (Venanzi and Rollo 1990). The proponents of this theory claim that what has been assumed to be DNA, composed of primarily (99%) fragmented and chemically modified molecules, is primarily RNA. Reduced thymine peaks in HPLC analysis and the alkali sensitivity exhibited by ancient DNA when compared with modern DNA (Pääbo 1989) has been presented as typical of DNA that has been chemically treated. Isolates from both ancient plant and human tissues were subjected to analysis by HPLC and also reacted with antibodies raised against recent DNA. The antibodies precipitated only about 1% of the total nucleic acids from both tissues, while DNase-free RNase degraded a large proportion of the sample. Examination of chromatograms previously published (Pääbo 1989) were reinterpreted by these authors and found to contain peaks which represented components of RNA molecules. The absolute identification of ancient DNA is difficult, and the possibility of RNA existing as a major component of ancient samples will be even more troublesome to prove unequivocally. Even though these samples have been shown to hybridize strongly with ribosomal RNA probes, an example of a processed RNA molecule (with intervening sequences spliced out) must first be identified (Rogan and Salvo 1990a).

In conclusion, the reports mentioned here show that nucleic acids can indeed be isolated from ancient tissue samples subjected to varied means of preservation. The analysis of these samples has provided interesting data regarding speciation and evolution and will undoubtedly become more important as methods and techniques improve. The advent of PCR has had a great effect on this emerging branch of science; so much of an effect that it appears deceptively simple to isolate and characterize DNA from ancient samples. In fact, contamination and false positives have proven to be complicating factors which have added an extra level of complexity to an otherwise straightforward set of protocols. The prevention of PCR contamination has itself generated a sizeable amount of research articles (Sarker and Sommer 1991). However, this does not lessen the importance and high degree of potential resulting from this work. This potential is immediately recognizable whether the readers be members of the scientific community or not. For example, the publication of DNA isolation from the extinct quagga provided a source of speculation in a short work of fiction (Farmer 1974). Seldom does an article in a refereed journal receive this type of a response.

Projects are being considered that would have been science fiction only a few years ago. Presently under consideration is the possibility of using these techniques to determine if Abraham Lincoln suffered from Marfan's syndrome, a condition resulting from a mutated collagen gene, by examining DNA extracted from his bone, blood, or hair (D. J. Prockop, personal communication). Another application of these techniques was the recent DNA typing of the skeletal remains of a murder victim (Hagelberg et al. 1991). This has become the first time that PCR-generated evidence has been acceptable to the

British courts (Sykes 1991). Clearly, usage of these protocols has future legal, moral and ethical implications. Fortunately, investigators seem to agree on directions for this type of research. Data can be used to estimate mutation rates, phylogenetic and nucleic acid data can be combined to examine relationships of extinct organisms, and familial, individual, biogeographic and physiological effects of speciation and relationships as well as the prevalence of genetic disease can be monitored in ancient groups and extrapolated to modern society.

REFERENCES CITED

Anderson, S., A. T. Bankier, B. G. Barrell, M. H. L. de Bruijn, A. R. Coulson, J. Drouin, I. C. Eperon, D. P. Nierlich, B. A. Roe, F. Sanger, P. H. Schreier, A. J. H. Smith, R. Staden, and I. G. Young
    1981 Sequence and Organization of the Human Mitochondrial Genome. *Nature* 290:457–465.

Baltz, R. H., P. M. Bingham, and J. W. Drake
    1976 Heat Mutagenesis in Bacteriophage T4: The Transition Pathway. *Proceedings of the National Academy of Science, USA* 73:1269–1273.

Battula, N., and L.A. Loeb
    1976 On the Fidelity of DNA Replication. *The Journal of Biological Chemistry* 251:982–986.

Benjamin, D. C., J. A. Berzofsky, I. J. East, F. R. N. Gurd, C. Hannum, S. J. Leach, E. Margoliash, J. G. Micheal, A. Miller, E. M. Prager, M. Reichlin, E. E. Sercarz, S. J. Smith-Gill, P. E. Todd, and A. C. Wilson
    1984 The Antigenic Structure of Proteins—A Reappraisal. *Annual Review of Immunology* 2:67–101.

Blanc, H., K. H. Chen, M. A. D'Amore, and D. C. Wallace
    1985 Amino Acid Changes Associated with the Polymorphic Hinc II Site of Oriental and Caucasian Mitochondrial DNAs. *American Journal of Human Genetics* 35:167–176.

Cann, R. L., M. Stoneking, and A. C. Wilson
    1987 Mitochondrial DNA and Human Evolution. *Nature* 325:31–36.

Chapel, T. A., A. H. Mehregan, and T. A. Rehman
    1981 Histologic Findings in Mummified Skin. *Journal of the American Academy of Dermatology* 4:27–30.

Clark, J. M., and G. P. Beardsly
    1987 Functional Effects of Cis-thymine Glycol Lesions on DNA Synthesis In Vitro. *Biochemistry* 26:5398–5403.

Daniels, F. Jr., and P. W. Post
    1970 Theories on the Role of Pigment in the Evolution of Human Races. *Advancements in the Biology of the Skin* 10:279–292.

Deininger, P. L., D. J. Jolly, C. M. Rubin, T. Friedman, and C. W. Schmid
    1981 Base Sequence Studies of 300 Nucleotide Renatured Repeated Human DNA Clones. *Journal of Molecular Biology* 151:17–33.

Doran, G. H., C. Dickel, W. E. Ballinger, O. F. Agee, P. J. Laipis, and W. W. Hauswirth
    1986 Anatomical, Cellular and Molecular Analysis of 8,000-year-old Human Brain Tissue from the Windover Archaeological Site. *Nature* 323:803–806.

Farmer, P. J.
    1974 'The King of the Beasts.' In *Science Fact/Fiction*, pp. 240–241. Scott, Foresman and Co., Glenview, IL.

Feinberg, A. P., and B. Vogelstein
    1983 A Technique for Radiolabelling DNA Restriction Endonuclease Fragments to High Specific Activity. *Analytical Biochemistry* 132:6–13.

Golenberg, E. M., D. E. Giannasi, M. T. Clegg, C. J. Smiley, M. Durbin, D. Henderson, and G. Zurawski
    1990 Chloroplast DNA Sequence from a Miocene *Magnolia* Species. *Nature* 344:656–658.

Hagelberg, E., I. C. Gray, and A. J. Jeffreys
    1991 Identification of the Skeletal Remains of a Murder Victim by DNA Analysis. *Nature* 352:427–429.

Hagelberg, S., B. Sykes, and R. Hedges
    1989 Ancient Bone DNA Amplified. *Nature* 342:485.

Hanni, C., V. Laudet, M. Sakka, A. Begue, and D. Stehelin
    1990 Amplification of Mitochondrial DNA Fragments from Ancient Human Teeth and Bones. *Comptes Rendus De L'Academie Des Sciences, Serie III (Paris).* 310(9):365–370.

Hansen, H. E., and H. Gurtler
    1983 HLA Types of Mummified Eskimo Bodies from the 15th Century. *American Journal of Physical Anthropology* 61:447–452.

Higuchi, R. G., B. Bowman, M. Freiberger, O. A. Ryder, and A. C. Wilson
    1984 DNA Sequences from the Quagga, an Extinct Member of the Horse Family. *Nature* 312:282–284.

Higuchi, R. G., L. A. Wrischnik, E. Oakes, M. George, B. Tong, and A. C. Wilson
    1987 Mitochondrial DNA of the Extinct Quagga: Relatedness and Extent of Postmortem Change. *Journal of Molecular Evolution* 25:283–287.

Horai, S., and E. Matsunaga
    1986 Mitochondrial DNA Polymorphism in Japa-

nese II, Analysis with Restriction Enzymes of Four or Five Base Pair Recognition Sites. *Human Genetics* 72:105–117.

Johnson, B. H., C. B. Olson, and M. Goodman
1985 Isolation and Characterization of Deoxyribonucleic Acid from Tissue of the Wooly Mammoth, *Mammuthus primigenius*. *Comparative Biochemistry and Physiology* 81:1045–1051.

Kochert, G.
1989 *Introduction to RFLP Mapping*. Department of Botany, University of Georgia, Athens, GA. Published by The Rockefeller Foundation.

Kornberg, A.
1980 In *DNA Polymerase*. W. H. Freeman, New York.

Lawlor, D. A., C. D. Dickel, W. W. Hauswirth, and P. Parham
1991 Ancient HLA genes from 7,500-year-old archaeological remains. *Nature* 349:785–788.

Lowenstein, J. M., V. M. Sarich, and B. J. Richardson
1981 Albumen Systematics of the Extinct Mammoth and Tasmanian Wolf. *Nature* 291:409–411.

Maniatis, T., E. F. Frisch, and J. Sambrook
1982 *Molecular Cloning: A Laboratory Manual*. 1st ed. Cold Spring Harbor Laboratory, New York.

Maxam, A., and W. Gilbert
1977 A New Method for Sequencing DNA. *Proceedings of the National Academy of Science*, USA 74:560–572.

Murray, H. G., and W. F. Thompson
1980 Rapid Isolation of High Molecular Weight DNA. *Nucleic Acids Research* 8:4321–4325.

Pääbo, S.
1985a Preservation of DNA in Ancient Egyptian Mummies. *Journal of Archaeological Science* 12:411–417.

1985b Molecular Cloning of Ancient Egyptian Mummy DNA. *Nature* 314:644–645.

1989 Ancient DNA: Extraction, Characterization, Molecular Cloning, and Enzymatic Amplification. *Proceedings of the National Academy of Science, USA* 86:6196–6200.

1990 Amplifying Ancient DNA. In *PCR protocols: A Guide to Methods and Applications*. Academic Press, Inc.

Pääbo, S., J. A. Gifford, and A. C. Wilson
1988 Mitochondrial DNA Sequences from a 7000-year-old Brain. *Nucleic Acids Research* 16(20):9775–9787.

Pääbo, S., R .G. Higuchi, and A. C. Wilson
1989 Ancient DNA and the Polymerase Chain Reaction. *The Journal of Biological Chemistry* 264:9709–9712.

Perkin Elmer Cetus, Norwalk, CT 06859.

Rainey, W. E., J. M. Lowenstein, V. M. Sarich, and D. M. Magor
1984 Albumen Systematics of the Stellers Sea Cow. *Naturwissenschaften* 71:586–588.

Reynolds, T. M.
1965 Chemistry of Nonenzymic Browning II. *Advances in Food Research* 14:167–183.

Rogan, P. K., and J. J. Salvo
1990a Study of Nucleic Acids Isolated from Human Remains. *Yearbook of Physical Anthropology* 33:195–214.

1990b Molecular Genetics of Pre-Columbian South American Mummies. *UCLA Symposium of Molecular and Cellular Biology* 122:223–234.

Rogers, S. O., and A. J. Bendich
1976 Extraction of DNA from Milligram Amounts of Fresh, Herbarium and Mummified Plant Tissues. *Plant Molecular Biology* 5:69–76.

Rollo, F., A. Amici, and R. Salvi
1988 Short but Faithful Pieces of Ancient DNA. *Nature* 335:774.

Saiki, R. K., D. H. Gelfand, S. Stoffe, S. J. Scharf, R. G. Higuchi, G. T. Horn, K. B. Mullis, and H. A. Erlich
1988 Primer-Directed Enzymatic Amplification of DNA with a Thermostable DNA Polymerase. *Science* 239:487–491.

Saiki, R. K., S. Scharf, F. Faloona, K. B. Mullis, G. T. Horn, H. A. Erlich, and N. Arnheim
1985 Enzymatic Amplification of Beta Globin Sequences and Restriction Site Analysis for Diagnosis of Sickle-cell Anemia. *Science* 230:1350–1354.

Sanger, F., S. Nicklen, and A. R. Coulsen
1975 DNA Sequencing with Chain-Terminating Inhibitors. *Proceedings of the National Academy of Science*, USA 74:5463–5467.

Sarkar, G. S., and S. S. Sommer
1991 Parameters Affecting Susceptibility of PCR Contamination to UV Inactivation. *Biotechniques* 10(5):590–594.

Scholer, G., J. F. Ward, and J. J. Weiss
1960 Mechanisms of the Radiation-Induced Degradation of Nucleic Acids. *Journal of Molecular Biology* 2:379–385.

Stoneking, M.
1986 Unpublished Ph.D. dissertation, University of California, Berkeley.

Stoneking, M., and A. C. Wilson
  1988 In *The Colonisation of the Pacific: A Genetic Trail*, edited by A. Hill and S. Serjeantson. Oxford University Press.

Sykes, B.
  1991 The Past Comes Alive. *Nature* 352:381–382.

Tabor, S., and C. C. Richardson
  1989 Selective Inactivation of the Exonuclease Activity of Bacteriophage T7 DNA Polymerase by in Vitro Mutagenesis. *The Journal of Biological Chemistry* 264:6447–6458.

Taylor, B., and K. J. Powell
  1982 Isolation of Plant DNA and RNA. *Focus* 4:4–6.

Tindall, K. R., and T. A. Kunkel
  1988 Fidelity of DNA Synthesis by the *Thermus aquaticus* DNA Polymerase. *Biochemistry* 27:6008–6013.

Venanzi, F. M., and F. Rollo
  1990 Mummy RNA Last Longer. *Nature* 343:25–26.

Vieira, J., and J. Messing
  1982 The pUC Plasmids, An M13mp7-Derived System for Insertion Mutagenesis and Sequencing with Synthetic Universal Primers. *Gene* 19:259–268.

Wallace, D. C., K. Garrison, and W. C. Knowler
  1985 Dramatic Founder Effects in Amerindian Mitochondrial DNAs. *American Journal of Physical Anthropology* 68:149–155.

Williams, S. R., J. L. Longmire, and L. A. Beck
  1990 Human DNA Recovery from Ancient Bone. *American Journal of Physical Anthropology* 81(2):318.

Wrischnik L. A., R. G. Higuchi, M. Stoneking, H. A. Erlich, N. Arnheim, and A. C. Wilson
  1987 Length Mutations in Human Mitochondrial DNA: Direct Sequencing of Enzymatically Amplified DNA. *Nucleic Acids Research* 15:529–542.

Linguistic Evidence for the Peopling of the Americas

MERRIT RUHLEN
4335 Cesano Court
Palo Alto, CA 94306

Recent work on the genetic classification of languages has found that (1) the aboriginal languages of the Americas fall into three distinct genetic groups, (2) each of these groups has a different Asiatic origin, thus implying three distinct migrations from the Old World to the New, and (3) South America, with minor exceptions, was populated by a single immigration from North America.

It has been known now for two centuries that language can be used to study the relationships among different ethnic groups and that from the study of these relationships (linguistic taxonomy), certain inferences can be made regarding the origin of the divisions in a population and the migrations that would account for the present distribution of languages. From the beginnings of comparative linguistics it was envisaged by men such as Thomas Jefferson that the study of the indigenous languages of the Americas might shed light on the relationships among, and the Asiatic origins of, Native Americans. Just two hundred years ago this year Jefferson wrote to James Madison: "I endeavor to collect all the vocabularies I can, of American Indians, as those of Asia, persuaded, that if they ever had a common parentage, it will appear in their languages" (Jefferson 1904:267). Despite such early hopes by visionaries like Jefferson, the goal of an overall classification of New World languages remained largely unachieved until recently, for reasons that are discussed in Ruhlen (1987). Furthermore, attempts to find Old World relatives of Native American languages are generally considered to have been unsuccessful or even, by some, to be impossible because of the alleged rapid changes in sound and meaning that all human languages constantly undergo. According to this view, even if the indigenous languages of the Americas were related to various Asiatic languages, the length of time since separation is so great that all trace of the original unity would long since have disappeared. Such a belief is today widely held, but I have sought to show in Ruhlen (1992) that it is incorrect. In the remainder of this paper I will summarize Joseph Greenberg's recent classification of New World languages and begin to explore its implications for the peopling of the Americas.

THE GREENBERG CLASSIFICATION

In 1956 Joseph Greenberg, having just completed his revolutionary classification of African languages, reported at the Fifth International Congress of Anthropological and Ethnological Sciences that, in his opinion, the native languages of the Americas were to be classified into three distinct families: (1) Eskimo-Aleut; (2) Na-Dene; and (3) Amerind. A summary of his classification was published four years later (Greenberg 1960), though without supporting evidence. Over the next quarter-century Greenberg continued to gather lexical and grammatical evidence from as many New World languages as possible and finally, in 1987, published his complete classification with supporting evidence. Since both the Eskimo-Aleut and Na-Dene families were well established and generally accepted by linguists, Greenberg devoted most of his book to a presentation of the evidence for the third New World family, Amerind. This evidence took the form of over 2,000 etymologies—lexical and grammatical—in support of Amerind and its eleven subgroups. Over three hundred of these etymologies connected multiple subgroups and thus were considered Amerind etymologies, rather than merely, say, Penutian or Hokan etymologies. Further study of the etymologies given in support of the Amerind subgroups has led me to conclude (Ruhlen 1989a) that at least another 150 Amerind etymologies can be discerned in Greenberg's book, bringing the total number of Amerind etymologies to around 500. A map of the Greenberg classification is shown in Figure 1.

Linguistic classifications such as Greenberg's are discovered on the basis of resemblances in sound and meaning in the basic vocabulary (e.g., pronouns, body parts, natural phenomena). One of the most salient traits of the Amerind family, which was remarked by both Alfredo Trombetti and Edward Sapir in the first decades of this century, is the presence of first-person *n-* and second-person *m-* throughout the languages of North and South America. Furthermore, not only does this trait connect all eleven Amerind subgroups, it also serves to distinguish the Amerind family from the world's other language families. In a recent study of personal pronouns in the world's languages (Ruhlen 1989b) I found that the Amerind pattern (*n-* 'I' vs. *m-* 'thou') is virtually nonexistent elsewhere in the world. By itself, then, a consideration of first- and second-person pronouns in New World languages leads directly to the Greenberg classification. When one adds to the equation the wealth of lexical and grammatical evidence presented in Greenberg's book, there can really be no doubt about the validity of the Amerind family. The shrill attacks on Greenberg's classification by some Amerindian scholars mirror those leveled at his African classification by Bantuists some four decades ago. Rebuttals to criticism of Greenberg's classification of New World languages may be found in Ruhlen (1988) and Greenberg (1989).

INTERNAL RELATIONSHIPS OF THE AMERIND FAMILY

Greenberg (1987) proposed etymologies in support of 11 Amerind subgroups: Almosan-Keresiouan, Penutian, Hokan, Central Amerind, Chibchan-Paezan, Andean, Macro-Tucanoan, Equatorial, Macro-Carib, Macro-Panoan, and Macro-Ge. The first four of these are found primarily in North America, the other seven predominantly in South America, as may be seen in Figures 2 and 3. Greenberg did not assume that all eleven Amerind subgroups were coordinate and as a first approximation proposed the subgrouping for the Amerind family shown in Figure 4.

In Ruhlen (1991) I reported the results of a statistical analysis of the matrix of Amerind traits (Appendix C of Greenberg 1987) that tended to support Greenberg's conclusions regarding the internal structure of the Amerind family. This study suggested that, in addition to the higher-level groupings proposed by Greenberg, all South American subgroups belong to a single higher-level grouping which I called Southern Amerind. Within this grouping there are indications that Chibchan-Paezan branched off first, followed somewhat later by Andean. There are also certain indications that Central Amerind is the most divergent branch of Amerind, but this question needs further study. I would now propose the Amerind subgrouping shown in Figure 5.

EXTERNAL RELATIONSHIPS OF NEW WORLD FAMILIES

Eskimo-Aleut

Lexical and grammatical similarities between Eskimo-Aleut and language families of Northern Eurasia have been noticed for centuries, though usually in terms of binary comparisons that revealed only part of the picture. Greenberg's multilateral approach to language classification has led him to propose a Eurasiatic family that encompasses most of the language families of Northern Eurasia: Indo-European, Uralic-Yukaghir, Altaic, Korean-Japanese-Ainu, Gilyak, Chukchi-Kamchatkan, and Eskimo-Aleut. In Eurasiatic the most common pronominal pattern is first-person *m-* and second-person *t-*, and Eskimo-Aleut shows reflexes of both pronouns. Furthermore, as Greenberg (1992) shows, the Eurasiatic family is characterized by two different first-person pronouns, *m-*, just mentioned, and *k-*, each serving a different function. Greenberg characterizes the *m-* pronoun as "active or ergative," while *k-* is basically "stative, absolutive,

Figure 1. Language families of the Americas. Reprinted from *A Guide to the World's Languages*, by M. Ruhlen (Stanford University Press, Stanford), 1987.

or passive." In Eskimo-Aleut the Eurasiatic pattern is reflected in ergative *m-* and absolutive *k-*. Accordingly, nouns that are the *subject* of transitive verbs use *-ma* as the first-person singular possessive ("my"), while nouns that are the *object* of transitive or the *subject* of intransitive verbs require the first-person singular possessive pronoun *-ka*. Greenberg has discovered over sixty grammatical and 500 lexical etymologies in support of the Eurasiatic family, and an examination of this evidence reveals that there is really nothing mysterious about the Eurasiatic affinity of Eskimo-Aleut. Rather the alleged isolation of Eskimo-Aleut is one more instance of beliefs engendered by the history of linguistics rather than by the principles of historical linguistics.

Na-Dene

As is well known, Edward Sapir concluded early in this century that the Na-Dene family of languages was most closely related to the vast Sino-Tibetan family of East Asia. Though he made a careful study of the relationship, none of his material was ever published and the proposed connection fell into disrepute, despite sporadic supporters (Shafer 1952, 1957; Swadesh 1952). Indeed, in recent years an attempt was even made to remove Haida from the Na-Dene family (Levine 1979), but Greenberg (1987) points out the many flaws in Levine's methods, which, if taken seriously, would do away with Indo-European as well. Greenberg did

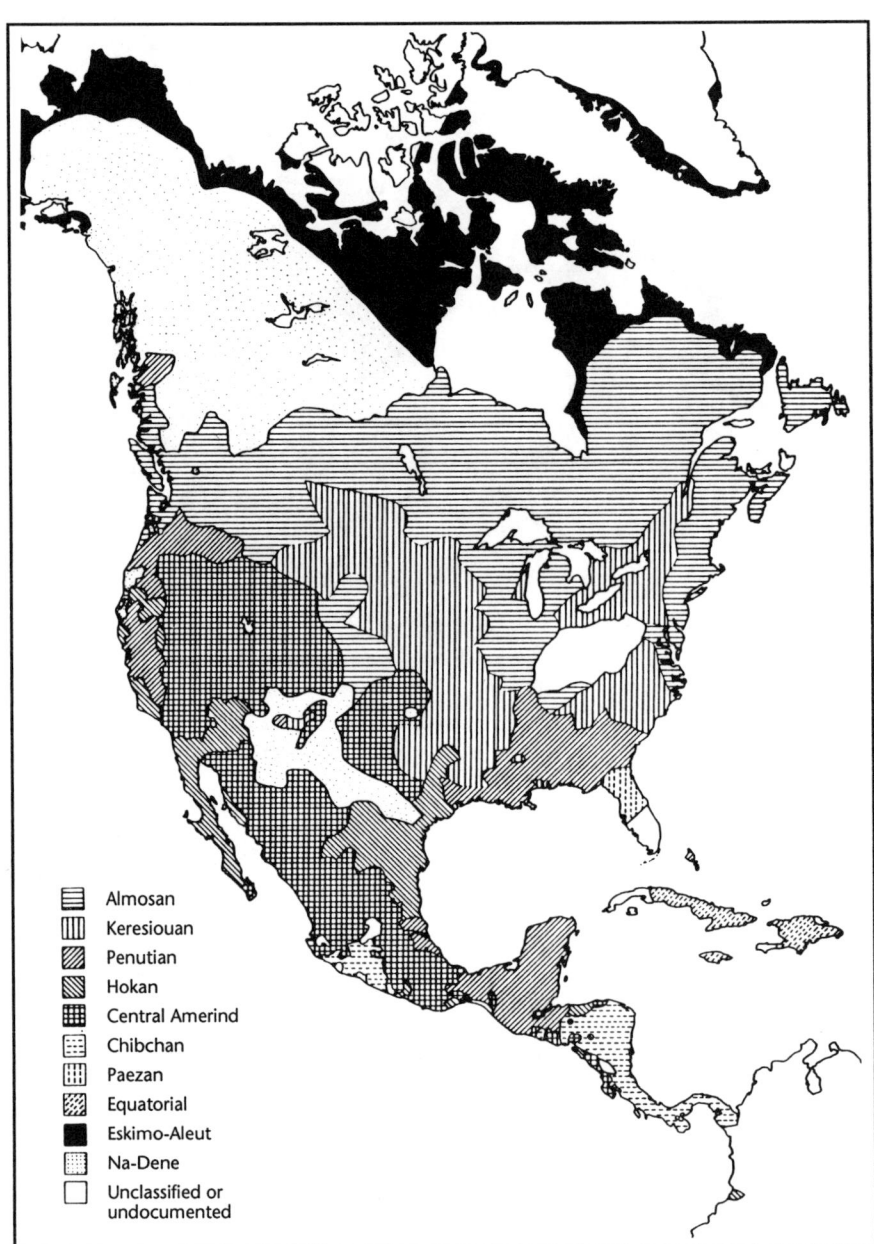

Figure 2. The Amerind family, North America. Reprinted from *A Guide to the World's Languages*, by M. Ruhlen (Stanford University Press, Stanford), 1987.

not propose any Na-Dene etymologies, arguing rather that Sapir had already made the case. He did, however, collect Na-Dene vocabularies during the course of his work. An examination of Greenberg's *Na-Dene Notebook* (Greenburg 1983), a copy of which is found in Stanford University's Green Library, provides abundant evidence that Haida is very much a part of Na-Dene, participating in numerous grammatical and lexical etymologies with the other members of Na-Dene (Tlingit, Eyak, Athabaskan).

Although Sapir's proposed connection between Na-Dene and Sino-Tibetan fell out of favor in this country in the second half of this century, Sapir himself had no doubts: "If the morphological and lexical accord which I find on every hand between Na-Dene and Indo-Chinese is 'accidental,' then every analogy on God's earth is an accident" (Golla 1984:374). Recently, Sapir's idea has been revived by Soviet scholars. Sergei Starostin proposed in 1984 that Sino-Tibetan was related to (North) Caucasian and Yeniseian in a family he named Sino-Caucasian. In 1986 Sergei Nikolaev proposed a substantial number of etymologies connecting Na-Dene with (North) Caucasian and renamed the family Dene-Caucasian (Nikolaev 1991). Presently Dene-Caucasian is taken to include (North) Caucasian, Sino-Tibetan, Yeniseian, Na-Dene, the extinct languages †Hurrian,

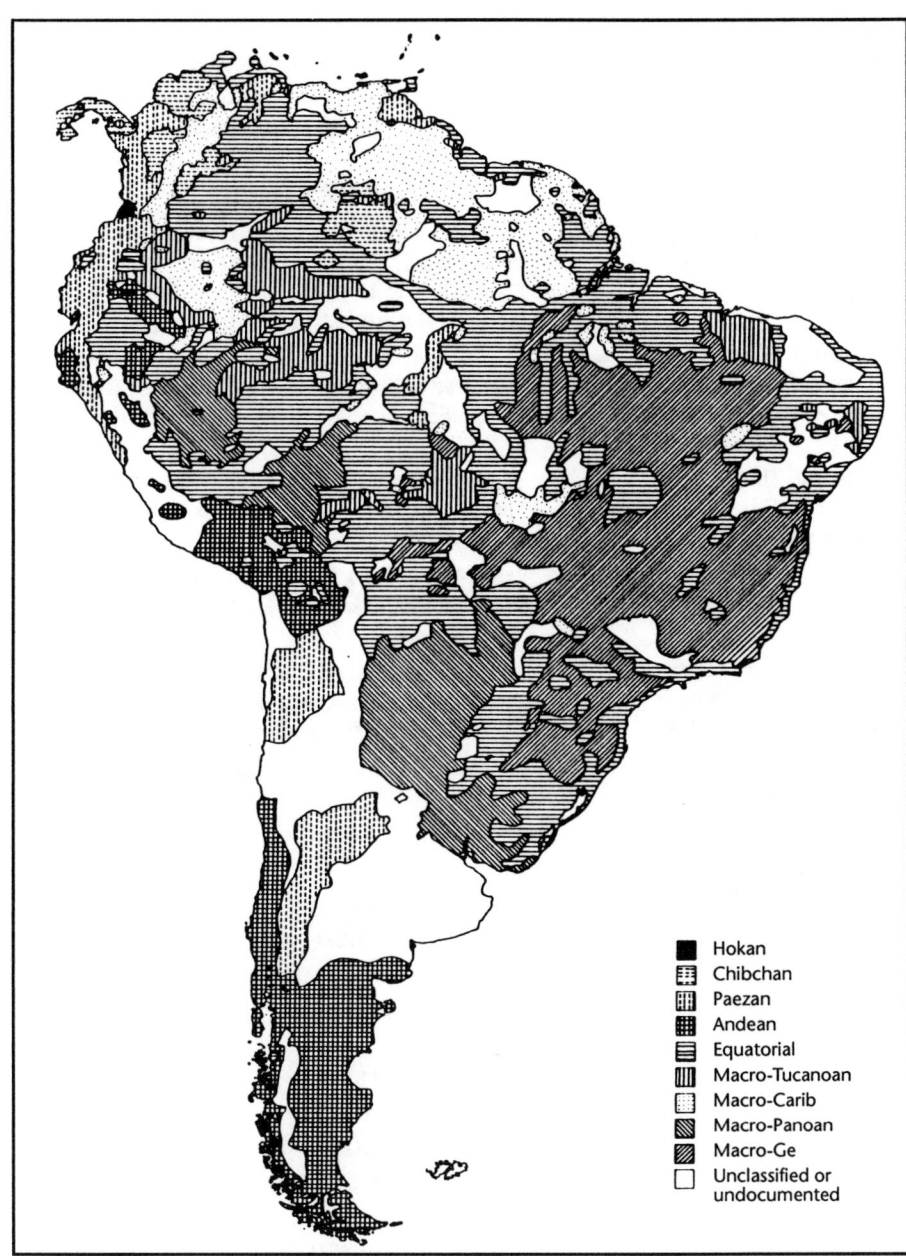

Figure 3. The Amerind family, South America. Reprinted from *A Guide to the World's Languages*, by M. Ruhlen (Stanford University Press, Stanford), 1987.

†Urartian, and †Hatti, and possibly the isolates Basque, Burushaski, and Nahali. Dene-Caucasian thus constitutes an expansion of Sapir's original idea.

As in the case of Eurasiatic and Amerind, pronouns provide important evidence for the validity of Dene-Caucasian. Starostin (1984) compared Proto-North Caucasian *z⁽ʷ⁾o 'I' (e.g., Chechen *suo*, Bats *so*, Abxaz *sa*, Kabardian *se*, Agul *zu*, Rutul *zı*, Lezgi *zun*, Archi *zon*,) with Proto-Yeniseian *ʔaẓ 'I,' while Diakonoff and Starostin (1986) added Urartian *ješə* (ergative) ~ *šo* (absolutive) 'I,' Hurrian *se-* 'I,' and Hatti *se-* 'I' to the comparison. Nikolaev (1986) compared these forms with Proto-Na-Dene *ṣʷí (e.g., Tanaina *ší?*, Galice *šii*, Navajo *ší*). Bengtson (1991) compares Burushaski *že ~ ža* 'I' with these forms and Nahali *ẓuo* 'I' would seem to belong here as well. For the second-person singular Starostin compared Proto-North Caucasian *wo 'thou' (e.g., Abxaz *wa*, Kabardian *we*, Xinalug *wı*, Lezgi *wun*, Archi *un*) with Proto-Yeniseian *ʔu ~ ʔəw 'thou,' and Diakonoff and Starostin added Hurrian *we- ~ -û*, Urartian *-w*, and Hatti *we-*, all second-person singular pronouns. To this comparison Nikolaev added Proto-Na-Dene *wĭ 'thou' (e.g., Tlingit *weh* 'thou'), and Bengtson, Burushaski *ūŋ* 'thou.' For first-person plural pronouns we may compare Haida *iit'* 'us,' Proto-Athabaskan **-ii'd* (< **iit*) 'we,' Navajo *-iid-* 'we' with similar forms in East Caucasian languages (e.g., Chamalal *iłi* 'we inc.,' Andi *iłi* 'we inc.,' Hunzib *ile* 'we').

In addition to the pronominal evidence enumerated above Nikolaev proposes many good lexical comparisons. Each of the etymologies given below is based on a comparison made by Nikolaev between Na-Dene and Caucasian languages. I have, however, added Haida forms (which were unavailable to Nikolaev), specific citations from Na-Dene languages taken from Greenberg's *Na-Dene Notebook* (Nikolaev gives only reconstructions in his article), or Sino-Tibetan forms taken from Starostin (1984) or Benedict (1972). I have also modified some of Nikolaev's reconstruction on the basis of the Haida material.

1. Proto-Na-Dene **q'al* 'skin,' Haida *q'al*, Tlingit *χas'*, Navajo *-kal* 'leather' = Proto-East Caucasian **q̄q̄ăt'V* 'skin, hide, bark' = Proto-Sino-Tibetan **qhrōw* 'bark.'
2. Proto-Na-Dene **k'ʷVnč* 'thumb,' Haida *(sli-)k* 'use,' Tlingit *guš* = Proto-Caucasian **k'⁽ʷ⁾Vṣ̌* 'finger, toe.'
3. Proto-Na-Dene **tuk'i* 'spit,' Tlingit *tuχ* 'spit,' Sarsi *zák'aʔ* 'saliva,' Ump-qua *seek'eʔ* 'saliva' = Proto-Nax **tük'* 'saliva' = Proto-Tibeto-Burman **(m-)tuk* 'spit' = Yeniseian: Kot *tuk* 'spit.'
4. Proto-Na-Dene **q'uti* 'armpit,' Haida *(s-)q'ut*, Chipewyan *-(n)k'ɛsí* = Proto-East Caucasian **q̄ʷV̂č̣'ʷV* 'elbow, armpit.'
5. Proto-Eyak-Athabaskan **šăNč'* 'father-in-law,' Galice *sāāt'eʔ* = Proto-East Caucasian **sʷĭč̣č̣V* 'father-in-law; first cousin (male).'
6. Proto-Na-Dene **lĭnh* 'woman, wife,' Hare *(t'e-)line* = Proto-East Caucasian **lɨnhV* 'woman, wife.'
7. Proto-Na-Dene **k'ălVg* 'butterfly' = Proto-East Caucasian **k'alVk'V* 'butterfly.'
8. Proto-Na-Dene **xăn?* 'water, river,' Haida *ʕan-t'* 'river, water,' Tlingit *hain* 'water,' Eyak *ʔā* 'river,' Tlatskanai *xonē* 'river' = Proto-East Caucasian **x̄ăn?ɨ* 'water, river.'
9. Proto-Na-Dene **q'ut'* 'bite,' Haida *q'usgat* 'bite,' Eyak *q'ət'*, Kato *gət'* = Proto-East Caucasian **q'at'ɨ* 'bite, piece.'
10. Proto-Na-Dene **t'ùxʷ* 'yellow, green,' Tlingit *sūhw* 'green,' Tanaina *t'ək* 'yellow,' Sarsi *t'úú* 'yellow,' Tututni *soh* 'blue,' Mattole *t'ow* 'yellow' = Proto-East Caucasian *čakʷV* 'yellow, green.'
11. Proto-Na-Dene **k'ʷaN(H)* 'dry,' Haida *k'a* = Proto-Tibeto-Burman **kaŋ* 'to be dry' = Proto-Caucasian **ʔiɢʷVrV* 'dry.'
12. Proto-Eyak-Athabaskan **šVʔgʷ* 'crooked' = Proto-Tibeto-Burman **guk ~ *kuk* 'crooked' = Proto-East Caucasian **č'Vkʷ V* 'crooked.'
13. Proto-Eyak-Athabaskan **k'ŭhlẓ̌* 'sour,' Chipewyan

Amerind:
  Northern:
    Almosan-Keresiouan
    Penutian
    Hokan
  Central:
    Tanoan
    Uto-Aztecan
    Oto-Manguean
    Chibchan-Paezan
    Andean
    Equatorial-Tucanoan:
      Macro-Tucanoan
      Equatorial
    Ge-Pano-Carib:
      Macro-Carib
      Macro-Panoan
      Macro-Ge

Figure 4. Subgrouping of the Amerind family (after Greenberg 1987)

Amerind:
  Northern:
    Almosan-Keresiouan
    Penutian
    Hokan
  Central:
    Tanoan
    Uto-Aztecan
    Oto-Manguean
  Southern:
    Chibchan-Paezan
    South American:
      Andean
      Southeast:
        Equatorial-Tucanoan:
          Macro-Tucanoan
          Equatorial
        Ge-Pano-Carib:
          Macro-Carib
          Macro-Panoan
          Macro-Ge

Figure 5. Subgrouping of the Amerind family (after Ruhlen 1991)

k'üz, Navajo *-k'ǫ́ǫ́ž* = Proto-Tibeto-Burman ***k(h)rok*** 'sour' = Proto-East Caucasian *q'⁽ʷ⁾Vlč̣'V* 'sour.'

14. Proto-Na-Dene ***kɨt'V*** 'child,' Haida *gɨɨt'(e)*, Tlingit *gít'a*, Eyak *qēt'* = Proto-Caucasian ***kənɬ'V*** 'small; puppy, child.'

Furthermore, the case for Dene-Caucasian can be strengthened beyond the evidence so far adduced by Starostin and Nikolaev. Since Starostin compared only three members of Dene-Caucasian (Caucasian, Sino-Tibetan, Yeniseian), and Nikolaev but two (Caucasian, Na-Dene), a great deal of evidence remains to be discovered in those families that have not yet been directly compared. In this regard all of the evidence connecting Na-Dene with Sino-Tibetan, which so impressed Sapir, remains to be integrated into the Dene-Caucasian etymologies. Thus, in all likelihood, the common Athabaskan second-person pronoun ***nan*** 'thou' (e.g., Galice *nan*, Hupa *niŋ*, Carrier *nen*, Kutchin *ɲã*) is cognate with Proto-Sino-Tibetan ***naŋ*** 'thou' (e.g., Burmese *naŋ*, Nung *na*, Chinese *njo*, Karen *na*). A lexical analogy between Na-Dene and Sino-Tibetan that has so far escaped notice is the following.

15. Proto-Na-Dene ***dzuC*** 'vagina,' Haida *chúu*, Sarsi *dzúz*, Tsetsaut *edju* 'vulva,' Galice *ǯoš* = Proto-Tibeto-Burman ***dźuk*** 'vulva,' Maru *dźok*, Atsi *dźu?*, Burmese *tsauk*, Chang Naga *sūk*, Lushei *tšhu*.

A multilateral approach to Dene-Caucasian, with the integration of Sapir's unpublished materials, will greatly strengthen the case for the affinity of Na-Dene with these Asian families, a case which is already founded on a substantial body of evidence.

Amerind

The Amerind family appears to be most closely related to a different set of Old World language families, namely, those found primarily in Northern Eurasia that Greenberg groups together in a Eurasiatic family (see above). While Eskimo-Aleut is simply one constituent of Eurasiatic, Amerind appears to be related to Eurasiatic as a whole, having presumably broken away from the Eurasiatic complex before it had begun to disintegrate.

Greenberg's Eurasiatic family is similar to the Nostratic family (see Kaiser and Shevoroshkin 1988) that has been postulated by Soviet scholars in the past several decades, but it differs in certain crucial respects. As defined by Vladislav Illich-Svitych (1967:1971–84) and Aron Dolgopolsky (1969, 1971, 1972, 1974, 1984), Nostratic is taken to include Afro-Asiatic, Kartvelian, Indo-European, Uralic, Dravidian, and Altaic. Greenberg does not deny that Eurasiatic is related to Afro-Asiatic, Kartvelian, and Dravidian, but he believes these relationships are more remote. Eurasiatic is based on a preliminary survey of all possibly related language families and is intended to be a valid linguistic taxon, whereas Nostratic was based largely on families for which reconstructions were available, and thus has little likelihood of constituting a valid linguistic taxon as currently conceived. Nonetheless, most of the over 700 Nostratic etymologies appear to be valid at some level of classification and there is great overlap with Greenberg's Eurasiatic etymologies. Perhaps the best way to view Nostratic is as a vast family, still not completely defined, of which Eurasiatic is but one subgroup. In any event it is now possible to compare Greenberg's Amerind etymologies with the Nostratic etymologies of Illich-Svitych and Dolgopolsky, as well as with Greenberg's Eurasiatic etymologies. On the basis of such a comparison, I have proposed over 100 etymologies connecting Amerind with Eurasiatic/Nostratic (Ruhlen 1989c). A few examples from these etymologies are given below. The following abbreviations are used.

PAA: Proto-Afro-Asiatic
PK: Proto-Kartvelian
PIE: Proto-Indo-European
PU: Proto-Uralic
PA: Proto-Altaic
PD: Proto-Dravidian
CK: Chukchi-Kamchatkan
EA: Eskimo-Aleut
AK: Almosan-Keresiouan
P: Penutian
H: Hokan
CA: Central Amerind
PUA: Proto-Uto-Aztecan
POM: Proto-Oto-Manguean
CP: Chibchan-Paezan
AN: Andean
EQ: Equatorial
MT: Macro-Tucanoan
MC: Macro-Carib
MP: Macro-Panoan
MG: Macro-Ge.

16. Nostratic ***č'ik'ʌ*** 'cut,' PK ***č'eč'k'-*** 'cut (finely),' PA ***čikʌ*** 'cut, chop,' Evenki *čikā-* 'cut, chop,' Even *čiki-* 'chop' = Amerind ***t'ik'a/t'ak'i*** 'hit,' Proto-Salish ***t'aqʷ*** 'break,' Snohomish *t'aq'* 'hit,' Lillooet *t'ikən* 'beat, whip,' Squamish *t'əxʷ* 'be hit,' Nootka *t'oqʷ* 'hit,' Quileute *t'ex* 'hit,' Kutenai *t'ik'* 'destroy,' Wichita *takʷi/tɨkʷi* 'hit,' Wiyot *tik* 'cut through,' Yurok *tikʷohs* 'hit,' Coos *tōh* 'hit,' Takelma *toj-k'* 'hit,' Wappo *təh* 'kill,' Aymara *tok'e* 'quarrel' (v.), Qawasqar *toks* 'fight,' Kahuapana *an-čiokma* 'fight,' Mascoy *tik* 'hit,' Moseten *-tak* 'hitting action,' Botocudo *čik* 'hit,' Kaingain *taik* 'hit.'

17. Nostratic ***da*** (locative), PAA ***d*** (locative), PK ***-da*** (allative), PIE ***-D/-eD*** (ablative), PD ***-ṭṭ/-tt(ʌ)*** (locative, ablative), PU ***-δa/-δä*** (ablative), Yukaghir *-da* (locative), PA ***-da*** (locative), Korean *it-te* 'now' (= demonstrative + locative), *te* 'place,' Japanese *-ta* (locative), Ainu *-ta/-te* (locative), Koryak *ti-te*

'when,' Aliutor *ti-ta* 'when' = AMERIND **te ~ *ta* (locative), Maidu *di* 'in,' Klamath *di* 'place of,' Catio *-de* (locative), Move *-te* 'in,' Lule *ta-* 'through, in.'

18. EURASIATIC **iri* 'be angry,' Sanskrit *irasyati* 'becomes angry,' Avestan *arəšyant-* 'envious,' Hittite *arsanija* 'to envy, be angry,' Ainu *iruska* 'become angry,' Greenlandic *irsivoq* 'is afraid' = AMERIND **iri* 'be angry,' Timucua *juru* 'be angry, afraid,' Warrau *jari* 'angry,' Itonama *jari-ʔna* 'be angry,' Chimu *iri* 'be afraid,' Millcayac *irrim* 'angry,' Surinam *erexko* 'be angry,' Trio *əire* 'fierce,' Uitoto *riie* 'angry.'

19. NOSTRATIC **jamʌ* 'water, sea,' PAA **jam* 'water, sea,' PU **jamʌ* 'sea,' PD **am(m)* 'water' = AMERIND **jume* 'water,' Wintun *mem* 'water,' Wappo *meʔ* 'water,' Atsugewi *jumē* 'river,' Chumash *ma* 'stream,' Esselen *imi-la* 'sea,' Washo *ime* 'water,' Yurimangui *jo-ima* 'saliva' (= 'mouth-water'), Tarascan *-ma-* (action on water), Cuitlatec *ʔumə* 'water,' Catacao *amum* 'sea,' Cholona *omium* 'wave,' Aguaruna *jumi* 'water, rain,' Yuracare *jumijumi* 'water,' Siracua *mama* 'water.'

20. NOSTRATIC **käjwʌ* 'chew,' PIE **ǵjeu-/gjeu-* 'chew,' PA **kābä-* 'chew,' Ainu *kui* 'chew,' Japanese *kui* 'bite into,' *kuu* 'eat, bite, chew,' Ryukyuan *kūyung* 'bite' = AMERIND **k'aiwa* 'bite,' Tsimshian *q'ai* 'bite,' Bodega *kawwu* 'bite,' Kiowa *k'ɔ* 'bite,' PUA **ko* 'chew,' Mura *kau(-assa)* 'eat,' Paez *koja* 'food,' Bribri *iku* 'bite,' Sabela *kæi* 'bite!,' Masaka *kaukæwi* 'bite,' Movima *kaiki* 'eat,' Miranya *me-ikoi* 'bite,' Uitoto *kai* 'gnaw,' Lule *kai* 'eat,' Vejoz *okua* 'to bite,' Marinahua *kiju* 'bite,' Proto-Tacanan **ika* 'eat, bite,' Meniens *kua* 'eat,' Proto-Ge **ku* 'eat.'

21. NOSTRATIC **K'apʼa* 'cover, close,' PAA **kp-/kʼp-* 'close, cover,' PU **kopa* 'bark,' Kamassian *kuba* 'skin, hide,' Estonian *kōba* 'fir bark,' Cheremiss *kuwo* 'shell, hull, husk,' PD **kapp-/kavʌ-* 'to close,' PA **k'apa-* 'cover,' Middle Korean *kəpcil* 'bark,' Japanese *kabur-* 'put on, cover,' *kapá* 'bark,' Ainu *sik-kap* 'eyelid,' Gilyak *xip* 'birch bark,' Greenlandic *qapuk* 'scum, froth' = AMERIND **k(ʼ)ap(ʼ)a ~ *q(ʼ)ap(ʼ)a* 'cover, close,' Squamish *qʌpʼ* 'close,' Chemakum *hap'ilii* 'cover,' Oowekyala *kapa* 'to lift a lid, blanket,' Haisla *kàpa* 'covered with frost,' Proto-Central Algonquian **kep* 'close,' Wiyot *kʷapl* 'be covered,' Catawba *kəpa* 'close,' Dakota *akaxpa* 'close,' Tonkawa *kapa* 'shut,' Cuna *akapa* 'close one's eyes,' Atacama *kʼaba* 'hide,' Mascoy *kjab* 'cover,' Panobo *kepui* 'close,' Coroado *kapo-em* 'to close.'

22. NOSTRATIC **Kʼarä* 'black, dark,' PAA **kʼr/kr* 'black,' PIE **ker-/ker-s* 'black, dark,' PD **kaṯ/kāṟ/kāṯ* 'black, dark,' PA **Karä* 'black,' Mongol *küreŋ* 'dark brown,' Manchu *kuri* 'dark brown,' Korean *kɨrɨnca* 'shadow,' Japanese *kuro-i* 'black,' Ainu *ekurok* 'black,' *kuru* 'shadow,' Gilyak *ıɣr-* 'black,' Eskimo *qirniq* 'black' = AMERIND **kʼara* 'black,' Wichita *kārʔi* 'black,' Mohawk *akara* 'dark,' Catawba *kare* 'dark,' Karok *ikxaram* 'night,' Ona *kar* 'charcoal,' Qawasqar *hakar* 'dark, black,' Araucanian *kuru* 'black,' Aymara *čʼiara* 'black,' Galibi *mekoro* 'black,' Opaie *kōra* 'black.'

23. NOSTRATIC **KʼüjnA* 'wolf, dog,' PAA **k(j)n/k(j)l/k(w)l* 'dog, wolf,' PIE **kwōn/kun-* 'dog,' PU **küjnä* 'wolf,' PA **kʼina* 'dog,' Old Turkish *qančiq* 'bitch,' Mongolian *qani* 'a wild, masterless dog,' Lamut *ŋen* 'dog,' Korean *kɑ̈* (< **kañi*) 'dog,' Gilyak *qan* 'dog,' Chukchi *käjŋən* 'dog,' Sirenik *qanaʁa* 'wolf,' = AMERIND **kʼuan* 'dog,' Achomawi *kuan* 'silver fox,' Tonkawa *ʔekuan* 'dog,' North Yana *kuwan-na* 'lynx,' Yurimangui *kwan* 'dog,' Towa *kiano*, Tiwa *kuijani(-dã)*, Zacapoaxtla *itskwiin-ti* 'dog,' Chatina *čuni, xnih*, Popoloca *kunija*, Ixcatec *ʔuniña*, Chocho *ʔuña*, Mazatec *naña*, Chilanga *akʼuan* 'deer,' Tarascan *axuni* 'deer, animal,' Similaton *aguingge* 'deer.'

24. NOSTRATIC **küni* 'wife, woman,' PIE **gʷen-* 'wife, woman,' PA **küni* 'wife,' Alaskan Eskimo *aganak* 'woman,' Greenlandic *arnaq* 'woman' = AMERIND **kuan* 'woman, wife, girl,' Tonkawa *kʷān* 'woman,' Seri *kuãam*, Tequistlatec *(l-)agaʔ-no*, Yokuts *kain*, Tsimshian *hanax*, Kamayura *kunja*, Yuracare *igūn* 'girl,' Cuica *kneu* 'female,' Guahibo *kvantua* 'first wife.'

25. NOSTRATIC **kʼutʼʌ* 'small,' PAA **k'(w)tʼ* 'small,' PK **kʼutʼ-* 'small,' PD **kuḍḍ-* 'small,' Turkish *küčük* 'small,' Uighur *kičik* 'small,' Evenki *köčaken* 'small,' Ryukyuan *kūt-ēng* 'be small,' Kamchadal *kižg* 'fine, small,' Kuskokwim *kituq* 'be small,' Inuit *-kuči* (diminutive) = AMERIND **kʼutʼi* 'small,' Wappo *kutʼija* 'small,' Wishram *kʼatʼ* 'small,' Klamath *kʼečča* 'small,' Proto-California Penutian **kut* 'little,' Huave *kičeeč* 'small,' Pokomchi *kʼisa* 'small,' Tequistlatec *guʔušu* 'narrow,' Quitemo *kuči* 'thin,' Arawak *kitʼke* 'narrow,' Botocudo *kuʃi* 'small,' Ingain *kutui* 'small.'

26. NOSTRATIC **KʼA* (allative), PAA **k* (allative), PU **-kkʌ/-kʌ* (allative), Yukaghir *-ge/-go* (allative), PD **-kkʌ/-kʌ* (dative, allative), PA **-kʌ* (dative, allative), Gilyak *-ak* (dative, allative), Aliutor *-ka* (allative), Chukchi *-ki* (locative), *-kjit* (direction of), *mi-k* 'where,' Greenlandic *-k* (locative), *na-k-it* 'whence' = AMERIND **k(ʼ)i* (allative), Wiyot *okʷ* 'in,' Yurok *-ik* 'in,' Seneca *-keh* 'in,' Maidu *-k* 'toward,' Alsea *k-* (locative), Yuki *kʼil* 'toward,' Totonac *k-* 'in,' Yana *-ki* 'hither,' Washo *-uk* 'toward,' Atsugewi *-k* (allative), Chimu *-ek* 'to,' Cuna *ki-* 'in, at, by.'

27. NOSTRATIC **-la* (collective), PU **-la* (collective), PD **-l* (plural), PA **-l(a)* (collective), Kamchadal *-al* (collective) = AMERIND **-le ~ *-la* (plural), Mataco *-el* (plural), Lule *mi-l* 'you' (cf. *mi* 'thou'), *-l* (personal plural, e.g., *kwe-l* 'children'), Mocovi *le-* (plural, cf. *i-tā* 'his father' and *le-tā* 'their father'), Guambiana *-ele* (noun plural), Colorado *-la* (plural of nouns and pronouns), Xinca *-li* (plural of nouns and pro-

nouns), Murire *-re* (pronoun plural), Bribri *-r* (noun plural), Paya *-ri* (plural verb subj.).

28. EURASIATIC **man* 'hand,' PIE **man-/mə-r-* 'hand,' Yurok *mana* 'finger,' Tungus *mana* 'paw,' Korean *manei* 'touch,' Ainu *amojn* 'hand,' *imeka* 'gift,' Gilyak *imy-* 'give,' *man-* 'measure by handspans,' *tuń-miń* 'finger,' Aliutor *məny-* 'hand,' Kerek *mənəqal* 'hand,' Itelmen *man Ze* 'palm' = AMERIND **man-/mak-* 'hand, give,' Proto-Central Algonquian *mī* 'hand,' Kwakiutl *maxwa* 'give potlatch,' Chinook *m-* 'hand (v.),' Maidu *ma* 'hand,' Central Sierra Miwok *amma* 'give,' Choctaw *ima* 'give,' Mixe *ma* 'give,' Totonac *makan* 'hand,' Akwa'ala *man* 'arm,' East Pomo *ma* 'hold,' Salinan *maa* 'hand,' Tequistlatec *mane* 'hand, arm,' *mage* 'five,' PUA **ma* 'hand,' **maka* 'give,' Proto-Chinantec **man* 'hand,' Kiowa *mã* 'hand,' *mē-ga* 'give,' Proto-Tanoan **ma-n* 'hand,' Colorado *manta* 'hand,' Ayoman *man* 'hand,' Mayna *mani* 'arm,' Quechua *maki* 'hand,' Ona *mar* 'arm, hand,' Ticuna *mi* 'hand,' Proto-Tupi **meʔeŋ* 'hand,' Caranga *maka* 'receive,' Pilaga *imak* 'left hand,' Lengua *amīk* 'hand,' Proto-Panoan **mɨkɨnɨ* 'hand,' Kamakan *mane* 'give,' Bororo *mako* 'give,' Kaingan *ma* 'bring.'

29. NOSTRATIC **mene* 'walk, step,' PIE **men-* 'trample, step on,' PU **mene* 'go, travel,' Yukaghir *män-* 'jump,' Old Turkish *man-* 'a step,' Tartar *maŋda* 'run,' Kamchadal *emeneŋ* 'a step' = AMERIND **mina* 'go,' Santa Ana *Ima* 'go!,' Chitimacha *ʔami* 'go, go away,' Kalapuya *maʔa* 'come,' Wappo *mi* 'go,' Taos *mē* 'go,' PUA **mi* 'go,' Bribri *mina* 'go,' Rama *mang* 'go!,' Matanawi *amī* 'go!,' Colorado *mai* 'go,' Araucanian *-me-* 'go to . . . ,' Pehuenche *amu* 'walk,' Auake *ma* 'walk,' Yuracare *ama* 'come!,' Moseten *mii* 'go, walk,' Chulupi *ma* 'go,' Umotina *a-menu* 'go,' Proto-Ge **mõ(r)* 'go, walk,' Dalbergia *mũ* 'go,' Kamakan *emang* 'go.'

30. Nostratic **mi ~ *ma* 'what,' PAA **m(j)* 'what, who,' PK **maj* 'what,' **mi-n* 'who,' PIE **mo-* 'how, if, when,' Hittite *maxxan* 'how,' PU **mi* 'what,' PA **mi-* 'what,' Korean *muəs* 'what,' Old Korean *mai* 'why,' Ryukyuan *mī* 'what,' *-mi* (interrogative enclitic), Ainu *mak* 'what,' *makan* 'what kind,' Chukchi *mɨkin* 'who,' *mi-k* 'where,' Kamchadal *min* 'which' = AMERIND **mi-n ~ *ma-n* 'who, what, where, when,' Central Sierra Miwok *minni* 'who,' San José *mani* 'where,' Patwin *mena* 'where,' Chickasaw *mano* 'where,' Cayapo *muŋ* 'who,' Guambiana *mu* 'who,' Paez *maneh* 'when,' Allentiac *men* 'who,' Kagaba *mani* 'where,' *mai* 'who,' Matagalpa *man* 'where,' Botocudo *mina* 'who,' Guayaki *ma* 'what,' Guajajara *mən* 'who,' Cofan *ma-ñi* 'where,' Maripu *manub* 'in which direction.'

31. NOSTRATIC **mo ~ *mu* 'this, he, other,' PAA **m(w)* 'they, this, he,' PK **m(a)-* 'this, he,' PIE **mo-* 'he, this,' PU **mū-/mō-* 'other,' PA **bū/bō* 'this' (oblique *mu-n*) = AMERIND **mo* 'that, he, the,' Maidu *mi* 'he,' *mō* 'that one,' *mɨ* 'this, that,' Atakapa *ma* 'that,' Proto-Algic **m-* (impersonal possessor), PUA **mo-* 'himself,' Taos *mo-* 'himself,' Guarani *amo* 'that,' Arara *mo* 'he,' Barama *mo(-ko)* 'he, she,' *mo(-ro)* 'it,' Waiwai *moro* 'that one,' Moseten *mo* 'that, he,' Chama *ma-* 'that,' Northern Cayapo *amu* 'he,' Guato *ma-* (stage III article).

32. EURASIATIC **ni* 'tooth,' Korean *ni* 'tooth,' Ainu *ni-* 'tooth,' Gilyak *nɨ-ɣs* 'tooth, teeth' = AMERIND **nene* 'tooth,' Cheyenne *-onen* '-toothed,' Kutenai *unān* 'tooth,' Cacaopera *nini* 'tooth,' Atacama *enne* 'tooth' Chilanga *ne* 'tooth,' Yanomamï *na* 'tooth,' Toyeri *ine* 'tooth,' Mekens *iñai* 'tooth,' Aguaruna *ñai* 'tooth,' Gualaquiza *naj* 'tooth.'

33. NOSTRATIC **ñiK'a* 'neck vertebra, neck,' PU **ñika* 'vertebra, neck,' Selkup *nukka* 'nape of the neck,' PA **ñika-* 'neck vertebra, neck,' Khalkha *nugas (-an)* 'spinal cord' = AMERIND *nuk' ~ nuq'* 'throat,' North Sahaptin *nuq' (-waš)* 'throat,' Chorti *nuk'* 'swallow,' Huastec *nuk'* 'throat,' Proto-Muskogean **nukkwi* 'neck,' Tequistlatec *nuk'* 'swallow,' San Antonio *(p-)ēnīk'a* 'throat.'

34. EURASIATIC **niu* 'see, eye,' Ostyak *niw-/ni-* 'see,' Mordvin *neje* 'see,' Finnish *näke-* 'see,' Yukaghir *nugie* 'I have seen,' Mongolian *nidün (< *ñundun)* 'eye,' Evenki *ñundun* 'eye,' Korean *nun* 'eye,' Japanese *na-mida* 'tear' (= EYE + WATER), Ryukyuan *nū-ng* 'see,' Gilyak *ñü-n* 'see,' *ñu-d* 'look,' *ñu-gu* 'show,' Kamchadal *nannin* 'eye' = AMERIND **neu* 'see,' Proto-Central Algonquian **nēw* 'see,' Yurok *new* 'see,' Cherokee *ni* 'look,' Catawba *nĩ* 'see,' Yuki *naw* 'see,' Choctaw *nowa* 'see,' Kekchi *nau* 'know,' POM **ni(n)* 'see,' PUA **ne* 'see,' Kariri *ne* 'see,' Campa *nie* 'see,' Wayana *ene* 'see,' Motilon *anu* 'eye,' Yagua *nuwātə* 'mirror,' Yameo *nutē* 'look at.'

35. NOSTRATIC **oñe* 'hand,' PU **oñe* 'hand, handmade,' PA **uñe* 'obedient' = AMERIND **ʔani/ʔoni* 'hand,' Tuscarora *-ʔohn* 'hand,' Kutenai *(ahq-)ʔān* 'handle,' Proto-Central Algonquian **-en-* 'hand,' Potowotami *-in* 'by hand,' Yuri *-enoo* 'hand,' Masaca *inæ* 'finger,' Proto-Panoan **ʔinã* 'give,' Toba *ane* 'give,' Lule *ni* 'give,' Mashubi *ni(-ka)* 'hand,' Proto-Ge **ñī-kra* 'hand,' Suya **ñi(-ko)* 'hand.'

36. NOSTRATIC **p'atʌ* 'wide,' PAA **pt'-/pt-* 'wide, to open,' PIE **pet(H)-* 'wide, to spread,' PD **pāt(t)ʌ* 'plot of land,' PA **pata-* 'field,' Ainu *para* 'broad, flat,' *pira* 'open, spread out,' Korean *pāl-* 'become broad,' Old Japanese *pïrö-i* 'broad,' Gilyak *p'al-* 'floor,' Kamchadal *p'(ă)l-xaŋ* 'cheek' = AMERIND **pat'a* 'broad, flat,' Haisla *patʰà* 'flat,' Proto-Salish **pʌt'* 'broad,' Proto-Siouan **pra* 'flat, broad,' Yurok *pel* 'broad,' Wiyot *bel* 'flat, wide,' Tsimshian *batˡ* 'broad,' Maidu *batbatpe* 'flat, planar,' Alabama *patʰa* 'broad,' Yahi *-d'pal* 'flat,' North Pomo *badō* 'flat,'

Quinigua *patama* 'broad,' Tequistlatec *spatʷ* 'broad,' Kiliwa *pataj* 'broad.'

37. NOSTRATIC **p'iγwʌ* 'fire,' PAA **pʕw* 'fire,' PK **px(w)* 'warm,' PIE *peHw-* 'fire,' PU *pīwe* 'hot, warm,' Korean *phi* 'burns,' Japanese *hi* 'burn,' Okinawa *fi* 'burn,' Ainu *api/abe* 'fire' = AMERIND **p'ixwa* 'fire, burn,' Proto-North Wakashan **pxa* 'warm (v.), heat, hot,' Proto-Maiduan **p'i-* 'hot,' Matlatzinca *pawi* 'hot,' Jicaque *pwe* 'burn,' Tequistlatec *bi* 'burn,' Proto-Arawakan **pawa(-ta)* 'to make fire.'

38. NOSTRATIC **p'ojʌ* 'child, baby,' PU **pojka* 'son,' PA **pö-/pi-* 'child, baby' = AMERIND **p'oj* '(younger) brother,' **p'ojp'oj* 'older brother,' Proto-California Penutian **bē* 'older brother,' Foothill North Yokuts *p'aj* 'baby,' *p'ajeeʔi* 'child,' Wappo *ʔepa* 'older brother,' Zuni *papa* 'older brother,' Shasta *ʔapu* 'older brother,' Salinan *pepeʔ* 'brother,' Taos *p'ōj* 'younger brother,' *popo* 'older brother,' PUA **pa* 'brother,' POM **po* 'younger brother,' **papi* 'older brother,' Cacaopera *pai* 'older brother,' Shiriana *aba* 'older brother,' Catio *amba* 'sister,' Tuwituwey *bibi* 'younger brother,' Papury *pui* 'younger brother,' Waikina *baī(-ga)* 'brother,' Yuracare *pe* 'younger brother,' Kariri *popo* 'older brother,' Hishcariana *pepe* 'older brother,' Yagua *rai-puipuin* 'brother,' Proto-Panoan **poi* 'sibling of opposite sex,' Proto-Tacanan **bui* 'son, daughter,' Moseten *voji* 'sister,' *voji-t* 'brother,' Botocudo *po* 'brother,' Kaingan *ve* 'sibling.'

39. NOSTRATIC **p'učw* 'body hair, down, feathers,' PK **pačw-* 'body hair, feather,' PIE **pous-* 'down, body hair,' PU *pučw* 'down' = AMERIND *p'utʸi* 'hair, feather, bird down,' Wappo *pučīš* 'hair,' Yuki *p'oti* 'feather,' Maidu *butu* 'hair,' Yokuts *pada* 'feather,' Tsimshian *p'əlk'wa* 'bird down,' Alsea *pəlupəlu* 'feather,' Tunica *-puli* 'plumage, hair,' PUA **po* 'body hair,' Taos *pʰo* 'hair,' Quechua *pʰuru* 'feather,' Jebero *ambolu* 'feather,' Tschaahui *amporo* 'crown of feathers,' Campa *biti* 'feather, hair,' Ipurina *piti* 'feather,' Kandoshi *poro* 'hair, feather,' Cayuvava *pote* 'feather,' Yuracare *pusi* 'feather,' Wayana *pot* 'feather,' Yagua *popejty* 'feather.'

40. NOSTRATIC **qot'i* 'fire; set on fire,' PD **otʌ-* 'kindle,' PA **ōti* 'spark, fire,' Korean *tha* 'burn,' Gilyak *t'a* 'burn,' Proto-Eskimo **uutï-* 'burn, boil, roast,' Kuskokwim *ɨtâ-* 'burn,' Aleut *ata* 'burn' = AMERIND **(ʔ)oti* 'fire; to burn,' Proto-Keresan **ʔɪrɪ* 'be hot,' Acoma *ɪdɪ* 'fire,' Seneca *aʔta* 'fire,' Blackfoot *ototo* 'to burn' (tr.), Wiyot *ad* 'fire,' *dōw* 'burn,' Proto-California Penutian **ʔitV* 'roast,' PUA **ta(h)i* 'fire; to burn,' POM **ntah* 'warm, fever,' Paez *otʸ* 'burn,' Tarascan *ete* 'burn,' Moseten *tʸi* 'fire,' Proto-Tacanan **ti* 'fire,' Proto-Panoan **čiʔi* 'fire,' Fulnio *to* 'burn,' Caraja *hæote ~ eoti* 'fire.'

41. NOSTRATIC **talHʌ* 'shoulder,' PD **tōḷ* 'shoulder, upper part of the arm,' PA **tālu* 'shoulder, shoulder blade' = AMERIND **ta(ʔ)la* 'shoulder,' Nisqualli *talakʷ* 'shoulder,' Songish *t'elaw* 'wing,' Musqueam *tʸɛleʔ* 'breast,' Quileute *tal* 'heart,' Shawnee *telja* 'shoulder,' Achomawi *tala* 'shoulder blade,' Salinan *itaʔl* 'shoulder,' North Yana *dul* 'neck,' Xinca *tali* 'neck,' Ulua *salax* 'shoulder,' Lenca *thala* 'neck,' Tarascan *teru(-nhe-kua)* 'chest,' Chimu *altærr* 'neck,' Catio *osorro* 'throat,' Proto-Carib **moo-tali* 'shoulder,' Uitoto *emodo* 'back,' Yagua *namatɔ* 'shoulder.'

In the Macro-Carib forms **mo-* appears to be the demonstrative discussed in No. 31 above.

42. EURASIATIC **tek* 'arrive,' PIE **tek-* 'reach,' Old Turkish *teg* 'reach, arrive,' Uighur *täg* 'arrive,' Korean *tah-* 'reach, arrive,' Japanese *tukú* 'arrive,' Inuit *tikippuq* 'arrive' = AMERIND **tek/tak/tok* 'return, come,' Tsimshian *adək* 'turn back,' Nez Perce *toq* 'return,' Cuna *taka* 'come,' Paya *tek* 'come.'

43. Eurasiatic **tuki* 'moon, sun, star,' Finnish *tähti* 'star,' Old Japanese *tukï* 'moon,' Ryukyuan *tsuchi* 'moon,' Ainu *touki* 'sun,' Aleut *tugidaq* 'moon' = AMERIND **tuki* 'sun,' Tsimshian *tʸius* 'sun,' Siuslaw *tʸuxtītʸ* 'early,' *tʸxajūwi* 'sun,' Wintun *ʔol-tik-al* 'dawn' (v.), *tuku* 'sun,' Proto-Costanoan **tuxi* 'day,' Santa Cruz *tuhe* 'day,' Zuni *jatokka* 'sun,' Tunica *tahčʼi* 'sun,' Chickasaw *čiiki* 'early,' Chol *zuka* 'dawn' (v.), Sierra Popoluca *tʸok* 'shine,' Sayula *taʔkš* 'shine,' Papantla *tuxkaket* 'light' (n.).

44. NOSTRATIC **t'umʌ* 'dark,' PAA **t'(w)m* 'dark,' PU **tumʌ/tümʌ* 'opaque, dark,' PA **t'umʌ-* 'darkness, haze,' Korean *ətu(u)m* 'dark' = AMERIND **t'umak* 'dark,' Nootka *tom* 'dark,' Yurok *tʸmej* 'be evening,' Kutenai *tamoxu-intʸ* 'be dark,' Keres *tʸamištʸ* 'dark,' Yokuts *čɨmʔēk* 'get dark,' Klamath *č'mog* 'dark,' Wappo *sum* 'evening,' Chitimacha *tʸima* 'night,' Atakapa *tem* 'night,' Koasati *tamoxga* 'night,' Tetontepec *tʸoʔm* 'midnight,' Huastec *tʸamul* 'night,' Yupultepec *ts'yəma* 'night,' Chiquimulilla *suʔmax* 'black,' Xinca *syma* 'night, black,' Caranga *sumči* 'dark,' Urupa *etim* 'night.'

45. NOSTRATIC **-t'ʌ* (causative), PAA **tʌ-/-t-* (reflexive), PD **-tt-* (causative), PU **-tt-/-t-* (causative, reflexive), Yukaghir *-te-* (denominative), PA **-t-* (causative), Korean *-tʰi* (causative), Japanese *-t* (causative), Ainu *-te* (causative), Gilyak *-d* (denominative), Chukchi *-et* (denominative), Kamchadal *t-* (causative), Eskimo *-ta/-ti* (causative), Aleut *-ti* (causative) = AMERIND **t(')u* (causative), Seneca *-ʔt-* (causative), Keres *-tʊ* (makes actions out of statives), Wiyot *-at* (transitivizer), Salish *-t* (transitivizer), Kutenai *-n't* (action by hand), Kwakiutl *-d* (transitivizer).

46. EURASIATIC **uni/ino* 'sleep,' Finnish *uni* 'sleep,' Izhor *uni(n)* 'sleep,' Dunshan *no* 'sleep,' Ainu *enunui* 'sleep,' Korean *nuul* 'lie,' Old Japanese *ne* 'sleep,' Ryukyuan *nun-ung* 'sleep,' *nī-bui* 'sleepy,' Gilyak *nax* 'sleeping place,' Proto-Eskimo **inaʁ* 'sleep'

= AMERIND *ino 'sleep,' Wappo hin 'sleep,' Mutsun one 'sit down,' Atakapa nI 'lie down,' Tunica na/nō 'lay down,' Zoque əŋ 'sleep,' Guayaki ñeno 'sleep,' Cofan anan-je 'sleep,' Uitoto inu 'sleep,' Bororo anu 'sleep,' Umotina inɔtu 'sleep,' Proto-Ge *nō 'lie,' Tibagi nan 'lie down,' Kamakan ha-nun 'bed.'

47. NOSTRATIC *ʔi/ʔe 'this, he,' PAA *j 'this, he,' PK *(h)i/(h)e 'that,' PIE *ʔei-/ʔe- 'this, he,' PU *i-/e- 'this,' PD *ĭ/ĕ 'this,' PA *i-/e- 'this, he,' Korean i 'this,' Japanese i-ma 'now,' Ainu i- 'his, him,' Gilyak i/e- 'his, him' = AMERIND *(ʔ)i 'he, this, the,' Chinantec ʔi 'he,' Tewa ʔiʔ 'he,' Mono ʔi-hi 'this,' Borunca i ~ iæ 'he,' j- 'his,' Lenca i(-na) 'he,' i- (indef. obj.), Cuna i- (indef. obj.), Bribri i- (indef. obj.), Chiquito i- 'his,' Kraho iʔ- 'his,' Guarani i- 'he, his.'

48. NOSTRATIC *ʕEK'u 'water,' PAA *ak'ʷ- 'water,' PIE *akʷa 'water, to drink,' Luwian aku- 'water,' Palaic aḫu- 'drink,' Ainu wakka 'water,' ku 'drink' = AMERIND *ʔokʷa ~ *ʔaqʷa 'water; to drink,' Proto-Central Algonquian *akwa 'from water,' Kutenai -qʷ 'in water,' Songish qʷaʔ 'water,' Chitimacha kuʔ ~ ʔak- 'water,' Chickasaw okaʔ 'water,' Hitchiti uki 'water,' Zoque ʔuhk 'drink,' Yucatec ukʷ 'be thirsty,' Kekchi uʔka 'drink,' Takelma ukʷ 'drink,' Nez Perce k'u 'drink,' Yuki uk'u 'water,' Wappo ʔuki 'drink,' Zuni k'a 'water,' Chimariko aqa 'water,' Cotoname ax 'water,' Kashaya ʔahqʰa 'water,' Seri ʔax 'water,' Tonkawa ʔāx 'water,' Yana xa(-na) 'water,' Yuma axa 'water,' Yamana aka 'lake,' Mapudungu ko 'water,' Aymara oqo 'swallow,' Auake okōā 'water, river,' Tucano oko 'water, rain,' Bahukiwa uku-mi 'he is drinking,' Guana uko 'rain,' Lule uk 'drink,' Mataco joke 'drink,' Guato ma-gŭng 'water,' Proto-Ge *ŋo 'water,' Coropo kuang 'river,' Kaingan goi/ngo 'water,' Bororo ku 'drink' (n.), Koraveka ako 'drink!'

CORRELATIONS WITH BIOLOGICAL TAXONOMY

A year after Greenberg published his classification of New World languages, a team of human geneticists published a phylogenetic tree of the human species that was based on the study of 120 alleles for 42 aboriginal populations of the world (Cavalli-Sforza et al. 1988). Cavalli-Sforza and colleagues found a very high degree of correlation between linguistic classifications and biological classifications in all parts of the world and, in what concerns us, the three linguistic phyla posited by Greenberg for the Americas each corresponds to a distinct biological cluster in the tree. Furthermore, they found that the Amerind family was most closely affiliated with the populations of Northern Eurasia, as has been argued on linguistic evidence in this paper. Dene-Caucasian groups were unfortunately not well repre-

sented in the biological study, and Na-Dene, which affiliated most closely with Amerind, was suspected of showing the diffusion of Amerind genes. Eskimo-Aleut was affiliated directly with Chukchi-Kamchatkan, and this grouping was one member of a larger North Asian cluster that corresponds to the Asian constituents of Greenberg's Eurasiatic family. Certainly the high degree of correlation between linguistic and biological classifications, arrived at independently of one another, provides additional support for Greenberg's classification of the languages of the Americas. The explanation for this parallelism is of course that the mechanisms underlying genetic and linguistic evolution are basically similar.

CONCLUSIONS

Recent work on the genetic classification of the world's languages has led to a number of important findings regarding the peopling of the Americas. First, the indigenous languages of the New World belong to three distinct linguistic families, Eskimo-Aleut, Na-Dene, and Amerind. Second, each of these families is most closely related to a different set of Old World language families, indicating that there were three distinct migrations from the Old World to the New. Third, the distribution and internal diversity of these three families strongly suggests that the first migration brought speakers of Proto-Amerind; the second migration probably brought speakers of Proto-Na-Dene; and the final migration brought speakers of Proto-Eskimo-Aleut. Fourth, the eleven Amerind subgroups defined by Greenberg seem to fall into three higher-level groupings, Northern, Central, and Southern Amerind. Fifth, South America appears to have been populated by a single immigration from the North (with a few minor exceptions) and Southern Amerind represents the linguistic reflection of this single migration.

REFERENCES

Benedict, P. K.
   1972 *Sino-Tibetan: A Conspectus*. Cambridge University Press, Cambridge, England.

Bengtson, J. D.
   1991 Notes on Sino-Caucasian. In *Sino-Caucasian Languages*, edited by V. Shevoroshkin. Bochum, Brockmeyer.

Cavalli-Sforza, L. L., A. Piazza, P. Menozzi, and J. Mountain
   1988 Reconstruction of Human Evolution: Bringing Together Genetic, Archeological and Linguistic Data. *Proceedings of the National Academy of Sciences U.S.A.* 85:6002–06.

Diakonoff, I. M., and S. A. Starostin
  1986 *Hurro-Urartian as an Eastern Caucasian Language.* R. Kitzinger, Munich.

Dolgopolsky, A.
  1969 Nostratičeskie osnovy s sočetaniem šumnyx Soglasnyx. *Etimologia* 1967:296–313. Moscow.
  1971 Nostratičeskie etimologii i proisxoždenie glagol'nyx formantov. *Etimologia* 1968:237–42. Moscow.
  1972 Nostratičeskie korni s sočetaniem lateral'nogo i zvonkogo laringala. *Etimologia* 1970:356–69. Moscow.
  1974 O Nostratičeskoj sisteme affrikat i sibiljantov: korni s fonemoj *ʒ. *Etimologia* 1972:163–75. Moscow.
  1984 On Personal Pronouns in the Nostratic Languages. In *Linguistica et Philologica,* edited by O. Gschwantler, K. Rédei, and H. Reichert, pp. 65–112. Wilhelm Braumüller, Vienna.

Golla, Victor (editor)
  1984 The Sapir-Kroeber Correspondence. Survey of California and Other Indian Languages. University of California, Berkeley.

Greenberg, J. H.
  1960 The General Classification of Central and South American Languages. In *Men and Cultures: Selected Papers of the 5th International Congress of Anthropological and Ethnological Sciences, 1956,* edited by A. Wallace, pp. 791–94. University of Pennsylvania Press, Philadelphia.
  1983 Na-Dene Notebook. Ms. on file, Green Library, Stanford University, Stanford.
  1987 *Language in the Americas.* Stanford University Press, Stanford.
  1989 Classification of American Indian Languages: A Reply to Campbell. *Language* 65:107–14.
  1992 *The Eurasiatic Language Family: Indo-European and Its Closest Relatives.* Stanford University Press, Stanford.

Illich-Svitych, V. M.
  1967 Materialy k sravnitel'nomu slovarju nostratičeskix jazykov. *Etimologija* 1965:321–96. Moscow.
  1971–84 *Opyt sravnenija nostratičeskix jazykov.* 3 vols. Nauka, Moscow.

Jefferson, T.
  1904 *The Writings of Thomas Jefferson,* vol. 7. The Thomas Jefferson Memorial Association, Washington, D.C.

Kaiser, M., and V. Shevoroshkin
  1988 Nostratic. *Annual Review of Anthropology* 17:309–29.

Levine, R. D.
  1979 Haida and Na-Dene: A New Look at the Evidence. *International Journal of American Linguistics* 45:157–70.

Nikolaev, S. L.
  1991 Sino-kavkazkie jazyki v Amerike, mss.

Ruhlen, M.
  1987 *A Guide to the World's Languages,* Vol. 1: Classification. Stanford University Press, Stanford.
  1988 Is Algonquian Amerind? Ms. in possession of author.
  1989a Additional Amerind Etymologies. Ms. in possession of author.
  1989b First- and Second-Person Pronouns in the World's Languages. Ms. in possession of author.
  1989c Linguistic Origins of Native Americans, Ms. in possession of author.
  1991 The Amerind Phylum and the Prehistory of the New World. In *Sprung from Some Common Source: Investigations into the Prehistory of Languages,* edited by S. Lamb and E. Douglas Mitchell. Stanford University Press, Stanford.
  1992 The Origin of Language: Retrospective and Prospective. In *Language Change and Biological Evolution,* edited by A. Piazza and L. L. Cavalli-Sforza. Stanford University Press, Stanford. Russian version in Voprosy Jazykoznanija (1991).

Shafer, R.
  1952 Athabascan and Sino-Tibetan. *International Journal of American Linguistics* 18:12–19.
  1957 Note on Athabascan and Sino-Tibetan. *International Journal of American Linguistics* 23:116–17.

Starostin, S. A.
  1984 Gipoteza o genetičeskix svjazjax sinotibetskix jazykov s enisejskimi i severnokavkazskimi jazykami. *Lingvističeskaja rekonstruktsija i drevnejšaja istorija vostoka* 4:19–38. Nauka, Moscow.

Swadesh, M.
  1952 Review of *Athapaskan and Sino-Tibetan* by R. Shafer. *International Journal of American Linguistics* 18:178–81.

The History and Classification of American Indian Languages: What are the Implications for the Peopling of the Americas?

IVES GODDARD
Dept. of Anthropology
Smithsonian Institution
Washington, D.C. 20560

LYLE CAMPBELL
Dept. of Anthropology
Louisiana State University
Baton Rouge, LA 70803-5306

Though the synthesis of linguistic and nonlinguistic data in hypothesized reconstructions of the peopling of the Americas is a complex task, it is one that can be useful to undertake, provided that the proper techniques are employed. The most important methodological prerequisite is the use of the well-established techniques of historical linguistics to establish and evaluate the linguistic data. Extreme caution should be exercised in using linguistic classifications, and conclusions derived from them, that are based on the comparison of superficially similar words and grammatical elements, such as the method of multilateral comparison employed by J. H. Greenberg and M. Ruhlen. The linguistic picture as presently known is compatible with a wide range of possible scenarios for the earliest peopling of the Americas. In exploring the best fit between linguistic and nonlinguistic hypotheses of New World prehistory, only explicitly historical hypotheses will prove to be of value.

INTRODUCTION

The history of the world's languages is obviously part of the history of the human race, in the Americas as elsewhere. Hypothesized reconstructions of the recent past have often relied on linguistic data and have typically attempted to encompass and to some extent to reconcile both linguistic and nonlinguistic aspects of human prehistory. The formulation of such syntheses is unfortunately, however, greatly complicated by many difficulties inherent in the correct utilization of linguistic data. Linguistic materials and their historical interpretation require specialized interpretation and evaluation, but at the same time they lend themselves to superficial treatment and specious argument to what seems a noticeably greater extent than other types of technical data used by prehistorians. It is our belief that, in spite of these difficulties, linguistic evidence can be brought to bear on questions relating to the first peopling of the Americas, and we attempt here to set out some of the methodological prerequisites for doing this. This is a particularly timely undertaking, since public dialogue on this subject has recently been dominated by a methodological approach that is inherently flawed and has led to conclusions that must be set aside if the general task of working out the prehistory of the Americas is to be placed on a sound basis. The methodological approach that we criticize is the one advocated by Greenberg (1987a) and by his associate and coworker Ruhlen (n.d.a, 1989, this volume; Ruhlen and Shevoroshkin 1989). We also want to make clear the limitations that any classification will have, given the current state of knowledge. Our conclusion is that the linguistic picture is compatible with a rather wide range of possible scenarios for the earliest peopling of the Americas, and that the current state of linguistic knowledge is of little help in trying to restrict that range of possibilities. We advise extreme caution in the development or utilization of any hypothesis of the first peopling of the Americas that relies on currently available deep-level classifications of American Indian languages, such as that propounded by Greenberg and Ruhlen.

The difficulties with the use of linguistic data flow in part from the fundamental question of the extent to which human linguistic history corresponds empirically to human nonlinguistic history. The relationship between linguistic history and other aspects of history is complex, and easy assumptions about this relationship are risky. People can learn and pass on new languages, but individuals cannot acquire new genes or teeth. Languages can become extinct in populations which survive genetically. As a consequence, attempts to correlate language groupings with human phylogeny or movements at deep time levels face major obstacles. It is well known that the language spoken by a group of people may come and go; it is likely that language replacement and extinction have been, over time, relatively common phenomena. To the extent that this has been the case, the preliterate linguistic history of the human race is unrecoverable. Judging from the known recent linguistic history of the world, it seems evident that the segment of human linguistic history which is recoverable is younger, probably much younger, than recoverable aspects of human biological history (cf. Boas 1940:212 and note 5 below).

Other difficulties with the use of linguistic data are inherent in the data itself. Any attempt to correlate linguistic history with other aspects of human prehistory must be based on reliable historical information on the languages being considered, which can be obtained only through the application of sound historical-linguistic techniques to correctly analyzed and understood features of the languages. Regrettably, the first language or languages spoken in the Americas are at present invisible to the generally accepted methods of historical linguistics, but this lack of knowledge cannot serve as a justification of the use of less reliable techniques.

APPROACHES TO THE CLASSIFICATION OF AMERICAN INDIAN LANGUAGES

Two approaches to the study of the relationships among American Indian languages were represented at this conference, which we refer to as 'word comparison' and 'standard historical linguistics'.[1] The word-comparison method is employed by Greenberg and Ruhlen, who call it "multilateral comparison"—an allusion to the large number of languages surveyed. The presentation of their data is in the form of lists containing numerous sets of words that are superficially "similar in sound and meaning" (Ruhlen 1987b:6)[2] and discursive considerations of similarities in grammatical morphemes. The aim of the method is classification, but the classification that results

---

[1] We intend these labels as easily understood, objective descriptions. A more technical term for 'word comparison' would be 'lexical comparison,' since this method includes the comparison of lexical items that are not whole words but grammatical morphemes. The word-comparison method does not, however, encompass the comparison of grammar, but only of grammatical elements treated as separate entities. Greenberg has referred to the classification of Indian languages based on standard historical linguistics as the "major alternative" (Greenberg et al. 1986:477; Lewin 1988:1632); Ruhlen (1987a:215–227; n.d. a) has referred to its practitioners as "Phase III linguists" and "Diffusionists" (the last an utterly false term presumably adopted for polemical effect).

[2] "Linguistic classifications such as Greenberg's are discovered on the basis of resemblances in sound and meaning in

from it is simply a codified statement of the judgments of similarity that have been made in assembling the sets of words. Greenberg (1987a:1–37, 1987b:647–650) expressly rejects historical linguistic techniques—there is no history in his book, only a classification that is presented as being a reflection of the history of the languages

The approach of standard historical linguistics employs techniques for formulating and testing hypotheses about the undocumented history of languages. These techniques have been developed and refined, over the last century and more, on the basis of the study by thousands of scholars of the historical changes undergone by a wide variety of languages. The goal of historical linguistics is to work out the linguistic history of languages and thereby to determine the principles and factors that govern the universal phenomenon of language change.

A fundamental fact on which there is general agreement is that there is extensive linguistic diversity in the Americas. A summary of the work of specialists employing the standard historical-linguistic approach (Campbell and Mithun 1979) found about 60 linguistic units (families and isolated languages) in North America, 15 in Middle America, and about 60 in South America—hence about 135 for the Americas as a whole. Greenberg's statement that this "major alternative [classification] . . . would involve the acceptance of something like 200 independent linguistic stocks" (Greenberg et al. 1986:477–478; Lewin 1988:1632) both exaggerates the number of entities and misstates what they are.[3] The linguistic units of the historical-linguistic classification are viewed by its proponents as a maximum number that reflects the progress so far of historical-linguistic scholarship. Many if not most supporters of the "major alternative" are sympathetic to the notion that all or nearly all American Indian languages may be related. Their classification simply reflects their belief that these deeper relationships cannot at present be demonstrated, owing to the great time depths involved and the inadequacy of linguistic methods to recover history after so much cumulative change has taken place. It is a commonplace to observe that it can never, in principle, be demonstrated that two American Indian (or other) languages are not related. At the same time, the burden of proof clearly falls on those who wish to claim closer affinity among some groups than among others. Greenberg et al. (1986:477) claim that "the Americas were settled by three separate population movements whose identity can be most precisely expressed in linguistic terms as Amerind, Na-Dene, and Aleut-Eskimo." Even if this is what happened at some remote time level, the tremendous linguistic diversity that came out of what is proposed as the single Amerind "population movement" would remain to be explained by any model of the peopling of the Americas.

LINGUISTIC CLASSIFICATION AND THE PEOPLING OF THE NEW WORLD

Greenberg and Ruhlen have postulated three independent migrations to the New World, separated in time, one for each of Greenberg's New World linguistic groups: Amerind, Na-Dene, and Aleut-Eskimo (Lewin 1988:1632; Ruhlen 1990). They are not, however, the first scholars to have adopted the approach that "the classification of modern American Indian languages can . . . be viewed in the context of the original settlement of the Americas" (Lewin 1988:1632). Edward Sapir's well-known opinion on this subject is so aptly framed as to be worth quoting at length. It shows how little progress has been made since his day in establishing a correlation between linguistic classification and the original peopling of the Americas:

> If the apparently large number of linguistic stocks recognized in America [can] be assumed to be due merely to such extreme divergence on the soil of America as to make the proof of an original unity of speech impossible, then we must allow a tremendous lapse of time for the development of such divergences, a lapse of time undoubtedly several times as great as the period that the more conservative archaeologists and palaeontologists are willing to allow as necessary for the interpretation of the earliest remains of man in America. We would then be driven to the alternative of assuming that the linguistic differentiation of aboriginal America developed only in small part (in its latest stages) in the new world, that the Asiatic (possibly also South Sea) immigrants who peopled the American continent were at the earliest period of occupation already differentiated into speakers of several genetically unrelated stocks. This would make it practically imperative to assume that the peopling of America was not a single historical process but a series of movements of linguistically unrelated peoples, possibly from different directions and certainly at very different times. This view strikes me as intrinsically highly probable. As the latest arrivals in North America would probably have to be considered the Eskimo-Aleut and the Na-dene (Haida, Tlingit, and Athabaskan) [Sapir 1949b:454–455].

---

the basic vocabulary. . . ." (Ruhlen, this volume). Greenberg and Ruhlen's reference to these sets of words as "etymologies" is misleading; in historical linguistics an etymology is an account of the history of a word (or other element) and its uses. The use of historical terminology for a set of contemporaneous data masks the fundamentally ahistorical nature of the word-comparison method.

[3] It is difficult to see anything but a polemical basis for Greenberg's (1987c:666) claim that "Chafe and Goddard . . .

Note that Sapir considers it "intrinsically highly probable" that "the peopling of America was . . . a series of movements of linguistically unrelated peoples," at the same time singling out Eskimo-Aleut (Greenberg's "Aleut-Eskimo") and Na-Dene specifically as the probable latest arrivals. Greenberg, on the other hand, has subjected the possibility of multiple migrations to exaggerated ridicule, declaring that if "each of these [supposed 200 linguistic units] represents a separate migration [they would have] requir[ed] a traffic controller at the Bering Strait" (Greenberg et al. 1986:478). Ruhlen (this volume) has firmly committed himself to the conclusion that the unity of Amerind implies a single migration for the ancestors of its speakers. "Something like 200" separate migrations and Greenberg's traffic controller are not, however, required by the fact that standard historical linguistics has so far not been able to reduce the linguistic diversity in the Americas to fewer than about 135 distinct units, and it is unfortunate that uncritical acceptance of this assertion has already started to show up in the secondary literature (e.g., Bray 1986; Fagan 1987:186). As Sapir points out, while progress so far in historical-linguistic classification permits the postulation of many migrations, it also gives grounds for the optimistic belief that some or even all these groups may ultimately prove to be related and hence to reflect few migrations to the New World, even perhaps only one. Thus far, however, valid linguistic methods provide no basis for choosing among the many alternatives. Notice, moreover, that even if Greenberg's tripartite view should ultimately prove to have merit, this would still leave the very large problem of the internal classification of his postulated Amerind family, which is the major topic of his book (Greenberg 1987a).

In contrast to Greenberg's insistence on three migrations, the conclusions of standard historical linguistics are compatible with several possibilities. This is because there is so much that we do not at present know that a number of scenarios are plausible or at least cannot yet be conclusively ruled out. We consider some of these possibilities, which are in part mutually exclusive and in part compatible. (1) If all or many American Indian languages form a genetic unit, it is possible that a single migration of this linguistic unit entered the New World and later diversified, producing the many language groups extant at the time of European contact. An important question for this hypothesis (raised already by Sapir) would be whether so much linguistic diversity could develop in the time since this migration (ca. 12,000 yr B.P.?).[4] (2) Under the same hypothesis of linguistic unity it is also possible that some linguistic differentiation took place in northeastern Asia, and that an indeterminate number of already distinct, descendant linguistic subunits crossed to the Americas over a period of time. This hypothesis would be compatible with a New World linguistic time depth that is greater than the date of first settlement; it would require assuming that any members of this linguistic unit that stayed behind in Asia were replaced by other languages (under the usual assumption that there is no language in Asia that is a member of a group of languages otherwise found only on the New World). (3) Another possibility is that there were multiple migrations, at different times, involving different languages that did not form a linguistic unit. This hypothesis raises the questions of how many migrations there were and what the evidence is for them, as well as increasing the probability that there should be evidence of linguistic connections between New World and Old World languages. (4) Yet another possibility is that there was a single migration in which more than one language was present, or a limited number of such multi-language migrations. This hypothesis raises questions similar to the previous one. (5) An additional possibility is that one or more of the linguistic units that migrated to the New World became completely extinct there. Although this is inherently likely, it would be extremely difficult to demonstrate other than, perhaps, by arguments derived from hypothetical models[5]. All of these hypotheses would have to deal with the generally observed fact that there is more linguistic diversity in the Americas than in Eurasia, in spite of the relatively recent peopling of the New World.[6]

As Meltzer shows, even setting aside the linguistic aspects of the Beringian migration problem, many possibilities remain:

> Coming to North America was not an event that was physically impossible except along circumscribed routes within narrow time windows. There was not one, but many possible routes . . . open at many different times. Beringia was a passageway through which there could have been hundreds, perhaps thousands of separate arrivals of small

---

both are absolutely prejudiced from the start against any attempt at deeper classification in the Americas;" in fact, Greenberg (1987a:163, 395) and Ruhlen (1987a:122, 242, 246) cite studies of deep-level linguistic relationship by Chafe (1964, 1973, 1976) and Goddard (1975).

[4] We hold no brief for this date; the present linguistic evidence cannot support any specific nontrivial conclusions about the date or dates of the peopling of the Americas. Since this paper was written we have seen an important paper by Johanna Nichols (1990), in which she demonstrates that the diversity of linguistic types in the new World would have required "tens of millenia" to have either filtered into the Americas or developed there.

[5] Lamb (1964:462), assuming 23 extant North American linguistic units with time depths of roughly 6000 to 7000 years, calculated that these continued only 11 to 15 percent of the total number of languages present at 6000 to 7000 yr B.P.

[6] Austerlitz (1974) calculated that there were 71 well-established aboriginal language families and isolates in

populations from Asia, and many movements back to Asia over tens of thousands of years. Even if we did know the precise timing of the Land Bridge ... or the timing of the ice-free corridor, which we do not ..., that would all be irrelevant if the earliest migrants had boats and traveled down the Pacific coast. [Meltzer 1989:474].

Indeed, the speculative literature that has attempted to enumerate how many migrations into the Americas there were does not even provide a consistent and methodologically precise definition of what "a migration" is. Acceptance of Hrdlička's more realistic picture of "dribbles" of people entering the Americas (Meltzer 1989:481) would leave few or no discrete migration events to count.

There are, of course, a number of less plausible, non-Beringian hypotheses and beliefs about how people arrived in the Americas. Some of these involve immigrants coming relatively recently and more or less directly from Europe, Africa, Japan, China, India, and Polynesia, including Lost Tribes of Israel, Egyptians, Phoenicians, Greeks, Romans, Welsh, and Vikings. To say no more about them, we can simply observe that there is no accepted demonstration that any such migrations have left an impact on the languages of the Americas. A general idea of this literature can be gained from Goddard and Fitzhugh (1979).

LINGUISTICS AND AMERICAN PREHISTORY

The standard historical-linguistic approach is compatible with a number of scenarios for the peopling of the Americas, but developments in the future should help to narrow the range of possibilities. There is every reason to hope that careful historical-linguistic research will find more and more American Indian groups to be linked, and archaeological and other evidence many help to narrow the scope further. Nevertheless, we must be prepared to accept the possibility that we may never know—the full story may be irretrievable owing to the amount of linguistic change that has taken place since, if not also before, the first movements to the Americas.

Even in our present state of knowledge, however, some of the specific claims that have been made for linguistic and human biological correlations can be shown to be misleading. For example, Greenberg (1989:113) emphasizes "that [his] linguistic classification shows an almost exact match with genetic classification by population biologists and with fossil teeth evidence." Greenberg et al. (1986:477) claim that linguistic, dental,

and genetic "lines of evidence agree that the Americas were settled by three separate population movements." And, "The following historical inferences may be derived from [Greenberg's] classification: There were three migrations.... The oldest is probably Amerind, since it centers farther to the south ... and shows greater internal differentiation.... Aleut-Eskimo is probably the most recent" (Greenberg et al. 1986:479). "For Amerind we are dealing with a time period probably greater than 11,000"[yr B.P.] (Greenberg et al. 1986:480). (Ruhlen [1987b:10] actually allows for the possibility of fewer migrations, insisting that "at most we can conclude that there were not more than three.") As noted above, however, there is no deterministic connection between language and gene pools. A single language can be spoken by a genetically diverse population; e.g., whites, blacks, American Indians, Asians and others speak American English. A genetically homogeneous group may speak more than one language, e.g., the many multilingual Indian communities of Latin America, speaking Spanish and the native language. That is, both language shift or loss and multilingualism are facts of linguistic life—genes neither cause nor cater to these phenomena. The principled basis for attempts to correlate human phylogeny and linguistic history has been severely criticized by evolutionary biologists (Bateman et al. 1990a, 1990b; O'Grady et al. 1989). Meltzer has concluded (cf. Zegura 1987:11):

> Genetic evidence from modern North American populations is somewhat equivocal.... The picture that emerges from comparing various gene distributions across those populations is one of 'discordant variation'—even within major groupings such as 'Amerind'. Genetic studies thus far cannot confirm conclusively how many major groupings there are of modern native North Americans, much less the presumed number of migrations [Meltzer 1989:481].

All this notwithstanding, Greenberg and his associates make claims based on assumed but unfounded genetic-linguistic correlations. For example, Turner's "Greater Northwest Coast or Na-Dene" dental cluster includes four population samples, "Southwest [United States, Northwest] United States and Canada, Gulf of Alaska, and Athapaskan," and is conceded not to match the ethnic or geographical distribution of the proposed Na-Dene linguistic grouping very well (Greenberg et al. 1986:483–485).[7] The Northwest Coast has few Na-Dene languages and many non–Na-Dene languages. It is notorious for intermarriage, slaving, linguistic and cultural diffusion, and multilingualism. The Northwest Coast is, therefore, precisely an area where one would not expect

---

North and Central America alone, as opposed to only 37 in all of continental Eurasia.

[7] Their choice of words is "the fit ... is not as precise;" we assume that the printer has dropped the bracketed words from the list of the population samples in the cluster, as there is not, and could hardly be, a "Southwest United States and Canada" sample.

linguistic and genetic traits to match, and in fact their claim that there is a match, even though slightly tempered, has been variously criticized by specialists. For example, Laughlin (1986:490) pointed out that "the dental evidence is displayed in a dendrogram that carries no hint of a triple division but rather is eloquent evidence of a single migration. Clearly dental evidence comprehends greater time depth than linguistic evidence.... Turner proves the Asiatic affinities of [all] Indians." Szathmary (1986:490) commented that "Turner's Greater Northwest Coast includes Kachemak, Kodiak and Alaska Peninsula samples that are likely Eskimoan.... Turner's 'Na-Dene' in fact includes representatives of what Greenberg calls 'Amerind' and 'Aleut-Eskimo'.... I found that the Nootka..., Haida, Tlingit, and Northern Athapaskan, and South Alaskan Eskimos... did not cluster together." With respect to genetic correlations, Laughlin (1986:490) calculated that "a chi-square test reveals no significant difference between right and wrong assignments [allocation of gene frequencies into language phyla] for these three groups [Greenberg's big three]"; and "the [genetic] differences between American populations are not large enough to postulate more than one migration." Weiss and Woolford (1986:492) noted that "isolation by distance among groups with a long history of habitation in a single local area can produce generally the same kind of [genetic] diversity as is observed, especially if a certain amount of population movement and expansion or contraction over long time periods occurs. Thus, even if there is a *general* three-way division of Arctic peoples, this proves neither that they have a three-part phylogenetic relationship nor that any such relationship as exists is due to separate waves of immigration." Even Greenberg et al. (1986:487) consider the hypothesis of three migrations as "still without strong confirmation" from their genetic data, which they therefore regard as "supplementary." Since, therefore, their claims about the genetic and dental history of the Americas are so far poorly supported, conclusions about correlations with postulated linguistic classifications and migrations would at best be premature, even if there were no problems with the hypotheses they rely on in these other areas.

In trying to correlate linguistic evidence and nonlinguistic evidence concerning the peopling of the New World, we need explicit, well-founded historical hypotheses, and we need crucially to pay attention to the interdependency of these hypotheses. For example, the Amerind linguistic hypothesis (that most of the New World's languages are related) requires a single and therefore brief influx of population for most of the New World. But if this influx lasted more than a short time, or if it came in more than one wave, say before and after the last glaciation, Greenberg's Amerind hypothesis would appear to be incompatible with the nonlinguistic facts.

Another early notion that still has some following is the coastal-entry model (most recently Gruhn 1988). This is offered in part as an explanation of an apparent anomaly in the distribution of languages in North America, the fact that eastern North America is dominated by a small number of language families (Algonquian, Iroquoian, Siouan, Muskogean, and not many more), while there is great linguistic diversity on the West Coast. Thus, for example, of Powell's (1891) famous 58 linguistic families in North America, 22 were represented in California. Under the coastal-entry hypothesis it is assumed that the earliest waves of immigrants moved down the West Coast, thus allowing more time for linguistic diversity to develop in that area, while other immigrants, perhaps hampered by glaciers (Rogers 1987), arrived in the East much later and had less time to differentiate linguistically.

There are serious problems with this notion, however. For example, the time depth for the language families of eastern North America is extremely shallow, not more than 4000 years (to take a high estimate for Iroquoian; [Lounsbury 1978:334]), and thus the relatively small linguistic diversity in the East can have little or nothing to do with events connected with the last glaciation. In fact, it must have come about long after the first peopling of this area. Between 12,000 and 4000 yr B.P., a great many languages could have come and gone in eastern North America, being replaced by other languages or becoming extinct with the deaths of their speakers. It is further discouraging to note that the correlation of even the recent and relatively accessible language families in the East with archaeological data has been notoriously difficult. Nevertheless, it is only by building explicit historical hypotheses addressed to specific problems that historically significant correlations between linguistics, archaeology, and other evidence can be discovered (cf. Gruhn 1990).

Meltzer considers other problems with the reasoning behind the coastal-entry hypothesis:

> There are more native American languages along the Pacific Northwest and California coasts than in any other area of North America, which is said to imply 'great time depth for human occupation' and thereby the corridor of entry (Gruhn 1988:84). The number of languages in any given region of North America, however, is hardly a function of time alone. There are a greater number of languages known from the Pacific Northwest and California primarily because it is one of the areas on the continent where indigenous populations weathered the deadly effects of European contact and disease and survived (though in an altered form) at least until the end of the nineteenth century when intensive linguistic fieldwork began in North America.... It is probably no more realistic to infer Pleistocene migration routes to North America by the number and distribution of modern language groups than it would be to infer Hernando de Soto's route by looking at the number

and distribution of Spanish dialects in the Southeast today—and at least we know that de Soto spoke Spanish [Meltzer 1989:475].

In fact, as Gruhn (1988:82) notes, there is good evidence that linguistic diversity comparable to that in California was present at the time of contact along the Gulf coast and in southern Texas (Goddard 1979), areas that are not candidates for the earliest migration routes.

METHODOLOGICAL CONSIDERATIONS

It is not just the correlations that have been claimed by Greenberg and his supporters between his American Indian language classification and other sources of information on prehistory that are weak. The linguistic classification itself and the methodology that underlies it have also been shown to be unreliable (e.g., Adelaar 1989; Campbell 1986, 1989; Chafe 1986; Goddard 1986, 1987, 1990; Mithun 1990:320–325). Here we present only a brief discussion, with an assessment of some examples repeatedly put forth by Greenberg and Ruhlen as particularly strong evidence.

Greenberg's classification is a codification of his judgments of inspectional similarity and is thus, in principle, ahistorical. It is well known, however, in historical linguistics and many other fields, that classifications based on inspectional resemblances are unreliable guides to history, and that this unreliability increases with the time depth of a putative relationship. After related languages have been separated for only a few thousand years, the resemblances between them that are due to their historical connections decrease, through normal linguistic changes, to the point where they become lost among the accidental or nonhistorical resemblances. The only way to determine which of these resemblances are historically genuine is to use the techniques of historical linguistics. Greenberg defends his ahistorical approach by pointing out that it gives correct results for the Indo-European languages, but success at a time depth of what can hardly be much more than 6000 years obviously does not guarantee success at the time depths that are involved in the early peopling of the Americas. A sorting of any entities based on judgments of similarity will always produce a classification, but the fact of a classification cannot be taken as an existential proof of its validity as a reflection of history.

Greenberg has estimated that "80 to 90% of linguists would probably agree with Campbell [1988]" (Lewin 1988:1632), probably an overly optimistic figure, and Ruhlen (n.d. a:12) concedes the truth of Bright's (1988) statement that "most scholars in native American comparative linguistics regard Greenberg's methodology as unsound." In fact, we are not aware of a single specialist working on American Indian historical linguistics who thinks that Greenberg has established the validity of his postulated Amerind phylum. Nor have the other deep-level groupings of languages proposed or revived by Greenberg attracted much of a following among practicing specialists. There is not, for example, any observable inclination by specialists to accept "Northern Amerind" as valid, or *its* component "Almosan-Keresiouan," or *its* subcomponent "Almosan," or *its* subcomponent "Mosan," the last two being 60-year-old proposals of Edward Sapir (1949a). To put it another way, if there really are similarities between, for example, the Algonquian and Iroquoian families that require an historical explanation, it should be possible to say what they are. These are well-known families, however, and the fact that no such similarities have caught the attention of the linguists who know them best must be considered significant. Furthermore, discussions of Greenberg's (1987a) book by specialists indicate that his word equations, such as those he proposes for Algonquian and Iroquoian, contain so many errors that they do not even provide a reliable data base that could be used to explore alternative hypotheses (Chafe 1987; Goddard 1987).

The differences between Greenberg's word-comparison approach and the standard historical-linguistic method are so vast that rational discussion between their respective proponents seems almost impossible. Consider, for example, some of the claims that have been repeatedly made about pronouns and pronominal markers. Ruhlen (1987b:10) has stated that "Amerind languages are characterized by first-person n and second-person m," following Greenberg (1987a:48–49), who wrote that "in Amerind languages . . . it would probably be easier to enumerate where nV- and mV- are not found than where they are" (see also Greenberg 1987b:650–651). More explicitly, Ruhlen (this volume) claims that "one of the most salient traits of the Amerind family . . . is the presence of first-person n- and second-person m- throughout the languages of North and South America. Furthermore, not only does this trait connect all eleven Amerind subgroups, it also serves to distinguish the Amerind family from the world's other language families." In his oral presentation Ruhlen stressed that "all eleven branches show" these pronouns. It should be noted that these observations about putative Amerind pronouns quoted from Greenberg and Ruhlen are not incidental comments but are put forth as particularly strong evidence supporting their claims.[8]

To evaluate these claims we may consider the first-

---

[8] Greenberg and Ruhlen usually write these affixes with a following hyphen, indicating that they intend them as prefixes. In some of their discussions, however, suffixes containing these consonants are included, but with no historical hypothesis relating the two types of affix. In supporting Greenberg's claim, Fleming (1987:196) presents it as refer-

and second-person singular pronouns in just one of the eleven subgroups proposed for Amerind by Greenberg, Almosan-Keresiouan (Table 1).[9] It would not occur to us to say that this set of languages is "characterized" by first-person *n*- and second-person *m*-, or that they exhibit this pair of prefixes (or affixes) as a "salient trait." Furthermore, we frankly find it hard to imagine that anyone examining these numerous and diverse sets of pronouns would want to claim that they are similar in this way. Such an assertion is simply too astonishing to warrant serious discussion. First-person *n* is no more common than second-person *n*. There is no second-person *m*- prefix, the only instances of second-person *m* being a suffix in a single sub-family, Ritwan, and the reflexive imperative in Kutenai, a category that has little likelihood of being historically equivalent to the simple second person. Four of the sets have *n* or *m*, or both, in both first- and second-person affixes (Algonquian suffixes, Cheyenne prefixes, Salish, and Kwakiutl). There are also vowels in most of these affixes, and often more than one consonant, but these additional segments appear to receive no systematic attention.

Greenberg and Ruhlen themselves admit more diversity in the pronouns of "Amerind" than might be implied by their repeated claims about *n*- and *m*-. Greenberg finds South America typified by first person *i*, second person *a*, and third person *i* (Greenberg 1987a:44–49, 273–275, 277–281), a totally distinct pattern, with second person *m* particularly absent. But if the *i/a/i* pattern is the hallmark of South America, the claim that the *n/m* pattern is a diagnostic for Amerind as a whole is weakened. Moreover, Greenberg (1987a:276) presents a first person *m* as characteristic of several groups, while several others have second person *ka* or *s* (Greenberg 1987a:278). Reflecting some of this diversity, Ruhlen (1989) reconstructs Amerind *naʔ*, *ʔi*, and *mai* as first-person singular and *ami ~ ama*, *a-*, and *ka ~ kai* as second-person singular. Far from offering an overall hypothesis of the history of New World pronominal systems, Greenberg and Ruhlen do not even have an explanation for the variation that they concede to exist.

Beyond refuting the claims of Greenberg and Ruhlen, however, there are some important lessons to be learned from the variety of pronouns that those of "Almosan-Keresiouan" illustrate. The first is that even this small segment of the languages of North America is astoundingly diverse. Any hypothesis of ultimate unity must postulate a time depth of many thousands of years to allow for the development of this diversity, and any historical-linguistic hypothesis worthy of the name must outline how these various sets of affixes could be derived from a single protogrammar. Secondly, under the hypothesis that the Almosan-Keresiouan languages form a genetic unit, it follows that its pronominal affixes have undergone a great deal of change since the time of their uniform protolanguage, resulting in entirely different systems of pronominal marking in putatively related languages. Almosan-Keresiouan would thus refute the assumption that pronominal morphemes are extremely stable through time, and it would demonstrate that new pronominal affixes have arisen repeatedly even in the last several thousand years of the linguistic history of the Americas.[10] But the assumption that, relatively speaking, pronouns are stable and not subject to replacement or renewal is a necessary premise of the claims of Greenberg and Ruhlen that consonants appearing in pronouns can be validly compared across all the languages of the world without doing historical-linguistic analysis. Thirdly, whether the diverse pronouns of Almosan-Keresiouan are relatively recent divergences or relatively old differences, they illustrate the independent use of the same consonants over and over again in different values. In the languages in Table 1, *m*, *n*, *t*, *k*, *c/č*, *s*, and *l/ł* are used sometimes for first person and sometimes for second person.

The repeated appearance in different languages of the same consonants in grammatical functions is a real phenomenon of human language and as such requires an explanation. One contributing factor is the well-known general linguistic trait that a single language typically uses only a fraction of its full complement of consonants to form its primary grammatical morphemes and hence must use the same consonants over and over in different functions (Floyd 1981). The consonants that are used tend to be the ones that are least marked from the perspective of phonological theory. Among other traits, the least-marked consonants are the most commonplace across languages and the most frequently used within each language; specifically, the least-marked consonants of the languages of the world include *m*, *n*, *t*, *k*, and *s* (cf. Ruhlen 1987a:11). As a result of this economy and, so to speak, lack of originality in the use of consonants, there is a much greater than chance agreement among the languages of the world on what consonants are used in grammatical elements. It is thus to be expected a priori that these consonants will show up again and again in different languages and language groups marking, say, first or second person, and many languages will therefore

---

ring to either prefixes or suffixes. Another variable is the presence of absence of a vowel (symbolized by V).

[9] Addition of the plural affixes for those languages in which they are distinct would increase the variety displayed but not the attestation of first-person *n*- or second-person *m*-. See note 16.

[10] We say "several thousand years" in allusion to the status of Almosan-Keresiouan as only a second-order subdivision of Amerind; since Greenberg and Ruhlen compare pronouns on a world-wide basis, however, the point here is valid on any specific hypothesis of the time depth of this putative tiny sliver of the totality of languages.

Table 1. First and Second Singular Pronouns in "Almosan-Keresiouan."

	Words and Prefixes		Suffixes	
	1sg	2sg	1sg	2sg
Almosan				
Algic				
Algonquian	*ne-	*ke-	*-(y)a·n, *-ak[1]	*-(y)an, *-at,[1] *-lwe[2]
Cheyenne	na-	ne-	-(t)ó, -o[1]	-(t)o, -os ~ -ot,[1] -ce[2]
Ritwan				
Wiyot	d-	kh-	-Ø, -ak[3]	-t, -am[3]
Yurok	ʔne-	ke-	-k̓	-ʔm
Kutenai	hu-, ka-[4]	hin-	-a(·)p[5]	-i(·)s,[4,5] -(e·)n,[2] -m[6]
Mosan				
Wakashan				
Kwakiutl			-ənɬ	-əns
Nootkan	*siy	*suw	*-s	*-suk
Chimakuan				
Quileute	lá·b; ʔal[7]	či; č[7]	-li, -s,[4] -sta[5]	-lič, -č,[4] -swo[5]
Salish	*ʔəncá; *n-[4]	*nəwí; *ʔən-[4]	*-(a)n, *-c,[5] *-mx[8]	*-(a)xʷ, *-ci,[5] *-mi[8]
Keresiouan				
Caddoan	*k-, *t-	*s-		
Caddo	ci-, ku-[5]	yahʔ-, si-[5]		
Iroquoian				
No. Iroqu.	*k-, *wak-[5]	*(-h)s-, *(-e)s(a)-[5]		
Seneca	k(e)-, wak(e)-[5]	s(e)-, sa-[5]		
Keresan				
Santa Ana	hínʊ; s-, tʰ-, kʰ-, n-[9]	híṣʊ; ṣ- ~ š-, çʰ- ~ cʰ-, pʰ-[9]		
Siouan-Yuchi				
Siouan	*w-	*r-		
Catawba	d- (~ n-)	y-	-naʔ⁴	-yaʔ⁴
Sioux	wa-, mã-[4,5]	ya-, nĩ-[4,5]		
Yuchi	di; di-, cɛ-[5]	cɛ; nɛ- ~ yo-, nɛnɜɛ-,[5] so-[10]		

Intransitive subject markers given first in sets; others are:
[1] Transitive subject.
[2] Imperative.
[3] Subjunctive.
[4] Possessor.
[5] Object (Siouan and Iroquoian: patient)
[6] Reflexive imperative.
[7] Conditional.
[8] Causative object.
[9] Indicative, dubitative, hortative, (first person) future hortative; single nonglottalized consonants only (there are many other class and modal allomorphs).
[10] Indirect object.

Omitted:
(1) Plurals, pluralizers, transitive combinations; in some languages these add many variants.
(2) Minor variants, especially if only vowels are involved or if additional material looks segmentable.

come to have similar pronominal systems by this factor alone.[11] An additional factor helping to explain the appearance of first- and second-person *m* and *n* in different languages with a frequency that is greater than chance is what might be called universal tendencies. Among the most likely sources of new pronouns is child language,

---

[11] Ruhlen (1989) reconstructs the first-person singular pronoun in Niger-Congo as *i ~ (m)i ~ (n)i* and the second-singular pronoun of another African linguistic phylum, Nilo-Saharan, as *i ~ (m)i ~ (n)i ~ (ñ)i*. Such cases make it clear that factors other than genetic relationship may be involved in making pronominal morphemes similar across languages.

and child-language expressions around the world abound in self-directed and other-directed words and vocables containing nasal consonants. The ultimate reason for this is a universal physical fact: a gesture equivalent to that used to articulate the sound *n* is the single most important voluntary muscular activity of a nursing infant (Goddard 1986:202). The accompanying oral gesture is a bilabial with lowered velum, which permits the epiglottis to interlock the nasal cavity with the raised larynx during ingestion (Laitman 1985:282); with voicing, this gesture produces an *m*. Also, the areal diffusion of pronouns among the various early groups which may have come into America—before, during, or after the crossing of Beringia—cannot be ruled out a priori. Diffusion of pronouns between languages is not excessively rare (Newman 1980:156; Thomason and Kaufman 1988:219–20, 223-8, 235, 293, 323). In any event, Greenberg (1989:113) greatly exaggerates when he asserts that the distribution of first-person *n-* and second-person *m-* in the Americas can only be explained by assuming either a single genetic unity for Amerind or "more than a hundred" instances of borrowing between the attested languages in their present locations, concededly "a highly improbable event."[12] Even under his assumptions, the maximum number of statistically probable borrowing events plus a number attributable to chance would be the maximum number of separate language groups in the Americas, a number that is certainly greater than one. But his underlying premise that genetic relationship and, however improbably, borrowing are the only positive factors that can result in languages having similar pronouns is simply false.[13]

It is easy to illustrate why, even in cases of apparently straightforward comparison, the method of historical linguistics produces valid hypotheses of relationship while the word-comparison method misses these valid hypotheses and leads instead to incorrect conclusions.[14] Three second-person prefixes in Table 1 are compared in Table 2 using each of these two methods. The word-comparison

---

[12] Greenberg (1989:113) seems to imply that he means his statement about borrowing to refer to the attested languages in their present locations when he says "over a distance far greater than that covered by IE" and "contacts of virtually every language with every other one." But surely if the languages could preserve traces of genetic inheritance dating back to a single migration through Beringia, they could preserve traces of borrowings from the same period.

[13] Another source of new consonants in pronouns is the resegmentation of concatenated elements, which may result in the incorporation into a pronoun of a consonant from another word or element that happened to be adjacent to the pronoun in some expressions (Campbell 1988:601-602). Starting in the seventeenth century Swedish *ni* replaced the old second-person plural pronoun *I*; the added *n-* was from the second-plural suffix *-en* on verbs, which preceded the pronoun in some constructions, but even this suffixal *-n* had

Table 2. Comparison of Three "Almosan-Keresiouan" Second-Person Pronominal Prefixes by Two Methods.

A. Word comparison:

Sioux *nĭ-* ≈ Cheyenne *ne-* || Ojibwa *gi-*

B. Historical linguistics:

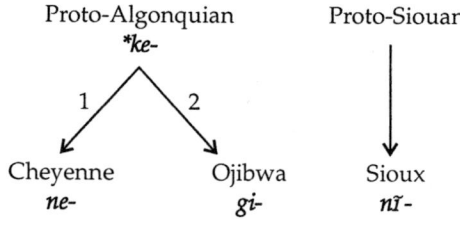

---

method would judge Sioux *n-* and Cheyenne *ne-* to be "similar in sound and meaning" and Ojibwa *gi-* to be dissimilar in sound (Table 2: A). Standard historical linguistics would approach these data within the framework of an attempt to work out the histories of these languages. The sequence of the hypotheses that were actually offered in this case shows how the understanding of Cheyenne increased as the historical hypotheses became more detailed and precise:

1. Cheyenne second person *ne-* is "analogical" or borrowed from Siouan (Goddard 1967:82; Michelson 1935:153).

2. Cheyenne *n-*[15] is a regular correspondence of *k-* in other Algonquian languages, e.g., Cheyenne *nehp-* 'covered' is the direct reflex of Proto-Algonquian **kep-* 'closed, covered', which is continued in Fox as *kep-* and in Cree as *kip-* (Leman 1980). It was previously established that Ojibwa *g-* comes from Proto-Algonquian **k-*. Thus Cheyenne *n-* is a regular

been a recent innovation (Haugen 1976:375, 304). Greenberg (1989:111) pleads that he was not misled by Campbell's specific example, but the point here is that the renewal of consonants in pronouns is a common feature in the historical development of languages and, as such, is a major potential source of error in ahistorical comparisons.

[14] Historical linguists often point out that a premise of relationship logically precedes the use of the comparative method to study linguistic history. Contrary to what Ruhlen (1987a:122) appears to argue, however, it does not follow from this that it makes sense to try to hypothesize an entire, detailed classification for hundreds of languages without doing any historical linguistics at all.

[15] By the standard notational convention used by linguists, ***n-*** (with a following hyphen) indicates any word-initial ***n***.

correspondence of Ojibwa *g-*, both reflecting Proto-Algonquian **k-*.

3. Cheyenne *n* regularly reflects Proto-Algonquian **k* before **e*, via the intermediate stages **ky* and **y* (Picard 1984; Proulx 1982b).

4. The development of Cheyenne *n-* from Proto-Algonquian **k-* is the result of a sequence of changes: Proto-Algonquian **ke* became pre-Cheyenne **kye*; then Proto-Algonquian **k-* disappeared in Cheyenne, leaving **ye-* from **kye-*; then pre-Cheyenne **y* became Cheyenne *n*. These postulated changes are part of a complex of partially interdependent innovations affecting Proto-Algonquian **k* and **e* in Cheyenne, and pre-Cheyenne **y* from various sources (Goddard 1988).

As a consequence of working out the phonological history of Cheyenne (Table 2: B, arrow 1) and the much simpler phonological history of Ojibwa (Table 2: B, arrow 2) it is possible to identify the second-person prefixes Cheyenne *ne-* and Ojibwa *gi-* as exact cognates, historical developments from an identical original form **ke-* inherited independently in two related languages. The Sioux prefix reflects a Proto-Siouan form. These results correspond to the fact that Cheyenne and Ojibwa are Algonquian languages and Sioux is Siouan. The equation between Cheyenne and Ojibwa is based on and accounted for by an explicitly reconstructed (that is, hypothesized) *history* of these languages, consisting of a complex of interconnected hypotheses of recurring patterns of change. Hypotheses of this type are absent from Greenberg's book. Instead, the word-comparison method would falsely equate the superficially similar Sioux and Cheyenne prefixes, while missing the real relationship between the Cheyenne and Ojibwa.

It is important to note also that using the word-comparison method, such incorrect equations cannot be refuted, even if they are inconsistent with the classification of the languages. The family relationships of the Algonquian and Siouan languages and the separateness of the two families from each other are obvious enough to be discovered by the word-comparison method. The discovery of these low-level relationships, however, does not invalidate incorrect equations between families. Using Greenberg's methodology, resemblances that cross the lines of language families (or of larger classificatory units), even isolated resemblances, can only be interpreted as historically significant similarities that result from deeper relationships between these lower-level groupings. Greenberg's (1987c:665, 1990) hints that such false equations can be identified in an objective way have not been accompanied by a formulation of a procedure by which this could be done, beyond his repeated assurances that the total mass of compared vocabulary would make the correct classification evident.

In fact, the acceptance of sporadic resemblances between language families as historically significant is the whole basis of the deeper levels of Greenberg's classification and the work Ruhlen (this volume) has erected on it. Consider again the claims about first-person *n-* and second-person *m-* in Almosan-Keresiouan. Greenberg's evidence that Algonquian reflects Amerind second-person *m-* is "Cree second-person plural, *-mwa*," and his evidence for second-person *m-* in Salish is "Kalispel . . . second-person plural subject *-m*" (Greenberg 1987a:49,54). His source for the Algonquian data was Sapir (1913:634), who correctly labels the suffix *-m ~ -mwa* as Ojibwa, and his source for Kalispel was presumably Vogt (1940:35), where *-əm* is listed as marking a second-singular object on resultative verbs. More recent publications on the historical grammars of Algonquian and Salish have established that *m* cannot be reconstructed as a second-person marker in either family (Goddard 1967, 1974; Newman 1977:304, 1980:156; Proulx 1982a:397–400); rather, an *m* characterizes some paradigms in both the first and second person.[16] In fact, Sapir (1915:193) himself already accepted as "very plausible" the refutation of his claim about Algonquian second-person **-m* by Michelson (1914:364).[17] Thus Greenberg is quite willing to accept the isolated testimony of a single language as valid for the family as a whole, if this language matches languages outside the family that he wishes to link up with it, and he is not dissuaded by counterevidence from historical

---

[16] Salish singular and plural second-person affixes with various functions contain the consonants *p, k, c, x^w, m, n, l*, and *ł* (Newman 1980:156). Kalispel second-person singular resultative object *-əm* reflects Proto-Salish second-person singular causative object **-mi* (Table 1), in which *m* is a marker of the causative-object paradigm appearing in all the first- and second-person endings. Although *m* is found in one set of endings (or perhaps two) in the second-person plural but not in the first-person plural, each of these second-person plural endings includes a *p* or an *l* in addition to *m*, and the *m* cannot be shown to be the primary marker of person. In the Proto-Salish independent pronouns, *m* is found only in the first-person plural, while the second-person plural contains both *p* and *l* (Newman 1977:304).

Taken together, these data would provide extremely weak support for the postulation of *m* as originally a mark of the second person in Salish. (We thank Paul Kroeber for help in interpreting Vogt's Kalispel data.)

[17] In the writings of Greenberg and Ruhlen the distinguished Algonquianist Truman Michelson (b. 1879, d. 1938) plays the role of bogeyman, a veritable ogre of hidebound historical linguistics. Only by recognizing that Michelson's name is expected to have this resonance can the reader appreciate the intended negative force of Ruhlen's (n.d. a) otherwise pointless description of Goddard as "like Michelson an Algonquianist with a Ph.D. from Harvard and effectively holding Michelson's 'chair' at the Smithsonian Institution."

Table 3. Stem-Formation Templates of Algonquian Forms Compared by Greenberg.

A) PA *naθkw- : Northern Wakashan nik- 'say' (ANSWER; Greenberg 1987a:165).
   Source: PA *naθkw- 'correspond, answer, hit on fly' (Bloomfield 1925:137), based on:
      PA *naθkw- + -m 'act on (anim.) by speech' → *naθkom- 'answer, say yes to';
      PA *naθkwe·- + *-eškaw- 'act on (anim.) by foot, body' → *naθkwe·škaw- 'go so as to encounter (anim.)'.
   Also occurring in:
      *naθkwe·- + *-en- 'act on (anim.) by hand' (cf. B) → *naθkwe·n- 'catch on the fly';
      *naθkw- + *-ete·- '(inan.) to be affected by heat, fire' (cf. C) → *naθkwete·- 'catch fire';
   And with abstract final: Cree naskwa·- 'retaliate'; reduplicated particle: Fox nana·hkawi 'in hostile manner'.

B) "Arapaho bæsæ, Fox ne-peʔšena 'I feel it' ": (Salish) Shuswap mu·s, Coeur d'Alene mus 'fumble, feel about' (FEEL; Greenberg 1987a:170).
   Sources: Arapaho ⟨bäsä-n-⟩ 'touch' (Kroeber 1916:116); Shawnee nipeʔšena 'I touch it' (Voegelin 1938-1940:85).
   Correctly: Arapaho besen- < PA *meš-en- (> Menominee 'get one's hand on, catch'; Maliseet 'catch').
      PA *meš- 'arrive at, reach, hit, hit upon' (Cuoq 1886:218, for Nipissing Ojibwa): *mešw- 'shoot at and hit (anim.)';
      *mešesi- 'be infected, afflicted by disease'; Ojibwa mišitto·- 'injure', mišikkaw- 'reach with the foot; (disease) to infect'; mišakkisse·- 'touch bottom'.

C) PA *kešy-, "Cree ... kis, Natick kussitau 'it is hot': Proto-Salish *kʷas 'hot, scorch' " (HOT; Greenberg 1987a:172).
   Sources: PA *kešite·wi 'it is hot' (Hockett 1957:258); Massachusett ⟨kussitteau⟩ 'it is hot' (Silver 1960:119).
   Analysis: PA *kešy- (intensive of heat, speed) + *-ete·- '(inan.) to be affected by heat, fire'.
   Cree kisite·w, Massachusett ⟨kussitt(e)au⟩ /kəsəta·w/ < PA *kešite·wi (PA *s, š > C, Ma s; PA *e > Ma ə).
   Cf. Massachusett ⟨kussitchuan⟩ /kəsəčəwan/ 'it flows in a rapid stream' (< PA *kešy- + *-čiwan- '(inan.) to flow';
      Munsee kší·te·w 'soup' (< PA *kešite·wi, nominalized); kšóte·w 'it is hot' (recomposition: |kəš-| + |-əte·-|);
      kší·la·n 'it's raining hard' (-əla·n 'rain'; old morphophonemics); kšó·xwe·w 'he walks fast' (-o·xwe·- 'walk').

Non-quoted italic forms are in phonemic transcription (in some cases updated and corrected), pointed brackets indicate unphonemicized forms written as in the source, and slashes mark their phonemicized equivalents.

PA = Proto-Algonquian
< = comes from (historically)
> = becomes (historically)
→ = makes, forms (as a derivational formation).

---

linguistics.[18] It is evident, however, that a methodology that accepts second-person *m* for Algonquian and Salish on the testimony of single languages in each will, if consistently applied, also accept second-person *n-* for Algonquian on the testimony of Cheyenne, given that it is "similar in sound and meaning" to the second-person *n-* of other putative Almosan-Keresiouan languages (Table 1). Any ad hoc principle that would eliminate the second-person *ne-* of Cheyenne as an inherited Algonquian feature would endanger a basic premise of Greenberg's methodology, that equations do not have to be consistent with the shallower levels of the classification to be valid for the deeper levels. In the present instance, an ahistorical argument that would reject Cheyenne second-person *ne-* as characterizing Algonquian would also have to reject Ritwan second-person *-m* as characterizing Almosan-Keresiouan.

Another way to evaluate the claims of Greenberg and Ruhlen about the saliency of pronominal similarities is to look at languages outside the Americas. Greenberg (1987a:49,54) repeatedly singles out the presence of Algonquian first-person *n-* and (he believed) "Cree second-person plural, *-mwa*" as a solid indication of the linkage of Algonquian to other languages having a similar pair of pronominal markers. Ruhlen (this volume) concluded that "the Amerind pattern . . . is virtually nonexistent elsewhere in the world." Consider, however, the implications for these claims of the fact that the Swahili

---

[18] Not surprisingly, the fact that he reaches his conclusions despite or in studied ignorance of the results of historical linguistics has drawn heavy criticism from historical linguists specializing in these languages; see the citations at the beginning of this section and the list of studies neglected by Greenberg in Campbell (1988:592, note 1).

subject prefixes include first-person singular *ni-* and second-person plural *m-*.[19] Exactly the same argument that would link Algonquian to the *n/m* pronoun set of "Amerind" on the supposed evidence of Cree would link Niger-Congo to it on the evidence of Swahili. Once again, other factors besides genetic relationship, or even borrowing, must be involved in producing similar pronominal marking in different languages.

A further demonstration of why reliable long-range comparison cannot be done without the historical-linguistic approach is presented by the problems that arise when comparing words between language families that have different stem-formation templates. In Table 3 (A, B, and C) we give three of Greenberg's Almosan-Keresiouan "etymologies." Each is followed by a summary of what is in the sources he apparently used for the Algonquian forms. From this one can judge how accurately Greenberg has conveyed the data in the sources, but the point here is not to illustrate his numerous errors on this score; in fact, we have tried to find examples which were not vitiated from the outset by miscues in the handling of the primary data. We then give additional data that show that the elements Greenberg takes as verb stems with concrete meanings are actually only parts of stems and have meanings that are quite abstract. This is because, as Table 3 illustrates, almost all Algonquian verb stems consist of at least two components, called the initial and the final (the only exceptions being a very few monosyllabic stems, mostly intransitives). This basic fact of the structure of Algonquian word stems presents a critical problem for attempts to relate Algonquian to other languages, since it means that Algonquian stems with the same meanings as unanalyzable, primary verbs in, say, English, Salish, or Wakashan typically have two lexical components, and that the meaning of an Algonquian stem cannot be ascribed to its initial alone. The initial that Greenberg takes as ANSWER has no necessary reference to speaking, which is what is required by his comparison. It is the use of this initial together with a final meaning 'speak to' that gives the combination the meaning 'answer'. The initial taken as FEEL is closer to English *get, get to* and can be translated 'touch' only in particular combinations, such as with the final meaning 'by hand, handle'.[20] The initial assumed to mean HOT is a general intensive used also for speed and the like. It only refers to heat when used with a final that specifies heat or fire as the cause of the condition or action being specified.[21] Thus, in each of these three cases the meaning assumed by Greenberg for the initial is found only when the initial is followed by a final that has that meaning. In fact, the first of the three initials (Table 3: A) can combine with any one of these three finals. Such examples show that for lexical items in different languages to be validly compared it is not sufficient for them to be "similar in sound and meaning"; they must be similar in sound, meaning, and grammar (or else, the historical linguist would say, the differences must be explicitly accounted for).

There is another significant aspect of Greenberg and Ruhlen's method of multilateral comparison that is illustrated in Table 3. In addition to citing Proto-Algonquian **kešy-* Greenberg (1987a:172) cites forms that are later historical developments from this: Cree *kis-* and Massachusett (**kussitau**).[22] In fact, the very sources from which Greenberg took these forms expressly cite Cree *kisite·w* and Massachusett (**kussitt(e)au**) as reflexes of Proto-Algonquian **kešite·wi* 'it is hot' (Hockett 1957:258; Silver 1960:119). The Cree and Massachusett forms add no information about Proto-Algonquian that is not already encompassed by the reconstruction of the Proto-Algonquian form. Their developments from Proto-Algonquian are entirely regular; for example, in both languages Proto-Algonquian **s* and **š* fall together to *s*. The reason for citing these descendant forms appears to be to provide a bridge between the Proto-Algonquian form and Proto-Salish **k̫as* 'hot, scorch': Cree and Massachusett have *s*, which can be compared with Salish *s*, and Massachusett has an orthographic ⟨u⟩ that can be compared with the labialization of the first segment in Salish.[23] This is a typical function of multilateral comparison, as Greenberg's (1987b:649) explication makes clear. But while such chaining together of partially similar

---

[19] No particular effort was needed to find this example. Swahili was simply the first language Goddard checked after Ruhlen's claim brought to mind Swahili *ni*.

[20] We ignore for present purposes the fact that the cited Fox word is actually a Shawnee word with an initial unrelated to the one in the cited Arapaho stem.

[21] This element shows up as an Amerind word for 'hot' in Ruhlen and Shevoroshkin (1989, ex. 40).

[22] Greenberg (1987a:172) uses the older name Natick for Massachusett. He also cites "Shawnee *kis*," but this is simply a mistake; Shawnee has *kiš-* in stems meaning 'hot', 'pain', 'angry', and 'fast' (Voegelin 1938–1940:301). The Blackfoot form he cites is not related; Blackfoot **(i)ksisto-** 'warm' reflects PA **ki·šow-* 'warm'. He also adds (after "cf.," hence perhaps with less confidence) Yurok *kecoyn hego·* 'sun', explained in his source as a derivative of *kecoy-* 'to be day' (Robins), 'to be daylight' (Berman), which literally means 'day traveler' (Robins 1958:204); a good case has been made by Berman (1982:418) that this is cognate with Proto-Algonquian **ki·š-*, appearing in **ki·šekwi* 'day, sky' and **ki·šo?θwa* 'sun'. It is not clear how a possible Proto-Algonquian **ki·š-*, apparently with an original meaning 'daylight, sky', might be related to **ki·šow-* 'warm', but in any event neither of these has anything to do with **kešy-* 'intensively'.

[23] Actually, as Silver (1960:119) makes clear, since Massachusett orthography is based on English rather than

words can lead to correct results when the words are in fact close cognates, as in Greenberg's example of the Indo-European words for 'tooth', it at best begs the question to apply it to sets of words whose relationship is in question, in the absence of explicit historical hypotheses. The use of historically secondary features to provide ostensible links of similarity, as in the present example, is entirely indefensible.[24]

The point is not simply that the equations of Greenberg's in Table 3 are incorrect, but that the method that leads to them is fundamentally flawed. It substitutes specious matchings for real history. From the perspective of historical linguistics it is clear that to validly compare verb stems with different structures requires a historical-linguistic hypothesis that accounts for the different structures. The comparison of Algonquian with any other language family faces this challenge (Goddard 1975:250). But this challenge can only be met by recognizing and approaching the problem of comparison as fundamentally a problem of reconstructing history, a problem that, being historical, can only be addressed by formulating explicit historical hypotheses. However sketchy and tentative such hypotheses may be to start with, they will only be worth our while if they have the triangular configuration of historical hypotheses rather than the linear configuration of ahistorical comparisons (B rather than A in Table 2). Since Greenberg (1987a), on principle, completely excludes from his book explicit hypotheses of history, his book contains no historical linguistics and has nothing to tell us about the linguistic history of the New World. There are no historical-linguistic hypotheses that can be compared with historical hypotheses from other fields of research on prehistory.

Finally, we may comment on the usefulness in principle of word comparisons of the sort Greenberg and Ruhlen have assembled. The fundamental problem with ahistorical word comparisons between languages, as with ahistorical grammatical comparisons (Table 2: A), is the absence of any principled basis for determining the extent to which the sets of words that are "similar in sound and meaning" are in fact the word sets that are each empirically the historical continuations of a single original, if indeed there are any. The word-comparison method has been defended by its proponents as overcoming this difficulty by the sheer weight of the numbers of languages compared, but it has never been satisfactorily demonstrated just how it does this in practice. The demonstration offered by Greenberg (1987a:24; cf. Ruhlen 1987a:10) is a table showing the classification of the languages of Europe, a problem that requires Indo-European and Finno-Ugric languages to be grouped and subgrouped correctly and separated from each other and from Basque. But these relationships and groupings are so obvious that they are, undeniably, easily discovered by the word-comparison method. After all, these groups of languages have been diverging for only a few thousand years, too short a time to mask their similarities but long enough to result in clearcut differences among their sub-branches. The question at issue, however, is whether the word-comparison method can correctly recover and rank language relationships at time depths that date back to the first peopling of the Americas and must therefore be at least twice as great as those of the language groupings of Europe. To demonstrate that the word-comparison method can accomplish this would require only the presentation of a table, like Greenberg's table of the languages of Europe, showing how the tabulation of words demonstrates the relationships of Amerind and its branches or, say, the connections and subgrouping of Almosan-Keresiouan. We imagine, however, that if it were possible to draw up such a table it would have appeared in Greenberg's book. The numerous sets of similar words Greenberg presents instead do not address the question of the validity of the method of multilateral comparison; they merely demonstrate the undoubted fact that using Greenberg's criteria and procedures many sets of ostensibly similar words can be assembled. The classificatory function of the method of multilateral comparison rests, in principle, on delineating language groups, each of which exhibits more similarities internally than it shares with other groups at the same level of the classification. Greenberg does not demonstrate that the new groupings he proposes have this property.

The problem of the evaluation of word comparisons is exactly the problem that historical linguistics addresses. The techniques of historical linguistics have been developed precisely in order to permit principled distinctions to be made between accidental and historically probative similarities. This is done by the postulation of a complex of historical hypotheses that provides the framework for evaluating proposed comparisons and discovering new historical connections. In contrast, the only validation possible for an equation produced by the word-comparison method is the equation itself. A telling example is furnished by Ruhlen (n.d. a), who singles out the following set of similar words as an "etymology" of bedrock certainty:

---

on continental alphabets, Massachusett (u) does not represent the rounded vowel [u] but the central vowel [ə] (the pronunciation corresponding to the apostrophe in English c'mon).

[24] Another example is Greenberg's (1987a:166) comparison of Algonquian and Iroquoian words for 'arm', which includes forms in Arapaho and Seneca that are accidentally convergent and hence only speciously similar (Goddard 1987:657). Ruhlen's (n.d. a) discussion of this example ignores Goddard's criticism of the illogical and methodologically illegitimate use of descendant forms in addition to their protoforms and instead argues other completely nongermane points.

Blackfoot *(mo-)kíts(-is)* 'finger', Wiyot *(mo-)kèc* 'fingers', Yurok *(cey-)ketew* '(little) finger'.

This is an updating, with some adjustments in the way the forms are cited, of a word set taken by Ruhlen and Shevoroshkin (1989:ex. 16) from Greenberg (1987a:172, Almosan-Keresiouan ex. 93) that incorporates a comparison between the Wiyot and Blackfoot words made by Sapir (1913:624). In fact, however, Blackfoot *mookítsis-* 'toe, finger, claw' regularly reflects Proto-Algonquian **-(x)kašy-* '(finger)nail, claw, hoof' (Proulx 1989:60). Wiyot *-ukhiʔs* 'finger(s)' (*-ukhiʔson-* before suffixes) is the noninitial form of *khiʔs (khiʔson-)*; it contains an element *-ʔson-* 'hand', found in a series of words referring to the arm, hand, and fingers (Teeter 1964:50).[25] Yurok *ceyketew* 'little finger' is made up of the well-attested elements *ceyk-* 'small' and *-etew* 'hand, finger' (Robins 1958:190, 222, 238, 239, 280, 293, etc.).[26] Thus correct analysis shows that the elements in these forms that have similar meanings are actually quite dissimilar in sound: Proto-Algonquian **-xkašy-* '(finger)nail, claw, hoof', Wiyot *-ʔson-* 'hand', and Yurok *-etew* 'hand, finger'. Of apparent similarities like that of the Wiyot and Blackfoot words for 'finger' Sapir asked rhetorically, "Are these 'accidents'?" and answered, "Fiddlesticks!" (cited with evident relish by Ruhlen n.d. a). A glance at the known facts about these forms shows, however, that the correct answer in this case was "Yes."[27] Ruhlen ridicules the idea that Greenberg's book could be largely a collection of coincidences, but examples like the foregoing show that this is not an unlikely possibility. In the present case the languages being compared are well enough known so that the falseness of the proposed comparison can be made immediately obvious. But the words in Greenberg's book are the end results of thousands of years of mostly unknown historical changes, often further distorted, at the final stage, by misapprehension and misinterpretation. It is thus indeed likely that errors and accidents have completely drowned out the differential proportions of whatever true cognate sets among linguistic groups of the Americas might, in principle, define a classification.[28]

It has been shown elsewhere that the method of word comparison cannot distinguish non-American Indian languages from languages of the Amerind grouping. For example, Finnish can be demonstrated to be a perfectly

---

[25] E.g., *-eʔson-* 'hand' in *doteʔsónił* 'his hands are large' (*dot-* 'large'; *-ił* 'third person'; Teeter 1964:39). Kroeber's *((m)okèc)* would be phonemically *-ukhiʔš*, with substitution of diminutive *š* for *s*; Reichard (1925:129) gives the presuffixal variant of this as the diminutive of a form equivalent to Teeter's *khiʔson-*.

[26] Perhaps Greenberg was misled by Robins' entry *cey(kel-)* 'to be small (human beings, etc.)', but according to standard linguistic conventions the parentheses mark a variable portion, not a separate element; the notation *cey(kel-)* abbreviates an alternation between *cey* (a complete word) and *ceykel-* (the form taken by *cey* before suffixes). The loss of word-final syllables and the simplification of word-final consonant clusters are common phonological processes in Yurok. The full form of *ceyk-* 'small' is attested in *ceykoh* 'to be small (round things)' and other words (for the segmentation of *-oh*, cf. *noʔoh* 'two (round things)', with *noʔ-* 'two'). For *-etew* 'hand, finger' compare *pletew* 'thumb, big toe' (*pl-* 'big') and *peʔwetew-* 'to wash the hands' (*peʔw-* 'wash'). But the point is not to criticize Greenberg and Ruhlen for not having checked the descriptive facts more carefully, but rather that such errors are inevitable when the comparison of languages is pursued using his methodology.

[27] Although Sapir at times showed great insight in proposing distant linguistic comparisons, he greatly overestimated the accuracy of his conjectures (Campbell 1988:593; Goddard 1986).

[28] For Ruhlen the word comparison discussed in this paragraph is an illustration of why Blackfoot words not found in other Algonquian languages can validly be used for comparisons outside of Algonquian. In this he states his opposition to the contrary view in Goddard (1987:656), though without direct counterarguments to the points made there regarding general methodological principles and the incompleteness of current knowledge of Blackfoot linguistic history. For any attempt to derive historical inferences from linguistic data to be useful, whatever lines of reasoning it employs must rest on only the most firmly established and best understood data. As Bray (1986) has written about archaeological data, "piling up dubious cases proves absolutely nothing." Judged from the perspective of the ordinary canons of reasoning, the defense of the use of poorly understood Blackfoot words is incomprehensible, but it is precisely the largely unique and obscure character of Blackfoot vocabulary (conveniently available in an extensive English-Blackfoot dictionary) that makes it an ideal language for use in multilateral comparison. Ruhlen and Shevoroshkin (1989) argue that the likelihood of there being an Algonquian source for words found only in Blackfoot is comparable to the likelihood of the inherited Indo-European status of words found in only one branch of Germanic (say, in Old Norse) but having other Indo-European cognates (say, in Greek). But in comparing Old Norse and Greek words, every step of the historical developments of the two languages is supported by detailed and explicit hypotheses of linguistic history, developed using historical-linguistic methods, while no such hypotheses exist for comparing Blackfoot alone to languages outside Algonquian. The example thus succinctly reveals the fundamental deficit of the word-comparison method, its absolute lack of a historical dimension, as well as the blindness of its defenders to the difference between the presence and absence of a historical-linguistic hypothesis.

good Amerind language using Greenberg's own techniques (Campbell 1988).[29] Indeed, Ruhlen's (this volume) paper for this conference, while unintentionally so, is in effect a clear admission of the inability of Greenberg's methodology to exclude many non-Amerind languages from Amerind. Specifically, he and Greenberg believe that Amerind and Eskimo-Aleut are related to their postulated Eurasiatic family (Indo-European, Uralic-Yukaghir, Altaic, Korean-Japanese-Ainu, Gilyak, Chukchi-Kamchatkan and Eskimo-Aleut), with Amerind related to Eurasiatic as a whole and Eskimo-Aleut as "simply one constituent of Eurasiatic." Their Na-Dene is paired with at least Sino-Tibetan and "Caucasian." Ruhlen (this volume) struggles to distinguish this vast (and to us incredible) array from the Nostratic hypothesis, which also includes a large quantity of far-flung languages, concluding that "[p]erhaps the best way to view Nostratic is as a vast family, still not completely defined, of which Eurasiatic is but one subgroup." To those less disposed to linguistic classifications as matters of faith, this Amerind-Eskimo-Aleut-Eurasiatic-Nostratic agglomeration simply constitutes the evidence that the methods and data used by Greenberg and Ruhlen are unable to exclude other, unrelated languages, a property which renders the postulation of Amerind as a linguistic unity a vacuous hypothesis.

CONCLUSION

We conclude that reliable knowledge of the linguistic history of the American Indians is currently so incomplete, for all but the shallowest levels, that it is compatible with a wide range of possible scenarios for the peopling of the Americas. This being the case, we urge caution in proposing hypotheses for the peopling of the Americas that are based on classifications of American Indian languages, even when they may have the attraction of appearing to help restrict that range of possibilities. We are particularly concerned that the classification presented by Greenberg (1987a) should not be accepted as a reasonable working hypothesis simply because there is nothing else with the same far-reaching scope. Greenberg's insistence that hypotheses of classification validly precede hypotheses of history has produced an indiscriminate mass of unverifiable conclusions. As Boas (1940:212) cautioned, "It should be borne in mind that the problem of the study of languages is not one of classification but that our task is to trace the history of the development of human speech." Explicit hypotheses of history will prove to be the only effective tool in the study of the history of languages and their speakers.

---

[29] A rebuttal of Greenberg's (1989) objections to this demonstration is in Campbell 1993.

REFERENCES CITED

Adelaar, W. F. H.
  1989 Review of *Language in the Americas*, by J. H. Greenberg. *Lingua* 78:249–255.

Austerlitz, R.
  1980 Language-Family Density in North America and Eurasia. *Ural-Altaische Jahrbücher* 52:1–10.

Bateman, R. M., I. Goddard, R. T. O'Grady, V. A. Funk, R. Mooi, W. J. Kress, and P. F. Cannell.
  1990a Speaking of Forked Tongues: The Feasibility of Reconciling Human Phylogeny and the History of Language. *Current Anthropology* 31:1–24.
  1990b On Human Phylogeny and Linguistic History: Reply to Comments. *Current Anthropology* 31:177–82.

Berman, H.
  1982 Two Phonological Innovations in Ritwan. *International Journal of American Linguistics* 48:412–220.

Bloomfield, L.
  1925 On the Sound-System of Central Algonquian. *Language* 1:130–56.

Boas, F.
  1940 *Race, Language and Culture*. Macmillan, New York.

Bray, W.
  1986 Finding the Earliest Americans. *Nature* 321:726.

Bright, W.
  1988 Review of *Language in the Americas*, by J. H. Greenberg. In *American Reference Books Annual*, vol. 19. p. 440.

Campbell, L.
  1986 Comment on *The Settlement of the Americas: A Comparison of the Linguistic, Dental and Genetic Evidence*, by J. H. Greenberg, C. G. Turner II, and S. Zegura. *Current Anthropology* 27:488.
  1988 Review of *Language in the Americas*, by J. H. Greenberg. *Language* 64:591–615.
  1993 The Classification of American Indian Languages and Its Implications for the Earliest Peopling of the Americas. In *Language and Prehistory in the Americas: An Examination of the Greenberg Classification*, edited by A. R. Taylor. Stanford University Press, Stanford. In press.

Campbell, L., and M. Mithun.
  1979 North American Indian Historical Linguistics in Current Perspective. In *The Languages of Native America: An Historical and Comparative Assessment*, edited by L. Campbell and M. Mithun, pp. 3–69. University of Texas Press, Austin.

Chafe, W.
1964 Another Look at Siouan and Iroquoian. *American Anthropologist* 66:852–862.

1973 Siouan, Iroquoian, and Caddoan. In *Current Trends in Linguistics*, vol. 10, part 2, edited by T. A. Sebeok, pp. 1164–1209. Mouton, The Hague.

1976 *The Caddoan, Iroquoian, and Siouan Languages*. Mouton, The Hague.

1987 Review of *Language in the Americas*, by J. H. Greenberg. *Current Anthropology* 28:652–653.

Cuoq, Jean-André
1886 *Lexique de la Langue Algonquine*. J. Chapleau and Fils, Montreal.

Fagan, B. M.
1987 *The Great Journey*. Thames and Hudson, London.

Fleming, H. C.
1987 Toward a Definitive Classification of the World's Languages. *Diachronica* 4:159–223.

Floyd, E. D.
1981 Levels of Phonological Restriction in Greek Affixes. In *Bono Homini Donum: Essays in Historical Linguistics, in Memory of J. Alexander Kerns*, edited by Y. L. Arbeitman and A. R. Bomhard, pp. 87–106. John Benjamins, Amsterdam.

Goddard, I.
1967 The Algonquian Independent Indicative. In *Contributions to Anthropology: Linguistics I*, pp. 66–106. National Museum of Canada Bulletin No. 214. Ottawa.

1974 Remarks on the Algonquian Independent Indicative. *International Journal of American Linguistics* 40:317–327.

1975 Algonquian, Wiyot, and Yurok: Proving a Distant Linguistic Relationship. In *Linguistics and Anthropology: In Honor of C. F. Voegelin*, edited by M. D. Kinkade, K. L. Hale, and O. Werner, pp. 249–262. Peter de Ridder Press, Lisse.

1979 The Languages of South Texas and the Lower Rio Grande. In *The Languages of Native America: an Historical and Comparative Assessment*, edited by L. Campbell and M. Mithun, pp. 355–389. University of Texas Press, Austin.

1986 Sapir's Comparative Method. In *New Perspectives in Language, Culture, and Personality: Proceedings of the Edward Sapir Centenary Conference, Ottawa*, edited by W. Cowan, M. K. Foster, and K. Koerner, pp. 191–214. Studies in the History of the Language Sciences, vol. 41. John Benjamins, Amsterdam.

1987 Review of *Language in the Americas*, by J. H. Greenberg. *Current Anthropology* 28:656–657; Errata 29:435.

1988 Pre-Cheyenne *y. In *In Honor of Mary Haas: From the Haas Festival Conference on Native American Linguistics*, edited by W. Shipley, pp. 345–360. Mouton de Gruyter, Berlin.

1990 Review of *Language in the Americas*, by J. H. Greenberg. *Linguistics* 28:556–58.

Goddard, I., and W. Fitzhugh
1979 A Statement Concerning America B.C. *Man in the Northeast* 17:166–172. (Also: *Biblical Archeologist* 41(3):85–88.)

Greenberg, J. H.
1987a *Language in the Americas*. Stanford University Press, Stanford.

1987b Language in the Americas. Author's Précis. *Current Anthropology* 28:647–656.

1987c Reply. *Current Anthropology* 28:664–666.

1989 Classification of American Indian Languages: A Reply to Campbell. *Language* 65:107–114.

1990 Comment on "Speaking of Forked Tongues: The Feasibility of Reconciling Human Phylogeny and the History of Language," by R. M. Bateman, I. Goddard, R. T. O'Grady, V. A. Funk, R. Mooi, W. J. Kress, and P.F. Cannell. *Current Anthropology* 31:18–19.

Greenberg, J. H., C. G. Turner II, and S. L. Zegura.
1986 The Settlement of the Americas: A Comparison of the Linguistic, Dental, and Genetic Evidence. *Current Anthropology* 27:477–497.

Gruhn, R.
1988 Linguistic Evidence in Support of the Coastal Route of Earliest Entry into the New World. *Man* 23:77–100.

Haugen, E.
1976 *The Scandinavian Languages: An Introduction to Their History*. Harvard University Press, Cambridge.

Hockett, C.F.
1957 Central Algonquian Vocabulary: Stems in /k-/. *International Journal of American Linguistics* 23:247-268.

Kroeber, A. L.
1916 Arapaho Dialects. *University of California Publications in American Archaeology and Ethnology*, vol. 12, No. 3, pp. 71–138. Berkeley.

Laitman, J. T.
1985 Evolution of the Upper Respiratory Tract: The Fossil Evidence. In *Hominid Evolution: Past, Present, and Future*, pp. 281–286. Alan R. Liss, New York.

Lamb, S. M.
- 1964 Linguistic Extinction in North America. In *Proceedings of the 35th International Congress of Americanists, Mexico, 1962*, vol. 2, pp. 457–464.

Laughlin, W. S.
- 1986 Comment on "The Settlement of the Americas: A Comparison of the Linguistic, Dental and Genetic Evidence," by J. H. Greenberg, C. G. Turner II, and S. Zegura. *Current Anthropology* 27:489–490.

Leman, W.
- 1980 Evidence for a PA *k: Cheyenne n Correspondence. *International Journal of American Linguistics* 46:316–318.

Lewin, Roger
- 1988 American Indian Language Dispute. *Science* 242:1632–1633.

Lounsbury, F. G.
- 1978 Iroquoian Languages. In *Northeast*, edited by B.G. Trigger, pp. 334–343. Handbook of North American Indians, vol. 15, W. C. Sturtevant, general editor. Smithsonian Institution, Washington, D.C.

Meltzer, D. J.
- 1989 Why Don't We Know When the First People Came to North America? *American Antiquity* 54:471–90.

Michelson, T.
- 1914 Two Alleged Algonquian Languages of California. *American Anthropologist* 16:361–366.
- 1935 Phonetic Shifts in Algonquian Languages. *International Journal of American Linguistics* 8:131–71.

Mithun, M.
- 1990 Studies of North American Indian Languages. In *Annual Review of Anthropology* 19:309–330.

Newman, S.
- 1977 The Salish Independent Pronoun System. *International Journal of American Linguistics* 43:302–314.
- 1980 Functional Changes in the Salish Pronominal System. *International Journal of American Linguistics* 46:155–167.

Nichols, J.
- 1990 Linguistic Diversity and the First Settlement of the New World. *Language* 66:475–521.

O'Grady, R. T., I. Goddard, R. M. Bateman, W. A. DiMichele, V. A. Funk, W. J. Kress, R. Mooi, and P. F. Cannell
- 1989 Genes and Tongues. *Science* 243:1651.

Picard, M.
- 1984 The Case Against Cheyenne *n* from PA *k*. *International Journal of American Linguistics* 50:111–117.

Powell, J. W.
- 1891 Indian Linguistic Families of America North of Mexico. Bureau of American Ethnology, Seventh Annual Report, pp. 1–142. Smithsonian Institution, Washington, D.C.

Proulx, P.
- 1982a The Origin of the Absolute Verbs of the Algonquian Independent Order. *International Journal of American Linguistics* 48:394–411.
- 1982b Proto-Algonquian *k in Cheyenne. *International Journal of American Linguistics* 48:467–471.
- 1989 A Sketch of Blackfoot Historical Phonology. *International Journal of American Linguistics* 55:43–82.

Reichard, G. A.
- 1925 Wiyot Grammar and Texts. *University of California Publications in American Archaeology and Ethnology*, vol. 22, No. 1, pp. 1–215. Berkeley.

Robins, R. W.
- 1958 *The Yurok Language: Grammar, Texts, Lexicon*. University of California Publications in Linguistics, vol 15. Berkeley.

Rogers, R. A.
- 1987 Review of *Language in the Americas*, by J. H. Greenberg. *Current Anthropology* 28:662–663.

Ruhlen, M.
- 1987a *A Guide to the World's Languages*. Vol. 1. Stanford University Press, Stanford.
- 1987b Voices from the Past. *Natural History* 96(3):6–10.
- n.d.a Is Algonquian Amerind? In *Genetic Classification of Languages*, edited by V. V. Shevoroshkin. University of Texas Press, Austin. In press.
- 1989 Materials for a Global Etymological Dictionary. 9. First- and Second-Person Pronouns in the World's Languages. Manuscript distributed to members of the World Summit Conference on the Peopling of the Americas, University of Maine, Orono.

Ruhlen, M., and V. V. Shevoroshkin
- 1989 Linguistic Origins of Native Americans. Manuscript distributed to members of the World Summit Conference on the Peopling of the Americas, University of Maine, Orono.

Sapir, E.
- 1913 Wiyot and Yurok, Algonkin Languages of California. *American Anthropologist* 15:617–646.
- 1915 Algonkin Languages of California: A Reply. *American Anthropologist* 17:188–194.
- 1949a Central and North American Languages [1929].

In *Selected Writings of Edward Sapir*, edited by D. G. Mandelbaum, pp. 169–178. University of California Press, Berkeley.

1949b Time Perspective in Aboriginal American Culture: A Study in Method [1916]. In *Selected Writings of Edward Sapir*, edited by D. G. Mandelbaum, pp. 389–467. University of California Press, Berkeley.

Silver, S.
1960 Natick Consonants in Reference to Proto-Central Algonquian. *International Journal of American Linguistics* 26:112–119, 234–241.

Szathmary, E. J.
1986 Comment on *The Settlement of the Americas: A Comparison of the Linguistic, Dental and Genetic Evidence*, by J. H. Greenberg, C. G. Turner II, and S. Zegura. *Current Anthropology* 27:490–491.

Teeter, K. V.
1964 *The Wiyot Language*. University of California Publications in Linguistics, vol. 37. University of California Press, Berkeley and Los Angeles.

Thomason, S. G., and T. Kaufman
1988 *Language Contact, Creolization, and Genetic Linguistics*. University of California Press, Berkeley.

Voegelin, C.F.
1938–
1940 Shawnee Stems and the Jacob P. Dunn Miami Dictionary. *Indiana Historical Society Prehistory Research Series*, 1:63–108, 135–167, 289–341, 345–389, 409–478. Indianapolis.

Vogt, Hans
1940 *The Kalispel Language*. Det Norske Videnskaps-Akademi, Oslo.

Weiss, K. M., and E. Woolford
1986 Comment on *The Settlement of the Americas: A Comparison of the Linguistic, Dental and Genetic Evidence*, by J. H. Greenberg, C. G. Turner II, and S. Zegura. *Current Anthropology* 27:491–492.

Zegura, S.
1987 Blood Test. *Natural History* 96(7):8–11.

Low-range Theory and Lithic Technology: Exploring the Cognitive Approach

DAVID E. YOUNG
Department of Anthropology
University of Alberta
Edmonton, Alberta T6G 2H4

ROBSON BONNICHSEN
Center for the Study of the First Americans
and the Department of Anthropology
Oregon State University
Corvallis, OR 97331

DIANE DOUGLAS
Dames and Moore
7500 N. Dreamy Draw Drive #145
Phoenix, AZ 85020

JILL MCMAHON
Department of Geology
University of Michigan
Ann Arbor, MI 48109

LISE SWARTZ
Department of Anthropology
University of Alberta
Edmonton, Alberta T6G 2H4

What can we hope to learn from the study of stone tools? The answer is a great deal. Since the inception of archaeology, prehistorians have recognized the importance of stone tools for making inferences about past human behavior (Grayson 1986).

The quality of the surviving archaeological record and our interpretive tools place limits on avenues that can be used to investigate "big-picture" problems such as the peopling of the Americas. Ericson (1984), for example, notes that critical methodological problems exist in quarry studies and lithic analysis and that these problems prevent us from making higher-level behavioral interpretations. Ideally, we need an arsenal of analyses that will allow us to: (1) discriminate the products of human behavior from those of nature, (2) isolate human groups in time and space, (3) characterize the organization and dynamics of prehistoric societies, (4) trace human dispersions and construct mobility models, (5) investigate adaptive strategies, (6) study the dynamics of cultural change through time, and (7) trace phylogenetic relationships among human groups through time.

In this paper we attempt to establish a framework for thinking about how prehistorians derive cultural information from the study of prehistoric technology. We review model-building procedures, examine assumptions of the normative and cognitive approaches, report on experiments designed to quantify behavioral data and to test some of the assumptions of the cognitive approach, and suggest directions for future research.

MODEL-BUILDING PROCEDURES

The scientific question that lithic analysts face is: How can we move from empirical observations of data collected in archaeological contexts to making valid statements about prehistoric cultural behavior? Making high-level abstractions concerning phenomena such as migration, adaptation, and cultural change must rely on hierarchal chains of linked inferences. These chains begin with empirical observations and build to increasingly higher levels of abstraction. Thus, our ability to make high-level statements about the past is dependent upon the quality and validity of low-level statements. This is particularly true for the analysis of flaked stone tools.

As scientists we use a variety of scientific methods, e.g., observations, sampling procedures, classifications, hypotheses, and theories, to explain the past. In addition to these, there are three methodological procedures and/or concepts that are basic to the investigation and explanation of flaked stone tools: (1) establishing procedures for the description and analysis of the material properties and morphological attributes of stone tools, (2) using analogical concepts to link experimental data and prehistoric tools and behavior, and (3) employing the theory of integrative levels to relate different kinds of data sets.

Establishing Procedures for Formal Analysis

Spaulding (1965) introduced the idea of dimensions to refer to the temporal, spatial, and formal boundary conditions of assemblages that must be controlled if we are to make legitimate comparisons between artifact assemblages. Stone tools are complex and multidimensional in nature. Because of this complexity, formal analysis should concentrate on the investigation of the two dimensions most amenable to empirical investigation: material properties and surface topography.

The study of material properties involves defining material properties that can be used as diagnostic signatures for material sources, characterizing material properties important to tool production and use, determining rates of material change useful for relative dating methods (e.g., obsidian hydration), and ascertaining how humans have modified the natural properties of raw materials to make them easier to work (e.g., heat treatment).

Analyzing the morphology of artifacts is complex and can be divided into three areas: macro-, meso-, and micro-analysis. Macro-analysis focuses on quantitative aspects of form (e.g., absolute length, width, and thickness) and the qualitative description of shape characteristics (e.g., deeply notched, V-shaped basal indention). Studies that emphasize only macro dimensions are coming under increasing criticism by specialists who feel that other kinds of information may be more important. For example, see Odell's (1988) discussion of the importance of use-wear studies for interpreting "projectile points" as cutting tools rather than as tips for hunting tools, and Flenniken's (1985) discussion of the importance of technology in classifying projectile points.

Meso-analysis focuses on the study of flake scars, the relationships between flake scars and stages of artifact production, and the linkage between morphology and behavior. Flake-scar studies provide information on production procedures and breakage due to use.

Micro-analysis concentrates on the study of edge-damage (micro-flakes and crushed areas), striae, and polishes on artifact surfaces and the processes whereby these phenomena are created (Hayden 1979; Keeley 1980; Newcomer et al. 1986; Odell 1986); and visual and microscopic examination of artifact surface alterations may provide clues concerning artifact production and use behaviors, and contribute to our knowledge about specific human adaptation patterns. Most use-wear specialists begin with the premise that surface modifications of tools suggest tool use, motor actions of prehistoric craftpersons, and something of the properties of the material that underwent modification. Despite important advances in this sub-field, several analytical problems are in need of clarification. Natural processes (Schnurrenberger and Bryan 1985) and tool production procedures result in damage, both microscopic and ascertainable by the human eye, that can be quite similar and readily confused with one another. Analogy provides one tool for sorting out these kinds of problems.

Analogy

The static topographical patterns invariably found during the analysis of flaked stone tools must be interpreted using a process known as analogical reasoning (see Young 1989). Whether we like it or not, all lithic studies rely on the use of the principle of uniformitarianism. In its simplest form, this principle holds that present-day processes are the key to understanding past events (cf. Dictionary of Geological Terms 1962).

There are several ways of generating modern analogs for reconstructing behavior patterns from the past. The most important of these are: (1) observations of modern tool-using primates (McGrew 1987), (2) observations of modern-day peoples making and using stone tools, (3) experimental studies (Crabtree 1972; Plew et al. 1985; Young and Bonnichsen 1984), which simulate in one way or another conditions thought to have existed in the past, and (4) the use of limited inference studies (Bonnichsen 1989). For example, ethnoarchaeologists who analyze abandoned camp sites in the light of information elicited from the modern-day hunters and gatherers who actually used the sites, provide models that are applicable to the past (Gould 1980; Gould and Saggers 1985).

Not surprisingly, lithic analysts seeking to explain their tool assemblages have looked to modern craftpersons for their analogs. The use of experimental analogs should be understood in terms of the historical circumstances that led to the development of this approach. Shortly after white contact in North America, native Americans lost the ability to make flaked tools. Avocational archaeologists who found stone artifacts wanted to know how these stone tools were made and began to experiment with a variety of methods, using trial-and-error procedures. Gradually these flintknappers developed a practical knowledge of how to make flaked stone tools. It is these individuals who are the founders and leaders in experimental lithic technology.

During the early 1960s, experimental lithic technologists caught the attention of professional archaeologists. Archaeologists seeking to construct better artifact classification systems were attracted by the insights experimental craftsmen could provide regarding tool making and using processes (Swanson and Butler 1962). As interest in flintknapping developed, field schools and ad hoc "flake outs" became common forums for the communication and practice of this folk art.

While many insights can be obtained by working with experimental craftpersons, much of what has been learned has yet to be framed in formal scientific terms. Given a paucity of sophisticated classification systems based upon experimental data, untested folk-knowledge assumptions are finding their way into archaeological classifications.

Theory of Integrative Levels

A third concept useful for developing an adequate method for analyzing prehistoric stone tools is Feibleman's (1954) theory of integrative levels. Over the last decade, middle-range theory has provided a focus for archaeological research (Binford 1981, 1983). While the goal of reconstructing the organization and dynamics of prehistoric societies is admirable, the methods for achieving this goal remain weak. We propose that Feibleman's (1954:59–64) theory of integrative levels provides a useful means for defining and linking the lowest levels of organization to the highest and vice versa. We also propose that the cognitive approach to lithic technology can contribute to the construction of low-, middle-, and high-range anthropological theory.

While it is not necessary to provide a full review of Feibleman's theory, a summary of statements for characterizing hierarchal organizations is germane. He proposes: (1) each level organizes the level or levels below it, plus one emergent quality—thus integrative levels are cumulative upward, (2) complexity of levels increases upward, (3) higher levels depend on lower levels, (4) lower levels direct the higher, (5) for any level in an organization, its mechanism lies at the level below and its purpose at the level above, (6) a disturbance introduced into any level reverberates at all levels, and (7) the higher the level, the smaller its population of instances.

From the above premises follow several rules of explanation. The most important of these are: (1) the reference of any organization must be at the lowest level which will provide sufficient explanation, (2) the reference of any organization must be at the highest level that its explanation requires, (3) every organization must be explained on its own level, and (4) no organization can be explained entirely in terms of a lower or higher level.

Scientific methods provide the means for reconstructing hierarchically structured linked systems from surviving physical remains. The development of models to explain flaked lithic remains begins with empirical observations of what survives, and making inferences about the systems that produced the observed patterning. This operation, here termed low-range theory, is the first building block in model construction, which serves as the foundation for higher levels of explanation.

Low-range theory focuses on investigating and reconstructing the following relationships: (1) artifact shapes and mental templates, (2) the morphology of individual flake scars (and flake-scar patterning) on artifacts and how the artifacts were made, and (3) wear patterns on artifacts and how the artifacts were used.

In contrast to low-range theory, middle-range theory focuses on understanding the organization and operational dynamics of past cultural systems. But it is constructed from the results of low-range theory. New meanings are attached to low-range statements. For example, inferences about artifact styles (patterns associated with mental templates) are transformed to middle-range theoretical statements by assuming that diagnostic shapes or attribute clusters are signatures produced by ethnic groups. Use-wear hypotheses represent another example. The proposed linkages between micro-flake scars, polishes, and striae and their inferred uses are assumed to represent activities that are adaptive in nature and thus allow statements to be made about human adaptation.

High-range theory draws on statements formulated in the construction of middle-range theory. It seeks to move beyond reconstructing paleo-socio, economic, and technological organizations to extra-societal questions. This level of investigation seeks answers to "big picture" questions such as: Why and how did the dispersion of modern humans occur? What does the peopling of the Americas tell us about this process? How are these events linked to changes in the earth's climatic, geologic, and biotic subsystems? High-range theory may also focus upon cultural change through time, and upon phylogenetic relationships among prehistoric peoples.

NORMATIVE VS. COGNITIVE ASSUMPTIONS CONCERNING LITHIC ANALYSIS

Lithic technology is a complex, multidisciplinary field. In fact, few if any specialists control the full range of skills and knowledge necessary to conduct holistic analyses of lithic assemblages. Research is fragmented and involves a variety of specialists including material scientists, geochemists, computer analysts, dirt archaeologists, and experimental flintknappers. As a consequence, this field is typified by many narrowly focused technical papers. With specialization and disciplinary fragmentation comes the problem of understanding how all the pieces fit together.

We see technology as an independent variable that directly or indirectly controls both the macro-shape parameters of artifact style and micro-shape parameters investigated by use-wear specialists. Conversely, macro- and micro-shape approaches rely upon technology and can be regarded as dependent sub-fields. For this reason, we believe that an understanding of stone tools should begin with an understanding of lithic technology.

The explanation of flaked-stone artifacts in terms of the processes that created them is complex. Modelers who seek to explain variation in artifact assemblages must take into account material, behavioral, and cultural variables as well as natural processes that can affect patterning of the surviving remains. In reviewing the literature, we note that there are two different sets of fundamental assumptions used to interpret prehistoric stone tool production patterns. These views can be summarized as the normative and cognitive approaches (Young and Bonnichsen 1984).

The Normative Approach

The normative approach views lithic technology as a vehicle for developing normative statements about the organization and operations of past lithic technology systems (Bradley 1985; Callahan 1979; Flenniken 1981; Muto 1971; Shafer 1985).

There are three major assumptions in the normative approach:

Assumption 1: all raw materials respond to flaking in much the same manner, and the application of a given technique will result in a consistent combination of attributes such as bulb configuration, lip size, etc. whose occurrence signifies a specific technique, e.g., hard hammer or soft hammer.

Assumption 2: the use of a given technique, e.g., hard hammer, always involves the same behavior, and scar patterns with specific constellations of attributes have an isomorphic relationship with the behavior patterns that produced them.

Assumption 3: modern and prehistoric craftpersons combine different techniques into lineal production strategies. These strategies can be divided into: (1) production stages to accommodate preforms abandoned early in the production process because of problems with the material; (2) artifacts that are broken in manufacture and therefore abandoned; (3) completed specimens; and (4) resharpened specimens.

The main problem with the normative approach is that it tends to ignore variation. Most lithic technologists, for example, recognize that raw materials are multidimensional in nature; that is, there are differences in their material properties, e.g., elasticity, plasticity, brittleness, grain size, bonding materials, and chemical elements. Yet, exactly how these differences affect fracture propagation and fracture-scar patterning is not a major concern among most experimental technologists.

Likewise, most craftpersons focus on the replication of artifact forms using techniques they feel comfortable with rather than replicating scar patterns that approximate those found in archaeological contexts. The details of production behaviors are seldom, if ever, recorded because it is impossible to document one's own behavior as a flintknapper while producing an artifact. Once again, many experimental flintknappers adopt a normative stance by ignoring behavior and decision-making strategies as sources of variation, which can confound interpretation of the archaeological record if not properly understood. Thus, there is a need for an empirical rather than an intuitive approach for relating flake-scar patterning to the decision-making process.

An additional problem of the normative approach is the use of lineal production models to classify prehistoric specimens. Analysts who use this method posit lineal production strategies that are divided into sequential stages. For the most part, production stages represent intuitive production types (often with overlapping boundaries) identified by a lithic craftperson on the basis of personal production knowledge. Lithic analysts sometimes adopt the stages suggested by experimental craftpersons. Thus, experimental production stages are given a new status, and become classification categories for sorting and classifying the items in archaeological assemblages.

Stage analysis is an intuitive, top-down, typological approach. The thesis that all artifacts produced by a human population were made by craftpersons using an identical series of stages organized sequentially in exactly the same manner is a topic worthy of further research. A comparative analysis of the production sequences on individual artifacts would provide an empirical means for determining the accuracy of the lineal-stage model. The detailed work of Young and Bonnichsen (1984), which examines the production behavior of two modern craftsmen, suggests that lineal-stage models do not accommodate feedback aspects of tool production nor do they reveal the generative processes that lie behind tool production.

The Cognitive Approach

The basic premises of the cognitive approach are that variation in materials, behavior, and cognition must be taken into account in developing models of stone tool production, and that this information can lead to more significant archaeological classifications. Several years ago, we began working with the premise that the morphological attributes of flake scars allow us to reconstruct at least part of the decision-making process involved in making a stone tool. The meaning of this claim needs to be unpacked. The claim also needs to be defended. First, let us consider some concepts, terms, and definitions essential for understanding the meaning of the claim.

We refer to an individual flake scar as a morpho-unit. A morpho-unit is a constellation of morphological attributes that results from the application of a behavior unit composed of a number of variables, including type of behavior employed (such as percussion or pressure), type of tool (such as hard hammer, soft hammer, or pressure flaker), and level of force (see Figure 1). Just as the behavior unit is a complex gestalt or patterning of interacting behavioral variables, the resulting flake scar is also a gestalt or pattern. The morphological pattern of the flake scar provides a record of how the behavioral gestalt was translated into energy, which traveled through the raw material in the form of force waves. Thus there is a correspondence between two gestalt patterns: the behavior unit and the morpho-unit, both of which can be observed and analyzed. What is difficult to observe or measure directly is the intervening force waves, which link the behavior unit and the morpho-unit. Ultimately, it is important to understand how a behavior unit is translated into energy, and how energy is translated into morphology (Tomenchuk 1985). Until this area of investigation becomes more sophisticated, however, we must rely primarily upon the simpler method of correspondence or correlation between behavior units and morpho-units.

By repeatedly correlating specific behavior unit inputs with resulting morpho-unit outputs, it is possible to learn to "read" a flake scar. "Reading" a flake scar involves a mental reconstruction of what kind of behavioral gestalt must have been involved in producing a specific morphological pattern. This is not a static affair, as no two behaviors are ever identical and no two flake scars are ever exactly the same. This means that the analyst must have a broad enough experience with seeing particular behavioral inputs produce specific morphological outputs to be able to account for morphological variation. In other words, when the analyst examines a morphological pattern, he/she must be able to simulate mentally the kind of behavioral gestalt that must have produced the patterned output. Gradually with experience, the analyst constructs a mental template of the range of both behavioral and morphological variation associated with a specific kind of behavior unit such as "moderate percussion thinning with a billet" or "substantial pressure shaping with a pressure flaker."

How does one gain this kind of analytic experience? There are only two ways: one can become a flintknapper, or one can watch flintknappers at work. It will be argued later in the paper that the second way may be the best because the flintknapper is too busy removing flakes to observe with sufficient detachment the connection between behavioral input and morphological output.

What does learning to "read" flake scars have to do with prehistoric artifacts? To some people, there seems to be very little connection between the experimental manufacture of stone tools by contemporary flintknappers and the analysis of prehistoric stone tools. They argue that prehistoric conditions were obviously different, particularly as we move back further and further in time. Physiological factors such as musculature may have been different, not just in terms of the normal range of variation among individuals, but in terms of differences among hominid species. Apart from well-preserved tools, generally made of stone, we don't know what kinds of manufacturing implements prehistoric craftpeople possessed; and we don't know how these tools were used. According to these critics, we can speculate about such matters on the basis of experimentation, but we were not present when the prehistoric artifact was made so there is no way to verify our reconstruction of the behavior units employed.

In our view, there is a bridge between the prehistoric flintknapper and contemporary experimental flintknapper. That bridge is provided by the raw material. A particular kind of rock, regardless of when and where it is flaked, provides an enduring record of the force that moves through it. Although the movement of the force cannot itself be seen, it is possible to experiment with different kinds of behavioral input until the desired morphological output is produced. In other words, if the experimental flintknapper wishes to understand the morphological pattern on a prehistoric flake scar, he/she must find a similar kind of material (from the same quarry if possible) and experiment with different kinds of flaking techniques (possibly inventing some along the way) until he/she is happy there is a good match. If a good match can be achieved, it is reasonable to assume that the moving force responsible for the prehistoric flake

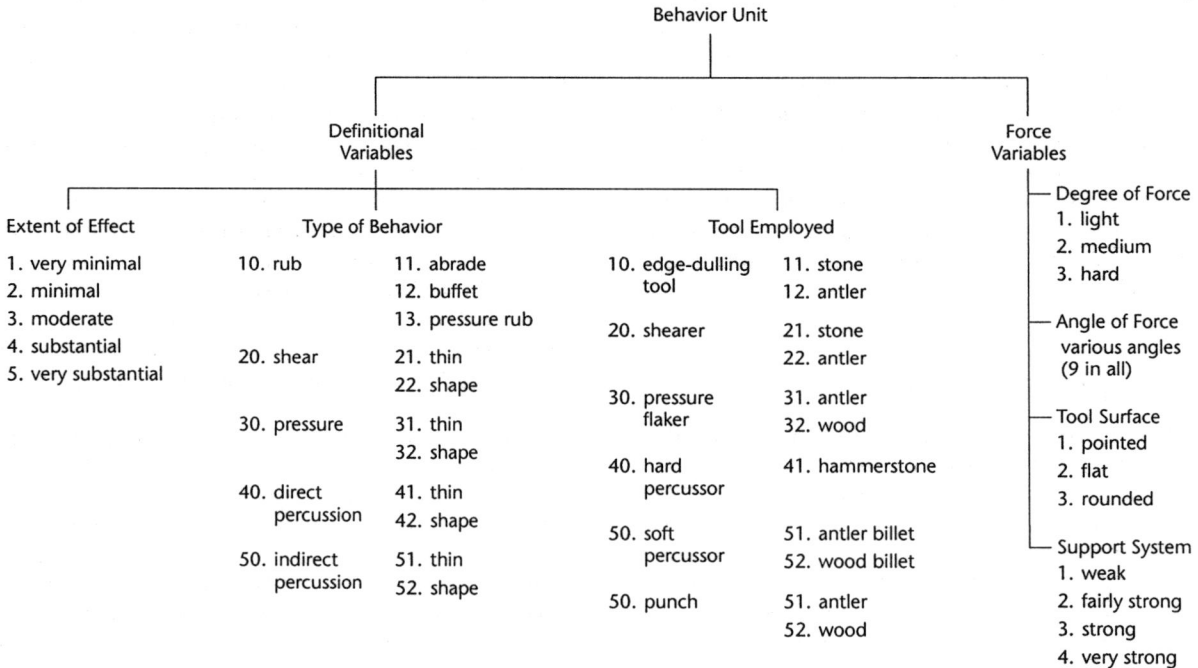

Figure 1. Variable involved in producing a behavior unit (from Young and Bonnichsen 1984).

scar has successfully been replicated. This is a reasonable assumption because experimental studies (Bonnichsen 1977) have shown that even small changes in behavioral input result in different morphological outputs. In other words, there appears to be a predictable relationship between force input and morphological output in the sense that one causes the other. The relationship is not arbitrary and is governed by mechanical principles that transcend time and space.

There are some pitfalls here, however. There is a good deal of variation within a particular kind of material such as flint, chert, or obsidian—sometimes even within material from the same quarry. There is often considerable variation even within the same piece of rock. This makes exact replication impossible, whether there is a time gap between the model and the replica of 100,000 years or five minutes. The best one can hope for is a close approximation.

It will also be noticed that although we have talked about a predictable relation between force input and morphological output, we have not claimed that there is only one constellation of behavioral variables that can produce a given type of force or stress distribution. While slight changes in behavioral input may produce consequent changes in morphology (which is why the relationship is predictable), it is theoretically possible to neutralize a change in one input variable with changes in other input variables so that the resulting force is similar even though the behavioral gestalts are different. For example, changing from a heavy to a light percussor can be offset by swinging the lighter tool with greater speed.

Neither have we claimed that a given type of force input always produces the same kind of fracture. For example, the same force applied to different artifacts can produce different fracture patterns because of differences in edge geometry, internal flaws in the material, etc. Although the relationship between force input and morphological output is predictable in a theoretical sense (assuming one is aware of all the factors that influence the distribution of stress in the material), the relationship is not constant and a given behavior unit may produce different flake scars. Just as a given behavior unit encompasses numerous slight variations in variables such as holding position and angle of force, resulting flake scars exhibit a range of variation in shape and morphological features.

What this means is that we can never be certain of the exact nature of prehistoric behavioral input variables such as tools, holding positions, and the like. For this reason, it is better to use general rather than specific terms when reconstructing prehistoric behavior. For example, the terms "hard hammer" and "soft hammer" are preferable to terms such as "cobble percussor" and "antler billet." It is not so important that we know what a billet is made of; it *is* important that we establish its elasticity, as elasticity has a direct bearing on morphological attributes such as degree of platform collapse or damage to the proximal margin of the flake scar. It might be possible to devise billets of antler, wood, or plastic, which would all be characterized by similar degrees of elasticity.

Analogical reasoning, under most conditions, is metaphorical rather than literal. In the case of stone tools, however, the fact that the relationship between force mechanics and rock is predictable (given the qualifications described above) means that we can transcend the limits of metaphor and argue that the relationship between a prehistoric artifact and its contemporary replica is one of identity rather than analogy (Young 1989). To the extent that he/she can obtain the same kind of rock used by a prehistoric ancestor, the contemporary craftperson can be reasonably sure that the successful replication of the morphological patterns exhibited by the flake scars on a prehistoric artifact provides a key to the general behavioral input employed by the prehistoric flintknapper.

We have attempted to establish that it is possible to learn to "read" prehistoric flake scars on the basis of observing the morphological patterns produced by different kinds of behavioral input in a contemporary, experimental situation. The experiments we have conducted in our own research involve having several different flintknappers apply different behavior units to a variety of materials. The resulting "experimental artifacts," for which the behavioral input conditions are known and recorded on video tape, are kept in a reference collection (Table 1).

Even if the analyst has a well-developed set of mental templates concerning the relationship between behavioral input and morphological output, it is useful to compare prehistoric flake scars with the reference collection when analyzing prehistoric artifacts. Comparison is enhanced if there are photographic blow-ups of both the prehistoric specimen and the "experimental artifacts" with which the prehistoric specimen is compared. Enlarging flake scars photographically frequently allows one to see morphological details that might otherwise be missed.

Identifying the probable behavior units responsible for the flake scars on a prehistoric artifact is only the first step in reconstructing the decision-making process of the prehistoric craftperson. The next step is to establish the purpose for which each behavior unit was used, as the same behavior unit can be used for more than one purpose. A good knowledge of flintknapping procedures

Table 1. Materials and Behavior Units Represented in the Reference Collection.

MATERIALS	
1. Georgetown Flint, Texas	6. Mt. Kineo Felsite, Maine
2. Norway Bluff, Maine	7. Spanish Diggings Quartzite, Wyoming
3. Munsungun Grey Chert, Maine	8. Lake Abitibi Welded Tuff, Ontario
4. Munsungun Black Chert, Maine	9. Knife River Flint, North Dakota
5. Munsungun Red Chert, Maine	10. Obsidian (control specimens), Burns and Glass Butte, Oregon

BEHAVIOR UNITS	
1. Rub abrade with cobble	17. Moderate pressure shape with antler pressure flaker
2. Rub buffet with cobble	18. Minimal percussion thin with antler billet
3. Rub buffet with antler billet	19. Moderate percussion thin with antler billet
4. Pressure rub with antler pressure flaker	20. Substantial percussion thin with antler billet
5. Minimal shear thin with antler pressure flaker	21. Minimal percussion shape with antler billet
6. Minimal shear thin with split cobble	22. Moderate percussion shape with antler billet
7. Moderate shear thin with antler pressure flaker	23. Minimal percussion thin with cobble
8. Moderate shear thin with split cobble	24. Moderate percussion thin with cobble
9. Minimal shear shape with antler pressure flaker	25. Substantial percussion thin with cobble
10. Minimal shear shape with split cobble	26. Minimal percussion shape with cobble
11. Moderate shear shape with antler pressure flaker	27. Moderate percussion shape with cobble
12. Moderate shear shape with split cobble	28. Moderate indirect percussion thin with punch
13. Minimal pressure thin with antler pressure flaker	29. Substantial indirect percussion thin with punch
14. Moderate pressure thin with antler pressure flaker	30. Fluting
15. Substantial pressure thin with antler pressure flaker	31. Resharpening
16. Minimal pressure shape with antler pressure flaker	

generally allows the analyst to determine whether the unit was used to thin the flake, move in the edges (referred to as "shaping"), contour the margins, prepare the platform, etc. Adding inferred purpose to a behavior unit transforms it into what we call a "production unit" (see Tables 4 and 5 at the end of the article for definitions of the variables used in constructing behavior and production units).

The third step is to reconstruct the sequencing of production units on the specimen. This is done by examining flake-scar overlap, considering both faces of the artifact. Flake scars removed early in the production process are usually obliterated by later work, so that the finished artifact may provide morphological evidence of only the last stage of the manufacturing process. Even so, a finished artifact usually exhibits between three and ten different kinds of production units.

After the flake scars (morpho-units) have been identified in terms of the probable behavior units that produced them, the behavior units transformed into production units (by adding inferred purpose), and the sequencing of production units established, the results are displayed in a flow diagram (see Figure 2 for an example of a flow diagram).

The intent of the flow diagram is not to document the exact sequencing of morpho-units for a particular artifact but to show that certain production units follow some kinds of production units and not others. In other words, the relationship among production units has a kind of grammatical structure in that certain types of sequential relationships are allowed, whereas others never occur.

Thus a flow diagram constructed for one artifact may serve equally well to describe the grammatical structure of another artifact even though the patterning of flake scars on the two artifacts is not identical. For example, if the sequence of production units on a particular artifact is $1 \rightarrow 2 \rightarrow 1 \rightarrow 3 \rightarrow 1 \rightarrow 4 \rightarrow 5$, the flow diagram will indicate that Production Unit 1 can be followed by 2, 3, or 4, but not 5, which must be preceded by 4. These same rules apply to the following sequence found on another artifact: $1 \rightarrow 3 \rightarrow 1 \rightarrow 2 \rightarrow 1 \rightarrow 4 \rightarrow 1 \rightarrow 3 \rightarrow 1 \rightarrow 4 \rightarrow 5$. Both sequences would follow the same rules and would thus be diagrammed the same way.

Based on one's knowledge of flintknapping, it is usually possible to describe what the rules seem to be and why they are there. For example, in the flow diagram represented in Figure 2, Behavior Unit 1 never precedes Behavior Unit 5 (at least in the same location) because both 1 and 5 are thinning units. A thinning unit can create an edge that is too thin to provide proper support for the removal of another thinning unit on the same spot. Trying to use another thinning unit on the same spot would probably crush the platform, resulting in a large notch rather than a thinning flake. Therefore, Behavior Unit 5 must be preceded by either 4 or 7. Behavior Unit 7 is an edge preparation unit that involves strengthening an

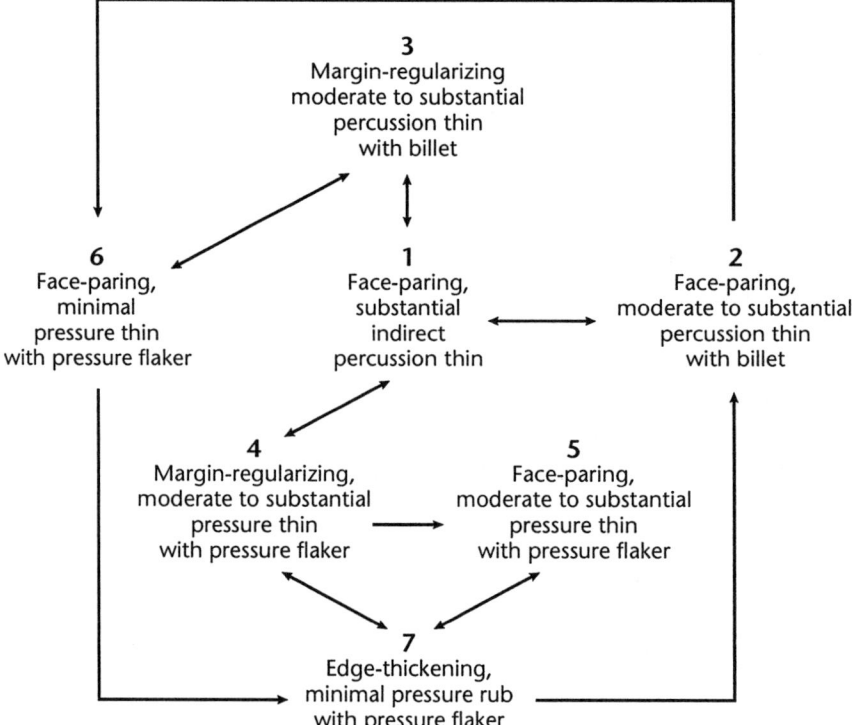

Figure 2. Example of a flow diagram showing inferred biface production units and their sequencing.

overly thin (sharp) edge by blunting the edge with the tip of the pressure flaker. Behavior Unit 4 is used to produce the proper curvature on the margin of the biface so that a subsequent thinning behavior will have a better chance of removing a long, thin flake. Ideally, both the edge and the margin of the biface are prepared before attempting to remove a large thinning flake. Thus a typical sequence might involve alternating between behavior units 4 and 7 along the edge of the biface (shown by the double-headed arrow), followed by Behavior Unit 5 (which can follow either Behavior Unit 4 or Behavior Unit 7).

By adding rules of this sort to a flow diagram, the analyst completes the grammatical analysis for a particular artifact and thereby reveals something of the underlying logic involved in its production. After a flow diagram has been prepared for each artifact in the assemblage or sample, one can then compare flow diagrams to see to what extent they overlap in terms of what production units are employed and how they are sequenced. If one artifact has five production units and another artifact has seven, four of which are shared in common, it is still possible, despite their differences, to see if the production units shared in common are sequenced in the same way. If they are, the two artifacts may have been produced by the same production grammar. By overlapping flow diagrams in this way, it is possible to build a more complete grammar than is exhibited by any particular artifact in the assemblage. Likewise, if some flow diagrams are compatible but others are not, it raises the possibility that the analyst may be dealing with a mixed assemblage—an assemblage in which more than one production grammar was employed to make the artifacts. This could be due to any number of reasons: artifacts could have been traded in; the "assemblage" represents occupation of the same site by different cultural groups at different times, etc. The purpose of the cognitive approach is not to answer these culture history questions but simply to classify the artifacts in such a way that meaningful culture-history and culture-change questions become possible.

To return to our original contention, we argue that it is more meaningful to classify prehistoric artifacts in terms of production strategies (or more accurately, production grammars) than in terms of easily observable and quantifiable attributes associated with size, shape, or gross technology. The logic of this claim should now be clear. It is possible to use the same production grammar to make artifacts of different sizes and shapes. If so, grouping artifacts in terms of size and shape would distort the situation and suggest erroneous interpretations. Likewise, some analysts claim they are doing a technological analysis when they distinguish artifacts in terms of whether they are fluted, hafted, etc. Fluted points across North America may be similar at the level of gross technology in that they all may have been hafted. The kind of technological analysis used in the cognitive approach indicates, however, that there are numerous ways of making fluted points and that there are a number of distinct fluted-point traditions, each with its own grammar. This, in turn, suggests that while hafting spread rapidly across North America because of its usefulness, fluting was executed in different ways by different groups with their own pre-existing technological traditions. If so, there may be no such thing as a "Clovis culture" (Bonnichsen 1991; Bonnichsen and Young 1980).

The above provides a brief description of the assumptions of the cognitive approach and how it can be used. For a fuller description, see the Young and Bonnichsen (1984) book, *Understanding Stone Tools: A Cognitive Approach*. In the methods developed in that book, the authors illustrate how to code the morphological attributes on flake scars using a qualitative or judgmental approach in which observations are assigned to mostly nominal categories. This qualitative approach was further developed in two graduate theses at the University of Alberta: *A Technological Analysis of Lake Abitibi Bifaces*, (1984), a Ph.D. dissertation by John Pollock; and *A Cognitive Analysis of Stone Tool Production* (1986), an M.A. thesis by Marjolaine Boutin-Sweet. Since that time, we have attempted to make the approach less subjective by relying more heavily on quantitative measurements. In the following section, we describe the results of this recent work and then turn to the question of how the accuracy of the cognitive approach in reconstructing past production behaviors might be tested.

EXPERIMENTS DESIGNED TO QUANTIFY BEHAVIORAL DATA AND TO TEST THE ACCURACY OF COGNITIVE RECONSTRUCTION

Quantifying Behavioral Input and Morphological Output

It has proven possible to quantify many aspects of both behavioral input and morphological output. In 1988, Jill McMahon finished an innovative M.S. thesis at the University of Maine that involved the quantification of flaking behavior. McMahon (1988, abstract) describes her experiments as follows:

> To study flaking behavior in detail, data recording and analytical techniques were borrowed from the field of biomechanics. A high-speed film record of expert and novice flintknappers performing some common direct percussion behavior units was analyzed to obtain detailed quantitative descriptions of the downswing movements of their striking arms. These data, combined with information about impacter mass and specimen edge angle, allowed the behaviors to be re-defined and compared in terms of the four mechanical variables:

edge angle, impacter mass, striking speed, and the direction of the applied force. Finally, the flake scars produced by the subjects were photographed, and their lengths and profile angles measured because both of these parameters respond directly to changes in the afore-mentioned mechanical variables (Cotterell and Kaminga 1979; Lawrence 1979).

We will return to the results of this study in the next section. Of importance here is the fact that McMahon was able to quantify certain aspects of behavior units. The high-speed film of flaking behavior could be slowed down or stopped on a particular frame, and the movements could be digitized to allow quantitative analysis. By and large, McMahon found that the actual behavior of the two flintknappers in the study conformed to Young and Bonnichsen's qualitative description of the behavior units the flintknappers were instructed to use.

The quantitative measurement of flake scar attributes was made possible at the University of Alberta by the purchase of a *reflex metrograph,* a three-dimensional digitizing apparatus that allows the researcher to move a small dot of light over the surface of a flake scar. Pushing a foot pedal instructs the machine to record the position of the dot of light in three dimensions. A computer program saves each set of three-dimensional measurements that are used to compute attributes such as edge angle (defined here as the angle formed by the intersection of two faces of a biface) or the height and spacing of ribs (undulations created by a force wave moving through the material). Working with magnifying glasses, the researcher is able to record minute differences (0.01 mm) in the surface of the flake scar.

A graduate student, Lise Swartz (1986), used the reflex metrograph to make quantitative measurements of the experimental reference collection, described in Table 1, housed at the University of Alberta. The goal of the research was to look for relationships between behavior units employed by experimental flintknappers and quantifiable attributes of the resulting flake scars. Information concerning the results of the reflex metrograph study (Swartz n.d.) are on file with the Project for the Study of Material Culture, Department of Anthropology, University of Alberta (David Young, director).

What follows is a summary of some of the more important findings for Georgetown flint (Texas), the material employed in the bifacial flaking experiments described in Young and Bonnichsen's (1984) book, and also employed in McMahon's study. The generalizations incorporate insights from both the Young and Bonnichsen book and from that portion of the reflex metrograph study that dealt with Georgetown flint. It should be kept in mind that these generalizations do not necessarily apply to other materials, which differ in key attributes such as density, elasticity, and grain size. It also should be kept in mind that the following generalizations are based upon a very small sample of morpho-units for each behavior unit studied. Because of the small sample (usually three to five morpho-units per behavior unit), no statistical tests were applied. As the number of flake scars associated with each behavior unit in the reference collection increases, the generalizations may have to be altered.

1. Removal of Platform and Proximal Margin Damage: the amount of platform (defined as the area of the edge on which force is applied by a percussor or pressure flaker) removed in the process of removing a flake is variable. Sometimes the platform is not strong enough to sustain the force and merely crushes, resulting in failure to remove the flake. Because none of the evidence of the crushing is removed, this condition often results in maximal proximal margin damage. Sometimes (particularly when the force is directed to much "downward" and not enough "inward") the force travels all the way from the dorsal to the ventral surface, resulting in a "notch" whose shape may resemble the shape of that portion of the tool that was used to apply the force. Thus, hammerstones tend to leave broad, flat notches, whereas pressure flakers tend to leave narrow U-shaped notches. When this happens, the entire platform area may remain attached to the flake that has been removed. This removes much (or all) of the evidence of damage caused by the application of force and leaves a "clean" flake scar with a relatively straight edge. This condition is considered ideal because it does not leave problems (such as a serrated edge or extensive proximal margin damage) to be solved in subsequent flake removal.

   At minimal and moderate force levels, soft-hammer flaking generally results in less platform removal and thus more proximal margin damage than pressure or hard hammer. At substantial force levels, however, a soft hammer is capable of leaving a clean flake scar (resembling a very large pressure flake scar in some ways).

2. Bulb of Force: Bulbs tend to be longer and deeper as the force level increases, for both pressure and percussion flaking. At substantial force levels, soft hammer tends to create deeper bulbs than pressure or hard hammer whereas pressure creates longer bulbs. At moderate force levels this is reversed, with percussion creating longer bulbs (in relation to overall flake scar length).

3. Slope: Soft hammer and pressure tend to create a more clearly demarcated, though not necessarily deeper, bulb of force than hard hammer, with the extra-bulbar portion (everything outside the bulb of force) of the flake scar following the curve of the biface. If skillfully executed, a hard-hammer flake can leave a curved surface, relatively unblemished by a distinctive bulb of force. Frequently, however, hard-hammer scars tend to be flat, often with a low-

pitched slope that "bites" too deeply into the material. This creates an overly thin artifact cross-section and frequently results in a distinctive hinge or step at termination.

4. Ribs (undulations on the surface of the flake scar): At minimal and moderate force levels, pressure and hard-hammer techniques often do not produce visible ribs unless the material is very fine grained. If ribs are visible, they tend to be relatively indistinct, more numerous, more closely spaced and evenly distributed across the flake scar, than is the case for soft-hammer techniques. This is particularly true for pressure. In contrast, soft-hammer flaking tends to produce more distinct but fewer ribs, which are often clustered on the distal half of the flake scar. For both pressure and percussion flaking, the distinctiveness of ribs increases with force levels. At substantial force levels, both pressure and percussion flaking can create distinctive ribs, but for pressure and soft hammer, the ribs tend to be concentrated near the termination of the flake scar, whereas in the case of hard hammer, there are often three major ribs (sometimes in association with a cluster of small ribs) more or less evenly spaced on the distal half of the flake scar, with the first rib marking the termination of the bulb of force, and the third rib marking the termination of the flake scar.

5. Thinning vs. Shaping: The above generalizations apply primarily to thinning, the intent of which is to reduce the thickness of the preform without significantly moving in the margins. In thinning, pressure is applied to the edge and directed toward the center of the preform in such a way that platform collapse (with its consequent moving in of the margin) is reduced. The intent of shaping, on the other hand, is to move in the margins by the application of force to the upper surface of the edge and in a downward movement (Figure 3).

Given the intent of thinning vs. shaping, it logically follows that platform collapse is undesirable for thinning. Therefore, a properly executed thinning flake will result in a less-distinct notch than in the case of shaping. One exception is the case of pressure thinning at moderate to substantial force levels. The build-up of force at the tip of the pressure flaker makes it difficult to avoid creating a U-shaped notch.

Because thinning normally creates less platform collapse, any damage that is done to the proximal margin (such as crushing) is not removed and extends further up the margin than in the case of shaping. Finally, thinning produces a more acute edge angle, a sharper edge, and a larger flake scar.

Since the goal of shaping is to move in the margins and thereby reduce the length and/or width of the artifact, platform collapse is desirable. In the case of isolated flake scars, shaping produces a distinct notch because of the

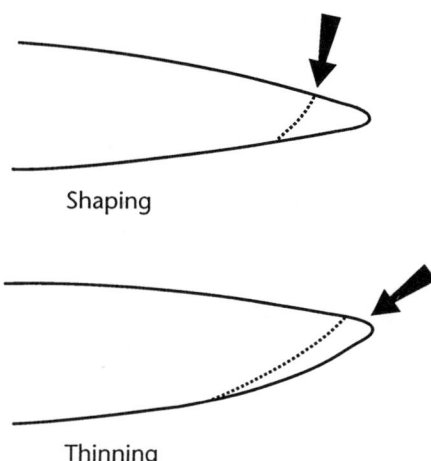

Figure 3. Shaping versus thinning. Arrows indicate angle of force; dotted lines indicate flake separation.

platform collapse. In the case of a series of overlapping flake scars, shaping tends to produce a scalloped edge. Shaping produces greater damage to the material impacted, but the evidence tends to be removed with the flake due to platform collapse. Therefore, there is frequently less evidence of proximal margin damage, which tends to be confined to the edge of the flake scar. Finally, shaping produces a steeper and smaller flake scar (see Figure 3), for a given force level, than in the case of thinning.

This section of the paper can be summarized by saying that over the past ten years, a good deal of time and effort has been expended to study the relationship between behavior units and morpho-units. Although the evidence has not always been consistent, there appears to be a general congruence of qualitative and quantitative data. Because of this congruence, it should be possible to construct attribute lists and analytic procedures that can be applied to prehistoric stone tools with some degree of confidence.

Testing Some Assumptions of the Cognitive Approach

Despite a growing sense of confidence in our ability to apply the cognitive approach to the analysis of prehistoric stone tools, there has been no way to demonstrate that our reconstructions of past behavioral events or decision-making processes are accurate. In an attempt to address the question of validity, the authors decided to engage in an experiment that would provide part of the answer. Three of the authors of this article, Young, Douglas, and Bonnichsen, agreed to use the cognitive approach to identify the behavior units employed in the experimental study conducted by McMahon, described above.

This "test case" is interesting in several ways. First, one of the two experimental flintknappers in the McMahon experiment was Bonnichsen. In other words, Bonnichsen was asked to identify flake scars, some of which he himself had produced several years earlier, in 1982. The other flintknapper involved in the McMahon experiment was Doug Schnurrenberger, who did his B.A. at the University of Maine and his Ph.D. at Alberta. A novice compared with Bonnichsen, who has flintknapped for much of his life, Schnurrenberger was included in McMahon's study to see if the behavior of an experienced flintknapper more nearly approximates the intent of the behavior units being employed, than is the case for a novice. This has obvious implications for the cognitive approach, as the archaeological record undoubtedly contains artifacts produced by novices.

Douglas at the time of this study was an archaeology major in the M.S. program at the University of Maine, having studied the cognitive approach with Young and actual flintknapping with Bonnichsen. Young is a cognitive anthropologist who (along with Bonnichsen) developed the analytic methods used in the cognitive approach to the study of stone tools. Although Young had a vague idea of McMahon's research problem and approach, he did not know which behavior units were actually employed in McMahon's study. Douglas had even less knowledge of what McMahon was doing. Bonnichsen, of course, had first-hand knowledge of McMahon's study, but since the study had been conducted a number of years earlier, he had forgotten the details of the research design.

McMahon sent the "experimental artifacts" produced by the two flintknappers in her study to the University of Maine, where the artifacts were photographed to aid in analysis (see Figures 5 through 16 at the end of the article). Three different conditions were set up in which Bonnichsen was provided with the least amount of data, Young with the most, and Douglas with an intermediate amount of data. The goal for all three analysts was to identify the probable behavior unit (as listed in Table 1) responsible for each of the flake scars included in the test case.

Bonnichsen examined the photographs, using an intuitive approach based upon his experience as a flintknapper, but without reference to the reference collection and without the use of formal analytic procedures.

In connection with her Honours Thesis (1988) at the University of Alberta, Douglas used Young and Bonnichsen's (1984) book, Boutin-Sweet's (1986) thesis, the results of Swartz's (1986) reflex metrograph study, and Tomenchuk's (1985) study of force mechanics to construct idealized flake scar profiles associated with the different behavior units defined by the cognitive approach (as listed in Table 1). She then coded the flake scars in the test case (referring to both the artifacts and the photographs) and compared the results with her idealized profiles, to obtain the best possible match. The idealized profiles and coding results for the test case flake scars are on file at the University of Alberta for those who would like to check the results.

Young (using a magnifying glass to examine both the artifacts and the photographs) coded the flake scars in the test case in terms of attributes suggested by the generalizations for Georgetown flint summarized above. He also had access to the reference collection, described above. Based on this coding, the distance among artifacts was plotted in terms of the number of shared attributes, considering all artifacts, two at a time. This mechanical operation (which could be performed by a computerized cluster-analysis program) produced several clusters. On the basis of his past experience in analyzing Georgetown flint "experimental artifacts," Young tentatively identified each cluster as being hard-hammer, soft-hammer, pressure, or edge-preparation units, and then further differentiated the members of each cluster in terms of amount and angle of force applied—to reconstruct specific behavior units. The details of this "cluster analysis" approach are on file at the University of Alberta. Suspicious of some of the results of the cluster analysis, Young then performed a more qualitative analysis, using all the data supplied to the other two analysts, in addition to the results of his own cluster analysis approach described above. This more qualitative approach resulted in different conclusions for some of the flake scars.

The results of the analyses by Bonnichsen, Douglas, and Young are summarized in Table 2. In the first column of Table 2 are shown the behavior units McMahon asked the two flintknappers to use. She was not specific in her directions of which edge-preparation units to employ, but merely allowed the flintknappers, if absolutely necessary, to modify the edges as they liked—in preparation for removing thinning and shaping flakes. Most of the edge preparation was obliterated by later work, but two examples remain intact: 1100 and 1300. The remaining morpho-units are all direct percussion, with either a hard or soft percussor. Because McMahon's research design was not set up specifically for the test case, she did not include examples of pressure or indirect percussion. This was, of course, unknown to the analysts. The remaining columns in Table 2 summarize the decisions made by Douglas, Young, and Bonnichsen, their scores, and their overall accuracy expressed as percentages. Table 3 summarizes the variables used to score the results of the test case.

Each analyst was given one point for correctly choosing between edge-preparation, pressure, direct percussion, and indirect-percussion flaking; and a second point for identifying the tool used: edge-rubbing tool, pressure flaker, direct-percussion tool (cobble or billet), or indirect-percussion tool (punch). The third point was given for distinguishing angle of force: force applied directly on the edge to prepare it for flaking, force applied at a right angle to the margin (behind the edge) to remove a shaping flake, or force applied at a 45-degree angle to the margin to remove a thinning flake (see Figure 3 for an illustration of the difference between shaping and thinning). The fourth point was given for determining degree of force employed: very minimal to very substantial.

As discussed above, McMahon did not record the type of edge-preparation units used (such as shearing or buffet). Therefore, it was impossible to judge the accuracy of the analysts' judgments concerning details such as the degree of force employed. For this reason, analysts were given a single point for recognizing an edge-preparation unit (Unit 1100 and Unit 1300), regardless of what kinds of more specific behaviors they thought were involved. All the other units could receive a score of up to 4 points each, as shown in the second column of Table 2. There are 50 possible points in all: four for each of the twelve direct-percussion units, and one for each of the two edge-preparation units. There is one exception. Since Bonnichsen did not analyze one of the edge-preparation units (Unit 1300) and one of the direct-percussion units (Unit 3100), the maximum score that he could achieve was 45 points instead of 50.

As might be expected, Bonnichsen, who was provided with the least amount of information, was the least accurate. This result illustrates a point that Bonnichsen has made for many years: that flintknappers are not necessarily the best-qualified individuals to analyze their own work.

Of the two more or less quantitative operations (those performed by Douglas and by Young's cluster analysis), that of Douglas proved to be more accurate. The highest level of accuracy was achieved by the qualitative operation performed by Young. The fact that Young was able to achieve a high score comes as no surprise, as he has had the most experience with applying the analytic procedures of the cognitive approach, and was also supplied with the greatest amount of data. The fact that Young's qualitative analysis was significantly more accurate than the cluster analysis, however, needs some comment. The human mind is unsurpassed as a computer. It is capable of performing a gestalt-type analysis in which morphological attributes are weighed in relationship to one another rather than mechanically tabulated. For example, hard-hammer thinning frequently produces a straight-edged flake scar termination, whereas pressure does not. If a given morpho-unit exhibits many of the attributes associated with pressure thinning but has a straight-edged termination, an analyst using a judgmental approach will overlook this apparent incongruity if it is noticed that termination of the flake scar coincides with a step or hinge produced by an underlying flake scar or by a flaw in the material. In other words, a gestalt judgment allows one to consider a number of factors in relationship to each other. To duplicate this feat a computer program would have to be endowed with artificial intelligence. The down side of a qualitative, gestalt approach is that not all aspects of the decision-making process are open to scrutiny. We will return to this problem at the end of the paper.

It should be emphasized, however, that the "qualitative" approach used by Young utilized systematic analytic procedures (such as independently coding each attribute on a flake scar and comparing the finished flake-scar profile with the reference collection). The approach is referred to as "qualitative" because the results of the formal analytic procedures were evaluated in light of the total context (the flake scar considered as a whole, including observation of flaws in the material, evidence of problems encountered in removing the flake, etc.). The final decision concerning behavior unit employed to create a morpho-unit was thus the result of both formal analytic procedures and gestalt judgment.

Evaluation of the Test Case Results

The results of the analytic operation can be compared with decisions made on the basis of chance. If someone were to randomly choose one option from each of the four variables shown in Table 3, he/she would have a 25% chance of choosing the correct type of behavior, a 20% chance of choosing the correct tool, a 33 ⅓% chance of choosing the correct angle of force, and a 20% chance of choosing the correct degree of force. Adding these percentages together and dividing by 4 produces an overall accuracy rate of 25% on average.

This assumes, of course, that the four variables are independent—in other words, that a choice concerning type of behavior does not influence one's choice concerning type of tool, etc. An analyst with even a little knowledge of flintknapping would know that not all the variables are independent. Thus, pressure flaking must be done with a pressure flaker instead of a billet or cobble, and indirect percussion (by definition) requires using a punch. There are some independent decisions that can be made at each level, however. For example, if the analyst decides that the type of behavior involved is direct percussion, he/she has a choice of hard or soft hammer (cobble or billet)—both of which can be used for either thinning or shaping. Finally, all the different types of behavior except edge preparation can involve all five force levels.

Because the four variables are not completely independent, it is very difficult to estimate the level of accuracy an analyst with a little knowledge of flintknapping might achieve. If the inexperienced analyst made the wrong choice on the first level of analysis, he/she could not hope to make a very high score overall. If, however, the analyst correctly selected direct percussion on the first level of analysis (which would be correct for 12 of the 14 units), he/she would then have a 50% chance of making a correct choice between hard and soft hammer on the second level of analysis. On the third level of analysis (angle of force), the analyst would have a 50% chance of correctly selecting thinning or shaping regardless of whether he/she had selected pressure, direct percussion, or indirect percussion on the first level of analysis. Likewise, with the exception of the edge-preparation units

Table 2. Test-case Decision by Analysts.

Behavior Unit Flintknappers Instructed to Use		Possible Score (No. Points)	Douglas	Score
Unit 1100:	Edge-preparation (tool, exact behavior, and knapper unspecified)	1	Edge preparation (shear shape with pressure flaker)	1
Unit 1200:	Moderate percussion shape with cobble (expert)	4	Moderate percussion shape with billet	3
Unit 1300:	Edge preparation (tool, exact behavior, and knapper unspecified)	1	Minimal pressure thin with pressure flaker	0
Unit 1400:	Moderate percussion shape with cobble (novice)	4	Moderate percussion thin with cobble	3
Unit 2100:	Moderate percussion shape with billet (expert)	4	Minimal to moderate percussion thin with cobble	2
Unit 3100:	Moderate percussion thin with billet (expert)	4	Moderate percussion thin with billet	4
Unit 3200:	Moderate percussion shape with billet (novice)	4	Moderate percussion thin with billet	3
Unit 3300:	Substantial percussion thin with cobble (failed) (expert)	4	Moderate percussion thin with billet	2
Unit 4100:	Moderate percussion thin with cobble (expert)	4	Substantial percussion thin with cobble	3
Unit 4200:	Moderate percussion thin with cobble (novice)	4	Substantial percussion thin with billet	2
Unit 5100:	Moderate percussion thin with cobble (novice)	4	Substantial percussion thin with billet	2
Unit 5200:	Moderate percussion thin with billet (novice)	4	Substantial percussion thin with billet	3
Unit 5300:	Substantial percussion thin with cobble (expert)	4	Substantial percussion thin with cobble	4
Unit 5400:	Substantial percussion thin with billet (expert)	4	Substantial percussion thin with billet	4
	Totals	50		36
	Accuracy			36/50 = 72%

(which involve very minimal to minimal force levels), any choice on the first level of analysis would provide a 20% chance of selecting the correct degree of force (fourth level of analysis) since all five force levels can be used with any of the percussion techniques. In brief, adjusting the formula to take account of connections between the four variables produces an average overall accuracy rate of 36.25% (25% on the first level + 50% on the second level + 50% on the third level + 20% on the fourth level divided by 4). This is a maximum accuracy rate in that the possibility of correct choices on the second level of analysis depends upon correct choices on the first level of analysis. Finally, it should be noted that for the two edge-preparation units, the four variables are almost completely interdependent. Thus edge preparation (first level) involves using an edge-rubbing tool (second level) to rub the edge (third level), usually using a very minimal degree of force (fourth level). An analyst with enough experience to recognize the interdependence of the levels for the edge-preparation units would be able to earn some "easy" points were it not for the fact that a maximum of one point was allowed for these units.

In summary, an analyst randomly selecting options from each of the four variables would, in a series of trials, achieve an accuracy rate of approximately 25% on average. An analyst with enough knowledge of flintknapping to recognize the connections between the variables (for example, that direct percussion requires use of a cobble or billet) might be able to raise this accuracy rate to 36%. To achieve a higher accuracy rate requires specialized knowledge such as how to distinguish thinning from shaping flakes. All the analysts in the experiment achieved significantly higher results than the base line range of 25 to 36% discussed above. It seems clear that an

Unit	Bonnichsen	Score	Young (1) Based Upon a Cluster Analysis	Score	Young (2) Based Upon a Qualitative Analysis	Score
1100	Edge preparation (minimal shear shape with pressure flaker)	1	Edge Preparation (minimal shear shape with pressure flaker)	1	Edge preparation (minimal shear shape with pressure flaker	1
1200	Minimal to moderate pressure shape	2	Moderate percussion shape with cobble	4	Moderate percussion shape with cobble	4
1300	Not analyzed	N/A	Edge Preparation (buffet)	1	Edge preparation (buffet)	1
1400	Edge preparation (buffet)	0	Edge preparation (buffet)	0	Minimal percussion shape with cobble	3
2100	Moderate percussion thin with billet	3	Moderate percussion shape with cobble	3	Moderate percussion shape with cobble	3
3100	Not analyzed	N/A	Moderate percussion thin with cobble	3	Moderate percussion thin with cobble	3
3200	Moderate pressure thin with pressure flaker	1	Moderate pressure thin with pressure flaker	1	Moderate percussion thin with cobble	2
3300	Moderate pressure thin with pressure flaker	1	Moderate pressure thin with pressure flaker	1	Moderate percussion thin with billet (failed)	2
4100	Moderate pressure thin with pressure flaker	2	Moderate percussion thin with billet	3	Moderate percussion thin with cobble	4
4200	Substantial pressure thin with pressure flaker	1	Moderate percussion thin with billet	3	Moderate percussion thin with cobble	4
5100	Substantial pressure thin with pressure flaker	1	Moderate percussion thin with billet	3	Substantial percussion thin with cobble	3
5200	Substantial percussion thin with billet	3	Substantial percussion thin with billet	3	Moderate percussion thin with billet	4
5300	Substantial percussion thin with cobble	4	Substantial percussion thin with billet	3	Substantial percussion thin with billet	3
5400	Substantial percussion thin with billet	4	Substantial percussion thin with billet	4	Substantial percussion thin with billet	4
	Totals	23		33		41
	Accuracy	23/45 = 51%		33/50 = 66%		41/50 = 82%

experienced flintknapper such as Bonnichsen can reconstruct past behaviors with an accuracy that far exceeds chance, and that applying cognitive analytic procedures can improve this accuracy rate further, as in the case of Young's approximately 80%. There were errors made, however. Before proceeding, it would be useful to consider the most frequent kinds of errors.

"Moderate percussion shape with cobble" executed by the novice was labeled as an edge-preparation unit (buffet) by Bonnichsen and by Young's quantitative approach. This is presumably due to the very small size and random patterning of the flake scars. Douglas, on the other hand, labeled one of the edge-preparation units "minimal pressure thin with a pressure flaker." This also is a readily comprehensible error, as one of the edge-preparation units ("pressure rub") produces a morphology very similar to minimal pressure thinning.

Bonnichsen mistook photographs of six of the eleven direct-percussion units that he analyzed for pressure flaking. Five of these mistaken units involved the use of a hard percussor, which frequently produces flat flake scars closely resembling those of pressure flaking. Young's cluster approach erroneously identified two of the twelve percussion units as pressure. Douglas correctly identified all the cobble and billet flakes as percussion, but confused cobble with billet flaking in five of the twelve cases. Young's "qualitative" analysis correctly identified all the cobble and billet flakes as percussion, but, like Douglas, confused cobble with billet flaking in five of the twelve cases.

It was relatively easy for the analysts to distinguish shaping from thinning for the 12 direct-percussion units. Young's quantitative approach made three errors, as did Douglas. Bonnichsen made three errors (for the 11 direct-

Table 3. Variables Used to Score the Results of the Test Case.

Type of Behavior
1. Edge preparation*
2. Pressure flaking
3. Direct percussion flaking
4. Indirect percussion flaking

Tool
1. Edge rubbing tool
2. Pressure flaker
3. Hard hammer (cobble)
4. Soft hammer (billet)
5. Punch

Angle of Force
1. Rub edge
2. Thin
3. Shape

Degree of Force
1. Very minimal
2. Minimal
3. Moderate
4. Substantial
5. Very substantial

* Note: Tool, angle, and degree of force were not specified for the edge-preparation units by McMahon. Analysts received one point for correctly distinguishing the edge-preparation units from other possible units.

percussion units analyzed), and Young's qualitative approach made only one error. The accuracy for estimating force levels was in the intermediate range. Young's qualitative and quantitative approaches both made only three errors; Douglas made six errors; and Bonnichsen made five errors (for the 12 units analyzed).

In summary, Bonnichsen was most likely to confuse percussion and pressure flaking, and Young and Douglas had some problems differentiating hard- and soft-hammer techniques. Otherwise, all three analysts attained a respectable level of accuracy in their reconstruction.

Assuming that cognitive analysts, or an automated system, could be trained or programmed to duplicate the accuracy of Young's qualitative approach (and it is not yet clear whether or not this can be done), is it reasonable to assume that Young's 82% accuracy rate might be further improved? For a partial answer to this difficult question, let us return to the results of the McMahon experiment described briefly above. The central questions in McMahon's research were: (1) Do differences in flake-scar morphologies accurately reflect differences in behavioral input? (2) Are the morpho-units produced by soft-hammer and hard-hammer techniques clearly distinguishable or do they overlap? (3) Are the morpho-units produced by thinning and shaping behaviors clearly distinguishable or do they overlap? (4) Are the behaviors of a novice and a skilled flintknapper, both trying to employ the same behavior unit, similar? To answer these questions, McMahon used digitizing techniques, combined with high-speed photography, to measure behavioral input; and she used a mechanical 3-D plotter (designed by David Tyler, Civil Engineering Department, University of Maine at Orono) to provide quantitative measurements of two flake-scar attributes: flake-scar profile angle and flake-scar length (see Figure 4 for definitions).

In answering the first question, McMahon concluded that flake-scar morphology does give an accurate representation of flaking behavior. In other words, the more similar the behaviors in terms of variables such as impacter selection, swinging speed and direction of applied force, the more similar the resulting flake scars—at least in terms of the morphological attributes used in her study: profile angle and flake-scar length.

The answer to questions 2, 3, and 4, considered together, is as follows:

(1) For the skilled flintknapper, there was almost no overlap between morphological attributes produced by hard- and soft-hammer thinning techniques, whereas there was considerable overlap

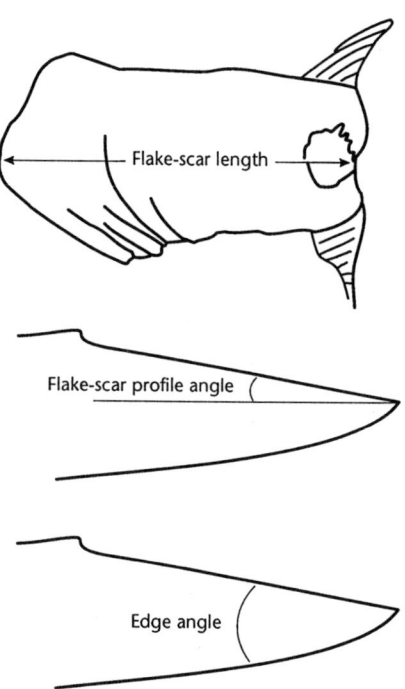

Figure 4. Flake scar length and flake scar profile angle (as used by McMahon 1988); edge angle as used by Young, Bonnichsen and McMahon.

between hard- and soft-hammer shaping techniques. For the novice, there was considerable overlap in morphological attributes produced by hard- and soft-hammer techniques, for both thinning and shaping.

(2) For both the skilled flintknapper and the novice, there was no overlap in morphological attributes between cobble thinning and shaping flakes, whereas there was considerable overlap between billet thinning and shaping flakes.

(3) Contrary to what might be expected, the range of variation in the morphological output of both the expert and the novice was approximately equal overall. For the expert, however, the morphological attributes associated with hard-hammer techniques produced more discrete clusters than in the case of the novice.

(4) Despite morphological overlap, there were some general trends on the part of both expert and novice: on average, the hard percussor produced thinning flake scars that were flatter and longer than for the soft percussor. Shaping flake scars produced by the hard percussor, on the other hand, tended to be steeper and shorter than in the case of soft-hammer shaping flakes.

(5) Despite the above generalization, there is enough morphological overlap in most cases to prevent an airtight distinction between hard- and soft-hammer morpho-units, and between thinning and shaping units, at least for the attributes analyzed in McMahon's study. Presumably, the same kinds of overlap occurred prehistorically, thereby making it impossible to distinguish hard- and soft-hammer techniques (or thinning and shaping techniques) in the archaeological record with 100 percent accuracy.

It should be emphasized that ambiguity arises, not in the relation between behavioral input and morphological output, because that appears to be relatively predictable. Rather, ambiguity arises from the fact that even for a skilled flintknapper, some billet thinning flakes are longer than some cobble thinning flakes (even though the reverse is true on average), and some shaping flakes are longer than some thinning flakes (even though the reverse is usually true). In other words, although morphology accurately represents behavior, behavior is not always consistent or in accordance with what is intended.

Let us return to the issue of the validity of the cognitive reconstruction. What needs to be made clear is that in the test-case experiment, the analysts studied the flake scars and made judgments about what kind of behaviors probably produced the flake scars. When the results were scored, however, the analysts' judgments were not compared to actual behavior but to the behaviors *intended* by the flintknappers, i.e., to the behaviors the flintknappers were instructed to perform by McMahon. As we have already seen, actual behavior does not always reflect intent. For this reason, some of the judgments made by the analysts were not necessarily wrong. Some hard-hammer morpho-units may look like those of soft hammer, or even pressure units, because the hard hammer is applied in such a way that the resulting force is not typical of the force usually produced by a hard hammer.

In other words, the morphology of a flake scar is not the result of a single variable such as "tool employed" but results from the interaction of a number of variables. Therefore, saying that a flake scar looks like it was produced by pressure thinning may be quite accurate even though a hammerstone was, in fact, used. What this all means is that the test case was not really as good an experiment as it should have been. An ideal experiment would supply three kinds of data: the intent of the flintknapper, the flintknapper's actual behavior (composed of numerous interacting input variables), and the resulting morphological gestalt. McMahon's study documented four behavioral attributes and two morphological attributes, but of course, there are many more. An ideal experiment would control for all the behavioral variables possible and analyze all the resulting flake scars—which could be in the thousands. Moreover, the ideal experiment would supply data on the nature of the connection between input and output variables, i.e., how the input gestalt was translated into forces and stresses that create flake-scar morphologies.

It should be apparent that an ideal experiment is not practical. Although individual variables can be controlled for, one at a time, using mechanical procedures (see Bonnichsen 1977), it is not realistic to attempt to control for all possible input conditions in a real-life situation. Even if the technological and financial resources were available, conducting comprehensive experiments would be complicated by the fact that the behavior of a flintknapper is not constant—in the sense that a given behavior unit is not always executed in the same way. Some of this variation is due to error or lack of control, but, paradoxically, it can also be due to skill. Part of the skill of a flintknapper lies in being able to adjust input variables such as angle and speed of impactor in accordance with changing feedback from emerging morphology.

Until more adequate experiments can be designed and implemented, we will have to settle for comparing flake-scar morphology with the intent of the experimental craftperson. This is not entirely unreasonable, because McMahon was able to show that actual behavior does approximate intent. Since we are dealing with approximations, however, we should not expect an analyst's score to be much higher than the 80% recorded in the experiment related above. Given the fact that a flintknapper's behavior does not always accurately reflect intent, and that behavior units are not necessarily discrete, it is perhaps surprising that the results of the test case were as good as they were.

This is not to say that we cannot further improve the accuracy of cognitive reconstruction. For example, Young and Douglas mistook hard-hammer and soft-hammer techniques nearly one-third of the time. Although some confusion of the two is understandable, given the fact that they produce flake scars that overlap morphologically, it should be possible to further improve our accuracy by using additional attributes. J. Tomenchuk (1985), for example, argues on the basis of his Ph.D. dissertation research that it is possible to distinguish between hard-hammer and soft-hammer techniques using attributes such as "fracture wings" and "Wallner lines."

Future Research

From the above, it is obvious that, despite the promising results obtained in the test case described above, we need to refine our analytic methods by developing better attributes and by devising better experiments. Because of the time and resources involved in this kind of research, it should involve a collaborative effort among those interested in experimental flintknapping and the reconstruction of past production systems.

For this to happen, there is a pressing need for standardization of concepts, definitions, and analytic procedures. Flintknappers tend to be individualists with their own flintknapping styles and methods of analysis developed over years of experience. Despite their obvious skills in fashioning beautiful artifacts, flintknappers do not necessarily possess the ability to analyze their own work objectively nor the theoretical skills to relate their analyses to the archaeological record. Thus, there must be collaboration, not only among flintknappers themselves, but among flintknappers, archaeologists, and cultural anthropologists.

We also need to find ways to translate qualitative judgments into programming instructions, which will allow video imaging equipment to perform coding and analytic operations involved in describing prehistoric stone tools. Although these aids may never equal the ability of the human mind to perform gestalt judgments, they can at least provide the analyst with systematic observations (and the more mechanical analytic operations). It is essential to automate the process as much as possible in order to maximize standardization and replicability—two essential ingredients if the cognitive approach, or any other approach, is to attain the status of a science. Qualitative observations made by an experienced and sensitive analyst may be hard to match, but if there are hundreds of analysts all using qualitative approaches, there is no hope of producing the cumulative results that allow a science to progress.

Automation of as many of the coding and analytic procedures as possible would also help make the cognitive approach usable by more people. At the present time, the analytic procedures are too time-consuming to be attractive to most archaeologists. It is essential to develop computerized aids simple enough to be used by archaeologists in the field. In addition, it would be desirable to have a centralized laboratory that would have the equipment necessary to perform more sophisticated descriptive and analytic procedures when desired. For example, the aircraft industry has visual-scanning devices capable of measuring and quantifying microscopic differences in the surface morphology of aircraft surfaces. This digitized information can then be used to reconstruct surface topologies for visual and statistical analysis on a computer. Such equipment, however, is far too expensive to be owned by individual analysts. Collaborative endeavors among both individuals and institutions is mandatory.

CONCLUSION

There appear to be grounds for assuming that a cognitive approach is capable of inferring behavior on the basis of flake-scar morphology, with a reasonably high degree of accuracy. Analytic models based upon such reconstructions, however, should be approached with caution due to the fact that there was probably a certain amount of overlap in both the behavior units and corresponding morpho-units of prehistoric craftpersons. What this means in terms of analysis is that the artifacts in prehistoric assemblages should not be separated into different groupings on the basis of superficial differences. Rather than focus upon minor differences in individual morpho-units (and the behavior units presumed to be responsible for the morpho units) exhibited by artifacts, it is wiser to focus upon inferred production grammars as a whole (represented in flow diagrams and attached rules).

In other words, armed with as much detailed information about the morphologies of individual flake scars on an artifact as possible, the cognitive researcher must move ahead to consider the *logic* behind the artifact as a whole. For example, two projectile points may be made by the same craftperson, using the same production grammar (repertoire plus rules) and the same type of material, and yet may exhibit differences in morpho-units. This is because two different pieces of rock, even if obtained from the same source, present different problems due to a variety of factors such as internal flaws or mistakes made by the craftperson.

Despite these differences, the skilled analyst should be able to reconstruct many of the specific problems encountered by the craftperson and explain why particular flake-removing strategies were formulated in response to these problems. Analyzing artifacts in this way means getting at the logic behind the morphologies of individual flake scars and their sequencing. In many cases, a similar logic will become evident for two or more artifacts whose morphologies appear to be different at a superficial level. Likewise, artifacts that exhibit considerable overlap in terms of presumed behavior units employed may nevertheless exhibit an overall logic that differs significantly.

Thus, although it is important to develop better attributes and to automate descriptive and analytic procedures for analyzing flake scars, there is an equal need to train analysts who know enough about flintknapping (either first hand or from working with flintknappers) to be able to understand the logic behind prehistoric artifacts. Only in this way can prehistoric artifacts be sorted into meaningful groupings suggestive of different production grammars—which in turn may be suggestive of different cultural affiliations.

To return to the issues raised in the first part of this paper, to the extent that the cognitive approach focuses upon reconstructing past production grammars on the basis of experimental analogs, it is an example of low-level theory. To the extent that the reconstruction of past production grammars allows prehistoric artifacts to be sorted into groups suggestive of cultural or ethnic affiliation, the cognitive approach makes a contribution to middle-range theory.

The cognitive approach by itself is not capable of reconstructing the number of cultural or ethnic groups represented in one assemblage, or group of assemblages. All the cognitive approach can do is to determine whether or not part of the variation represented in an assemblage, or group of assemblages, may be due to differences in underlying production logic—as opposed to variation resulting from differences in material, function, use, or natural processes. If there is a suggestion that the artifacts under analysis exhibit different patterns of underlying logic, it is then possible to ask the question of "why"? Are these differences in production logic due to the introduction of "foreign" items through trade? Are they due to the fact that more than one group occupied the same camp site? Or are they due to the fact that the group may have been sufficiently large or complex to tolerate different production grammars within the same community? The latter possibility does not seem likely on the basis of ethnographic evidence, but it cannot be ruled out. The lithic data alone cannot answer these questions. At this point, more traditional types of archaeological data, such as use-wear data, information on flora and fauna found in association with the artifacts, etc., must be introduced.

Despite the inability of the cognitive approach to answer mid-range theoretical questions on its own, it has a vital role to play in the sense that mid-range theory is only as good as the classification systems upon which it is built. The primary contention of this paper is that classifying lithic artifacts on the basis of size, shape, and gross morphology is not good enough. One of the characteristics of an ethnic or cultural group, if it is to be distinguished meaningfully from other groups, is some degree of uniqueness in how it structures the world. Differences in how the world is structured are expressed in the grammars that members of the group use to produce appropriate behavior, to speak appropriately, and to manufacture appropriate artifacts. Most of these grammars do not leave a tangible trace and cannot be reconstructed. Fortunately, production grammars are an exception because they leave traces in finished artifacts. Although considerations such as size and shape play a role in the decision-making process, much more detailed information is provided by the subtle details of flake-scar morphology and the patterning of flake scars on an artifact. If one of the goals of mid-range theory is to reconstruct the existence of prehistoric ethnic or cultural groups on the basis of material evidence, it is essential to describe and classify the material evidence in an appropriate manner.

In other words, classification systems can be constructed in a variety of ways—depending upon the purposes for which they are intended. If the concept of grammar is essential to defining culture (and cultural groups), it seems appropriate that artifact classification systems should also be based upon grammatical concepts. In brief, the cognitive approach to lithic analysis provides a theory and a methodology for linking low-range and mid-range approaches to the interpretation of prehistory. It is only one tool among many, but it deserves serious consideration.

Table 4. Definition of Variables Used in Defining Behavior Units (from Young and Bonnichsen 1984).

Column 1 (Extent of Effect)

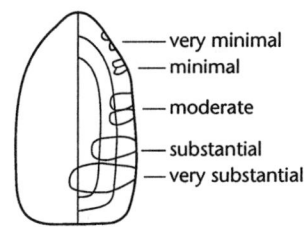

1. *Very minimal* — Restricted to edge rubs (abrade buffet, or pressure rub), results in a dulling or blunting of the edge
2. *Minimal* — Flake scars restricted to margin of artifact—that portion of a face extending from the edge approximately one-third toward the midline
3. *Moderate* — Flake scars extend not less than one-third and not more than two-thirds towards the midline.
4. *Substantial* — Flake scars extend not less than two-thirds toward the midline and no farther than the midline.
5. *Very substantial* — Flakes extend over the midline

Table 4 (continued)

Column 2 (Type of Behavior)

10. *Rub*		Edge rub units involve rubbing the edge of the artifact to blunt it slightly and thereby strengthen the platform in preparation for subsequent flaking activity. Edge rubs can also be used to isolate a platform or to smooth the edge after flaking activity has occurred. In either case, the amount of material removed is very minimal.
20. *Shear*		Shearing involves pressing the flat side of a tool against the artifact edge and slowly twisting it (either perpendicularly or diagonally) across the edge.
30. *Pressure*		Pressure is the type of force that occurs when the top of a pointed tool is set on the edge of the artifact and then pushed either inward or downward (or both) with increasing force.
40. *Direct percussion*		Percussion refers to a blow with a tool such as a hammerstone or billet to the topside (from the craftperson's view) or edge of the artifact.
50. *Indirect percussion*		Indirect percussion (not encountered in this case study) involves placing a tool such as an antler on the edge of the artifact and hitting it with another tool.

Column 2, Second-order distinctions

Abrade	Rubbing the edge of the artifact with a back and forth movement, parallel to the edge, with an abrasive tool such as a rock (grinder).
Buffet	Dragging a tool such as the flat side of an antler across the edge of an artifact.
Pressure rub	Rubbing across the edge with the top of a pointed tool such as a pressure flaker; usually the artifact is held flat so the pressure rub can be applied downward; if the tip of the pressure flaker is applied in an upward motion it can be referred to as a "pressure flick."
Thin	Thinning involves the removal of relatively long thin flakes from the underside of the artifact by the application of force at an acute angle to the edge of the specimen. Although the top face is slightly affected by the total or partial removal of the platform, the underside is much more drastically affected. The result is to thin the specimen much more rapidly than the margins are moved in.
Shape	Shaping, on the other hand, involves the more or less perpendicular application of force behind the edge of the top face of the specimen. This rapidly and efficiently removes large chunks of material we call shaping flakes. The result is to move the margins in at a much faster rate than the specimen is thinned.

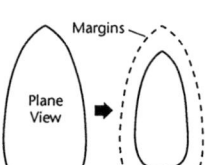

Column 3 (tool employed)

10. *Hammerstone*	A rounded rock used in percussion work.
20. *Grinder*	A smooth stone or split cobble used to rub the edge of an artifact; Callahan uses the edge (formed by splitting a cobble) for shearing, and may occasionally use the rounded portion for percussion.

Table 4 (continued)

30. *Pressure flaker*	A pointed tool used to concentrate and deliver the force to a highly specified point with a pressure technique.	
40. *Billet*	A blunt, relatively resilient tool, such as antler or wood, used in percussion work, direct or indirect.	

Table 5. Definition of Prefixes Used to Transform Behavior Units into Production Units (from Young and Bonnichsen 1984).

Series A: Core

01 *Face-creating*	Removing a material such as cortex from a core to create a face from which flakes can be struck (for making artifacts) or which can be used as a striking platform; it is often necessary to create two adjacent faces: one to be used as a platform and the other to be used for flake removal.	
02 *Edge-dulling*	Blunting an overly thin edge so that it will not crush when used as a platform for the removal of flakes; can also be used to smooth an edge after the removal of flakes; involves rubbing the edge.	
03 *Edge-thickening*	Removing the overly thin edge with a pressure, percussion, or shear technique so the edge will not crush when used as a platform for the removal of flakes; the difference between units 02 and 03 is in the technique used (rubbing vs. flaking or shearing) and in the amount of material removed.	
04 *Margin-contouring*	Removing material on the margin(s) of an artifact in order to achieve the desired thinness and curvature near the edge; margin-contouring may involve reducing the edge angle (if the margin near the edge is overly thick); if, however, the margin is too flat, contouring may require increasing the edge angle.	
05 *Face-paring*	Removing thinning flakes from a face of a core after cortex has been removed; goal is to strike off flakes suitable for making into artifacts.	

Series B: Flake Edge

20 *Edge-dulling*	See Unit 02 above.
21 *Edge-thickening*	See Unit 03 above.

Table 5 (continued)

22	*Edge angle-reducing*	Thinning the margin on one or both faces in order to reduce the angle at which the two faces meet; edge angle correction of this sort is usually preparatory to the removal of substantial thinning flakes; it can also precede edge shearing.
23	*Edge-centering*	Removing material on the margins of both faces so that when viewed in cross-section, the edge where the two faces meet wavers as little as possible and is equidistant between the two faces.
24	*Edge-straightening*	Removing projecting material so that when viewed from the top (rather than in cross-section), the edge wavers as little as possible.
25	*Edge-regularizing*	Edge strengthening, reducing, straightening, and centering—all in one operation; this is most efficiently accomplished with a shearing movement around the edge from one face to the other; it can also be accomplished by techniques such as bifacial thinning and shaping.

Series C: Flake Margin

30	*Margin-regularizing*	Removing irregularities on the margin of an artifact; a primary source of such irregularities is the inter-flake scar ridges left by the previous removal of flakes; may also be used to eliminate step fractures or flake scars with abrupt terminations on margin.
31	*Margin-contouring*	See Unit 04 above.
32	*Margin-beveling*	Removing short, flat flakes on the margin of an artifact in order to create a solid platform for the removal of thinning flakes; margin beveling is created on the underside (from the craftsman's view) and usually involves the use of minimal shaping or thinning units.
33	*Margin-moving*	Removing a portion of the margin in order to move the margins inward—thereby shaping the artifact and decreasing the area enclosed by the outline form.
34	*Platform-isolating*	Removing small notches on either side of area to be used as a platform for removal of a thinning flake; notching helps direct the force so it moves toward the center of the artifact rather than spreading out; sometimes a notch is used to provide a place to set the tip of a pressure flaker so that it will not slip off the edge.

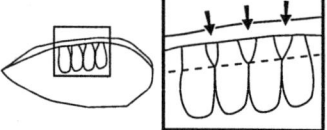
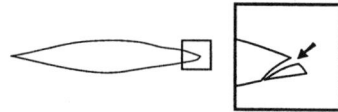
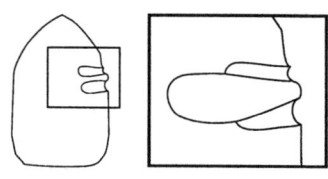

Table 5 (continued)

35 *Ridge-creating*	Removing material on the margin of an artifact in order to create a straight ridge that can be used to provide access to the interior of the artifact.	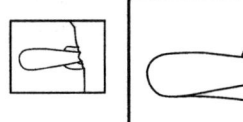

Series D: Flake Face or Side

40 *Face-paring*	Removing flakes from the underside in order to thin the artifact; although face-paring may also remove a portion of the top face (thereby moving in the margins of the artifact), a thinning flake is at least twice as long as the depth of the platform area; this means the artifact is thinned faster than the contours are moved in.	
41 *Side-reducing*	In addition to the upper and lower face, a flake can also have a side (often consisting of the platform); side-reduction involves removing this third face in order to achieve a flake with two faces only.	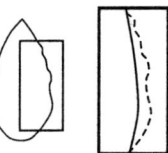

Series E: Flake Finishing

50 *Notch-creating*	Removing material from both faces in order to create a notch—presumably for hafting purposes.	
51 *Flute-creating*	Removing a thinning flake from the base toward the tip (or vice versa) so as to cross-cut the intersection of flakes originating on both lateral edges; a flute may extend only part way along the length of the artifact or it may extend the entire distance.	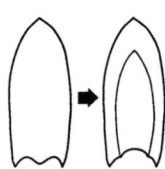
52 *Contour-correcting*	Final correcting of the edge (plane view) in order to create a symmetrical artifact.	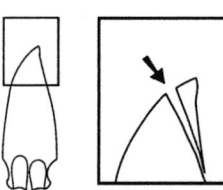
53 *Edge-dulling*	Abrading or buffeting the edge of the artifact so that the finished edge is dull to the touch; presumably, edge-dulling is to prevent damage to hafting materials; edges most commonly dulled for this purpose are the base and stem (or notches).	 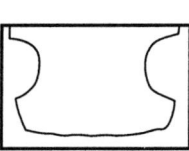

Table 5 (continued)

54 *Base/stem-paring*	Final thinning of base and/or stem, presumably for hafting.	
55 *Face-regularizing*	Final flake removals designed to regularize flake-scar patterning on faces of artifact.	

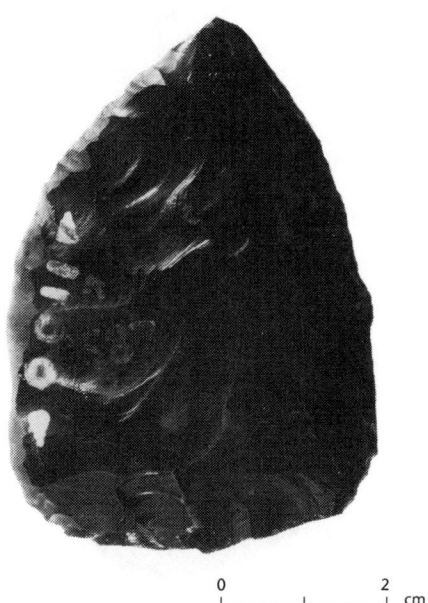

Figure 5. 1100 Edge preparation (unspecified).

Figure 6. 1200 Moderate percussion shape with cobble (expert).

Figure 7. 1300 (left) Edge preparation (unspecified).

Figure 8. 1400 Moderate percussion shape with cobble (novice).

Figure 9. 2100 Moderate percussion shape with billet (expert).

Figure 10. 3100 (left) Moderate percussion thin with billet (expert). 3200 (right) Moderate percussion shape with billet (novice).

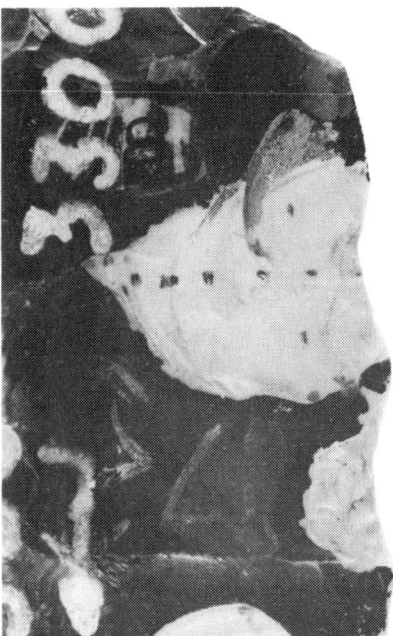

Figure 11. 3300 Substantial percussion thin with cobble (failed)(expert).

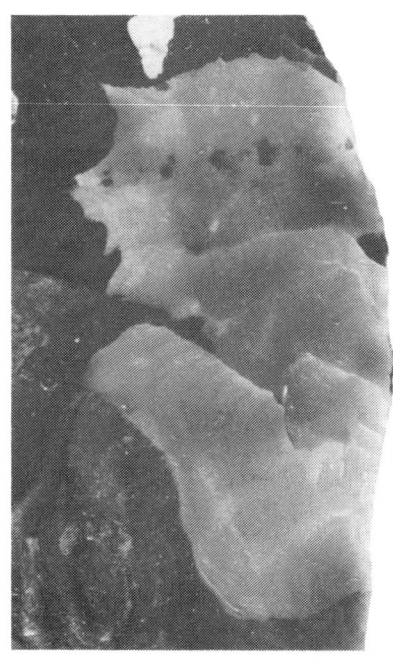

Figure 12. 4100 Moderate percussion thin with cobble (expert).

Figure 13. 4200 (top) Moderate percussion thin with cobble (novice). 5100 (bottom) Moderate percussion thin with cobble (novice).

Figure 14. 5200 Moderate percussion thin with billet (novice).

Figure 15. 5300 (top) Substantial percussion thin with cobble (expert).

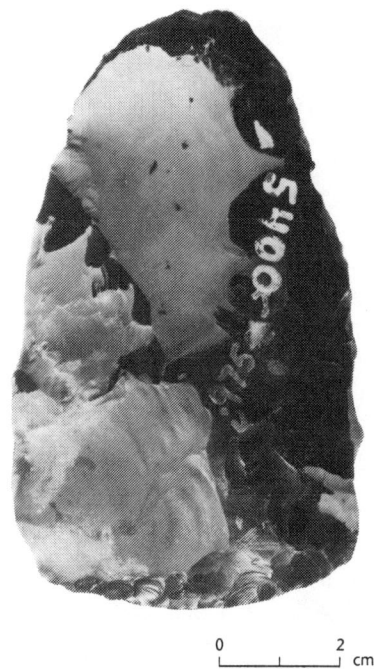

Figure 16. 5400 Substantial percussion thin with billet (expert).

REFERENCES CITED

Binford, L. R.
- 1981 *Bones: Ancient Men and Modern Myths.* Academic Press, New York.
- 1983 *In Pursuit of the Past.* Academic Press, New York.

Bonnichsen, R.
- 1977 *Models for Deriving Cultural Information from Stone Tools.* National Museum of Man, Archaeological Survey of Canada, Mercury Series 60, Ottawa.
- 1989 Construction of Taphonomic Models: Theories, Assumptions and Procedures. In *Bone Modification,* edited by R. Bonnichsen and M. H. Sorg, pp. 515–526. Center for the Study of the First Americans, University of Maine, Orono.
- 1991 Clovis Origins. In *Clovis Origins and Adaptations,* edited by R. Bonnichsen and K. Turnmire, pp. 309–330. Center for Study of the First Americans, Oregon State University, Corvallis.

Bonnichsen, R., and D. E. Young
- 1980 Early Technological Repertoires: Bone to Stone. *Canadian Journal of Anthropology* 1(1):123–128.

Boutin-Sweet, M.
- 1986 *A Cognitive Analysis of Stone Tool Production.* Unpublished M.A. thesis, Department of Anthropology, University of Alberta, Edmonton.

Bradley, B. A.
- 1985 Lithic Reduction Sequences: A Glossary and Discussion. In *Lithic Technology: Making and Using Stone Tools,* edited by E. H. Swanson, pp. 5–13. The Hague.

Callahan, E.
- 1979 The Basics of Biface Knapping in the Eastern Fluted Point Tradition: A Manual for Flintknappers and Lithic Analysts. *Archaeology of Eastern North America* 7:1–179.

Cotterell, B., and J. Kaminga
- 1979 The Mechanics of Flaking. In *Lithic Use-Wear Analysis,* edited by Brian Hayden, pp. 97–112. Academic Press, New York.

Crabtree, D. E.
- 1972 An Introduction to Flintworking. *Occasional Papers of the Idaho State University Museum* 28. Pocatello.

Dictionary of Geological Terms
- 1962 Prepared by American Geological Institute. Dolphin Books, Doubleday & Company, Inc., Garden City.

Douglas, D.
- 1988 *Lithic Technology and Artifact Morphology: An Analysis of Correlations between Decision-Making, Behavior, Force, and Artifact Morphology in Stone Tool Production.* Unpublished honors thesis, Department of Anthropology, University of Alberta, Edmonton.

Ericson, J. E.
- 1984 Toward the Analysis of Lithic Production Systems. In *Prehistoric Quarries and Lithic Production,* edited by J. E. Ericson and B. A. Purdy, pp. 1–9. Cambridge University Press, Cambridge.

Feibleman, J. K.
- 1954 Theory of Integrative Levels. *British Journal for the Philosophy of Science* 5:59–66.

Flenniken, J. J.
- 1981 Replicative systems Analysis: A Model Applied to the Vein quartz Artifacts from the Hoko River Site. *Washington State University Laboratory of Anthropology Reports of Investigations,* No. 59.
- 1985 Stone Tool Reduction Techniques as Cultural Markers. In *Essays in Honor of Don E. Crabtree,* edited by M. G. Plew, J. C. Woods, and M. G. Pavesic, pp. 265–276. University of New Mexico Press, Albuquerque.

Gould, R. A.
- 1980 *Living Archaeology.* Cambridge University Press, Cambridge.

Gould, R. A., and S. Saggers
- 1985 Lithic Procurement in Central Australia: A Closer Look at Binford's Idea of Embeddedness in Archaeology. *American Antiquity* 50:117–135.

Grayson, D. K.
- 1986 Eoliths, Archaeological Ambiguity, and the Generation of "Middle-Range" Research. In *American Archaeology Past and Future,* edited by D. J. Meltzer, D. D. Fowler, and J. A. Sabloff, pp. 77–134, Smithsonian Institution Press, Washington D.C.

Hayden, B.
- 1979 *Lithic Use-Wear Analysis,* edited by B. Hayden, pp.113–121, Academic Press, New York.

Keeley, L. H.
- 1980 *Experimental Determination of Stone Tool Uses: A Microwear Analysis.* University of Chicago Press.

Kriger, A.
- 1944 The Typological Concept. *American Antiquity* 3:271–288.

Lawrence, R.
- 1979 Experimental Evidence for the Significance of Attributes Used in Edge-Damage Analysis. In *Lithic Use-Wear Analysis,* edited by B. Hayden, pp. 113–121 Academic Press, New York.

McGrew, W. C.
   1987 Tools to Get Food: the Subsistence of Tasmanian Aborigines and Tanzanian Chimpanzees Compared. *Journal of Anthropological Research* 43:247–258.

McMahon, J. P.
   1988 *A Biomechanical Study of Flintknapping.* M.A. thesis, University of Maine, Orono.

Muto, G. R.
   1971 A Stage Analysis of the Manufacture of Stone Tools. In *Great Basin Anthropological Conference 1970: Selected Papers,* edited by C. M. Aiken, pp. 109–118 University of Oregon Anthropological Papers 1. Eugene.

Newcomer, M. R., Grace and R. Unger-Hamilton
   1986 Investigating Microwear Polishes with Blind Tests. *Journal of Archaeological Science* 13:207–217.

Odell, G. H.
   1986 Review of Use-Wear Analysis of Flaked Stone Tools, by Patrick C. Vaughan. *Lithic Technology* 15:115–120.
   1988 Addressing Prehistoric Hunting Practices through Stone Tool Analysis. *American Anthropologist* 90:335–355.

Plew, M. G., J. C. Woods, and M. G. Pavesic (editors)
   1985 *Stone Tools Analysis: Essays in Honor of Don E. Crabtree.* University of New Mexico Press, Albuquerque.

Pollock J.
   1984 *A Technological Analysis of Lake Abitibi Bifaces.* Unpublished Ph.D. dissertation, Department of Anthropology, University of Alberta, Edmonton.

Shafer, H. J.
   1985 A Technological Study of Two Maya Workshops at Colha, Belize. In *Stone Tools Analysis: Essays in Honor of Don E. Crabtree,* edited by M. G. Plew, J. C. Woods, and M. G. Pavesic, pp. 277–315. University of New Mexico Press, Albuquerque.

Schnurrenberger, D., and A. L. Bryan
   1985 A Contribution to the Study of the Naturefact/Artifact Controversy. In *Stone Tool Analysis: Essays in Honor of Don. E. Crabtree,* edited by M. G. Plew, J. C. Woods, and M. G. Pavesic, pp. 133–159. University of New Mexico Press, Albuquerque.

Spaulding, A. C.
   1964 The Dimensions of Archaeology and Archaeology. In *Physical Anthropology and Archaeology,* edited by P. B. Hammond, pp. 209–223. MacMillan, New York.

Swanson, E. H., Jr., and B. R. Butler
   1962 The First Conference of Western Archaeologists on Problems of Point Typology. *Occasional Papers of the Idaho State College Museum* Number 10. Pocatello.

Swartz, L.
   1986 *Quantitative Analysis of Experimental Lithic Material.* Unpublished manuscript on file with the Project for the Study of Material Culture (D. Young, director), Department of Anthropology, University of Alberta, Edmonton.

Tomenchuk, J.
   1985 *The Development of a Wholly Parametric Use-Wear Methodology and its Application to Two Selected Samples of Epipaleolithic Chipped Stone Tools from Hayonim Cave, Israel.* Unpublished Ph.D. dissertation, University of Toronto, Toronto.

Young, D. E.
   1989 How Powerful are Archaeological Inferences Based Upon Experimental Replication? In *Bone Modification,* edited by R. Bonnichsen and M. H. Sorg, pp. 53–63. Center for the Study of the First Americans, University of Maine, Orono.

Young, D. E., and R. Bonnichsen
   1984 *Understanding Stone Tools: A Cognitive Approach.* Center for the Study of the First Americans, University of Maine, Orono.

An Application of Nitrocellulose Membrane for the Identification of Blood Residues on Artifactual Materials

DAVID C. HYLAND
Director, Organic Residues Laboratory
Mercyhurst Archaeological Institute
Erie, PA 16546

JAMES M. ADOVASIO
Professor and John E. Boyle, Chair
Departments of Anthropology/Archaeology and Geology
Mercyhurst College
Erie, PA 16546

JEAN M. TERSAK, M.D.
Childrens Hospital
Pittsburgh, PA

MICHAEL I. SIEGEL
Professor and Chair
Department of Anthropology
University of Pittsburgh
Pittsburgh, PA 15260

Recent progress in laboratory analyses has enabled researchers to examine and identify blood antigen residues adhering to artifactual materials present in the archaeological record. This capability is dependent upon the biological activity of the sample. While the taphonomic processes affecting hemoglobin and its "lifespan" are yet to be fully understood, current research demonstrates that detection and identification procedures can be successfully employed to analyze blood-bearing materials several millennia old.

To date, a number of different methods have been utilized to determine the species of origin of residual blood: Ouchterlony double immunodiffusion (Downs 1985), crystallography (Loy 1983, 1987a), isoelectric focusing (Loy 1987a, 1987b; Loy and Nelson 1987; Nelson et al. 1986; Sinclair and Slattery 1982), cross-over immunoelectrophoresis (Barr 1989; Newman and Julig 1989), and radioimmunoassay (Lowenstein 1985, 1986).

The enzyme immunoassay (EIA), as developed by the authors, utilizes a nitrocellulose protein-binding membrane and affinity-absorbed antibodies. This procedure has shown that it is possible to retain both specificity and sensitivity in a technique conducive to the rigors of archaeological field work and the vicissitudes of differential preservation.

However, due to shared-reactivity, species identification of blood residue using immunological techniques can be problematic when it is necessary to distinguish individual species within a single genus or family. Recent work has shown that careful refinement of antisera can reduce shared-reactivity, thereby increasing specificity (Berkeley Antibody Company, personal communication 1987). This refinement is accomplished by absorbing any antibodies from the antisera that may cross-react with antigenic sites held in common by closely related species. Experimental work with known samples has demonstrated that these enzyme immunoassays can distinguish taxa below the rank category of family (i.e., genus and species).

The ramifications of the successful, wide-scale implementation of this technique are discussed in terms of Paleoindian artifact function as well as paleoeconomic, paleoenvironmental, and paleodietary reconstruction, using case studies from various portions of the Americas.

INTRODUCTION

Discussions of the current status of American archaeology often dichotomize the field by suggesting that it is proceeding along two distinct lines of investigation: theoretical refinement and furtherance of methodology. While it is understandable that these two scientific realms might be treated synthetically as separate entities, it is a commonplace that methodological progress is necessary to progress in theory and vice versa. Science consists of both the accumulation of facts and the eduction of principles (Youmans 1874). Comprehensive histories of science do not often present a scientifically balanced composition, however. In general, most attention is paid to theory. This is true of American archaeology as well (e.g., Willey and Sabloff 1980), and this tendency is comprehensible in light of the great strides made in archaeological theory in the past 40 years. Nevertheless, a good argument can be made that progress in field data-recovery methods and laboratory analyses has outstripped progress in theory-building. Archaeology has always been a heavily derivative pursuit, and it has borrowed widely from many other disciplines. The incorporation of methods and procedures developed in other fields into the suite of archaeological investigation strategies has never been greater than it is today. Even within the analytical realm, however, most technical treatises rely upon procedures derived from physics and chemistry (e.g., Leute 1987; Parkes 1986). This is probably a function both of the length of time that particular techniques have been employed and an emphasis on artifact age determination in many archaeological projects. A wealth of new procedures, developed in the fields of biochemistry and molecular biology, are rapidly becoming available today, however, that have important applicability in archaeological studies. For example, a number of techniques have been developed in recent years to determine the species of origin of blood residues found on artifactual materials (Downs 1985; Hyland et al. 1989; Lowenstein 1985; Loy 1983; Nelson et al. 1986; Oates et al. 1983). The implications of this work are many and varied. These techniques can provide both corroborative and direct evidence on tool manufacture and function, faunal environment, and animal utilization. They therefore deserve the serious consideration of contemporary archaeologists.

Successful detection and identification of blood antigen is dependent upon the biological activity of the sample. Sensabaugh et al. (1971) have reported the retention of significant levels of enzymatic and immunochemical activity in an eight-year-old sample of dried human blood. Others have noted that proteins have remained biologically active in 20-year-old freeze-dried specimens, in whole blood solutions stored for over 40 years, and in germinating seeds that have been dormant for 2000 years (Sensabaugh et al. 1971). The enzyme immunoassay (EIA) procedure described in this report successfully identified (with 100% accuracy) prepared test samples of three different, known species of blood that were incubated for eight hours at temperatures up to 51° C. Due to extensive denaturation, only the experimental group that was boiled failed to show any reactivity (Tersak and Hyland 1988). Thus, mounting experimental evidence indicates that proteinaceous material can remain relatively stable for many years under a variety of environmental and depositional regimes.

While the persistence of reactive proteins in the archaeological record may be quite astounding, at present it is not known to what degree proteins are inherently stable or whether particular preservation factors might account for their long-term endurance. This issue requires additional research, the results of which may necessitate changes in methods of artifact recovery. Loy (1983) suggests that electrostatic interactions with soil clay particles are responsible for the protection of proteins from microbial attack and removal by ground water. The experimental work of Gurfinkel and Franklin (1988), which indicates that hemoglobin does bind to soil and clay particles, tends to confirm Loy's (1983) hypothesis. Thus, removal of adherent soil from the surface of an artifact may result in a substantial loss of blood antigen. However, in the case of Gurfinkel and Franklin (1988), it should be noted that hemoglobin solutions were applied directly to soil and clay particles and allowed to dry. Further testing is needed to determine the extent to which proteins that have dried on the artifact surface prior to deposition can be preserved via electrostatic interactions.

In their detailed analysis of a dehydrated sample of blood, Sensabaugh et al. (1971) suggest that dried blood proteins are continually and gradually modified through aggregation, whereby proteins covalently cross-link to form a single proteinaceous mass with a high molecular weight. This physicochemical modification results in markedly decreased solubility, thus protecting the protein from removal by water (Sensabaugh et al. 1971). Sensabaugh et al. (1971) also state that cross-linked proteins have lowered levels of biological activity, making difficult the detection and identification of blood antigen. However, the utilization of immunosorbent preparation techniques has demonstrated that cross-linked antigens retain their ability to react with complementary antibodies (Tijssen 1985:112). Other simulation experiments indicate that organic material suffers substantial and rapid degradation until only low-molecular–weight fragments remain, which then stabilize and form durable, long-lasting residues (Gurfinkel and Franklin 1988). Loy (1983) reports that hemoglobin is protected from degradation by the denaturation of serum proteins, and that exposure to air reduces the oxygenated hemoglobin to a more stable form. Finally, we hypothesize that protein molecules may be conjoined with fatty tissues, resulting in an insoluble complex that is secure against dissolution by water. While many means of protein preservation have been suggested, further experimentation is required to confirm the preservation efficacy of these mechanisms, particularly under various taphonomic conditions. The results of such research will yield crucial information for the construction of archaeological data-recovery programs in the future.

While consideration of blood antigen taphonomy is important, the central problem of blood identification is species determination. At present, five different methods have been employed to determine blood antigen identity. All of these methods depend upon the remarkable ability of protein to retain a level of biological activity over a long period of time. Three of these assays are immunologically based, one utilizes techniques of crystallography, and a fifth technique is based on electrophoretic principles.

Isoelectric focusing is a fairly recent addition to the repertoire of biochemical techniques employed to identify prehistoric blood residues (Loy 1987; Loy and Nelson 1987; Nelson et al. 1986). Originally developed to isolate and prepare particular proteins (Righetti 1983:9), this electrophoric procedure is particularly amenable to the identification of blood samples because of its capability for high-resolution separations (Righetti 1983:10). Isoelectric focusing can separate out and distinguish between different protein macromolecules much more ably than can a classical electrophoretic system (Righetti 1983:338). Thus, low taxonomic distinctions are possible. Nelson et al. (1986) employed isoelectric focusing to identify blood residues eluted from a 1000-year-old limestone spall-flake found in British Columbia. By comparing the isoelectric points (pI) of known reference samples to those of the unknown blood residue, the species of origin is determined. However, problems of cost and mass-utility remain. While this method has been used with success, further development will be required before it can be used routinely in the study of archaeological materials. Needless to say, this is not a procedure amenable to field operations.

Loy (1983) describes a method that relies on precipitation by "salting-out" crystalline hemoglobin. Hemoglobin crystals are characterized by size, shape, surface charge, rate of growth, and attributes of solubility and precipitation. These properties are genetically determined by amino acid sequences and, therefore, are species-specific. Identification is accomplished by comparing crystals grown from blood film on an artifact to those prepared from known specimens. Thus, in this method multiple testing for different species requires only a single sample. However, it should be noted that a sizable sample is needed for effective and sufficient crystallization of the hemoglobin, and this requirement may result in a lower level of detectability (Table 1).

Although the hemoglobin crystalline properties of numerous species have been determined (Loy 1983; Washino 1977), results from the examination of archaeological materials are often obscured by environmental contaminants such as salt crystals (J. Custer, personal communication 1988). Thus, particular care in the interpretation of the results is necessary as crystalline forms other than hemoglobin may be present in the sample. All other blood identification techniques take advantage of the great utility of immunoassays. Developed in the 1960s, immunoassays were originally used to identify antigens present in histological samples (Tijssen 1985:2). Further developments have dramatically expanded the range of application of these powerful procedures. The effectiveness of immunoassays is primarily due to the nature of the antibody/antigen reaction. Antibodies, produced by the immune system in response to the intrusion of foreign, non-self compounds (antigens), have an extremely high affinity for complementary antigens. Specifically, antibodies have a high affinity for particular antigenic sites or determinants, called epitopes, which are located on the antigen. Careful control of this immunoreaction allows the positive identification of antigens and, by inference, the species of antigen origin.

Several immunoassay methods have been utilized for the study of residual blood. Ouchterlony double-diffusion (Ouchterlony 1968) is a technique that depends upon the diffusion of antigen and antibody through a gel matrix. If immunoreactive, the resulting antigen/antibody complex precipitates in the zone of optimum concentration and forms an opaque line. The identity of an unknown antigen is thus revealed by directly observing the product of its positive reaction with a known antibody. Unfortunately, this method is

Table 1. Comparison of Blood Antigen Identification Techniques.

Technique	Advantages	Disadvantages
Comparative Crystallography	Unlimited comparison with known specimens.	Lowered objectivity. Low detectability.
Ouchterlony Double-Diffusion	—	Low detectability.
Isoelectric Focusing	Multiple species identification possible from from one sample. High detectability.	Potential health hazards (toxins).
Radioimmunoassays (RIAs)	High specificity. High detectability. High sensitivity.	Expensive equipment. Short reagent shelf-life. Potential health hazards (toxins). Radioactive waste disposal. Immunoreactive consumption.
Enzyme Immunoassays (EIAs)	High specificity. Very high detectability. High sensitivity. Inexpensive. Applicable under field conditions.	Potential health hazards (toxins).

subject to low detection limits. The Ouchterlony plates restrict the volume of sample that can be diffused, and amplification procedures are not easily applied, as is possible with radioimmunoassays (RIAs) and enzyme immunoassays (EIAs). (See Table 1.)

As utilized by Lowenstein (1985, 1986), RIAs have offered an effective and reliable means of identifying blood antigen residues. RIAs rely on the reaction between antigen and corresponding antibody, as does Ouchterlony double-diffusion, but they utilize radioactive tracers (labeled to the reactants) as indicators for the detection of that reaction. RIAs have potentially higher detectabilities via the application of secondary antibodies, which effectually amplify the initial reaction (Figure 1). However, while the method employed by Lowenstein has higher levels of detectability, sensitivity, and specificity, this technique has some significant drawbacks. Expensive equipment is required for measuring radioactivity, the reagents have a short shelf life, the plastic used in this procedure is immunoreactive consumptive (necessitating the use of large amounts of reactants), and the disposal of radioactive wastes can be problematic (Tijssen 1985:1). (See Table 1.)

EIAs make use of the "discriminatory" ability of antibodies and employ enzymes conjugated to secondary antibodies as immunoreactant labels (Tijssen 1985:1). The high catalytic power of enzymes confers potentially higher detectabilities than is possible with RIAs (Tijssen 1985:1) and facilitates the identification of nanogram (10^{-9}) to picogram (10^{-12}) quantities of blood antigen. In addition, the equipment required for EIAs is relatively inexpensive, the assays are feasible under archaeological field conditions, and there are no radiation hazards (Tijssen 1985:2). (See Table 1.)

All immunological identification techniques are based on the "discriminatory" power of antibodies. This ability is predicated upon specific structural attributes. As multichain proteins that belong to the immunoglobulin class, antibodies share basic structural features but are physicochemically heterogeneous. The antigen binding fragments (Fab) of an antibody each contain a hypervariable region that creates diversity and specificity (D. R. Davies, personal communication 1988). This region, known as the binding site or paratope, accounts for the heterogeneity of immunoglobulin and permits recognition of and combination with all possible antigenic configurations. Native antisera produced against foreign antigens are polyclonal, that is, they recognize many different epitopes, some of which will certainly be shared by a number of evolutionarily related species. Conversely, monoclonal antibodies are hyperspecific, or capable of recognizing only one epitope; however, they are equally reactive with different antigens bearing an identical, complementary epitope. In other words, epitopes held in common by two or more species cannot be distinguished by monoclonal antibodies, nor is this shared reactivity removable. Monoclonal antibodies can be developed, however, that are capable of recognizing unique, species-specific epitopes. Thus, the desired goal of absolute species specificity is attainable. Removal of shared reactivity exhibited by polyclonal antibodies requires another tactic. (See Discussion for more on polyclonal antibody production.) Utilizing techniques of affinity chromatography, antibodies that recognize non-specific antigenic sites are absorbed out; the result is an affinity-purified polyclonal antibody that is directed against species-specific proteins.

Affinity-purified polyclonal antibodies show great promise for increasing the resolution of hemoglobin identification assays. Likewise, these assays also can be used to identify other proteinaceous residues recovered from archaeological contexts. Unfortunately, affinity-purified polyclonal antibodies, such as those prepared under contract by Berkeley Antibody Company for subsequent projects undertaken by the authors (e.g., Hyland and Anderson 1990), could not be utilized for the present study. The methods employed to elicit and purify these affinity-purified polyclonal antibodies are, nonetheless, described below. The methods employed by BABCo in the purification process are as follows. Fresh red blood cells are first taken from each species presumed to be represented by artifactual blood stains. They are washed with physiological saline, and all serum proteins are removed. Next, the washed erythrocytes are suspended in sterile, distilled water and allowed to lyse. The cell membranes are then removed by centrifugation. The resultant hemoglobins contained within the supernatant are then utilized as immunogens. These immunogens are used to inoculate laboratory rabbits to induce antibody formation. Crude antisera generated against the hemoglobins are then withdrawn from the rabbits and purified using affinity chromatography matrices, which consist of purified hemoglobin from various species closely related to the species used in creating the original immunogen (Figure 2).

By passing the antisera over species-related hemoglobins, cross-reactive antibodies become bound to antigenic sites that are shared by sibling species. The resultant non-cross-reactive antibody is thus species-specific. The antibody is then passed over an affinity matrix bearing the appropriate complementary antigen. This process concentrates and further purifies the antibody. The antibody is finally eluted from the column, and the immunoreactive amount of the antibody (titers) is then determined.

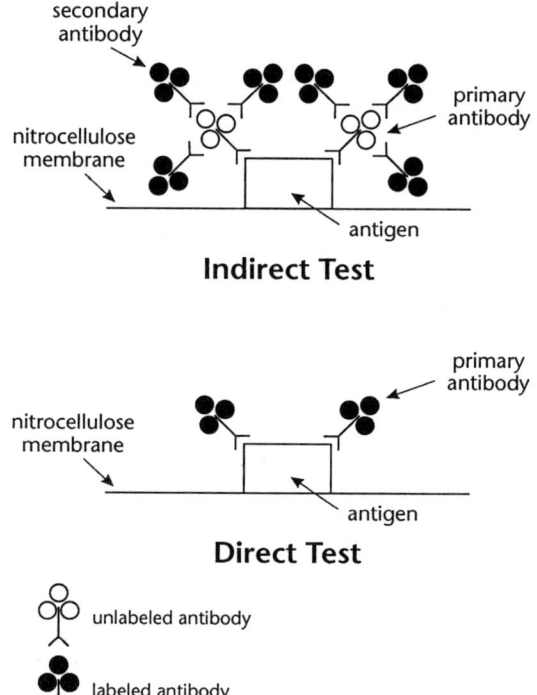

Figure 1. Schematic of indirect and direct tests for detection of antigen/antibody complex, comparing the quantities of enzyme-labeled antibody associated with antigen. Higher detectabilities are possible with the indirect test. (Adapted from Roitt 1984:156, Figure 6.11.)

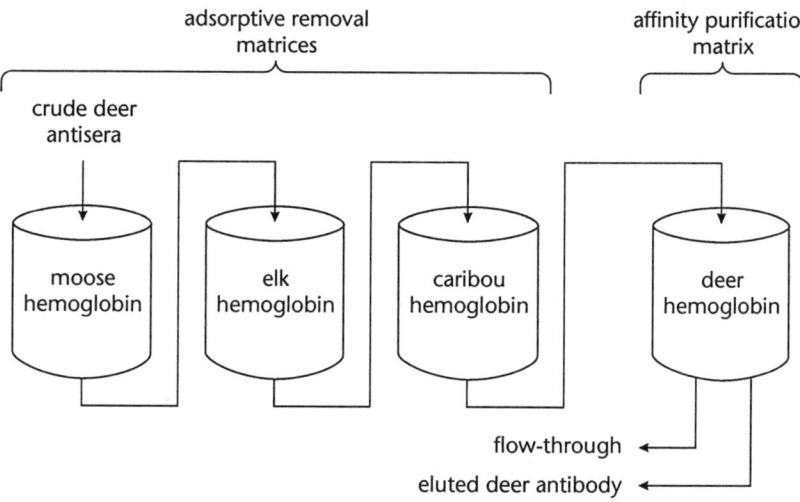

Figure 2. Production of polyclonal deer-specific antibodies. A crude antiserum generated against deer hemoglobins is passed over columns bearing hemoglobin derived from moose, elk, and caribou. After adsorption to each of the columns, the antibody is applied to a column bearing deer hemoglobin. The column is extensively washed, and specific antibodies are eluted with 0.1 M glycine HCl, pH 2.8. (Adapted from Berkeley Antibody Company 1988:11, Figure 3.)

The nemesis of all immunologically based species identification techniques is shared reactivity. While careful control over production and purification of antibodies can eliminate spurious antigenic reactions, the researcher must rigorously and routinely check all antibodies used for species identification purposes against a battery of control specimens.

METHODS

The authors have developed a technique for the detection and identification of blood antigen residues that employs purified polyclonal antibodies and EIAs. This program consists of four phases.

The first phase involves a listing of all fauna temporally and spatially associated with the artifact assemblage to be tested. A representative species of antibody is then selected from this list for use in the identification assay. The second phase is a process designed to extract the blood residue. Initially, all artifacts are scanned for the presence of blood residue under low-power magnification (<10X). Next, using a pipette, a small amount (<100 µl) of Tris buffered saline (1XTBS: 20mM Tris, 500mM NaCl, pH 7.5) is applied to the surface of the artifact, particularly edges and crevices. The solution is agitated with the tip of the pipette during application and is subsequently withdrawn. This sample can be dispensed repeatedly, applied to the artifact, and drawn up before proceeding to phase three. The researcher may also repeat this step using additional quantities of fresh saline.

Phase three tests for the presence of hemoglobin. A minute portion (10–12 µl) of the eluted solution is applied to a Hemastix reagent strip (Miles Laboratories 1980). Due to the effects of auto-oxidation, the test area is compared with the color chart supplied with Hemastix 40 seconds after application, as recommended in the technical notes provided with the reagent strips. The heme group of hemoglobin catalyzes a reaction on the reagent strip, resulting in a color change from orange to dark blue. Although the Hemastix reagent strip also reacts with other substances exhibiting peroxidase-like activity (e.g., chlorophyll), all samples that test positive are subjected to the species identification procedure. Since the EIA is immunologically based, samples testing positive which are in fact false positives due to the presence of chlorophyll or some other environmental contaminant, do not react with the antisera and are recorded as negatives. This eliminates the need for a separate step to distinguish plant from animal residues in the procedure.

The fourth phase of this procedure is the immunoassay. Species identification is accomplished by incubating the antigen with samples of known blood antisera utilizing a vacuum-assisted microfiltration apparatus and a nitrocellulose protein-binding membrane (Figure 3). Subsequent steps involve blocking (blocking solution; 20mM Tris, 500 mM NaCl, 0.75% evaporated milk, pH 7.5) any nonspecific antibody-binding sites and washing the membrane with Tween-20 (1XTTBS; 20mM Tris, 500mM NaCl, 0.05% Tween-20, pH 7.5) to reduce background activity in the assay (Tersak and Hyland 1988). Incubation continues following the application of an enzyme-labeled secondary antibody that reacts with the bound primary antibody. When incubated with the proper chemicals (60 mg 4-chloro-1-napthol in 20ml ice-cold methanol, plus 60 µl ice-cold hydrogen peroxide in 100 ml 1XTBS), the horseradish peroxidase-conjugated antibody catalyzes a colorific reaction. Thus, positive antigen/antibody reactions can be viewed directly and in comparison with positive and negative controls. The identity of the immunoreactive primary antibody indicates the species of origin of the unknown blood residue.

RESULTS

The efficacy of the procedure outlined above was demonstrated in tests using known blood samples that were experimentally baked on lithic material (Tersak and Hyland 1988).

Dilutions of deer, dog, and human blood were applied to 40 artifacts divided into four groups. Group one was allowed to dry at room temperature. Groups two and three were incubated at 37°C and 51°C, respectively, for eight hours. The fourth group was boiled for five minutes. EIAs correctly identified the species of origin of all blood types in groups one, two, and three. Group four showed no immunoreactivity with complementary or noncomplementary antiserum. These results also demonstrate the survivability of blood antigen at ambient temperatures.

A 45-specimen set of lithic artifacts collected from the Shoop Paleoindian site was provided for analysis by K. W. Carr, Bureau for Historic Preservation, Harrisburg, Pennsylvania, and was used for the first archaeological application of this technique. The entire sample was subjected to the initial blood detection procedure. After removing all residue from the tool surface microcrevices, Hemastix reagent strips were used to detect the presence of blood. Positive results were obtained from 13 of the 45 artifacts. Next, controlled EIAs were conducted to test for deer antigen. The primary antibody (deer globulin antiserum produced in rabbit, cat. no. 2433-50-2) employed in the assays was obtained from Difco Laboratories and, unfortunately, proved to be cross-reactive with antigen common to other cervids, in particular, caribou. Experimental assays demonstrated that caribou antigen and anti-deer serum are immunoreactive. Of the 13 specimens tested, colorimetric assays revealed one positive reaction, which is discussed further under Summary and Implications. Four explanations are offered for the negative cases: (1) dirt and other

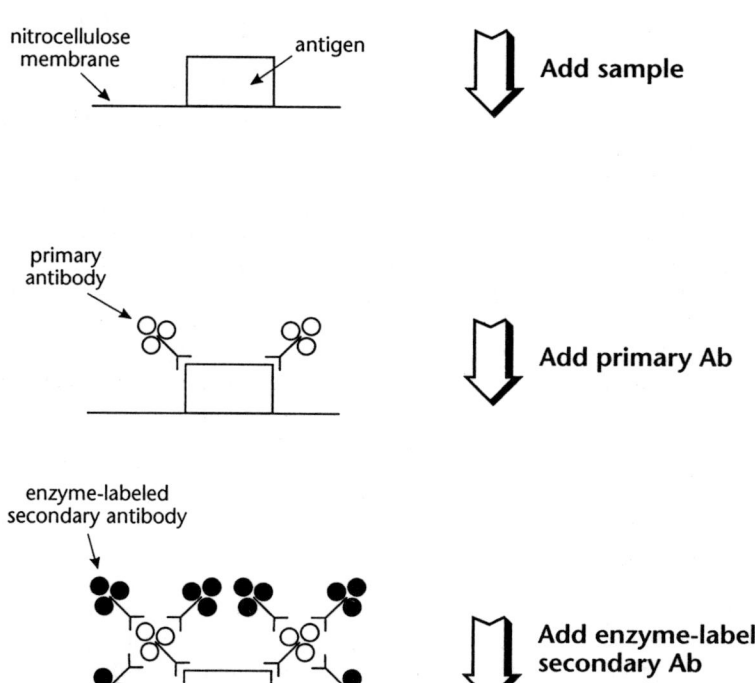

Figure 3. Application of sample and antibodies in the enzyme immunoassay showing the sequential addition and binding of primary and secondary antibodies. Also shown here is the detection-enhancing capability of the secondary antibody.

sediment extracted from the tool may have sufficiently stained the Hemastix reagent strip to be interpreted as hemoglobin positive; (2) environmental contaminants containing cationic substances may have produced false positive reactions with Hemastix; (3) blood antigen of species non-reactive with anti-deer serum may have been present; and (4) immunological activity of the antigen may have been reduced to levels beyond the limits of detectability.

DISCUSSION

This project was initiated in order to test the feasibility of examining a fixed percentage of all lithics recovered from cultural resource management (CRM) localities for the presence of blood antigens. While EIAs have proven effective as presently employed, many aspects of this procedure warrant improvement. Attempts to refine the techniques are currently in progress, and a number of these problems and suggested solutions are discussed below.

Utilizing affinity chromatographic strategies, recent purification efforts designed to eliminate cross-reactivity contained in bison-, antelope-, and elephant-specific antibodies demonstrate that only a minority of the total antibody is species-specific (Berkeley Antibody Company, personal communication 1988). This is due to the overwhelming number of homologous proteins contained in the sera of mammalian species, against which the total antibody is produced. Refinement efforts are further confounded at the family level of relatedness. At this level the number of serum proteins common to all member species is of such magnitude that the absorptive purification process consumes the entire complement of antiserum. In short, the procedure yields no species-specific antibody. Previous attempts at removing from whole anti-deer serum antibodies that are cross-reactive with homologous proteins of elk, moose, and caribou have seen similar results (Berkeley Antibody Company, personal communication 1988). Presently, efforts to overcome these limitations are concentrated on refining antibody produced against hemolysate rather than antibody produce against whole blood (Berkeley Antibody Company, personal communication 1988). This will eliminate the "swamping" effect of homologous serum proteins and produce a species-specific antibody.

Another area under scrutiny is the identification of extremely small quantities of antigen. Although very high detectabilities are associated with EIAs, efforts to expand beyond current limits are merited. It has been suggested (Tijssen 1985:377) that the use of 4% polyethylene glycol (PEG) in the assay both increases detectability and accelerates immune reactions. This procedure may facilitate the identification of blood residues on washed artifacts, thus enhancing the potential to recover valuable information from scrupulously clean museum collections.

As noted in the Results section, Hemastix may indicate absence of blood when the quantity of antigen is meager; however, these minute quantities can be examined using enzyme immunoassay. In other words, the detection limits of Hemastix, as used in the initial antigen-detection phase, are not equipotent with those of the immunologically based species-identification assay. Differential detection levels between these two assays require an antigen-recognition test with detectability limits at least equal to those of the identification procedure itself. An immunologically based presence/absence test is one obvious means of increasing the ability to detect small quantities of antigen. This could be accomplished by the production of an antibody immuno-reactive with a pan-mammalian antigen. Although such a particular antigen has yet to be identified, it theoretically exists based on evidence that a majority of serum proteins are held in common by member-species of mammalian families (Berkeley Antibody Company, personal communication 1988). As always, cost and on-site applicability must be borne in mind and weighed against the need or desirability of high-resolution analyses, especially in the case of contractual and cultural resource management research projects.

Also of concern is the method utilized to extract blood residues from various artifacts. In an effort to increase the amount of residue fixed in solution, a new extraction method is suggested. Present extraction techniques consist of applying small quantities of buffering solution to the surface of an artifact, agitating the mixture with a probe, and then withdrawing the solution via pipette. We propose that the entire artifact be submerged in an ultrasonically agitated bath of buffered saline. This would aid removal of antigen particularly in those cases where blood residue is sparse and thinly dispersed on the surface of an artifact. While this process requires larger volumes of buffering solution, the subsequent speciation procedure is not sensitive to the concentration level of the antigen solution. Only protein is captured by the membrane as the supernatant filters through. Thus, the amount of buffering solution required in the extraction process is of little consequence. This is an important advantage offered by the use of nitrocellulose membrane.

In all probability, the greatest disadvantage of EIAs as a vehicle for species identification is the inability to identify multiple species from a single sample unless the sample size permits repetitive assays. This may be critical in cases where the sources of the artifactual blood stain are many and varied. Such a scenario is easily imagined, for it is very likely that artifacts employed in animal-processing activities became stained time and again with blood from different species. Meticulous analyses of tool function may thus be impaired by the incomplete recovery of available evidence. The other side of this invidious coin dictates that with small samples the researcher must employ the "correct" antibody on the first trial. With the exception of this provision, the source of the antigen under study cannot be specified.

Obviously, the drawbacks associated with destructive testing are multifarious. Two possible solutions for the multiple-species testing problem are suggested for future research. First, a variety of species-specific primary antibodies could be simultaneously, not individually, incubated with the sample. Each type of primary antibody is paired with an appropriate complementary secondary antibody possessing a unique enzymatic label. The respective labels, when properly developed, would indicate the presence of blood from particular source species. For this scheme to be fulfilled, a separate and discernible enzyme is needed for every presumed species. These enzymes must be able to be developed singly or in conjunction with others and yet retain the ability to be examined individually.

An alternative solution is based on nucleic acid research (Berkeley Antibody Company, personal communication 1989). After binding to the nitrocellulose membrane, the unknown antigenic sample is permanently fixed to the substrate. This permits the application, removal (using appropriate separation techniques), and reapplication of a number of primary antibodies. Consequently, this design requires the sequential application of an array of antibodies demanding substantial laboratory time. This strategy is nondestructive, however, and permits the identification of any number of species represented in the artifact sample.

Finally, there is a need for objective, quantifiable results at the output end of the assay. The intensity of the color developed from the enzyme/substrate reaction is proportional to the quantity of bound antibody. Currently, this result is recorded simply as positive or negative, based on visual comparison with the known antigens that are used as controls in the assay. Far more objective results could be obtained with a densitometer or spectrophotometer and would allow for computation and standardization of many statistical parameters.

SUMMARY AND IMPLICATIONS

The data summarized here clearly indicate that EIAs provide an effective means of detecting and identifying blood antigen residues with a high level of sensitivity, detectability, and specificity. Additionally, EIAs are relatively inexpensive, flexible, amenable to manipulation, and may even be performed in the field. EIAs also provide quantifiable and replicable results. The implications of the widespread use of this technique are thus immediately apparent.

Using only the lithic assemblage from the Shoop site as an example, it is clear that EIAs can provide high-resolution information that is directly relevant to tool function and use as well as to dietary and environmental reconstruction.

The solitary "hit" from the Shoop site is an end uniface or endscraper, which is not only one of the dominant tool forms at the site but is also a "major player" in several competing scenarios of site use. One of these scenarios alleges that these items, on the basis of configuration and macro-edgewear, were chiefly employed in the working/shaping of wood. Their profusion is therefore interpreted to represent a major emphasis on wood processing at this site. According to another "script", these end unifaces were principally employed in defleshing the hides of either now locally non-resident (e.g., caribou) or currently resident, medium-sized to large animals (e.g., deer, elk). In yet another view, these end unifaces are multipurpose tools with many potential functions. Confounding the function issue even further are widely contrasting opinions about the prevailing climate and flora at the time this site was utilized. (See Carr 1987, 1988 for views on these subjects.) The resolution of these competing perspectives has not been easy.

While edgewear studies have progressed substantially in the 35 years since Semenov's (1964) seminal publication, in and by themselves studies cannot completely resolve questions about tool function at Shoop or other sites. Neither can they directly address matters of human diet or paleoclimatic parameters of site use. However, EIAs can address all of these matters, and even in their present incipient state of application and refinement, they have demonstrated that at least one Paleoindian uniface was used on a cervid. If this knowledge proves to be applicable to a broader sample of unifaces from Shoop, then the hunting and processing of cervids was a major activity at this site. Furthermore, depending on the type of cervid ultimately identified, very different environmental reconstructions may be able to be developed for this part of central Pennsylvania. In any case, EIAs have opened a new window on the interpretations of aboriginal tool function and site use. The potential of this technique, once it is refined, extends not only to Shoop and to other localities in Pennsylvania, but quite possibly to archaeological sites throughout the world.

ACKNOWLEDGMENTS

The success of the project in this paper and continued support for ongoing research in this area of inquiry would not have been possible without the generous assistance and cooperation of a number of individuals and organizations. First of all the authors wish to express their gratitude to Texas Eastern Gas Pipeline Company for funding this project. We also would like to thank those who donated materials essential to the completion of this work, especially to K. W. Carr, Bureau for Historic Preservation, Pennsylvania Historical and Museum Commission, Harrisburg, Pennsylvania, who made available the artifactual materials from the Shoop site. Frank H. Wright, D.V.M., Minnesota Zoological Garden, Apple Valley, Minnesota; Penny Miller and Eric Tradgen, Good Zoo, Wheeling, West Virginia; Robert A. Wagner, D.V.M., Pittsburgh Zoo, Pittsburgh, Pennsylvania; and Norman Smith, D.V.M., Veterinary Associates, Shippenville, Pennsylvania, all generously provided the authors with blood samples of the various species of mammals without which all testing would have come to a standstill. In addition, the authors acknowledge the invaluable assistance of Stephanie S. Luck and Thomas R. Anderson of the Berkeley Antibody Company, Inc., Richmond, California.

REFERENCES CITED

Barr, S. J.
1989 *Blood from Stones: Blood Residue Analysis of the Dietz Site Clovis Artifacts.* Presented at the 54th annual meeting of the Society for American Archaeology, April 5–9, 1989, Atlanta, GA.

Berkeley Antibody Company, Incorporated
1988 *Immunoassays for Identification of Blood Residues on Archaeological Samples.* NSF Grant No. ISI-8860654. Richmond, CA.

Carr, K. W.
1987 Continuing Research at the Shoop Site—A Paleoindian Occupation in the Ridge and Valley Section of Central Pennsylvania. Paper presented at the Eastern States Archaeological Federation Annual Meeting, Charleston, S.C.

1988 Environmental Reconstruction at a Paleoindian Site in Central Pennsylvania. Paper presented at the Fifty-Ninth Annual Meeting of the Society for Pennsylvania Archaeology, Inc., Morgantown, PA.

Downs, E. F.
1985 An Approach to Detecting and Identifying Blood Residues on Archaeological Stone Artifacts: A Feasibility Study. Ms. on file, Center for Material Research in Archaeology and Ethnology, M.I.T., Cambridge, MA.

Gurfinkel, D. M., and U. M. Franklin
1988 A Study of the Feasibility of Detecting Blood Residue on Artifacts. *Journal of Archaeological Science* 15(1):83–98.

Hyland, D. C., and T. R. Anderson
1990 Blood Residue Analysis of the Lithic Assemblage from the Mitchell Locality, Blackwater

Draw, New Mexico. In A. T. Boldurian: Lithic Technology at the Mitchell Locality of Blackwater Draw: A Stratified Folsom Site in Eastern New Mexico. *Plains Anthropologist*, Memoir 24. 35:105–110.

Hyland, D. C., J. M. Tersak, J. M. Adovasio, and M. I. Siegel
1989 Identification of the Species of Origin of Residual Blood on Lithic Material. *American Antiquity* 55(1):104–112.

Leute, U.
1987 *Archaeometry: An Introduction to Physical Methods in Archaeology and the History of Art.* VCH, Weinheim, Federal Republic of Germany.

Lowenstein, J. M.
1985 Molecular Approaches to the Identification of Species. *American Scientist* 73:541–547.
1986 Evolutionary Applications of Radioimmunoassay. ABL, Nov.–Dec. 1986:13–15.

Loy, T. H.
1983 Prehistoric Blood Residues: Detection on Tool Surfaces and Identification of Species of Origin. *Science* 220:1269–1271.
1987a Recent Advances in Blood Residue Analysis. In *Archaeometry: Further Australasian Studies*, edited by W. R. Ambrose and J. M. J. Mummery, pp. 57–65. The Australian National University, Canberra.
1987b Elk Creek Lake Project: Residue Analysis of 50 Artifacts from Three Sites. In *Data Recovery at Sites 35JA27, 35JA59, and 35JA10, Elk Creek Project, Jackson County, Oregon*, eds., R. M. Pettigrew and C. G. Lebow, pp. 55–62. Eugene: INFOTECH Research.

Loy, T. H., and D. E. Nelson
1987 Potential Applications of Organic Residues on Ancient Tools. In *Proceedings of the Twenty-Third International Archaeometry Symposium*, edited by J. Olin and J. Blackmun, pp. 179–185. Smithsonian Institution Press, Washington, D.C.

Miles Laboratories
1980 Hemastix Reagent Strips. Ames Division, Miles Laboratories, Elkart, IND.

Nelson, D. E., T. H. Loy, J. S. Vogel, and J. R. Southon
1986 Radiocarbon Dating Blood Residues on Prehistoric Stone Tools. *Radiocarbon* 28(1):170–174.

Newman, M. E., and P. J. Julig
1989 The Identification of Protein Residues on Lithic Artifacts from a Stratified Boreal Forest Site. *Canadian Journal of Archaeology* 13:119–132.

Oates, D. W., C. A. Jochum, K. A. Pearson, and C. A. Hoilien
1983 Field Technique for the Identification of Deer Blood. *Journal of Forensic Science* 28(3):781-785.

Parkes, P. A.
1986 *Current Scientific Techniques in Archaeology.* Croom Helm, London.

Righetti, P. G.
1983 *Isoelectric Focusing: Theory, Methodology, and Applications.* Laboratory Techniques in Biochemistry and Molecular Biology, vol. II, edited by T. S. Work and E. Work. Elsevier Science Publishers, Amsterdam.

Roitti, I. M.
1984 *Essential Immunology.* 5th ed. Blackwell Scientific Publications, Oxford.

Semenov, S. A.
1964 *Prehistoric Technology.* Translated by M. W. Thompson. Barnes and Noble, New York.

Sensabaugh, G. G., A. C. Wilson, and P. L. Kirk
1971 Protein Stability in Preserved Biological Remains, Parts I and II. *International Journal of Biochemistry* (2):545–568.

Sinclair, A., and W. Slattery
1982 Identification of Meat According to Species by Isoelectric Focussing. *Australian Veterinary Journal* 58:77–80.

Tersak, J. M., and D. C. Hyland
1988 Application of Nitrocellulose Membrane: A New Method for Identification of Residual Blood on Lithic Material. Ms. on file, Department of Archaeology/Anthropology, Mercyhurst College, Erie, Pennsylvania.

Tijssen, P.
1985 *Practice and Theory of Enzyme Immunoassays.* Laboratory Techniques in Biochemistry and Molecular Biology, vol. 15, edited by R. H. Burdon and P. H. van Knippenberg. Elsevier Science Publishers, Amsterdam.

Washino, R. K.
1977 *Identification of Host Blood Meals in Arthropods.* U.S. Army Medical Research and Development Command, Washington, D.C.

Willey, G. R., and J. A. Sabloff
1980 *A History of American Archaeology.* 2nd ed. W. H. Freeman, New York.

Youmans, E.
1874 Herbert Spencer and the Doctrine of Evolution. *Popular Science Monthly* 6(1874-75):20–48.

The Pacific Coast Route of Initial Entry: An Overview

RUTH GRUHN
Department of Anthropology
University of Alberta
Edmonton, AB, Canada T6G 2H4

The Pacific coast route of initial entry of human populations into the New World merits serious consideration as a viable alternative to the interior route. Several questions will be addressed in this review of the model. (1) Was the North Pacific coastal route feasible at an early time, both in terms of environmental conditions and human adaptability?; (2) What concrete evidence is there to testify that the coastal route was indeed the initial path of entry?; and (3) Why does the coastal-entry model have greater explanatory power than the conventional interior route model?

1. Recent geological, geomorphological, and paleoenvironmental studies indicate that environmental conditions were most severe on the southern edge of Beringia and in southern Alaska during the phases of maximum Wisconsinan glaciation; but environmental conditions on the North Pacific coast may have been much like modern times during the last major interstadial (middle Wisconsinan), more than 50,000 yr B.P., the probably minimal time of entry as now indicated by very early radiocarbon dates from archaeological sites in South America. Descriptions of the ethnographic Yahgan of coastal Tierra del Fuego can be drawn upon to support the contentions that sparse, littoral-adapted populations may successfully survive in cold, stormy, rugged coastal environments with minimum material culture.

2. The lack of any concrete archaeological evidence in the form of very early dated occupation sites in north Pacific coastal areas is the major weakness of the coastal entry model. Such evidence cannot be expected, given the devastation rendered the middle Wisconsinan land surfaces by subsequent large-scale tectonic and isostatic level changes, massive tidal and storm scouring of coastlines, and extensive erosion and deposition of sediment by expanding ice caps and valley glaciers in southern Alaska and western British Columbia. Better luck may be expected in the coastal zones south of the glaciated areas; that is, in southwestern Washington, western Oregon, and California. Land forms and sedimentary deposits of middle and late Wisconsinan age in these areas must be searched, and possible archaeological sites thoroughly investigated by professional archaeologists and paleoenvironmental specialists. Meanwhile, the evidence of aboriginal language-group distributions in the Americas lends support to the coastal-entry–route model.

3. Recent archaeological research in South America has made it clear that any model of the initial entry of populations into the New World must explain the presence of unspecialized lithic industries in several remote areas of the southern continent by at least 33,000 yr B.P. and even 40,000 yr B.P. The conventional model of an initial entry of Upper Paleolithic-style hunters through the interior corridor no earlier than

12,000 yr B.P. fails completely. The coastal-entry model provides for an early entry of littoral-adapted populations with unspecialized lithic traditions which could have rapidly expanded lineally down the west coast of North America and into South America long before the continental interior of North America was populated.

INTRODUCTION

A North Pacific coastal route of initial entry into the New World, first suggested by Chard (1963, 1974:44), has long been advocated by Knut Fladmark, since his detailed study of late Pleistocene geological and paleoenvironmental conditions on the British Columbian and southeast Alaskan coasts (Fladmark 1975, 1978, 1979, 1983). Most recently Gruhn (1988), following studies by Rogers (1985a, 1985b), argued that the distribution and internal diversification of major groups of aboriginal American languages also supported the coastal-entry model.

Three salient questions about the initial coastal-entry model will be addressed in this paper. One is whether the coastal route was really feasible, in terms of the environmental conditions in the North Pacific area during the Upper Pleistocene and in terms of human adaptability to such conditions at an early time. Another question is whether there is any concrete evidence that the coastal route was indeed the initial path of New World settlement. The third question relates to the explanatory power of the initial coastal-entry model—why this model appears to be preferable to the conventional model of an entry route through the interior of Alaska and northwestern Canada. I hope to demonstrate that, all factors considered, the coastal-entry model is a quite viable alternative to conventional thought about the initial peopling of the New World.

FEASIBILITY OF THE COASTAL ROUTE

The time frame in which to consider the feasibility of the coastal route in terms of environmental conditions and human adaptability is at minimum the latter part of the Upper Pleistocene period. The earliest definite radiocarbon-dated archaeological sites now known for the New World—the lower occupation levels at Monte Verde in south-central Chile (Dillehay and Collins 1988, Dillehay, this volume) and at Toca do Boqueirão da Pedra Furada in northeastern Brazil (Delibrias and Guidon 1986; Guidon 1986; Guidon and Delibrias 1986, Guidon and Parenti 1989; Guidon et al. this volume)—indicate that we must seriously consider a minimum date of 50,000 years ago for the earliest passage of human populations across the Bering Straits. This minimum timing of the initial entry requires an examination of environmental conditions in the North Pacific area during the middle Wisconsinan interval, calculated to date between approximately 60,000 and 30,000 years ago (Hopkins 1982:7).

To date most paleoenvironmental research on Upper Pleistocene Beringia has been concentrated in the interior zones, and there is relatively little information about conditions on the North Pacific coastline. A large part of the problem, of course, is the marked fluctuation in the position of this coastline over the past 100,000 years. The estimated worldwide eustatic decrease in sea level during phases of maximum glaciation would indicate the expansion of the coastal zone out to the present 100-meter isobath (Cronin 1983). Sea level was apparently lower than now even during the middle Wisconsinan interstadial: Hopkins (1982:13–14) indicates that the eustatic sea level in the southern Bering Sea area fluctuated between perhaps 70 and 20 m below present sea level in the course of the Boutellier interval, the middle Wisconsinan. However, identifying the position of the North Pacific coastline in any particular locality during the course of the middle Wisconsinan interval is a difficult task indeed, especially considering the clear evidence for isostatic uplift as well as the sporadic but pronounced local tectonic movements in the North Pacific area.

Very little information is available to me concerning environmental conditions in the Soviet North Pacific area during the period of interest. Bespalyy (1984:32) mentions the Karginskiy interglaciation on the Chukchi Peninsula, with two radiocarbon dates of approximately 40,000–42,000 yr B.P. and the corresponding Penzhina interglaciation in the northeastern Okhotsk region, with several radiocarbon dates ranging between 44,600 and 26,440 yr B.P. It is said that the climate warmed about 50,000 years ago and that there was birch in a now-treeless area in Kamchatka. Glaciation was apparently restricted in the mountainous areas at the time. One may tentatively conclude from this limited report that environmental conditions were relatively moderate, perhaps even somewhat milder than at present, along the Soviet North Pacific coast during this interstadial. Exactly where the coastline was at the time is unknown; and there is no information about coastal conditions, especially the extent of sea ice.

For the east side of the Bering Sea area, details about changes in environmental conditions are provided by a study of a deep-sea core collected from the edge of the submerged Umnak Plateau in the southeastern Bering Sea (54° 51' north latitude, 170° 41' west longitude) by Sancetta and associates (Sancetta et al. 1985). Analyses were made of stratigraphic changes in fossil diatoms, oxygen isotopes from diatom silica, pollen, and clay minerals within this 14.5-m-long core. The core was divided into four units. The lowest, Unit 4, is a clayey silt correlated with the early Wisconsinan glacial advance (isotope Stage 4), a time of low sea level, with evidence of a moss-sedge tundra environment on the exposed continental shelf, and much sea ice. Unit 3, overlying Unit 4, is a silty diatom ooze. Fluctuation in diatoms, oxygen isotopes, pollen, and clay minerals in this complex depositional unit are believed to correlate with alternating stades and interstades of the middle Wisconsinan interval (isotope Stage 3). The lower part of Unit 3 is suggested to represent a time of warmer interstadial climate, with a rise in sea level, although below that of today; and a sedge-grass tundra cover of the coastal shelf. There was only occasional sea ice. Unit 2, overlying Unit 3, was a diatom-bearing silt representing the late Wisconsinan glacial maximum, with a marked drop in sea level and extreme glacial conditions with complete sea-ice cover. Unit 1, a diatom ooze, represents the Holocene interval.

The results of analysis of this long deep-sea core from the edge of the continental shelf in the southeastern Bering Sea area suggest that environmental conditions were more favorable for movement of human populations along the south edge of the Bering Land Bridge in the middle Wisconsinan interval than before or after this time. According to Sancetta (personal communication), during this interval "there was sea ice in winter but meltback in late spring and a very productive marine ecosystem for the open season." However, passage through the area during the later Wisconsinan, in the phase of maximum glaciation and continuous sea ice, would have been very difficult indeed.

Farther east, in southern Alaska, studies also indicate that very severe conditions characterized the coastal zone during the phase of maximum glaciation in the late Wisconsinan. The Alaska Peninsula was covered by an almost continuous ice sheet (Detterman 1986); and thick ice caps covered most of the Aleutian Islands and a considerable portion of the adjacent Aleutian Platform, with extensive floating ice shelves in the Bering Sea adjacent on the north and probably on the Pacific side as well (Thorson and Hamilton 1986). The Gulf of Alaska region farther east also featured very extensive valley and piedmont glaciation at this time; indeed, it is believed that much if not all of the continental shelf in this area may have been covered with glacial ice (Molnia 1986). Given the geological evidence for extensive glaciation and ice cover from the area of the Alaska Peninsula east to Yakutat Bay, a distance of over a thousand kilometers, it would be reasonable to say that the coast of southern Alaska would have presented an impassable barrier to any human population during the late Wisconsinan maximum. The late Wisconsinan glacial erosion is so extensive and severe throughout this large region that, to date, no deposits of the middle Wisconsinan interval have been definitely identified by geologists in the coastal zone of southern Alaska. If human populations traveled along the south coast of Alaska during the middle Wisconsinan interval, the traces of their passage were obliterated in that area during the subsequent glacial advance.

To the southeast, in the rugged fiord country of the Alaska Panhandle and the northwest coast of British Columbia, there is more geological evidence preserved of the middle Wisconsinan interval. In the Juneau area, a peat deposit at Montana Creek dated greater than 39,000 yr B.P. may be assigned to the middle Wisconsinan interval (Mann 1986:256). The pollen spectrum from this peat bed, which is overlain by glacial-marine deposits, is dominated by *Artemesia* and sedge, with a minor component of arboreal pollen. A cooler climate than today is indicated; but glaciers had receded out of the inner fiords of southeast Alaska at this time, and the extent of glaciers in the area is thought to have been similar to modern times (Mann 1986). Farther south, there is a peat deposit of middle Wisconsinan age at Yokoun River on east-central Graham Island in the Queen Charlottes, with bracketing dates of 45,700 ± 970 yr B.P. (GSC 3534-2) and 27,500 ± 400 yr B.P. (GSC-3530), featuring pollen of subalpine forest vegetation (*Picea, Tsuga mertensiana, Abies*) and wetlands (Warner et al. 1984). It is estimated that mean annual temperatures were 1°-2° C lower than at present, although precipitation was higher, and that the east-central part of Graham Island was ice-free until after 27,500 years ago.

Farther south along the British Columbia coast, deposits of middle Wisconsinan age have been identified in coastal-bluff or gravel-pit exposures at several localities in the Straits of Georgia area and the lower Fraser valley. The Cowichan Head Formation, stratified between thick glacial deposits and dated between 59,000 and 25,000 yr B.P., is assigned to the Olympia nonglacial interval (Armstrong and Clague 1977; Clague 1981). This formation, which may be up to 17 m thick at exposures in the eastern coastal lowlands of Vancouver Island, consists of a lower marine member and an upper member of horizontally bedded fluvial or estuarine gravel, sand, or silt, which is rich in organic material. Analyses of the pollen record from three localities in eastern Vancouver Island by Alley (1979) indicated that during the interval from 50,000 to 29,000 years ago the pollen spectrum was dominated by arboreal species, indicating a closed forest analogous to the modern Coastal Douglas Fir vegetation zone. Armstrong and Clague (1977) indicate also that fossil beetle species identified in deposits of the Cowichan Head Formation are similar to modern types in the region. Clague (1981) concludes that before 29,000 yr B.P. the environment of southern coastal British Columbia was much like the present, with widespread forest and glaciers confined to the mountains; the climate may have been somewhat cooler than at present, with minor fluctuations.

The Olympia nonglacial interval is followed by the late Wisconsinan Fraser glaciation, in which a major ice sheet covered the lower Fraser area and Vancouver Island, the Olympic Peninsula was extensively glaciated, and ice flowed throughout the Puget Sound area as far south as 47° north latitude (Clague et al. 1980; Thorson 1980). South of the major meltwater channel in the Chehalis valley, however, the Pacific coast west of the Cascades was clear, down into southwest Washington, Oregon, and California.

In summary, the middle Wisconsinan paleoenvironmental record, although sparse in the North Pacific area due to subsequent severe glacial erosion and changes in sea level, currently indicates that environmental conditions were similar to or only somewhat cooler than at the present time. We may imagine that early human groups expanding along the North Pacific coast in the course of this interval of relatively moderate climate, before 40,000 years ago, would have faced conditions much like the present: in most of the area, a cool maritime climate; probably a rugged coastline in Kamchatka; a featureless coastal plain in Beringia; and, to the east and south in Alaska and British Columbia, steep rocky shorelines, islands, deep fiords, and the occasional valley glacier extending to the sea. The next major issue concerns the feasibility of this coastal route in terms of early human adaptability to such environmental conditions.

In response to this question, I propose to draw upon the ethnographic analogy of the historic Yahgan of coastal Tierra del Fuego (Cooper 1946; Gusinde 1937), people who were adapted to a climate and environment which may be comparable to the middle Wisconsinan environment of the North Pacific coast. At the start it must be emphasized that the ethnographic Yahgan are *not* seen here as the direct unmodified cultural descendants of the initial population of the New World. Indeed, the archaeological record for southern Tierra del Fuego (summarized in Orquera 1987) indicates that the ancestors of the Yahgan arrived on the Beagle Channel by about 6500 yr B.P., with a fairly sophisticated bone and stone industry that continued to late prehistoric times; but even the meager technology recorded for the Beagle Channel peoples in the ethnographic present was obviously sufficient to provide for a successful littoral adaptation in a high-latitude maritime climate.

The southern coast of Tierra del Fuego at 54°–56° south latitude is very rugged fiord country, with steep, thickly forested mountain slopes running into the sea and valley glaciers descending to the shoreline. As described by Cooper (1946), the climate is very cool, with the summer mean temperature about 10° C and the winter temperature normally close to freezing, with a winter minimum of -12° C. Early European mariners have vividly described the wet, stormy weather characteristic of the area—windy and cool with frequent severe gales, rainstorms or sleet, and snowfalls even in summer. They were amazed at the minimal clothing and shelter of the natives. The Fuegian Indians seen by Charles Darwin (1889:212–213) during December 1832 and January 1833 on the Beagle Channel wore only short otterskin or sealskin cloaks and were often observed virtually naked. Darwin (1889:212) described the temporary dwellings as small flimsy huts with a framework of broken branches set in the ground and bent over, covered simply by piles of brush or sealskins; Cooper (1946) adds that the floor of the hut might be scooped out to a depth of several feet, and a fire was kept in the center of the hut.

The Yahgan were dependent upon littoral food sources. Mussels collected from rocky areas at low tide were the major food reported in early historic accounts, although seals and guanacos seem to have been more important in the late prehistoric period (Orquera 1987:404–406). The Yahgan also fished, hunted otters, exploited stranded whales, snared or clubbed sea birds, and collected bird eggs. As described by Darwin (1889:236), a large edible tree fungus was collected; otherwise the Yahgan found very little vegetable food in the forest.

The Yahgan bark canoe was noted in 1578 by Sir Francis Drake (1628:37) and observed by Darwin (1889). As described by Cooper (1946:88), the canoe was made of several wide strips of southern beech bark (*Notofagus*) removed from the tree with a bone chisel or mussel-shell knife. The strips of bark were sewn together with lashing of whale bone or shredded saplings. The canoes leaked badly, but were adequate for the frequent movement of families along the coastline.

The rest of the inventory of Yahgan material culture, as described by Cooper (1946:89–90), included string made of a variety of fibers, used to make bird snares, fishing lines, lashings, and bow strings; coiled baskets; cylindrical bark buckets; and skin pouches. Pronged sticks were used to collect sea urchins and crabs. The most common weapon was a wooden spear with bone point. More limited in use were harpoons (spears with detachable bone points secured by a cord), wooden clubs, and stone-tipped arrows. By the historic period, very few stone artifacts were in use. The common cutting and scraping tool, noted even by Drake (1628:38), was a large mussel shell; according to Drake, these were strong enough to cut wood. Not much would be preserved of ethnographic Yahgan material culture on most archaeological sites.

The ethnographic example of the Yahgan of coastal Tierra del Fuego, then, indicates that a littoral-adapted population could survive in a cool, humid high-latitude maritime climate with a minimal material culture. Whereas a specialized and elaborate (Upper Paleolithic-like) technology would be required for survival in a high-latitude interior continental zone with at least a seasonally severe arctic climate in wintertime even during interstadial periods, a simple technology could be sufficient for a year-round littoral adaptation on the North Pacific coast. In sum, one could surmise that even a population as poorly endowed with material culture as the ethnographic Yahgan could have made it into the New World along the North Pacific coast during the middle Wisconsinan interval.

CONCRETE EVIDENCE FOR THE COASTAL ROUTE

The next question to be addressed is whether there is any concrete evidence that the North Pacific coastal route was indeed the initial path of entry for the New World aboriginal population. For most prehistorians, archaeological evidence is preferable to any other; and it is of great concern that the likelihood of finding any archaeological sites of middle Wisconsinan age preserved in the North Pacific coastal zone is so minute. The eustatic sea level then was lower than at present, so the coastline of the time is now under water. The entire south coast of Beringia is now flooded. In southern Alaska, massive glacial ice of the maximum late Wisconsinan advance apparently covered at least the present coastline for over a thousand kilometers, eroding away any middle Wisconsinan land surface in the present coastal zone. Even farther south, in the Alaska Panhandle and along the west coast of British Columbia, only a mere handful of localities which preserve any middle Wisconsinan terrestrial deposits are known. In sum, finding an archaeological site of middle Wisconsinan age preserved anywhere on the present North Pacific coast would be simply incredible luck. We cannot expect it.

If archaeological evidence of an initial coastal-entry route is to be found, it must be sought in the coastal area south of the zone directly affected by the maximum late Wisconsinan glaciation. The areas to search for archaeological evidence (with due regard for sea-level changes) are southwestern Washington State, coastal Oregon, and California. To date, it seems, regional archaeologists in Washington and Oregon have not even dreamed of systematically checking middle or late Wisconsinan sedimentary deposits for possible archaeological remains. In California, archaeological research into the question of pre-Holocene settlement has been inhibited by a historical development: the known, possibly really early sites—Calico (Leakey et al. 1972), Texas Street (Carter 1957), Buchanan Canyon (Minshall 1976), the Brown Site (Minshall 1981), Santa Rosa Island (Berger 1982; Orr 1968)—were first discovered and explored by researchers who advanced claims which were not documented and substantiated by the production of full, detailed, scientific site reports. Professional archaeologists have rejected these claims, but only through superficial inspection of the evidence as it has been presented by these claimants. Not one of the sites has been thoroughly and systematically investigated by a modern professional archaeologist. This situation may change only with recognition by professional archaeologists of the real possibility of middle and late Wisconsinan archaeological sites in California.

As the matter stands at the moment, there are several known sites in southern California which may be middle or late Wisconsinan in age, but these sites have not been scientifically documented. North of California, no possible early sites have been reported. At present, then, there is no concrete archaeological evidence of the North Pacific coastal route of initial entry.

There is, however, another line of concrete evidence which is supportive: historical linguistic evidence. I have dealt with this evidence at length elsewhere (Gruhn 1988), so here I will simply summarize the picture.

Supporting the Pacific coastal-entry model is the fact that the area of greatest diversification of aboriginal languages, in terms of the location of the major subdivisions of widespread language stocks and the number of isolates (languages or language families which are not clearly demonstrated to be genetically related to others), is the west coast of North America—specifically, in the Alaska Panhandle and western British Columbia, western Washington, western Oregon, California, and western Mexico. The implication of the language distributions is a much greater time depth of populations on the west coast than in the interior of the continent (Gruhn 1988:78–79).

Archaeologists dealing with the question of earliest settlement of the Americas are now well aware of Joseph Greenberg's sweeping, large-scale classificatory scheme in which all native American languages except Eskimo-Aleut and Na-Dene are incorporated into a great phylum termed Amerind (Greenberg 1987a; Greenberg et al. 1986). Archaeologists should also be aware that Greenberg's methodology and the strength of his evidence have been the subject of heated debate among linguists (for example, Campbell 1988 vs. Greenberg 1989; see also Greenberg 1987b). Even with the Greenberg classification, however, the fact still remains that the greatest diversification of aboriginal languages is on the west coast of North America; indeed, all of the major North American Amerind groups that Greenberg proposes—Almosan-Keresiouan, Hokan, Penutian, and Central Amerind—are centered in or very near the west coast zone.

THE EXPLANATORY POWER OF THE COASTAL ENTRY ROUTE

In any scholarly analyses of a historical problem, the model of events preferred is that which best incorporates established fact. The fact to be explained in any acceptable model of earliest New World prehistory is that there are in South America well-stratified and radiocarbon-dated human occupation sites of an age of 34,000 years ago or greater. These earliest archaeological sites feature very simple, unspecialized lithic technologies. Researchers maintaining the model of the North American Clovis complex as representing the earliest peopling of the New World, with entrance via an interior Beringia/ice-free corridor route no earlier than 12,000 years ago, simply cannot believe the South American sites (e.g., Fagan 1987; Lynch 1989; Martin 1987). How could people with a very simple, unspecialized lithic technology make it through Beringia; and how could the population expand down into South America so long ago without leaving obvious traces in North America?

The coastal-entry model resolves both these questions. It proposes that the initial American population did not pass through the arctic rigors of interior Beringia but along the North Pacific Coast, where a more moderate climate and rich and diverse littoral food resources did not require the development of a complex and sophisticated lithic technology. Indeed, the example of the ethnographic Yahgan indicates that a human population may survive in a high-latitude maritime environment with a minimum material culture. For the second question, a littoral-adapted population would expand lineally along a virgin coastline, with population growth and migration limited to a very narrow spatial front. One would expect that the front of population expansion moved fairly rapidly down along the western coastline of North America, and human groups passed through the Isthmus of Panama to reach south-central Chile and northeastern Brazil long before settlement of the continental interior of North America.

While we cannot expect to find archaeological remains of an early coastal-entry route in the North Pacific area, nevertheless the model may be tested by archaeological research, in that several predictions may be derived from it. The model would be supported if an archaeological site of middle Wisconsinan age is demonstrated in western Oregon, California, or Mexico. The model would be discredited if an archaeological site dated 50,000 yr B.P. or older is discovered on the northern Great Plains, at the southern end of the Ice-Free Corridor.

CONCLUSION

To conclude, I will restate the responses to the primary questions about the coastal-entry route raised at the beginning of this paper. The route was indeed feasible, in terms of known environmental conditions in the North Pacific coastal zone during the middle Wisconsinan period and in terms of ethnographically demonstrated human capacity to adapt to such environmental conditions by means of a littoral economy with a minimum material culture. There is no demonstrated archaeological evidence along the route, but concrete historical-linguistic evidence supports the model. Finally, the model provides an adequate explanation for the archaeological record of human populations with simple, unspecialized lithic technologies in peripheral areas of South America by 40,000 years ago, long before the settlement of the continental interior of North America. It predicts that archaeological sites of middle Wisconsinan age will be found in the western coastal zones of North America, while sites older than 50,000 yr B.P. will not be located on the northern Great Plains. The coastal-entry model is certainly a viable alternative to the conventional model of an interior early route, and it merits archaeological research specifically to test it. Perhaps the Center for the Study of the First Americans will need a new logo: not fur-clad folk trudging through the tundra, but a woman paddling the family canoe down the coast of beautiful British Columbia.

ACKNOWLEDGMENTS

I am indebted to Charles Schweger for initial references on the paleoenvironment of the North Pacific area; and to John Clague, Rolf Mathewes, Constance Sancetta, and Robert Thorsen for their informative letters and reprints.

REFERENCES CITED

Alley, N. F.
    1979 Middle Wisconsin Stratigraphy and Climatic Reconstruction, Southern Vancouver Island, British Columbia. *Quaternary Research* 11:213–237.

Armstrong, J. E., and J. J. Clague
    1977 Two Major Wisconsin Lithostratigraphic Units in Southwest British Columbia. *Canadian Journal of Earth Sciences* 14:1471–1480.

Berger, R.
    1982 The Woolley Mammoth Site, Santa Rosa Island, California. In *Peopling of the New World*, edited by J. E. Ericson, R. E. Taylor, and R. Berger, pp. 163–170. Ballena Press, Los Altos.

Bespalyy, V. G.
    1984 Late Pleistocene Mountain Glaciation in Northeastern USSR. In *Late Quaternary Environments of the Soviet Union*, edited by A. A.

Velichko, H. E. Wright, Jr., and C. W. Barnowsky, pp. 31–33. University of Minnesota Press, Minneapolis.

Campbell, L.
1988 Review of *Language in the Americas* by Joseph H. Greenberg. *Language* 64:591–615.

Carter, G.
1957 *Pleistocene Man at San Diego*. Johns Hopkins Press, Baltimore.

Chard, C.
1963 The Old World Roots: Review and Speculations. *Anthropological Papers of the University of Alaska* 10(2):115–121.

1974 *Northeast Asia in Prehistory*. University of Wisconsin Press, Madison.

Clague, J.
1981 *Late Quaternary Geology and Geochronology of British Columbia, Part 2: Summary and Discussion of Radiocarbon-Dated Quaternary History*. Geological Survey of Canada Paper 80-35. Ottawa.

Clague, J. J., J. E. Armstrong, and W. H. Mathews
1980 Advance of the Late Wisconsin Cordilleran Ice Sheet in Southern British Columbia Since 22,000 yr BP. *Quaternary Research* 13:322–326.

Cooper, J.
1946 The Yahgan. In *Handbook of South American Indians*, vol.1, edited by J. H. Steward, pp. 81–106. Smithsonian Institution, Washington, D.C.

Cronin, T. M.
1983 Rapid Sea Level and Climatic Change: Evidence from Continental and Island Margins. *Quaternary Science Reviews* 1:177–214.

Darwin, C.
1889 *A Naturalist's Voyage: Journal of Researches into the Natural History and Geology of the Countries Visited During the Voyage of H.M.S. "Beagle" Round the World*. 2nd edition. London.

Detterman, R. L.
1986 Glaciation of the Alaska Peninsula. In *Glaciation in Alaska: The Geologic Record*, edited by T. D. Hamilton, K. M. Reed, and R. M. Thorson, pp. 151–170. Alaska Geological Society, Anchorage.

Delibrias, G., and N. Guidon
1986 The Rock Shelter Toca do Boqueirão do Sitio da Pedra Furada. *L'Anthropologie* 90:307–316.

Dillehay, T. D., and M. Collins
1988 Early Cultural Evidence from Monte Verde in Chile. *Nature* 332:150–152.

Drake, F.
1628 *The World Encompassed*. London.

Fagan, B.
1987 *The Great Journey. The Peopling of Ancient America*. Thames and Hudson, New York.

Fladmark, K. R.
1975 *A Paleoecological Model for Northwest Coast Prehistory*. Archaeological Survey of Canada Paper No. 43 Mercury Series. National Museum of Man, Ottawa.

1978 The Feasibility of the Northwest Coast as a Migration Route for Early Man. In *Early Man in America from a Circum-Pacific Perspective*, edited by A. L. Bryan, pp. 119–128. University of Alberta, Edmonton.

1979 Routes: Alternate Migration Corridors for Early Man in North America. *American Antiquity* 44:55–69.

1983 Times and Places: Environmental Correlates of Mid-to-Late Wisconsinan Human Population Expansion in North America. In *Early Man in the New World*, edited by R. Shutler, pp. 13–41. Sage Publications, Beverly Hills.

Greenberg, J. H.
1987a *Languages of the Americas*. Stanford University Press, Stanford.

1987b Languages in the Americas. *Current Anthropology* 28:647–667.

1989 Classification of American Indian Languages: A Reply to Campbell. *Language* 65(1):107–114.

Greenberg, J. H., C. R. Turner II, and S. L. Zegura
1986 The Settlement of the Americas: A Comparison of the Linguistic, Dental, and Genetic Evidence. *Current Anthropology* 27:477–497.

Gruhn, R.
1988 Linguistic Evidence in Support of the Coastal Route of Earliest Entry into the New World. *Man* 23(1):77–100.

Guidon, N.
1986 Las Unidades Culturales de São Raimundo Nonato—Sudeste del Estado de Piau—Brasil. In *New Evidence for the Pleistocene Peopling of the Americas*, edited by A. L. Bryan, pp. 157–171. Center for the Study of Early Man, University of Maine, Orono.

Guidon, N., and G. Delibrias
1986 Carbon-14 Dates Point to Man in the Americas 32,000 Years Ago. *Nature* 321:769–771.

Guidon, N., and E. Parenti
1989 Toca do Boqueirão do Sitio da Pedra Furada: Escavações 1987. In *Dédalo*, pp. 57–67. Publ. Avulsa. No. 1. Universidade de São Paulo, São Paulo.

Gusinde, M.
   1937 Die Feuerland-Indianer. Vol. 2:*Die Yamana*, Mödling.

Hopkins, D. M.
   1982 Aspects of the Paleogeography of Beringia during the Late Pleistocene. In *Paleoecology of Beringia*, edited by D. M. Hopkins, J. V. Matthews, Jr., C. E. Schweger, and S. B. Young, pp. 3–28. Academic Press, New York.

Leakey, L. S. B., R. D. Simpson, T. Clements, R. Berger, and J. Witthoft
   1972 *Pleistocene Man at Calico.* San Bernadino County Museum, Redlands.

Lynch, T.
   1989 Comment on "Hominid Use of Fire in the Lower and Middle Pleistocene: A Review of the Evidence." *Current Anthropology* 30:15–16.

Mann, D. H.
   1986 Wisconsin and Holocene Glaciation of Southeast Alaska. In *Glaciation in Alaska: The Geologic Record*, edited by T. D. Hamilton, K. M. Reed, and R. M. Thorson, pp. 237–265. Alaska Geological Society, Anchorage.

Martin, P. S.
   1987 Clovisia the Beautiful! *Natural History* 96(10):10–13.

Minshall, H. L.
   1976 *The Broken Stones.* Copley Press, San Diego.
   1981 The Geomorphology and Antiquity of the Charles H. Brown Archaeological Site at San Diego, California. *Pacific Coast Archaeological Quarterly* 12:39–57.

Molnia, B. F.
   1986 Glacial History of the Northeastern Gulf of Alaska—A Synthesis. In *Glaciation in Alaska: The Geologic Record*, edited by T. D. Hamilton, K. M. Reed, and R. M. Thorson, pp. 219–235. Alaska Geological Society, Anchorage.

Orquera, L. A.
   1987 Advances in the archaeology of the Pampa and Patagonia. *Journal of World Prehistory* 1(4):33–413.

Orr, P.
   1968 *Prehistory of Santa Rosa Island.* Santa Barbara Museum of Natural History, Santa Barbara.

Rogers, R. A.
   1985a Glacial Geography and Native North American Languages. *Quaternary Research* 23:130–137.
   1985b Wisconsinan Glaciation and the Dispersal of Native Ethnic Groups in North America. In *Woman, Poet, Scientist: Essays in New World Anthropology Honoring Dr. Emma Lou Davis*, edited by T. C. Blackburn, pp. 105–113. Ballena Press, Los Altos.

Sancetta, C., L. Heusser, L. Labeyrie, A. S. Naidu, and S. W. Robinson
   1985 Wisconsin-Holocene Paleoenvironment of the Bering Sea: Evidence from Diatoms, Pollen, Oxygen Isotopes, and Clay Minerals. *Marine Geology* 62:55–68.

Thorson, R. M.
   1980 Ice-Sheet Glaciation of the Puget Lowland, Washington, During the Vashon Stade (Late Pleistocene). *Quaternary Research* 13:303–321.

Thorson, R. M., and T. D. Hamilton
   1986 Glacial Geology of the Aleutian Islands (Based on the Contributions of Robert F. Black). In *Glaciation in Alaska: The Geologic Record*, edited by T. D. Hamilton, K. M. Reed, and R. M. Thorson, pp. 171–191. Alaska Geological Society, Anchorage.

Warner, B. G., J. J. Clague, and R. W. Mathewes
   1984 Geology and Paleoecology of a Mid-Wisconsin Peat from the Queen Charlotte Islands, British Columbia, Canada. *Quaternary Research* 21:337–350.

General Index

12-Mile Creek site 31
^{14}C See also C-14 3–4, 27–41, 49–51
Abxaz 181
accelerator (atomic) mass spectrometry 3, 27–28, 33–35, 45–46, 48
Achomawi 184, 186
acid 14, 30–33, 36–39, 45–53, 74, 165, 168, 170, 173, 241, 246
    aspartic 32, 39, 46, 48–53
    fulvic 38–39, 47, 49–53
    glutamic 32, 39, 48–53
    total amino 31–32, 36, 38–39
acid treatment 30–32
affinity chromatography matrix 242–243, 245
affinity-absorbed antibodies 239
Africa, Africans 5, 8, 77, 100, 103, 127, 131–136, 144, 170, 178, 193, 197
African classification 178
Afro-Asiatic 183
Agattu 85, 109
Aguaruna 184–185
Agul 181
Ainu 80–82, 86–90, 99–103, 105–107, 109, 120, 123, 124, 183–187
Akwa'ala 185
Alabama 185
Alaska Peninsula 5, 59, 81–82, 86, 88, 93, 95–100, 102–104, 106–109, 120, 122–124, 126, 138, 144, 184, 193–194, 249–253
Aleut, Aleutian tradition 4, 79–110, 127, 131–132, 144, 146–149, 156, 158, 186, 191–194, 251
Algonquian 11, 123–124, 184–185, 187, 194–203
Aliutor 184–185
allele 85, 119, 137
    enzyme 119
    protein 119
Allentiac 185

Almosan-Keresiouan (AK) 123–124, 178, 180, 182–184, 187, 195–203, 253
Alsea 184, 186
Altaic 178, 183, 204
Amaknak 84, 86, 91–94, 96, 98, 103
Amerind 5, 18, 79, 81, 92, 99–103, 105–108, 118, 120, 124–127, 178–187, 191–196, 198–204, 253
AMS 3–4, 27–28, 33–40, 45–53
analyzing magnet 34–35, 66
Anangula core 108
ancient biological divergence hypothesis 81, 110
Andean (AN) 178, 181–183
Angmagssalik 120–122, 125
antibody/antigene 170, 172, 239–247
antler 29–30, 214–215, 228–229
Apache 82, 91, 95–96, 100, 102, 117, 120–121, 125–126
apatite structure 30–32, 46, 49
Arara 185
Araucanian 184–185
Arawak 184
Archi 181
Arctic Mongoloid 80–81, 105–106, 108
Arctic Small Tool tradition (ASTt) 107, 109
Arctic village 120
Arikara 101–102, 144, 146–150
Assiniboin 82, 90–92, 102, 107
Atacama 184–185
Atakapa 185–187
Athapaskan 79, 82–84, 86–93, 95–103, 105, 107–109, 117–118, 120–121, 123–127, 193–194
Atsugewi 184
Attu 85, 109
Auake 185, 187
Augpilagtok Island 120–123, 125–126
Australia, Australian 77, 133–134, 136, 144, 146–147, 149, 151, 153–155, 157–158
Avestan 184

Aymara 183–184, 187
Ayoman 185

Bahukiwa 187
Barama 185
base insoluble 31
base soluble 31
basic vocabulary 178, 191
Basque 8, 181, 202
bat 11, 13, 19, 83, 103, 118, 120, 136, 167, 181, 185, 189, 193, 244, 246
beaver 120
Berg Norwegians 101
Bering Land Bridge 110, 251
Bering Sea 80, 82, 95, 97, 105, 107–109, 120, 250–251
Bering Strait 95, 100, 107, 157, 192
Beringia 1, 81, 118, 127, 158, 192, 198, 249–250, 252–254
beta particle emissions 34
Bezdanjaca Cave 32–33
binary comparison 178
binding site 242
biochemistry 31, 39, 165, 240–241
biogeochemistry 31–33, 36, 38, 41
biological classification 187
bipartite genetic difference model 126
Bison antiquus 29
bivariate comparison 103
bizygomatic breadth 145, 149, 152, 156
Blackfoot 82, 90–92, 102, 107, 186, 201, 203
blade site 106, 108
blood antigen, technique for detection and identification 136, 239–242, 244–246
Bodega 184
Bonferroni alpha protection 145
Bonner Springs 143
Bororo 185, 187
Borunca 187
Botocudo 183–186
brachycephalic 85, 90, 103–104, 158
brachycranic 141, 148, 157
Bribri 184–185, 187
Briord 32–33
Bristol Bay 82, 86, 91–92, 95, 97
Browns Valley 142, 150, 152, 157
burial-mound complex 82, 90, 98
Buriat 101, 146–147
Burmese 183
Burushaski 181

C-14 See also ^{14}C 45–53, 76
C-558 29
C-score 101
Cacaopera 185–186
California 4, 8, 19, 27, 31, 35, 41, 45, 48, 50, 102, 135, 194–195, 247, 249, 252–254
Campa 185–186

Canada 3, 30, 79, 102, 110, 117, 120–121, 135, 144, 193, 249–250
Caraja 186
Caranga 185–186
carbon isotope ratio 34
carbonates 29–33, 37, 46, 66
Carrier 183
Catacao 184
Catawba 184–185
Catio 184, 186
Caucasian 180–183, 204
Cayapo 185
Cayuvava 186
Central Amerind (CA) 178, 183, 253
Central Sierra Miwok 185
cephalic index 103
Chaluka 81–82, 84, 108
Chama 185
charcoal 28–30, 33, 52, 184
charge-to-mass ratio 34
Chatina 184
Chechen 181
Chemakum 184
Cheremiss 184
Cherokee 185
Cheyenne 82, 90–92, 102, 107, 185, 196–200
Chibchan-Paezan (CP) 178, 180–183
Chickasaw 185–187
Chilanga 184–185
Chimu 184, 186
China 3–4, 73, 75–78, 81, 134138, 143–144, 158, 193
Chinantec 187
Chipewyan 117, 120–123, 125–126, 182
Chiquimulilla 186
Chiquito 187
Chitimacha 185–187
Choctaw 185
Chol 186
Cholona 184
chord distance 119
Chorti 185
chromatography 31, 33, 38, 47, 242–243, 245
Chukchi 80–82, 85–90, 92–94, 96, 98, 100–103, 106, 120–123, 125–127, 136, 144, 146–147, 184–186, 250
Chukchi-Kamchatkan (CK) 178, 183, 187, 204
Chukotkan 84, 92, 93, 95, 99–102, 105, 107, 108, 120
Chulupi 185
Chumash 184
Classic Mongoloid 80–81, 105
clinoid bridge 84, 92
Clovis 2–3, 5–6, 18–19, 28, 45, 47, 51, 58, 60–68, 149, 217, 254
cluster analysis 79, 83, 91, 99–101, 107, 137, 220–221, 223
Cody tradition 143
coefficient of divergence 77, 80
Cofan 185, 187

collagen 27, 31–33, 38–39, 41, 45–53, 168, 172
collagen-degraded bone 39
collector 34
Colorado 45, 47, 60, 184–185
concomitant reduction 152
Coos 183
Coroado 184
Cotoname 187
cranial index 76–78, 103, 105, 153
craniofacial structure 78, 101, 142, 145, 157–158
craniometric analysis 80, 83, 98, 101, 103–104, 106, 108, 143, 146–147, 156
Cree 117, 120–125, 198–201
cross-linked protein 241
crystallography 239, 241–242
Cuica 184
Cuna 184, 186–187
cyclotron 34

Dakota 82, 90, 107, 144, 184, 215
Dakota Sioux 91–92, 102, 104
Dalbergia 185
decay counting 27, 33–34, 36–38
demic expansion 109
Dene-Caucasian 180–181, 183, 187
Deneid variety 104, 106
dental morphology 80–81, 118, 131, 133, 137
diachronic comparison 80
diagenesis 30–33, 36–40, 47, 66
direct counting 34, 36–38, 203
DNA polymerization 128, 166–167
Dogon Zulu 156
Dogrib 82, 117, 120–126
dolichocranic 104, 153, 157–158
Domebo 38–39, 47–49, 63
Dravidian 136–137, 183
Dunshan 186

early Archaic 141, 143
East Pomo 185
ecozone 106
Eden tradition 135, 143
Egyptian 8, 101, 133–134, 144, 146–147, 166, 168, 193
electrophoretic principles, procedure 127, 136, 166, 172, 241
enzymatic activity 6, 119, 166–169, 171, 239–240, 242–246
enzyme immunoassay (EIA) 6, 239–240, 242, 244–246
epitopes 241–242
Equatorial (EQ) 178, 180–183
Escapule Mammuthus sp. 39
Eskimo, Eskimoan language 4–5, 9, 11, 78–110, 117–118, 120–127, 136, 144, 146–150, 178–179, 183–184, 186–187, 191–192, 194, 204, 253
Eskimo-Aleut (EA) 4–5, 81, 103–106, 108, 117–118, 178–180, 183, 187, 191–192, 204, 253
Esselen 184

Estonian 137, 184
etymology 178–180, 182–183, 191, 201–202
Eurasia 5, 105, 131, 136–138, 142, 178–179, 181, 183–187, 192–193, 204
Europe 7–12, 14, 32, 73, 77, 101, 120–122, 125, 127, 131–138, 141, 143–144, 149, 151, 154–158, 192–194, 202, 252
Evenki 82, 183–185
Eyak 5, 180, 182–183

facial height 143, 145–147, 149, 152, 156
Finnish 80, 137, 185–186, 202–203
Firstview tradition 143
fluted-point tradition 16, 143, 217
Folsom site 7–8, 15–19, 28–29, 62
Foothill North Yokuts 186
fox 184, 198, 200–201
Freeman-Tukey inverse sine transformation 83
Ft. Yukon 120
Fulnio 186

Galibi 184
Galice 181–183
Gallup Navajo 120–123, 125
gas scintillation system 34
gel matrix 241
gelatin, gelatinization 31–33, 38, 47, 49–52, 169
gene flow 5, 77, 79, 81, 84, 105, 107–109, 119, 121–123, 125, 127, 142
gene frequency 80, 109, 118–120, 123–128, 194
genetic classification 177, 187, 193
genetic distance 83, 117–119, 121–127, 145
genetic drift 83, 86, 119, 125, 137
Georgia 105, 144, 146–147, 156, 251
Gilyak 178, 184–187, 204
glycine/aspartic ratio 31–32
glycine/glutamic ratio 31–32, 50–51
Gm frequency 120–125
Gordon Creek 142, 150
graphite 36, 47, 50–53
grasses 29, 132
Greeks 8, 193, 203
Greenberg classification 5, 178, 253
Greenland 80, 101–103, 109, 120–122, 125, 144
Grotte Patrone 32–33
Guahibo 184
Guajajara 185
Gualaquiza 185
Guam 101, 106
Guambiana 184–185
Guana 187
Guarani 185, 187
Guato 185, 187
Guayaki 185, 187
Gulf of Alaska 107, 193, 251

Haida 5, 82, 84, 86–102–103, 106–107, 117–118,

120–121, 123–126, 179–183, 191, 194
hair 29, 105, 172, 186
Haisla 184–185
hare 32, 82, 182
Hatti 181
Hawaii 106, 134, 144
Hemastix reagent strip 244–245
hemoglobin 239–241, 243–245
high-energy mass spectrometry (HEMS) 34
high-vacuum pathway 34
Hishcariana 186
Hitchiti 187
Hittite 184–185
HLA 119, 127, 171
Hokan (H) 178, 180–183, 253
Holocene 1, 4, 30–32, 45–47, 49, 52, 57–60, 62, 64–65, 67, 132, 137, 141, 143, 145, 157–158, 251
Hopewell 79, 82–83, 86–95, 98–100, 102–104
Hopi 117, 120–122, 125
Horn Shelter 142–143, 150, 152
Huastec 185–186
Huave 184
humic compound 33, 39
humin 39
Hungarian 101
Hupa 183
Hurrian 180–181
hydroxyproline 31–32, 38, 48–52

Igloolik 120–123, 125
immunochemical activity 240
immunogen 243
Immunoglobulin 119, 242
Immunoglobulin Gm haplotype 4, 5, 117, 118, 120, 125, 126
immunological identification technique 239, 241–242, 244, 246
immunosorbent preparation technique 241
India 101, 133, 137, 193
Indo-European 178–179, 183, 195, 202–204
infraorbital suture 84, 92–93
Ingain 184
Inuid variety 104, 107
Inuit 184, 186
Inupiaq group 82, 85–104, 107, 110
ion source technology 27, 34, 36
Ipurina 186
Iroquoian 194–195, 197, 202
isoelectric focusing 239, 241–242
isotopic exchange 29, 31
Itelmen 185
Itonama 184
Izhor 186

J-shaped profile 40
Japan, Japanese 80–82, 86–90, 100, 102–103, 105–107, 109–110, 133–134, 143–144, 146, 158, 170, 183–187, 193

Jebero 186
Jicaque 186
Jomon 80–82, 86–90, 99–103, 105–107, 143–144, 146, 149, 151, 154–155, 157–158
Kabardian 181
Kachemak 108, 194
Kagaba 185
Kagamil 82, 84, 86–94, 97–98, 102–103, 105
Kahuapana 183
Kaingan 185–187
Kalapuya 185
Kamakan 185, 187
Kamassian 184
Kamayura 184
Kamchadal 184–186
Kamchatka Peninsula 8, 109, 120, 250, 252
Kandoshi 186
Karen 183
Kariri 185–186
Karok 184
Kartvelian 183
Kashaya 187
Kato 182
Keams Canyon 120
Keams Navajo 120–122, 125
Kekchi 185, 187
Kerek 185
Keres 186
Khalkha 185
Kiliwa 186
Kiowa 184–185
Klamath 184, 186
Km frequency 120–121, 123
Koasati 186
Kodiak 80, 82–83, 86–88, 90–91, 93–95, 97–99, 104–105, 107–109, 134, 194
Kodiak early 82, 86–92, 95–98, 100, 102–103, 106
Kodiak Island 80, 82, 86, 91, 93, 95, 98, 104
Kodiak late 82, 86–92, 95, 97–98, 100, 102–103
Koniag 82, 86, 103–104, 107–108
Korean-Japanese-Ainu 136, 178, 204
Koryak 183
Kot 182
Kraho 187
Kuskokwim 82, 91–92, 97, 184, 186
Kutchin 82, 120, 123–124, 183
Kutenai 183, 185–187, 196–197
Kwakiutl 185–186, 196–197

Lakotid variety 104
Lamut 184
late Archaic 152
late Prehistoric 82, 85, 95, 152, 252
late Woodland 79, 82–83, 86–94, 96, 98–100, 102, 107
Laurentide ice sheet 127
Lenapid-Walcolid hybrid 104
Lenca 186–187

Lengua 185
lexical etymology 179–180
Lezgi 181
Lillooet 183
Lindenmeier 29
linguistics 3, 5–7, 18–19, 81, 83, 86, 91, 100–104, 106–107, 109, 118, 135, 137, 177–179, 183, 187, 189–200, 202–204, 253
liquid scintillation system 34
Lombard 144, 146–147, 156
Longin technique 32–33, 38
Lost Tribes of Israel 8, 193
Loy's hypothesis 240, 241
Lubbock Lake 29, 64–66
Lule 184–185, 187
Luwian 187

Mackenzie MMD 90
Macro-Carib (MC) 178, 181–183, 186
Macro-Ge (MG) 46–47, 168, 178, 181–183, 244
Macro-Indian 81, 95, 99, 101
Macro-Panoan (MP) 178, 181–183, 185
Macro-Tucanoan (MT) 142, 178, 181–183, 185, 215
Maidu 184–186
mammoth 1, 38–39, 45, 47–52, 63, 170
mandibular ramus 103
Maori 106
Mapudungu 187
marble 36
Marinahua 184
Maripu 185
Masaka 184
Mascoy 183–184
Mashubi 185
mass spectrometer 3, 27–28, 33–35, 45–46, 48
Massachusett 200–202
Mataco 184, 187
Matagalpa 185
Matanawi 185
Matlatzinca 186
Mattole 182
Mayna 185
mean measure of divergence (MMD) 79, 83–90, 92–96, 98–100, 102, 105, 109, 133–134
Mekens 185
Melanesia 133–134, 136, 144, 149
Mendelian pattern 80
Meniens 184
Mescalero Apache 120–122, 125
metric traits 103
Mexico 3–4, 15, 28, 45, 48, 51–52, 101, 127, 135, 144, 253–254
microcore 39, 106
midden cultures 81–82, 108
middle Korean 184
Middle Paleolithic Skhul V, Israel 152
Millcaya 184

Minatogawa 77, 143–144, 146–151, 154–155, 157
Mississippi Valley 60, 90
mitochondrial DNA (mtDNA) 5, 101, 127, 135, 166, 168–171
Mixe 185
Mocovi 184
Mohawk 184
Mongol, Mongoloid 76–77, 80–81, 99, 101, 103, 105–106, 108, 118, 120, 123–124, 133–138, 157, 184–185
monoclonal antibodies 242
monoenergetic ionized beam 34
Mordvin 185
morphometric analysis 137, 141–143, 158
Moseten 183, 185–186
Motilon 185
Movima 184
multichain proteins 242
multilateral comparison 189–190, 201–203
multivariate analysis 103, 143, 145, 158
mummy 82, 84, 168, 170
Mura 184
Murire 185
Muskogean 194
Musqueam 186
mutation 80, 119, 167, 172–173
Mutsun 187
mylohyoid bridge 84, 92

Na-Dene 4–5, 79–82, 84, 90–93, 95, 97–102, 104–106, 108–109, 117–118, 120–121, 125, 136, 178–180, 182–183, 187, 191–194, 204, 253
Nahali 181
Namu 79, 81–83, 86–100, 102–103, 105–106
nasiomalar angle 103
nasofacial complex 101
Navajo 82, 91, 95–96, 100–102, 117, 120, 125, 181–183
Near Islands 91–92, 100, 103, 108
Nenets 120–126
Neo-Aleut 85, 104–105
Neoarctic 79, 107–109
Neoarctic Amerind 79, 107
Neolithic 79, 106–107, 131, 137, 144
Neolithic Jomonese 81
neutron flux 36
New Chaplino 120
New York 60, 102
Nez Perce 186–187
Nganasan 120–123, 125
Niger-Congo 197, 201
Nisqualli 186
nitrocellulose protein-binding membrane 239, 244
nitrogen concentration 31
noncollagen proteins 27, 38–39
nonmetric cranial traits 79–81, 83–84, 86, 91, 95, 97, 101, 104, 106, 108–109
Nootka 118, 183, 186, 194

North Pomo 185
North Sahaptin 185
North Yana 184, 186
Northern Cayapo 185
Norton 59, 79, 107–109
Nostratic 183–187, 204
Nung 183
Nunivak 82, 86–94, 97–98, 100, 102–103, 107
Nushagak River 86, 91–92

Ob River 120, 144
Ojibwa 117, 120–126, 198–200
Okinawa 143–144, 186
Old Bering Sea phase 82, 95, 97
Old Crow Basin 30
Ona 184–185
Oowekyala 184
Opaie 184
osteocalcin 27, 39, 46
osteometrics 141–142
Ostyak 185
Ouchterlony double-diffusion technique 241–242
Oxford AMS Laboratory 38
Pacific Rim 6, 142, 157–158
Paez 180–181, 184–186
Palaic 187
Paleo-Aleut 84–85, 91–93, 103, 107–108
Paleo-Indian wave 2–5, 16–17, 28, 46, 52, 57–68, 117–118, 131–132, 135, 137–138, 141–143, 145–147, 149–150, 152–153, 156–158, 240, 244, 247
Paleoarctic 5, 79–80, 96, 106–109
Paleoarctic Amerind 79, 106–107
Panobo 184
Papago 117, 120–123, 125
Papantla 186
Papury 186
paratope 242
Patagonia 101
Patwin 185
Paya 185–186
peat 9, 29–30, 67, 251
pebble-tool industry 106
Pecos Pueblo 144, 146–150, 156
Pehuenche 185
Pelican Rapids 142, 150
Penutian (P) 5, 8, 14, 16–20, 28–29, 32–33, 39, 45–53, 59, 75, 79–82, 86, 90, 93, 95–96, 98, 100, 104–110, 123–124, 137–138, 142–144, 146–147, 157, 165, 178, 180–186, 192–194, 199, 204, 249–254
peptides 38, 46
Peru 101, 135, 144, 146–150, 171–172
Phoenicians 8, 193
phonology 107, 196, 199, 203
phylogeny 4–5, 11, 118–119, 131, 135, 137, 170, 173, 187, 190, 193–194, 209, 212
Pilaga 185
Pima 117, 120–123, 125, 127

Pleistocene 1–2, 4, 7–12, 14–19, 28, 32–33, 37, 40, 46, 52, 57, 59–65, 68, 73, 76–77, 81, 96, 106–107, 132–133, 135, 137–138, 143–144, 158, 194, 250
Point Barrow 90–92, 96–97, 100, 102, 107
Pokomchi 184
polyclonal antigenes 242, 243
Polynesia 101, 133, 136, 144, 193
Popoloca 184
porotic hyperostosis 152
Port Moller Aleutian tradition 108
Potowotami 185
pre-Aleut 102, 104, 144, 146–150, 158
pre-Clovis 2–3, 17–18, 28
pre-Mongoloid 157
precipitation by salting-out crystalline hemoglobin method 241
principal components analysis (PCA) 145, 148, 156–158
protein 27, 31, 33, 38–39, 45–48, 50, 119, 123, 166, 168, 170–171, 239–246
Proto-Afro-Asiatic (PAA) 183–187
Proto-Algonquian 198–201, 203
Proto-Altaic (PA) 20, 183–187, 200–201, 239
Proto-Arawakan 186
Proto-California Penutian 184, 186
Proto-Carib 186
Proto-Caucasoid 157, 182–183
Proto-Chinantec 185
Proto-Costanoan 186
Proto-Dravidian (PD) 183–187
Proto-Eyak-Athabaskan 182
Proto-Indo-European (PIE) 183–187
Proto-Kartvelian (PK) 183–187
Proto-Mongoloid 80–81, 106, 157
Proto-Muskogean 185
Proto-Na-Dene 181–183, 187
Proto-Nax 182
Proto-Oto-Manguean (POM) 183, 185–186
Proto-Panoan 185–186
Proto-Salish 183, 185, 199–201
Proto-Sino-Tibetan 182–183
Proto-Siouan 185, 198–199
Proto-Tacanan 184, 186
Proto-Tanoan 185
Proto-Tibeto-Burman 182–183
Proto-Tupi 185
Proto-Uralic (PU) 183–187
Proto-Uto-Aztecan (PUA) 183–186
Proto-Yeniseian 181
pull-push process 34
Punuk 79, 82–83, 86–91, 93–96, 98–100, 102–103
purified proteins 31, 33

Q-mode correction 145, 148, 153
Quechua 185–186
Queen Charlotte Islands 117, 123
Quileute 183, 186, 197
Quitemo 184

radioimmunoassay (RIA) 170, 239, 242
Rama 185
Rancho La Brea 142, 150
Reindeer Chukchi 121–125
Ritwan 196–197, 200
Romans 8, 193
Russians 3, 109
Rutul 181
Ryukyuan 184–186

Sabela 184
Salinan 185–186
Salish 186, 196–197, 199–201
Samurai 101
San Carlos Apache 120–123, 125–126
San José 185
Sanskrit 184
Santa Ana 185, 197
Santa Cruz 101, 186
Sarsi 182–183
Sauk Valley 142, 150, 152
Sayula 186
Scottsbluff tradition 143
Selkup 185
Seneca 184, 186, 197, 202
Seri 184, 187
serine 39, 48–50
serum protein system 123, 241, 243, 245–246
Shasta 186
Shawnee 186, 200–201
Shiprock 82, 84, 91–94, 96, 98, 102
Shiriana 186
Siberia, Siberian 82, 102–103, 106–108, 121–125, 135, 137–138, 144
Siberian Eskimo 80–82, 86–90, 92–93, 95–96, 98–103, 121, 126
Siberian Nenets 121, 123
Sierra Popoluca 186
Similaton 184
Sino-Caucasian 180
Sino-Tibetan 179–180, 182–183, 204
Sinodonty 81, 118
Sioux, Siouan family 102, 104, 194, 197–199
Siracua 184
Sirenik 184
Siuslaw 186
skeletal analysis 48, 109, 143
Smith Sound 101
Snohomish 183
solvent extraction technique 31, 38
Songish 186–187
Southwest culture area 117
species-specific epitopes 242
species-specific proteins 243
spectrometer 3, 27–28, 33–35, 45–46, 48
Squamish 183–184
St. Lawrence Island 91–92, 100, 103, 120–121, 123–126

standard distance 119, 121–124, 126
statistical analysis 131, 178, 226
Subarctic culture area 117
subsistence economy 143
Sundadonty 81
Surinam 184
Suya 185

t-test 145–147
Takelma 183, 187
TAMS-type instruments 34
Tanaina 82, 181–182
tandem particle accelerators 34
Tanoan 182
Taos 185–186
Tarascan 184, 186
Tartar 185
Tasmania 109, 144, 146–147, 149, 156, 170
Taymyr Peninsula 120
Taz River 120
Tennessee Woodland 144, 148–149, 156
Tequistlatec 184–186
Tewa 187
Texas 1, 7, 29, 57–62, 65–66, 141, 144, 148, 150, 152, 157, 165, 195, 215, 218, 247, 253
Thermal Maximum 106
three-migration model 4–5, 95, 105, 117–118, 120–121, 123
threonine 39, 48–49
Thule 79, 95, 100, 107–109, 120–122, 125
Tibagi 187
Ticuna 185
Timucua 184
titers 243
Tiwa 184
Tlatskanai 182
Tlingit 5, 82–84, 86–96, 98–103, 106–107, 109, 118, 120, 125, 180–183, 191, 194
Tonkawa 184, 187
Totonac 184–185
Towa 184
Toyeri 185
trait-by-trait analysis 104
triangular matrix 83
tripartite classification 118
triple division 194
Tschaahui 186
Tsimshian 184–186
Tucano 187
Tungus 80–83, 86–90, 100–103, 105–107, 185
Tunica 186–187
Tuscarora 185
Tututni 182
Tuwituwey 186
tympanic dehiscence 84, 92

UCR Radiocarbon Laboratory 41

Uighur 184, 186
Uitoto 184, 186–187
Ulua 186
Umnak, Umnak Island 81–82, 84–94, 96–99, 102, 104, 106–108, 251
Umotina 185, 187
univariate comparison 92–93, 103, 105, 133, 144–145
unweighted pair group method (UPGMA) 119
Upper Cave, China 76–78, 143–144, 146–151, 153–155, 157–158
upper Paleolithic Predmost 3, Czechoslovakia 152
upper Pleistocene 106, 144, 250
Uralic 136–137, 183
Uralic-Yukaghir 178, 204
uranium series 36, 48, 50, 74–76
Urartian 180–181
Urupa 186
Uto-Aztekan 120, 132, 134, 182
Uyak site 80, 82, 86, 105

Vancouver Island 118, 251–252
Vejoz 184
Vikings 193
Vindija Cave 32–33

Waikina 186
Waiwai 185
Wajin 109
Wakashan 186, 196, 200, 201
Walapai 117, 120–123, 125–126
Wappo 183–187
Warrau 184
Washo 184
Wayana 185–186
Welsh 8, 193
West Siberian Plain 120

whale 33, 252
Whitewater Draw 142–143, 150
Wichita 183–184
Wilson-Leonard 142, 150
Wintun 184, 186
Wisconsinan 249, 251–253
Wisconsin times 15, 117–118, 127, 249–254
Wishram 184
Wiyot 183–186, 197, 203
Woodland-Plains subcluster 91, 98
word comparison method 190, 202–203

Xinalug 181
Xinca 184, 186

Yagua 185–186
Yamana 187
Yameo 185
Yanomamï 185
Yeniseian 180, 182–183
Yokuts 184, 186
Yuki 184–187
Yukon River 91, 103
Yuma 187
Yupik Eskimo 82, 85, 91, 101, 108
Yupultepec 186
Yuracare 184–186
Yuri 185
Yurimangui 184
Yurok 183–186, 197, 201, 203

Zacapoaxtla 184
Zoque 187
Zuni 117, 120–123, 125, 186–187
zygomaxillary angle 103